Knopf Publications in Psychology

THE CORE SERIES

David Krech and Richard S. Crutchfield
ELEMENTS OF PSYCHOLOGY

Kenneth R. Hammond and James E. Householder
INTRODUCTION TO THE STATISTICAL METHOD

Leo Postman, Editor
PSYCHOLOGY IN THE MAKING
Histories of Selected Research Problems

THE GENERAL SERIES

Catherine Landreth
THE PSYCHOLOGY OF EARLY CHILDHOOD

PSYCHOLOGY
in the Making

Histories of
Selected Research Problems

KNOPF CORE SERIES

Contributors

Richard S. Crutchfield

William F. Dukes

Harrison G. Gough

Julian E. Hochberg

Marjorie P. Honzik

David Krech

Gerald E. McClearn

John P. McKee

Donald W. MacKinnon

Leo Postman

Donald A. Riley

Mark R. Rosenzweig

Theodore R. Sarbin

Read D. Tuddenham

PSYCHOLOGY
in the Making

Histories *of*
Selected Research Problems

EDITED BY

Leo Postman

UNIVERSITY OF CALIFORNIA

Alfred·A·Knopf · NEW YORK

1964

L. C. catalog card number: 62–12131

THIS IS A BORZOI BOOK,
PUBLISHED BY ALFRED A. KNOPF, INC.

REPRINTED 1963, 1964

Preface

IT IS OUR HOPE that the essays in this book will help the student to see some of the theoretical and methodological problems of present-day psychology in historical perspective and to become acquainted with the excitements, frustrations, and rewards which accompany the growth and development of psychological science. The importance of historical sophistication for the cumulative and orderly progress of a science, and especially of a young discipline like psychology, needs hardly to be defended. Without such sophistication, Boring warned us more than thirty years ago in the preface to his *History of Experimental Psychology*, the investigator "sees the present in distorted perspective, he mistakes old facts and old views for new, and he remains unable to evaluate the significance of new movements and methods." As the volume of psychological research expands at an accelerated rate, this judgment is more valid than ever.

The chapters of this book do not add up to a comprehensive history of psychology, nor do we wish to claim that our selected case histories of research encompass the range and diversity of problems which have led to the development of different fields of specialization within psychology. The variety of substantive and theoretical issues is, however, sufficiently great to drive home the fact that the intellectual antecedents of contemporary psychology are to be found in many different scientific disciplines and philosophical traditions. Today psychology has more histories than one.

The present project was planned and organized by a group of faculty members in the Department of Psychology at Berkeley who found that they shared an interest in the historical development of psychological ideas. All but two of the contributors are colleagues at Berkeley; Dr. Hochberg and Dr. Dukes may be claimed by us as alumni. As even a cursory reading of a few of the chapters will show, however, the book is far from representing a common point of view toward the theoretical and methodological issues of psychology. It would be idle to pretend that our historical analyses and evaluations are free of bias, and we have made no attempt at compromise or accommodation. Whatever measure of unity there is comes from an interest in the intense examination of the historical antecedents which shape our current concerns.

It is a pleasure to record our sincere gratitude to Mrs. Katherine Eardley, who prepared the illustrations, and to Mrs. Anne Lipow for her careful editorial assistance. Dr. Pauline Austin Adams worked patiently and faithfully on the preparation of the Index.

L . P .

Berkeley, California
July 7, 1961

Contents

INTRODUCTION

CHAPTER I

Some Guides to the Understanding of the History of Psychology

RICHARD S. CRUTCHFIELD
AND DAVID KRECH

THERE IS PERHAPS no human enterprise whose development is as dependent upon its past achievements as is science, and whose practitioners can so easily—and often to their benefit—ignore its past. The resolution of this paradox is quite simple and it serves to illuminate the role of the study of the history of science in the education of the scientist.

What we know today about a scientific topic—whether it be a theory, an hypothesis, or a collection of facts—is clearly the end product of a long period of past accumulation of knowledge. This dependence on the past no scientist would deny. But it is equally true that we know more today than yesterday because of the scientist's willingness and eagerness to uproot, destroy, and disregard the legacy of his past. The scientist is always on the alert to seek out error. And he seeks out errors and inadequacies most assiduously in the accumulated knowledge within his own discipline. When he finds them he casts them off. To look forward to the new findings of tomorrow rather than to revere the "truths" of yesterday is the mark of the creative scientist. This, too, no scientist would deny.

3

And so it comes about that if we are interested in teaching the student of the humanities, or the non-scientist in general, something *about* the nature of science, we teach him the history of science; when we are interested in teaching the student how to *be* a scientist—a botanist, physicist, or chemist—we often do not bother to teach him the history of his science at all. This is reflected in the internal organization of university departments of research and instruction. The "History of Science" may be found as a separate discipline, organized within the humanities division of the university, and staffed by men who are specialists —historians of science—but not themselves primarily scientists. The science departments rarely offer courses of the history of their own science, nor are any of the staff members of a genetics department, for example, likely to be historians of genetics first and geneticists second.

THE STUDY OF HISTORY OF PSYCHOLOGY

BUT THE ABOVE PICTURE is not true of psychology. In the offerings of almost every large (and of many a small) psychology department there is a course called "History of Psychology" or some equivalent thereof. And there have been renowned psychologists whose eminence was almost entirely due to their scholarship as historians of psychology. There are numerous reasons why psychology is almost unique among the sciences in this respect. Let us briefly examine but three of them.

(1) Psychology is still close enough in time and in subject matter to its ancestral home—philosophy—to reflect the parental interests and predilections. And philosophy, as indeed all the humanities, has ever been concerned with history. In this sense, psychology's concern with its history might be termed vestigial.

(2) Psychology probably ranks above all other sciences in the persistence with which it has engaged the attention of mankind over the ages. Man, no matter what else he observed and wondered about, seems always to have observed and wondered about himself and his fellows. The accumulated lore about the behavior of man, passed down from generation to generation, sifted (somewhat) and tested (somewhat) by time, has in it a considerable number of fairly respectable generalizations and insights. All this has enabled man, long, long ago, to pose some fairly simple but basic questions about himself. And because the simple and basic questions are often the most difficult to answer in any science—and especially in so complex a science as psychology—many of these questions of the past are still with us. The concern of today's psychologists about the nurture of the creative process is a concern which probably antedated the first pedagogue and the first schoolboy's stylus. Today's psychologists are intrigued by the locus of the controlling mechanisms of emotions, of intellect, of wants and desires. So were the

ancients—and the ancients before them. Already by the time of Aristotle this was a question of dispute among the physicians and philosophers (and one where Aristotle seemed to have pulled his greatest "boner" by placing the seat of the intellect in the heart). When animal psychologists today conduct experiments to determine whether the ability to perceive the spatial aspects of our environments is learned or innate, they are merely the latest entrants in a debate of many centuries' duration—as Hochberg in his chapter in this book reminds us when he points out that this very issue "remains a challenge today, after some 360 years of dispute" (p. 255).

It is probably true that problems persist longer in psychology than in most other sciences. When the psychologist reads the history of his science (perhaps the longest, uninterrupted intellectual history of any science) he reads of questions and attempted answers to questions with which he is struggling in his laboratory today. He finds very little of the "musty," the quaint, and the foolishly outmoded there. This may be why the history of psychology continues to attract the psychologist, more so, for example, than does the history of chemistry attract the chemist.

(3) Finally, nothing which is behavior can be foreign to the psychologist. Because psychology is concerned with all of man's behavior, it must not only *be* a science, but it must also *study* science as an important kind of human behavior. In the grammar of science, psychology must be in both the nominative and the accusative case. It must, in other words, study itself as it studies behavior. This means being self-conscious about the processes of science. It is therefore apparent why psychology seeks to study, carefully and analytically, the development and history of psychology. Psychology's concern with scientific history can be understood as a concern with what is part of its own proper scientific subject matter.

But quite aside from these special considerations, there are a number of general reasons why students of psychology should (and sometimes do) study the history of their science. And these general reasons apply to students of other sciences with equal force. These general factors influence the vigor with which the scientist will pursue his science and the attitude he will adopt toward his science. Again we might look at three such factors.

It has often been said that a knowledge of the history of one's science teaches the scientist humility and tolerance for opposing views. The succeeding chapters of this book are replete with instances of scientists who, certain of the truth of their formulations, lived only to see these formulations abandoned by science; the succeeding chapters are filled, too, with instances of scientific hypotheses derided as silly, inane, and beyond the pale by the scientific authorities of the day—hypotheses which today live on in respectability while their authoritative detractors have been consigned to oblivion. One might draw the moral from this that error will out—eventually. But another moral would seem to be that truth *can* be and sometimes is suppressed for long periods by the scientist who lacks humility and tolerance. Humility and tolerance, in other words, are not only good for the soul, but also good for the advancement of science. Studying history is not the only way to achieve these admirable attributes, but it can be a very effective way.

It has also been said that the history of science not only teaches one to be humble about his own achievements and scientific notions, but also teaches one to take pride in scientific endeavors, and to have courage in the face of immediate difficulties and frustrations. Each of the eleven narratives in this book tells a story of significant progress and of great achievement, but progress and achievement which are rarely without interruption, rarely without repeated and sometimes long and costly stumblings into blind alleys. The moral seems to be—science will get there, don't give up the ship! And so again, the history of science can help inculcate desirable traits, traits of pride, of courage, and of perseverance, which are not only good for the character, but also good for the progress of science.

And finally, of course, study of the history of one's science helps make the scientist a complete man. From what we can surmise about man's motivations and needs, he cannot live and function at his best except when he sees his life and his functions as an essential part of something of lasting value, except when he identifies himself with something greater, more durable than his mortal self. For a scientist to know the history of his science is to see his laboratory, and his tables of data, and his journal articles, and his scientific meetings as his participation and involvement in an ancient and honorable activity—an activity which has shaped and turned the world, which has engaged the great minds and noble men of countries and times distant from his own, and which will probably continue to do so for ages to come. He becomes a part of these eternal strivings. It may well be that, in studying the history of his own science, he will find therein the moral equivalent of religion, the moral equivalent of clan and national loyalty. And if this helps him function well, it helps science grow.

PURPOSE OF THIS BOOK

IT IS FOR THESE general reasons as well as the specific ones previously listed that the study of the history of psychology is to be commended to the student—whether he be a student who wants to know *about* psychology, or whether he be a student who wants to *do* psychology. The present book, it is hoped, will make a contribution to such study. In this book we present, in the form of "case studies," the histories of eleven quite specific research problems in psychology. This form of writing scientific history, while not entirely novel (see, for example, Conant, 1947), is also not entirely the orthodox way of writing it. But we feel that in the light of our discussion of the role of history in the education and training of the scientist, this form is a highly suitable one. Let us explain.

Perhaps the most important generalization which can be made about the history of science is that it is not a static affair. Science's *past*, no less than its present, is dynamic and ever-changing. Each generation must rewrite the history of science. History, everyone will agree, cannot be the complete and orderly recording of *every* past event. Even the least discerning of historians must pick and discard among the events he is to record in his history. He chooses his events on the basis of their importance or significance for other events. An event which made no difference to what else was happening at the time, or to what happened later, would merit little attention by the historian. But in science (and most probably elsewhere too) the importance of a past event may change from century to century, decade to decade, or even year to year.

As we read the case studies in this book we are struck with the fact that discoveries, hypotheses, and theories may pass through a whole series of cycles in terms of their "importance." Today's discovery may remain of little interest to anyone (except, perhaps, its discoverer) until, many years later, it "comes into its own." And when that happens it is clear that the history of that science needs to be rewritten, and the neglected discovery of the past given its "proper" place. For example, Rosenzweig (p. 135) points out that when Boring wrote his history in 1942, he gave little place to early central hypotheses of hunger and thirst. He "cited these hypotheses, but only briefly, because there was no way of knowing then where they were to lead." However, in Rosenzweig's account, as we shall see, these early hypotheses figure more prominently because "experimentation of the 1940's and 1950's has partially confirmed them, and favored their elaboration." To say that science's past is an ever-changing one is merely another way of saying that the doctrines, data, and discoveries of science are ever-changing.

If this is true, how are we best to write the history of science? There probably is no single "best" way. Certainly the general historian of science has a crucial contribution to make. He attempts to look at all of science or at a specific science—its antecedents, origins, and its social milieu—and he tells a tale of growth, development, and achievement. But this, we think, is not enough. If we are to rewrite the history of psychology, to bring it up to date, it would appear from our argument that one way of doing this would be to start out from the vantage point of *today's* doctrines, data, and discoveries.

But to write a history solely from the vantage point of today may lead to grievous error and bad history. Such an account may turn out to be too bland, too simplified, too much concerned with what *today* appear to be the successes, and too little concerned with what *today* appear to be the failures; in other words, written too much from the perspective of the present, looking backward, and not enough from the perspective of the then contemporary situation. Not only would such a history be "naive history," it would also fail to inculcate all the virtues we have suggested that the history of science can promote. What we wanted, in other words, was a history, as written from the perspective of the working scientist (himself intimately involved in the problems of today), and also as written from the perspective of the historian. We decided that such an enterprise would require the participation of men representing diverse fields of psychological science, and, if possible, men of science having some taste for the pursuits of the scholar. Whether we have succeeded in finding such men, only the reader can decide. But the scientists who have written this book have sought to reflect the two perspectives we have indicated.

NATURE OF THE BOOK

EACH OF THE ELEVEN succeeding chapters in this book is a narrative history of *a specific problem important in current psychology*. Each chapter is written by an active research worker specializing in the area of his chapter's concern. Each of these psychologists has looked back upon the history of *his* problem and has sought to trace its development. He begins with the earliest modern statement of the problem and its first "solution." He describes the reaction of the scientific world to this solution. Briefly, and in simple language, he then provides the reader with the successive highlights of the history of the problem up to recent times. The author identifies, for the reader, the key figures in this history; he recounts the tale of these key figures as they have walked proudly into blind alleys and stumbled blindly into breakthroughs. The reader sees new answers replacing old ones; he sees the "same" problem subtly changing; he sees rival theories in prolonged conflict. Liberal quotations from original sources are given, so that the reader can recapture the experiences associated with some of the great names and events in psychology, as well as put the achievements and failures of the past in their proper historical context in the *then* contemporary situation. By this technique, it is hoped, the reader can better appreciate how day-to-day results are obtained, new experimental techniques and methods come into being, further experiments are planned, conducted, and then revised—and through all this he can see psychology slowly, slowly developing.

These narratives, or case studies, can be seen as providing "working papers" for the student of psychology and the history of science. From these accounts it is hoped the student will gain incentive and encouragement to undertake research on his own challenging problems in the field of psychology. And from these accounts, it is hoped, he will be able to derive some general principles about the enterprise which is science.

We have put these hopes to examination in the following pages of this chapter. What morals, generalizations, and principles about scientific history *do* appear in these case studies? Of course each reader will tend to arrive at a somewhat different set of such principles, but it might be of interest and value to the reader to see what has impressed those of us who have been intimately involved in this enterprise. In other words, we have taken our own advice literally. We have examined the following chapters as though they were indeed working papers for a history of psychology, and in the next few pages we present some of our findings.

CONCEPTIONS OF SCIENTIFIC HISTORY

IN HIS HISTORY of cosmology Arthur Koestler (1959) has described contrasting conceptions of the nature of scientific history in these words:

> We are in the habit of visualizing man's political and social history as a wild zig-zag which alternates between progress and disaster, but the history of science as a steady, cumulative process, represented by a continuously rising curve, where each epoch adds some new item of knowledge to the legacy of the past, making the temples of science grow brick by brick to ever greater height . . . In fact, we have seen that this progress was [not] "continuous." . . . The philosophy of nature evolved by occasional leaps and bounds, alternating with delusional pursuits, *culs-de-sac*, regressions, periods of blindness and amnesia. The great discoveries which determined its course were sometimes the unexpected by-products of a chase after quite different hares. At other times, the process of discovery consisted merely in the cleaning away of the rubbish that blocked the path, or in the rearranging of existing items of knowledge in a different pattern.[1]

In the chapters that follow we shall encounter numerous events in the development of various psychological research problems that fit the above picture of the history of science. We shall find, too, that neither this nor any other single picture does justice to the variety of trends that do occur.

Just as in the study of the growth of individual learning psycholo-

[1] From Arthur Koestler, *The Sleepwalkers*, p. 513, copyright 1959, and used by permission of The Macmillan Company, New York.

gists have found it useful to describe the process in several quite different
ways, so, too, there are several ways of describing the process of growth
in psychological research. And, interestingly enough, these several ways
bear at least some superficial resemblance to ways of describing different
phases of the individual learning process. Sometimes scientific progress
—like learning—does take the form of a *gradual increment*, a slow amass-
ing of detailed facts about a scientific phenomenon. (See, for instance,
McClearn, p. 186, and McKee and Honzik, pp. 623ff.) Sometimes it
takes the form of *trial-and-error*, a process of successive trying out of
various possibilities, most of which prove fruitless, and a few of which
get gradually strengthened through proving useful. And finally, it sometimes takes the form of *sudden insight*, a process of partial or complete
restructuring of scientific thinking, a short-cutting of the processes of
gradual increment and trial-and-error through major breakthroughs.

Which of these pictures is most authentic for a given case depends
on the concrete nature of the particular psychological problem; it depends also upon the stage of development of the scientific work on that
problem—whether early or late, whether in the pioneering stage of
groundbreaking, exploration, and general mapping, or in the more
settled stage of intensive cultivation, consolidation, and refinement of
details of the map.

The Spiral of History

As we survey the course of scientific work on a psychological problem over a considerable period of time, we often discern a pattern of
recurrent return to earlier conceptions. We seem to detect a tendency
for thinking on the problem to go full circle. But this usually turns out
to be not really a circle, not simply a regression to an earlier stage. Instead, there is a kind of spiral, a recurrence of older conceptions but at a
more advanced level of complexity and sophistication. In the chapters
that follow there are numerous illustrations of this *spiral of history*.
In the recent history of research on intelligence the emergence of a limited number of fundamental factors derived from factor analysis brings
us back—though in a far more complicated form—to the much earlier
and subsequently discredited notion of mental "faculties" (Tuddenham, p. 512). Thorndike's concept of spread of effect suffered what
was an apparent demise at the hands of its experimental critics, and
then more recently the spiral of history brought a resuscitation of the
concept (Postman, p. 386). In the work on cortical localization of function there was a continuous spiraling from the notion of specificity to
the notion of generality (Krech, Chap. 2). It is not only concepts and
theories that show this spiraling phenomenon; experimental *methods* do
so too, as we shall see, for example, in the vicissitudes of the method

of successive reproduction in studying memory for visual form (Riley, p. 452).

This does not mean to say, of course, that it is possible to detect this grand spiral design in the history of every problem. Sometimes progress is not through such an ebb and flow of theories but by a "continuous Donnybrook of rival views" (Tuddenham, p. 471; Gough, pp. 548*ff*.). And sometimes the problem may be in such an early phase of growth that the turn of the spiral has not yet commenced. (This indeed is one of the main morals to be drawn by the scientist as a student of scientific history: he must remain always alert to the possibility that the old and discredited notion still possesses some unsuspected life and may once again have its day.) Often, too, the rebirth of older conceptions may occur without the scientist's being aware that these *are* mere modern versions of older ideas. This is clearly shown in Cannon's revival of "local" theories of thirst which had been put forth decades and generations earlier (Rosenzweig, p. 113). In the field of perception there have been repeated "rediscoveries" of elegant arguments with renewed philosophical flurry—flurry which might have been avoided by a little knowledge of history (Hochberg, p. 264). As Santayana phrased it: "He who would ignore history must be prepared to repeat it."

One of the basic reasons why such incessant spiraling of scientific ideas does occur is the tendency toward antinomies in the theories and approaches to a problem—a given theory may contain within itself the germ of its opposite. Moreover, a dominant theory, unopposed, tends to go too far, to be stated too extremely, and a corrective swing of the pendulum ensues (for example, see McKee and Honzik, p. 595). The very fact that science is a "public" rather than a "private" enterprise vastly facilitates this effect: the constant critical appraisal of one's data and theories by other scientists, the immediacy of the response to the challenge of new scientific contributions, necessarily makes for effect and counter-effect. It is precisely these factors which help account for the generalization we have already discussed—that *scientific history is not static, but dynamic.* The scientific story of any given problem is never done. No matter how far it has progressed, no matter how "final" the solution may appear, it always turns out that the story is "continued." Sometimes this is a matter of extending the problem or the theory so that it embraces more and more; sometimes it is a matter of coming to see how the specific explanation can fit into a larger conceptual scheme.

In order to understand more concretely just how and why the scientific history of psychological research does have the general characteristics we have discussed, we shall now consider (1) the influence of the social and cultural context on psychology, (2) the influence of other sciences on the work of psychology, (3) the effect of the continuous interaction of theory, method, and findings in psychology, (4) the factors that tend to inhibit scientific progress, (5) the capitalization on error, ambiguity, and accident in scientific work, and (6) the characteristics of scientists and their ways of work that help determine the path of scientific history.

THE CONTEXT OF CULTURE

THE PARTICULAR FORM of a science at any given time in history, the kinds of problems with which it concerns itself, the new directions it takes—all these are markedly influenced by the total cultural context, the particular historical period in which the scientific work is embedded. As Boring (1950) has so persuasively shown, the effect of the *Zeitgeist* —the spirit of the times—is ever present.

Partly this reflects the fact that the scientist—like every person—is a member and product of his society. Certainly no psychologist can escape this influence, no matter what his experimental problem, and no matter how thick and soundproof are the walls of his laboratory cubicle. As Sarbin points out (p. 775), Clark Hull fully realized this even when working with a purely laboratory approach to the problem of suggestibility. After presenting his carefully accumulated data and rigorously argued theory, Hull concludes, in the last paragraph of his book, that his work would necessarily be found wanting in the future if for no other reason than that "no worker can wholly escape the ideology of his time."

The Ideological Climate

The effect of the *Zeitgeist* on science is most obviously felt through the general ideological climate of the times. The effect is not only from the more formal philosophical thinking, but also from the values and outlook that characterize the popular beliefs of the literate people of the culture.

There are endless examples. Philosophical treatments of the classical Mind-Body problem have insistently influenced psychological inquiry. Thus Charcot's and Bernheim's different theories about hypnosis and different kinds of research on hypnosis reflected differences in their conceptions about the Mind-Body problem (Sarbin, p. 766). As Hochberg points out (pp. 257*ff*.), the basic nature-nurture question in perception was in its early stages influenced greatly by the common views about man and the cosmos in the so-called "age of reason." So, too, was the stress on environmentalism fostered by the prevailing democratic political philosophy (McKee and Honzik, p. 640).

This does not mean, of course, that scientific psychological concepts are merely the prevailing beliefs of a culture writ in "scientific" terms. The scientific statement of a problem has its own requirements, and when there is a translation from the philosophical or the common-sense statement to a scientific one there may occur a shift in the basic nature of the concept. Where philosophy, for example, may eschew the heuristic, or convenient, for the absolute truth, and where common sense may prefer the blacks and whites to grays, science may content itself with compromise or working statements. Thus, though philosophers lined up into mutually exclusive camps of Nativistic or Empiricistic explanations of perception, *scientific* formulations were suggested and defended which could accommodate an interaction of *both* nativistic and empiricistic determinants (Hochberg, Chap. 5).

Social Needs

The economic and social support of science depends heavily upon the needs, interests, and good will of other members of the society. Thus all sorts of extrascientific factors and forces may stimulate, direct, or limit the work of science. These forces may be political, economic, religious, military, moral, aesthetic, etc.

Often science may be supported mainly because of society's belief that science will ultimately "pay off" in practical applications. And, of course, this has been true to an astonishing degree, even for many of those explorations into "pure" science and abstract theory that seemed to have no possible connection with the practical world. We are reminded of Kurt Lewin's dictum: "There is nothing so practical as a good theory."

And though we often find that society's demand for immediate practical results tends to handicap the work of science, we often also see a beneficial consequence. There is a constant fertile interplay between application and theory. Applied problems often set new and significant scientific problems (see, for example, Gough, p. 526). A well-known illustration of this was the case in which the practical needs of the Paris school authorities shaped the mental test research of Binet. In discussing this example, Tuddenham (p. 515) concludes that ". . . the history of research upon intelligence provides an instructive example of the close link between science and the society in which it is rooted. The idea that intellectual discovery proceeds in an ivory tower is largely myth; in those instances in which scientific innovations seem to bear little relationship to the social matrix, they run a serious risk of being neglected and misunderstood until emerging human needs provide the circumstances necessary for acceptance and exploitation." And one can also point to the interesting observation that scientific work in behavioral genetics was given added impetus by the desires of the eugenicists to promote their programs of improving the human race (McClearn, p. 236).

The needs of the society do not necessarily *create* the scientific problem—which may have existed beforehand—but may serve, rather, to *redirect and spur* the work on the problem. This was, for example, the case with Binet; he had actually begun his scientific investigation of intelligence before the practical school needs were brought to his attention. Or, to take another example, new advances in thinking about the classical problem of perceiving space and distance were stimulated by the pressure of military needs in the landing of aircraft (Hochberg, p. 315).

Such beneficial interaction between application and "pure" science is especially noteworthy in psychology, owing to the richness and diversity of its subject matter, the complexity of its problems, and the variety of its techniques. For example, observations in the clinic have repeatedly come to have important impact on what went on in the psychological laboratory. Krech (pp. 46*ff*., 62*ff*.) shows how this occurred in the development of research on brain functioning. Other instances are found in the study of repression (MacKinnon and Dukes, Chap. 11) and in research on the physiological bases of hunger and thirst as motives (Rosenzweig, p. 84). Observations of behavior in the clinic and in other applied settings not only help to pin-point problems, and to provide fuel for scientific ideas, but they also serve as valuable correctives to a tendency toward oversimplification of human behavior in the thinking of the "pure" scientist (Krech, p. 46).

The frequent close interplay between application and theory does not, of course, imply that the two are *always* closely connected. Sometimes progress can be made in practical problems without any substantial benefit to theory. Thus the work on intelligence of foster children and foster parents may have obvious practical value, but may not—because of complicating variables—have basic scientific value (McClearn, p. 204). Conversely, scientifically valuable research may often best proceed in a way that is deliberately far removed from the "real life" situation. As Riley (p. 413) reminds us: "In general, laboratory experiments are not set up to imitate the most typical case found in nature. Instead, they are intended to answer some specific question of interest to the experimenter." (See also MacKinnon and Dukes, p. 678.)

THE CONTEXT OF OTHER SCIENCES

JUST AS A SCIENCE exists within some kind of general cultural context, so does it exist within a general *science* context. That is, no science exists—for very long—in isolation from other sciences. What happens to one science is partly a function of the state of affairs existing in other sciences. And it is to the interpenetration of ideas among the sciences that we now turn, briefly examining our case studies for what light they can throw on this aspect of the history of psychology.

Boundary Crossers

Almost every chapter in this book testifies to the importance of other sciences—particularly physics, physiology, medicine, and genetics —for the growth of psychological science. This has not been altogether a one-way street. Occasionally, psychology has also made its mark on other sciences. For example, as can be seen in McClearn's chapter (p. 230), behavioral questions arising in psychological inquiry played a role in the study by geneticists of the Lamarckian hypothesis. An interesting sidelight on one concrete avenue through which this interpenetration of ideas occurs is the very considerable frequency in the history of psychology with which physicians and surgeons, physiologists and physicists, have "passed" as psychologists. They have done this by contributing signally to psychological research and either becoming full-fledged psychologists, or becoming "honorary psychologists," as it were.

Among the many physicians and surgeons who were, or became, psychologists and who are discussed at some length in the following chapters are such different men as Binet, Freud, Spurzheim, Mesmer, and William James. Among physicists and physiologists are Helmholtz, Fechner, and Hering.

In science, as in international law, there is the doctrine of "hot pursuit": a scientist in the hot pursuit of a solution to a problem does not hesitate to cross the boundaries of other sciences. Psychology has benefited greatly from this doctrine.

Scientific Analogies

A somewhat less direct way in which other sciences have influenced the course of psychological theory has been through the kinds of physical and biological *analogies* that have been used in thinking about psychological processes. The prime role that analogical thinking can serve in creative scientific work has been discussed by many writers (see, for example, Oppenheimer, 1956). Its effect, they note, can be both beneficial and detrimental. It would appear that the positive value lies in the stimulus given the creative thinker by such analogies—the calling to his attention of new questions about psychological processes. The detrimental effects seem to lie in an uncritical overacceptance of the analogy—taking it over, not as an instructive resemblance, but as an identity. Thus, when such physical and biological analogies became crystallized into conceptual models of psychological processes, they often proved misleading. Numerous examples are found in our case studies: hypnosis conceived in terms of the "flow of fluid," of "magnetism," of a "telegraph wire model" (Sarbin, pp. 750–1, 782), etc.

Scientific Authority

A still more subtle way in which other sciences have influenced the course of scientific psychology has been through the *authority* they provide concerning the "proper" scientific methods, the "proper" kinds of scientific models, etc. Inasmuch as there exists a kind of status hierarchy among the sciences (with the older and more highly developed, e.g., physics, the more prestigeful), psychology and psychologists have tended to identify with and imitate these higher-ranking sciences. This has had profound value for psychology in that it was able to benefit by the past experiences of these other sciences. But it has also sometimes resulted in a slavish copying of the particular methods and particular orientations of these other sciences where such methods and orientations, being unsuitable for the unique problems of psychology, proved handicapping to the progress of scientific psychology.

THE INTERACTION OF THEORY, METHOD, AND FINDINGS

PERHAPS THE MOST impressive thing we find as we read the account of the developmental course of scientific work on a psychological problem is *the continuous reciprocal interaction of theory, method, and findings*. Everyone will recognize, of course, that each of these aspects plays an essential role in the scientific undertaking, but there may be misconceptions about the particular way they fit together. Outlines of scientific method may tend to convey too rigidly systematized a prescription of the "logical" order of steps in a scientific inquiry, to wit: (1) A theoretical statement of the problem is first made; this then leads (2) to the derivation of explicit hypotheses, which determine (3) the design of experiment to be carried out; this design (4) dictates what specific techniques are used; (5) the resulting research findings confirm or reject the initial theory, which, being now (6) revised or extended, commences the cycle once again, with new experiments leading to new findings, etc.

This "idealized" picture of orderly sequential progress rarely describes the reality of research work. The direction of functional interdependence in theory, method, and findings is not one-way, but two-way. Not only does theory lead to method, and method to findings; contrariwise, method may lead to theory, and findings to methods. "Where do I start?" asked Alice in Wonderland, and the disconcerting answer was, "Why, at the beginning, of course." And this is the case with a piece of scientific research. It starts at the beginning, but there are many different possible beginnings—the advent of a new theoretical idea, the invention of a new technique, the observation of a new fact.

The crucial point to remember is that developments in theory, in technique, in experimentation, in findings are all likely to be going on *simultaneously*. Techniques do not necessarily wait in their development until they are "logically" required, nor do empirical findings necessarily stem from theoretical questions. Often in science tools are invented before there is any use for them, data accumulated before they fit into any theoretical scheme. Partly this reflects differences in types of interest among different scientists. As we shall later note, some scientists are primarily interested in theory, others in doing experiments, still others in inventing new techniques. And they may work away in their own right, unconcerned with the possible relevance of what they are doing for the other aspects of the science.

Let us now look more specifically at the way in which each of these different main components of the scientific enterprise is shaped by and in turn helps shape the others.

Theory and Findings

It is almost too obvious to merit special discussion that there is constant interplay of theory and data. The particular theory will, by directing the investigator's attention toward certain questions, lead to the collection of certain kinds of data rather than others. Conversely, the availability of certain data will lead the scientist to formulate theories especially tailored to incorporate just these facts rather than others. A good example is found (Krech, pp. 39ff.) in Flourens' theoretical formulation of cortical function designed to accommodate *his* facts, a formulation which differed from the phrenologists' theory which had been designed to cover quite a *different* set of facts.

Perhaps it should be added that despite this frequent close interplay of theory and data, there are often cases in science where theory goes its own way for considerable periods of time unchecked by and "uncontaminated" by fact. (See, for instance, Gough, p. 565.) And, too, there may be long periods of sheer data accumulation, "unhampered" by theory. McKee and Honzik made this quite clear in their account of the psychology of sucking behavior (p. 623). Indeed, it is worth noting that it is often possible to make good use of such facts for the purpose of accurate prediction, even though no adequate theories are available to account for the facts. Thus Hochberg (p. 317) points out how a good deal could be understood and predicted about space perception, even though the theoretical nature-nurture controversy was unsettled. And Tuddenham (p. 516) notes that great research advances occurred in the problem of intelligence, even though adequate theories of intelligence were lacking.

Theory and Method

It is not surprising that the theoretical persuasions of the investigator may influence his choice of experimental methods for testing his theories, and that opposing theorists may favor methods that differ markedly and thus offer little common basis for comparison of results. (See, for example, Postman's discussion of Thorndike's methods of studying the Law of Effect, pp. 353ff.) More particularly, an influential prevailing theory may come to dictate the nature of new techniques developed in the field. Thus, for example, Spearman's notion of a unitary "g" had marked effects on techniques of mental test construction and the development of IQ measures (Tuddenham, p. 504).

What may not be so obvious, on the other hand, is that the development and use of a particular research *method* may come significantly to shape the further *theoretical* progress on a problem. (In this connection see the effect of Hull's use of laboratory techniques in research on hypnosis in emphasizing certain theoretical issues—Sarbin, p. 775.) Indeed, the method used in investigating an issue can sometimes become a vital part of the theoretical controversy itself (see Hochberg, p. 298, and Gough, p. 528).

Method and Findings

As the French neurologist, Pierre Flourens, phrased it, "It is the method which gives the results" (Krech, p. 40). This essential interdependence of methods and findings has several sources. For one thing, a measuring instrument tends to place *limits* on the kind of data that can be obtained. The use of Flourens' cortical-ablation technique for the study of brain localization of functions limited him to work on lower animals, and therefore to relatively simple behavior. Another example: The small sex differences obtained in scores on intelligence tests are partly a necessary result of the fact that in the development of these tests, items tending to differentiate the sexes were excluded (Tuddenham, p. 499).

For another thing, obtained data are often the *artifacts* of the method of recording. This is nicely illustrated by the investigations which sought to determine the relations between stomach contractions and hunger pangs through the well-known method of introducing a balloon into an "empty" stomach. Later investigations have quite clearly indicated that the very introduction of the balloon increases the activity of the stomach and therefore, concludes Rosenzweig (p. 112), "the early results on stomach contractions were partly artifacts of the method of researching."

Finally, not only can we agree with Flourens that the method gives the results, but the history of science is replete with illustrations that the method also shapes the very questions (theoretical and empirical) which the scientist can ask or even is interested in asking. (See Krech, p. 40.) Here we have theory, method, and data interacting. No instrument, in the hands of the scientist, is strictly a "neutral" one. The very choice of that instrument or method already betrays the scientist's theoretical orientation. The psychologist who uses a structured personality inventory rather than a "depth interview," or a Skinner-box rather than a memory drum, is choosing his method partly because of his *theoretical* preferences or biases.

Optimal Timing of Theory, Method, and Findings

Of crucial importance for their role in science is the *timing* in the appearance of new facts, new ideas, new techniques. Sometimes these come along at just the right strategic moment, exactly when most needed at the given stage in the research enterprise and when they can have optimal effect. Sometimes, on the other hand, the critically needed ideas or facts or methods are *delayed*, and progress on the problem is thereby hindered; or sometimes they come *too early*, before they can have their full impact, the prevailing climate not being auspicious for the new ideas, facts, or methods. As Krech points out in connection with the early theorizing on brain localizations by the phrenologists, "A theory—a very good theory—may be premature for many reasons. The spirit of the times may not be conducive for a favorable hearing; the older theory, already in the field, may not yet have outlived its usefulness; or the new theory may be premature because no valid supporting data can be adduced to spell out its implication in any specific manner and to discipline its speculations. The very same general theory, proposed at a later date, may be welcomed enthusiastically by the scientific world" (p. 35).

We find in psychological history many such instances of early anticipations of later ideas (for example, Schopenhauer as precursor of Freud —MacKinnon and Dukes, p. 664). Often these early ideas, which seem surprisingly "modern" to us now, remained neglected for a long time. A dramatic instance of this is found in Rosenzweig's account (p. 80) of Robert Whytt's anticipation of the findings on the conditioning of responses. In 1763 Whytt wrote: "We consider . . . that the remembrance or *idea* of substances formerly applied to different parts of the body, produces almost the same effect as if those substances were really present. Thus the sight, or even the recalled *idea* of grateful food, causes an uncommon flow of spittle into the mouth of a hungry person; and the seeing of a lemon cut produces the same effect in many people." This observation waited 134 years before Pavlov's work on the conditioned salivary response to food and acid elaborated this age-old observation into the foundation for a whole new system of psychology. Another classic case in scientific history was the disappearance for about thirty-five years of Mendel's fundamental ideas and observations on genetics (McClearn, p. 160), though here perhaps it was not so much a matter of later neglect of his work as a matter of failure of initial impact because of publication of his writings in an obscure journal. (Here, by the way, we see the crucial role of *communication* in science.)

Another reason that scientific ideas may sometimes occur prematurely is that the new hypotheses outstrip the contemporary possibilities of testing them. The required techniques may not yet be available, as we see in the case of research on the psychology of hunger, where hypotheses alternative to the "local" hypothesis had to await techniques which would permit "conducting experiments in the depths of the living body" (Rosenzweig, p. 134). What may at one time be thought of by the theorist as a purely "imaginary" experiment, impossible in fact, turns out much later to be an experiment that is actually feasible; and being done, it may serve to throw crucial empirical light on the earlier untested speculation. So it was with the "imaginary experiment" of Locke and Berkeley more than two centuries before von Senden's actual experiments on restored vision in cataract cases (Hochberg, pp. 265, 322).

Sheer technological advances are often the key to scientific progress. Until more refined instruments, cheaper research methods, etc., are invented, basic progress on a problem may be stymied. Sometimes it is technological advance in an apparently remote field that proves crucial for a scientific breakthrough in another field. McClearn cites several such examples: the new steps in chromosome theory made possible by advances in the chemistry of dyes (p. 161); the stimulus to research on hereditary and environmental factors in psychological characteristics produced by improved physiological techniques for differentiating identical from fraternal twins (p. 195).

INHIBITING FACTORS ON SCIENTIFIC PROGRESS

ANOTHER USEFUL APPROACH to understanding some of the events described in the case narratives in this book is through an analysis of the factors which *inhibit* scientific progress on a problem. There are many such factors, some having to do with the stultifying effects of prevailing theories or the inadequacies of alternative theories, some having to do with the effects of various kinds of biases and errors in methods and thinking.

The Constraints of Prevailing Theory

It is perfectly obvious that continued progress in a field of inquiry is heavily indebted to the earlier theories that previous investigators have gradually evolved. It may not be quite so obvious that prior theories can also exercise a negative, restraining influence by standing in the way of

further progress. One general and far-reaching way in which this sometimes occurs is when existing theoretical orientations so thoroughly
dominate a discipline that entire new fields of inquiry are thereby inhibited. McClearn, for example, points out how the development of the
whole field of behavioral genetics was impeded for a considerable period
by the widely accepted "environmentalism" and radical Behaviorism
that denied the role of hereditary factors (p. 236). And then there was
the well-known resistance of academic psychology to even an *investigation* of whether Freud's highly original psychoanalytic notions had anything to contribute (MacKinnon and Dukes, pp. 670–3).

Another constraining effect of a prevailing theory stems from the
fact that the theory may determine the particular way that the phenomena relevant to the problem are categorized by the scientist. And this
may prevent him from "seeing" phenomena in new ways, necessary for
further scientific progress on the problem. Sometimes the very *names*
by which phenomena are customarily categorized may tend to inhibit
an insightful reorganization of the scientist's thinking about the problem: "Old names conceal new problems" (Hochberg, p. 327).

The Survival Value of Outworn Theories

Why *do* certain scientific theories often hang on for long periods of
time, continuing to exercise their inhibiting influence on new advances
even though the theories may be poor or inadequate or downright
wrong? One important generalization about this is that an inadequate
theory tends to persist if no better alternative theory is available. As
Hochberg comments in regard to the "astonishing" survival of classical
associationism in perception, "It would seem that its greatest virtue is
the absence of any really plausible, specific, systematic alternative"
(p. 271). We often find cases in which a theory advanced by one worker
may pre-empt the field because of the default of other workers in not
offering explicit alternative theories. Thus Tuddenham (p. 504) notes
how Spearman's "g" theory of general intelligence—despite its clear
shortcomings—came to dominate a great deal of research in the field
partly because Binet had failed to provide explicit theories to accompany his research findings, and into this theoretical vacuum Spearman's
views expanded.

Moreover, it is not infrequently the case that a theoretical "explanation" may resist attack and continue to survive even though there
are recognized facts to contradict it (see Rosenzweig, p. 134, in connection with the "local" hypothesis of hunger and thirst). Sometimes this is
because the particular theory or "explanation" has an elegance of form
or the simplicity of a "single cause," and such theories are indubitably
attractive to the scientist trying to make sense of complex phenomena.

Thus, not only did Spearman's theory of "g" fill a vacuum, it also had the compelling virtues of simplicity and elegance. Sometimes the contradicted theory persists because it makes "good common sense," or because voices of authority "from Plato and Aristotle on" support it.

Uncritical Appraisal of Theories

The general attractiveness of a theory, whatever the reason, makes for a readiness for uncritical acceptance of the whole theory on the basis of insufficient evidence, sometimes indeed on the basis of a single allegedly "crucial" experiment. This seems to have been partly true, for example, of the reaction of many "Gestaltoid" psychologists to Wulf's hypothesis and classical experiment (Riley, Chap. 7). Sometimes this involves what Postman (p. 377) refers to as the "error of partial fit"—a *whole* hypothesis is considered confirmed on the basis of its ability to account for *some* of the facts about the phenomenon.

The opposite also occurs: a whole theory may be uncritically rejected on the basis of a negative finding in a "crucial" experiment that in fact is not really capable of testing the theory. An illustration given by Tuddenham (p. 480) was the over-reaction against the whole notion of mental testing caused by the Wissler and Sharp studies, which in fact merely emphasized individual differences in test scores and questioned the notion that all tests intercorrelate highly.

The very enthusiasm with which a theory is acclaimed may carry the seeds of its own destruction. A theory uncritically embraced by the nonscientific public can suffer the kiss of scientific death. (See Krech, p. 34, regarding the effect of public enthusiasm for phrenology.) Moreover, repudiation of a theory may also mean an unwarranted rejection or neglect of the observations or data on which the theory was based. For example, Sarbin describes (p. 755) how the justified repudiation of the theory of "animal magnetism" was accompanied by an unjustified rejection of certain dramatic facts about hypnotic phenomena.

The Effect of Bias and Error

Various kinds of biases and errors that inevitably creep into scientific work on a problem are another potent source of interference with progress on the problem. We have already discussed how the very phenomena studied may be selected, distorted, suppressed, or produced by the approach taken, by the particular samples of subjects studied, by the method used, etc. Thus the fact that Charcot carried on all his studies of hypnosis exclusively with female hysteric patients caused him to observe only special and limited data and led him to distorted conceptions about the problem; Liébeault dealing with more "normal" samples of French peasants was led to quite different conclusions (Sarbin, p. 764). A research method may inadvertently result in the suppression or masking of critically relevant facts or questions. A particularly significant illustration in psychological history was the blindness of early experimentalists to the crucial importance of *individual differences* in psychological functions, brought about by their insistence on treating individual variation as "error"—a nuisance to be gotten rid of by the use of proper experimental controls (Tuddenham, p. 474).

It goes almost without saying, of course, that it is through the exercise of proper controls and other essentials of the scientific method that scientific progress is made possible. Failure to use such controls plus other shortcomings in research design and execution have frequently in the history of psychology been the source of difficulties in the progress on a problem. The accounts by Riley (Chap. 7) and by Postman (Chap. 6) provide specific documentation here. Another illustration is the misuse of the "experience table" in research on psychological prediction (Gough, pp. 559ff.).

There is also sometimes an inhibiting effect on scientific progress owing to the perpetuation of certain errors of fact, for example, errors that may creep into a textbook and be parroted by succeeding textbooks. Words and names in science sometimes immortalize such mistakes. Thus the small, oval endocrine gland attached to the base of the brain is still called the "pituitary gland" because Galen, about 1800 years ago, made the mistake of assuming that this gland secretes mucus (*pituita*) from the brain into the nose and throat (Rosenzweig, p. 78).

CAPITALIZING ON ERROR AND ACCIDENT

THE PROGRESS OF SCIENCE, our narratives in this book tell us, is not smooth sailing. The scientist navigates a perilous and tortuous course, seeking to avoid the shoals of factual error, the whirlpools of biased theory. He often gets accidentally driven far off course. He may end up totally lost or may founder. But he may also thus be led, against his will, despite his ignorance, and without any forethought, to the discovery of great new continents. One of the most striking facts about the history of science is that scientific progress is often made through *capitalizing on misconception, error, ambiguity, and accident.*

The positive role of *error* in science has been discussed by Boring (1950) in connection with the contribution made by the phrenologists: "No scientist consciously cultivates error; yet the truth—a scientific truth which may last for a century before some flaw in its formulation is discovered—is often the mean between an established misconception and an hyperbole which has been built up to overcome the inertia of tradition" (Krech, p. 42). Error may lead the investigator on a false trail, but this may be a trail that he would never have otherwise explored and on this trail he may eventually discover a different truth.

Not only error but also *ambiguity* or lack of clarity in the formulation of theory may come paradoxically to serve good ends. For example, Riley (Chap. 7) describes the extensive research and theorizing which grew out of Wulf's provocative but imprecisely stated notions about memory for visual form. This is not, of course, to argue that ambiguity ought to be deliberately cultivated; much wasted time and misguided effort have doubtless occurred in the history of psychological work owing to confusion of concepts and terms.

The Positive Value of Accident

The vital role of *accident* in the physical and biological sciences has been widely recognized. In psychological history, too, we see instances of such happy accidents. For example, Postman (p. 378) describes how Jenkins and Sheffield, while experimenting on quite a different hypothesis, discovered evidence on the role of guessing habits in the spread of effect. Another instance: in the course of neurological ablation studies aimed at destroying the "hunger center," it was unexpectedly discovered that there was a center for *satiation* of hunger (Rosenzweig, p. 116). Finally, a more dramatic example given by Krech (p. 62): the lucky accident of the unlucky patient whose "ulcerating brain" provided the surgeon with the first opportunity to stimulate man's cortex electrically and to observe the behavioral effects.

Unfortunate sufferers have contributed much to the development of the science of psychology. In addition to the patient just mentioned, there were the French patients, Bache and Leborgne, whose cerebral strokes, well-timed deaths, and prompt autopsies helped establish the cortical localization of certain speech functions (Krech, pp. 46*ff*.). And then there was the famous unfortunate, Alexis St. Martin. He was a French-Canadian hunter whose stomach wall was opened by the accidental discharge of a shotgun, thus enabling the first systematic observations of the process of digestion. This observation proved to be of great value in initiating research into the problem of the physiology of hunger (Rosenzweig, pp. 84*ff*.).

But the mere occurrence of accidents is not enough; the scientist must be prepared to capitalize on the accident, to see its possible implications. In short, the scientist must be liberally endowed with *serendipity*—the art of discovering the unexpected when seeking for something else. In order to understand better just why some scientists under some circumstances will exhibit serendipity and some will not, we must turn our attention now to the characteristics of scientists and the conditions of their work.

THE SCIENTIST

As WE HAVE SEEN, scientists are subject to human frailties, succumb to error and emotional bias. Like all people, scientists are driven by diverse motivations, egocentric as well as truth-seeking; like all people, scientists show extreme diversity in temperamental traits. Understanding of the course of scientific history requires an understanding of these aspects of the personalities of scientists and of their characteristic ways of working.

Scientific history, like all history, can be written in two quite different ways. It can be written on the one hand as a story of the massive achievements of certain giant figures, geniuses such as Freud whose impact on the path of science is plain for all to see (MacKinnon and Dukes, p. 662). This might be thought of as the "Great Scientist" theory of scientific history. This theory finds one of its minor but revealing expressions in the eponymous proclivities of scientists—the labelling of anatomical structures, physiological processes, scientific laws with a specific scientist's name. In psychology we have "Broca's area," "Weber's Law," the "James-Lange Theory," etc. It seems to be the fate of most eponyms, however, that their legitimacy cannot bear too close examination. Thus the study of the circumstances leading to the discovery of the cortical speech center would seem to suggest that the eponym, "Auburtin's area," would be as appropriate as, or even more appropriate than, "Broca's area" for that center (Krech, pp. 46–7). That the attempt to credit the discovery of almost any phenomenon to a single person is an enterprise of dubious merit is seen when we consider that usually it is not the *first* scientist making the observation who gets the credit for it, but rather the scientist who *systematically exploits* such an observation. This seems to have been the case, for example, in the "discovery" of the conditioned response (see Rosenzweig, pp. 80, 88, 90).

At the other extreme the scientific story can be written in terms of an "inevitability" theory of history. What counts in this view is not the particular scientist, however great, but the surrounding context of his work, the particular stage of a science, the whole body of influences that would inevitably at a certain point produce a theory of evolution, or a heliocentric conception—if not by Darwin or Copernicus, then by someone else. In support of this "inevitability" theory one could cite the many instances of *simultaneous discovery* in science—the discovery of the same phenomenon or the formulation of essentially the same theories by scientists distant from each other, and sometimes by scientists who are unaware of each other's work. An interesting variant of this common phenomenon is recounted in McClearn's chapter (p. 160) when he points out that in 1900 three different investigators almost simultaneously and completely independently *rediscovered* Mendel's work. If one scientist won't do it, then another will; or if one scientist does it at the wrong time, three others will do it at the right time!

The truth obviously lies somewhere between these two extremes of the "great scientist" theory and the "inevitability" theory. We have already discussed the vital role of contextual influences on the course of a science. It is also plain to see that at certain crucial points in scientific history, a decisive influence is produced by a *particular* scientist; the particular step taken in theory, the particular experiment done, the particular technique invented reflect his particular personality.

Personality Differences

Clearly, there are distinctive temperamental differences among scientists which get reflected in their work. Some psychologists have a preference for "general" theory, others prefer "specific" theories; some eschew theory altogether and prefer to concentrate on collection of empirical data. Some psychologists spread their work over a wide spectrum: an example is Binet, of whom Tuddenham remarks, "There is scarcely an area or type of approach in modern psychometrics in which it cannot be said 'Binet was first,' yet his wide-ranging investigations were the antithesis of superficial" (p. 481). Another would be Sir Francis Galton, who worked in psychometrics, is seen as the "father of behavioral genetics" by McClearn (p. 155), was a creative statistician, worked on the nature of imagery, etc. Other psychologists, equally influential, specialize in a much narrower range.

Scientists differ also in their characteristic style of thinking. Some have a strong predisposition toward caution, a reluctance to stray very far from the safety of data, an insistence on precision and definiteness that may—carried to an extreme—render the individual so intolerant of ambiguity that he cannot be creative. Other scientists have a strong predisposition toward the seeking of all-embracing explanations; they may tend to overgeneralize, to overstate their case, and these tendencies carried to an extreme may impair their creativity through a lack of sufficient discipline in their thinking. Sometimes such an overstatement of a position can, however, be beneficial to the progress of the field. Thus, as Boring (1948) has pointed out, Gall's extreme arguments on brain functioning stimulated Flourens to productive research that he might not otherwise have done.

The fact that many scientists are likely to develop strong emotional attachments to their own ideas can have both positive and negative consequences. The necessity of defending their views may lead them into surprising blindnesses about possible alternative interpretations of their data. In this way, Goddard's strong dedication to a hereditarian view of intelligence blinded him to a possible environmental explanation of the feeblemindedness of the Kallikak family (McClearn, p. 181). But the necessity of defending their theories can also force scientists into creative reformulations. Some theorists, let it be noted, *can* and *do* change their imperfect theories in the light of their own new facts or the facts of others. A good example is that of Thorndike who was able, in the light of new evidence, to make basic revision in his law of effect by abandoning the "punishment clause" (Postman, p. 349).

Scientific creativity often requires that the individual be temperamentally capable of inventing, making use of, and being comfortable with *idiosyncratic* ideas and methods. Scientists obviously differ widely in this capability; for some of them anything but fairly orthodox approaches is "disturbing," while for others no approach is "out of bounds." Thus one physiologist, bent on experimental study of the physiological mechanism of hunger, did not hesitate to employ the phenomenological method of a "public opinion poll" to gather data on people's experiences of hunger (Rosenzweig, p. 94).

*   *   *

The foregoing pages, then, present some of the conclusions we have come to as we have examined and probed and "sounded" for the meaning of the events covered by the scientific case studies in this book. All we can add is our hope that the reader will find these introductory observations of some value, and our trust that as he reads the next eleven chapters he will discover other—and personally more useful—guides. For the well of history is bottomless, and he may probe as deeply as he wills.

REFERENCES

BORING, E. G. *Sensation and perception in the history of experimental psychology.* New York: Appleton–Century, 1942.

————. *A history of experimental psychology,* 2nd ed. New York: Appleton–Century–Crofts, Inc., 1950.

CONANT, J. B. *On understanding science.* New Haven: Yale Univ. Press, 1947.

KOESTLER, A. *The sleepwalkers.* New York: The Macmillan Company, 1959.

OPPENHEIMER, R. Analogy in science. *Amer. Psychologist,* 1956, *11,* 127–35.

PART I

Biological Foundations
of Behavior

CHAPTER 2

Cortical Localization of Function

DAVID KRECH

GALL AND SPURZHEIM

IF THE CONDITION of being puzzled is an effective motivating state for the scientist, then the problem of cortical localization of function has served the neurologist, brain anatomist, psychiatrist, and psychologist well. For there is perhaps no single experimental problem which has so intrigued and puzzled these scientists for so long a period of time as this "great question of differentiation of function in the cerebral cortex"—to use David Ferrier's characterization. And this condition of puzzlement continues even unto this day.

The modern story of research in cortical localization starts with some very simple observations made by the youthful Franz Joseph Gall.

> From earliest infancy, I lived in my family surrounded by brothers and sisters, and in the midst of a large number of comrades and fellow-pupils. Each of these individuals possessed something particular, a talent, an inclination, a faculty, which distinguished him from others . . . In the course of our studies some were distinguished by the beauty of their handwriting, others by their facility in arithmetic, still others by their aptitude for the study of history . . . some devoted their leisure to painting or to cultivating a garden, while their comrades enjoyed themselves in boisterous games. . . . In this manner

each one of us maintained his individual character [Gall and Spurzheim, 1810, p. 1].

Thus wrote Franz Joseph Gall in 1810. In his youth these differences in character and talent were a vexing concern for Gall, for he had
been repeatedly annoyed by schoolmates who were able to learn by
heart—with little effort—lessons which they did not in the least understand, while he found difficulty in memorizing even the smallest passages.

Born in Tiefenbronn Germany in 1758, he was sent at the age of
nine to study with his uncle, a curé in the Black Forest. It was there that
he first earned frequent criticisms for his failure to memorize his assign-
ments as well as did his companions. Later, at school in Baden, then at
Brûshal, and finally at the medical schools in Strasbourg and Vienna,
these facile memorizers "often took away from me the rank I had earned
in the written compositions" (*ibid.*, p. ii). Salient and annoying figures, Gall observed them carefully, and finally he discovered their secret:
"I noticed then that they all had large and protruding eyes, and I remembered that so had my rivals in the first school" (*ibid.*, p. ii). This
was a satisfying discovery, because it meant to Gall that this talent which
he lacked was a matter of bodily structure and his failure to memorize
his lessons was a fault of this sort and not a fault of understanding or of
effort.

Quite aside from the value that this idea may have had for Gall's
self-respect, his "discovery" of a relation between the ability to memorize and the structure of the head initiated a life-long search for the
structural basis of all individual differences in talents or abilities. This
search culminated in his doctrine of brain localization of function, a
doctrine which troubles and divides neurologists and psychologists even
today.

By training Gall was an anatomist. He and his pupil, J. G. Spurzheim (1776–1832), were responsible for many important and lasting discoveries in neuro-anatomy and neuro-physiology. Gall's neurological
work was primarily responsible for the first modern views of the function
of the cortex. Where formerly the cortex was considered as an inert "covering" of the brain (and hence its name), Gall realized that the cortex
consisted of functioning neural cells and surmised that these cortical
cells had contact with the brain below and participated in the function
of the subcortical brain. The demonstration of the crossing of the pyramids, the analysis of brain and spinal cord into gray and white matter,
and the recognition that the two hemispheres of the brain are symmetrical and united by the commissures are further examples of the neurological contributions of Gall and Spurzheim.

But Gall was not content with the study of anatomy. He wanted to know the functions of the brain as well.[1] And the answer to brain function, Gall and Spurzheim felt, was to be found by seeking correlations among brain structure, brain physiology, and behavior—a formula which still is the best guiding principle for research in this area.[2]

"An exact knowledge of the functions of any organic part," wrote Spurzheim, "requires an examination of its structure; for physiology without anatomy is unfounded, while anatomy without physiology is useless. We therefore never separate anatomy and physiology" (1815, pp. v, vi). This belief in the interdependence of structure and function served as *a priori* support for their thesis of brain localization. Their argument reduced to three basic principles: (1) The brain is the sole organ of the mind. (2) The basic character and intellectual traits of man are innately determined. (3) Since there are differences in character and intellectual traits among individuals as well as differences in various intellectual capacities within a single individual, there must exist differentially developed areas in the brain, responsible for these differences! Where there is variation in *function*, there must be variation in the controlling *structures*.

To put these principles to the test, an additional assumption was necessary—that there was a correlation between the shape of the skull and the conformations of the brain. With this assumption, one could measure differences of development in various brain areas and relate these differences to differences in behavior.

Although the general notion that the brain is the organ of the mind is an ancient one (Pythagoras held this view), Gall and Spurzheim were among the first neuro-anatomists to champion it, and they found it necessary to devote much of their writing to its defense. From their time on (although not necessarily because of their work alone) most scientists have willingly worked within that assumption.

Their second principle, that the behavior and personality of man were composed of innately given "faculties," found more resistance. The ideas of Gall and Spurzheim differed from those of the accepted faculty psychology of their day in two ways: In the first place, a good deal of the current psychology was empiricistic—the individual was what he was because of his *training and environment*. Gall, on the other

[1] Gall complained that in medical school "one would say much about the functions of muscles, of viscera, etc.; but no one told me anything about the functions of the brain and its various parts" (*ibid.*, p. iii).

[2] Note Spurzheim's "modern" comment on what has become known as the "interdisciplinary" approach: "The chief of the artificial impediments to the improvement of psychology was the blamable method . . . employed in the study of human nature. . . . The useful example of the Greek philosophers is neglected. Anatomy, physiology, medicine, philosophy, education, religion and legislation, instead of uniting their mutual influence, constitute so many particular doctrines or sciences" (1815, p. 8).

hand, insisted that the distinctive traits which set one individual apart from others were determined by *inherited neurological structure*. In the second place, Gall felt that the faculties of the accepted psychology ("intelligence," "attention," etc.) were too vague to be useful. Impressed as he was with individual differences, he wanted faculties, ". . . the different proportions of which . . . explain differences in individuals." Borrowing liberally from the Scotch and English psychologists and making whatever changes seemed to be necessary, Gall ended up with a long list of fairly specific faculties—"verbal memory," "memory for persons," "mechanical aptitudes," "self-esteem," "cautiousness," etc. Spoerl (1936) suggests that Gall's faculties are very similar to today's notion of personality traits as "units or elements which carry the distinctive behavior of a man." Whatever the merits of Gall's faculties, our major concern is not with their fate at the hand of science, but rather with the fate of phrenology's third and most enduring principle—the principle of brain localization of function.

Until Gall's time the brain was considered to act as a whole, a single unit without functional differentiation. Occasional suggestions of brain localization had been made from time to time (some as early as the thirteenth century), but the overwhelming scientific consensus was opposed to such views. The immediate reaction of the scientific world to Gall's doctrine that "the brain is composed of as many individual and independent organs as there are fundamental forces of the soul" (Spurzheim, 1815, p. 272) was ridicule and abuse.

In reading Gall and Spurzheim one must be impressed with the soundness and sophistication of their philosophy of science and the reasonableness of their general argument. Furthermore, their major proposition—brain localization of function—is one which later investigation seems to have supported. Why, then, did they find so little acceptance at the hands of their contemporaries? One might venture several reasons. In the first place, the nonscientific public quickly took over the whole doctrine of phrenology and made of it a quick and easy method of prognostication and of "personality analysis." As Boring points out, "Phrenology had a tremendous popular appeal. The most important and greatest puzzle which every man faces is himself, and secondarily, other persons. Here seemed to be a key to the mystery, a key fashioned in the scientific laboratory and easy to use . . . Quite early it came to occupy the position of psychic research today, looked at askance by most men of science because unproven" (1950, pp. 56-7). To have taken phrenology seriously would have put the scientist in the camp of the palmist, astrologer, and "crackpot." Every new scientific idea which appeals to the imagination of the uncritical enthusiast runs the risk of this kiss of death.

Secondly, and perhaps more importantly, while the general argument in support of brain localization was presented by Gall and Spurzheim in a reasonable manner, the specification of the details of the theory and the supporting data (mostly anecdotal, as we shall soon see) did not meet even the minimum requirements of validity, reliability, and objectivity which science was already beginning to demand. The difference between the theoretical arguments of Gall and Spurzheim in favor of brain localization, and their data and inferences in support of their theory, is quite astounding. As we read them, we almost get the feeling that we are reading two quite different sets of authors. (Note the difference between the tone of pages 252–69 and 277ff. of the following excerpts.) It would appear that their theory was premature and wildly overstated. This has happened many times in science. A theory—a very good theory—may be premature for many reasons. The spirit of the times may not be conducive for a favorable hearing; the older theory, already in the field, may not yet have outlived its usefulness; or the new theory may be premature because no valid supporting data can be adduced to spell out its implication in any specific manner and to discipline its speculations. The very same general theory, proposed at a later date, may be welcomed enthusiastically by the scientific world.

And now let us turn to Gall and Spurzheim "in person."

THE PHYSIOGNOMICAL SYSTEM OF DRS. GALL AND SPURZHEIM; FOUNDED ON AN ANATOMICAL AND PHYSIOLOGICAL EXAMINATION OF THE NERVOUS SYSTEM IN GENERAL, AND OF THE BRAIN IN PARTICULAR: AND INDICATING THE DISPOSITIONS AND MANIFESTATIONS OF THE MIND.[3]

INTRODUCTION (p. 1)

This system is commonly considered as one according to which it is possible to discover the particular actions of individuals: It is treated as an art of prognostication. Such however is not the aim of our inquiries. . . . The object of this new psychological system . . . is to examine the structure, the functions and external indications of the nervous system in general, and of the brain in particular.

[3] This is the title of Spurzheim's 1815 English publication from which the succeeding excerpts are taken. This publication represents an early and faithful account of their system in a less wordy style than does the six-volume *Anatomy and Physiology of the Nervous System* of Gall and Spurzheim, published over a period of ten years from 1810 to 1820. That Spurzheim's book presents a "faithful" account is testified by Gall's complaint in 1818 (referring to Spurzheim's French edition of this book): "Of one hundred and twenty pages . . . one hundred and twelve are copied from my own works. . . . He will say that he has the right to do this, because he is supposed to be the collaborator . . . At least he could have indicated the source of his riches. . . . Others have already accused him of plagiarism; it is, at the very least, quite ingenious to make up books by means of scissor snips" (1818, p. x). The reference page numbers given in the excerpts reproduced here are from the second edition (London).

THE BRAIN IS AN AGGREGATION OF ORGANS (pp. 166–80)

As it is demonstrated that the brain is exclusively the organ of the manifestations of the mind, it is to be investigated whether it is composed of as many particular and independent organs as there are particular and independent manifestations of the mind. . . .

Let us first examine, in a general way, the proofs which induce us to think that the brain must be considered as composed of different organs.

The beaver which builds its hut, the dog which hunts, the blackbird which sings, the swallow which migrates, cannot have similar brains. . . . Even individuals of the same variety do not possess all faculties in the same degree . . . hence the organization of their brains cannot be equally perfect. . . .

In the same individual, moreover, certain propensities, sentiments and intellectual faculties manifest themselves with great energy, while others are scarcely perceptible. . . . Hence the same mass of the brain cannot preside over the same functions. . . .

The propensities and intellectual faculties do not manifest themselves simultaneously. . . . Certain faculties are very energetic in children, and others appear only in adult persons. . . . Now if the manifestations of all faculties were dependent upon the same organ, they ought to appear and disappear simultaneously.

The state of disease proves also the plurality of the cerebral organs: for how is it possible to combine partial insanities with the unity of the brain?

He then takes up several objections to the thesis of plurality. Among these is the objection that ". . . by this separation of the organs the unity of organization would be destroyed." This he answers in the following way:

It is certainly impossible to deny the mutual influence and dependence of the different organs; and in fact none can insist upon this truth more than we do. There is, however, a great difference between the correct assertion, that the different organs exert a mutual influence upon each other, and the incorrect one, that each part does not exert its particular function.

METHOD OF STUDYING PHYSIOGNOMY, OR, RATHER, THE FACULTIES OF THE HUMAN MIND [4] (pp. 252–69)

In this study, as in every other, our leading principles are observation and induction. We, therefore, begin by observing what man is, and not what, according to the prejudiced opinions of some philosophers, he ought to be. The first thing, then, to be observed and generally know is, that . . . each individual differs from another by his peculiar character.

[4] The term "phrenology" was not introduced until after 1815 (Boring, 1950, p. 59).

Let me now state the means which are fit for determining the organs of the manifestations of the mind. Gall compared all energetic actions with the greatest development of any part of the brain; and when he found that a greater development of any cerebral part corresponded with any given energetic action, he supposed that this part of the brain might be the related organ. The probability then increased in the same proportion as the number of observations was multiplied. Moreover, if the head of any individual presented any protuberance, which was evidently the result of cerebral development, Gall endeavoured to be acquainted with the talents or the dominant character of the person. . . . In these two ways did he determine all the organs he discovered [See Figure 1].

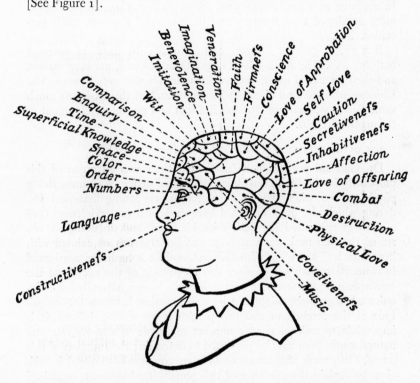

FIGURE 1. Diagram of cranial representation of Gall's system. This drawing was made from a leaflet announcing one of Spurzheim's lectures in London. (From D. Krech and R. S. Crutchfield, *Elements of Psychology*, p. 481. Published by Alfred A. Knopf in 1958, and used with their permission.)

We have been able to collect innumerable facts by our visits to establishments for education, to hospitals for idiots and madmen, to houses of correction and to prisons, and by our intercourse with different nations and with all classes of society.

Gall soon felt the necessity of making a collection of casts of indi-

viduals remarkable for any quality, whether talent or moral sentiment.
. . . By these means he was enabled to multiply and rectify his observations.[5]

As the arrangement and position of all parts which are common to
man and animals are the same, it is very useful to compare with each
other animals which are endowed with the same faculties, and also to
compare them with animals which are destitute of these faculties.
. . . Thus, the comparative anatomy and physiology of the brain may
contribute greatly to determine the organs. . . .

The diseased state of the brain and its accidental injuries may also
be taken advantage of, in order to determine particular organs. . . .
In madmen with partial insanities, the respective organs are commonly
more developed than the rest, and their external signs are easily perceived. . . .

It is of the greatest importance to consider the heads of different
nations. . . . The foreheads of negroes, for instance, are very narrow,
and their talents of music and mathematics are also very limited. The
Chinese, who are fond of colours, have the arch of the eye-brows much
vaulted, and we shall see that this is a sign of a greater development of
the organ of colour.

ORGAN OF AMATIVENESS (physical love) (pp. 277–85)

Dr. Gall did not originally think that there was an organ of this
propensity in the brain; but discovered its existence by chance. Being
physician to a widow who was subject to very strong hysterical fits,
during which she drew her head backward with great violence, Gall
sometimes supported her head with his hand, and, in doing so, observed that her neck was very large and hot. He was acquainted with
her character [6] as well as with this fact, and he accordingly considered
in connection with her passion, this magnitude of the neck, and the
consequent development of the cerebellum: he was naturally led to inquire whether there might not be some relation between the magnitude of the cerebellum and this particular propensity. Indeed, it is
impossible to unite a greater number of proofs to demonstrate any
natural truth, than may be presented to determine the function of this
organ. First, none of the causes which are commonly admitted is sufficient to explain the existence of this propensity. Moreover, organized
beings which are propagated by buds, slips, or by cuts, have neither

[5] Bentley (1916) quotes Möbius to the effect that as early as 1802 Gall was said
to possess over three hundred skulls of persons whose mental characteristics he knew,
and one hundred and twenty casts of distinguished living persons. In subsequent years
these collections were largely increased. It is interesting to note that Gall's skull was
placed in the museum of the Jardin des Plantes in Paris, where Gall died in 1828.
Spurzheim, who died in Boston about five years later, left his skull to the Harvard
Medical Museum, ". . . its surface markings giving no clue to the splendid anatomical mind that was his" (Stookey, 1954, p. 565).

[6] Gall's case-history description of this patient makes it quite clear why she was
later referred to as "Gall's passionate widow."

brain nor cerebellum. . . . I think, indeed, that this organ and its special faculty are fairly established.

ORGAN OF COMBATIVENESS (pp. 301–4)

Dr. Gall, having called together boys from the streets, occasionally made them fight: there were of course some who were fond of it, and others who, on the contrary, were peaceable and timid. In the former, that part of the head which corresponds to the posterior inferior angle of the parietal bone, behind the mastoid process (or, in grown-up persons, generally about one inch and a half behind the ear) was prominent, and in the latter, the same place was flat or depressed. . . . The courageous animals have the head between and behind the ears very large. . . . This is an unfailing sign to distinguish or recognize if a horse be shy and timid, or bold and sure.

ORGAN OF SELF-ESTEEM (pp. 332–3)

Gall first found this organ in a beggar: in examining the head of this person, he observed in the midst of the upper posterior part of the head, an elevation which he had not before observed in so high a degree: he asked him the cause of his mendicity; and the beggar accused his pride as the cause of his present state, he having considered himself too important to follow any business: he therefore only spent money, and did not think of earning a livelihood. We have a great number of proofs as to this organ, and can establish its existence. Proud persons and those who, alienated by pride, imagine themselves to be emperors, kings, ministers, generals, etc. possess it in high degree.

ORGAN OF CAUTIOUSNESS (pp. 335–7)

Two persons at Vienna were known to be remarkable for their extreme irresolution; and therefore, one day in a public place, Gall stood behind them and observed their heads. He found them extremely large on the upper posterior part of both sides of the head; and this observation gave the first idea of this organ.

*   *   *

PIERRE FLOURENS (1794–1867)

ALMOST EVERYONE who was anyone in the scientific world of the early nineteenth century opposed Gall's and Spurzheim's phrenology. Logical arguments, experimental data, ridicule, and even governmental persecution were employed. But the one man who is given the major credit for "demolishing" Gall and Spurzheim was the French experimental neurologist, Pierre Flourens. As late as 1943, J. F. Fulton, the eminent physiologist, could write (in his historical note on the work on the frontal association areas) with some fervor about Flourens' achievement: "The earliest experiments were those of the French neurologist Flourens (1824), who, on the basis of ablation studies, cast to the four winds the phrenological doctrines of Gall and Spurzheim. Flourens denied the existence of functional localization, except in the most general sense . . . and he also rendered an important service in the history of Neurology by overthrowing the naive concepts of phrenology" (1943, p. 413).

Flourens' attack took the forms of logical and *ad hominem* arguments and experimental counter-evidence. Flourens preferred Descartes' philosophy of the unity of the soul to the phrenologists' "specificity" doctrine, and in his major attack on phrenology he "brought forth Descartes to confound Gall's doctrine" (Boring, 1950, p. 63). But contrary to Boring's characterization of Flourens as a man who "had the gift of annihilating an opponent . . . in fair play and without bitterness" (*ibid.*, p. 63), Flourens regarded Gall and Spurzheim as fair game for all kinds of demeaning practical jokes. Thus in Flourens' little popular book, *Comparative Psychology*, he repeats with relish such stories as the following:

> The famous physiologist, Magendie, preserved with veneration the brain of Laplace. Spurzheim had the very natural wish to see the brain of a great man.
>
> To test the science of the phrenologist, Mr. Magendie showed him, instead of the brain of Laplace, that of an imbecile.
>
> Spurzheim, who had already worked up his enthusiasm, admired the brain of the imbecile as he would have admired that of Laplace [1864, p. 234].

Our major concern, however, is with Flourens' brilliant and original experimental attack. His most significant achievement was the substitution of evidence from the laboratory for the phrenologists' uncontrolled observations of clinical and anecdotal material. He did this by developing a new experimental technique, the ablation experiment, in which specific areas of the brain are surgically destroyed or "ablated." This experimental innovation of Flourens has proved to be a most fruitful technique in neural-behavioral science. However, in bringing neural-behavioral studies into the laboratory and applying the ablation technique to them, Flourens *radically changed the original Gall-Spurzheim question and thereby altered the nature of the answer.* This is a recurrent pattern in the history of science. We might here recall the words of Flourens himself: "It is the method which gives the results" (1842, p. 502)—and perhaps add, "the method having first shaped the question."

The use of Flourens' laboratory technique limited him, of course, to work on the lower animals—pigeons, chickens, rabbits, etc. This meant several things. In the first place, since hens and pigeons have almost no cortex to speak of, insofar as Flourens' work and conclusions were largely based on experimentation with hens and pigeons, his work was irrelevant to the major point at issue: the function of the cortex. In the second place, since Flourens' work was entirely restricted to the lower animals, the behavior to be studied could not concern itself with specific mental "faculties" like "memory for persons," "pride," "music," "mathematics," "wit," "ambition," etc.—faculties and traits which were of major concern for Gall and Spurzheim. Instead of such faculties, ". . . the major proportions of which . . . explain differences in individuals," Flourens studied such general faculties (disregarding individual differences) as "perception," "intelligence," "will," and "coordination of the movements of locomotion"—behavior categories which Gall had deliberately discarded. And from the time of Flourens until very recently, the more ambitious search of Gall and Spurzheim—the search for the neurological basis of the personality and intellectual traits of man—was dropped in favor of Flourens' more limited and "manageable" objective, i.e., the search for the neurological basis of seeing, hearing, walking, etc.

Finally, quite aside from the unique human functions which Flourens could not (or would not) study, the results of his animal experiments were prejudiced by the lack of methods for recording, measuring, and distinguishing behavior patterns and capacities. Flourens could determine only whether this or that ablation resulted in stupor, wakefulness, inability to fly or to eat, and so forth. What effect such ablations had upon more particular functions could not be determined but only guessed at. This, of course, cannot be taken as a criticism of Flourens—we could hardly expect him to invent and develop a new science of animal behavior in addition to a neurological technique.[7] This development was to come only some eighty years later.

His experimental results led Flourens to two major conclusions. First: "The encephalon, according to my experiments, is a *multiple* organ, because it is composed of several organs, each distinct from the others by its function: the cerebrum, seat of the intelligence; the cerebellum, seat of the principle which coordinates locomotor motions; the medulla oblongata, seat of the very principle of life, etc., etc." (1864, pp. 247–8). Secondly: "The unity of the cerebrum proper . . . is one of the most important results of my experiments. . . . Indeed, not only do all perceptions, all volitions, in a word, all the intellectual faculties reside exclusively in this organ, but they all reside there coextensively, and without any one being separable from the others" (p. 249). In addi-

---

[7] As we have already noted, Flourens did publish, in 1864, a book entitled *Comparative Psychology* in which he argued for the principle that "psychology embraces all intelligent beings"; but in this book there is no suggestion that the *behavior* of animals can be experimented with in the laboratory. Here he bases all his conclusions on general observation, philosophical and rational arguments, and opinions of authorities. The only laboratory observations he refers to are his own ablation experiments.

tion to these two major conclusions, he arrived at a number of auxiliary generalizations—generalizations which were to be rediscovered and re-affirmed by Lashley a hundred years later. Among these were: (1) While the various sense organs might have separate and localized projection areas in the cortex, the *functional* value of this localization (the ani-mal's "perceptions") is dependent upon the cerebral cortex *as a whole*. (2) Loss of function is correlated with extent of ablation of cortical tis-sue. (3) If sufficient cortical tissue is left intact, the remaining tissue may take over the functions of the entire organ, i.e., there is restitution of function.

Flourens, in his differentiation of the functions of the cerebellum, the medulla oblongata, the corpora quadrigemina, and the spinal cord, does not completely deny the principle of localization, but redefines the functions with respect to which there is localization. It is because of this that E. G. Boring, the historian of psychology, sees Flourens as a beneficiary of Gall! Thus Boring writes:

> Gall's extremely specific psychophysiology accomplished two things. In the first place, it forced the problem of the correlation of mind and brain to the fore. . . . In the second place, by going to extremes, Gall made a radical but less extreme view actually seem conservative. With-out a Gall, Flourens might never have conceived the problem of find-ing different functions for the cerebrum, the cerebellum, the medulla and the cord; and Flourens' position was much strengthened because he could appear as a conservative correcting the pseudo-science of Gall and Spurzheim. It is the familiar case where the truth is more nearly approximated because a traditional belief that deviates from the truth in one direction is offset by the dramatic and vigorous exaggeration that deviates in the other direction. No scientist consciously cultivates error; yet the truth—a scientific truth which may last for a century be-fore some flaw in its formulation is discovered—is often the mean be-tween an established misconception and an hyperbole which has been built up to overcome the inertia of tradition [1950, pp. 61–2].

And now Flourens speaks:

RECHERCHES EXPERIMENTALES SUR LES PROPRIETES ET LES FONCTIONS DU SYSTEME NERVEUX DANS LES ANIMAUX VERTEBRES.[8]

EXPERIMENTS RELATIVE TO THE DETERMINATION OF THE ROLE AND FUNCTIONS OF THE CEREBELLUM [pp. 37–43]

I have removed, by successive layers, the cerebellum of a pigeon. During the ablation of the first layers, there appeared only a little weakness and disharmony in movements.

[8] This is the title of Flourens' major report of his experimental studies, first pub-lished in Paris in 1824. The page references given in these excerpts refer to the second edition of this work, published in 1842. In his book Flourens reserves a general discus-sion of his method for his last chapters, and this accounts for the failure of the ex-cerpts to follow an obvious logical development.

With the removal of the middle layers, an almost general agitation appeared, although there were no signs of convulsion; the animal performed abrupt and disordered movements; it heard and saw.

With the extirpation of the last layers, the animal, whose faculty of jumping, flying, walking, standing had been more and more disrupted by the preceding mutilations, lost this faculty entirely.

From all these facts combined, it follows: [pp. 48–50]

That the faculty of coordinating movements into walking, jumping, flying, or standing depends exclusively on the cerebellum.

On the other hand, once the cerebral lobes are removed, vision is lost, since the animal does not see; volition is lost, since it does not will; memory is lost, since it does not remember. It bumps twenty times against the same object, without having the idea of turning away from it; it flutters if it is struck, but does not think of fleeing.

If a movement is begun, the animal continues it, but never originates it spontaneously; it flies only if thrown up in the air, walks only when pushed, swallows only if the food is pushed into its beak. But, and this cannot be too much admired, flying, walking, or swallowing, once begun, are continued, and are accomplished with a perfect regularity and correctness.

All phenomena of intelligence and will have disappeared, yet all the phenomena of movement persist nevertheless.

It is not volition any more which determines the animal's movements; but some external irritation can replace volition and determine them just as well.

Surely nothing can better prove how completely *intelligence* and *volition* are distinct from *excitability*, and the parts wherein they reside from those that excite *contraction*.

GENERAL CONCLUSIONS [pp. 55–9]

The nervous system is not a homogeneous system. The cerebral lobes do not act like the cerebellum, nor the cerebellum like the spinal cord, nor the spinal cord like the nerves.

But it is a single system.

All its parts concur, conspire, consent. What distinguishes them is some particular and determinate mode of action; what unites them is a reciprocal action on their common energy.

The animal that has lost its cerebral lobes has not lost its *sensitivity*; it preserves it entire; it has lost only the *perception* of its sensations, it has lost only its *intelligence* [footnote, p. 79].

NEW RESEARCHES ON THE PROPERTIES AND FUNCTIONS OF THE VARIOUS PARTS WHICH MAKE UP THE CEREBRAL MASS [pp. 85–110]

Animals deprived of their cerebral lobes have therefore neither perception, nor judgment, nor memory, nor volition: for there is volition only if there is judgment, and judgment only if there is memory, and memory only if there has been perception. The cerebral lobes are therefore the exclusive seat of all the perceptions and all the intellectual faculties.

But do all these perceptions and all these faculties occupy the same seat in these organs, or is there, for each of them, a seat different from that of the others?

Here are a few experiments which fully resolve, it seems to me, this difficulty.

I carefully removed the whole anterior portion of the right cerebral lobe of a pigeon in successive layers, and the whole superior and middle of the left.

Vision weakened more and more, very gradually, as the extirpation progressed, and was finally lost on both sides only when the layers, near the central node of both lobes, were removed.

But, as soon as vision was lost, so was audition; and, together with vision and audition, all intellectual and perceptual faculties.

I removed on another pigeon, by equally careful and successive ablations of layers, the whole exterior and posterior of both cerebral lobes, up to a few millimeters from the central node of these lobes.

As the ablation progressed, vision diminished gradually and noticeably; audition weakened just as did vision; all the other faculties in the same manner; and as soon as one of these was completely lost, so were they all.

Finally, on a third pigeon, I completely exposed the central node of the two lobes by the successive and gradual ablation of all the superior, posterior and anterior layers.

With each new removal, vision lost some of its energy; and as soon as the animal saw no more, it also heard no more, willed no more, remembered no more, judged no more, and was exactly in the same situation as an animal totally deprived of its lobes.

Therefore, (1) it is possible to remove, either in front, or in back, or on top, or on the sides, a rather extensive portion of the cerebral lobes, without their functioning being lost. A rather restricted portion of these lobes suffices therefore for the exercise of their functions.

(2) As this removal progresses, all the functions weaken and die out gradually; and, past certain limits, they are completely gone. The cerebral lobes contribute therefore in their totality to the full and entire exercise of their functions.

(3) Finally, as soon as one perception is lost, all are lost; as soon as one faculty disappears, all disappear. There are not, therefore, different sites for the different faculties, nor for the different perceptions. The faculty to perceive, to judge, to will one thing resides in the same place as the faculty to perceive, judge, will another; and consequently this faculty, essentially one, resides essentially in a single organ.

Each of the various sense organs has its distinct origin in the cerebral mass. . . .

One can, therefore, by destroying separately each of these particular origins, destroy separately each of the four senses, at least all their effects, at one blow, by the sole destruction of the central organ where their sensations are transformed into perceptions.

· ·

We have just seen that it is possible to remove a certain portion of the cerebral lobes without these lobes losing their functions completely; there is more: they can recover them in their entirety after having lost them completely.

I uncovered a pigeon's central node by stripping off gradually successive layers of the two lobes; I stopped as soon as, by the effect of this removal, the animal had lost the use of all its senses and all its intellectual faculties.

From the very first day, the two mutilated cerebral lobes became enormous; their tumefaction diminished on the second day; it had almost disappeared on the third. Beginning then, the pigeon gradually reacquired sight, hearing, judgment, volition, and the rest: after six days it had recovered all; and what must be especially noticed is that as soon as it had recovered one of its faculties, it had recovered them all.

On another pigeon, I carried this on by stripping off a little further: this animal, like the preceding one, lost all its intellectual and perceptual faculties; but it recovered them only imperfectly.

On a third pigeon, I carried this removal further yet: and, this time, all these faculties were lost forever.

Thus, so long as the loss of substance suffered by the cerebral lobes does not go beyond certain limits, these lobes recover, after a certain time, the exercise of their functions; past these limits, they recover them only imperfectly; and past these limits, they do not recover them at all.

· ·

As a final result, then: such an immediately complete incapacitation of the organ by the loss of only one of its parts; such a complete restitution of its function by only a part of the organ; all this shows very well that each of these organs is nothing but a single organ: for the disturbance of a single point disturbs the whole, and the preservation of a single point restores all.

· ·

Unity is the grand principle which reigns.

*   *   *

The Clinic, the Autopsy Table, and the Laboratory (1861–76)

For about fifty years Flourens' ideas remained dominant, despite some opposition, notably from Bouillaud (1796–1881), a psychiatrist and neurologist who continued to champion the doctrine of specificity. Significantly, the opposition to Flourens' laboratory-supported doctrine of nonspecificity came from clinical medicine with its observed correlations between limited paralysis and limited cerebral lesions—correlations which seemed to demand differentiation of function in the cerebral hemispheres. If anecdotal data characterized Gall's period, and animal experimentation the Flourens era, then it can be said that an interaction between clinical observations and laboratory experimentation distinguished the next period—the period of the Clinicians Broca (1824–80) and Hughlings-Jackson (1835–1911) and the experimenters Fritsch (1838–1927), Hitzig (1838–1907), and David Ferrier (1843–1928)—French, English, and German champions of the localization hypothesis.

This period starts in 1861 with a series of lively debates before the Paris Anthropological Society and with "fresh" evidence from Broca's autopsy table which pointed toward a localized "speech center" in the third frontal convolution of the dominant hemisphere. The story then shifts to the English clinician, John Hughlings-Jackson, with his inspired guesses about separate motor centers in the brain, guesses based on his observations of the recurrent patterns of epileptic seizures among the patients of the National Hospital for the Paralyzed and Epileptic. These clinical guesses are then dramatically supported by the experimental work of the Germans, Fritsch and Hitzig—work which involved the invention of a radically new experimental approach to the problem of brain localization. And finally we turn our attention to Ferrier, a colleague of Hughlings-Jackson at the National Hospital and one of the great experimentalists in neurology, who almost immediately took up and extended the work of Fritsch and Hitzig, and after some four years in the laboratory ventured to report to the Royal Society that "*a scientific phrenology*" was now possible. Flourens' adage, "the method gives the results," which helped us understand his nonlocalization position, helps us now see why the localization hypothesis again gained ascendance.

For the opening chapters of this period we turn to Professor Stookey's (1954) revealing account: [9]

> During February, March, and April, 1861, a notable series of meetings of the Anthropological Society took place in Paris, in which Pierre Gratiolet, Ernest Auburtin, and Paul Broca participated, which culminated finally in the recognition and establishment of the principle of cerebral localization.
>
> This was a great debate . . . carried on primarily by Pierre Gratiolet, the fame of whose contribution in anatomy carried such tremen-

[9] The following excerpts are all taken verbatim from Professor Stookey's paper (1954), which offers a new interpretation of the role played by Broca, the French surgeon, in the discovery of the speech center.

dous weight . . . Nevertheless, undaunted, Ernest Auburtin, thirty-
six years old, Chief of Clinic at Charité, devoted pupil and son-in-law
of Bouillaud, repeatedly rose in the various meetings to disagree with
Gratiolet's concept that the brain acted as a whole and that localized
functional centers did not exist.

Auburtin, opposing the views of Gratiolet, insisted that the opinion
first expressed by Gall, and subsequently elaborated by Bouillaud,
namely that the faculty of speech was to be found in the anterior lobe,
had been adequately demonstrated clinically. To this Gratiolet replied that research thus far had failed to find any localization of faculties in the brain.

In order to bring the discussion which had taken place at length to a
final conclusion, Auburtin on April 4 challenged those who opposed
cerebral localization by saying, "On the service of M. Bouillaud, I
have studied for a long time a patient named Bache who has lost his
speech, who nevertheless understands all that is said to him. . . .
This man will die, without doubt, in a short time. In view of the
symptoms which he presents, I have made a diagnosis of the softening
of the anterior lobes. If at autopsy the anterior lobes are found intact,
then I shall renounce the ideas which I have sustained. . . ."

Five days after this challenge, a patient, Leborgne, having been admitted at the age of twenty-one, was transferred from the medical
service of Bicetre where he had been for thirty-one years [having developed a critical leg infection] to the surgical service of Broca. . . .
During thirty-one years Leborgne had lost his speech, being only able
to say "Tan," and was known by that name throughout the hospital.
On admission, Tan's intelligence was normal. . . . Since this patient
apparently presented the symptoms described by Auburtin in the debate before the Anthropological Society and it was obvious that the
patient could not survive, Broca invited Auburtin to examine the
patient to determine if the patient fulfilled the criteria set forth by
Auburtin, so that the challenge made by Auburtin could be settled.

Broca stated: "In view of the fact that M. Auburtin only a few days
before had declared that he would renounce the idea of cerebral localization if a single case in whom the loss of the faculty of articulate
language were demonstrated to him without a lesion in the anterior
lobes, I invited him to see my patient, to know above all what would
be his diagnosis and if this observation would be one of those whose
findings he would accept as conclusive. In spite of the complications
which had supervened during the last eleven years, my colleague found
the present condition sufficiently clear to conclude without hesitation
that the lesion had had its origin in the anterior lobes."

At autopsy the left frontal lobe was adherent to the dura, was soft,
the convolutions destroyed, resulting in a cavity the size of an egg
filled with fluid in the posterior part of the second and third frontal
convolutions.

At the April session of the Anthropological Society, Broca merely
placed Leborgne's brain in evidence. . . .

It was recognized that the duration of the disease in Leborgne and the gradual progressive extension of the disease process perhaps did not permit of a precise determination of the point of origin of the primary focus. However, on October 27, Broca fortunately had a second patient come to autopsy named Lelong, eighty-four years of age, who had had a sudden loss of speech a year and a half before, during which interval he had been able to say only three or four words. Death followed a fracture of the neck of the femur.

As soon as the brain was placed on the table, it was at once apparent that a superficial circumscribed lesion occupied the left frontal lobe immediately below the anterior extremity of the sylvian fissure. . . . The lesion was far more circumscribed than the one that existed in the brain of Leborgne; in comparing the two specimens it was apparent that the center of the lesion was identical in the two cases. The right hemisphere was perfectly normal.

. . . .

This discovery of 1861 provided an effective impetus for the search for localization of function in the brain. Three years later Hughlings-Jackson noted an association between speech defects and right-sided chorea, and suggested that there was "no more difficulty in supposing that there are certain convolutions superintending those delicate movements of the hands which are under the immediate control of the mind, than there is one, as Broca suggests, for the movements of the tongue in purely mental operations." [1]

Some of Hughlings-Jackson's guesses were more specific. For a brief description of these, and for an introduction to the story of their experimental verification, let us turn for a moment to David Ferrier's account as presented in his famous report, *The Functions of the Brain* (first published in 1876): [2]

Hughlings-Jackson, from a minute and careful study of the phenomena of unilateral and limited epileptiform convulsions, arrived at the conclusion that they were due to irritation, or discharge, of certain convolutions of the opposite cerebral hemisphere functionally related to the corpus striatum and muscular movements. Though he furnished many arguments in favour of his hypothesis, since verified, his views were regarded merely as ingenious speculations, and devoid of any actual proof . . . The determination of these functions of the hemispheres and of the different parts had to be founded only on the results of vaguely established experimental lesions in the lower animals, or on the complex assemblage of phenomena met with in connection with

[1] Quoted from Penfield and Boldrey (1937, p. 390).

[2] It is instructive to note that this famous work of an experimentalist was dedicated to "Dr. Hughlings-Jackson who from a clinical and pathological standpoint anticipated many of the more important results of recent experimental investigation into the functions of the cerebral hemispheres."

the fortuitous and indefinite experiments of disease in man. Everywhere doubt and discrepancy prevailed. A new era in cerebral physiology was inaugurated by the discovery by Fritsch and Hitzig in 1870 that the application of the galvanic current to the surface of the cerebral hemisphere in dogs gave rise to movements on the opposite side of the body—movements which varied with the position of the electrodes [1886, pp. 222–3].

What Fritsch and Hitzig had done was to apply a galvanic current ("of sufficient intensity to cause a distinct sensation when applied to the tip of the tongue") through bipolar electrodes to various areas of the dog's hemisphere. From the anterior half they obtained movements of muscle groups in the opposite half of the body. In this area they were able to map five different motor points. From the posterior half of the brain they secured no motor movements. This seemed to demonstrate, quite clearly, some degree of specification of a "motor center" in the brain. Again we had localization—this time from the laboratory. And again, it was a new method which seemed responsible for the change in the scientific acceptance of the doctrine. This new method of Fritsch and Hitzig no longer necessitated "vaguely established experimental lesions" and could be applied (as it was, for the first time in 1874) to experimentation upon conscious man.[3] Ferrier assessed the value of the method (in the second edition of his book) in these terms: ". . . the indications furnished by the electrical irritation of the hemispheres have so guided and directed experimental and clinical research, that the physiology of the brain has made greater advances during the last ten years than in all the previous years of physiology and pathology together" (1886, p. 223)—a judgment which would find confirmatory evidence for the next seventy years.

Ferrier, "primarily in order to test the views of Hughlings-Jackson," quickly took up this method and soon published the results of repeated cortical stimulation in several species, among them being monkeys, dogs, jackals, cats, rabbits, rats, guinea pigs, pigeons, fish, and frogs. The net result of Ferrier's work was the final (to date) establishment of the principle of localization of *sensory* and *motor* function in the brain. With the publication of his book (and other subsequent supporting work by many scientists), the "great question of differentiation of function in the cerebral cortex" came to the end of one phase and was now ready for another major reformulation—a reformulation which was to be made this time by psychologists—and a reformulation which again was to bring on "doubt and discrepancy." But before taking up this next period, let us read in Ferrier's great classic.

[3] The account of work with electrical stimulation of man's cortex will be given in a later section, pp. 62–8 of this chapter.

THE FUNCTIONS OF THE BRAIN [4]

FUNCTIONS OF THE CEREBRUM [pp. 220–9]

Though it is by means of the cerebrum that we feel and think and will, the question is whether, by physiological or pathological investigation, we can throw a light on psychological manifestations; whether the cerebrum, as a whole and in each and every part, contains within itself, in some mysterious manner inexplicable by experimental research, the possibilities of every variety of mental activity, or whether certain parts of the brain have determinate functions.

Up to a comparatively recent date, if we except the cumbrous cross-divisions and fanciful localization of "faculties" of the phrenological system, the results of experimental physiology and human pathology had been considered as opposed to the localization of special functions in distinct regions of the cerebral hemispheres. . . . The doctrine of Flourens met with very general acceptance. . . .

A new era in cerebral physiology was inaugurated by the discovery by Fritsch and Hitzig. . . . I verified and extended the facts first indicated by Fritsch and Hitzig. . . .

The great and significant feature of the reactions produced by electrical excitation of the cortex is that they are definite and predictable, and vary with the position of the electrodes. As will be seen in the following chapter, areas in close proximity to each other, separated by only a few millimeters or less, react to the electrical current in a totally different manner. If there were no functional differentiation of the areas under stimulation the diverse effects would be absolutely incomprehensible. . . . [5]

EXPERIMENTS ON MONKEYS [pp. 235–56]

The surface of the cerebral hemispheres in macaques, the species of monkeys usually employed in these experiments, is divided into certain lobes and convolutions by certain primary and secondary fissures or sulci. . . .

The points of electrical irritation are indicated on the accompanying figures [See Figure 2] by areas or circles which mark the extent of the regions stimulation of which gives rise to certain more or less definite and constant movements. . . . The boundaries are deter-

[4] The following excerpts are taken from the second edition of the book, London, 1886, and are restricted to a discussion of the functions of the cerebrum.

[5] In 1906 Charles S. Sherrington dedicated his great *Integrative Action of the Nervous System* to "David Ferrier in token of recognition of his many services to the experimental physiology of the central nervous system" and continued to express admiration and astonishment at the precision of Ferrier's results: ". . . it is surprising that by our relatively imperfect artifices for stimulation we should be able to obtain clear evidence. . . . Remarkable that electrical stimuli applied to the organ of mentality yield with regularity certain localized movements from certain restricted areas of its surface" (pp. 269–71).

mined by frequently repeated application of the electrodes on and around these areas. . . .

The following are the phenomena most constantly observed:

(1) On the superior or postero-parietal lobule. *The opposite hind limb is advanced as in walking* . . .

(2) On the upper extremity of the ascending parietal, and adjoining portion of the ascending frontal convolution. *Flexion with outward*

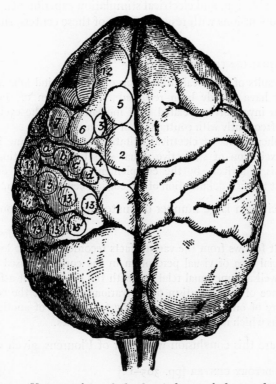

FIGURE 2. Upper surface of the hemispheres of the monkey. The circling and included numerals are explained in the text. This figure is a reproduction of Ferrier's Figure No. 69 found in his *Functions of the Brain,* 1886.

rotation of the thigh, rotation inwards of the leg, with flexion of the toes.

. . . .

(5) On the ascending frontal convolution at the base of the superior frontal. *Extension forwards of the opposite arm.*

. . . .

(12) Including the posterior half or two-thirds of the superior and middle frontal convolutions. *The eyes open widely, the pupils dilate, and head and eyes turn to the opposite side.*

. . . .

OCCIPITAL LOBE

I have never obtained any reactions on stimulation of the occipital lobes, while at the same time, and with the same strength of current, the reactions above described were one or all readily obtained.

. . . .

For his investigations of "sensory centers" Ferrier has recourse to anatomical, ablation, and electrical stimulation experiments. We excerpt his major conclusions with respect to two of these centers, the visual and auditory.

THE VISUAL CENTER [pp. 270–305]

The results of electrical stimulation of the occipital lobe and angular gyrus have already been recorded . . . irritation of the angular gyrus was invariably associated with movements of the eyeballs . . . and very frequently with contraction of the pupils.

The phenomena of electrical irritation appeared to me indicative of the excitation of subjective visual sensation, and, acting on this hypothesis, I arrived, by the complementary method of destructive lesions, at the first delimitation of the cortical center of vision.

After citing a large number of anatomical and ablation studies, he concludes:

. . . It follows from the various facts recorded that the localization of a special area of visual perception in the cortex is based on structural as well as functional relations with the eyes; so that a functional equivalence of indifferentism of the various regions of the cortex and the theory of one region compensating for the loss of another are assumptions which involve anatomical impossibilities.

Compare this conclusion with that of Flourens, given earlier.

THE AUDITORY CENTER [pp. 305–12]

. . . In addition to the strong presumption furnished by the character of the electrical reactions that the superior temporo-sphenoidal convolution in the monkey is the center of hearing, the results of localized destruction of this convolution are such as to prove this beyond all doubt.

Again he cites the results of various experiments, concluding with an account of "experiment 13":

In this animal the superior temporo-sphenoidal convolution was cauterized in both hemispheres; and, as was found on careful examination, the lesions were accurately confined to this convolution . . . without inflammation or secondary extension. . . .

Six weeks after the operation the animal was exhibited before the physiological section of the International Medical Congress in London, 1881, along with another monkey affected with right hemiplegia from lesion of the motor area of the left hemisphere. While it was climbing about, and disporting itself before the audience, a percussion cap was exploded, causing the hemiplegic monkey to start suddenly, while this one remained perfectly unconcerned, and gave not the slightest indication of having heard anything. All present admitted that the animal was undoubtedly deaf; it was defective in no other respect. . . .

Further proofs of the localization of the auditory centers in the superior temporo-sphenoidal convolutions are almost superfluous. . . .

THE HEMISPHERES CONSIDERED PSYCHOLOGICALLY [pp. 424–68]

Hitherto we have considered the brain chiefly in its physiological aspects, and the conclusion has been arrived at that the hemispheres consist of a system of sensory and motor centers. . . .

That the brain is the organ of the mind is a universally admitted axiom. We have no proof of subjectivity or modifications of consciousness apart from the action of the cerebral hemispheres. . . .

We have therefore many grounds for believing that the frontal lobes, the cortical centers for the head and ocular movements, with their associated sensory centers, form the substrata of those psychical processes which lie at the foundation of the higher intellectual operations. . . . Intelligence and will have no local habitation distinct from the sensory and motor substrata of the cortex generally. There are centers for special forms of sensation and ideation, and centers for special motor activities and acquisitions, in response to and in association with the activity of sensory centers.

There may be highly developed sensory centers and defective sensory apparatus, and highly developed motor centers and defective executive apparatus—conditions which must materially influence mental development. [Note, in the following concluding sentences, how closely Ferrier comes to the original Gall and Spurzheim position.] But other things being equal—if such a postulate can ever be reasonably made—there are grounds for believing that a high development of certain regions will be found associated with special faculties of which the regions in question are the essential basis. . . . That such a relation will be found to exist is more than probable, but on this point and many others, in the absence of rigidly determined data, I forbear to speculate.

*   *   *

FRANZ AND LASHLEY

AND THEN CAME the psychologist, with his interest in relatively complex animal as well as human behavior and his concern that *behavior* be studied objectively and measured quantitatively—a new emphasis in science.

The progress in neural-behavioral research had thus far spiraled around significant advances in *neurological* techniques—from the careful anatomical studies of Gall and Spurzheim, through the skillful ablation procedures of Flourens, to the electrical stimulation techniques of Fritsch and Hitzig and of Ferrier. The development of the other variable —behavior—lagged behind. To be sure, the protocols of the clinical neurologist were better than Gall's casual and fanciful observations, but in the laboratory no advances in the measurement of behavior had been made since the time of Flourens. Impressionistic observation of behavior was still the custom in the laboratory.

With the growth of the new science of animal psychology—at the very end of the nineteenth century—this one-sided development was changed. Now, for the first time, methods became available for the objective and quantitative differentiation of behavior patterns in experimental animals—of sensory and motor capacities, of learning and remembering processes, of motivational and instinctive patterns. The significance of these new methods was clearly foreseen by Sherrington. In his 1906 publication, in the very same chapter in which he had displayed so much admiration for Ferrier's work, he wrote: "The results before you must appear a meagre contribution toward the greater problems of the working of the brain; their very poverty may help to emphasize the necessity for resorting to new methods of experimental inquiry in order to advance in this field. New methods of promise seem to me those lately followed by Franz, Thorndyke [sic], Yerkes, and others; for instance, the influence of experimental lesions of the cortex on skilled actions recently and individually, i.e., experientially, acquired. . . . By combining methods of comparative psychology (e.g., the labyrinth test) with the methods of experimental physiology, investigation may be expected ere long to furnish new data of importance toward the knowledge of movement as an outcome of the working of the brain" (p. 307).

With the publication in 1902 of Sheperd Ivory Franz's (1874–1933) study (*On the Functions of the Cerebrum: The Frontal Lobes in Relation to the Production and Retention of Simple Sensory Habits*), this new phase in the history of the "great question" was officially opened. This first experimental paper on the question to be published by a psychologist had two epoch-making features:

(1) The major objective of the research was the examination of the relation of cortical functioning to "mental processes." [6] From now on, learning and problem-solving behavior was to be the concern of many of the brain-localization studies—rather than the traditional simple sensory reactions or motor reflexes.

[6] "The present research was undertaken to determine, if possible, the relation of the various so-called association areas . . . to simple mental processes" (Franz, 1902, p. 1).

(2) The major methods are twofold: "surgical procedures" and "determination of habits." From now on, neural-behavioral studies were increasingly to present objective and quantitative data on both the neural *and* behavioral side.

With this new method Franz obtained data which seemed inconsistent with Ferrier's brain-localization principles. Franz found that after a bilateral lesion in the frontal lobes, the newly formed habits were lost, but the "inherited and long-standing habits seemed to be retained" (p. 21). "Habits once lost after removal of the frontals may be relearned. After a second operation they are again lost, and may be regained a second time" (*ibid.*). No one part of the brain seemed to be the locus of learned habits. With further experiments Franz changed from holding a questioning attitude toward brain localization, to an aggressive and determined antilocalization position. By 1911, in his presidential address to the Southern Society for Philosophy and Psychology, Franz raised anew the banner of Flourens and lashed out against the "new phrenology"—his term of contempt for those who held to the localization doctrine. In this speech he was especially critical of the histological evidence in support of cortical localization:

> . . . It is within the past few years that our latest contributions to the doctrine of phrenology have appeared. These may be described in brief as the histological localization of mental processes.
>
> It was discovered that certain areas of the cerebrum differ both macroscopically and microscopically from other areas. . . .
>
> Brodmann has given the clearest pronouncement regarding the supposed value of these observations. He has written: "Physiologically unlike parts have unlike structure," and "parts of organs which differ structurally must have different functions." In these statements we have the entering wedge for a more complete phrenology than has been advocated since the time of Gall.
>
> . . . This view, however, cannot be accepted . . . we may say that mental processes are not due to the independent activities of individual parts of the brain, but to the activities of the brain as a whole. . . . We have no facts which at present will enable us to locate the mental processes in the brain any better than they were located fifty years ago . . . it would appear best and most scientific that we should not adhere to any of the phrenological systems, however scientific they may appear to be on the surface [1912, p. 328].

Thus was the same issue joined once again. For the next forty years this view and this method were to prevail in the monumental work of Karl S. Lashley (1890–1959), one of the most influential and productive psychologists who has worked in the field of neural-behavioral studies.

Lashley, a student of John B. Watson, early in his career worked with Franz, published with him, and then continued, on his own, the study of the effects of brain lesions on "intelligence"—using the white rat as his experimental subject. An indefatigable worker, he published studies of brain anatomy, founded several laboratories in psychophysiology, and through his many students and by his example set the pattern for much of the experimental work in that field for many years. Lashley's position on the question of brain localization is very clear. He could accept the work of Ferrier—as far as localization of sensory and motor centers was concerned—but saw very little relationship between such localization and the "major question"—the problem of the locus of "centers of control." Writing in 1937 he was to say:

> The principal sensory and motor areas have been delimited . . . [but] increasing knowledge of the facts of cerebral localization has only emphasized ignorance of the real reason for any gross localization whatever. . . . The separation of the sensory fields of the cortex may have no further significance than that the neuroblasts in the thalamic nuclei differentiate at different times. . . . On anatomic grounds alone there is no assurance that cerebral localization is anything but an accident of growth. . . . It has been assumed that the properties of experience are represented at the level of some simple nervous activity or in single loci: sensation in the sensory area, volitional pattern in the motor regions or particular forms of intelligent behavior in restricted coordinating centers. Such conceptions of localization are oversimplified and must be abandoned. . . . The position of Goldstein that the functions of every center are dependent on its relations to the rest of the intact nervous system, cannot be too strongly emphasized in considering problems of neuro-psychology [pp. 371, 375–6, 386].

Since he was interested primarily in learning behavior, and with his training in psychology, Lashley's work was to have an influence not only on the problem of brain localization, but on such more specifically psychological problems as the *nature of intelligence* (where he argued that his experiments "lend support to the theory which conceives intelligence as a general capacity" [1929, p. 173]), and the *nature of the learning process* (where he felt that his data "oppose theories of restricted reflex conduction").

Feeling that the doctrine of localization of function (in terms of his restatement of the problem) was untenable, Lashley proposed two major substitute principles (principles which are reminiscent of some of Flourens' conclusions). These were: (1) equipotentiality of parts, and (2) mass action.

> The term "equipotentiality" I have used to designate the apparent capacity of any intact part of a functional area to carry out, with or without reduction in efficiency, the functions which are lost by destruction of the whole. This capacity varies from one area to another and with the character of the functions involved. It probably holds only for

the association areas and for functions more complex than simple sensitivity or motor coordination.

Mass Function— . . . the equipotentiality is not absolute but is subject to a law of mass action whereby the efficiency of performance of an entire complex function may be reduced in proportion to the extent of brain injury within an area whose parts are not more specialized for one component of the function than for another [1929, p. 25].

These two principles, as well as his notions of the learning process, were criticized for their vagueness. Lashley acknowledged this criticism and replied: ". . . it seems better to admit ignorance and to be guilty of vagueness rather than to blind ourselves to significant problems" (p. 172).

And now let us hear Lashley's story in his own words:

BRAIN MECHANISMS AND INTELLIGENCE [7]

PREFACE [pp. ix–xi]

The experiments reported in the following pages are a continuation of a program, outlined some years ago, for an analysis of the neural mechanisms which play a part in learning. As the work has progressed, it has become increasingly clear that the associative or mnemonic process cannot be sharply distinguished . . . from other psychological processes. . . . In many ways they suggest the behavior which we designate as "intelligent," and it has seemed worth while to attempt to relate the results of the present experiments to the broader problems of intelligence. . . .

OBJECT OF THE PRESENT EXPERIMENTS [pp. 14–15]

The experiments to be reported are an attempt to sample the activities of the rat, to determine the correlations among them, and to test the influence of certain neurological variables upon them. . . .

The great majority of recent discussions of learning in animals have developed under the influence of the doctrine of random activities and the elimination of useless movements. Habits are conceived as successions of movements . . . as simple concatenations of conditioned reflexes.

I began the study of cerebral function with a definite bias toward such an interpretation of the learning problem. The original pro-

[7] This book, published in 1929, was Lashley's major work and his most influential contribution to the field. In terms of method, posing of problems, research results, and provocative theories, it represents a significant turning-point in the history of the experimental approach to the problem of brain localization of function. Much has happened since the publication of this book, and many of Lashley's methodological procedures now seem "obvious"—but at the time, they were revolutionary innovations. History has proceeded at a rapid pace within the last several decades. The following excerpts are used by permission of the University of Chicago Press.

gram of research looked toward the tracing of conditioned-reflex arcs through the cortex. . . . The experimental findings have never fitted into such a scheme. Rather they have emphasized the unitary character of every habit, the impossibility of stating any learning as a concatenation of reflexes, and the participation of large masses of nervous tissue in the functions rather than the development of restricted conduction-paths.

GENERAL METHODS [pp. 16–26]

The experiments to be reported include training of rats in a variety of problems either before or after destruction of parts of the cerebral cortex, with retention tests to determine the influence of lesions upon previously formed habits or upon retention of habits formed after injury.

THE INFLUENCE OF CEREBRAL LESIONS UPON THE CAPACITY TO LEARN [pp. 27–76]

Ten problems were finally selected for study. To test the influence of complexity of problem on degree of deterioration three mazes were used; and for the permanence of the defect, a fourth. For diversity of sensory components the brightness habit and the incline box were included. Retention tests for two mazes and the brightness habit, and a test for the ease of substituting one habit for another, completed the series.

We shall first consider the average effects of cerebral lesions, disregarding locus and magnitude. . . .

(A) Comparison of the massed records of the normal and operated animals brings out two facts clearly. (1) The operated animals are significantly inferior to normals trained under similar conditions in the learning and retention of a variety of mazes. (2) The inferiority is not uniform but is statistically reliable for all mazes. In contrast to this, there is no evidence of any inferiority in the formation or retention of the habit of brightness discrimination. . . . The results justify the conclusion that cerebral lesions may produce a marked reduction in the ability to learn and to remember some problems and at the same time leave the capacity with respect to other problems entirely unaffected. . . .

. . . .

The series of cases includes animals with lesions in various parts of the cerebrum. [See Figure 3] . . . We must first consider the influence upon learning of lesions in the different cortical areas. . . .

The range in extent of the lesions in the series of operated animals was from 1.5 to 81.2 per cent of the total surface area of the cerebrum. . . . Correlations between the magnitude of the injury and the amount of practice required for learning have been computed. . . . With one exception, retention of Maze I, the correlations are positive and in most cases in excess of three times their probable errors. . . .

The approximately equal correlations within the single fields further show that the retardation is dependent solely upon the extent of destruction, irrespective of its locus within the cerebral hemispheres.

Three of the problems used, Mazes I, II, and III, involve, insofar as one can determine, the same kind of sensory and motor processes. They differ in the length of the true path, in the number of turns to be made, and in the relative position of the turns, but present strictly comparable sensory situations.

For normal animals an increase in the number of culs-de-sac to be learned did not proportionately increase the difficulty of the problem. For the operated animals, on the contrary, increase in the number of culs-de-sac resulted in a disproportionate increase in the difficulty of

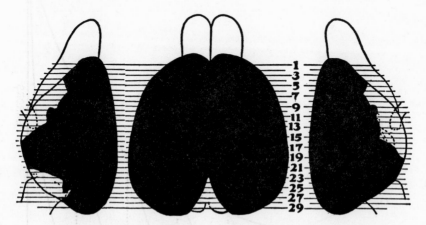

FIGURE 3.   The total area of the cortex explored in the rat for tests of the effect of lesions on mass learning and retention. This figure is a reproduction of Lashley's Figure No. 21 found in his *Brain Mechanisms and Intelligence*, 1929. Used by permission of the University of Chicago Press.

the problem . . . as the magnitude of the lesion increases, the difficulty of the problem becomes progressively greater [See Figure 4].

THE EFFECTS OF CEREBRAL LESIONS SUBSEQUENT TO THE FORMA-
TION OF THE MAZE HABIT: LOCALIZATION OF THE HABIT [pp. 86–
108]

The questions at issue may be summarized as follows: (1) Is the maze habit "localized" in any particular part of the cerebral cortex, i.e., is the habit abolished by the destruction of any particular area? (2) Is there any correlation between the degree of amnesia and the extent of the lesion either within a functional area or within the cortex as a whole? (3) Are qualitative differences in the character of the amnesia demonstrable, and do these correlate with variations in the position of the lesions within the general field of localization of the habit?

Approximately 75 animals were trained in the maze, subjected to

operations of the cerebral cortex, and subsequently tested for retention.

After presenting the data and their analysis, Lashley comes to the
following conclusions:

. . . This evidence . . . is opposed to the localization of the maze
habit in any single part or parts of the cortex. It supports, rather, the

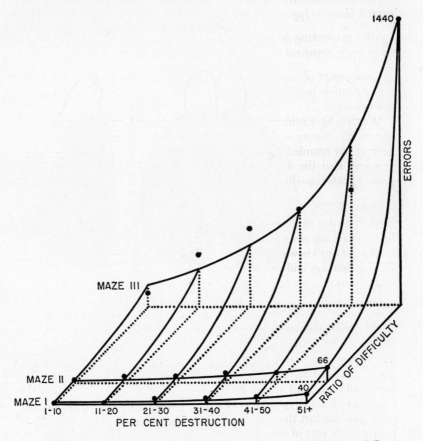

FIGURE 4. The relation between the extent of cerebral lesion, difficulty of the problem to be learned, and degree of retardation in learning. The separation of the three maze curves represents the relative
difficulty of the problems for normal animals; the abscissae of the
curves, the percentage destruction; and the ordinates, the number of
errors made during learning. This figure is based upon Lashley's (1929)
Figure No. 17. Used by permission of the University of Chicago Press.

view that any lesion which exceeds 15 per cent of the total cortex, irrespective of its locus, may produce a loss of the habit. This is in accord with the findings for retardation in initial learning.

. . . It is less certain, though probable, that all parts of the cortex participate equally in the performance of the habit and that lesions of equal size produce equal loss of the habit, irrespective of their locus.

We must now turn to the question of the qualitative effects of the lesions. Is the function of all parts of the cortex the same in kind or does each contribute special functions, such as visual or kinesthetic memories, which are summated in the normal functioning of the habit? . . . This will be the task in the following section.

THE RELATION OF REDUCED LEARNING ABILITY TO SENSORY AND MOTOR DEFECTS [pp. 109–19]

After presenting additional data from his brain-injured animals and from animals deprived of vision by blinding, Lashley concludes:

Comparison of the data on the cases enumerated above show little if any relation between the locus of injury and the type of post-operative behavior. . . .

We thus have evidence that the maze habit is not interfered with by any purely sensory or motor defect, that the formation of a sensory habit is not retarded by absence of the corresponding cortical sensory area, and that the deterioration following lesions in different cortical sensory fields is qualitatively the same for all fields.

COMPARISONS OF THE RAT WITH OTHER FORMS [pp. 142–56]

It is possible that the cerebral functions in the rat are not typical of the mechanisms at work in the higher forms. . . .

Most of our knowledge of cerebral function is based upon studies of the dog, monkey and man. I shall review briefly some of the work with these forms. . . .

After doing so, he concludes:

This brief summary of literature on other forms than the rat shows the similarity of problems which arise at all levels of complexity and the narrow limitations of our actual knowledge of cerebral mechanisms. Specialization of function of different parts of the cortex occurs in all forms, but at best this is only a gross affair, involving general categories of activity rather than specific reactions. The more complicated and difficult the activity, the less the evidence for its limitation to any single part of the nervous system, and the less the likelihood of its disintegration into subordinate physiological elements. . . .

. . . there is little evidence of a finer cortical differentiation in man than in the rat.

* * *

THE BRAIN SURGEONS

AT ABOUT the very time Franz and Lashley were challenging the localization thesis, the clinician returned to the field with new and effective support for localization. Actually, of course, the clinician had never left the field, but had continued in the pattern established by Hughlings-Jackson and Broca—studying the behavioral effects of disease in the human cortex. The experimentalist, however, placed little reliance on localization founded on the effects of cortical lesions induced by disease. Such lesions could not be clearly circumscribed and no means were available for discriminating between the direct and indirect effects of pathological processes. Ferrier had cautioned that such "experiments of disease in man" could "be made to support almost any doctrine, however absurd" (1886, p. 270). And yet it was impossible, so it seemed, to carry out precise, controlled, experimental manipulation of the living human cortex.

With the discovery by Fritsch and Hitzig of the electrical irritability of the cortex, however, a new method suddenly became available to the clinician—and from a passive observer he became an *active experimenter*, for within four years after the Fritsch and Hitzig report appeared, the method had been extended to the human cortex.

The first surgeon to stimulate man's cortex electrically and to observe the behavioral effects was Dr. Roberts Bartholow, "Professor of Materia Medica and Therapeutics and of Clinical Medicine in the Medical College of Ohio." We quote from his own account of the case of:

MARY RAFFERTY, *aet. 30;*
Born in Ireland; present residence, Cincinnati;
Occupation, domestic.
Admitted to the Good Samaritan Hospital, January 26, 1874

Mary is a woman of medium height . . . rather feeble-minded. . . . Thirteen months ago . . . a small ulcer appeared on the scalp, produced as she supposed by the friction of a piece of whalebone in her wig.

The skull is eroded and has disappeared over a space of two inches in diameter, where the pulsations of the brain are plainly seen.

Although rather feeble-minded, Mary returns correct replies to all questions.

As portions of brain-substance have been lost by injury or by the surgeon's knife, and as the brain has been deeply penetrated by incisions made for the escape of pus, it was supposed that fine needles could be introduced without material injury to the cerebral matter. . . .

The method of procedure was proposed to consist in tentative experiments with both currents (*a Galvanic and a Faradic*) on different parts of the brain. . . .

Observation 1. *Needles were inserted at various points into the dura mater and brain.* Mary declared, in answer to repeated questions, that she felt no pain. . . .

Observation 3. Passed an insulated needle into the left posterior lobe. . . . When the circuit was closed, muscular contraction of the right upper and lower extremities ensued. . . . Mary complained of a very strong and unpleasant feeling of tingling in both right extremities.

In order to develop more decided reactions, the strength of the current was increased . . . her countenance exhibited great distress, and she began to cry . . . left hand was extended . . . the arms agitated with clonic spasms; her eyes became fixed, with pupils widely dilated, lips were blue, and she frothed at the mouth.

Three days after this "experiment," Mary Rafferty died and Dr. Bartholow concludes: "It has seemed to me most desirable to present the facts as I observed them, without comment" (Bartholow, 1874).

Dr. Bartholow and Mary Rafferty (with a skull eroded, "as she supposed by . . . a piece of whalebone in her wig") had made several significant discoveries: (1) No pain was experienced by a conscious human being from weak electrical stimulation of the exposed cortex; (2) these weak currents applied to localized areas could produce fairly specific muscular contractions; (3) the patient whose cortex was being stimulated could report upon the accompanying "subjective" sensations. With these three discoveries the great era of the *surgeon-experimenter* was to begin. From now on, every human brain exposed for medical treatment was an open invitation to experiment. And many of these invitations were accepted.

Numerous surgeons soon verified Bartholow's observations, and in 1909 Harvey Cushing, at the Johns Hopkins Hospital, succeeded in producing *sensation without movement*. In a series of "second-stage" operations on two patients—"a sturdy and intelligent boy of 15 years of age" and "an intelligent man, aged 44"—Cushing was able to find a cortical area which seemed to produce only subjective "experience"— divorced from any motor components. The search for sensory functional areas could now be undertaken with as much precision as for motor areas. No longer was the surgeon to be limited to observation of gross movements—he could ask for detailed "introspective" reports from his patients, and the effects of limited and clearly localized cortical stimulation could now be studied upon the perceptual and "mental" processes available only through verbal reports of man.

From that point on a large body of evidence has been gradually accumulating in support of the localization doctrine. Perhaps one of the most productive and influential surgeon-experimenters in this field has been Wilder Penfield (1891———), Professor of Neurology and Neurosurgery at McGill University. Born within a year of K. S. Lashley, he has followed in his work the best tradition of Hughlings-Jackson and David Ferrier—combining the clinical and experimental study of localization of function. All told, he and his associates have reported on approximately 400 cases—operations carried out from 1928 (about the very time Lashley was preparing his famous monograph) to about 1950. And as was true for Hughlings-Jackson and Ferrier, Penfield found that his data supported a localization doctrine. With his new technique and with his human subjects, Penfield not only brings evidence of detailed sensory and motor localization (which Lashley could willingly grant), but also evidence of fairly precise cortical localization of visual and auditory *imagery*, of speech *skills*, of complex and integrated *memories, dreams, illusions*, and *hallucinations*—the very phenomena which Lashley was insisting were not localizable but were functions of the brain as a whole.

Penfield differentiates four major functional zones in the human cortex: (1) sensory and motor areas (along either side of the fissure of Rolando); (2) "elaboration areas" (adjacent to the sensory and motor areas) where stimulation produces arrest of the mechanism of an acquired skill, as in speech; (3) areas in which memories, hallucinations, illusions, and dreams are stored (temporal region); and (4) the anterior frontal areas in which epileptic discharge produces unconsciousness. The "seat of consciousness," where "the most important means of coordinating the functions of the cortical areas" are stored, Penfield places in the subcortical centers "which must lie within the mesencephalon and the diencephalon" (1950, p. 235). See Figure 5.

For a fragmentary indication of some of the most astounding and fascinating observations in the whole history of cortical localization research, we now turn briefly to Penfield and his patients:

THE CEREBRAL CORTEX OF MAN [8]

PREFACE [pp. ix–x]

During a period of nineteen years, one of us, W. P., has endeavored to make adequate records of brain operations which were carried out under local anesthesia. . . . These surgical procedures are not experiments, for we are dealing with human beings. But from time to time conditions present themselves which would satisfy the most exacting requirements of a critical investigator. . . . We shall draw upon the material of approximately 400 craniotomies under local anesthesia.

[8] This volume by Penfield and Rasmussen is dedicated by the authors to ". . . the succession of patients who have helped them understand many things, and to the physiologists whose basic work has guided them in this clinical study." Published in 1950, this book presents Penfield's most exhaustive analysis of his cases in support of his localization hypotheses. (Copyright 1950 by The Macmillan Company, New York; the following selections used with their permission.)

DESCRIPTION OF ROUTINE OPERATIVE PROCEDURES [pp. 4–9]

A brief description of the operative procedure in one case may serve to illustrate the conditions under which much of the data to be reported were collected.

Case G. C. A boy of 18 years gave a history of focal epileptic seizures which began with sensation in the left side of the body. . . . It was decided to carry out an osteoplastic craniotomy.

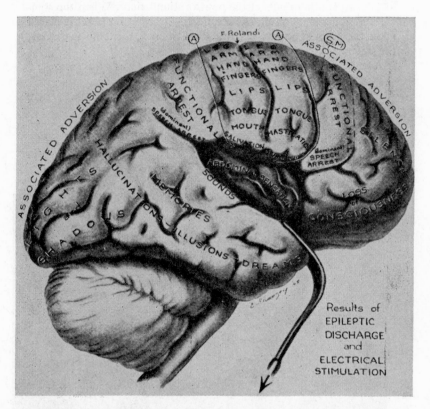

FIGURE 5. This figure is a reproduction of Penfield's Figure No. 120 found in his *The Cerebral Cortex of Man*, copyright 1950 by The Macmillan Company, New York, and used with their permission. It represents Penfield's view of cortical localization in the human brain. Compare this figure with Spurzheim's figure (Figure 1, page 37).

. . . The scalp was sterilized and Nupercaine was injected to produce analgesia. . . . After making the scalp incision, a bone flap was cut and turned downward upon the reflected scalp and temporal muscle. The dura was opened and the brain kept moist during the succeeding procedures by spraying it with Ringer's solution. . . . A small intracerebral tumor presented itself on the surface of this boy's cortex.

The surgical problem was to remove the tumor without damage to the precentral gyrus. . . . Consequently, the motor and sensory areas were mapped out carefully by stimulation. For this purpose a bipolar electrode was used with the points separated about 3 mm. . . . It is our custom to begin stimulation with a frequency of 60 cycles per second and a voltage of ½ a volt. The voltage is gradually increased until the first response is obtained.

During the stimulation a secretary sits in the viewing stand, separated completely from the operating room by glass, and the operator dictates to her the results of the positive stimulations. When the stimulation produces no result, she records this fact but no ticket is placed upon the brain. The first positive stimulation is therefore marked 1, the second 2. . . .

A few of the positive responses to stimulation . . . in this case:

Point 4 (1 volt)—Tingling, upper part of left leg.

7 (1 volt)—"Contraction of my left hand and arm." There was closure of the hand and pronation of the forearm.

25 (1 volt)—Sensation in tip of tongue.

27 (1 volt)—Sensation in left side of tongue.

Photographs were then taken of the brain with the numbers in place [See Figure 6].

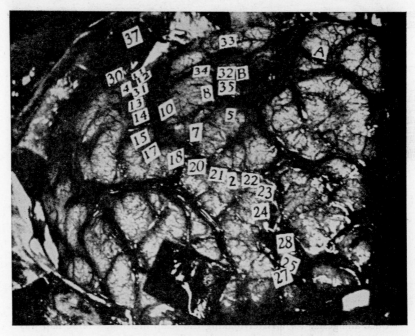

FIGURE 6.   Case G. C. Numbered tickets placed on each point where stimulation produced a positive response. At A and B the electrocortico-gram showed abnormality, and a small tumor is shown presenting between these tickets. This figure is a reproduction of Penfield's Figure No. 8 found in *The Cerebral Cortex of Man*, copyright 1950 by The Macmillan Company, New York, and used with their permission.

SOMATOSENSORY RESPONSES [pp. 21–5]

Sensory responses were elicited primarily from the cortex adjacent to the central fissure. . . .

The conclusion is that the major cortical representation of somatic sensation (proprioceptive and discriminatory) is in the postcentral gyrus. . . .

The *sequence of sensory responses* is almost invariable. . . .

The sensory cortex is thus apparently organized so that various bodily regions are represented in an orderly, constant manner, with, however, a variable degree of overlapping so that at any one spot on the sensory cortex there is represented a functional unit pertaining to some region of the body and possessing a low threshold to electrical stimulation.

SPEECH ARREST AND APHASIA [pp. 93–108]

Patients talk quite freely during cortical stimulation except when it is carried out in sensorimotor areas devoted to word articulation or in areas of cortex related to speech. Arrest of speech was recorded 74 times in the course of 35 operations. . . . The usual practice was to carry out stimulation without the patient's knowledge either while he was talking or counting. . . .

Case E. P. Left craniotomy. Second operation.

For details and corresponding figures, see pages 102–4 of Penfield and Rasmussen.

Objects, or pictures of objects, were shown to the patient one after another. . . . During the process, stimulation was carried out with the following results:

Point 31 (1½ volts)—Prevented naming, although it had not stopped counting. A child's top was shown to patient during stimulation. He said, "One of those things that goes." When the electrode was withdrawn, he said immediately, "Top."

32 (1½ volts)—Unable to name. After withdrawal, he said at once, "It's a bird," which was correct. This was repeated after an interval, using a comb. He was unable to name it, but explained afterward, "I knew it was a comb but I could not say it."

MEMORY, SENSORY PERCEPTIONS AND DREAMS [pp. 157–81]

This chapter will be devoted to the temporal lobes.

Hallucinations . . . may be produced by electrical stimulation of the temporal cortex. . . .

Case J. V. This patient was a girl of 14 years who had suffered from epileptiform seizures. . . .

Her attacks were characterized by sudden fright and screaming. . . . On careful questioning, it was learned that during the preliminary period of fright she invariably saw herself in a scene that she remembered to have occurred at the age of 7 years.

The scene is then described. For details of this case see pages 164–7 of Penfield and Rasmussen.

> . . . She occasionally had nightmares during her sleep and in the dream the scene was re-enacted. . . .
>
> *Operation.* An osteoplastic craniotomy was carried out under local anesthesia, exposing the posterior half of the right hemisphere . . . the exposed cortex was . . . explored with stimulating electrodes.
>
> Stimulation of points on the lateral aspect of the temporal lobe . . . produced in the patient different portions of her "dream" as follows:
>
> At a point near to 14 and 16 . . . stimulation had the following effect. She stared suddenly and then cried: "Oh, I can see something come at me! Don't let them . . ."
>
> Stimulation farther anterior caused the patient to cry out that she heard a large number of people shouting. . . .
>
> In summary . . . when the cortex was stimulated, this neurone pattern *referring to the "scene"* could be activated from different points although the cortex surely served as repository of innumerable other patterns. . . . When the electrodes were held in place for a longer period, the hallucination progressed like a story or memory unfolding.
>
> . . . .
>
> It is obvious that within the temporal cortex there are mechanisms which somehow play an important role in the act of remembering. . . .
>
> The organization of the temporal cortex is evidently different from that of other areas inasmuch as here alone electrical stimulation . . . activates acquired synaptic patterns. The fact that it is only in this region that such stimulation produces complex psychical illusions and hallucinations argues for some degree of localization of intellectual function.
>
> Although dreams have been analyzed hopefully and sometimes profitably from the day when Pharaoh called Joseph . . . little attention has been payed to their mechanism. . . . We have stumbled unexpectedly upon the location of the neuronal patterns "which dreams are made of" and have glimpsed other mechanisms within the humming loom of the mind.

*   *   *

POSTSCRIPT

THE STORY OF THE "great question of differentiation of function in the cerebral cortex" does not, of course, end with Penfield's patients confronting Lashley's rats, each bearing contradictory witness. At the present writing it would not even be correct to say that the evidence from the animal laboratory and that from the clinic are contradictory. Since Lashley's time other experimenters employing other animals have expended hundreds of man-hours in a continued search for the answer to the problem raised by Gall and Spurzheim. And the findings of these experimenters do not altogether agree with those of Lashley.

The equipotentiality and mass action hypotheses of Lashley were based primarily upon the results of experimental work with rats. But it was soon realized that what is true of the rat brain may not be true of the more highly developed brains of monkeys and men. As Herrick, the eminent neurologist, was wont to point out, "Men are bigger and better than rats."

Shortly after Lashley's work was published, ablation experiments were extended to the monkey. It was soon discovered that the monkey's cortex showed more specificity of function than did the cortex of the rat. For example, a task necessitating a high degree of directed attention seems to be interfered with when lesions are produced in the frontal areas of the monkey's brain. Lesions in other areas do not show the same degree of interference with this kind of problem-solving. Typical of the position of many animal experimenters is that taken by H. F. Harlow (1905————), one of the pioneers in the use of monkeys for neurobehavioral research. In summarizing a series of studies which investigated the effects of lesions on the anterior and posterior association areas in the cortex, Harlow writes: ". . . different kinds of intellectual functions are differentially susceptible to lesions located in the frontal and posterior association areas. . . . In no cortical association area have we found a lesion that completely destroys any intellectual function" (1952, p. 252). In other words, some kinds of problem-solving can be localized to some degree, but no kind of problem-solving can be localized completely.

In addition to increased experimental work with the higher animals, clinical observations on human beings have also been expanded. These clinical studies have found their subjects not only among the brain tumor patients and brain-injury accident cases (the traditional sources for such studies since the days of Broca and Bartholow) but in two additional "modern" sources. The first of these are patients suffering from gunshot wounds incurred in one of the many wars which have characterized the twentieth century, and secondly there are the schizophrenic patients who have had large parts of their cortex removed or connections of whole areas with the rest of the brain severed (operations performed in a therapeutic effort for which there has never been an adequate rationale).

The study of these numerous human cases corroborates in general the studies of the subhuman primate laboratory. The two sets of results point to some degree of specificity in the cerebral cortex. The exact nature and degree of this specificity is in dispute—as it has always been throughout the history of this "great question." Some research workers believe that in the frontal lobes are to be found the centers for "reasoning," or for the "elaboration of conscious thought," or for "attentiveness." Other experimenters refuse to commit themselves either to any specific list of "functions" or specific loci. Perhaps the following two propositions come close to a possible consensus:

(1) *No one kind of learning or mental process or function is dependent solely upon one area of the cortex.* Almost every part of the cortex seems to be involved in every kind of learning, mental process, or function. This is especially true of the complex behavior of man—the very kind of behavior which concerned Gall and Spurzheim. To this extent the general positions taken by Flourens and Franz and Lashley are corroborated.

(2) *The different areas of the cortex seem to play unequal roles for different kinds of learning, mental processes, or functions.* The various parts of the cortex do not contribute equally to every different learning task, or mental operation. We can "spare" certain cortical areas more readily than others. To this extent the positions of Broca and Ferrier and Penfield are corroborated.

It might appear, therefore, that the 150-year-old dispute between Gall and Flourens is finally going to end in a compromise. But this view, in the light of the history of this question, may be premature. The laboratories and clinics are still hard at work on this problem—and hard at work with many new techniques. Among these new techniques are the electroencephalography techniques, which permit the recording of evoked and spontaneous potentials from the central nervous system; the development of stereotaxic instrumentation, which permits accurately controlled stimulation and electrolytic destruction of focal regions deep within the substance of the brain; the implanted electrode techniques, which make possible electrical stimulation and measurement of the brain of a "free" and moving animal; the biochemical techniques which now make possible accurate and quantitative analyses of the biochemical composition of brain tissue. From the laboratories and clinics and through the use of these new techniques have come a number of new hypotheses—many of which are being put to rigorous test right now. Some of these hypotheses "reverse the field" and suggest that "centers" should be sought in subcortical areas rather than in the traditional cortical regions. Some hypotheses seek to correlate the control of behavior with differences in metabolic activity of the cortex rather than seeking relationships between structural areas and behavior patterns.

While these and many other hypotheses are still too recently arrived on the scientific scene for evaluation at the present time, it would be most imprudent if we were now ready to write finis to this story with the pious statement that a compromise seems to be in the offing. As every historically oriented student of science knows, new methods and new theories almost inevitably mean new formulations of the problem, new data, and new answers. The field of brain localization is not in short supply of either new methods or new theories. And as long as the laboratories and clinics are still hard at work on this problem, completely novel and unexpected answers and rebuttals are the only things we can safely expect. The history of the doctrine of specificity provides us with sufficient reason for this expectation. We have seen how Gall's specificity theory was first reformulated and then completely demolished by Flourens' careful and beautiful experimental work; some fifty years later, under a new formulation, and supported by new data from Broca's clinic and Ferrier's laboratory, the theory was revived and became the most respectable and fruitful of scientific hypotheses. After another fifty years or so, it was again vigorously attacked by the studies of Franz and Lashley—studies which introduced a new and vitally important concept in experimental design and which again reformulated the problem. And within the last several decades, in the hands of animal experimenters, brain surgeons, and clinicians, the doctrine has again been elevated to the position of an "obvious scientific truth." The story of scientific research in this, as in so many other areas, is a continuous, spiraling repetition of challenge and response.

REFERENCES

BARTHOLOW, R. Experimental investigation into the functions of the human brain. *Amer. J. Med. Sciences*, 1874, 67, 305–13.

BENTLEY, M. The psychological antecedents of phrenology. *Psychological Monographs*, 1916, 21, 102–15.

BORING, E. G. A *history of experimental psychology*, 2nd ed. New York: Appleton-Century-Crofts, Inc., 1950.

FERRIER, D. *The functions of the brain*, 2nd ed. London: Smith, Elder and Company, 1886.

FLOURENS, P. *Recherches experimentales sur les proprietes et les fonctions du system nerveux dans les animaux vertebres*, 2nd ed. Paris: J. B. Bailliere, 1842.

————. *Psychologie comparee*, 2nd ed. Paris: Garnier Freres, 1864.

FRANZ, S. I. New phrenology. *Science*, 1912, 35, 321–8.

————. On the functions of the cerebrum: the frontal lobes in relation to the production and retention of simple sensory habits. *Amer. J. Physiol.*, 1902, 8, 1–22.

FULTON, J. F.   *Physiology of the nervous system,* 2nd ed. New York: Oxford University Press, 1943.

GALL, F. J.   *Anatomie et physiologie du system nerveux en general, et du cerveau en particulier.* Vol. III. Paris: D'Hautel, 1818.

GALL, F. J., AND SPURZHEIM, G.   *Anatomie et physiologie du system nerveux en general, et du cerveau en particulier.* Vol. I. Paris: Haussman et D'Hautel, 1810.

HARLOW, H. F.   Functional organization of the brain in relation to mentation and behavior. In *The biology of mental health and disease.* New York: Paul B. Hoeber, Inc., 1952.

LASHLEY, K. S.   *Brain mechanisms and intelligence.* Chicago: University of Chicago Press, 1929.

——.   Functional determinants of cerebral localization. *Archives of Neurology and Psychiatry,* 1937, 38, 371–87.

PENFIELD, W., AND BOLDREY, E.   Somatic motor and sensory representation in the cerebral cortex of man as studied by electrical stimulation. *Brain,* 1937, 60, 389–443.

PENFIELD, W., AND RASMUSSEN, T.   *The cerebral cortex of man.* New York: The Macmillan Company, 1950.

SHERRINGTON, C. S.   *The integrative action of the nervous system.* New Haven: Yale University Press, 1906.

SPOERL, H. D.   Faculties vs. traits: Gall's solution. *Character and personality,* 1936, 4, 216–31.

SPURZHEIM, J. G.   *The physiognomical system of Drs. Gall and Spurzheim.* London: Baldwin, Cradock, and Joy, 1815.

STOOKEY, B.   A note on the early history of cerebral localization. *Bull. of the New York Acad. of Med.,* 1954, 30, 559–78.

CHAPTER 3

The Mechanisms of Hunger
and Thirst

MARK R. ROSENZWEIG

HUNGER AND THIRST affect behavior so broadly and pervasively that they have been studied over the centuries in attempts to improve understanding, prediction, and control of behavior. In this chapter we will consider questions about the bodily mechanisms that control eating and drinking: What mechanisms start a person or animal eating or drinking on a particular occasion? What stops it? What regulates the amount ingested? How do eating and drinking reinforce behavior?

Psychologists are currently working actively on these questions, as we shall see. Naturalists, physicians, and physiologists have contributed to this area from ancient times, and they continue to do so. At present, modern behavioral techniques coupled with modern physiological techniques are producing rapid advances in our knowledge of the mechanisms of hunger and thirst. Reviewing this area can therefore show us how the same behavioral problems were conceived and attacked at different periods in history.

First, however, let us note briefly some of the many ways in which hunger and thirst are taken up by the behavioral sciences. The description of the behavior of a species must include its food-getting activities; such description is the province of ethnologists, zoologists, and comparative psychologists. Anthropological descriptions of human behavior

73

have shown the rich diversity of customs and ceremonies surrounding eating and drinking among various cultures. In the molding of personality, situations involving hunger have often been considered vital. As an extreme case, the Siriono Indians of Bolivia are reported to be "a society in which the drive of hunger is so constantly frustrated as to have become the dominant motivating force in shaping habit and custom" (Holmberg, 1950, p. 93). ". . . The personality of the adult Siriono is itself a logical consequence of a lifelong struggle to secure enough to eat" (p. 98). Characteristic changes in personality have also been found to accompany starvation (Keys, Brozek, Henschel, Mickelsen, and Taylor, 1950).

In his laboratory the psychologist is often vitally concerned with hunger and thirst. The physiological psychologist may study them in their own right, as basic motives whose physiological mechanisms need to be understood. The experimental psychologist may use hunger and thirst as tools in order to determine the effects of motivation on behavior. Thus, human performance on perceptual and problem-solving tasks has been found to vary with time elapsed since the previous meal. With animal subjects, food and water are the most common of all incentives and rewards used to secure performance in experimental situations. As we will see in later sections, recent discoveries give promise of more direct and precise experimental control of motivation and reinforcement than has ever before been possible.

"LOCAL," "GENERAL," AND "CENTRAL" HYPOTHESES

THE FIRST MAIN PROBLEM to be tackled was how the body detects its needs. Many ingenious investigators have proposed different hypotheses to explain how depletion of food and water is detected. We will survey the development of the main hypotheses in roughly chronological order. Before starting our survey, we should note three main groups into which most hypotheses of hunger or thirst can be classified. This threefold classification was used by Luciani (1906). It consists of (1) local hypotheses, (2) general hypotheses, and (3) central hypotheses. These types of hypotheses have appeared and reappeared during the history of investigation.

The meaning of each of these types can be explained with the aid of Figure 7. Both the local and the general hypotheses are *peripheral* hypotheses. That is, they hold that hunger arises from changes detected "out in the body" rather than in the central nervous system. *Central* hypotheses, on the contrary, hold that hunger reflects changes detected within the brain. Local hypotheses were proposed by the earliest investigators of the problem (and by some recent ones, as well). They suggested that hunger arises in the stomach or its vicinity. Because they as-

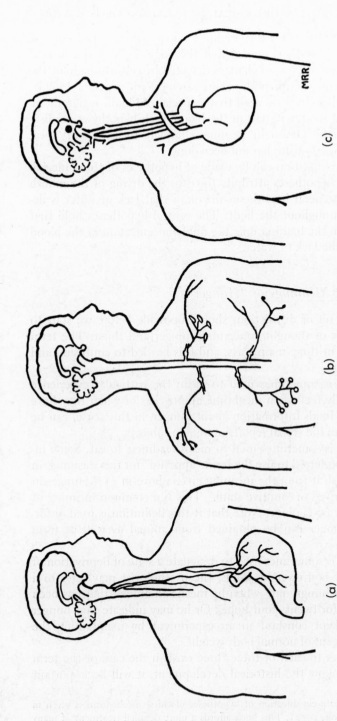

FIGURE 7. Diagrams of (a) local, (b) general, and (c) central hypotheses of hunger.

(a) According to the local hypothesis, "the stomach is the sense organ for hunger." In the figure, the stomach is shown connected to the brain by the vagus nerve.

(b) According to the general hypothesis, hunger is detected by changes in cells throughout the body. In the figure, a few different types of cells in various parts of the body are indicated schematically along with the afferent nerves that carry their messages to the central nervous system.

(c) According to the central hypothesis, a specialized center in the brain monitors the food supply in the blood. The figure indicates both a center in the basal region of the brain and part of the circulatory system.

signed a precise location for the origin of hunger, their hypotheses are often called "local." Others denied that the origin is local and instead ascribed hunger to widespread changes detected by cells throughout the body; for this reason, their hypotheses are often called "general." Finally, still other researchers hypothesized that a specialized brain region monitors the supply of food materials in the blood; such hypotheses are usually called "central." (It might be more complete to call them "local central" hypotheses, but this has not been done.)

The same classification can be made of hypotheses of thirst mechanisms. The local hypotheses attribute thirst to the drying of the mouth and throat. The general hypotheses maintain that lack of water is detected by cells throughout the body. The central hypotheses hold that specialized cells in the brain sample the fluid concentration of the blood and thus detect the lack of water.[1]

Different Meanings of "Hunger"

One further set of distinctions should be made before we start to survey the history of thought concerning hunger and thirst. The term "hunger" is used in three main ways, and this has led to confusion and misunderstanding:

(1) Hunger is sometimes used to mean the particular experience that people usually feel when meal-time approaches or when they have been deprived of food. Information about hunger, in this sense, can be obtained only from the verbal reports of human subjects.

(2) Hunger is sometimes used to mean readiness to eat. Some investigators have preferred to use the term "appetite" for this meaning, in order to distinguish it from the meaning given above in (1). Hunger in this sense is a "drive" or "motive state." This is a common meaning of hunger in current psychology. Note that if this definition is used, information about hunger can be obtained from animal as well as from human subjects.

(3) Hunger is sometimes used to designate a state of deprivation of food or deficit of body weight. Thus, the psychologist may refer to a "twenty-four-hour hungry rat" when he means an animal that has been deprived of food for twenty-four hours. Or he may indicate that hunger motivation was kept constant in an experiment by maintaining the animals at 80 per cent of normal body weight.

Parallel usages to each of these three exist in the case of the term "thirst." As we follow the historical development, it will be important

---

[1] A more elaborate classification of hypotheses of thirst mechanisms is given in the book *Thirst* (Wolf, 1958). This book affords a more detailed treatment of many aspects of thirst than can be presented here.

to see what usage each person employs (and sometimes to see what confusion among usages he shows.)

EARLY LOCAL HYPOTHESES OF HUNGER AND THIRST

Teachings of Antiquity

PLATO.   Investigators in antiquity had made some progress in the study of hunger, relying chiefly upon medical experience and upon comparative behavior and anatomy of animals. They discussed both the sensation of hunger and readiness to eat. In the ancient Academy of Athens, some held that hunger occurs whenever the alimentary canal is empty. Plato (429–347 B.C.) referred to this teaching in his dialogue *Timaeus*. The main speaker in this dialogue claimed that men could not have become philosophers if their long and capacious intestines had not freed them from constant hunger!

> They who framed our kind knew what would be our incontinence in the matter of meat and drink, how greed would move us to consume much more than need and due measure call for. Since, then, they foresaw this . . . they appointed what is called the abdomen to be a receptacle for the future surplus of meat and drink and made the guts wind and coil within it, lest quick transit of nutriment through them should force the body to crave fresh nutriment too quickly, make it ravenous and so render the whole tribe of us, through gluttony, incapable of philosophy and music, deaf to the voice of our divinest part [Taylor, 1929, p. 76].

(This passage anticipates by over two thousand years Claude Bernard's famous dictum, "Stability of the internal environment is the essential condition of the free life.")

ARISTOTLE.   Aristotle (384–322 B.C.), also a member of the Academy of Athens, made intensive studies of comparative behavior and anatomy. He found support for the hypothesized relationship between hunger and emptiness of the alimentary canal. In a discussion of the eating habits of different species of animals, he attributed gluttony to particular anatomical characteristics of the stomach and intestines:

> Now in all such animals as it behooves to be more temperate in the consumption of food than those we have been considering, the lower stomach presents no wide and roomy spaces, neither is their gut ever straight, but has numerous convolutions. For amplitude of space causes desire for ample food, and straightness of the intestine causes quick return of appetite. And thus it is that all animals whose food receptacles are either simple or spacious are of gluttonous habits, the latter eating enormously at a meal, the former making many meals at short intervals [Ogle, 1882, p. 90].

GALEN.   It remains to tell how the emptiness of the alimentary canal is translated into hunger. A partial answer was provided considerably later by the great Graeco-Roman physician Galen (A.D. 138–201). Galen localized responsibility for the sensation of hunger in the stomach. He pointed out that the stomach is well supplied with sensory nerves which convey information to the brain. The following passage, from a section on the nerve supply of the stomach, indicates much of Galen's views about hunger:

> Some doctors claim that the organs attached to the stomach have an equally precise sensation and hold that the desire for food is as great in them as in the stomach. It seems to me that the sensation is feeble in those organs but strong in the stomach and particularly at its entrance where most of the nerves seem to end. Thus this part of the stomach is the most sensitive, and it is especially in this place that persons seized by violent hunger feel contractions and, so to speak, pangs and gnawing. . . . [Daremberg, 1856, p. 591].

In view of much later developments, it is interesting to note that Galen spoke of *contraction* of the stomach in hunger.

In his many books, Galen summarized the medical and physiological knowledge gained up to his time, and he made original contributions that have led some to call him the founder of experimental physiology. Thus, he added greatly to the knowledge of the nervous system by making experimental lesions in the brains of animals and by transecting various nerves. At the same time he reached many erroneous conclusions. For example, he taught that the pituitary gland secretes mucus from the brain into the nose and throat. The name "pituitary" still reflects this misconception (pituita = mucus). There is no opening between the pituitary and the nose or throat, but in this case truth did not overtake error for 1,500 years. The long lag occurred when scientific investigation in the West dwindled away during the decline of the Roman Empire and throughout the period when the Church ruled over education. Not only did investigation stop, but much of the knowledge gathered by the Greek scientists was lost during the Dark Ages, which extended from about the third to about the eleventh century A.D. Western Europe finally recovered Galen's works from Arabic sources during the twelfth century. When anatomical dissection began again, in the thirteenth century, it was employed largely to demonstrate Galen's teachings. Although Galen was not a Christian, his anatomical and physiological teachings were favored by the Church during the Middle Ages, and they remained the unshakeable authority until the Renaissance. Résumés of Galen's writings were used as medical textbooks throughout the Middle Ages and even into the seventeenth century.

Local Hypotheses Survive the Renaissance

With the coming of the Renaissance, anatomy and physiology began to stir again, but it was the seventeenth century before experimental studies of digestion were performed. From this time onward, however, there is a steady progress of investigation and hypothesis to report.

HALLER'S LOCAL HYPOTHESES. Extensive consideration was given to hunger and thirst by Albrecht von Haller, the most eminent physiologist of the eighteenth century. Haller's *Primae Lineae Physiologiae* (1747) has been called the first textbook of physiology. In it he related both hunger and thirst to sensations arising from parts of the alimentary canal, thus continuing the peripheral approach of the ancient authors. Here are some key passages of his work, as given in an American translation of 1803:

> We are induced to take food, both from the sense of pain which we call hunger, and from that of the pleasure imparted by the sense of taste. The first of these proceeds undoubtedly from the folds of the stomach, which possess great sensibility, being rubbed against each other, by the peristaltic motion, and by the pressure of the diaphragm and abdominal muscles, so that naked nerves being rubbed against naked nerves excite an intolerable degree of pain [p. 313].
>
> Thirst is seated in the tongue, [throat], oesophagus, and stomach. For whenever these parts, which are very sensible, and naturally are moistened by their mucus and salival juices, grow dry from a deficiency in the secretion of those humours, or from muriatic or alkalescent salts adhering to them, a much more intolerable sensation is produced, as thirst is attended by much greater danger, and does not abate until the abundance of water, being restored to the blood, and the obstruction removed from the secreting vessels in the parts mentioned, they are again moistened [p. 314].

These hypotheses offered explanations for two aspects of hunger and thirst. In the first place, they gave direct explanations for the *sensations* of hunger and thirst. Secondly, it was assumed that these unpleasant sensations led the person to eat and drink, since these acts offered the only means of ending the sensations of hunger and thirst. Thus the *urge to ingest* was explained as well as the sensation of need.

In the case of thirst, Haller's account indicated that the need varies with circumstances. Working brings on thirst, he noted, because it causes perspiration which removes water from the body. Thirst abates only when water is again made abundant in the blood. In the case of hunger, there was no such approach to a quantitative treatment. Hunger would be felt, according to this hypothesis, whenever the stomach was empty, because then its inner folds would rub against each other.

ROBERT WHYTT ANTICIPATES SALIVARY CONDITIONING.   Haller
mentioned, without elaboration, that hunger makes saliva flow. His contemporary, Robert Whytt (1763), gave a much fuller account which
anticipated later work on hunger and conditioning of responses:

> We consider . . . that the remembrance or *idea* of substances for-
> merly applied to different parts of the body produces almost the same
> effect as if those substances were really present. Thus the sight, or
> even the recalled *idea* of grateful food, causes an uncommon flow of
> spittle into the mouth of a hungry person; and the seeing of a lemon
> cut produces the same effect in many people [1763, p. 280].

It must have been age-old knowledge that the mouth may water at
the thought or sight of food. Many physiologists were to mention this
phenomenon during the eighteenth and nineteenth centuries—Erasmus
Darwin (1796), Dumas (1803), Müller (1838), Bidder and Schmidt
(1852), and Bernard (1856, 1872). Nevertheless, it seems that no one
bothered to study this effect until Pavlov began to elaborate the concept of the conditioned reflex, 134 years after Whytt's account. As we
shall see later, Pavlov came to study conditioning through his research
on digestion and the neural control of gastric secretion.

ERASMUS DARWIN'S LOCAL HYPOTHESES.   Erasmus Darwin (the
grandfather of Charles Darwin) agreed with Haller that the sensation of
hunger is due to the state of the stomach. He disagreed, however, concerning the actual state, since he attributed hunger to the *inactivity* of
the empty stomach. Darwin set forth his views in a book on "laws of
organic life" (1796). He attributed both hunger and thirst to a lack
of proper stimulation:

> Hunger has been fancifully ascribed to the sides of the stomach rub-
> bing against each other, and to the increased acidity of the gastric
> juice corroding the coats of it. If either of these were the cause of hun-
> ger, inflammation must occur, when they had continued for some
> time; but, on the contrary, coldness and not heat are attendant on hun-
> ger; which evinces, that like thirst it is owing to the inactivity of the
> membrane, which is the seat of it . . . [1796, p. 125].

During the next century a number of authorities asserted that the
empty stomach is quiescent, and several others asserted that it is active.
Little was done to investigate this question directly until the very end of
the nineteenth century.

Darwin also observed that learning could affect both the timing of
hunger and the amount of food required. This sort of observation was
soon to be used to support the hypothesis of central control of hunger.
Darwin, however, merely set these facts down without noting that they
seem to impair the adequacy of a local theory:

The sense of hunger as well as of thirst is liable to acquire habits in respect to the times of its returning painfulness, as well as in respect to the quantity required to satiate its appetency, and hence may become diseased by indulgence, as well as by want of its appropriate stimulus. Those who have been accustomed to distend their stomach by large quantities of animal and vegetable food, and much potation, find a want of distention, when the stomach is empty, which occasions faintness, and is mistaken for hunger, but which does not appear to be the same sensation. I was well informed, that a woman near Lichfield, who eat [2] much animal and vegetable food for a wager, affirmed, that since distending her stomach so much, she had never felt herself satisfied with food; and had in general taken twice as much at a meal, as she had been accustomed to, before she eat so much for a wager [p. 126].

AN EARLY PAIR OF GENERAL HYPOTHESES

THE VARIOUS LOCAL hypotheses that had been suggested by the start of the nineteenth century were all rejected as "miserable explanations" by the physiologist C. L. Dumas (1803). For example, he claimed that "the walls of the stomach, however they may approach and touch, cannot produce a painful rubbing from which the feeling of hunger has been supposed to come. Furthermore, what is there in common between this vague rubbing, this irregular shock, and the fixed, constant sensation, of need for food?" (1803, pp. 53–4).

Dumas hypothesized that hunger and thirst both depend upon changes in the nervous system and that both types of change reflect information from sensory systems distributed widely throughout the body:

> We explain the cause of hunger by the absorbant action of the lymphatic vessels which, after having exhausted the nutritive juices, act upon the organs themselves and produce a sort of weak suction whose stimulating effect [is] communicated to the nervous system. . . . The cause of thirst is explained by the dominant action of the vascular system which, charged with caloric and blood, produces a sort of inflammatory irritation which affects the nervous system . . . [pp. 65–6].

Both hunger and thirst are thus of *general* origin, since the lymphatic and vascular systems ramify so widely through the body.

Partly because of the prevailing stress upon sensation, the local theories remained dominant. Critics of Dumas suggested that he confused the local feelings that cause us to eat and drink with the general bodily states that result from lack of food and water (Chaussier and Adelon, 1814). After Dumas' hypotheses were dismissed, relatively little

---

[2] Here Darwin was using the old past tense, pronounced "et."

was to be heard of general hypotheses until the very end of the nineteenth century.

EARLY NEUROLOGICAL OBSERVATIONS AND HYPOTHESES

Tests of the Local Hypothesis of Hunger

Since it was generally accepted early in the nineteenth century that the state of the stomach determines hunger (Chaussier and Adelon, 1814), several French investigators began to experiment on the nerve supply of the stomach. They removed the pneumogastric nerves in animal subjects; these are nerves that carry impulses from the stomach to the central nervous system. This treatment, Leuret and Lassaigne found, did not reduce eating in horses, and Sedillot obtained the same result in dogs (Milne-Edwards, 1879, p. 492). The result was seen as incompatible with the hypothesis that the urge to eat originates in the stomach. It was noted, however, that the horses seemed to have an impaired control over cessation of eating, for after the operation they would eat even when the stomach was full.

Flourens' Experiments on the Brain

The pioneer neurophysiologist, Pierre Flourens, removed parts of the central nervous system in animals and studied the effects on a variety of behaviors. He delivered a renowned series of lectures on this work in 1822–3 (Flourens, 1842). Removal of the cerebral hemispheres in birds, he reported, produced the loss of all sensation and all volition. Such birds would not take food or water by themselves and would starve in the midst of plenty. They could, however, be kept alive for many months if food and water were put in their mouths. Flourens believed that he had demonstrated from the effects of partial ablation of the hemispheres that "all perception and all volition occupy the same seat in these organs; the faculty of perceiving, of conceiving, of will thus constitutes an essentially unitary faculty" (p. 109).

Magendie and "General Laws of Organization"

Another pioneer of neurophysiology, François Magendie, also attributed the primary control of hunger and thirst to the central nervous system. (Magendie and Charles Bell are familiar to students of physiology and psychology as the two independent discoverers of the law of spinal roots; i.e., that the ventral spinal roots are motor and the dorsal roots are sensory.) Magendie's important text, *Précis elémentaire de physiologie*, came out in a number of editions from 1817 on and was widely translated. On hunger and thirst, his position remained unchanged from the first edition on. He stated that he had never seen the stomach in a contracted state during starvation, although he had looked for this in several experiments. He attacked vigorously each of the local hypotheses that had been advanced to explain hunger. Magendie's own hypothesis was a vague central one—apparently a "general central" hypothesis. This passage summarizes his position:

> Hunger results, like all other internal sensation, from action of the nervous system; it has no other seat than this system itself, and no other causes than the general laws of organization. Proofs of the truth of this assertion are that hunger continues sometimes, though the stomach be full of food; that it may not develop though the stomach be empty for a long while; finally, that it be ruled by habit to the point of stopping spontaneously when the usual hour for eating is past. This is true, not only of the feeling that occurs in the region of the stomach, but also of the general weakness that accompanies it . . . [1838, p. 274].

Magendie's position on thirst was similar to his position on hunger: "Thirst is an instinctive sentiment; it comes essentially from organization . . ." (p. 274).

Curiously, in considering the mechanism of satiation, Magendie referred only to the stomach and not to the nervous system. The accumulation of food in the stomach leads first to an agreeable feeling of satisfaction of a need. Continued eating leads to a feeling of fullness, and, if further continued, leads eventually to nausea. The volume of food is not the only factor: "All other things being equal, a nutritive food leads more quickly to the feeling of satiety" (p. 286).

In asserting that hunger originates in the central nervous system, Magendie anticipated later workers. It is clear, however, that he could offer little direct evidence to support his assertion. It may be that he was influenced by the discovery of the brain center that regulates respiration—a discovery made by his student Legallois in 1812. As we shall see later, another student of his, Moritz Schiff, was to propose a detailed central hypothesis of hunger in 1867.

Johannes Müller's Views

Johannes Müller considered hunger and thirst and many other topics of psychological interest in his renowned *Handbuch der Physiologie des Menschen* (1838). Müller is now best known to psychologists for his formulation of the law of specific nerve energies in the *Handbuch*. This law states that each type of sensory nerve can serve only one type of sensation, no matter how the nerve is stimulated; thus, whether the optic nerve is stimulated by pressure, by electricity, or by radiant energy, we have a visual sensation in each case—we perceive only the state of our

sensory nerves. Müller's work (and that of his students, such as Helmholtz) was of great importance in the development of both physiology
and psychology. Müller was a master of several disciplines and urged the
coordination of different fields as, for example, in this aphorism: "No
one can be a psychologist without being a physiologist."

Müller did not adopt a clear-cut hypothesis about the hunger mechanism, but he stressed the role of the nervous system. The local lack of
the stimulus of food in the digestive organs, he believed, is made known
by the nerves to the sensorium (the perceptual region of the brain).
This localized sensation of hunger can be relieved by affecting neural
activity at any of several levels, from the stomach to the brain: ". . . the
sensation of hunger is put an end to, by the change which the assumption of food produces in the state of the gastric nerves, by strong impressions on the sensorium and the active states of it excited by passions or
meditation, and by the change produced in the brain itself by taking
opium, etc." (1838, p. 485). Müller distinguished these localized sensations from more general effects of fasting that are felt throughout the
body. Magendie had made the same distinction, and many subsequent
writers continued to consider separately the localized and the generalized sensations of both hunger and thirst.

DIRECT OBSERVATION OF THE STOMACH IN ACTION

Beaumont's Observations on Alexis St. Martin

A curious accident now made it possible to observe the stomach in
action—the first major American contribution to physiology. In 1822
Alexis St. Martin, a young French-Canadian hunter at Fort Mackinac
on the American frontier, was gravely injured by the accidental discharge
of a shotgun. A large hole was torn in his side, and the stomach wall was
opened. An Army surgeon, Dr. William Beaumont, nursed the injured
man slowly back to health during the next two years. The aperture in the
body wall narrowed down to become a tube or fistula. Food no longer
escaped, but the fistula could easily be pushed open to allow access to
the stomach. Dr. Beaumont tried by every means to make the fistula
heal over, even suggesting an operation, which his patient refused. Only
when it became clear that the fistula was permanent did Beaumont
gradually realize that he had the opportunity to experiment on many of
the perplexing problems about digestion. He had already made some
unsystematic observations, but now he undertook several lengthy series
of experiments on his recovered but not always cooperative patient.[3]

[3] "Not always cooperative" is probably an understatement. After the first brief
series of experiments in 1825, St. Martin disappeared. When Beaumont finally learned
of his whereabouts four years later, St. Martin was working in Canada; he had married
and had two children. Beaumont hired him to return to the United States with his

Beaumont's first article on this case was published in 1824, and he wrote a full account of his research in 1833. The unusual opportunity for dis' covery and Dr. Beaumont's thorough use of it quickly made this case a classic in medical and physiological history.

PHYSIOLOGICAL, PSYCHOLOGICAL, AND PSYCHOSOMATIC DISCOVERIES. Beaumont not only observed the process of digestion within the stomach, but, with gastric juice obtained through the fistula, he was also able to reproduce digestion outside the body. Many of his observations are important for psychology as well as for physiology: Anticipating much later observations of Pavlov, Beaumont noted that the swallowing of food excited the secretion of gastric juice much more than did direct stimulation of the stomach (1833, p. 207). He also observed that emotional conditions affected gastric secretion and activity (a basic "psychosomatic" discovery). For example, when St. Martin became angry the flow of gastric juice stopped; when he became calm, the flow started again (pp. 86 and 107). Of direct importance for the study of hunger was the discovery that putting food directly into the stomach allayed hunger and stopped the motions of the stomach:

Experiment 65

To ascertain whether the sense of hunger would be allayed without the food being passed through the oesophagus, he fasted from breakfast time till 4 o'clock, p.m., and became quite hungry. I then put in at the aperture, three and a half drachms of lean, boiled beef. The sense of hunger immediately subsided, and stopped the borborygmus, or croaking noise, caused by the motion of air in the stomach and intes-

---

family and kept them for three years. St. Martin did not always take well to the dietary restrictions sometimes imposed on him, but even his anger was of value to posterity—it allowed Beaumont to observe various effects of emotion on the stomach. In 1832 St. Martin's wife persuaded him to return to Canada from Fort Crawford where Beaumont was then stationed. St. Martin took his family in an open canoe by the Mississippi and Ohio Rivers, by Lakes Erie and Ontario, and finally down the St. Lawrence; the trip to Montreal took about three months. Beaumont got St. Martin to return again in the fall of 1832. To help Beaumont with the rather heavy expenses of maintaining St. Martin and his family, the Surgeon-General had St. Martin enrolled in the Army as a sergeant. Late in 1833, St. Martin left for good, and Beaumont was never able to persuade him to return for any price. St. Martin did in later years exhibit his fistula to physicians and scientific groups, but he refused to return to Beaumont, although he often wrote Beaumont for money. When St. Martin died near Montreal in 1880, his family carried on the tradition of uncooperativeness. Dr. William Osler, then residing in Montreal, wrote to try to obtain St. Martin's stomach for the United States Army Medical Museum. He is said to have received this telegram in reply: "Don't come for autopsy; will be killed." To avoid an autopsy, the family kept the body until it was in such an advanced stage of decomposition that it had to be left outside the church during the funeral services. As a final measure, they buried the body in a grave eight feet below the surface of the ground.

tines, peculiar to him since the wound, and almost always observed when the stomach is empty [p. 208].

As we will see in a later section, psychologists have recently been extending this sort of observation with animal subjects. They have been attempting to determine the relative amounts of reinforcement obtained by the passage of food through the mouth and throat and by its placement in the stomach.

BEAUMONT'S LOCAL HYPOTHESIS OF HUNGER.   Considering the causes of the sensation of hunger, Beaumont took up the local hypotheses that Magendie had also enumerated and gave reasons for rejecting each of them. He rejected Magendie's own central hypothesis as well:

> Magendie, convinced that all the theories on this subject were unsatisfactory, comes to the following comprehensive conclusion: that "Hunger is produced like all other internal sensations, by the action of the nervous system, and it has no other seat than in this system itself, and no other causes than the general laws of organization." I cannot perceive that such explanations bring the mind to any satisfactory understanding of the subject. . . . When we can arrive at the exact interpretation of an author, who says that hunger has "No other causes than the general laws of organization," it will then be time to give reasons for an assent to or dissent from the proposition [pp. 55–6].

Beaumont set forth his own local hypothesis, "anxious mainly to elicit investigation on the subject," and "believing it to be as reasonable, to say the least, as any that has been propagated." His suggestion was that "*hunger* is the effect of *distention* of the vessels that secrete the gastric juice" (p. 276). In support of this he noted that there is no secretion when the stomach is empty; he supposed that the distention of the glands due to storage of gastric juice would be painful; and he noted that "quiescence and relief from the unpleasant sensation of hunger . . . are experienced as soon as the vessels are emptied" (p. 59).

Beaumont's hypothesis was exactly the opposite of an earlier one proposing that gastric secretion is the cause of the hunger pangs (Sömmerring, 1801). Beaumont's observation that there is no secretion in the empty stomach refuted Sömmerring's hypothesis, although it was not sufficient evidence to prove his own hypothesis.

BEAUMONT'S LOCAL HYPOTHESIS OF THIRST.   Concerning thirst, Beaumont supposed that when the body lacks water, the blood becomes more viscid; this retards salivary secretion in the mouth and throat, giving rise to the characteristic feelings of dryness there. "The sensation of dryness, or thirst, is supposed to be the effect of evaporation, the mouth and throat being constantly exposed to the atmosphere. When there is sufficient fluidity of the blood, the secretion is so much more copious than the evaporation, that a constant moisture is preserved" (p. 61).

These two sentences of 1833 give the substance of the "theory of thirst" that Cannon was to state in 1918; they are similar to Haller's explanation of 1747.

Again Beaumont disagrees sharply with Magendie's explanation in terms of "organization":

> The sensation of thirst resides in the tissues; and it is no more "an instinctive sentiment" than any other sensation of the economy. To say that it is the "result of organization" gives no explanation, amounts to nothing, and is certainly, to say the least, a very unsatisfactory way of disposing of the question [p. 61].

Beaumont's displeasure with vague explanations in terms of "organization" is reminiscent of certain current controversies.

Enthusiastic Reception of Beaumont's Work [4]

Beaumont's early articles had received favorable comment in European journals and his book created considerable excitement among European physicians when it appeared in 1833. A German translation was published in 1834, and a Scottish edition in 1838 made the work more readily available to British physicians. The acceptance of Beaumont's observations was aided by the great importance that Johannes Müller ascribed to them in his outstanding *Handbuch*. Müller concluded that Beaumont had proved beyond a doubt the existence of the gastric juice, a subject about which there was still controversy. Relating at length the story of St. Martin's wound, Müller repeated Beaumont's description of the process of digestion, and he reproduced some of Beaumont's tables showing the different times required to digest various foods. Claude Bernard later called Beaumont's research "epoch-making."

Beaumont's hypotheses about the mechanisms of hunger and thirst received less attention than his experimental observations; it was the observations that influenced the course of research on digestion and hunger. Although it is sometimes stated that Beaumont was the first to observe stomach activity through a fistula, the medical literature reveals over a dozen earlier cases (Myer, 1912; Kisch, 1954). The importance of Beaumont's observations lies in their extensiveness and excellence and in their influence upon later work.

Research with Experimental Gastric Fistulas

Soon after Beaumont's work came an American contribution of even greater general importance—the discovery of chemical anesthesia

[4] This topic is treated in detail in the monograph, *The Reception of William Beaumont's Discovery in Europe* (Rosen, 1942).

in 1840. Surgery for medical and experimental purposes was enormously facilitated by this discovery. The danger of infection was still present, however, whenever surgery was performed. After Lister inaugurated antiseptic precautions in 1867 this scourge was largely overcome, and the depths of the living body could be explored with relatively little risk.

TASTING IS SHOWN TO STIMULATE GASTRIC SECRETION.   Within ten years after Beaumont published his observations, two physiologists— Blondlot, a Frenchman, and Bassov, a Russian—were inspired by his work to make artificial gastric fistulas in animals. Thus they could study directly, and at will, the chemical and mechanical processes of digestion. Blondlot (1843) carried out extensive observations with this technique. Among other results, he found that much more gastric juice is secreted when food is swallowed than when it is introduced directly into the stomach through the fistula. His interpretation of this observation was that tasting food "stimulates sympathetically" the stomach and disposes it to prepare its secretion. "Another more general consequence which I believe one can deduce from the experiment is this: The preliminary acts of tasting, chewing, salivating and swallowing have, apart from their role in digestion, the further effect of provoking sympathetically a certain degree of overexcitation in the lining of the stomach. Thus they are not without influence on the secretion of gastric juice" (1843, p. 224).

THE SIGHT OF FOOD IS SUFFICIENT TO STIMULATE GASTRIC SECRETION.   A further striking observation in this direction was published by Bidder and Schmidt in their book on digestion (1852). They found that simply *showing* food to the dog could provoke the flow of gastric juice (p. 35). They also stated that casual introspection demonstrates that the sight or even the mere thought of food can provoke the flow of saliva (p. 13). The main interest of Bidder and Schmidt was in the secretions that aid digestion, and they did not carry these behavioral observations further. Richet in 1878 confirmed the observations of Bidder and Schmidt; he reported that when a dog with a fistula was allowed to smell meat, the lining of the stomach became red, and gastric juice began to flow.

A colleague of Richet went further and made an artificial gastric fistula in a human subject—for therapeutic reasons, of course (Richet, 1878). The patient was a young man who had accidentally burned his esophagus so badly with a caustic solution that it closed completely. Emboldened by the success of the St. Martin case, the surgeon made a gastric fistula through which his patient could be fed. It worked perfectly, and Richet conducted experiments with this subject during the year that followed the operation. Because there was no connection between the mouth and the stomach, Richet could obtain pure gastric juice, unmixed with food. The subject had only to put tasty food in his mouth to start the gastric juice flowing. Once again, stimuli acting on sense organs at a distance from the stomach could elicit gastric secretion.

Pavlov was to make this same observation around the turn of the century. He, too, as we shall see in a later section, was chiefly interested in the physiology of digestion when he made this observation. But, unlike his predecessors, he was to follow up the problem of "psychical secretion." Thereby he not only made discoveries of great importance for understanding the controls of eating and drinking, but he also helped to open up a whole new approach to psychological research.

SALIVATION AND THIRST

Now LET US TURN from gastric secretion and hunger to some related contemporary work on salivary secretion and thirst. Although Haller (1747) and Beaumont (1833) had suggested that salivary secretion is important in preventing thirst, not much was known about salivation in their time. The three main pairs of salivary glands had been described anatomically. No distinction was made among the secretions of these glands until 1780, when an investigator obtained the pure secretion from the duct of the parotid gland. It was not until 1847 that the great physiologist Claude Bernard, the favorite student of Magendie, similarly obtained the pure secretions of the submaxillary and sublingual glands. Bernard devoted several lectures of his physiology course in 1854–1855 to salivation (Bernard, 1856). He demonstrated that the secretions of all three glands differ somewhat from each other and are produced under somewhat different situations. Thus, for example, the parotid gland secretes especially during chewing. The submaxillary gland is excited to secrete by taste stimuli—"It is this secretion which runs from the human mouth and is expelled in jets at the sight of a tasty morsel" (p. 74). Carl Ludwig had shown in 1851 that salivation is controlled neurally, and Bernard extended the knowledge of the separate neural control of the parotid and submaxillary glands.

Interfering with Salivation Affects Thirst

In order to collect and measure salivary secretion, Bernard diverted the parotid secretion of horses to the outside of the cheek. He found that the drier the food, the more saliva was secreted. He also observed that the experimental horse was much thirstier than the normal; that is, it drank about half again as much as a normal animal. But Bernard insisted that the increased thirst was due to the body's loss of fluid through the cheek and was not due to the local drying of the throat.

He opposed the local hypothesis and probably supported a general hypothesis, although he did not spell out his preference:

> You must not believe, gentlemen, that the exaggerated thirst after section of the parotid ducts occurs because there is an increased dryness of the throat that causes the feeling of thirst. This feeling is actually the expression of a general need caused by the diminution of the quantity of liquid in the body. If you transect the esophagus low in the neck, in a horse whose parotid ducts have been sectioned, and then you have the animal drink, the water is expelled forcefully, at each swallow, between the forelegs; it cannot be absorbed in the intestine. Now, in these circumstances, the thirst of the animal is not appeased, although it wets its throat. It continues to drink until it is fatigued, and starts again until fatigue again forces it to stop, and so forth . . . [Bernard, pp. 50–1].

We will see this "sham drinking" technique employed again in the twentieth century.

An observation of Bidder and Schmidt (1852) suggested that interference with salivary secretion could increase thirst even though there was no loss of water in the body. They tied shut the ducts of the parotid and submaxillary glands on both sides of the mouth in dogs, preventing secretion from the glands:

> The first consequence of tying off the four large salivary ducts is a striking decrease in the fluid which the mucous membrane needs, so that only by keeping the mouth closed can the mucous membrane be kept moist. However, when some air is allowed to enter, a real drying out can scarcely be prevented. Not only dry food, like bread, but even sufficiently moist food, like fresh meat, is swallowed only with difficulty and with obvious strain. The thirst of such animals is accordingly also greatly increased, so that they are always ready to drink [Bidder and Schmidt, pp. 3–4].

This observation of Bidder and Schmidt seems to afford at least as strong support for a local hypothesis of thirst as Bernard's observation affords against it. Nevertheless, Bernard's experiment was to be more often cited than that of Bidder and Schmidt. Perhaps this was because of Bernard's eminence in physiology. Perhaps it was because Bernard was directing his argument to an issue, while Bidder and Schmidt were merely reporting an observation without emphasizing its importance for theory.

Bernard's Anticipation of Salivary Conditioning

We saw in the last section how work with *gastric* fistulas in the mid-nineteenth century anticipated the discovery of conditioning. Bernard's work with *salivary* fistulas led to an even fuller anticipation. In a

popular article, Bernard (1872) added both an important generalization and an important observation to the earlier description of his experiment on the parotid fistula:

> . . . Saliva flows abundantly when a tasty substance stimulates the
> nerves of the mucous membrane of the mouth, and . . . gastric juice
> forms when food touches the sensitive lining of the stomach. This me-
> chanical stimulation of the peripheral sensory nerves . . . can, how-
> ever, be replaced by purely psychic or cerebral stimulation. A simple
> experiment demonstrates this. Taking a fasting horse, you expose the
> duct of the parotid gland on the side of the jaw; you open the duct,
> and no saliva flows. If you then show the horse some oats or, even bet-
> ter, if you do not show him anything but make a motion which indi-
> cates to the animal that you are going to feed him, immediately a jet
> of saliva flows continuously from the parotid duct. . . . Dr. Beau-
> mont observed similar phenomena on his Canadian patient. The
> thought of a succulent morsel not only led to secretion of the salivary
> glands but it also provoked an immediately increased flow of blood
> into the mucous membrane of the stomach [1872, p. 378].

Here we have a clear description of one stimulus taking the place of
another in evoking a salivary or gastric response. The only way in which
this falls short as a description of conditioning is that it does not indicate the process by which one stimulus comes to replace another. Had
this question occurred to Bernard, perhaps he could have answered it
—twenty-five years before Pavlov was to do so.

Hunger and Thirst as Sensations

ALTHOUGH SOME investigators were already studying the control of eating and drinking, as we have seen, others were interested only
in the sensory aspects of hunger and thirst. This sensory approach is
exemplified in the mid-nineteenth century writings of the physiologists
E. H. Weber and Carl Ludwig.

Weber (of Weber-Fechner law fame) wrote briefly about hunger
and thirst in his chapter, "Cutaneous sense and common feeling," in
Wagner's *Handwörterbuch der Physiologie* (1846). This chapter is a
foundation stone of psychophysics. Concerning hunger and thirst, however, Weber made no innovations. His suggestions were almost identical with the local hypotheses that Haller had offered one hundred
years before and that Cannon was to offer about seventy years later.
Two sentences give the gist of the local hypotheses that he set forth:

> I consider it probable that the strong contraction of the muscle fi-
> bers of the completely empty stomach, whereby its cavity disappears,
> is connected with the sensation . . . that we call hunger [1846, pp.
> 580–1].

Thirst is perhaps caused by modification of secretion occurring on many areas of the mucous membrane, this in turn being due to a deficiency in the large proportion of water in the blood [p. 586].

LUDWIG—"EATING IS NOT EVIDENCE OF HUNGER."   Ludwig was emphatic that investigation of intake of food had nothing to do with the study of hunger. In his textbook of physiology (1861), he granted that many experiments had shown that animals continue to eat eagerly after the nerves from the stomach have been transected. "But," he insisted, "these observations in no way refute the assumption that the experience of hunger is connected with these nerves, for many other causes—and, in particular, psychic ones—can lead to the taking of food" (1861, p. 580). This was an argument that Cannon was to cite in defense of his local hypothesis in 1912, giving the example that appetite, rather than hunger, leads people to eat dessert. The question at issue here seems to be which definition of hunger shall be used. If hunger is defined in terms of experience that people report, then animal experiments are indeed beside the point. Most twentieth-century investigators have not accepted this restrictive definition. (In addition, as we shall see, the twentieth century has produced evidence that a person with no stomach does in fact feel hunger.)

GROWTH OF CENTRAL HYPOTHESES

Basal Regions of the Brain Implicated

As knowledge of the nervous system continued to increase, some physiologists found the basal regions of the brain a likely seat for regulation of hunger. This was the opinion of F. A. Longet in his Traité de physiologie (1861). Taking it almost for granted that the brain controls hunger, he argued that the hunger centers were probably in the basal regions rather than in the cerebral hemispheres:

. . . The role which we believe the basal portions of the brain centers to play in man suggests that they are not unrelated to sensations of hunger. It is not possible to agree with [the phrenologists] Combes, Spurzheim, Hoppe and Broussais that there is an organ of alimentivity, situated in the lateral and median fissures of the base of the skull and belonging to the cerebrum proper. For the sensation of hunger, which is shown by the fact of taking food, manifests itself in animal species lacking a real cerebrum. Also, in the human species there have been cases of acephaly, with complete absence of the cerebrum and cerebellum, where the fetuses lived for several days and showed by their cries and their sucking movements that they felt hunger. In these fetuses there remained, of course, those basal parts of the neural centers (pons and medulla) without which life is impossible for a single instant [1861, p. 21].

Many succeeding workers similarly argued that the seat of hunger is in the brain stem; they employed the same evidence of food-taking by animals with primitive brains and by babies lacking most of the brain.

It is worthy of note that Longet, although writing in the same year as Ludwig, took an opposite position from Ludwig on the definition of "hunger." For Longet, eating or readiness to eat were sufficient evidence of hunger. Most subsequent investigators were to take the same view; i.e., they were primarily interested in the regulation of behavior rather than in experience.

The regions of the brain mentioned by Longet are shown in Figure 8. This diagram also indicates other brain regions that will be mentioned in later sections when we come to further hypotheses about the location of centers that regulate eating and drinking.

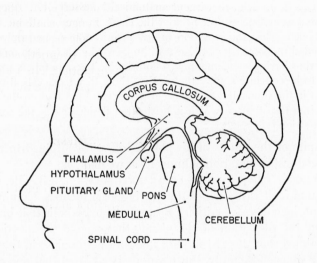

FIGURE 8. The brain is shown in an outline of the head. The left half of the brain has been removed, and you are looking at the medial surface of the right half. Structures that lie on the midline have been cut in half; these include all the structures named in the figure except the thalamus and hypothalamus. The thalamus and hypothalamus lie on both sides of a midline ventricle which is filled with cerebrospinal fluid.

Schiff's Central Hypotheses

A much more precise central hypothesis was offered by Moritz Schiff.[5] His *Leçons sur la physiologie de la digestion* (1867) shows the

---

[5] Schiff was a German student of Magendie and Longet who had a distinguished international career. Forced to leave Germany after serving as physician to a revolutionary army in 1848, he became Professor of Comparative Anatomy at Bern and then was Professor of Physiology at Florence, 1863–76. He is best known for research in neurophysiology and for pioneer work in endocrinology.

advanced state of knowledge about digestion and related processes in the mid-nineteenth century. The book is a series of thirty-eight lectures which were accompanied by animal demonstrations. Chapters 2 and 3 deal with hunger and thirst. Since they anticipate many important later accounts, Schiff's points are worth examining in some detail. They are close to our current understanding in several respects. (In his account, note that Schiff used "hunger" both in the sense of human experience and in the sense of readiness to eat.)

Schiff could find no support for the local hypotheses which made hunger dependent upon changes in the stomach. In fact, on the basis of an early public opinion survey, he doubted that most people feel hunger in the stomach:

> I had occasion to question some soldiers on this point, keeping by preference to individuals without anatomical knowledge. . . . Several indicated to me vaguely the neck or the chest, 23 the breastbone, four could not localize the sensation in any definite region, and only two designated the stomach as the seat of hunger. These were two medical aides, thus having some anatomical knowledge. These numbers are too small to be conclusive; nevertheless they show that the localization of hunger in the stomach does not occur in everyone and that on the contrary, it is the stomach which is least often designated as the seat of the sensation [1867, p. 31].

In spite of the results of his poll, Schiff still continued to refer to "the special gastric sensation of hunger," as we shall see.

SCHIFF'S CRITICISMS OF LOCAL HYPOTHESES.   Like Beaumont, Schiff found fault with each of the existing local theories. Coming after Beaumont, he could also criticize Beaumont's hypothesis that hunger is caused by the distention of the glands that secrete the gastric juice. Schiff claimed that the gastric juice does not accumulate in the glands while the stomach is empty. Furthermore, he asserted that one can irritate the stomach walls and cause abundant secretion without making hunger stop. On the last point Schiff was in error, for many workers have substantiated Beaumont's observation that very little gastric juice is secreted upon purely mechanical stimulation of the stomach.

As further evidence against local theories of hunger, Schiff showed that removal of all nerves to the stomach does not prevent normal eating. He could cite several experiments of other investigators, and he had seen the facts himself: "In rabbits I have cut the two pneumogastrics, the two sympathetics, and removed the celiac ganglia. I have often kept the animals five or six days during which they ate and digested very well" (p. 37).

SCHIFF'S CENTRAL HYPOTHESIS OF HUNGER.   Schiff favored what he called a "general" hypothesis of hunger; we shall see that it should more appropriately be called a *central* hypothesis. Schiff stated that the blood is always being modified because the body removes from it the materials necessary for metabolism and for rebuilding of tissue. "This modification, when it reaches a certain degree, cannot fail to influence what we call the *general state*; in other terms, the neural centers must be affected by the impoverished blood and react by a particular sensation of general nature" (p. 30).

The fact that people usually localize their feelings of hunger somewhere in the trunk was not accepted by Schiff as evidence against a central theory. He attempted to show that although hunger is perceived in a peripheral location, it may actually originate in the central nervous system. He noted that tumors in the brain often cause patients to feel localized pain out in the body:

> Now, it is not necessary that the irritation of the centers be mechanical [as in the case of a tumor]. It can also come from a chemical alteration, from a change in the composition of the blood. Consequently, the diminution of elements in the blood which makes us feel the need to eat may also show itself by changes in local sensitivity, and the locality where we perceive that change need not be directly affected. Support is given to this conjecture by the fact that it is not excessively rare to observe extensive lesions of the stomach . . . in which the patients still perceive the special gastric sensation of hunger [p. 47].

What part of the brain is primarily responsible for hunger? Schiff believed it was the brain stem, and he used arguments similar to those of Longet, with whose work he was familiar. More precisely, he located it ". . . in the central regions where the nerves come together from the various localities that can seemingly be affected by hunger; that is, in the medulla, a little above the roots of the pneumogastric nerves" (p. 48).

EVIDENCE FOR THE CENTRAL HYPOTHESIS. Finally, Schiff detailed a number of further arguments in support of his central hypothesis of hunger. We can only indicate some of them very briefly here:

> Some animal species such as the guinea pig and the rabbit never have an empty stomach in normal living, yet they eat regularly. Therefore hunger cannot depend upon emptying of the stomach [p. 32].
>
> Once the stomach is empty in man, its state does not change further, but hunger continues to increase during fasting [p. 40].
>
> There may be abnormally strong hunger, although digestion is normal, if the food is not absorbed properly by the blood. This may occur in clinical cases when the duodenum is bypassed or when the intestine is too short [pp. 43 *et seq.*].
>
> Injection of properly treated food into the blood stream appeases hunger. Animals can be nourished perfectly in this way, without their having to eat [p. 46].

Thus the over-all picture of the regulation of eating was this: The blood loses its supply of nutritive materials to the cells. The nervous system, and especially centers in the brain stem, are affected by these changes in the blood. This chemical stimulation of the centers results in awareness of the need to eat. This need involves sensations which are referred by the individual to the gastric region, although they do not necessarily involve the digestive organs in any direct way.

Thirst, like hunger, was considered by Schiff to be of central origin, the nervous system detecting the lack of water in the blood. He marshaled considerable experimental evidence in favor of this hypothesis.

It should be noted that none of Schiff's evidence for his central hypotheses was drawn from direct experiments upon the brain. Fifty years were to pass before surgical techniques developed to the level of experimentation upon presumed centers for hunger and thirst. This experimentation was to justify Schiff's theorizing in some respects, but to indicate the need for modification in others.

GENERAL HYPOTHESES OF HUNGER AND THIRST

AT THE BEGINNING of the nineteenth century the physiologist C. L. Dumas had set forth general hypotheses of both hunger and thirst, as we have seen. At the time, local hypotheses were entrenched, and general hypotheses tended to be disregarded. During most of the rest of the century, general hypotheses were mentioned only infrequently, but they reappeared prominently at the very end of the nineteenth century.

Roux on Hunger

ORIGIN GENERAL. "After having brilliantly refuted the doctrine of gastric origin [of hunger], Schiff fell into an equally great error. He believed that the sensation of hunger is caused by direct action upon brain centers of blood that is lacking in nutritive material" (Roux, 1897, p. 412). The writer of this statement was the psychologist-physician, Joanny Roux. The statement appears in his "physiopsychological" study of hunger. Against Schiff's hypothesis, Roux claimed that modern physiology has shown that the nervous system never functions spontaneously in the normal state. All cerebral activity starts with stimulation at the periphery. If the nervous system is activated by a condition of the blood, this is a pathological phenomenon, and it cannot be the origin of normal hunger. With both local and central hypotheses thus ruled out in his thinking, Roux backed a general hypothesis of hunger:

All the cells of our organism are strictly interdependent. . . . When a cell feels a need which, because of its specialization, it cannot satisfy by itself, it appeals to other cells by means of the nervous system. This is the origin of all nutritive reflexes, and we will show that, *in the sensation of hunger, there is nothing but a nutritive cortical reflex, a reflex still not completely adaptive and therefore giving rise to consciousness as an epiphenomenon* . . . [p. 413].

He emphasized that "hunger originates in all the cells of our organism."

SATIATION LOCAL. Roux also considered how hunger can be appeased. He noted that eating stops hunger immediately, before absorption of food into the blood can take place. He also noted that filling the stomach with indigestible material can check hunger for a while. Filling the stomach, Roux conjectured, inhibits the sensation of hunger. Such inhibition is important, he noted, since without it we would eat continuously until absorption of food remedied the bodily need; without inhibition arising from the full stomach, we would eat too long and too much. Thus Roux, like Magendie, referred satiation to the stomach, although he sought elsewhere for the origin of hunger.

Changes in Osmotic Pressure as the Stimulus of Thirst

Three years after Roux had stated his general hypothesis of hunger, the physiologist André Mayer proposed a general hypothesis of thirst (1900). Mayer proposed that the physiological correlate of thirst is the osmotic pressure of the blood. (The osmotic value of a solution depends upon its concentration. If a bodily cell is placed in a *hypertonic* saline solution—a solution that has a higher concentration of sodium than the cell—water leaves the cell and the cell shrinks. If the cell is placed in a *hypotonic* saline solution—one with a lower-than-usual concentration—water enters the cell and it swells.) In 1900 it was thought that peripheral cells might thus serve as receptors for changes in osmotic pressure during water deprivation, shrinking in size as the water content of the blood decreased. More recently "osmoreceptors" have been sought in the brain.

MAYER'S EVIDENCE. Mayer presented much evidence to support his hypothesis that thirst is caused by elevation of the osmotic pressure of the blood. He demonstrated that the osmotic pressure rises in conditions that are known to produce thirst. For example, he placed rabbits in a hot, dry sweat box for two hours. At the end of this period each rabbit showed an increase in osmotic pressure of the blood. (Dumas [1803] had reported that artificial fever always produced thirst in animals.) In another experiment he deprived dogs of water for periods ranging from four to seven days. Each dog showed an increase in osmotic pressure over its earlier control value. Mayer also tested whether thirst would disappear when the osmotic pressure was restored to normal. After depriving a dog of water for several days, he gave it an injection of hypotonic saline solution. When it was then offered water to drink, the dog took very little. "The hypertonicity was removed, and he was no longer thirsty" (1900, p. 47). With another deprived dog, Mayer injected a solution with a saline concentration as high as that of the blood. "After injection of 2 litres of solution in 2 hours, he drank two and a half litres of water. The injection did not change or perhaps even increased his osmotic pressure, and he was still thirsty" (p. 47).

Mayer acknowledged that some clinical cases showed striking changes in water intake after injuries to the medulla. He pointed out that this did not necessarily mean that there is a center for drinking in the medulla. Rather, he felt, the medulla contains a center for regulating the osmotic pressure of the blood, and it thereby influences thirst (p. 83). At the same time, he suggested that the change in osmotic pressure excites the medulla particularly, as well as causing generalized stimulation throughout the body (p. 148). Thus his hypothesis was a general one, but with central components as well.

A MODIFIED GENERAL OSMOTIC HYPOTHESIS.   As often happens, another scientist had independently undertaken a similar study at the same time. This investigator, H. Wettendorff (1901), confirmed Mayer's observations in part, but he also suggested an important modification. It was true that osmotic pressure of the blood increased during water deprivation of several days' duration, but no change could be found during the first few days of deprivation. Thus, thirst developed while the blood was apparently still normal. Mayer, it seemed, had not followed the changes closely enough in time. Furthermore, Wettendorff suggested, the initial changes should not be sought in the blood. He claimed that the blood and the brain probably keep their normal osmotic properties as long as possible, the other tissues and fluids yielding water to them during deprivation. He concluded that thirst is the result of a general change in the tissues. The cells are sensitive to changes in osmotic pressure of the fluid that bathes them, and such changes are reported to the brain. He did not specify any particular location in the brain. Finally, Wettendorff distinguished between the "apparent thirst" felt in the mouth and throat and the "real thirst" of the tissues:

. . . It is easy to understand that the perception of thirst is localized in the mouth and throat, because, as we have stated earlier, these areas are exposed to continuous ventilation; their dehydration must therefore be rapid and extensive. . . . Finally, we have also noted that an association of ideas must occur during our individual development between *real thirst*, resulting from the state of the deep tissues, and the *painful sensation,* resulting from the drying of the mouth and throat, which always accompanies the general phenomenon [1901, p. 474].

Both Mayer and Wettendorff thus agreed on these points: (1) Deprivation of water leads to changes in osmotic pressure. (2) These changes are detected by receptors situated throughout the body. (3) Information about changes in osmotic pressure is relayed to the brain, thus causing thirst.

PAVLOV'S RESEARCH ON DIGESTION AND CONDITIONING

IN 1904 IVAN PETROVITCH PAVLOV was awarded the Nobel Prize for his research on digestion. In his address at the award ceremonies in Stockholm, he outlined the new direction his research was taking—the study of conditioned reflexes. Actually, Pavlov's work on conditioning grew out of his work on digestion, and both phases of his research are important for the understanding of hunger and eating behavior.

The Discovery of "Psychic Secretion" of Gastric Juice

The first phase of Pavlov's research was summarized in his book, *The Work of the Digestive Glands* (cited in the German translation as Pawlow, 1898). Pavlov utilized the artificial gastric fistula (derived ultimately from Beaumont). He combined this with another operation in which the esophagus was divided and both ends were made to heal at the skin (like Claude Bernard's "sham drinking" horse). Thus the mouth and stomach were separated completely (as in the patient that Richet had studied). Figure 9 diagrams the experimental preparation. Dogs so operated had to have food placed directly into the stomach; with good care they could live for many years in excellent health.

> With such animals one can make the following interesting experiment: If the dog is given meat to eat, the food drops out again from the upper segment of the divided esophagus. However, from the completely empty stomach, previously washed out with water, an active secretion of gastric juice soon commences; it continues for as long as the animal eats, and even for a short time longer. . . . From a dog thus operated upon, you can collect on any day, or even daily, a couple of hundred cubic centimeters of gastric juice without apparent injury to its health; that is to say, you can procure gastric juice from these dogs almost as milk is obtained from a cow [1898, pp. 13–14].[6]
> . . . We may feed the dog as long as we wish; the secretion will flow at the same rate for one, two or more hours. We have had dogs so greedy that they did not tire of eating for five or six hours in this fash-

[6] Many dogs were, in fact, kept as "cows"; Pavlov helped to support the laboratory by selling gastric juice for therapeutic purposes.

ion, secreting up to 700 cc of the purest gastric juice. The meaning of this experiment is clear. It is obvious that the effect of feeding is transmitted by nervous channels to the gastric glands [p. 64].

PERCEPTION AIDS DIGESTION.   Pavlov and his collaborators next measured a phenomenon that had been reported by Blondlot half a century earlier in 1843, but that had remained largely unknown. This was that swallowing food produces greater gastric secretion than placing it directly in the stomach. Here Pavlov made a significant further observation: In order to measure the effect of placing food in the stomach, it

FIGURE 9.   Dog prepared with esophageal and gastric fistulas. Food taken by mouth falls out of the esophageal fistula into a container. Food can be put into the stomach through the lower portion of the esophagus, by-passing the mouth and throat. Gastric juice drops out through the gastric fistula and its secretion can thus be measured. Pavlov observed that taking food by mouth elicits gastric secretion even though the food never reaches the stomach. Food put directly into the stomach, Pavlov found, does not stimulate gastric secretion—unless the dog sees that it is being fed in this way!

had to be concealed from the animal! If the dog noticed that food was being placed in its stomach, this alone would cause the gastric glands to secrete. This observation is clearly related to the earlier one of Bidder and Schmidt (1852)—cited by Pavlov—that the mere sight of food can cause gastric secretion.

Digestion was found to be markedly slower when food was placed in the stomach (without the dog's knowledge) than when it was swallowed normally. Digestion of food placed directly in the stomach could be aided by "sham-feeding," i.e., by letting other food pass through the mouth and drop out the cut esophagus. "This," concludes Pavlov, "represents the digestive value of the passage of food through the mouth, the value of a strong desire for food, the value of appetite" (1898, pp. 107–8). He referred to the effect as a "psychic" one. One might characterize this effect by saying that perception affects digestion. Pavlov's way of putting it was that the reflex of gastric secretion can become connected to new stimuli.

Conditioning the Salivary Reflex

After writing his book on the digestive glands, Pavlov turned to an intensive investigation of "psychical secretion." He now used the salivary glands almost exclusively, finding them more convenient for this purpose than the gastric glands. Because the "psychical secretion" depends upon many conditions, it appears capricious unless all the factors are controlled. Pavlov therefore referred to it in 1903 (see 1928) as "conditional." (Somehow this was translated into English as "conditioned," whence the term "conditioned reflex.") In the same paper Pavlov spelled out the main behavioral procedures necessary for establishing a conditional reflex. The description of conditioning in current textbooks of psychology derives ultimately from Pavlov's papers of this period.

Underlying the appearance of the conditional reflex, Pavlov suggested, was the formation of temporary connections between the cortical areas representing the conditional stimuli and the salivary center of the brain. In a more detailed paper the next year, he noted that the amount of salivary secretion varied with the state of hunger or satiety. This he explained as being due to changes in excitability of the salivary center of the brain. The excitability, in turn, he believed to be influenced by the chemical composition of the blood which he asserted to differ between the hungry and satiated states.

The Hunger Center

Pavlov soon came to regard salivation as being under the control of a hunger center in the brain which also influences gastric secretion and movements of the skeletal musculature. In a 1910 lecture entitled "The Hunger Centre" (see 1928), he maintained that this center is just as real as the respiratory center of the brain, although the hunger center is rarely mentioned in any textbook. In a sentence that might be taken as the motto of the book you are now reading, he stated, "When you light upon some interesting question, paradoxically enough, it is not to be found in new but old books!" (1928, p. 147). Pavlov maintained that the stimulation of the hunger center is "automatic," i.e., that it occurs through changes of blood chemistry. He thus supported a central hypothesis like that of Schiff:

> . . . It is clear that the first impulse to the activity of the food centre —by which it secretes saliva and gastric juice—arises from the chemical composition of the blood of the animal which has not eaten for several hours. In such an animal the blood acquires "hungry" properties. This finds a close analogy in the respiratory centre. . . . If it is admitted that the chief stimulator of the respiration centre is an internal

automatic stimulus, then the same must be accepted in regard to the food centre. Besides the analogy there are facts which support this view.

. . . Although various nerves leading from the gastro-intestinal tract have been cut, no one has ever seen a disappearance of the positive movement reaction of the animal to food, or, using the usual terminology, a loss of appetite. . . .

Consequently, the chemical composition of the blood of a hungry animal is a stimulus for the food centre . . . [1928, p. 148].

PAVLOV'S PERIPHERAL APPROACH TO CENTRAL PROCESSES.   It is less important to determine the location of the food center, Pavlov felt, than to investigate its functions. His experimental program rarely employed surgical intervention in the brain, although he had operated extensively on the alimentary canal. In the search for the food center, others were soon to show the creative inventiveness in brain surgery that Pavlov had shown in surgery of the alimentary canal. Pavlov did maintain that the food center must be situated in more than one part of the nervous system. Part of the center must lie below the cerebral hemispheres, since a decerebrated pigeon, although it will not eat, becomes more active the longer it is deprived of food. When food is put in its crop, the pigeon becomes quiet again. (About ninety years earlier, Flourens had reported that the decerebrated pigeon will not eat, but he did not mention any increase in activity with deprivation.) Part of the food center, and the taste center, Pavlov felt, must lie in the cerebral hemispheres.

Significance of Pavlov's Research for Understanding of Hunger

In showing that conditioning can affect physiological processes, Pavlov provided a way of dealing with the effects of learning on ingestion. Such effects had been noted long before Pavlov. For example, Erasmus Darwin had written in 1796 that habit affects both the timing of hunger and thirst and the amount required for satiation. After Pavlov's research, work on learned aspects of hunger became more prominent. It was later shown that learning also affects the choice of food and that learned preferences may even predominate over the influence of bodily needs on selection of food. Thus the control of eating does not operate in a completely preestablished fashion, but rather it is capable of modification through training. Conditioning has also been suggested to play a role in satiety, since eating normally stops before any food can be absorbed from the alimentary tract.

In writing of the hunger center and its stimulation by changed conditions of the blood, Pavlov helped to keep the central hypothesis before the attention of investigators.

In attempting to invent and apply quantitative measures of both physiological processes and behavior, Pavlov helped to bring precision into both fields. One of the novel physiological methods employed in his laboratory was the recording of the movements of the stomach. This work was soon to lead to Cannon's local hypothesis of hunger.

ABANDONMENT OF THE SUBJECTIVE APPROACH. Pavlov's research illustrates the trend toward objective study of behavior early in the twentieth century, and, by its success, probably helped to accelerate this trend. At the start of the research on conditioning, however, Pavlov and his collaborators tried to employ the typical psychological methods of the time. The observer, in such studies, attempted to grasp the mental state of his subject, whether human or animal. Pavlov found these methods fruitless:

> . . . Does not the eternal sorrow of life consist in the fact that human beings cannot understand one another, that one person cannot enter into the internal state of another? . . . In our "psychical" experiments on the salivary glands (we shall use provisionally the word "psychical"), at first we honestly endeavored to explain our results by fancying the subjective condition of the animal. But nothing came of it except unsuccessful controversies, and individual, personal, incoordinated opinions. We had no alternative but to place the investigation on a purely objective basis. The first and most important task before us, then, is to abandon entirely the natural inclination to transpose our own subjective condition upon the mechanism of the reaction of the experimental animal, and instead, to concentrate our whole attention upon the investigation of the correlation between the external phenomena and the reaction of the organism . . . [1928, p. 50].

Pavlov therefore gave up the subjective methods which he believed to be the only approach of psychology, and he contrasted objective physiology with subjective psychology. Later he found that his information about psychology had been too restricted, and in 1923 he acknowledged graciously the priority of psychologists:

> Some years after the beginning of the work with our new method I learned that somewhat similar experiments had been performed in America, and indeed not by physiologists but by psychologists. Thereupon I studied in more detail the American publications, and now I must acknowledge that the honour of having made the first steps along this path belongs to E. L. Thorndike. By two or three years his experiments preceded ours, and his book [*Animal Intelligence—An Experimental Study of the Associative Processes in Animals*, 1898] must be considered a classic, both for its bold outlook on an immense task and for the accuracy of its results [1928, pp. 39–40].

In the behaviorist movement that began in 1913, Watson used the conditional reflex as a substitute for association, and Pavlov's research provided a strong support for behavioristic psychology.

ON THE TRAIL OF THE BRAIN CENTERS FOR EATING AND DRINKING

THE BASE OF THE BRAIN is probably the best protected, most inaccessible region in the entire body. A special socket of bone encloses the pituitary gland which hangs by its stalk from the hypothalamus (see Figure 10). It was toward this region that the search began to narrow down as investigators sought the centers controlling ingestion of food and drink.

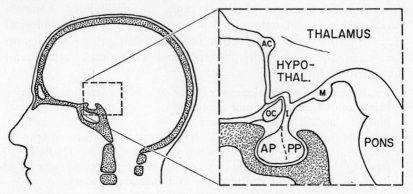

FIGURE 10. The pituitary gland hangs down from the base of the brain into a recess in the floor of the skull. The left side of the figure shows the skull, with the region of the pituitary indicated by the central rectangle. To the right this region has been enlarged to show the pituitary gland, its stalk, and neighboring structures. (*AP*, anterior pituitary gland; *PP*, posterior pituitary gland; *I*, infundibulum or stalk of the pituitary; *M*, mammillary body; *OC*, optic chiasma; *AC*, anterior commissure.)

The Pituitary Is Implicated in Control of Growth and Weight

AN ORGAN OF UNKNOWN FUNCTION.   Galen's assertion that the gland secretes mucus into the nose and throat was, as we have seen, responsible for the name "pituitary." Renaissance investigators at first accepted this view but then abandoned it when they could find no passages for such secretion. A more neutral name was then proposed for the pituitary—"hypophysis cerebri" (outgrowth of the brain); similarly, the stalk was called "infundibulum cerebri" (funnel of the brain) because of the way the third ventricle narrows down and ends in the stalk. Currently both sets of names are used for the gland and stalk.

Early in the nineteenth century the function of the pituitary body was still a matter for speculation. Most authors considered it to be neural, but Magendie suggested that the pituitary body was a lymphatic organ absorbing cerebral fluid and pouring it into the blood (Livon, 1909). In the second half of the century, there was greater conservatism. Longet stated flatly that the function of the pituitary was unknown. After Darwin's *Origin of Species* in 1859 it became clear that some organs are merely vestigial and have no function in the present state of evolution. William James was merely voicing a current view when he stated in his *Psychology:* "[The pituitary body] has no known function and is probably a 'rudimentary organ' " (1891, p. 82).

FIRST CLINICAL OBSERVATIONS ABOUT PITUITARY FUNCTION.   The first steps toward solving the puzzle of the pituitary had already been taken when James wrote. An isolated observation in 1840 had described a pituitary tumor in a case where obesity had a rapid onset (Brobeck, Tepperman and Long, 1943). A few similar reports were made before 1900. In the 1880's Pierre Marie called attention to a peculiar syndrome (acromegaly) in which a disfiguring overgrowth of bone occurs in adults. In 1886 Marie announced that cases of acromegaly had tumors of the pituitary. Somewhat later it was found that skeletons of human giants show an enlarged bony socket for the pituitary. A growth hormone was hypothesized, and it was later isolated from the anterior pituitary. In an article that was to stimulate much research, Fröhlich (1901) reported a case involving obesity and genital underdevelopment which he believed to be due to a pituitary tumor. Thus it appeared that the pituitary might be responsible for growth and for maintenance of body weight.

Pituitary or Hypothalamus?

Careful clinical investigators soon found that pituitary tumors often damage the hypothalamus as well as the pituitary. They attempted to determine whether some symptoms could be attributed to the pituitary and others to the hypothalamus. The physician J. Erdheim suggested in 1904 that there is such a separation of function. After examining many clinical cases and studying reports of others, he agreed with Fröhlich that obesity often occurs in cases of pituitary tumors, but he did not agree that the obesity was caused by a change in endocrine function:

> Putting the evidence together, we find it very probable that adiposity occurring with tumors of the hypophysis . . . should not be attributed to faulty endocrine function of the hypophysis but rather to an undefined region in the base of the brain which is directly influenced (stimulated or injured) by the tumor. Our assumption is supported by the fact that the base of the brain is found to be destroyed or greatly compressed in these cases, and certainly by a tumor that came either from the hypophysis or its vicinity [1904, pp. 700–1].

Obesity is not the only symptom that may arise from the tumors in this region. Erdheim noted the occurrence of its opposite—lack of appetite and undernourishment—and also cases of abnormal thirst and drinking (polydipsia), and abnormally great excretion of urine (polyuria). "Thus, in those cases of tumors of the hypophysis or its vicinity that are accompanied by obesity, there is damage to the base of the brain by the tumor; but not all tumors so located and injuring the base of the brain are accompanied by obesity" (p. 700).

Lively controversy developed over the respective roles of the pituitary and the hypothalamus. Some investigators preferred to consider them as forming one compound system, so that differentiating their function was unnecessary and, in fact, improper. Physiologists soon attempted to solve this problem by making experimental lesions in animal subjects, trying to impair only small regions and to leave the surrounding tissue intact. (It should be noted that these investigators did not share Pavlov's belief that the physiologist need not concern himself about the location of neural centers. If a center can be located, then it can be experimented upon directly. Many valuable discoveries have been obtained in this way, as we will see in later sections.)

Hypothalamic Lesions Alter Intake of Food and Water

The technical difficulties were gradually overcome, until small lesions could be made in the hypothalamus without impairing the pituitary stalk or body. One of the first successful experiments of this sort was performed by Bailey and Bremer (1921). They exposed the hypothalamus from the side and then stabbed a fine probe into its base. This small lesion was sufficient to produce abnormalities of water and food intake:

> A lesion, even extremely minute, of the para-infundibular region of the hypothalamus provokes with certitude (in thirteen of thirteen dogs) a polyuria which appears in the first two days. According to the extent of the lesion it varies from a transient one lasting from six to eight days to an apparently permanent polyuria [1921, p. 803].

In the cases in which the animal was not comatose after the operation, the dogs increased their intake of water about a day before the polyuria appeared; this indicated that the increased drinking, and not ths increased urination, was the primary effect of the hypothalamic lesion.

In the cases with the largest lesions of the hypothalamus there were other symptoms such as general ill health, obesity, and genital atrophy. Two cases of experimental obesity appear in the report of Bailey and Bremer. We must wait until 1931, ten years later, to see further cases of obesity produced experimentally by lesions in the hypothalamus, and we must wait until 1940 to see accurate localization of the hypothalamic nucleus involved in this effect.

The experiments of Bailey and Bremer, corroborated by others on water regulation done at about the same time (Camus and Roussy, 1922), demonstrated that parts of the hypothalamus influenced consumption of water and food. Thus localization experiments on the animal brain confirmed hypotheses drawn from the clinical study of the human brain. The precise mapping of the centers involved was still more than twenty-five years away. It awaited development of a practical technique for making extremely small, accurately localized lesions in the brain.

The experiment of Bailey and Bremer did not by itself put an end to the pituitary-hypothalamus controversy. Fröhlich himself recognized the role of the hypothalamus in 1939 at a symposium where he was an honored participant:

> The discussions that I have attended in the past two days have established the fact that we were wrong in 1901, that it was not the pituitary body but the hypothalamus, but I must remind you that all we knew at that time was that the hypothalamus was an anatomical region lying beneath the thalamus. That is all that we knew [1940, p. 723].

CANNON'S SALVO OF LOCAL THEORIES

ALTHOUGH EVIDENCE was steadily accumulating in favor of central hypotheses, the local hypotheses did not fade away before them. Rather, local hypotheses shot into prominence again, beginning in 1912.

Activity of the Empty Stomach

As we have seen, it had long been argued whether the empty stomach is active, as Haller (and Galen) supposed, or whether it remains quiescent, as Erasmus Darwin had insisted. At the turn of the century this old problem was revived and apparently settled. Several Russian investigators claimed that the earlier opinion was correct when they observed contractions in the "empty" stomachs of experimental animals. A detailed report was given by Boldireff (1905) who worked in Pavlov's laboratory. His technique was to record changes in the volume of a rubber balloon placed in the stomach through a fistula. The experimental arrangements are shown in Figure 11. When the stomach contained no food, periods of activity would occur lasting for twenty to thirty minutes. During such a period, there would be a contraction every minute or two. Between periods of activity, the stomach would be quiet for one and a half to two and a half hours. The contractions stopped whenever gastric juice flowed, whether the flow was spontaneous or was evoked by showing the dog food. At first Boldireff considered that hunger might cause the stomach contractions. "Later we

had to abandon this opinion and we were unable to refer these phenomena to a common cause, since certain relations between them are
absolutely contradictory; thus the secretion of gastric juice which is
evoked by inanition, causes the periodic phenomena to disappear"
(1905, pp. 96–7). Also, he found that the contractions became weaker,
rather than stronger, during fifteen to twenty hours of deprivation.

These arguments against relating hunger and stomach contractions do not appear very convincing. It is not starvation but the signal of
food that elicits secretion of gastric juice. Therefore, if stomach contractions are related to hunger, they might well be expected to stop

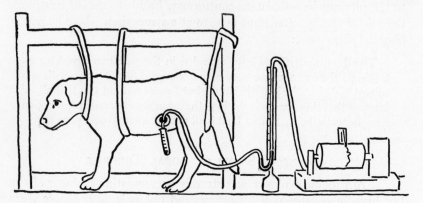

FIGURE 11.   Experimental set-up used in Pavlov's laboratory to measure the movements of the stomach. Through a fistula in the body wall,
tubes can be inserted into the stomach. The upper tube ends in a small
balloon in the stomach. As the stomach contracts, it presses on the balloon. The pressure is transmitted through the tube and causes both a
displacement on the manometer gauge and an inflection in the curve
being recorded on the cylinder at the right. (After Boldireff, 1905,
Figure 3.) The movements of the stomach were soon to be recorded in
human subjects, using a modification of this technique (see Figure 12).

when the arrival of food is signaled. The observation that the contractions weakened during deprivation need not be considered conclusive, since they were made on three animals in poor health. Clearly,
Boldireff's report was an invitation to further work on this subject.

Cannon's Local Theory of Hunger

The physiologist W. B. Cannon soon undertook a similar experiment upon a single human subject, his collaborator Washburn (Cannon and Washburn, 1912). Washburn could swallow without difficulty
a small balloon at the end of a tube. The balloon was inflated in the
stomach, and stomach contractions could then be recorded; the experimental arrangements are shown in Figure 12. During the recording
of stomach movements, the subject was asked to press the key whenever

he felt pangs of hunger. The records showed a "concomitance of contractions and hunger in man." Figure 12 presents an example of the
experimental recordings. Reports of hunger can be seen to coincide
with the peaks of stomach contractions. On the basis of his observations, Cannon argued strongly that stomach contractions are the cause
of hunger. Certainly the observations supported the stomach-
contraction hypothesis as against three other local hypotheses that were
still in the running: (1) contact of the walls of the empty stomach
(Haller), (2) lack of activity of the empty stomach (Erasmus Darwin),

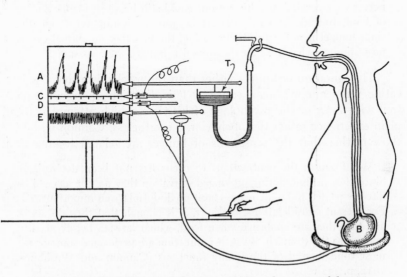

FIGURE 12. Recording stomach contractions and reports of hunger
pangs in the human observer. Changes in pressure in the stomach are
represented in trace A on the revolving drum. Reports of hunger pangs
are made by pressing the key; these are recorded as trace D on the drum.
Gastric contractions and reports of hunger pangs are seen to coincide
rather closely on the record. (From D. Krech and R. S. Crutchfield,
Elements of Psychology, p. 329. Published by Alfred A. Knopf in 1958,
and used with their permission.)

and (3) distention of the gastric glands during storage of gastric juice
(Beaumont). Since Cannon's hypothesis has been accepted, or at
least mentioned, in psychology textbooks for over forty years, it is
worth our careful examination.

"HUNGER PANGS" AND EATING. Cannon's claim that stomach
contractions are the cause of hunger was somewhat more modest than
it might appear. He meant only that "hunger pangs," the peculiar sensations that some people feel periodically after several hours of deprivation, are due to stomach contractions. Eating that is not associated
with hunger pangs, Cannon attributed to "appetite":

Hunger . . . is a dull ache or gnawing sensation referred to the lower mid-chest region and the epigastrium. . . . It may exist separately from appetite, as, for example, when hunger forces the taking of food not only distasteful but even nauseating [Cannon and Washburn, 1912, p. 441].

Because animals eat, sometimes eagerly, when the gastro-intestinal tract is wholly separated from the nervous system [reference to Schiff], the conclusion has been drawn that hunger must be a general sensation and not of peripheral [i.e., local] origin. But appetite as well as hunger leads to eating. As Ludwig stated many years ago, even if all afferent nerves were severed, psychic reasons could still be given for the taking of food. Indeed, who eats dessert because he is hungry? Evidently, since hunger is not required for eating, the fact that an animal eats is no testimony whatever that the animal is hungry . . . [p. 443].

The sensation of hunger rather than the mechanism that regulates eating was Cannon's main concern. This direction of his work fitted well with most of the psychology of his time, which attempted to explain experience rather than behavior. Nevertheless, Cannon wished to show further that the sensations of hunger are related to ingestion:

What causes the contractions to occur has not been determined. Since they decline during prolonged starvation they do not seem to be directly related to bodily need. Habit no doubt plays an important role. For present considerations, however, it is enough that they do occur, and that they are abolished when food, which satisfies bodily need, is taken into the stomach. By such indirection are performed some of the most fundamental of the bodily functions [Cannon and Washburn, 1912, p. 452].

Admitting stomach contractions as the cause of hunger explains several characteristics of hunger—its sudden onset, its periodicity, and its decline during starvation.

Carlson Supports Cannon's Hypothesis

Cannon's observations were soon corroborated and extended by A. J. Carlson in an impressive series of experiments. Carlson published an integrated account of his work in a book, *The Control of Hunger in Health and Disease* (1916). He and his collaborators used over fifty adult human subjects and found that "when the empty stomach shows strong contraction, the subject invariably signals that he feels hunger, and, on being questioned, he invariably replies that he feels hunger in his stomach" (Carlson, 1916, p. 64). Healthy newborn infants were also found to have stomach contractions, before any food had entered the stomach. Stomach contractions were also studied in several animal forms—dogs, rabbits, guinea pigs, pigeons, frogs, turtles, and a goat. In all these forms, deprivation of food led to increased gastric contractions and increased general bodily activity.

Nevertheless, in Carlson's view, the stomach was not yet established as the basic source of hunger. Perhaps the central nervous system governed stomach contractions and was itself the ultimate source of hunger. Carlson therefore removed all neural connections to the stomach in dogs, in order to determine whether stomach contractions would still occur. After the operation typical rhythmic contractions still occurred when the animal was deprived of food. This excluded the nervous system as the origin of stomach contractions. (*Inhibition* of stomach contractions is, nevertheless, controlled reflexly, as Carlson reported in 1913. Tasting or chewing food, he found, promptly stops both the sensation of hunger and stomach contractions. He speculated that this reflex might be conditional but concluded that it is probably innate.)

Next, Carlson sought to determine whether changes in blood chemistry might stimulate the stomach to contract. After a series of experiments, he concluded that some local factor in the stomach is chiefly responsible for the rate of contraction, although the rate can be modified somewhat by neural and chemical factors.

In order for the "gastric hunger contractions" to affect sensation and elicit reflex responses, they must be reported to the central nervous system, Carlson noted. The main afferent pathway from stomach to brain is the vagus nerves. "The primary hunger center is therefore the sensory nuclei of the vagi nerves in the medulla (fasciculus solitarius). Some of the more direct hunger reflexes (such as salivation, vasomotor fluctuations, etc.) may be carried out via these medullary centers alone" (1916, p. 214). (This is very close to the location that Schiff had designated fifty years before, although Schiff, it will be recalled, had proposed a central hypothesis and had denied the importance of stomach activity for hunger.)

By the time of Carlson's book, psychology textbooks—for example, Pillsbury's (1916)—were already referring to Cannon and Carlson's work as explaining the cause of hunger.

Reservations about the Stomach-Balloon Experiments

Certain other experimenters did not agree that "hunger pangs" were caused by strong contractions of the empty stomach. Boldyreff (1916) insisted that, although stomach contractions could be felt, they have no relation to the sensation of hunger. Furthermore, it was pointed out later that ". . . contractions seen by the users of balloons should not be spoken of as contractions of an *empty* stomach . . ." (Alvarez, 1940, pp. 397–8). When activity of the empty stomach was recorded without the use of a balloon, little activity was observed (Gianturco, 1934). Moreover, it was found that the introduction of a balloon into the previously empty stomach increased its activity! (Gianturco, 1934; Martin and Morton, 1952.) In other words, the early results on stomach contractions were partly artifacts of the method of recording.

Cannons's Local Theory of Thirst

In 1918 Cannon gave an influential lecture entitled, "The Physiological Basis of Thirst." As in the case of hunger, he distinguished between an appetite for fluids and true thirst. According to Cannon, most investigators had accepted a "general theory" of thirst, such as that stated by Schiff. (We would now call this a *central* hypothesis.) However, Cannon argued that the evidence for such a hypothesis is not conclusive. Furthermore, he considered it essential to account for the "universal" experience of dryness in the mouth and throat, and he felt that most investigators had neglected the sensation in favor of the bodily need which accompanies it.

The mouth and throat of land animals, Cannon noted, become dry as air traverses these passages during respiration. During the course of evolution, as air replaced water in the gullet, the land animals developed salivary glands which secrete a fluid that is normally more than 97 per cent water. In keeping with these facts, Cannon proposed his hypothesis:

> . . . that the salivary glands have, among their functions, that of keeping moist the ancient watercourse; that they, like other tissues, suffer when water is lacking in the body—a lack especially important for them, however, because their secretion is almost wholly water, and that, when these glands fail to provide sufficient fluid to moisten the mouth and throat, the local discomfort and unpleasantness which result constitute the feeling of thirst [1918, p. 295].

EVIDENCE FOR THE LOCAL THEORY OF THIRST.   To support his hypothesis, Cannon cited research of various investigators; for example, that of Pavlov showing that more saliva is secreted for dry food than for moist food. (Claude Bernard, we have noted, had demonstrated this considerably earlier.) Cannon also reported results of some experiments that he had done on himself. In one experiment he deprived himself of water and measured his salivary output once an hour. Thirst appeared about the time that salivation decreased, four hours after the start of the experiment. In another experiment he injected himself with a drug, pilocarpine, that prevents salivation, and he observed that he felt thirsty after the injection. The feeling of thirst could be abolished by washing the mouth and throat with an anesthetic solution, presumably because this prevented information about the local dryness from reaching the nervous system.

> From the evidence presented . . . it seems to me that we are now in a position to understand the mechanisms by which all three of the essential supplies from the outer world are provided for in our bodily economy. The oxygen supply is arranged for by the control which changes in the blood, brought about mainly by variations in the carbon dioxide content, exert on the centre for respiration. The proper food supply ultimately is assured, because we avoid, or check, by taking food, the distressing pangs of hunger which powerful contractions of the empty stomach induce unless food is taken. And the water supply is maintained because we avoid, or abolish, by taking water or aqueous fluid, the disagreeable sensations which arise and torment us with increasing torment if the salivary glands . . . fail . . . to pour out their watery secretion in sufficient amount and in proper quality to keep moist the mouth and pharynx [1918, p. 301].

This explanation of thirst is clearly similar to those of Haller (see p. 79), Beaumont (see p. 86), and Weber (see p. 92), but Cannon was evidently not aware of any of these anticipations of his hypothesis.

It is worth noting that Cannon accepted the central detection of a bodily need in the case of oxygen. Pavlov, as we have seen, argued that detection of the lack of food must operate in a similar way to detection of lack of oxygen. Cannon, however, believed that in the cases of lack of food and water the strong local sensations provide the ultimate guarantee of their satisfaction.

The Fate of Cannon's Local Hypotheses

INITIAL WIDESPREAD ACCEPTANCE. Cannon's hypotheses won immediate attention because their correlation of psychological need and physiological process could be so readily demonstrated. Besides, the local hypotheses seemed both simpler and more complete than hypotheses that involved the mysteries of the brain. The central hypotheses that had been prominent in physiological writing since the 1860's had received little attention in psychological texts. Now Cannon's local hypotheses were given wide currency in textbooks of both physiology and psychology.

Cannon's hypotheses were given even wider prominence among psychologists when he wrote the chapters on hunger and thirst in Murchison's *Handbooks of Experimental Psychology* in 1929 and 1934. In the first of these volumes, he countered proponents of central hypotheses with a number of arguments. One was that the brain does not normally respond to any chemical changes except changes in oxygen content of the blood. We have seen that Roux had advanced a similar argument in 1897. This statement would appear to contradict Cannon's recognition, in 1918, that the respiratory center of the brain responds to variations in the carbon dioxide content of the blood. This particular argument against central hypotheses did not appear in the 1934 edition.

REFUTATION OF CANNON'S LOCAL HYPOTHESES.   Meanwhile, further evidence in support of central hypotheses was accumulating. Eventually decisive evidence against the local hypotheses was also found. It will be recalled that many proponents of local hypotheses were not inclined to accept animal experiments as being relevant, since these investigators defined hunger in terms of reportable experience. To find human test cases must have seemed almost impossible—it would require a person without a stomach and a person without salivary glands. Eventually such cases were found, and they provided evidence that seemed to refute the local theorists, and under the conditions that they had demanded:

(1) Schiff had noted long before that patients with extensive lesions of the stomach often continued to feel hunger normally. With the progress of surgery in the twentieth century, larger and larger portions of the stomach could be removed. L. R. Müller (1915), arguing against the local hypothesis, reported that patients with practically total excision of the stomach continued to feel hunger just as before. Eventually it became possible to remove the stomach completely, and such patients were found still to perceive hunger normally. In a case reported in 1931 the patient "was emphatic in stating that the sensation of hunger was now 'just the same' as when he had a stomach." "Unfortunately he could not recall ever having had either before or after operation any sensation he would describe as a hunger pang. To him the sensation was one of emptiness in the stomach, followed by a feeling of general weakness" (Wangensteen and H. A. Carlson, 1931, p. 545). To test the local hypothesis thoroughly in this case, a recording balloon was put into the intestine to see whether the intestine might have taken over this function of the excised stomach. Nothing similar to stomach contractions was observed.

(2) The case of a man who had never had salivary glands was reported in 1936 (Austin and Steggerda). This man was accustomed to relieve the dry feeling in his mouth by taking a few small swallows of water nearly every hour. He reported that about four times a day he became actually thirsty; on these occasions he drank about 250 cc. (eight ounces) at a time. His total daily intake was about that of normal subjects living in the same environment.

The cases in (1) and (2) demonstrated that hunger can occur and eating be regulated without a stomach and that thirst can occur at normal intervals and drinking be regulated without salivary glands.

Cannon seems never to have abandoned his belief in his local hypotheses. In his book, *The Wisdom of the Body* (1939), he stated the local hypotheses along with much evidence in favor of them, and he did not mention other hypotheses.

Carlson held to the local hypothesis of hunger right through the final edition of his textbook, *The Machinery of the Body* (Carlson and Johnson, 1953). Concerning the local hypothesis of thirst, however, he felt impelled to do some tinkering as early as the first edition of the text (Carlson and Johnson, 1937). "Dryness of the surface of the mouth and throat," Carlson stated, "may cause a desire to moisten the parts; but unless the surface dryness is also accompanied by a water deficiency in the deeper tissues as well, true thirst is not experienced" (1937, p. 290). He therefore shifted the origin of thirst by a fraction of an inch to the deeper tissues of the throat, "which thus appears to be a sense organ for thirst, just as the stomach is for hunger" (1937, p. 290).

Although it has become clear that local hypotheses do not give the complete story of hunger and thirst mechanisms, it is possible that local sensations do normally play a role in the regulation of eating and drinking. In experimental work, many physiologists have continued to use stomach contractions as an index of the occurrence of hunger. One recent reviewer (Soulairac, 1958) concludes that any attempt at a complete theory of the regulation of hunger must take account of the gastric sensations.

PINPOINTING BRAIN CENTERS THAT CONTROL BEHAVIOR

DURING ALL THE DEBATE over the local hypotheses revived by Cannon, research continued on the central mechanisms of hunger and thirst. The local hypotheses were not able to hold back the rising tide of evidence. More and more exacting work was done to destroy or stimulate precise regions of the brain. This was coupled with continually refined measurements of eating and drinking and related behavior. Because of the great increase in physiological and psychological research in recent years, our account will be even more selective and fragmentary than in the earlier sections.[7]

The Stereotaxic Technique

The technique of Bailey and Bremer (1921) sufficed to prove that centers in the hypothalamus influence the intake of food and water. It was not precise enough, however, to map the hypothalamic nuclei and find exactly which ones were responsible. The hypothalamus is a cluster

[7] A detailed review of recent work on mechanisms of control of eating is given by Soulairac (1958).

of tiny nuclei, and recent research has demonstrated that different hypothalamic nuclei are responsible for different motive states—hunger and satisfaction of hunger, thirst and satisfaction of thirst, body temperature, lactation, and mating. To find this out, it was necessary to make very small localized lesions and to study the effects on behavior. The problem was complicated by the fact that in most cases the lesions must be exactly symmetrical in the two sides of the brain for any behavioral effect to occur.

A technique capable of such precision had been developed around 1905 by Horsley and Clarke. They fitted a calibrated frame around the head of the experimental animal and guided a fine electrode into the brain, controlling the position of the tip in three dimensions. With brain maps prepared in advance, they could reach any desired locus within the brain. Then an electrical current could be put through the electrode, to destroy the tissue just around the electrode tip. Or the electrode could be used to stimulate brain centers. Several studies were done with this technique before the First World War, but great skill and patience were required to use it. Stimulation experiments were continued by the Swiss physiologist Hess and others. Stereotaxic production of lesions was largely abandoned for about twenty years, "perhaps because the electrodes were very fragile and expensive and because the chart sections for localization were inadequate" (Ranson, 1934, p. 272). In the early 1930's the technique was revived and made practical by the development of strong inexpensive electrodes and the preparation of improved maps of the brain (Ranson).

A Center That Inhibits Eating

The first center to be located definitely was not one for hunger or thirst but rather was a center for the *satisfaction* of hunger. The initial observation was that destruction of this region led to development of obesity. It will be recalled that obesity following hypothalamic damage had been reported in humans by Erdheim in 1904 and had been demonstrated in two of the dogs of Bailey and Bremer in 1921. Smith produced obesity in rats by means of hypothalamic injuries, but he noted that "structural studies upon the hypothalamus of the rat are so difficult that the localization of the injuries inducing obesity . . . has not been determined" (1931, p. 57). Finally Hetherington and Ranson (1940, 1942), using the improved Horsley-Clarke technique, located the effective area—it was the ventromedial nuclei of the hypothalamus (see Figure 13). Other investigators soon confirmed that destruction of similar locations in the monkey and the cat produced obesity.

Hetherington and Ranson coupled their accurate lesions with more adequate behavioral measures than had previously been used in this field. They measured both spontaneous activity and food intake in operated and control animals (1942). For a few hours after the operation, rats showed overactivity, but then a lasting inactivity set in. The operated animals consumed large amounts when offered soft palatable food, but a diet of hard dry pellets discouraged high intake. From their observations, Hetherington and Ranson hypothesized that both the excessive eating and the reduced activity were only symptoms of the primary cause. This primary deficiency, they suggested, was a partial inability to use the body's store of food. According to this hypothesis the operated rats accumulated fat because they could not readily metabolize it; they overate because the cells actually lacked nutriment.

OVEREATING IS A PRIMARY EFFECT OF THE BRAIN LESION.   Another research team, working at the same time, put its emphasis directly on the overeating. These investigators, Brobeck, Tepperman, and Long (1943), termed the condition produced by the lesions "hypothalamic hyperphagia" (hyperphagia = overeating). They noted that "the rats appeared to be ravenously hungry almost immediately after the operation, eating two or three times the normal amount of food daily. . . . When they were fed normal quantities of food, they frequently ate a 24-hour portion within a few hours" (p. 851). As the rats became obese, the hyperphagia gradually disappeared. Some rats were then fasted; they metabolized their fat and lost weight. When their weight was down to normal, they were again given food freely. There had been no recovery from the effects of the lesion, for the rats again showed hyperphagia and again became obese. These and other observations convinced Brobeck *et al.* that "the adiposity does not cause, but rather follows, the increased appetite" (p. 849).

If destruction of this hypothalamic area causes overeating, then presumably the area normally functions to inhibit eating. It was several years before this point was made explicitly, however, and the discovery of a center which normally promotes eating helped to clarify the picture.

Another inhibitory area has been pointed out recently—the amygdaloid complex (Green, Clemente, and de Groot, 1957). This complex is composed of nuclei lying in the base of the temporal lobe, to the side of the hypothalamus (see Figure 13). It receives fibers from the cortex of the frontal lobe and sends fibers to the ventromedial nucleus of the hypothalamus (Adey and Meyer, 1952). Thus the amygdaloid nuclei may act as a way station, transmitting cortical messages to the hypothalamic inhibitory center. Without these messages, the inhibitory center may fail to function adequately.

The Hypothalamic "Feeding Center"

A BRAIN LESION THAT ABOLISHES EATING.   In 1951 Anand and Brobeck announced that bilateral destruction of a small region in the lateral hypothalamus leads to complete and permanent cessation of eating. They noted that some earlier workers had reported incidental cases of inhibition of eating after hypothalamic lesions. Nevertheless, theirs was the first study directed toward localizing the center involved. Rats with lesions in the "feeding center" never ate in spite of attempts to put food near them or even in the mouth. Until they became emaciated and lethargic through starvation, the operated rats looked normal and showed a normal amount of activity.

RELATIONS BETWEEN INHIBITORY AND EXCITATORY CENTERS. Anand and Brobeck attempted to define the relation between the two hypothalamic regions that affect eating. In some rats they first made medial lesions, producing obesity (e.g., the center lesions in Figure 13). Then a single lateral lesion was made; it had no effect on eating (the lesion to the left in the illustration). Finally, the second lateral lesion was made, and thereafter the animal stopped eating and never ate again. It was concluded that the lateral feeding center "may be responsible for the central hunger reaction or the urge to eat, while the ventromedial nucleus or some structure in its neighborhood may be capable of exerting an inhibitory control over the 'feeding center' . . ." (Anand and Brobeck, 1951, p. 138).

Anand, Dua, and Shoenberg (1955) reported similar effects in cats and monkeys. Two of the six aphagic monkeys would eat, however, if food was placed in their mouths. Since they had not observed such an effect in rats or cats, the investigators speculated that control of eating might show a greater influence of the neocortex in higher animals.

Electrical Stimulation of Centers for Satiety and Feeding

While lesions show what happens in the absence of the destroyed brain center, the normal activity of the center may be revealed by stimulating it electrically. This technique has been employed ever since Fritsch and Hitzig used it in 1871 to study the motor cortex. The Swiss physiologist Walter Rudolph Hess explored the functions of the hypothalamus for over twenty years by means of this technique. He implanted electrodes in the hypothalamus and, after the animal had recovered from the operation, the hypothalamus could be stimulated while the animal moved about freely. Hess was awarded the Nobel Prize in 1949 for this work. Hunger and thirst were not principal subjects of his research, but another investigator studied the records of Hess in this regard and found a number of experiments from 1928 to 1942 in which localized stimulation led to ravenous eating and drinking (Brügger, 1943).

Swedish workers later employed the methods of Hess to study eating in the goat. They reported in 1954 (Larsson) that stimulation in the lateral hypothalamus often produced hyperphagia, sometimes accompanied by an unusual amount of licking and chewing. Sometimes only the licking and chewing occurred. In two cases hyperphagia was also obtained upon stimulation of the nucleus of the vagus nerve

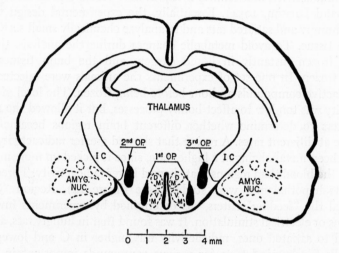

FIGURE 13. Section cut across the rat brain, running through the hypothalamus. Lesions are shown as black areas. After small bilateral lesions just to the side of the ventromedial nuclei of the hypothalamus (1st op.), the animal began to eat excessively and became obese. A unilateral lesion in the lateral hypothalamic area (2nd op.) produced no further change. Following a symmetrical lateral lesion (3rd op.), the animal stopped eating, and it never ate again. Such experiments suggest the existence of localized control over satiety and hunger. (Placement of lesions after Anand and Brobeck, 1951.) *IC*, internal capsule; *Amyg. Nuc.*, amygdaloid nuclei; *DM*, dorsomedial nucleus of the hypothalamus; *VM*, ventromedial nucleus of the hypothalamus.

in the medulla. Stimulation of the hypothalamus was also accomplished by injecting small amounts of salt solution through hypodermic needles implanted in the brain; this type of stimulation was also effective in producing hyperphagia.

Both the medial (satiety) and lateral (feeding) centers of cats have been stimulated electrically (Delgado and Anand, 1953; Anand and Dua, 1955). Increased intake was produced by stimulation of the lateral feeding region; in many cases the increase persisted for a day or two after the stimulation. Stimulation of the medial hypothalamus decreased intake but never led to complete cessation of eating. When stimulation produced no changes in eating, the electrodes were later found to be outside of the food centers. Thus the results of stimulation experiments agreed well with the results of lesion experiments.

Brain Biochemistry in Hunger

Creation of lesions clearly removes the brain from its normal state, and electrical stimulation does not leave it completely normal either. In an attempt to study the mechanism of hunger without disrupting brain activity, biochemical methods have recently been used (Forssberg and Larsson, 1954). Essentially, the experimental design was to take hungry and satiated rats and to analyze chemically small sections of brain tissue. To avoid metabolic changes during the analysis, the rats were frozen instantly in liquid oxygen, and the brain tissues were kept frozen. In one set of experiments the animals were injected with radioactive compounds an hour before being frozen. The level of radioactivity was too low to affect bodily processes, but it allowed the experimenters to determine whether different brain regions became radioactive at different rates. A region that showed greater radioactivity must have been metabolizing at a higher rate, since it picked up more material from the blood than regions that showed lower radioactivity. Three parts of the hypothalamus were studied (see Figure 14). Region "C" included the "feeding centers," as determined by experiments involving lesions or electrical stimulation. It was found that in hungry rats, as compared to satiated ones, radioactivity was higher in C and lower in A and B. Biochemical tests for various compounds important in carbohydrate metabolism yielded similar results. Thus it appears that during hunger, Region C becomes more active than usual, while the surrounding regions become less active. The biochemical techniques therefore corroborate the localization determined by experiments involving lesions and electrical stimulation.

"HUNGRY BLOOD"

WHILE SOME INVESTIGATORS were trying to find the brain centers that regulate eating, others were attempting to determine what characteristics of the blood are monitored by the hunger centers. What differences between the blood of hungry and satiated organisms are important in determining hunger and satiety?

The level of glucose (blood sugar) was an obvious candidate for consideration. Glucose is the primary fuel of the cells; other sugars, as well as fats and proteins, must be transformed into glucose before they can provide energy to the cells. Soon after insulin was discovered in 1921, it was found that large doses, which reduce greatly the level of blood sugar, cause hunger. Bulatao and Carlson (1924) suggested that low levels of blood sugar provoke gastric contractions and thus cause hunger. Other experimenters were unable to correlate spontaneous fluctuations in blood sugar either with gastric contractions (Quigley and Hallaran, 1932; Scott, Scott, and Luckhardt, 1938) or with reports of hunger (Janowitz and Ivy, 1949). The level of glucose in the blood is kept rather constant, and fluctuations in it tend to be small and brief.

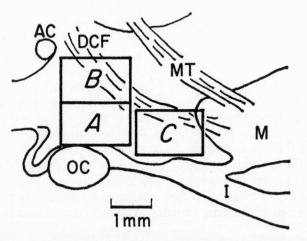

FIGURE 14. Section cut through the rat hypothalamus parallel to the midline. (This is similar to the section of the human brain shown in the right half of Figure 10. Note, however, that in the rat brain the stalk of the pituitary, *I*, slants almost horizontally to the rear rather than hanging almost straight down as in the human brain.)

Radioactively tagged compounds were injected into hungry and satiated rats. Blocks of tissue were then removed for chemical analysis. Block *C* included both the medial and lateral hunger centers shown in Figure 13. Hungry rats showed greater radioactivity in *C* and less in *A* and *B* than did satiated rats. (After Forssberg and Larsson, 1954, Figure 14.)

AC, anterior commissure; OC, optic chiasma; M, mammillary body; I, infundibulum; DCF, descending column of the fornix; MT, mammillothalamic tract (tract of Vicq d' Azyr).

Recently Jean Mayer [8] and his associates have suggested that food intake is regulated by the rate of passage of glucose into cells in the ventromedial hypothalamus (Mayer, 1953). The rate of entrance of glucose into hypothalamic cells could not be measured directly, but it was suggested that the *difference* of glucose levels between the arteries and the veins gives an index of utilization of glucose. It is quite possible for a high level of glucose to exist in the blood without passing readily into the cells; this may occur, for example, in sugar diabetes. In this case the arterio-venous difference in glucose remains small, and the cells

[8] Jean Mayer is the son of André Mayer whose osmotic hypothesis of thirst we have noted and who did much subsequent research on food and water regulation.

are actually short of glucose, starving in the midst of plenty. The hypothesis that hunger and ingestion are regulated by cells that monitor the arterio-venous difference in glucose has been termed the "glucostatic theory."

Evidence Concerning the Glucostatic Hypothesis

Human subjects have been found to have their hunger satiated when they had relatively large arterio-venous differences in glucose; the existence of small differences was a necessary condition for the occurrence of hunger, but hunger did not always accompany small arterio-venous differences (Van Itallie, Beaudoin, and Mayer, 1953; Stunkard and Wolff, 1956). An attempt to test the hypothesis by injection of glucose did not yield clearcut results (Bernstein and Grossman, 1956). Another attempt involved injections of a hormone, glucagon, that promotes both formation of glucose and utilization of glucose by the cells; it also increases the arterio-venous difference markedly. Injection of this hormone promptly checked both gastric contractions and reports of hunger (Stunkard, Van Itallie, and Reis, 1955). Injection of glucagon over a two-week period also reduced significantly the amount of food eaten (Schulman, Carleton, Whitney, and Whitehorn, 1957).

CHEMICAL DESTRUCTION OF CELLS THAT CONTROL HUNGER.   Evidence of a different sort has come from the injection of gold thioglucose in mice and rats (Mayer, 1957). This compound is toxic, and a large proportion of the animals who survive the injection become obese. Examination of the brains reveals damage especially in the ventromedial region of the hypothalamus. Related compounds containing sugars other than glucose are equally toxic, but they do not induce hypothalamic lesions nor cause obesity. It appears that it is the affinity of cells in the ventral hypothalamus for glucose that leads them to take in the toxic gold thioglucose. Not all cells in this region are affected, as histological examination of the lesions indicates. Furthermore, animals made obese in this way do not show associated symptoms, such as gonadal dysfunction or disturbance in water balance, to the degree found in rats made obese by destroying all cells in the region. Thus it appears that cells monitoring glucose utilization are interspersed with other cells in the ventral hypothalamus.

While the glucostatic hypothesis is attractive, it is still in the process of being weighed and tested (see Soulairac, 1958, pp. 727–33).

Evidence for a Fat Hormone

Short-term monitoring of the body's supply of nutrients may be accomplished in terms of the availability of glucose, but the body's long-term stores of energy are held in the form of fat (Kennedy, 1953). Recent research has produced evidence for a hormone whose level in the blood would reflect the store of fat and help determine the rate of intake of food (Hervey, 1959). Pairs of young rats were joined surgically so that some exchange developed between their bloodstreams; they can be considered to be artificial Siamese twins. Several months later, one rat of each pair would then be made hyperphagic by means of a hypothalamic lesion, and it would grow obese. Within a few months, the fat deposits of such an animal would reach fifty per cent of its body weight. Meanwhile the partner would become thin, lose almost all its fat, and in some cases would die of malnutrition. These results can be interpreted by hypothesizing that the fat deposits of the first animal caused liberation of a hormone that signals the presence of large amounts of fat. Presumably the brain of this animal no longer detected the fat hormone after destruction of the ventromedial nuclei (the regions that are also thought to monitor the glucose difference). In the partner with the normal brain, however, the circulating fat hormone was detected and this led to reduced intake of food. It should be noted that the cross-circulation did not carry large amounts of material from the obese rat to its undernourished partner. While the amount of food materials transferred was obviously slight, the amount of hormone in the cross-circulation was sufficient to be effective, and hormones are known to be active in minute amounts.

THE CENTRAL REGULATION OF DRINKING

INVESTIGATION OF THE CONTROL of drinking has progressed in parallel with the studies of the control of eating that we have just reviewed. The experiment of Bailey and Bremer (1921), it will be recalled, showed that both excessive drinking and excessive eating can be caused by small lesions in the hypothalamus. In the case of thirst, however, the primary stimulus condition was found before the brain centers were localized accurately.

The Stimulus That Initiates Thirst

Lack of water in the body is the obvious condition that arouses thirst and drinking, but where in the body does the effective lack occur? André Mayer (1900) had supposed that hypertonicity—a relative lack of water—occurred in the blood and thus in all the cells; Wettendorff (1901) believed that it must be in fluids and tissues other than the blood and the brain. The osmotic hypothesis received support when Leschke (1918) reported that intravenous injection of a hypertonic saline solution in human subjects immediately caused intense thirst. However, this had to be qualified later when it was found that not all hypertonic solutions had this effect (Arden, 1934). By proper choice of injected solutions, water could be moved in or out of the cells, while keeping constant the total water content of the body. Thus Gilman (1937) injected either sodium chloride or urea solutions into dogs, making the osmotic pressure of the blood rise to the same extent in both cases. Since sodium does not readily pass through cell membranes, water left the cells; urea passes through the membranes, so no shift of water occurred in this case. When the dogs were allowed to drink a half hour after the injection, those given saline solution drank more than twice as much as those given urea solution. In another experiment, water was driven into the cells. Despite the signs of dehydration, "the strikingly dry appearance of the oral mucous membranes and the probable lack of salivary secretions, these dogs did not experience the sensation of thirst." They shunned water. "It is tempting to attribute this to the low electrolyte and high water content of the cells" (Gilman, 1937, p. 327). It seemed clear, therefore, that lack of water in the *cells* was the primary stimulus to drinking.

The sensitivity of detection of water deficit was shown by Adolph and his collaborators. Dogs were found to start drinking whenever their water loss reached about ½ per cent of the body weight; they did not sip frequently but drank only when the threshold water loss had occurred (Robinson and Adolph, 1943). Moreover, if greater deficits were produced by withholding water, the dog made up the deficit quite exactly when it was allowed to drink freely. Within four minutes, the amount of the deficit was ingested—long before the water could be absorbed into the blood (Adolph, 1939). It is as if the mechanism had been preset to take in the needed amount.

The signal that stops the drinking may be the quantity of "water messages" sent by the taste receptors, according to recent evidence of Deutsch and Jones (1960). These investigators referred to the finding of Zotterman (1956) that in the rat one type of nerve fiber can indicate either water or salt. It indicates water by a *decrease* in the rate of spontaneous firing, whereas it indicates a hypertonic salt solution by an *increase* in the rate of firing. A hypotonic salt solution will decrease the rate of firing, but not so greatly as will pure water. Several studies have shown that rats drink large quantities of hypotonic saline solution even where water is freely available, and this had been taken as evidence for a preference for salt. However, Deutsch and Jones showed that when thirsty rats were allowed to run to one arm of a T-maze for water or to the other arm for salt solution, the rats clearly preferred the water. Deutsch and Jones therefore suggest that when a rat starts drinking saline solution, it drinks more saline than it would drink water because it receives less "water messages" per unit of volume. A hypotonic salt solution is, in effect, diluted water!

The Thirst Centers

Granted that the hydration of bodily cells controls drinking, do all cells participate equally in this regulation? As in the case of hunger centers, experiments involving small lesions helped to localize the centers controlling drinking.

HYPOTHALAMIC LESIONS THAT CAUSE EXCESSIVE DRINKING. Although it had been demonstrated that lesions at the base of the hypothalamus led to excessive drinking (Bailey and Bremer, 1921), controversy continued because excessive output of urine also occurred in such experiments. Many investigators maintained that the lesion caused the polyuria directly and that the polydipsia was only a secondary effect. In order to solve this problem, Bellows and Van Wagenen (1938) decided to separate drinking from water content of the body by using dogs with esophageal fistulas (the same sort of preparation that Pavlov had used to study gastric secretion). After the fistulas were established and the dogs became accustomed to having food and water placed directly into the stomach, they rarely drank. Whatever water they did drink only flowed out through the upper fistula without reaching the stomach. Then lesions were made in the tuber cinereum—the base of the hypothalamus just behind the pituitary stalk (see Figure 15). The dogs soon began to drink enormous quantities of water, all of which passed out through the fistula. Their urinary excretion remained normal. Dogs without fistulas, subjected to the same hypothalamic lesion, developed both polydipsia and polyuria. Thus the excessive drinking was shown to be the primary result of the lesion; the polyuria occurred only when the water content of the body became too great. Bellows and Van Wagenen concluded, "The production of a persistent 'unjustified' thirst, or primary polydipsia, by an injury to the hypothalamus suggests that this region of the brain is the center of the thirst function" (1938, p. 469).

Searching for possible "osmoreceptors" that might monitor water metabolism, Verney (1947) noticed peculiar fluid-filled cells in the supraoptic region of the anterior hypothalamus. He speculated that these cells might have stretch receptors attached to their surface, thus providing for conversion of changes of osmotic pressure into nerve impulses. Although little evidence has been offered to support this speculation, it has remained rather popular.

HYPOTHALAMIC LESIONS THAT ABOLISH THIRST. The progress of experimentation on hunger centers next stimulated further work on thirst. In some experiments it was found that a *reduction* of drinking accompanied hypothalamic obesity; it was suggested that centers for drinking might be so close to centers for eating that they could not completely escape damage when the centers for eating were destroyed (Stevenson, Welt, and Orloff, 1950). This would mean that the excitatory center for drinking is located close to the inhibitory center for eating. In other experiments, when the entire anterior hypothalamus was removed in dogs, they stopped drinking completely and soon died unless water was administered. "The absence of thirst is evidenced by a complete lack of interest in water, even to the point of critical dehydration; yet when water is baited slightly with milk or meat juice, the animal drinks it ravenously, i.e., as food but not as water. Thirst continues to be absent in the presence of physiological stability maintained by therapy" (Witt, Keller, Batsel, and Lynch, 1952). (It is interesting to note that normal suckling animals refuse water but drink milk eagerly.) Andersson and McCann (1956) found that medial hypothalamic lesions, not involving the anterior hypothalamus, can also produce stoppage of drinking. Although their dogs shunned water, they readily drank milk or broth. Most animals showed partial recovery of drinking within about two weeks after the operation.

EXPERIMENTAL STIMULATION OF THIRST CENTERS.   Electrical and chemical stimulation of the hypothalamus have also been used to localize the centers that regulate water intake. Stimulation with hypertonic saline solution anywhere within a fairly wide region of the medial hypothalamus produced prompt and excessive drinking (Andersson and McCann, 1955). Electrical stimulation allowed a much more precise localization of the site giving the maximal polydipsic effect— just between the descending column of the fornix and the tract of Vicq d'Azyr (see Figure 15). Stimulation here evoked drinking in ten to thirty seconds, and drinking continued until two or three seconds after the current was stopped. Experimental goats could be made to drink up to 40 per cent of their body weight within a short period, causing marked signs of water intoxication. The stimulation evoked approach to water as well as drinking; i.e., if the water was placed in the far corner of the pen, the animal would go to it and start drinking when the stimulation was turned on. One observer commented that Andersson knows how to lead an animal to water *and* make it drink!

Electrical recording techniques may also be helpful in locating the centers and following the neural processes that control drinking. In an initial study of this sort, von Euler (1953) recorded the potentials of the supraoptic region of the hypothalamus in anesthetized cats. When he injected a hypertonic salt solution into the carotid artery, a long slow change of potential developed; when he injected tap water (which is, of course, hypotonic), a response of the opposite polarity was evoked. Such

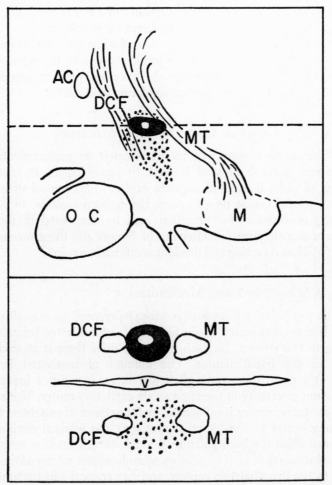

FIGURE 15. Sections through the hypothalamus of a goat, to show a region controlling drinking. (The upper section is similar to that of the human brain shown in Figure 10 and of the rat brain in Figure 14.) The dotted area represents the region of the hypothalamus where microinjections of hypertonic salt solutions elicited drinking. The black area represents the region where electrical stimulation caused drinking, and the central white circle shows where the most pronounced effect was obtained.

The brain was cut through horizontally at the level of the dotted line, and this section is shown in the lower part of the figure. Here you are looking down on the section, and the ventricle (V) runs along the midline. The region responding to microinjections has been indicated on one side and that responding to electrical stimulation on the other, but both types of stimulation are, of course, effective on both sides of the hypothalamus.

AC, anterior commissure; DCF, descending column of the fornix; MT, mammillothalamic tract (Tract of Vicq d'Azyr); OC, optic chiasma; I, infundibulum; M, mammillary body; V, third ventricle. (After Andersson and McCann, 1955, Figures 1 and 2.)

differential reactivity is one of the requisites of a center regulating water intake on the basis of changes of the internal environment.

Much progress has thus been made in finding regions that excite or inhibit drinking. Nevertheless, the localizations and the relationships among centers regulating water intake have not yet been detailed to the extent that is true of the centers regulating food intake.

Central Control of Motivation

THE RAPID PROGRESS of recent research on centers controlling hunger and thirst is of vital interest to psychologists. It raises the prospect of more direct and accurate experimental control of motivation and reinforcement than has ever before been possible. In evaluating these possibilities, two questions will be considered in the final section of this chapter: (1) How do the hunger and thirst mechanisms work? (2) How do eating and drinking reinforce behavior?

A Schema of Drive Mechanisms

The psychologist Eliot Stellar (1954) proposed an over-all physiological scheme that he felt might fit all types of motivated behavior. According to this scheme, for each motive or drive there is an excitatory center in the hypothalamus. The amount of motivated behavior shown at a given time, for a particular drive, is a direct function of the amount of activity in the appropriate excitatory center. The activity of the excitatory center is influenced by four classes of variables: (1) an inhibitory center in the hypothalamus, (2) the internal environment which can affect the hypothalamus through its rich vascular supply and the cerebrospinal fluid, (3) sensory stimuli which set up afferent impulses to the hypothalamic centers, and (4) cortical and thalamic centers which can exert excitatory and inhibitory influences on the hypothalamic centers. Let us see how well this scheme encompasses the facts so far discovered about hunger and thirst. Let us also see where it must be extended or modified.

THE HUNGER MECHANISM.   An *excitatory center* has been localized in the lateral nucleus of the hypothalamus. Both lesions and electrical stimulation have demonstrated this. Nevertheless, this cannot be the sole seat of excitation, for Teitelbaum and Stellar (1954) have demonstrated that it is possible to get rats to eat again after destruction of this region. The rats were kept alive by force-feeding and they were offered highly palatable foods; they recovered normal eating behavior within six to sixty-five days after the operation. It is not yet known where in the brain the residual excitatory activity may be centered.

An *inhibitory center* has been localized in the ventromedial nucleus of the hypothalamus. When this is destroyed, the animal becomes hyperphagic and gains weight rapidly. Similar effects occur with lesions in the amygdaloid nuclei; it is possible that the amygdaloid nuclei serve to funnel impulses into the ventromedial nucleus. Two sorts of evidence show that the ventromedial nucleus (and the amygdaloid complex) cannot be the sole seat of inhibition: (1) Hypothalamic hyperphagic rats do not gain weight without limit; their weight finally reaches a plateau. Thus there must still be some avenue through which obesity can check intake. (2) Obese hyperphagic rats are more finicky than normal animals about their diet; they refuse hard or unpalatable food that a normal rat would eat. It appears that destruction of the ventromedial nucleus abolishes the inhibition that normally arises from ingestion but leaves intact the inhibition that arises from other sources. It is not yet known where the inhibitory controls are located that continue to function after the ventromedial nucleus has been destroyed.

The *internal environment* certainly affects the hypothalamus, although it is not yet clear what characterizes "hungry blood." Recent evidence indicates that it is the arterio-venous difference in glucose. Glucose seems to be taken up especially rapidly in the ventromedial region of the hypothalamus. There may also be a hormonal indication of the body's store of fat, this too being monitored by the ventromedial hypothalamus.

Sensory stimuli are no longer considered to be the origin of hunger, as the local theorists had long maintained. On the other hand, the stimuli occurring as a consequence of eating have long been considered important in allaying hunger (Magendie, 1838; Roux, 1897), and recent work offers some support for this view. The stimulation arising from ingestion provides a rapid feedback, which is later supplemented by a delayed feedback as the internal environment is modified by absorbed food. Attempts have been made to assess separately the effectiveness of stimulation of the mouth and throat and of the stomach on allaying hunger. Experiments on dogs with esophageal fistulas demonstrate that they will swallow much more food than they need (Pawlow, 1898; Janowitz and Grossman, 1949). Thus the consummatory acts of passing food through the mouth and throat are not an important source of inhibition. Placing food directly in the stomach through a gastric fistula inhibits real feeding, but it does not inhibit sham-feeding through an esophageal fistula. The most effective way found to inhibit sham feeding was to place food into the stomach while the dog was sham feeding (Janowitz and Grossman, 1949). Apparently this reproduces the *pattern* of stimulation which normally checks eating.

Cortical and thalamic centers can also be shown to influence eating, and other brain regions may also be important. Removal of the frontal cortex may lead to overeating in rats (Richter and Hawkes, 1939) and in men. Destruction of cortical and thalamic areas that are important in form perception will obviously handicap a person or animal in finding food. Even if forms are perceived, objects may not be recognized if the temporal-lobe cortex is destroyed bilaterally; this has led to attempts by monkeys (Klüver and Bucy, 1939) and by men to eat inedible objects. The great importance of learning for selection of foods and for scheduling meals has long been noted; this may be taken as indirect evidence for the participation of nonhypothalamic centers in the control of eating behavior.

The five-part mechanism we have examined can encompass most of the facts we have reviewed. It has some gaps and limitations, as in the case of the residual controls which continue even after destruction of the known "centers." These limitations serve to show the work still to be done before the complete story is known.

THE THIRST MECHANISM.   There seem to be two *excitatory centers* for thirst in the hypothalamus. One is somewhere in the anterior hypothalamus; the other is in the lateral medial hypothalamus. Destruction of either leads to cessation of drinking water, although milk and broth are still accepted. The presence of two such regions is a complication not foreseen in Stellar's scheme. Furthermore, at least in the case of the medial location, animals show partial resumption of drinking if kept alive for about two weeks. Perhaps the other excitatory area can take over completely in this case.

An *inhibitory center* for thirst has been found in the tuber cinereum at the base of the hypothalamus. More accurate localization of this center is needed.

The *internal environment* seems to be monitored by the changes it produces in cellular hydration.

Sensory stimuli must be important in the identification of water; it will be recalled that animals which refused water after hypothalamic lesions nevertheless continued to accept milk or broth. Stimuli from the mouth and throat also serve to allay thirst and inhibit drinking. An animal with an esophageal fistula will pass through its mouth and throat an amount of water closely equal to its deficit. It is as if the excitatory mechanism were prepared to call out a certain amount of consummatory behavior or to require a certain number of "water messages." Gastric sensations are less effective in dogs; putting water in the stomach will also check drinking, but only after a delay of ten minutes (Bellows, 1939) or thirty minutes (Holmes, 1941). The latter delay is great enough to allow almost complete absorption into the bloodstream to take place, minimizing the importance of the gastric sensory factor. In the rat, putting water directly into the stomach leads to a prompt reduction in drinking (Miller, Sampliner, and Woodrow, 1957; O'Kelly and Falk, 1958). It should be noted that in the rat water is absorbed from the digestive tract more rapidly than in larger animals. Again, it is not clear whether gastric stimulation alone can allay thirst before changes occur in the internal environment.

The role of *other brain regions* has not been studied as extensively in the control of drinking as in the control of eating. There seems to be no evidence that nonhypothalamic regions influence the drive to drink. Nevertheless, insofar as perceptual mechanisms and learning influence the search for water and the scheduling of drinking, it is probable that nonhypothalamic regions participate as they do in the case of hunger.

For thirst, there are clearly gaps in the data as well as limitations in the five-part scheme.

How Do Eating and Drinking Reinforce Behavior?

In many learning situations, food or water are used as rewards. It has often been supposed that since hunger and thirst are basic needs, the substances which reduce these needs are primary reinforcements. Clark L. Hull (1943) considered, however, that the long delay between ingestion and reduction of need in the cells made it improbable that ingestion is a primary reinforcement. Nevertheless, the presentation and mastication of food is a powerful reinforcing combination. "These considerations strongly suggest that *the eating of food brings about learning through secondary reinforcement rather than through primary reinforcement*" (1943, p. 99).

Hull suggested that this hypothesis could be tested upon animals with esophageal fistulas. (He knew of the work of Bellows and Van Wagenen, although he did not cite it here.) In the experiment, one type of food could be eaten and allowed to fall from the upper fistula. For another type of food, a tube could connect the two fistulas, so that the food would reach the stomach. ". . . A dog sham fed on one kind of food and really fed on another kind of food should, after a time, show a distinct preference for the food which mediates nutrition and so primary reinforcement; after much training it might even refuse to eat the sham food since, not being reinforced, this activity should suffer experimental extinction" (1943, p. 99). Tolman also suggested the same experiment several years later (Tolman, 1949, p. 147).

LEARNING NOT TO EAT.   Hull never carried out exactly this experiment, but he did an interesting pilot study on a single dog and published it several years later (Hull, Livingstone, Rouse, and Barker, 1951). In one part of this study the dog was allowed to sham feed on gruel once a day; the session was continued until the dog made a pause of five minutes in his eating. The question was whether experimental extinction would occur. During the first few days, the dog "ate" gruel equal to three-quarters of its body weight in each session. Thereafter the amount taken diminished rapidly, and on the eighth day the dog took only a few licks. Outside the experimental room, it would still sham feed. The experimental extinction found here (and the extinction of drinking in the fistulous dogs of Bellows and Van Wagenen) stands in unresolved contrast to the dogs of Pavlov who apparently did not show extinction of sham eating (see p. 99). The results of the American investigators suggest that the sight, smell, and taste of food and the consummatory responses may afford secondary rather than primary reinforcement.

Other evidence nevertheless suggests that the stimulation arising from consummatory acts may afford primary reinforcement, and this may be an innate characteristic—at least of mammals. It is clear that newly born mammals must nurse *before* food is ever absorbed into the body from the digestive tract. The problem of the sucking reflex is complicated, however, and McKee and Honzik discuss its history and present status in their chapter (see pp. 585–661).

CENTRAL VERSUS PERIPHERAL REINFORCEMENT.   The reward value of placing food directly into the stomach was also tested in Hull's pilot experiment. The dog learned to go to the side of the maze where gruel was put into the lower fistula through a tube rather than to the other side of the maze where an empty tube was put into the fistula. Experiments on this question were soon reported by other psychologists at Yale. They compared the reduction of hunger in rats after three treatments: (1) swallowing a fixed amount of milk, (2) receiving the same amount of milk directly in the stomach, and (3) receiving this amount of saline solution directly in the stomach. Hunger was measured by the rate with which the animal would press a panel to obtain milk (Kohn, 1951), or by the amount of milk it would drink from a graduate (Berkun, Kessen, and Miller, 1952). In both experiments, milk injected into the stomach reduced hunger more than did saline, but milk drunk normally was even more effective. Miller and Kessen (1952) similarly found that rats learned a T-maze faster when they were rewarded by being allowed to drink milk than when milk was injected into the stomach. Bellows (1939) had shown that there is a rapid temporary reduction in thirst when water is passed through the mouth and a more slowly acting but longer reduction when water is put directly into the stomach. (It will be recalled that Alexis St. Martin's hunger could be satisfied by food placed directly into the stomach; nevertheless, he preferred normal eating.)

A further step in by-passing the normal alimentary channels was taken in an experiment where the reward was intravenous injection of glucose solution (Coppock and Chambers, 1954). Rats were restrained in a snugly fitting cage so that almost the only response available was turning the head to one side or the other. During an initial period, the side preferred by the rat was determined. Then during the training period, the rat was rewarded by glucose injection whenever he turned his head to the initially non-preferred side. Rats given the glucose reward showed a significantly greater preference for the rewarded side than did the controls. These and related results (Chambers, 1956) indicate that reinforcement need not involve peripheral stimulation, consummatory responses, or even gastric stimulation.

An even more advanced step in tracing the process of reinforcement would be to stimulate directly the brain centers that signal satisfaction of cellular need. The experiments in which the satiety regions were stimulated, reducing intake of food (Anand and Dua, 1955), suggest that this can be done. It has not yet been demonstrated, however, whether such stimulation can be used to reinforce behavior. An unexpected discovery is the finding of Olds and Milner (1954) that there may be a "reward region" of the brain. Electrical stimulation within this region can apparently be used to reinforce any aspect of performance that the experimenter selects. More recently Olds has reported that parts of this reward region show interaction with the level of hunger, so that a hungry animal can be "rewarded" by a lower voltage of stimulation than a satiated animal (Olds, 1958). Research in this area is being actively pursued by many investigators.

SUMMARY AND CONCLUSIONS

Now THAT WE HAVE brought our survey down to the near present, what main themes stand out in retrospect? How can we characterize a century and a half of active research on the mechanisms of hunger and thirst?

First of all, it may be well to recall that experimentation on hunger and thirst did begin only in the early nineteenth century, although recorded speculation about their origins goes back to classical antiquity. The ancient speculation quite naturally referred hunger to the stomach, both because food was known to go to the stomach and because it is in this general region that many people feel special sensations when mealtimes approach or when they have been deprived of food. These local hypotheses were revived after the Renaissance. The first experimenters logically sought to test such hypotheses by cutting the nerves that carry information from the stomach to the central nervous system. The unexpected result of these experiments was that animals could regulate their eating in normal fashion after the nerves of the stomach were transected or removed. In spite of this "decisive" experimental attack, we have seen that local hypotheses of hunger continued and even flourished for over a century. Similarly, the local hypothesis of thirst remained popular long after it was shown that thirst is not abolished by removal of the nerves of the throat.

Why Discredited Hypotheses Persisted

Why did the local hypotheses last so long after experimental refutation? Several reasons seem likely:

(1) Partly it was because the local hypotheses fitted in well with both common sense and the psychological schools of the nineteenth century. For the introspective and phenomenological approaches (as well as for common sense) sensation and perception—conscious experience —determine behavior. "Sensation is the guide of life." Conscious experience in the case of hunger seemed to arise from the region of the stomach, and no further questions occurred. Problems of hunger drive and control of ingestion were beyond the scope of these experience-oriented approaches.

(2) The voices of authority, from Plato and Aristotle on, supported local hypotheses.

(3) While it was easy to show shortcomings in the local hypotheses, it was difficult to spell out a better hypothesis in detail. Some explanation was needed for the occurrence of hunger and thirst, and having an inadequate one was perhaps more reassuring than possessing none at all. Thus the existence of an unsolved problem was covered over by a plausible hypothesis, one supported both by common sense and by the voice of authority.

Our historical examination has also shown why it was so difficult to work out a better hypothesis in detail. To do so required conducting experiments in the depths of the living body. The history of physiology is almost synonymous with progess in recording and influencing internal bodily processes: Beaumont and his successors watching the stomach in action; later investigators measuring changes in the blood during hunger and thirst; making precise lesions in the brain; stimulating small regions of the brain electrically; analyzing chemical changes in tiny brain centers.

It is of course true that hypotheses often outstrip the current possibilities of testing. Some far-seeing scientists have been able to predict the results of later experiments long before the experiments had become possible technically. It is just as true that others, equally confident, have made assertions that were not borne out by later experiments. Whatever the reputation of a prophet when he speaks, only later fact shows him to have been true or false. Thus the history of a given period will be written differently at different times. For example, Boring had relatively little to say about early central hypotheses when he wrote about hunger and thirst in 1942. He cited these hypotheses, but only briefly, because there was no way of knowing then where they were to lead. The early central hypotheses figure more importantly in our account because experimentation of the 1940's and 1950's has partially confirmed them and favored their further elaboration.

Conditions of Current Progress

Experimentation accomplishes more than testing hypotheses; it often uncovers unexpected facts which stimulate scientists to extend existing hypotheses and to produce new ones. Throughout all the latter part of this history, we have seen hypotheses guiding experiments and newly discovered facts in turn leading to the formulation of new hypotheses. Thus the older central hypotheses furnished one reason for experimental attempts to destroy the hunger center. These attempts resulted in the unexpected discovery of a center for satiation or inhibition of hunger. This, plus the subsequent discovery of an excitatory center, has led to more detailed hypotheses involving a balance of activity among brain centers. Again, the older hypothesis of regulation of hunger in terms of the level of blood sugar was not verified by experimentation. Measures were made of sugar in arterial and in venous blood, and neither could be correlated with hunger. Eventually it was noticed that while the raw measures did not correlate with hunger, the arterial-venous difference could be correlated with hunger. A new avenue of attack was thus opened. Progress seems to come both from skillfully calculated, well-instrumented tests of hypotheses and from recognition and exploitation of unforeseen results that may (happily) turn up in the best planned experiments.

Behavioral as well as physiological methods had to be elaborated for the prosecution of this research. Essentially it is only since the establishment of psychology as a separate discipline that investigators have attempted precise, reliable measurement of behavior. Measurement of drive strength still poses problems, and different measures do not always agree. For example, an observation of the early 1940's, extended by more recent research, showed that rats with hypothalamic lesions overate when given a preferred food but ate less than normal control animals when given a less desired food. There is now a tendency to use a combination of measures in the attempt to disentangle drive strength from complicating factors.

Thus the twin characteristics of the most advanced current research on mechanisms of hunger and thirst are these: (1) precise recording and influencing of bodily processes, coupled with (2) accurate, reliable measurement of behavior. The research is therefore a combination of modern physiology and modern psychology. Since it is going on vigorously, the present version of history (completed in 1959) will, in its turn, soon be subject to change.

REFERENCES

ADEY, W. R., AND MEYER, M.   Hippocampal and hypothalamic connexions of the temporal lobe in the monkey. *Brain*, 1952, 75, 358–84.

ADOLPH, E. F.   Measurements of water drinking in dogs. *Amer. J. Physiol.*, 1939, 125, 75–86.

ALVAREZ, W. C.   *An introduction to gastro-enterology*, 3rd ed. New York: P. E. Hoeber, 1940.

ANAND, B. K., AND BROBECK, J. R.   Hypothalamic control of food intake in rats and cats. *Yale J. Biol. Med.*, 1951, 24, 123–40.

ANAND, B. K., AND DUA, S.   Feeding responses induced by electrical stimulation of the hypothalamus in cats. *Indian J. med. Res.*, 1955, 43, 113–22.

ANAND, B. K., DUA, S., AND SHOENBERG, K.   Hypothalamic control of food intake in cats and monkeys. *J. Physiol.*, 1955, 127, 143–52.

ANDERSSON, B., AND MCCANN, S. M.   A further study of polydipsia evoked by hypothalamic stimulation in the goat. *Acta physiol. Scand.*, 1955, 33, 333–46.

————.   The effect of hypothalamic lesions on the water intake of the dog. *Acta physiol. Scand.*, 1956, 35, 312–20.

ARDEN, F.   Experimental observations on thirst and on potassium overdosage. *Aust. J. exp. Biol. med. Sci.*, 1934, 12, 121–2.

AUSTIN, V. T., AND STEGGERDA, F. R.   Congenital dysfunction of the salivary glands with observations on the physiology of thirst. *Illinois med. J.*, 1936, 69, 124–7.

BAILEY, P., AND BREMER, F.   Experimental diabetes insipidus. *Arch. int. Med.*, 1921, 28, 773–803.

BEAUMONT, W.   *Experiments and observations on gastric juice and the physiology of digestion.*   Plattsburg, N.Y.: F. P. Allen, 1833.

BELLOWS, R. T.   Time factors in water drinking in dogs. *Amer. J. Physiol.*, 1939, 125, 87–97.

BELLOWS, R. T., AND VAN WAGENEN, W. P.   The relationship of polydipsia and polyuria in diabetes insipidus. *J. nerv. ment. Dis.*, 1938, 88, 417–73.

BERKUN, K. J., KESSEN, M. L., AND MILLER, N. E.,   Hunger-reducing effects of food by stomach fistula versus food by mouth measured by a consummatory response. *J. comp. physiol. Psychol.*, 1952, 45, 550–4.

BERNARD, C.   *Physiologie expérimentale.* Vol. 2. Paris, 1856.

———. Des fonctions du cerveau. *Revue des deux Mondes*, 1872, 98, 373–85.

BERNSTEIN, L. M., AND GROSSMAN, M. I.   An experimental test of the glucostatic theory of regulation of food intake. *J. clin. Investig.*, 1956, 35, 627–33.

BIDDER, F., AND SCHMIDT, C.   *Verdauungssäfte und Stoffwechsel.* Leipzig: Mitau, 1852.

BLONDLOT, N.   *Traité analytique de la digestion.* Nancy: Grimblot and Raybois, 1843.

BOLDIREFF, W. N.   Le travail periodique de l'appareil digestif en dehors de la digestion. *Arch. du Sci. biol.*, St. Petersbourg, 1905, 11, 1–157.

BOLDYREFF, W.   Fonction periodique de l'organisme chez l'homme et les animaux. *Quart. J. exper. Physiol.*, 1916, 10, 175–201.

BORING, E. G.   *Sensation and perception in the history of experimental psychology.* New York: D. Appleton-Century, 1942.

BROBECK, J. R., TEPPERMAN, J., AND LONG, C. N. H.   Experimental hypothalamic hyperphagia in the albino rat. *Yale J. Biol. Med.*, 1943, 15, 831–53.

BRÜGGER, M.   Fresstrieb als hypothalmisches Symptom. *Helv. physiol. pharmacol. Acta*, 1943, 1, 183–98.

BULATAO, E., AND CARLSON, A. J.   Influence of experimental changes in blood sugar level on gastric hunger contractions. *Amer. J. Physiol.*, 1924, 69, 107–15.

CAMUS, J., AND ROUSSY, G.   Les syndromes hypophysaires: Anatomie et physiologie pathologiques. *Rev. neurol.*, 1922, 38, 622–37.

CANNON, W. B.   The physiological basis of thirst. The Croonian Lecture of the Royal Society, London. *Proc. Roy. Soc.*, 1918, 90, 283–301.

———. Hunger and thirst. In C. Murchison (Ed.), *The foundations of experimental psychology.* Worcester, Mass.: Clark University Press, 1929. Pp. 434–48.

———. Hunger and thirst. In C. Murchison (Ed.), *Handbook of experimental psychology.* Worcester, Mass.: Clark University Press, 1934. Pp. 247–63.

———. *The wisdom of the body.* New York: Norton and Co., 1939.

CANNON, W. B., AND WASHBURN, A. L.   An explanation of hunger. *Amer. J. Physiol.*, 1912, 29, 441–54.

CARLET, G.   Faim et soif. In A. Dechambre (Ed.), *Dictionnaire encyclopédique des sciences medicales.* Vol. 37. Paris: G. Masson, 1877. Pp. 155–60.

CARLSON, A. J. Contributions to the physiology of the stomach. III. The contractions of the empty stomach inhibited reflexly from the mouth. *Amer. J. Physiol.*, 1913, 31, 212–22.

————. *The control of hunger in health and disease*. Chicago: University of Chicago Press, 1916.

CARLSON, A. J., AND JOHNSON, V. *The machinery of the body*. Chicago: University of Chicago Press, 1937.

————. *The machinery of the body*, 4th ed. Chicago: University of Chicago Press, 1953.

CHAMBERS, R. M. Some physiological bases for reinforcing properties of reward injections. *J. comp. physiol. Psychol.*, 1956, 49, 565–8.

CHAUSSIER, F. AND ADELON, N. P. Digestion. In C. L. F. Panckoucke (Ed.), *Dictionnaire des sciences medicales*. Vol. 9. Paris: C. L. F. Panckoucke, 1814. Pp. 354–451.

COPPOCK, H. W., AND CHAMBERS, R. M. Reinforcement of position preference by automatic intravenous injections of glucose. *J. comp. physiol. Psychol.*, 1954, 47, 355–7.

DAREMBERG, C. *Oeuvres anatomiques, physiologiques et medicales de Galien*, Vol. 2. Paris: J. B. Baillière, 1856.

DARWIN, E. *Zoonomia; or, the laws of organic life*. Vol. 2. London: J. Johnson, 1796.

DELGADO, J. M. R., AND ANAND, B. K. Increased food intake induced by electrical stimulation of the lateral hypothalamus. *Amer. J. Physiol.*, 1953, 172, 162–8.

DEUTSCH, J. A. AND JONES, A. D. Diluted water: An explanation of the rat's preference for saline. *J. comp. physiol. Psychol.*, 1960, 53, 122–7.

DUMAS, C. L. *Principes de physiologie*. Vol. 4. Paris: Déterville, 1803.

ERDHEIM, J. Ueber Hypophysenganggeschwülste und Hirncholesteatome. *Sitzungsb. Akad. Wissensch, Math., -naturwissensch. Klasse, Wien*, 1904, 113:3, 537–726.

EULER, C. VON. A preliminary note on slow hypothalamic "osmopotentials." *Acta physiol. Scand.*, 1953, 29, 133–6.

FLOURENS, P. *Recherches expérimentales sur les propriétés et les fonctions du système nerveux dans les animaux vertébrés*, 2d ed. Paris: J. B. Baillière, 1842.

FORSSBERG, A., AND LARSSON, S. On the hypothalamic organisation of the nervous mechanism regulating food intake. Part II. Studies of isotope distribution and chemical composition in the hypothalamic region of hungry and fed rats. *Acta physiol. Scand.*, 1954, 32, suppl. 115, 41–63.

FRÖHLICH, A. Ein Fall von Tumor der Hypophysis cerebri ohne Akromegalie. *Wien. klin. Rundschau*, 1901, 15, 883–906.

————. Discussion following paper by P. Bailey. *Res. Publ. Ass. nerv. ment. Dis.*, 1940, 20, 713.

GIANTURCO, C.   Some mechanical factors in gastric physiology. *Amer. J. Roentgenology*, 1934, 131, 735–44.

GILMAN, A.   The relation between blood osmotic pressure, fluid distribution and voluntary water intake. *Amer. J. Physiol.*, 1937, 120, 323–8.

GREEN, J. D., CLEMENTE, C. D., AND DEGROOT, J.   Rhinencephalic lesions and behavior in cats. *J. comp. Neurol.*, 1957, 108, 505–45.

HALLER, A. V.   *First lines of physiology.* Troy, N.Y.: O. Penniman and Co., 1803. (Translation from original published in 1747.)

HERVEY, G. R.   The effects of lesions in the hypothalamus in parabiotic rats. *J. Physiol.*, 1959, 145, 336–52.

HETHERINGTON, A. W., AND RANSON, S. W.   Hypothalamic lesions and adiposity in the rat. *Anat. Rec.*, 1940, 78, 149–72.

————.   The spontaneous activity and food intake of rats with hypothalamic lesions. *Amer. J. Physiol.*, 1942, 136, 609–17.

HOLMBERG, A. R.   *Nomads of the long bow; the Siriono of Eastern Bolivia.* Washington: Smithsonian Institution, 1950.

HOLMES, J. H.   *A study of thirst.* Unpublished doctoral dissertation, Columbia University, 1941. (Cited in C. T. Morgan and E. Stellar, *Physiological psychology.* New York: McGraw-Hill Book Co., 1950. P. 386.)

HORSLEY, V., AND CLARKE, R. H.   The structure and functions of the cerebellum examined by a new method. *Brain*, 1908, 31, 45–124.

HULL, C. L.   *Principles of behavior.* New York: Appleton-Century, 1943.

HULL, C. L., LIVINGSTONE, J. R., ROUSE, R. O., AND BARKER, A. N.   True, sham, and esophageal feeding as reinforcements. *J. comp. physiol. Psychol.*, 1951, 44, 236–45.

JAMES, W.   *Psychology.* New York: Henry Holt and Co., 1891.

JANOWITZ, H. D., AND GROSSMAN, M. I.   Some factors affecting the food intake of normal dogs and dogs with esophagostomy and gastric fistula. *Amer. J. Physiol.*, 1949, 159, 143–8.

JANOWITZ, H. D., AND IVY, A. C.   Role of blood sugar levels in spontaneous and insulin-induced hunger in man. *J. appl. Physiol.*, 1949, 1, 643–5.

KENNEDY, G. C.   The role of depot fat in the hypothalamic control of food intake in the rat. *Proc. Roy. Soc., Ser. B.*, 1953, 140, 578–92.

KEYS, A., BROZEK, J., HENSCHEL, A., MICKELSEN, O., AND TAYLOR, H. L.   *The biology of human starvation.* Minneapolis: University of Minnesota Press, 1950.

KISCH, P.   Jacob Helm's observations and experiments on human digestion. *J. History of Med.*, 1954, 9, 311–28.

KLÜVER, H., AND BUCY, P. C.   Preliminary analysis of functions of the temporal lobes in monkeys. *Arch. Neurol. Psychiat., Chicago*, 1939, 42, 979–1000.

KOHN, M. Satiation of hunger from food injected directly into stomach vs. food ingested by mouth. *J. comp. physiol. Psychol.*, 1951, 44, 412–22.

LARSSON, S. On the hypothalamic organisation of the nervous mechanism regulating food intake. Part I. Hyperphagia from stimulation of the hypothalamus and medulla in sheep and goats. *Acta physiol. Scand.*, 1954, 32, suppl. 115, 1–40.

LESCHKE, E. Ueber die Durstempfindung. *Arch. Psychiat. Nervenkr.*, 1918, 59, 773–81.

LIVON, C. Hypophyse. In C. Richet (Ed.), *Dictionnaire de physiologie.* Vol. 8. Paris: F. Alcan, 1909. Pp. 789–874.

LONGET, F. A. *Traité de physiologie.* Paris: Victor Masson et Fils, 1861. 3 vols.

LUCIANI, L. Sulla genesi della sensazioni della fame e della sete. *Arch. Fisiol.*, 1906, 3, 541–6.

LUDWIG, C. *Lehrbuch der Physiologie des Menschen.* Vol. 2. Leipzig and Heidelberg: C. F. Winter, 1861.

MAGENDIE, F. *Précis élémentaire de physiologie*, 5th ed. Brussels: Société Typographique Belge, 1838.

MARTIN, W. G., AND MORTON, H. S. Clinical studies with the electrogastrograph. *AMA Arch. Surg.*, 1952, 65, 382–96.

MAYER, A. *Essai sur la soif. Les causes et son mecanisme.* Paris: Jouve et Boyer, 1900.

MAYER, J. Glucostatic mechanism of regulation of food intake. *New England J. Med.*, 1953, 249, 13–16.

———. Correlation between metabolism and feeding behavior and multiple etiology of obesity. *Bull. N.Y. Acad. Med.*, 1957, 33, 744–61.

MILLER, N. E., AND KESSEN, M. L. Reward effects of food via stomach fistula compared with those of food via mouth. *J. comp. physiol. Psychol.*, 1952, 45, 555–64.

MILLER, N. E., SAMPLINER, R. I., AND WOODROW, P. Thirst-reducing effects of water by stomach fistula vs. water by mouth measured by both a consummatory and an instrumental response. *J. comp. physiol. Psychol.*, 1957, 50, 1–5.

MILNE-EDWARDS, H. *Leçons sur la physiologie.* Vol. 13. Paris: G. Masson, 1878–9.

MÜLLER, J. *Elements of physiology.* (Trans. W. Baly.) Vol. 1. London: Taylor and Walton, 1838.

MÜLLER, L. R. Ueber die Hungerempfindung. *Deutsch. med. Wochenschr.*, 1915, 41, 1297–1301.

MYER, J. S. *Life and letters of Dr. William Beaumont.* St. Louis: C. V. Mosby, 1912.

OGLE, W. *Aristotle, on the parts of animals.* London: Kegan Paul, Trench and Co., 1882.

O'KELLY, L. I., AND FALK, J. L. Water regulation in the rat: II. The effects of preloads of water and sodium chloride on the bar-pressing performance of thirsty rats. *J. comp. physiol. Psychol.*, 1958, 51, 22–5.

OLDS, J. Selective effects of drives and drugs on "reward" systems of the brain. In G. E. W. Wolstenhome and C. M. O'Connor (Eds.), *Ciba Foundation symposium on the neurological basis of behaviour.* London: J. and A. Churchill, 1958. Pp. 124–41.

OLDS, J., AND MILNER, P. Positive reinforcement produced by electrical stimulation of septal area and other regions of rat brain. *J. comp. physiol. Psychol.*, 1954, 47, 419–27.

PAVLOV, I. P. *Lectures on conditioned reflexes.* (Trans. W. H. Gantt.) New York: International Publishers, 1928.

PAWLOW, J. P. *Die Arbeit der Verdauungsdrüsen.* (Trans. A. Walther.) Wiesbaden: J. F. Bergmann, 1898.

PILLSBURY, W. B. *The fundamentals of psychology.* New York: The Macmillan Company, 1916.

QUIGLEY, J. P., AND HALLARAN, W. R. The independence of spontaneous gastro-intestinal motility and blood sugar levels. *Amer. J. Physiol.*, 1932, 100, 102–10.

RANSON, S. W. On the use of the Horsley-Clarke stereotaxic instrument. *Psychiatrische en neurologische Bladen*, 1934, 3–4, 270–9.

RICHET, C. Des propriétés chimiques et physiologiques du suc gastrique chez l'homme et les animaux. *J. de l'Anatomie et de la Physiologie*, 1878, 14, 170–333.

RICHTER, C. P. Factors determining voluntary ingestion of water in normals and in individuals with maximum diabetes insipidus. *Amer. J. Physiol.*, 1938, 122, 668–75.

RICHTER, C. P., AND HAWKES, C. D. Increased spontaneous activity and food intake produced in rats by removal of the frontal poles of the brain. *J. Neurol. Psychiat.*, 1939, 2, 231–42.

ROBINSON, E. A., AND ADOLPH, E. F. Pattern of normal water drinking in dogs. *Amer. J. Physiol.*, 1943, 139, 39–44.

ROSEN, G. *The reception of William Beaumont's discovery in Europe.* New York: Schuman's, 1942.

ROUX, J. La faim, étude physio-psychologique. *Bulletin de la Société d'Anthropologie de Lyon*, 1897, 16, 409–55.

SCHIFF, M. *Leçons sur la physiologie de la digestion.* Vol. 1. Florence and Turin: H. Loescher, 1867.

SCHULMAN, J. L., CARLETON, J. L., WHITNEY, G., AND WHITEHORN, J. C. Effect of glucagon on food intake and body weight in man. *J. appl. Physiol.*, 1957, 11, 419–21.

SCOTT, W. W., SCOTT, C. C., AND LUCKHARDT, A. B. Observations on blood sugar levels before, during and after hunger periods in humans. *Amer. J. Physiol.*, 1938, 123, 243–7.

SMITH, P. E. Disorders induced by injury to the pituitary and the hypothalamus. *J. nerv. ment. Dis.*, 1931, 74, 56–8.

SÖMMERRING, S. T. *Vom Baue des Menschlicken Körpers*, Vol. 5:2. Frankfurt-am-Main: Barrentrapp and Wenner, 1801.

SOULAIRAC, A. Les régulations psycho-physiologiques de la faim. *J. de Physiologie*, 1958, 50, 663–783.

STELLAR, E. The physiology of motivation. *Psychol. Rev.*, 1954, 61, 5–22.

STEVENSON, J. A. F., WELT, L. G., AND ORLOFF, J. Abnormalities of water and electrolyte metabolism in rats with hypothalamic lesions. *Amer. J. Physiol.*, 1950, 161, 35–9.

STUNKARD, A. J., VAN ITALLIE, T. B., AND REIS, B. B. The mechanism of satiety: effect of glucagon on gastric hunger contractions in man. *Proc. Soc. exp. Biol. Med.*, 1955, 89, 258–61.

STUNKARD, A. J., AND WOLFF, H. G. Studies on the physiology of hunger. I. The effect of intravenous administration of glucose on gastric hunger contractions in man. *J. clin. Investig.*, 1956, 35:7–12, 954–63.

TAYLOR, A. E. *Plato: Timaeus and Critias.* London: Methuen, 1929.

TEITELBAUM, P., AND STELLAR, E. Recovery from the failure to eat produced by hypothalamic lesions. *Science*, 1954, 120, 894–5.

THORNDIKE, E. L. Animal intelligence—an experimental study of the associative processes in animals. *Psychol. Rev.*, 1898, 2, 1–106. (Monogr. Supplements, whole No. 8.)

TOLMAN, E. C. There is more than one kind of learning. *Psychol. Rev.*, 1949, 56, 144–55.

VAN ITALLIE, T. B., BEAUDOIN, R., AND MAYER, J. Arteriovenous glucose differences, metabolic hypoglycemia and food intake in man. *Amer. J. clin. Nutrition*, 1953, 1, 208–17.

VERNEY, E. B. The antidiuretic hormone and the factors which determine its release. *Proc. Roy. Soc.*, 1947, 135, 25–106.

WANGENSTEEN, O. H., AND CARLSON, H. A. Hunger sensations in a patient after total gastrectomy. *Proc. Soc. exper. Biol. Med.*, 1931, 28, 545–7.

WEBER, E. H. Der Tastsinn und das Gemeingefühl. In R. Wagner (Ed.), *Handwörterbuch der Physiologie*. Vol. 3. Braunschweig: F. Vierweg, 1846.

WETTENDORFF, H. Modification du sang sous l'influence de la privation d'eau. *Travaux de Laboratoire de Physiologie: Instituts Solvay, Bruxelles*, 1901, 4, 353–484.

WHYTT, R. *An essay on the vital and other involuntary motions of animals*, 2d ed. Edinburgh: J. Balfour, 1763.

WITT, D. M., KELLER, A. D., BATSEL, H. L., AND LYNCH, J. R. Absence of thirst and resultant syndrome associated with anterior hypothalectomy in the dog. *Amer. J. Physiol.*, 1952, 171, 780.

WOLF, A. V. *Thirst*. Springfield, Ill.: C. C. Thomas, 1958.

ZOTTERMAN, Y. Species differences in the water taste. *Acta physiol. Scand.*, 1956, 37, 60–70.

CHAPTER 4

The Inheritance of Behavior

GERALD E. McCLEARN[1]

To ILLUSTRATE A POINT concerning the inheritance of gestures, Darwin (1872) quoted an interesting case which had been brought to his attention by Galton.

> A gentleman of considerable position was found by his wife to have the curious trick, when he lay fast asleep on his back in bed, of raising his right arm slowly in front of his face, up to his forehead, and then dropping it with a jerk so that the wrist fell heavily on the bridge of his nose. The trick did not occur every night, but occasionally. . . .

Nevertheless, the gentleman's nose suffered considerable damage, and it was necessary to remove the buttons from his nightgown cuff in order to minimize the hazard.

> Many years after his death, his son married a lady who had never heard of the family incident. She, however, observed precisely the same peculiarity in her husband; but his nose, from not being particularly prominent, has never as yet suffered from the blows. . . . One of his children, a girl, has inherited the same trick [pp. 33f.].

Probably everyone could cite some examples, perhaps less dramatic than Mr. Galton's, where some peculiarity of gait, violence of temper, degree of talent, or similar trait is characteristic of a family, and such phrases as "a chip off the old block," "like father, like son," and "it runs in the family" give ample evidence of the general acceptance of the no-

[1] The author is indebted to Drs. D. S. Falconer, J. Hirsch, R. C. Roberts, and C. Stern for their helpful advice and criticism. They are, of course, blameless for any remaining errors. This chapter was completed while the author was a National Academy of Sciences–National Research Council Senior Postdoctoral Fellow in Physiological Psychology, at the Institute of Animal Genetics, Edinburgh, Scotland.

tion that behavior traits may be inherited in the same manner as physical ones. The central purpose of this chapter is to consider the history of scientific inquiry into these matters.

Behavioral genetics may be informally defined as that discipline concerned with elucidating the degree and nature of genetic determination of similarities and differences in the behavior of individuals. Progress in this endeavor has necessarily depended upon prior progress of genetics as well as of psychology. It will also be necessary, therefore, to examine, in a modest way, the growth and development of the field of genetics.

ANCIENT CONCEPTS

IT IS USUALLY extremely difficult, if not impossible, to pinpoint the earliest expression of a view concerning any subject matter. The present topic is no exception, but as a matter of general interest, we may note that its origins must be very remote indeed.

The concept that "like begets like" has had great practical importance in the development of domesticated animals, which have been bred as surely for behavioral as for physical characteristics. By extrapolation, it might be suggested that a glimpse of the notion of inheritance, including inheritance of behavior traits, may have appeared in human thought as early as 8000 B.C., to which date the domestication of the dog has been traced.

The workings of inheritance have been of great interest to men all throughout recorded history, and many interesting conjectures were made (Zirkle, 1951). Most of these notions have little direct continuity with the present topic, however, and we may turn shortly to the nineteenth century, pausing only to mention briefly some examples of early Greek thought on the subject.

One of the most familiar of the early statements is that of Theognis (Roper, 1913, p. 32), in the sixth century B.C., who commented on contemporary mores:

> We seek well-bred rams and sheep and horses and one wishes to breed from these. Yet a good man is willing to marry an evil wife, if she bring him wealth: nor does a woman refuse to marry an evil husband who is rich. For men reverence money, and the good marry the evil, and the evil the good. Wealth has confounded the race.

By implication, at least, Theognis believed that such marriages with "evil" spouses would not generate "well-bred" offspring.

The Spartans, as is well known, took direct and positive action to eliminate those who were not "well-bred," by the practice of infant exposure. This infanticide was designed to eliminate those of unsound soul as well as those of defective body, for as Roper (1913, p. 19) points out, "To the Greeks, believing only in the beauty of the spirit when reflected in the beauty of the flesh, the good body was the necessary correlation of the good soul."

In *The Republic* (Davis, 1849, p. 144), Plato suggested a course of action whereby the principles of inheritance of behavior could be used to develop a more ideal society:

> It necessarily follows . . . from what has been acknowledged, that the best men should as often as possible form alliances with the best women, and the most depraved men, on the contrary, with the most depraved women; and the offspring of the former is to be educated, but not of the latter, if the flock is to be of the most perfect kind. . . . As for those youths, who distinguish themselves, either in war or other pursuits, they ought to have rewards and prizes given them, and the most ample liberty of lying with women, that so, under this pretext, the greatest number of children may spring from such parentage.

The age of parents was also seen as an important factor, and Plato suggested that men should procreate when thirty to fifty-five years of age, while women should bear children when between the ages of twenty and forty. If, by chance, children should be conceived past the prime periods, they should be exposed at birth.

Aristotle offered less counsel on these matters than did Plato, but he had some definite ideas concerning the proper age of parents and the optimal season of the year for procreation. Eighteen and thirty-seven were the recommended ages, for women and men respectively, to begin reproduction.

> It is extremely bad for the children when the father is too young; for in all animals whatsoever the parts of the young are imperfect, and are more likely to be productive of females than males, and diminutive also in size; the same thing of course necessarily holds true in men; as a proof of this you may see in those cities where the men and women usually marry very young, the people in general are very small and ill framed . . . And thus much for the time which is proper for marriage; but moreover a proper season of the year should be observed, as many persons do now, and appropriate the winter for this business. [Ellis, 1912, pp. 233–4.]

Thus we see that both Plato and Aristotle, who contributed so much to subsequent philosophical thought, attached great importance to the circumstances surrounding mating, including the nature of the parents themselves.

ADVANCES IN BIOLOGY

BIOLOGICAL THOUGHT during the ensuing centuries was dominated by Aristotle's pronouncements on natural history, and by the teachings of the Roman, Galen, concerning anatomy. Progress in understanding biological phenomena was virtually halted during the general stagnation of nontheological intellectual pursuits which typified the Middle Ages. Then came the Renaissance. For biology, the Renaissance may well be described as beginning with Vesalius's brilliant work on anatomy in 1543 which, in contrast to the earlier work, was based on actual painstaking dissection of the human body. Harvey's momentous discovery of the circulation of the blood followed after a considerable interval, in 1628. This finding was of far-reaching importance, for it opened the way to the mechanistic as opposed to the vitalistic viewpoint, and thus to empirical research on phenomena of life.

The pace of biological research quickened, and many fundamental developments in technique and in theory ensued in the following century. One of the cornerstones of biology was laid by Linnaeus in 1735, when in *Systema Naturae* he described over 4,000 species of animals and plants. Subsequent work in taxonomy, showing at the same time the great diversity of life and the extent to which many groups appeared to be variants of a common theme, suggested to some that various types of organisms had developed or evolved from other types.

One of the dominant figures of this period was Lamarck, who argued that the deliberate efforts of an animal could result in modifications of the body parts involved, and that the modifications so acquired could be transmitted to the animal's offspring. For example:

> . . . we perceive that the shore bird, which does not care to swim, but which, however, is obliged (*a besoin*) to approach the water to obtain its prey, will be continually in danger of sinking in the mud, but wishing to act so that its body shall not fall into the liquid, it will contract the habit of extending and lengthening its feet. Hence it will result in the generations of these birds which continue to live in this manner, that the individuals will find themselves raised as if on stilts, on long naked feet; namely, denuded of feathers up to and often above the thighs [Packard, 1901, p. 234].

For various reasons, Lamarck's and similar theories concerning evolution were unsuccessful. However, the cumulative thought set the stage for the most fundamental contribution to biological science yet made—the evolutionary theory of Charles Darwin.

THE ERA OF DARWIN AND GALTON

Darwin's Theory of Evolution

NATURAL SELECTION.   It was in 1859 that Charles Darwin yielded to the persuasions of friends and published his monumental *The Origin of Species by Natural Selection* as an "abstract" of his theory of evolution. The essence of this theory was that species and genera had been differentiated as a consequence of the "struggle for life."

> Owing to this struggle for life, any variation, however slight and from whatever cause proceeding, if it be in any degree profitable to an individual of any species, in its infinitely complex relations to other organic beings and to external nature, will tend to the preservation of that individual, and will generally be inherited by its offspring. The offspring, also, will thus have a better chance of surviving, for, of the many individuals of any species which are periodically born, but a small number can survive [Darwin, 1869, p. 61].

This principle was called Natural Selection, and it is clear that Darwin considered that behavioral characteristics are just as subject to natural selection as are physical traits. In *The Origin of Species* an entire chapter is devoted to a discussion of instinctive behavior patterns, and in the later *The Descent of Man and Selection in Relation to Sex*, detailed consideration is given to comparisons of mental powers and moral senses of animals and man, and to the development of intellectual and moral faculties in man. In these discussions Darwin was satisfied that he had demonstrated that the difference between the mind of man and the mind of animals "is certainly one of degree and not of kind" (Darwin, 1873, p. 101)—an essential point, since one of the strongest objections to the theory of evolution was the qualitative gulf which was supposed to exist between the mental capacities of man and of lower animals. All the behavior traits cited in support of this idea must be, by implication, inherited, since, for Darwin, it is only the inheritable traits which have long-range evolutionary significance.

In an explicit summary statement, based largely on observations of "family resemblance," Darwin said:

> So in regard to mental qualities, their transmission is manifest in our dogs, horses, and other domestic animals. Besides special tastes and habits, general intelligence, courage, bad and good temper, etc., are certainly transmitted. With man we see similar facts in almost every family; and we now know through the admirable labors of Mr. Galton that genius, which implies a wonderfully complex combination of high faculties, tends to be inherited; and, on the other hand, it is too certain that insanity and deteriorated mental powers likewise run in the same families [1873, Vol. I, pp. 106f.].

SOURCES OF VARIABILITY.   It was most crucial for the evolutionary theory that heritable variation be present in each generation, or evolution could not continue. But, by the commonly accepted principle that characteristics merged or blended in offspring, it was apparent that variability of a trait would be roughly halved in each generation, and would rapidly diminish to a trivial level, were it not replenished in some manner. Darwin devoted much attention to the causes of variability (Darwin, 1868) and concluded that changes in the conditions of life in some way altered the reproductive systems of animals in such a manner that their offspring were more variable than they would have been in stable conditions. Ordinarily, this enhanced variability would be random—natural selection would then preserve those deviants which by chance happened to be the better adapted as a consequence of their deviation. Sometimes, however, particularly if continued for a number of generations, an environmental condition might induce *systematic* change—the environment directly inducing changes making organisms more adapted to it.

Another source of variability was presumed to be the effects of use and of disuse:

> Increased use adds to the size of a muscle, together with the blood-vessels, nerves, ligaments, the crests of bone to which these are attached, the whole bone and other connected bones. So it is with various glands. Increased functional activity strengthens the sense-organs. Increased and intermittent pressure thickens the epidermis; and a change in the nature of the food sometimes modifies the coats of the stomach, and increases or decreases the length of the intestines. Continued disuse, on the other hand, weakens and diminishes all parts of the organisation. Animals which during many generations have taken but little exercise, have their lungs reduced in size, and as a consequence the bony fabric of the chest, and the whole form of the body, become modified [1868, Vol. II, p. 423].

Likewise, with respect to behavioral characteristics, ". . . some intelligent actions . . . after being performed during many generations, become converted into instincts, and are inherited" (1873, Vol. I, p. 36) and "It is not improbable that virtuous tendencies may through long practice be inherited" (1873, Vol. II, p. 377).

It should be noted that Darwin was not completely satisfied with the doctrine that characters acquired by use, disuse, or environmental modification could be transmitted to subsequent generations (see Fisher, 1958, pp. 607). Yet such a mechanism seemed to be necessary to explain some of the facts. As we shall see, a vigorous controversy has persisted over this theory, which is generally described as Lamarckian.

Galton's Contribution

The *Origin of Species* caused a violent reaction. Fierce denunciation came from those whose sensibilities were shocked by this contradiction of the Biblical account of creation. There was opposition, too, from other scientists, whose favorite theories were challenged by the new conceptions. There were, however, some scholars to whom the arguments were immediately compelling. Among this latter group was Francis Galton, Darwin's half-cousin.

The *Origin* directed Galton's immense curiosity and talents to biological phenomena, and he soon developed what was to be a central and abiding interest: the inheritance of mental characteristics.

HEREDITARY GENIUS.   In 1865 two articles by Galton, jointly entitled "Hereditary Talent and Character," were published in *Macmillan's Magazine*. Four years later a greatly expanded discussion was published with the title, *Hereditary Genius: An Inquiry into its Laws and Consequences.*

The general argument presented in this work is that among the relatives of persons endowed with high mental ability is to be found a greater number of other extremely able individuals than would be expected by chance; furthermore, the closer the family relationship, the higher the incidence of such superior individuals.

Applying Quetelet's "law of deviation from an average," at the time a fairly recent development, but later to become familiar as the normal curve, Galton distinguished fourteen levels of human ability, ranging from idiocy through mediocrity to genius.

No satisfactory way of quantifying natural ability was available, so Galton had to rely upon reputation as an index. By "reputation" he did not mean notoriety from a single act, nor mere social or official position, but "the reputation of a leader of opinion, of an originator, of a man to whom the world deliberately acknowledges itself largely indebted" (1869, p. 37). The designation "eminent" was applied to those individuals who comprised the upper 250 millionths of the population (i.e., one in 4,000 persons would attain such a rank), and it was with such men that the discussion was concerned. Indeed, the majority of individuals presented in evidence were, in Galton's estimation, the cream of this elite group, and were termed "illustrious." These were men whose talents ranked them one in a million.

On the basis of biographies, published accounts, and direct inquiry, Galton evaluated the accomplishments of eminent judges, statesmen, peers, military commanders, literary men, scientists, poets, musicians, painters, Protestant religious leaders and Cambridge scholars, and their relatives. (Oarsmen and wrestlers of note were also examined to extend the range of inquiry from brain to brawn.) In all, nearly 1,000 eminent men were identified in the 300 families examined. With the over-all incidence of eminence only 1 in 4,000, this result clearly illustrated the tendency for eminence to be a family trait.

Taking the most eminent man in each family as the reference point, the other individuals who attained eminence (in the same or in some other field of endeavor) were tabulated with respect to closeness of family relationship. Table 1, in which each entry is expressed in percentage form, gives the principal results. These data give a uniform picture of decreasing likelihood of eminence as the degree of relationship becomes more remote.

Galton recognized the possible objection that relatives of eminent men would share social, educational, and financial advantages, and that the results of his investigation might be interpreted as showing the effectiveness of such environmental factors. To demonstrate that reputation is an indication of *natural* ability, and not the product of environmental advantages, three arguments were presented. First, Galton stressed the fact that many men had risen to high rank from humble family backgrounds. Second, it was noted that the proportion of eminent writers, philosophers, and artists in England was not less than that in the United States, where education of the middle and lower socioeconomic classes was more advanced. The educational advantages in America had spread culture more widely, but had not produced more persons of eminence. Finally, a comparison was made between the success of adopted kinsmen of Roman Catholic Popes, who were given great social advantages, and the sons of eminent men, and the latter were judged to be the more distinguished group.

TABLE 1

INCIDENCE OF EMINENCE IN RELATIVES OF EMINENT MEN *

NATURE OF KINSHIP	Judges	Statesmen	Commanders	Literary	Scientific	Poets	Artists	Divines	All Classes
Father	26	33	47	48	26	20	32	28	31
Brother	35	39	50	42	47	40	50	36	41
Son	36	49	31	51	60	45	89	40	48
Grandfather	15	28	16	24	14	5	7	20	17
Uncle	18	18	8	24	16	5	14	40	18
Nephew	19	18	35	24	23	50	18	4	22
Grandson	19	10	12	9	14	5	18	16	14
Great-grandfather	2	8	8	3	0	0	0	4	3
Great-uncle	4	5	8	6	5	5	7	4	5
First cousin	11	21	20	18	16	0	1	8	13
Great-nephew	17	5	8	6	16	10	0	0	10
Great-grandson	6	0	0	3	7	0	0	0	3
All more remote	14	37	44	15	23	5	18	16	31

*These figures express the incidence of eminence per 100 families. From Francis Galton, *Hereditary Genius*, p. 317. Published in 1869 by MacMillan of London, and used with their permission.

In Galton's view, men of mediocre talents might be supressed by environmental obstacles, but inherited genius will out, regardless of adversity, and no amount of social or educational advantage can serve to raise a man to eminence unless he possesses inherited natural ability.

POLITICAL AND SOCIAL IMPLICATIONS OF THE INHERITANCE OF EMI-NENCE.   Galton was keenly aware of the powerful implications of his arguments. In introducing *Hereditary Genius*, he announced:

> I propose to show in this book that a man's natural abilities are derived by inheritance, under exactly the same limitations as are the form and physical features of the whole organic world. Consequently, as it is easy, notwithstanding those limitations, to obtain by careful selection a permanent breed of dogs or horses gifted with peculiar powers of running, or of doing anything else, so it would be quite practicable to produce a highly-gifted race of men by judicious marriages during several consecutive generations [1869, p. 1].

Improvement of mankind in this way, by the application of principles of heredity, was given the name "Eugenics" (Galton, 1883, p. 24) and the furtherance of eugenic goals became the underlying theme around which most of Galton's work was oriented.

PIONEERING RESEARCH IN PSYCHOLOGY AND STATISTICS.   To be sure, the "highly gifted race" Galton envisaged would need to be physically sound, and much attention was given to measurements of health and physique; but Galton was primarily concerned with the sound mind, and focused his efforts on the problems of assessing mental characteristics. In a prodigious program of research, he developed apparatus and procedures for measuring auditory thresholds, visual acuity, color vision, touch, smell, judgment of the vertical, judgment of length, weight discrimination, reaction time, and memory span. In addition, a questionnaire technique was employed to investigate mental imagery, and association of ideas was studied by introspection. One particularly intriguing, although not especially successful, investigation involved the use of composite portraiture, whereby the photographs of a number of individuals could be superimposed to yield their common features. These composite photographs were then used in an effort to determine what relationship, if any, existed between the facial characteristics of certain groups and various attributes of their intelligence, personality, morality, and health.

The problems of properly expressing and evaluating the data obtained from such researches were formidable, and Galton also turned his remarkable energies to statistics, pioneering in the development of the concepts of the median, percentiles, and correlation.

It was, of course, desirable to have data from large numbers of individuals, and various stratagems were employed to this end. For example, Galton arranged for an "Anthropometric Laboratory for the measurement in various ways of Human Form and Faculty" to be located at an International Health Exhibition. Some 9,337 people paid fourpence each for the privilege of being measured for various bodily and sensory characteristics! On another occasion a contest was sponsored in which awards of £7 were given to those submitting the most careful and complete "Extracts from their own Family Records." Thus did Galton obtain a large number of pedigrees which he could examine for evidence of human inheritance.

TWINS AND THE NATURE-NURTURE PROBLEM. Of special relevance to the present topic is Galton's introduction (Galton, 1883) of the twin-study method to assess the effectiveness of *nature* (inheritance) and *nurture* (environment). The essential question in this examination of twins was whether twins who were alike at birth became more dissimilar as a consequence of any dissimilarities in their nurture, and conversely, whether twins unlike at birth became more similar as a consequence of similar nurture. Galton acknowledged two types of twins: those arising from separate eggs, and those arising from separate germinal spots on the same egg, yet he did not distinguish between the two types in his discussion, except as they fell into his "alike at birth" or "unlike at birth" categories. Gathering his evidence from answers to questionnaires and biographical and autobiographical material, Galton observed that, in thirty-five cases of twins who had been very much alike at birth, and who had been reared under highly similar conditions, the similarities persisted after they had grown to adulthood and gone more or less separate ways.

In twenty cases of originally dissimilar twins, there was no compelling evidence that they had become more alike through being exposed to similar environments.

> There is no escape from the conclusion that nature prevails enormously over nurture when the differences of nurture do not exceed what is commonly to be found among persons of the same rank of society and in the same country. My fear is, that my evidence may seem to prove too much, and be discredited on that account, as it appears contrary to all experience that nurture should go for so little [1883, p. 241].

GALTON'S WORK IN PERSPECTIVE. The ten years between *Origin of Species* and *Hereditary Genius* had not been sufficient for the idea of man as an animal to be digested. For many of those who accepted Darwin, of course, Galton was a natural and logical extension: man differs from animals most strikingly in mental powers; man has evolved as have other animals; evolution works by inheritance; mental traits are inheritable.

For those whose faith in the special creation of man remained firm, Galton was unacceptable, atheistic, and reprehensible.

Even among those not arguing primarily on theological grounds, there were wide differences of opinion as to the proper frame of reference for the study of man. In psychiatric theorizing, for example, some views were based upon the concept that human behavior is determined by biological processes, and that no adequate theory of mental functioning or malfunctioning could disregard man's fundamentally animal nature. On the other hand, there were those who chose to regard the "psyche" as capable of investigation in and of itself, with organic processes ignored as irrelevant (see White, 1948).

There were also scholars whose inquiries stemmed, not from interest in psychiatric problems, but from a general desire to understand "mind." The philosophical approach was dominated by the British philosophers, whose emphasis was clearly on experience and thus on "nurture," having been inspired by Locke's seventeenth-century *tabula rasa* dictum that ideas are not inborn, but come from experience. The role of experience was also emphasized by experimental psychology, which is usually dated from Wundt's establishment of the *Psychologisches Institut* in 1879, just prior to Galton's major works. In spite of the fact that Wundt had come to psychology from physiology, his approach was not biological in the same sense as Galton's, and the goal at Wundt's institute was the identification, through introspection, of components of consciousness. Individual differences, which formed the very heart of Galton's investigations, were nuisances in this search for principles which had general application to all. One notable exception to this general trend was provided by an American named J. McK. Cattell, who, as a student of Wundt, insisted on studying individual differences. After Cattell left Leipzig, he worked for a while with Galton, and had his belief in the importance of individual differences strengthened and confirmed. Cattell had an important influence on the development of American psychology, and, as we shall see later, inspired some of the earliest experimental work in behavioral genetics.

From the foregoing it may be seen that Galton's work was neither completely in step nor completely out of step with the times. As it happened, Galton lived in the greatest period of intellectual turmoil which had occurred in biology. His work was both a product and a causal factor of the advances made. Galton was not the first to insist upon the importance of heredity in traits of behavior. We have seen explicit statements on this matter by the ancient Greeks. Nor was Galton the first to place his conclusions in an evolutionary context. Spencer had introduced an "evolutionary associationism" in 1855 (Boring, 1950, p. 240). But it was Galton who championed the idea of inheritance of behavior, who vigorously consolidated and extended it, and who gave it a substance and direction it had hitherto lacked. If it ever becomes of moment to designate the "father" of behavioral genetics, Galton will have no real competition for the title.

Theories of Inheritance

For Darwin and Galton the transmission of characteristics from generation to generation was an essential concept. There was substantial evidence of the importance of heredity, but its laws had proved extremely resistant to analysis. In particular, a vast amount of data had been accumulated from plant and animal breeding. Offspring frequently resembled one of the parents, or were perhaps intermediate to both parents. But two offspring from the very same parents could be quite unlike. As Lush described the situation even considerably later, the first rule of breeding was that "like produces like," while the second rule was that "like does not always produce like" (Lush, 1951, p. 496).

PANGENESIS. The theory of heredity most successful in explaining the confusion of facts at the time was the "provisional hypothesis of pangenesis" as described by Darwin. On this view, the cells of the body,

> . . . besides having the power, as is generally admitted, of growing by self-division, throw off free and minute atoms of their contents, that is gemmules. These multiply and aggregate themselves into buds and the sexual elements; . . . [1868, p. 481].

Gemmules were presumably thrown off by each cell throughout its course of development. With the uniting of gemmules from the male and female parents, gemmules of the various developmental periods would come into play at the proper times, and thus direct the development of a new organ like that from which they had arisen.

If a body part were modified by use or disuse, the gemmules cast off by the cells of the body part would also be modified, and thus acquired characteristics could be transmitted to the offspring. Of specific interest to our present topic, we may note Darwin's statement:

> With respect to mental habits or instincts, we are so profoundly ignorant on the relation between the brain and the power of thought that we do not know whether an inveterate habit or trick induces any change in the nervous system; but when any habit or other mental attribute, or insanity, is inherited, we must believe that some actual modification is transmitted; and this implies, according to our hypothesis, that gemmules derived from modified nerve-cells are transmitted to the offspring [1868, p. 472f.].

Galton took issue with some of the features of pangenesis, and performed a long-range study which was a direct attempt to determine if gemmules from one breed of rabbit would affect the progeny of another breed when transfused in the blood. This experiment, which, incidentally, was performed in collaboration with Darwin, had a quite negative outcome. Galton also doubted the inheritance of acquired characteristics. A substantial, but on the whole friendly, disagreement grew up between Darwin and Galton on these issues, with the latter publishing extensively on a revised theory. Galton's revision foresaw many of the later developments, but to Gregor Mendel must go the credit for providing the basic answer to the riddle of inheritance.

MENDEL'S EXPERIMENT AND THEORY.   Mendel was an Augustinian monk who conducted his critical researches on pea plants in the garden of a monastery at Brunn, Moravia.

Much of the information concerning heredity available at the time had been based on experiments on "plant hybridization" involving the crossing of plants of different species. Among the difficulties of this approach, two of the most important were that the offspring were frequently sterile or semi-sterile, so that succeeding generations were difficult or impossible to obtain, and that the features which had been investigated were generally too complex for clear analysis. Mendel's success can be attributed in large part to his method of dealing with these problems. By crossing different varieties within the same species, Mendel got viable and fertile offspring, and thus was able to proceed to hybrids of the second generation. By concentrating his attention on simple dichotomous characters, he was able to make a thorough analysis, uncluttered by problems of measurement or distinction of categories. Curiously, Mendel's greatest innovation was evidently his insistence on *counting* all the progeny, and not being content with an attempt at a verbal summary of the typical result. This was, of course, made convenient by dealing with dichotomous characteristics.

In all, some seven morphological characters were investigated, and uniform results were obtained with respect to all. In the first-generation hybrid offspring (later named the F_1 or first filial generation) between plants differing with respect to any one of the characters, all plants were uniform, and like one of the parents. That parental character which appeared in the F_1 was called dominant; the parental character which was not expressed was called recessive. When the F_1 plants were allowed to self-pollinate, plants showing the dominant trait and plants showing the recessive trait were found among the offspring (the F_2, or second filial generation) in a definite 3:1 ratio, but no plants were found which were intermediate. Furthermore, it was found that the recessive plants "bred true"—their offspring always showed the recessive character. One third of the dominant plants also bred true, but two thirds yielded both types of progeny.

To account for these results, Mendel postulated that each parent possessed two elements which determined the particular trait. Each parent would transmit one of its elements to its offspring. In the case where the parents differed in respect to a characteristic, an element contributed by the one parent might be dominant over that contributed by the other parent, and the offspring would resemble the former. Nonetheless, the recessive element would not be contaminated in any way by its association with the dominant element. When the individual offspring in turn had offspring, it would pass on the element which it had received from each of its own parents to one half of its progeny—and the nature of the recessive element passed on would not differ in any way from its nature when transmitted from the original parent. Thus, the gametes (sex cells) were regarded as pure and essentially inviolable. Now, when such a hybrid offspring (F_1) is self-pollinated (or more generally, when two such hybrids are mated), the male and female germ cells (gametes) will each contain one of the elements only. The gametes will unite at random. Thus if A represents the dominant element and *a* the recessive, each hybrid is A*a*, but each gamete produced by the hybrid will be either A or *a*. When two hybrids are crossed, yielding an F_2 generation, the following combinations can occur: AA, A*a*, and *aa*, and these will occur in a 1:2:1 ratio. Because of dominance, the AA will not be distinguishable from the A*a*, except by examination of their offspring, so that the observable character will be displayed in a 3:1 ratio. This was Mendel's first law, the "law of segregation." Figure 16 shows the relationships graphically.

The second major law was the law of independent assortment. This principle was discovered when parents differing in two or more characteristics were crossed. For example, a pea plant having yellow, round seeds was crossed with one having green, wrinkled seeds. The first generation hybrid plants uniformly had yellow, round seeds, since these elements are dominant. In the generation resulting from the self-pollination of these plants, the characteristics were combined at random. The elements for yellow and round were not bound together simply because they were associated in that combination in the "grandparents." The elements, indeed, were sorted out at random, hence the name "independent assortment." A schematic illustration of this feature of Mendel's theory is shown in Figure 17.

DEVELOPMENT OF MODERN GENETICS

MENDEL'S RESULTS AND THEORY were read to the Brunn Society of Natural Science in 1865, and were later published in the proceedings of the Society. The crucial experiments had therefore been done and reported prior to Darwin's most complete statement of pangenesis, and

The "big" parent is characterized by the two A elements. The "small" parent has two a elements.

Each gamete formed can contain only one element, and, in this case, each parent can form only one kind of gamete.

The gametes unite to form F_1 individuals. Because of dominance of A over a, the F_1 individuals are all like their "big" parent.

The F_1 individuals can each produce two kinds of gamete, A or a, and these will be formed in equal numbers.

If mating occurs between two F_1 individuals, the gametes will combine at random to form several combinations.

Three kinds of zygote occur in the F_2, in the ratio $1:2:1$. Because of dominance, however, AA cannot be distinguished from Aa, and the ratio actually observed will be $3:1$.

The "small" and one third of the "big" individuals can produce only one kind of gamete. The other two thirds of the "big" individuals can produce two kinds of gamete, as was true of the F_1. An a gamete from one of the latter will not be different from the a gamete from the "small" individual of the F_2.

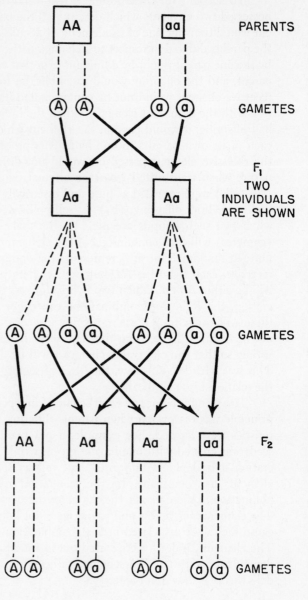

PARENTS

GAMETES

F_1
TWO
INDIVIDUALS
ARE SHOWN

GAMETES

F_2

GAMETES

FIGURE 16.   A schematic illustration of the Law of Segregation when one element is dominant. The hypothetical character is indicated by the size of the squares. Gametes are shown as small circles.

The *AA* combination results in a "big" individual, and the *aa* combination results in a "small" individual. *BB* results in a "square," and *bb* results in a "diamond." *A* is dominant over *a*, and *B* is dominant over *b*.

With regard to these characters, each parent can produce only one kind of gamete.

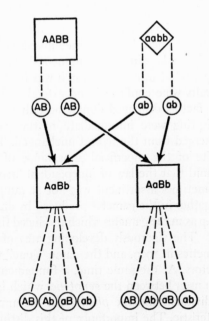

F₁ individuals are all alike: "big" and "square."

Each F₁ individual can form four kinds of gamete with regard to these characters.

This diagram shows the result of random combination of the gametes of a female and of a male F₁ individual. All possible combinations of "big," "small," "square," and "diamond" appear. The grandparental combinations of *AABB* and *aabb* occur no more often than expected by chance.

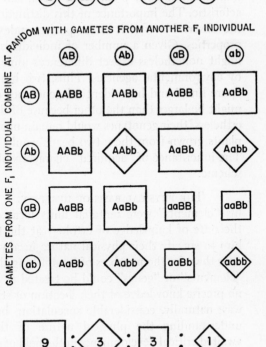

Note that the ratio of F₂ phenotypes is:

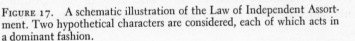

FIGURE 17. A schematic illustration of the Law of Independent Assortment. Two hypothetical characters are considered, each of which acts in a dominant fashion.

before *Hereditary Genius*. But Darwin and Galton were not alone in overlooking Mendel's ideas. For thirty-four years, the "Versuche über Pflanzen-Hybriden" (Mendel, 1865) remained almost completely unheeded. Then, in 1900, three investigators—Correns, de Vries, and von Tschermak—almost simultaneously "rediscovered" Mendel's work, and a period of intensive research was inaugurated in which the Mendelian results were confirmed and extended. Some modifications ensued. Not all factors displayed dominance; there were cases in which the hybrid offspring were intermediate to the parents. Nonetheless, the factors emerged from the hybrid unchanged. The "purity of gametes" held in spite of the superficial appearance of blending. Furthermore, it was found that the law of independent assortment did not hold absolutely. Sometimes assortment was not at random, but factors tended to stick together in the gametes produced by an individual in the same relationship as in the gametes which produced the individual.

The vigorously developing area of research came to be known as genetics in 1909, and the name "gene" was proposed for the Mendelian factors. At the same time, a fundamental distinction was made by Johannsen between the *genotype*, which is the genetic composition of the individual, and the *phenotype*, the apparent, visible, measurable characteristic. The importance of this distinction is that it makes clear that the observable trait is not a perfect index of the individual's genetic properties. Given a number of individuals of the same genotype, one might nonetheless expect differences among them—differences caused by environmental agencies. Thus, two beans might be from the same "pure line," and have identical genotypes with respect to size, yet one might be larger than the other because of differences in "nurture." Nevertheless, their genotypes would remain unaffected, and the beans of the plants grown from these two beans would be of the same average size. The inheritance of "acquired" characters obviously has no place in this scheme.

THE PHYSICAL BASIS OF HEREDITY.   Mendel was convinced that his "elements" were material units located in the gametes, but with the state of knowledge of cytology at the time, it was not possible for him to specify their physical nature in any greater detail. It was fortunate that, for the purposes of establishing the basic Mendelian laws, the "elements" or "genes" could be treated as hypothetical constructs, and no precise knowledge of their location or structure was necessary. There was, naturally, considerable speculation, but the real breakthrough in understanding the physical nature of the determiners of heredity awaited critical developments in the field of cytology.

CYTOLOGICAL DISCOVERIES.   The study of the cell and its contents had progressed rapidly since the general acceptance, in the mid-nineteenth century, of the doctrine that cells are the structural and functional units of living organisms. Aided in no small degree by advances in the chemistry of dyes, cytologists were able to develop means of staining the contents of cells to render them more visible for study. It was soon found that a portion of the cell, the *nucleus*, contains a number of small rod-shaped bodies which are called *chromosomes* (colored bodies) because of their capacity to be stained by particular dyes. The number of chromosomes, with some exceptions that need not concern us now, are the same in all somatic cells of an organism, and all individuals of a species have the same number. The number of chromosomes, however, varies greatly from species to species. It was known that in the process of growth the cells divide into two "daughter cells," each of which then later divides into two more, and so forth. Study of the chromosomes revealed that a remarkable series of changes takes place during this process of cell division, or *mitosis*. Prior to the splitting of the cell, the chromosomal material doubles, and during the cell division, half of the material goes into one daughter cell, half into the other. The chromosomes are somewhat distinctive in shape and size, so that it was possible to determine that each daughter cell receives an equivalent chromosomal complement. This distinctiveness of chromosomes also permitted the observation that chromosomes are present in pairs, and that the chromosomal material in a cell could be viewed as consisting of two comparable or *homologous* sets.

Quite independently of knowledge of the Mendelian laws, evidence was obtained that the chromosomes are, in some way, concerned with heredity, and it was concluded that one *set* of chromosomes is contributed by each parent. The process by which this is accomplished (meiosis) consists essentially of the splitting of a cell into two without the prior doubling of chromosomal material which is found in mitosis. One member of each pair of chromosomes is drawn into each daughter cell before the division is complete. The set included in any one gamete, however, is not necessarily the complete set which the individual had received from its mother or from its father. A reshuffling takes place, so that an individual transmits to its offspring some of the chromosomes it received from its own mother along with some received from its own father.

CHROMOSOMES AND GENES. This interesting behavior of the chromosomes was seen to parallel the behavior of Mendel's "elements": two elements, paired chromosomes; one element in each gamete, one of each pair of chromosomes in each gamete. On this, and other evidence, it was suggested that the genes are in fact particulate physical bodies residing at specific *loci* on the chromosomes.

The advances in understanding of the chromosomal basis of heredity also allowed explanation of the exceptions to the law of independent assortment which had been noted (see p. 160). It was evident that there are more genes than there are chromosomes, and that therefore each chromosome must contain a number of genes. If two characteristics under study are determined by genes on the same chromosome, it is clear that these genes cannot assort independently. Such *linkage* was experimentally demonstrated, but it was also discovered that linkage is not a permanent, unbreakable bond. During one stage of gamete formation, the chromosomes line up pair by pair. Each member of each pair separates into two. The adjacent members of this *tetrad* frequently come into contact and exchange parts. This mutual exchange is usually done with such precision that equivalent sections are traded—each of the members participating in the exchange receiving the same loci that it gives.

Figure 18 is a diagrammatic illustration of this process for one pair of chromosomes only. It should be remembered that the same events may be occurring at the same time for all other chromosome pairs. In Figure 18A are shown the two members of the chromosome pair. The maternal chromosome, carrying the genes A, b, and C, is shown as white, and the paternal chromosome with the genes a, B, and c is shown as gray. At one stage in meiosis each of the chromosomes can be seen to be duplicate, as shown in Figure 18B. In Figure 18C the adjacent members are shown as crossed over one another. During this stage the chromosomes may break and rejoin, yielding the configuration of Figure 18D. Each one of these four members will be transmitted to one gamete. Consider only the A-a and B-b locus for the moment. As shown in Figure 18E, one gamete will carry the genes A and b as in the grandmother, one will carry a and B as in the grandfather, and the other two will carry A with B and a with b. For these last, recombination has taken place. Crossing over of this kind does not always occur at the same place, and the probability that recombination will occur is a function of the distance between the genes involved. In Figure 18, for example, the crossing over has not affected the relationship between the A-a and the C-c loci. All gametes are either AC or ac, as in the grandparental combinations, since the crossover did not occur between these loci. Crossing over could occur between the A and C loci, but would be less frequent than between A and B. Because of this, the crossover gametes frequently occur less often than the non-crossover, and this forms an exception to the law of independent assortment. Genes located on different chromosomes do, of course, assort at random.

AUTOSOMES AND SEX CHROMOSOMES.   Detailed examination of the chromosomes revealed that one pair was exceptional, in that the

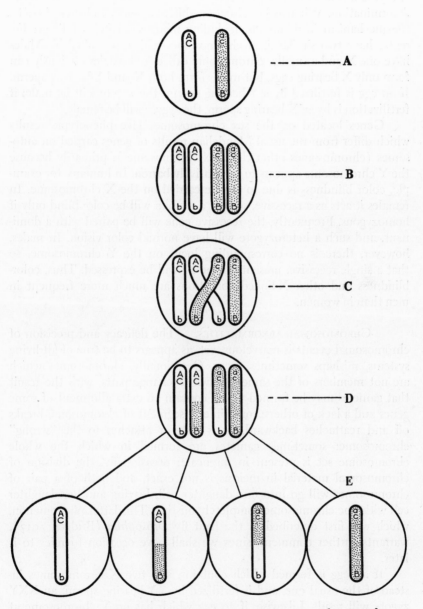

FIGURE 18. Diagrammatic illustration of crossing over—the mutual exchange of material by homologous chromosomes.

members of the pair were of obviously different size and shape. Eventually, it was possible to relate this atypical pair of chromosomes to sex determination. Whereas the situation differs in birds and some insects, the mechanism in mammals, including man, is briefly as follows: Females have two similar-sized chromosomes which are called X. Males have one X and a smaller chromosome called Y. Females obviously can form only X-bearing eggs, but males form both X- and Y-bearing sperm. If an egg is fertilized by a Y-bearing sperm, the zygote will be male; if fertilization is by an X-bearing sperm, the zygote will be female.

Genes located on the sex chromosomes give phenotypic results which differ from the usual Mendelian results of genes carried on autosomes (chromosomes other than sex chromosomes), primarily because the Y chromosome appears to be relatively barren. In humans, for example, color blindness is due to a gene carried on the X chromosome. In females it acts as a recessive, so that a woman will be color-blind only if homozygous. Frequently, the recessive gene will be paired with a dominant, and such a heterozygote will have normal color vision. In males, however, there is no corresponding locus on the Y chromosome, so that a single recessive, present on the X, will be expressed. Thus, color-blindness and other X-linked conditions are much more frequent in men than in women.

CHROMOSOMAL ABNORMALITIES.   The delicacy and precision of chromosomal events is marvelous, yet, as appears to be true of all living systems, mishaps sometimes occur. Occasionally, chromosomes which are not members of the same pair will exchange parts, with the result that gametes may be formed which contain an extra allotment of some genes and a lack of others; sometimes a segment of chromosome breaks off and reattaches backward, or is lost, or attaches to the "wrong" chromosome; sometimes gametes are formed in which the whole chromosome set is present in duplicate; occasionally, the division of chromosomal material in meiosis is not exact, and both of a pair of chromosomes will go into one daughter cell, leaving another daughter cell with one chromosome completely missing. This latter phenomenon, which was first described in the fruit fly Drosophila (Bridges, 1913), warrants further comment, since we shall have occasion to refer to it later.

If an egg is formed which contains, say, two X chromosomes instead of the usual one, and is fertilized by a Y-bearing sperm, an XXY zygote will result. Likewise, if an egg which has no X chromosome at all is fertilized by a Y-bearing sperm, the resulting zygote will be YO (where O represents absence of a chromosome). In like manner, XXX and XO gametes will be formed if eggs of these respective constitutions are fertilized by X-bearing sperm. In Drosophila, XXX and YO flies usually die, but XXY are viable, fertile females, and XO are viable but sterile males. These abnormalities of chromosomal distribution can occur with respect to autosomes as well as to sex chromosomes, and occur in male as well as in female gametogenesis.

MODIFIABILITY OF THE GENES.   Mendel's conclusion concerning the "purity of the gametes," and Johannsen's demonstration that environmental modification of a phenotype does not alter the genotype, present a view of the genes as being highly stable and well insulated from the effects of environment. There were, however, many observations which showed that the stability of the genes is a relative matter. On occasion, a given gene might undergo a more or less permanent change, called a mutation. The reasons for this alteration in the nature of genes are still incompletely understood, but significant advances have been made since the discovery in 1927 by Muller that irradiation of corn and barley increases the rate of gene mutation. Since this discovery of the *mutagenic* effect of X-rays, other means of experimentally inducing mutations have been discovered, including certain chemical compounds and the application of extreme temperatures, and the mutability of the hereditary material of other species has been demonstrated. Thus, *certain environments* can bring about changes in genotype, but this situation differs greatly from the old notion of inheritance of acquired characters. Under that scheme, the environment was thought capable of bringing about systematic changes, or else the organism, by use or disuse of body parts, caused a change, which made the organism *more adapted to the environment*, and this adaptation could be transmitted to subsequent generations. The mutations, however, induced by X-ray and other mutagenic agents, as well as those occurring "spontaneously," are apparently random—the mutation might affect eye color or wing shape or any of a large number of such characteristics, but the organisms are not made more adapted for example, to an X-ray environment. Actually, the mutations which occur seem much more likely to be deleterious than advantageous to the organism.

The capability of experimentally inducing mutations has proved to be of marked value in genetic research, and has contributed greatly to the elucidation of the molecular structure of genes and of the biochemistry of gene action.

Progress in the understanding of mutations has also been of importance to evolutionary theory. It may be recalled that Darwin took great pains in considering the possible sources of heritable variation, and somewhat reluctantly concluded that Lamarckian mechanisms are among the important factors. Contemporary evolutionary theory views mutation as an important (and perhaps the only) source of the genetic variability upon which natural selection operates.

MECHANISM OF GENE ACTION.   At one level, gene action may
be described in terms of dominance, recessiveness, or additivity. Further
insights into the mechanism of gene action have been obtained by
certain experiments with fruit flies. In *Drosophila melanogaster* there
are four chromosomes and, of course, each fly has two of each. By proper
techniques, however, it is also possible to obtain flies with abnormal
numbers of a given chromosome. The effect of varying "dosages" of
genes can then be studied. An example of the results of this kind of research is given by the mutant gene "shaven," which reduces the number
of abdominal bristles on the fly (see Wagner and Mitchell, 1955). Representing the normal gene by S and the "shaven" by s, and letting $<$
mean "has fewer bristles than," we may describe the three possible
types of normal flies (each possessing two chromosomes) as follows:
$ss < Ss < SS$. By adding or subtracting chromosomes containing the s
gene, the following is obtained:

$$s < ss < sss < Ss < SS$$

An interpretation of these findings is that the mutant gene is working in the same direction as the normal gene, but is simply less effective.
This kind of mutant is described as a *hypomorph*. By similar experiments (see Wagner and Mitchell), other types of mutants have been
described: *antimorphs*, which have an effect contrary to the normal
gene; *hypermorphs*, which have an effect greater than the normal gene;
neomorphs, which have an effect unrelated to the normal gene; and
amorphs, which have no effect at all. All of these can be incorporated
into an explanatory scheme if one assumes that genes produce some substance, and that it is through the substance produced that they have
their effect. The key role of enzymes in biochemistry early led to the
notion that genes produce enzymes, and a great amount of research
brought forth the "one gene—one enzyme" hypothesis which stated
that each gene produces a single enzyme. This is now thought to be an
oversimplification, but it is clear that genes confer specificity upon enzymes, although several genes may be involved in determining specificity
of a given enzyme (Davis, 1954, p. 29). The enzymes, of course, are centrally involved in the metabolic processes resulting in development and
functioning of the sensory, associative, and effector organs, and thus can
influence behavior through any or all of these systems. Figure 19 gives
a diagrammatic indication of the complexity of the intermediate steps
between the initial gene action and the phenotypic expression. Here it
may be seen that alteration of any one of a number of different pathways may result in change of a given phenotype, and that, conversely,
alteration of any one pathway may have consequences for a number of
different phenotypes.

In view of the complexities suggested in Figure 19, it is no surprise that, in numerous cases, "modifier" genes have been described which alter the effect of a major gene upon some character. Indeed, it is clear that describing any gene as *"the"* gene determining a character is only a convenient short-hand expression. All genes exert their influence in the context of the total genetic system, and identifying the gene for "shaven," for example, is simply an expedient way of saying that the gene occupies a particularly strategic location in the network of the genetic factors acting upon the formation of abdominal bristles.

THE COLLABORATION OF GENES AND ENVIRONMENT.   One of the most important principles to emerge from genetics research is that a phenotype is the joint product of genetic and environmental factors.

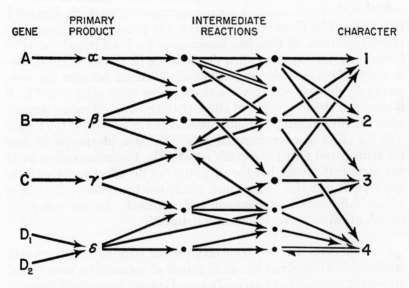

FIGURE 19. Diagrammatic representation of the complexity of gene interaction in the production of a character. (By G. Ledyard Stebbins.)

This is easily made apparent by a *reductio ad absurdum:* if there is no environment, no organism can develop to display any phenotype whatsoever. Likewise, without a genetic constitution, there will be no organism. It is clear that a question asking if a trait is due to heredity or to environment is nonsense. Without both, there would be no trait at all. A meaningful answer, however, may be sought to a question concerning the *relative* contributions of genetic *differences* and environmental *differences* to the *variability* of a characteristic. We must not then seek absolute answers to the question of the importance of heredity or of environment in determining a characteristic. The answer obtained will depend upon the extent to which relevant genetic variability exists within the group being considered and upon the range of environmental differences to which the individuals are exposed. If genetic variability is eliminated, or reduced drastically, and environment allowed to vary, then environmental agencies will appear important. The average and the variability of the phenotype will depend, however, on the nature of the common genotype. If environment is held constant and genotype allowed to vary, then genotype will be seen as important, but the average and the variability of the phenotype will depend upon the nature of the common environmental conditions. Hogben (1933, pp. 96f.) presented a discussion of Krafka's data on eye mutants which succinctly demonstrates these principles. Two different mutants, "low-bar" and "ultra-bar," reduce the number of facets in a fly's eyes. The extent of reduction, however, depends upon temperature. Figure 20 shows this interaction. The distance AB represents the phenotypic difference between two stocks of flies, one homozygous for low-bar and the other homozygous for ultra-bar, when the fly larvae developed at 16° C. The distance CD represents the phenotypic difference between the same genetically different stocks, when development takes place at 25° C. It is clear that the magnitude of effect of the genetic difference depends upon the environment. The drops from A to C and from B to D represent the effect of environmental difference upon phenotype for low-bar animals and ultra-bar animals respectively. Environment has an affect upon both stocks, but the magnitude of the effect varies with the genotype. It may also be seen that, at any one temperature, the role of genetic differences is emphasized, and conversely, for any one stock, the role of environmental differences is stressed.

THE EXTENSION OF MENDELIAN THEORY TO QUANTITATIVE CHARACTERISTICS.   Throughout the early period of enthusiastic research following the rediscovery of Mendel's laws, Galton's biometrical approach to problems of the inheritance of continuously varying characteristics had been pursued vigorously, notably by Pearson. Rather than finding mutual support in each other's work, the Mendelians and the biometricians came into acute conflict. It was difficult for the Mendelians to reconcile continuous variation with the type of qualitative, discrete difference, mediated by particulate genes, with which they had worked. The biometricians, on the other hand, supported the blending hypothesis, and were inclined to regard the Mendelian type of inheritance as an unimportant exception to the general rule. With justification, they pointed to the obvious importance of the smoothly continuous, quantitative characteristics, such as height, weight, intelligence, and so on. It was apparent, to the biometricians, at least, that the type of thing investigated by Mendelians—causing qualitative differences, and usually

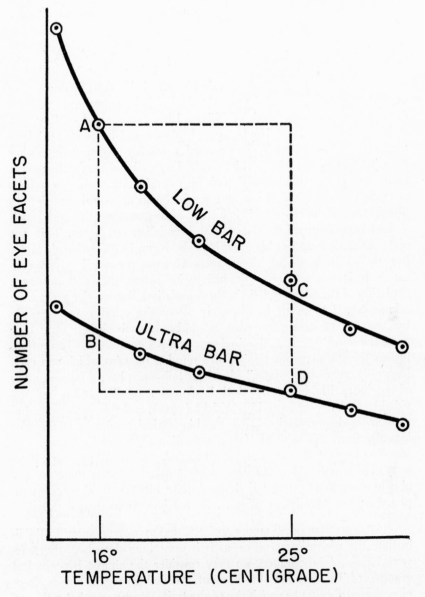

FIGURE 20.   Hogben's plot of Krafka's data, showing gene-environment interaction in the production of eye facet number in *Drosophila*. (From L. Hogben, *Nature and Nurture*, Figure 2. Published in 1933 by George Allen & Unwin Ltd., and used with their permission.)

abnormalities—could not possibly account for such continuous distributions.

THE MULTIPLE FACTOR HYPOTHESIS.   The groundwork for the resolution of this conflict had been provided, in fact, by Mendel himself, when he suggested that a certain characteristic might be due to two or three elements. General acceptance of this idea, however, was not forthcoming until the work of Nilsson-Ehle (1908) and of East and collaborators (East and Hayes, 1911; Emerson and East, 1913). These researchers showed that if one assumed a *number* of gene pairs, rather than just one pair, each of which exerted a small and cumulative effect upon the same character, and took into consideration also the effects of environment, the final outcome would be an apparently continuous distribution of the characteristic instead of dichotomous categories such as had been featured in the typical Mendelian researches. This was quite different from the blending hypothesis for, in this *multiple factor* hypothesis, the hereditary determiners were not presumed to vary continuously in nature from individual to individual, thus determining a gradation of the characteristic in the population. Rather, the genes were acknowledged to occur in discretely alternative conditions (typically two, sometimes more), but when a number of such discrete units bear upon the same character, the final outcome is a continuous distribution, just as the simultaneous tossing of a number of coins which can each have only one of two "states"—heads or tails—can have a large number of outcomes. Elaborate statistical development of this notion was provided by Fisher (1918) and by Wright (1921), and this work presented convincing demonstrations that the biometrical results in fact follow logically from this multiple factor extension of Mendel's theory. The blending hypothesis was gradually discarded, and as early as 1914 Bateson could remark, "The question is often asked whether there are not also in operation systems of descent quite other than those contemplated by the Mendelian rules . . . none have been demonstrated." [2]

AN ILLUSTRATIVE MODEL OF POLYGENIC INHERITANCE.   To illustrate the multiple factor, or, as it is sometimes described, the *polygenic* [3] type of inheritance, we may consider the simple hypothetical example of Table 2. For the moment, we shall disregard any environmental contribution to variability of the trait. We assume that a characteristic is influenced by genes at two loci (in actual cases many more loci

[2] From K. Mather, "The Progress and Prospect of Biometrical Genetics" in L. C. Dunn, ed., *Genetics in the 20th Century*, p. 111. Copyright 1951 by The Macmillan Company, and used with their permission.

[3] There are certain distinctions made between the terms "multiple factor" and "polygenic" in some usages. For present purposes, they may be considered synonymous.

may be involved). Furthermore, we assume that two alleles, or alternative gene states, exist at each locus, i.e., A or a and B or b, and that the alleles act additively within a locus and also between loci. If each allele represented by a capital letter adds one unit to the trait, the various gene combinations will yield the phenotypic values shown in Table 2a. Now, suppose an AABB individual, with a score of 4, to be mated with an aabb individual, with a score of 0. All the offspring will be AaBb, and all will have scores of 2. Each such F_1 individual will be able to generate 4 kinds of gamete. The genetic combinations which could result from a mating of two F_1 individuals are shown in Table 2b, where the possible

TABLE 2a

PHENOTYPIC VALUES FOR VARIOUS GENOTYPES ASSUMING ADDITIVE
GENE ACTION

(See text for explanation)

GENOTYPE	AABB	AABb	AaBB	AAbb	AaBb	aaBB	Aabb	aaBb	aabb
PHENO-TYPIC VALUE	4	3	3	2	2	2	1	1	0

TABLE 2b

GENOTYPES OF OFFSPRING OF MATING OF TWO F_1 INDIVIDUALS
PHENOTYPIC VALUES SHOWN IN PARENTHESES

GAMETES PRODUCIBLE BY FEMALE F_1 PARENT

		AB	Ab	aB	ab
GAMETES PRODUC-IBLE BY MALE F_1 PARENT	AB	AABB(4)	AABb(3)	AaBB(3)	AaBb(2)
	Ab	AABb(3)	AAbb(2)	AaBb(2)	Aabb(1)
	aB	AaBB(3)	AaBb(2)	aaBB(2)	aaBb (1)
	ab	AaBb(2)	Aabb(1)	aaBb(1)	aabb(0)

gametes are shown in the margins, and the entries in the body of the table show the genotypes which would result from the random combination of the gametes. It can easily be seen that variability will exist in this F_2 generation. Tables 2c and 2d show the results of *backcrossing* F_1 individuals to the AABB parent and to the aabb parent, respectively. Under the simple model we have been using, the parents and F_1 have no variability, while the backcross groups have some variability, but less than the F_2. With respect to averages, the F_1 is located halfway between the parents, the F_2 mean is at the same point, and the backcross means are intermediate between the F_1 value and that of the parent to which the backcross mating was made. Figure 21a compares the different groups with respect to these statistical features.

The very simple situation we have considered may be complicated

TABLE 2c

GENOTYPES OF OFFSPRING OF BACKCROSS OF F_1 TO *AABB* PARENT
PHENOTYPIC VALUES SHOWN IN PARENTHESES

GAMETES PRODUCIBLE BY F_1 PARENT

		AB	Ab	aB	ab
GAMETE PRODUCIBLE BY *AABB* PARENT	AB	AABB(4)	AABb(3)	AaBB(3)	AaBb(2)

TABLE 2d

GENOTYPES OF OFFSPRING OF BACKCROSS OF F_1 TO *aabb* PARENT
PHENOTYPIC VALUES SHOWN IN PARENTHESES

GAMETES PRODUCIBLE BY F_1 PARENT

		AB	Ab	aB	ab
GAMETE PRODUCIBLE BY *aabb* PARENT	ab	AaBb(2)	Aabb(1)	aaBb(1)	aabb(0)

TABLE 2e

PHENOTYPIC VALUES FOR VARIOUS GENOTYPES WITH ADDITIVE GENE ACTION
AT ONE LOCUS AND DOMINANCE AT THE OTHER LOCUS

GENOTYPE	AABB	AABb	AaBB	AAbb	AaBb	aaBB	Aabb	aaBb	aabb
PHENOTYPIC VALUE	4	3	4	2	3	2	2	1	0

in various ways. Let us consider, for example, what would result if the B alleles acted additively, while the A alleles displayed dominance. The phenotypic values for the possible genotypes would be as shown in Table 2e. The F_1 of the cross between *AABB* (4) and *aabb* (0) would, of course, be *AaBb*, as before, but under these conditions the phenotypic value of such individuals would be 3 instead of 2. The F_2 and backcross generations would also have the same genotypes as those shown in Table 2b for the first example, but different phenotypic values would result for many of the genotypes. Figure 21b shows the distribution of the trait in the various generations for the new hypothetical case. The differences in statistical values—means, standard deviations, skewness—under the two conditions are apparent.

Another complicating feature, and one of paramount importance, is that environmental factors will also contribute to the variability of the

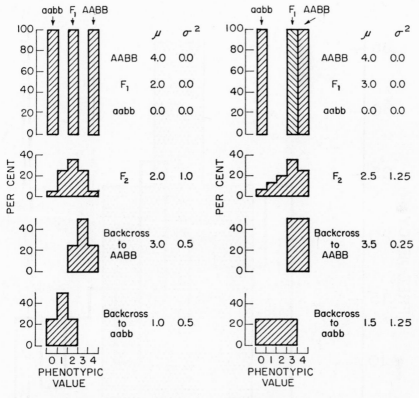

FIGURE 21a. Distributions of *AABB* and *aabb* parents and various derived generations, assuming additive gene action and negligible environmental influence.

FIGURE 21b. Distribution of *AABB* and *aabb* parents and various derived generations, assuming additive gene action at one locus, and dominance at the other. Environmental influence is assumed to be negligible.

trait. When the environmental contributions are added to, or subtracted from, the value that we would expect on the basis of genotype alone, the result is a blurring of the boundaries between adjacent score values. The distribution of the trait may be less symmetrical, may encompass a greater range, and may in various other ways differ from the diagrammatic neatness of Figures 21a and 21b. The effect of a simple pattern of environmental action on the genotypic situation depicted in Table 2b is shown in Figure 21c. The latter was constructed by assuming a population of ninety-six individuals, composed of six representatives of each genotype in Table 2b. It was further assumed that randomly acting environmental forces could affect the scores by ±2.0, ±1.5, ±1.0, ±0.5, or o units. Assigning these environmental effects randomly to the ninety-six individuals gave the outline frequency distribution of Figure 21c. For comparison, the shaded frequency distribution shows the result to be expected on genotypic value only. It is easily seen that the environmental effects have blurred the symmetry of the genotypic distribution.

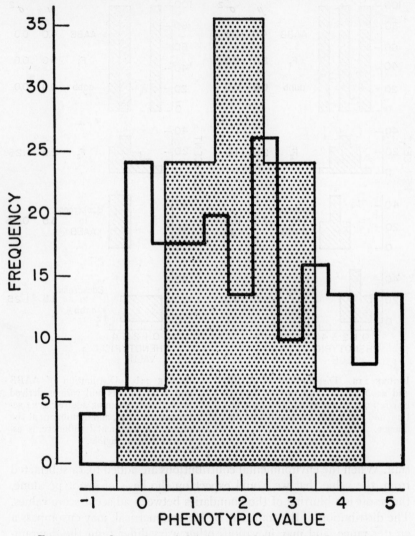

FIGURE 21c. Comparison of distributions of hypothetical F₂ population ignoring environmental effect (shaded distribution), and assuming random environmental effect described in text (outline distribution).

Other complications include the possibility of one locus contributing more to the trait than others, linkage of loci, and *epistasis*, or interaction between loci, in which the effect of an allele at one locus is dependent upon the nature of the alleles at some other locus.

As is readily apparent, the Mendelian procedures for investigating single major genes are inappropriate in analyses of polygenic inheritance. The theoretical developments by Fisher and Wright, and subsequently elaborated by them and by other workers, have made possible a statistical approach to the problem. By the analysis of various statistics, particularly correlations among relatives and variances of groups of different genetic constitution, it is possible to assess the relative contributions of genetic and environmental factors, and the nature of action (additive, dominant, epistatic, etc.) of the genes involved. (For recent statements of the statistical approach to quantitative genetics, see Falconer, 1960; Lerner, 1958; Mather, 1949; and Wright, 1952.)

MAJOR GENES, POLYGENES, AND BEHAVIOR. The success of the polygenic interpretation of quantitative characters is of crucial importance for behavioral genetics. A very large proportion of psychological phenotypes is of the quantitative variety, and with reference to Figure 20, must be regarded as being well over toward the right margin. At least on the level of description and analysis permitted by current knowledge, intelligence and personality characteristics, for example, must surely be resultants of the action of a large number of organ systems, and consequently will be products of the genes influencing the various contributing systems.

Searching for *the* gene of intelligence or temperament, then, is likely to be a fruitless task, although the various subcomponents of such phenotypes may quite possibly be subject to fairly simple genetic determination. This is not to say that single gene effects are never to be expected. Even in phenotypes well established as polygenically determined, it is sometimes found that a single gene pair may have potent influence. In the case of normal variation in human stature, for example, there is little doubt that a number of loci is involved. Yet a single gene is known which causes chondrodystrophic dwarfism (see Stern, 1960, p. 99). The same situation probably obtains in the case of intelligence, with several known conditions of feeble-mindedness (to be discussed in some detail later) providing examples of single genes overriding the polygenic system which determines the "normal" variation in intelligence.

DEVELOPMENT. Any particular trait chosen for study is susceptible to change during the life of the organism. Genetic and environmental forces begin their interaction at conception. The chemical nature of the cytoplasm of the fertilized egg, and later the adequacy of the placental attachment, for example, play equally indispensable roles, and are just as much part of the environment as the postnatal food the organism eats and the air it breathes.

Analysis of the long-term development of a characteristic may provide insights into the operation of the hereditary and environmental forces which would be unattainable by study at only one selected developmental period.

Salient features of the developmental process have been summarized schematically by Waddington (1957) with reference to tissue development. In Figure 22 an "epigenetic landscape" is presented. The

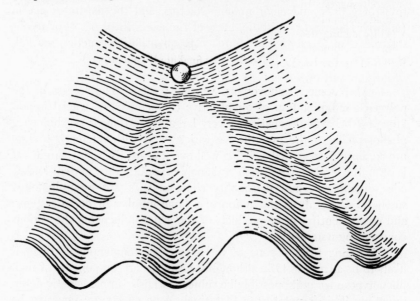

FIGURE 22. Waddington's "epigenetic landscape"—a hypothetical model describing gene-environment interaction in development. For interpretation, see text. (After C. H. Waddington, *The Strategy of the Genes*, Figure 4, p. 29. Published in 1957 by The Macmillan Co. and George Allen & Unwin Ltd., and used with their permission.)

background corresponds to conception and the foreground shows different phenotypic values at some point in development. The path of the ball, as it rolls downhill, represents the development of some particular part of the egg. The landscape is characterized by valleys and hills, and the particular contour of the landscape may be considered to be determined by genotype. Each individual of different genotype may thus have a different contour. Environmental forces act to move the ball laterally, and may thus switch development from one channel to another if applied at a critical juncture.

Concerning this model, Waddington says:

Although the epigenetic landscape only provides a rough and ready picture of the developing embryo, and cannot be interpreted rigorously, it has certain merits for those who, like myself, find it comforting to have some mental picture, however vague, for what they are trying to think about. For instance, it makes one reflect that there may be regions at upper levels which are almost flat plateaus from which two or three different valleys lead off downwards. These, in fact, correspond to what we know as states of competence, in which embryonic tissues are in a condition in which they can be easily brought to develop in one or other of a number of alternative directions. Again, the model immediately suggests that one ought to consider the degree of canalisation of any particular path of development. Has the valley a flat bottom and gently sloping sides? If so, there will be only a rather slight tendency for a developmental trajectory, when displaced from the valley centre, to find its way back there again; the final adult character will be easily caused to vary by minor fluctuations in the conditions under which development occurs. On the other hand, if the valley bottom is very narrow and the sides steep, it will be more difficult to push the trajectory away from its normal course and it will quickly return there, unless indeed it has been pushed over the brow of a watershed either into another valley or on to a plateau which represents some aberrant conditions intermediate between one organ and another [4] [1957, pp. 30–1].

In addition to its heuristic value, Waddington's model provides an instructive summary, for with this schema in mind, it is difficult to forget the complexity of interactions, among genetic factors and between genetic and environmental factors, which lead to the development of a characteristic.

SUMMARY OF DEVELOPMENTS IN GENETICS. The foregoing account has been necessarily simplified, and vast areas of genetic theory and research have been ignored completely. The attempt has been made to present a reasonably contemporary picture of those aspects of genetic theory that appear to be most salient in relation to phenotypes of behavior.

In the short span of half a century, genetics has metamorphosed from a minor area on the outskirts of biological research to a central area of paramount importance to all the biological and related fields.

We may now turn to a consideration of the import of genetics for psychology. For convenience, the subject matter is divided into human research and research on experimental animals. Within each of these categories, the emphasis will be on the earlier research, from the turn of

[4] From C. H. Waddington, *The Strategy of the Genes.* Published by The Macmillan Company and George Allen & Unwin Ltd. and used by their permission.

the century until about 1930, with a briefer treatment of the subsequent work.

HUMAN RESEARCH

ALTHOUGH MOST of the major advances in genetics resulted from research on plants and lower animals, many studies were made of the inheritance of a wide variety of characteristics in humans. Most of the characteristics studied were abnormalities of one kind or another, and in time, hereditary defects were identified in almost all organ systems (see Gates, 1946). Now, practically any organ or tissue, and particularly components of receptor, effector, and associative systems, may play a role in behavior, so that in a very real sense the discovery of the genetic basis for color-blindness, deaf-mutism, and certain forms of ataxia, for example, have been contributions to behavioral genetics. At present, however, we shall emphasize the developments in respect to those traits that fall within the customary definitions of intelligence, aptitude, mental deficiency, psychosis, neurosis, and personality.

Several general approaches to the problem may be distinguished: pedigree analyses and family histories, correlations among relatives, twin studies and foster-child studies. Some researchers have used combinations of these methods, but insofar as possible, we shall consider the developments within each technique separately.

Studies on Eminent and "Degenerate" Families

EMINENT AND ROYAL FAMILIES.   Several extensive surveys followed Galton's procedure of investigating the accomplishments of relatives of notable people. Royal families provided particularly convenient source material, owing to the easy availability of their genealogical records (Woods, 1906; Gun, 1930a, 1930b). One disadvantage of this line of inquiry, however, was the sometimes dubious correspondence of legal and biological parentage. For example, Gun (1930b, p. 195) in discussing King James I, remarks, "his characteristics have but little resemblance to those of any of his ancestors. This fact was so obvious that from an early period doubts arose as to his parentage, some considering that he was the son of Mary by David Rizzio, while others contended that he was a changeling." Nevertheless, Gun was convinced that the family histories clearly showed the inheritance of certain traits. Thus the Stewarts were said to be characterized by tactless obstinacy, which "ran like a thread down the direct male line . . ." (1930b, p. 201). The Tudors, on the other hand, were thought to be hereditarily endowed with love of learning.

THE "JUKES" FAMILY.   Dugdale, on the other hand, had concerned himself with the other end of the scale of social merit. As a member of the executive committee of the Prison Association of New York, Dugdale was named a committee of one to inspect county jails. In one county he was impressed by finding six of the prisoners to be related. Undertaking an intensive survey of this family, he was able to trace the lineage back to six sisters, to whom he gave the pseudonymous label "Jukes." One of the six had left the country and was not traceable. The remaining five had provided a most striking posterity, characterized by criminality, immorality, pauperism, and feeble-mindedness. Dugdale was primarily a social reformer, and was rather cautious in assigning the causal role in this pedigree of sordidity to nature or to nurture. That there was a social problem was clear enough. Dugdale (1877) estimated the cost to the state, in welfare relief, institutional care, etc., to exceed one million dollars over a seventy-five-year period. In 1911 some of Dugdale's original manuscripts were found, which gave the real name of the Jukes family. Estabrook (1916), acting upon this information, was able to trace the family history over the forty years ensuing since the first study. Estabrook summarized his study as follows:

> For the past 130 years they have increased from 5 sisters to a family which numbers 2,094 people, of whom 1,258 were living in 1915. One half of the Jukes were and are feeble-minded, mentally incapable of responding normally to the expectations of society, brought up under faulty environmental conditions which they consider normal, satisfied with the fulfillment of natural passions and desires, and with no ambition or ideals in life. The other half, perhaps normal mentally and emotionally, has become socially adequate or inadequate, depending on the chance of the individual reaching or failing to reach an environment which would mold and stimulate his inherited social traits. . . . Heredity, whether good or bad, has its complemental factor in environment. The two determine the behavior of the individual [1916, p. 85].

This conclusion was reasonably modest, assigning importance to both heredity and environment, but the findings of the study were enthusiastically endorsed by the more ardent eugenicists, and came to be regarded as proof of "morbid inheritance."

Various criticisms have been leveled at the Jukes study, and at a number of similar studies which followed. Perhaps the most cogent objection raised was that members of the families shared similar environments as well as a common lineage. Thus, while the more or less anecdotal evidence could be accepted as presenting a dismaying picture of human degradation, there was no means of determining the relative contributions of environment and heredity.

THE "KALLIKAKS."   In 1912 Goddard published an account of a family which, in his view, provided a clear-cut resolution of the problem of disentangling nature and nurture. This family consisted of two branches, each of which could be traced back to the same man. According to the report, "Martin Kallikak" (again, a pseudonym), while a soldier in the Revolutionary War, had an affair with a feeble-minded girl whom he met in a tavern. When the girl gave birth to a son, she named him "Martin Kallikak, Jr." After the war, Martin, Sr. returned home, married a girl of good family, and began the other branch of the family. Among 480 descendants of the illicit affair, a very "Jukes"-like picture was presented. Among the descendants of the marriage, almost all were normal, good members of society.

These results were taken to demonstrate that feeble-mindedness, which was regarded as the root of all the family difficulties, was inherited. A discussion of Mendelian principles was provided in the report, but judgment was reserved as to whether feeble-mindedness is a unit character, caused by a single gene.

The investigation of the Kallikaks was carried out largely by a field worker interviewing members of the family and people who knew members of the family. In discussing the general methodology, Goddard stated that although the evidence was occasionally ambiguous, and judgment had to be withheld, the field worker could usually decide easily the mentality of the persons interviewed. He also defended the assessment of the intellect of deceased individuals by interview of acquaintances, which was part of the procedures used in the study.

CRITICISM OF FAMILY STUDIES.   As with the Jukes, the Kallikak findings were widely hailed in some circles, and vigorously criticized in others. In 1942 Goddard wrote a defense of the study, replying to some of the principal critics. To the criticism that assessment by a field worker was unreliable, Goddard replied that the field worker was well trained, and from familiarity with institutionalized cases, could adequately judge mental level. Furthermore, if doubt remained, a case was marked undetermined. To the objection that the evidence that Martin, Sr. was the father of Martin, Jr. was scant, and would not be acceptable in a court case, Goddard simply replied, "A strange statement. Courts have always accepted such evidence and still do. In this case there was not even a doubt" (1942, p. 575).

These answers were not very satisfying, and one of the strongest critics, Scheinfeld (1944), retorted in detail. Particularly, he remained unconvinced that the evidence for Martin, Jr.'s paternity, "a single short sentence, *unaccompanied by any documentation or supporting evidence*" (p. 262), could serve the purposes of a scientific investigation. If this particular point is not adequately demonstrated, of course, the whole study becomes meaningless. Scheinfeld also remained unimpressed by the unsupported claim of accuracy in diagnosing the mental condition of the living, not to mention the dead, Kallikaks.

But even if the above could all be allowed, there remained another fundamental, and indeed a vitiating, problem. This concerns Goddard's failure to consider seriously the possibility that differences in environment might have been strong factors in creating at least some of the disparity between the two Kallikak branches. "This possibility he dismissed lightly by saying that the bad Kallikaks . . . are not open to this argument," and ". . . that we are dealing with a problem of true heredity no one can doubt" (Scheinfeld, 1944, p. 262). Such a major issue cannot be so easily disposed of, and, in fact, the impossibility of separating genetic and environmental effects renders the whole study pointless.

The objections raised to the studies of eminent and degraded families are telling, and by current standards we must judge that, whatever their worth as sociological documents, these studies merely serve to confuse the problem of determining the relative influence of nature and nurture.

Pedigree Studies on Mental Defects [5]

Aside from the large-scale efforts described above, there were numerous smaller pedigree studies involving the investigation of many families with relatively fewer individuals studied per family. In a review of the literature to 1912, Davenport (1912) was in fact able to present data on musical ability, artistic composition, literary composition, mechanical skill, calculating ability, memory, temperament, handwriting, pauperism, narcotism, criminality, and feeble-mindedness.

Most of these studies are susceptible to the same type of criticism as was applied to the Kallikaks, but in the subsequent research on one of the topics, feeble-mindedness, the pedigree approach achieved its most substantial success as applied to the problems of behavioral genetics.

One of the most influential of the early publications was that of Tredgold (1908). In examining the family histories of some 200 cases of "every grade and variety of amentia," he concluded that there were two basic causal factors: intrinsic (hereditary) and extrinsic (environmental), and he regarded the former to be of "immense importance," accounting for some 80 per cent of the cases. The roles of age of parents and of intoxication at the time of conception were specifically examined and judged to be of trivial importance. Other conditions, however, were thought to be very effective in bringing about deterioration in the

---

[5] The terms "mental defect," "feeble-mindedness," and "amentia" are employed interchangeably in this discussion.

germ cells. After discussing the Mendelian hypothesis that gametes are unaffected by environment, Tredgold (1908, p. 36) rejected it as being inconsistent with the experiences of physicians.

> With regard to the causation of amentia, I believe that there are certain diseases which bring about a deterioration of the germ plasm. The chief of these are alcoholism and consumption. . . . In consequence, there results a pathological change in that part of the offspring which is at once the most elaborate, the most vulnerable, and of most recent development—namely, the cerebral cortex. This change consists in a diminished control of the higher, and increased excitability of the lower, centres, and is manifested clinically as neurasthenia, hysteria, migraine, and the milder forms of epilepsy. We may say that a neuropath has been created. Should the adverse environment continue, or should such a person marry one similarly tainted, then the nervous instability becomes accentuated in the following generation, and insanity, the graver forms of epilepsy, and early dementia, make their appearance [1908, p. 37].

Thus the various traits mentioned, ranging from neuroses through insanity to profound mental deficiency, were regarded to be all the outcome of successive stages in a hereditary deterioration set in action by some environmental factor.

Two years after his study of the Kallikaks was published, Goddard (1914) presented an extensive collection of pedigrees of mentally defective patients at the Vineland Training School. The Binet-Simon Measuring Scale of Intelligence was administered to a number of the inmates, but the remainder of the pedigrees were primarily studied by field-worker interviews. After studying the pedigrees, Goddard concluded that, of 327 families investigated, the mental defectiveness was inherited in 164, and probably inherited in another 34 cases. The remaining cases were described as due to accident (57), having no determined cause (8), unclassified (27) and neuropathic (37). The latter group was composed of families in which there was little or no history of feeble-mindedness per se (apart from the institutionalized patient), but many other conditions, such as alcoholism, paralysis, suicidal tendency, nervousness, etc., were prevalent. For Tredgold this was the typical picture in inherited mental deficiency. Goddard thought that the feeble-mindedness in these families was probably *not* transmissible, and suggested that some might be due to adverse influences on the mother's "power of nutrition."

In what Goddard called the hereditary cases, he concluded:

> Since our figures agree so closely with Mendelian expectation and since there are few if any cases where the Mendelian formula does not fit the facts, the hypothesis seems to stand: viz. normal-mindedness is, or at least behaves like, a unit character; is dominant and is transmitted in accordance with the Mendelian law of inheritance.

The writer confesses to being one of those psychologists who find it hard to accept the idea that the intelligence even *acts like a unit character*. But there seems to be no way to escape the conclusion from these figures [1914, p. 556].

In the ensuing years, a number of further pedigree studies were published. Gates reviewed the evidence to 1933, and concluded:

. . . it may be stated that feeble-mindedness is generally of the inherited, not the induced, type; and that the inheritance is generally recessive. Most often a single recessive gene appears to be involved; but, as with other abnormalities, occasionally the inheritance is of a different type [1933, p. 265].

By this time the Mendelian principles dominated the conceptual approach to the problem, but were still not universally accepted. Tredgold (1937), for example, in a revision of his earlier text, considered some of the evidence that feeble-mindedness was a recessive condition, and acknowledged that this might be the case in certain special types of defect, but maintained that for mental defect in general, it had not been demonstrated.

We also find evidence of the still-lingering Mendelian-biometrician dispute in a 1930 lecture by Pearson (published in 1931):

Attempts have been made on very inadequate data, most inadequately handled, to fit insanity and feeble-mindedness into the Mendelian theory. Of these attempts I shall hardly find time to say anything in this lecture; in my opinion they fail hopelessly, for they overlook essentially the fact that insanity and feeble-mindedness are far from being simple unit characters. The boundary between sanity and insanity is a perfectly indefinite one. . . . There is no mental test which will separate the normal from the feeble-minded child, the measurements of intelligence show no breaks from one end of the scale to the other [1931, p. 366].

To support the last point, Pearson presented his analysis of Jaederholm's data, which showed that when intelligence test scores of normal children and of children classed as mentally deficient were superimposed, the result was a smooth continuous distribution. There was no gap, no separation into two discrete groups. Pearson saw the problem as even more complicated, for not only was it impossible to separate clearly the feeble-minded from the normally intelligent, but feeble-mindedness was also confounded with other defects. In a conclusion reminiscent of Tredgold, Pearson stated:

. . . in feeble-minded stocks mental defect is interchangeable with imbecility, insanity, alcoholism, and a whole series of mental (and often physical) anomalies [1931, p. 375].

Here, indeed, is a serious problem. If the different phenotypes cannot be adequately distinguished, how can a pedigree study possibly yield any valuable result?

At about the same time, Crew (1932) reviewed the status of work on the genetics of mental defect, and he, as did Pearson, called attention to the continuous distribution of intelligence.

Pearson had concluded that the Mendelian approach was doomed to failure because of the absence of a clear dichotomy. Crew did not question the applicability of Mendelian theory, but emphasized that there were probably many different genetic types of mental defect, and that genetic analysis would need to consider the various types separately. Furthermore, he stressed that the various types need not be subject to the same type of genetic action—some might be dominant, some recessive, some due to multiple factors.

As a matter of fact, there had been an increasing attention to this possibility with a growing tendency to investigate distinct syndromes, and, especially in those conditions which involved gross nervous system damage, there were encouragingly good "Mendelian" results. (See Gates, 1946; Böök, 1953.)

PHENYLKETONURIA.   In 1934 Penrose published an essay the purpose of which was to examine the available methods for the study of human heredity. To illustrate a principle concerning the relatively high frequency of cousin marriages among parents of offspring showing rare recessive conditions, he presented some data which he had collected on an "unspecified type" of mental defect. In the same year Fölling announced (1934) that the urine of some feeble-minded persons contained an abnormally large amount of phenylpyruvic acid. Penrose (1935a) thereupon tested 500 feeble-minded patients and found one case in which phenylpyruvic acid was excreted. This patient had a brother who was also feeble-minded, although not institutionalized. The biochemical peculiarity was also found in this brother, but not in two normal sibs or the parents. Returning to the first family, Penrose (1935b) then tested the urine of the one surviving feeble-minded individual, and found phenylpyruvic acid. By 1937 Jervis (1937) was able to confirm the recessive nature of the condition, as had been suggested by Penrose's data, and numerous studies have since explored one aspect or another of the condition, known variously as Fölling's disease, phenylketonuria, or phenylpyruvic oligophrenia. A number of hypotheses have been put forward to account for the excessive phenylpyruvic acid in the urine and some other related biochemical anomalies (Jervis, 1954). Jervis (1947, 1953) has provided strong evidence that the basic biochemical deficiency is a reduction in the ability to convert phenylalanine into tyrosine, due to a loss or deficiency of the enzyme involved in that reaction. The reaction has been localized in the liver (Udenfriend and Cooper, 1952), and the relationship of the reaction to other biochemical substances has been traced (see Neel and Schull, 1954; Wagner and Mitchell, 1955). Recently, there have been several clinical investigations into the effect of reducing the phenylalanine content of the diet of phenylpyruvics (e.g., Bickel, Gerrard, and Hickmans, 1954). These studies have shown a reduction in biochemical defect while the special diet is given, and a recurrence when an ordinary diet is reintroduced. Observations on general behavior and tests of mental age give promising indications that an improvement in intelligence also accompanies the special diet.

Another recent contribution to the understanding of phenylketonuria has been the demonstration (Hsia *et al.*, 1956) that persons of normal intelligence, who must nevertheless be heterozygous for the gene causing phenylketonuria (e.g., parents of an affected child), are distinguishable from homozygotic normals by the chemical constitution of certain body fluids. Apart from practical applications in genetic counselling, this finding illustrates a most important principle, namely, that the mode of gene action may differ at different levels of analysis. At the level of mental defect, phenylketonuria provides a clear example of a recessive condition, yet at a biochemical level, the mode of gene action must be at least partial dominance, for the heterozygotes are discriminable from the normals.

Thus, in phenylketonuria, we find the most complete genetic analysis of a human behavioral phenotype: the mode of gene action is known on the "Mendelian" level (i.e., homozygous recessives show the trait), heterozygotes are identifiable biochemically, the gene action is known to affect an enzyme involved in a specific reaction, the organ in which the crucial reaction occurs has been identified, the relationship to other biochemical processes has been described, and an environmental alteration which modifies the trait has been discovered, offering a reasonable hope that a full cure may some day be found.

In 1954 a review article (Jervis, 1954) listed 312 identified cases. In terms of the reference defective populations, this represents about sixtenths of one per cent.

OTHER TYPES OF MENTAL DEFECT. The great progress in analyzing phenylketonuria has inspired vigorous examination of other varieties of feeble-mindedness, and, while none other has as yet been as well described, a substantial amount of information has been acquired (see Böök, 1953). Jervis (1952), in a review of the literature, discussed some twenty types of mental deficiency concerning which some genetic information is available. Some conditions appear to be dominant, some recessive, and for others various irregularities are reported. This same author has also shown that the various syndromes can be classified according to the tissue affected (i.e., cutaneous or osseous) or the type of biochemical deficiency involved (metabolism of lipids, amino acids, carbohydrates, or pigments).

There remains, apart from these delineated conditions, a large number of "undifferentiated" mental defectives. It is likely that refined searches on the biochemical level might identify other unitary conditions with a simple pattern of inheritance. Other conditions (as in the case of Mongolism, to be discussed later) might prove to be due to quite unusual genetic irregularities. There will probably remain a "hereditary" group, below the arbitrary division point in the distribution of intelligence, which resists analysis by the pedigree method. These individuals undoubtedly represent the lower tail of the distribution generated by assortment of the polygenes underlying "normal" intelligence, and should no more be considered abnormal than those whose intelligences are an equal distance above the mean.

Finally, we must not disregard the cases of environmental origin. Unquestionably, a variety of environmental factors acting either postnatally (such as severe head injuries), or prenatally (such as infection of the mother by rubella during pregnancy) can eventuate in mental defect. Advancement in understanding genetic factors in mental defect, as well as in therapeutics and preventive measures, depends upon the study of the "environmental" as well as the "genetic" conditions.

From the vantage point of current knowledge, we may judge that Tredgold was correct in concluding that some cases of mental deficiency were attributable to hereditary factors, and others due principally to environmental factors, but his ideas about the origin of the germ-plasm damage and progressive degeneration must be judged wrong. Goddard was right in that some mental deficiency was a single-locus recessive effect, but wrong in overgeneralizing to all feeble-mindedness, and incorrect in concluding that normal intelligence was necessarily due to a single locus if defective intelligence was. Pearson had a major and valid point in the lack of a discrete gap between normal and abnormal, but was too willing to judge therefrom that Mendelian analysis could not succeed in any degree. Gates assessed well the evidence on hand, but was overoptimistic concerning the likelihood of finding all cases of mental deficiency to be of the Mendelian variety.

Thus, in this brief account of the development of theories concerning inheritance of mental defect, we may see that the progress was not made by a single penetrating discovery or pronouncement, but rather proceeded by increments, with the contributors at various stages frequently being both correct and incorrect in varying degrees.

Correlations Between Relatives

The biometricians concentrated their investigations on quantitatively varying characteristics, and developed and employed the correlation technique for use in their studies. The chief spokesman for this approach was Pearson, who assumed that, since Galton's work, the fact of inheritance of mental characteristics could not be denied. The next step was to determine if heredity is as potent in determining mental as in determining physical characters. Arguing the impossibility of comparing adult moral and mental traits with those of children, Pearson settled upon the measurement of correlation between sibling pairs. Through an appeal in a professional journal, Pearson got the cooperation of a number of teachers in supplying measurements or ratings of sibling pairs with respect to certain physical characteristics—health, eye color, cephalic index, etc., and with respect to certain "psychical" characters—vivacity, assertiveness, introspection, popularity, conscientiousness, temper, and ability. The average correlation for the physical traits was slightly in excess of .50 and the same was true for the psychical traits.

> We are forced absolutely to the conclusion that the degree of resemblance of the physical and mental characters in children is one and the same. It has been suggested that this resemblance in the psychical characters is compounded of two factors, inheritance on the one hand and training or environment on the other. If so, you must admit that inheritance and environment make up the resemblance in the physical characters. Now these two sorts of resemblance being of the same intensity, either the environmental influence is the same in both cases, or it is not. If it is the same, we are forced to the conclusion that it is insensible, for it cannot influence eye colour. If it is not the same, then it would be a most marvellous thing, that with varying degrees of inheritance, some mysterious force always modifies the extent of home influence, until the resemblance of brothers or sisters is brought sensibly up to the same intensity! Occam's razor will enable us at once to cut off such a theory. We are forced, I think literally forced, to the general conclusion that the physical and psychical characters in man are inherited within broad lines in the same manner, and with the same intensity [Pearson, 1904, pp. 155–6].

The logic of this procedure seemed at the time to be clear and straightforward. The correlations between siblings on various mental traits could be compared to the empirical value for physical traits (presumed to be highly hereditary), and with each other, and the relative degrees of hereditary control of the various mental traits could thereby be determined. It was with essentially this orientation that several studies on intelligence were conducted. These represented an improvement over Pearson, in that objective measures of performance were obtained rather than ratings. Starch (1917), for example, measured the resemblance of siblings on a variety of "mental traits," some of which were presumably directly affected by school work (e.g., reading ability, vocabulary, spelling, arithmethical ability) and some presumably not so affected (e.g., canceling of "A's" in a page, rate of tapping). Large differences in correlation values were obtained for the different tests, but the values for traits supposed to be influenced by direct tuition were not, on the average, higher than those for traits less subject to training. This result was interpreted as support for the hereditary interpretation, "since the resemblance is no greater in those traits which are more directly affected by environment" (Starch, 1917, p. 237). Thorndike likewise used Pearson's value of .50 as a benchmark. Employing data obtained from Institute of Educational Research Tests, applied to ninth through twelfth grade pupils, he concluded that the sibling correlation in the whole population would be about .60.

> If we may accept Pearson's results for the resemblance of siblings in eye color, hair color, and cephalic index (.52, .55, and .49), and regard .52 ± .016 as the resemblance in traits entirely free from environmental influence, we may infer that *the influence upon intelligence of such similarity in environment as is caused by being siblings two to four years apart in age in an American family today is to raise the correlation from .52 to .60* [Thorndike, 1928, pp. 52–3].

Fisher's classic 1918 paper, and various contributions following it, provided a theoretical basis for Pearson's empirically obtained value, for it was shown that, under certain conditions, the assortment of Mendelian factors would generate a value of .50 for parent-offspring as well as for sibling correlations. This would occur when (1) the genes involved acted additively (i.e., heterozygotes were intermediate to homozygotes), (2) mating between parents was random with respect to the trait, and (3) environment had no effect upon the trait.

A substantial number of correlations was subsequently published, and while there were differences from study to study, the values reported tended to cluster around .50. Jones (1928), for example, presented parent-child and sibling correlations of .51 and .49, respectively, on Army Alpha and Stanford-Binet test scores. Roberts (1941) obtained a sibling correlation of .53 in intelligence measures.

It is very tempting to interpret these findings as indicating that the genetic mechanism underlying intelligence is that specified in the assumptions by which the theoretical value of .50 was obtained. Indeed, this is one possible interpretation, but as we shall see, it cannot be rigorously shown to be the correct one.

SOME DIFFICULTIES OF THE CORRELATIONAL APPROACH IN THE STUDY OF HUMANS.   Consider first the assumption of additive gene action. If in fact this assumption does not hold, the predicted correlation is changed, and the amount of change depends upon the degree of dominance, the magnitude of epistatic effects, and the relative frequencies of the alternative alleles in the population. If dominance is complete, and the alleles are equally frequent, for example, and the other assumptions are valid, the predicted parent-offspring correlation (r_{PO}) is .333 and the sibling correlation (r_{OO}) is .416 (see Li, 1955).

Next, consider the assumption of random mating. This demands that the correlation between parents be zero, which has been definitely shown to be incorrect with respect to intelligence. Conrad and Jones (1940) found a husband-wife correlation of .52 with respect to Army Alpha scores, and Willoughby (1928), who administered eleven different tests, found husband-wife correlations ranging from .20 to .65. This positive association between parents will tend to raise both r_{PO} and r_{OO}, and the amount of increment will depend upon the magnitude of the parental correlation.

Finally, we may examine the assumption that environment has no effect upon the trait. Although the empirical evidence on the effects of enriched or impoverished environments is rather ambiguous (see Thompson, 1954, p. 220) it would be rash to argue dogmatically that the assumption is valid for the kind of characteristic we have been considering. If the effective environmental factors are distributed randomly, the correlation will be reduced to an extent dependent upon the magnitude of the environmental effect. But even this assumption that effective environmental factors are randomly distributed throughout the population is an improbable one. From general considerations it seems likely that environmental factors are more similar within families than between families. Furthermore, on objective grounds, it has been found repeatedly that a substantial correlation exists between children's intelligence and various economic and cultural attributes of the home. Burks (1928a) found a correlation of .48 between children's IQ and a rating of the home cultural level. Leahy (1935) found correlations of .51, .52, and .45 between the IQ of the child and a cultural index, an economic index, and the father's occupational level, respectively.

It has been argued that such values demonstrate the efficacy of the environment in determining intellectual level. It is just as defensible to argue that the parents with the better inherent intelligence provide better environments for their children.

Such a correlation between genotype and environment, if it exists, has rather complicated effects upon the correlations among relatives, depending upon the proportion of additively acting genes and the degree of genotype-environment correlation. Generally, r_{PO} and r_{OO} will be raised.

An additional possible complication was pointed out by Gray and Moshinsky (1932–3), who found sister-sister correlations to be higher than either brother-brother or brother-sister correlations. They suggested that this difference might be attributed to a greater uniformity of early environments of female sibs than of mixed pairs or of pairs of brothers.

There are further pitfalls in the correlational approach, which are not directly related to genetic theory. We may illustrate some of these by again referring to the literature on intelligence.

Thorndike (1928) gave clear expression to one of the difficulties—biased sampling—in his study. In this project, two forms of a test battery were administered, one year apart, to brothers and sisters in school. There was a tendency to eliminate the poorer students from the sample, because data could only be used from those who remained in school during the one-year interval. Any such elimination of extremes will, of course, have an effect on the correlation coefficient by virtue of restriction of the range of scores.

Another biasing effect was due to the fact that only children in high schools were measured, and only the intellectually abler students proceeded that far in their education.

Furthermore, since dull children could fail promotion, and bright children could be accelerated, there would be a tendency for brighter younger brothers and duller older brothers to be included in the survey. This factor would tend to reduce within-family resemblance.

Jones (1928) overcame some of these sampling problems by administering tests to whole families, rather than just to pupils in school. Alert to the possibility that what was found in one population might not apply to another population, Jones's concern was to obtain a representative and homogeneous New England rural population. But selection of a sample of restricted range may, in general, be expected to have a depressing effect on a correlation coefficient. Cattell and Willson (1938) therefore attempted to get a broad sample covering the total range of intelligence. The mid-parent–mid-child correlation thus obtained was .70.

The correlational technique poses other vexing problems of a statistical nature (see Burks, 1928c), and corrections are frequently required. Many of the coefficients discussed earlier were, in fact, corrected for one reason or another. The study of Cattell and Willson provides an illustration of the types of correction used and of their effect upon the final reported value. Beginning with the raw correlation of .70, corrections were made to compensate for age differences, lack of normality of the distribution, range, and attenuation. The final correlation value reported was .91. Obviously, the adequacy of the corrections made in the various studies will have an important effect on their comparability.

The value of .91 is greatly in excess of the general trend of the previously cited results. Cattell and Willson provided other corrected correlations, as follows: one parent–one child, .84; pairs of siblings, .77;

husband-wife, .81. These values are all greater than those previously obtained, and the authors regard them to be nearer to the "correct" values, because of the greater sampling range in their study, and because more adequate corrections were made. Thorndike (1944) tested 409 pairs of brothers at Columbia College, and found a raw correlation of .41. When this value was corrected to estimate correlation in the general population, a value of .73 was obtained. The data of the 1928 study were also re-examined, and a sibling correlation of .69 was obtained. Thorndike concluded, in agreement with Cattell and Willson, that the true value of family correlations is considerably higher than was previously thought to be the case.

The greater part of the research employing correlations of relatives has been directed toward intelligence, but a number of specific apitudes and personality traits have also been investigated. As examples, we may note the studies of May and Hartshorne (1928) and of Crook (1937). May and Hartshorne studied cheating and deception by use of a number of task situations where deception could be detected. Correlations between siblings ranging from .21 to .70 were obtained. Rejecting common environment as the sole factor in determining the similarity in tendency to cheat, the authors concluded that genetic factors are about as important in determining tendency to deceive as they are in determining intelligence.

Crook performed a study on certain personality characteristics, and, drawing his conclusions from his own and previous work, concluded that, with respect to traits of neuroticism, introversion, dominance, and self-sufficiency, the best estimate of parent-offspring correlation was .16, and of sibling correlation, .18. These values were taken to indicate the relatively lesser importance of genotype in determining individual differences in these personality traits than in intelligence.

From the above discussion, it is clear that the interpretation of correlations among relatives is not a simple matter. If an adequate sample is available, and random mating within the population assured, or the extent of husband-wife correlation known; if environmental factors are known to be random, or their relationship to genotype known; and if the test itself has adequate reliability—then empirically obtained correlation coefficients could be used to reach conclusions concerning the nature of the gene action.

Theoretically, these matters are all capable of accomplishment. Practically, however, there are formidable difficulties. One fundamental problem may be singled out for special mention: it is practically impossible to list exhaustively, let alone measure adequately, *all* the *relevant* environmental variables.

As it stands, then, a large number of different conclusions may be deduced from the same obtained correlation values.

Twin Studies

DEVELOPMENT OF TWIN-STUDY LOGIC.   Another principal technique which has been utilized in the study of the inheritance of mental characteristics in man has been the investigation of twins, a procedure first introduced by Galton.

The first major study to follow Galton's example was that of Thorndike (1905), who published a paper entitled "Measurements of Twins," several years after taking his doctorate under J. McK. Cattell.

A fairly lengthy discussion of the nature of twinning was presented, and specific attention was given to the suggestion that there are two kinds of twins; those arising from the same egg and always of the same sex ("duplicate twins"), and those arising from separate eggs and either like-sexed or of different sexes ("fraternal twins"). After assessing the evidence, Thorndike rejected this hypothesis, and proposed that all twins are of the same kind, but on a continuous distribution of degree of resemblance. Therefore, in handling the data of this investigation, all the twins were considered together. Fifty pairs of twins were located from the New York public schools, and they were tested on efficiency in arithmetic computations, naming word opposites, finding misspelled words, and crossing out letters. The possibility of assigning quantitative scores to each individual represented an advance over Galton's original work, where anecdotal evidence was relied upon. The logic of this investigation, however, was essentially the same as Galton's; if environment is important to the traits measured, twins should become more alike the longer they are exposed to the same environment. Therefore the correlation between twin pairs should be higher for twins twelve to fifteen years old than for twins nine to twelve years old. Furthermore, the less the difference between the correlation of sibling pairs and the correlation of twin pairs, the greater the effect of environment. Finally, nurture is important to the degree that the correlation between twins in respect to traits judged "subject to home training" exceeds that for traits not so easily subject to training. The results showed the twins to be more similar to each other than were siblings, the older twins being actually somewhat less similar rather than more similar than the younger, and the correlations for traits subject to training were no greater than for traits not susceptible to training. These results

. . . are easily, simply and completely explained by one simple hypothesis: namely, that the natures of the germ cells—the conditions of conception—cause whatever similarities and differences exist in the original natures of men, that these conditions influence body and mind equally, and that in life the differences in modification of body and mind produced by such differences as obtained between the environ-

ments of present-day New York City public school children are slight
. . . [Thorndike, 1905, p. 9].

Thorndike cautioned, however, against confusing

. . . two totally different things: (1) the power of the environment,
—for instance, of schools, laws, books and social ideals,—to produce
differences in the relative achievements of men, and (2) the power of
the environment to produce differences in absolute achievement. It has
been shown that the relative differences in certain mental traits which
were found in these one hundred children are due almost entirely to
differences in ancestry, not in training; but this does not in the least
deny that better methods of training might improve all their achievements fifty per cent, or that the absence of training, say in spelling and
arithmetic, might decrease the corresponding achievements to zero
[1905, p. 11].

Twin study was then largely neglected for about twenty years, following which a spate of studies was published within a short period.

Merriman, by 1924, was able to employ more refined test procedures than had previously been used, and administered the Stanford-
Binet, Army Beta, and National Intelligence Test, in addition to obtaining teachers' estimates of the intellectual capacity of the subjects. Using
the same type of comparison as Thorndike, Merriman found that the
correlations between twin pairs ten to sixteen years of age were not
greater than those between twin pairs five to nine years of age. Moreover, Merriman reopened the question of whether there were two types
of twins. After reviewing current biological evidence, and relevant aspects of his own research, he concluded, Thorndike to the contrary notwithstanding, that there are two classes. fraternal and duplicate. From
this, a new type of comparison was suggested:

The fraternal, being of the two-egg origin, should show no greater
resemblance than ordinary siblings, since each individual of the pair
develops from a wholly independent arrangement of the factors for
heredity in the germ cells. . . . The duplicate being of the one-egg
origin, should show a very much higher degree of resemblance than the
fraternal because each member of the pair develops from substantially
the same arrangement of the factors for heredity in the germ cells
[Merriman, 1924, p. 3].

Now, a real difficulty was that, while all unlike-sexed twins could
be clearly identified as fraternal, some like-sexed twins would be fraternal and some duplicate. But, lacking a clear way of distinguishing the
two kinds of like-sexed twins, Merriman accepted the error that was
entailed, and compared the like-sexed pairs, consisting of fraternal and
duplicate cases, with the unlike-sexed pairs, composed solely of frater-

nals. The correlations for like-sexed pairs were in every case higher than for unlike-sexed pairs, and the latter quite reasonably approximated the value of .50 which Pearson had found to be characteristic of sibling correlations. Clearly, greater intellectual similarity accompanied greater genetic similarity. Indeed, the correlations obtained for like-sexed twins were in the neighborhood of .90, leaving apparently little variability to be explained by environmental differences.

Lauterbach's (1925) study followed almost immediately. The results on a number of intelligence tests confirmed Merriman's findings nicely, in that the correlations between older and younger twins did not differ, and the correlations between like-sexed twins exceeded those between unlike-sexed twins. Wingfield (1928) contributed more evidence confirming Merriman and Lauterbach, and went the further step of separating out a group of like-sexed twins which appeared, to himself and to the subjects' teachers, to be physically identical. These "identicals" were much more similar to each other than were the remaining non-identicals.

In the same year Tallman (1928) presented her results on Stanford-Binet IQ scores of twins. As in the previous studies, like-sexed twins were more similar than unlike-sexed twins. An "identical" group was separated out from all the like-sexed twins, and the comparison of this group with the non-identicals confirmed Wingfield's results.

TWIN DIAGNOSIS.   It is obvious that general and subjective impressions of similarity do not provide an adequate criterion for the classification of twins. A refinement was offered by Siemens, who, in 1924, published his *Die Zwillingspathologie*, a book which inaugurated a long series of twin studies on human pathological conditions by German workers. Essentially, Siemens' scheme (see Siemens, 1927) was to determine various characteristics which almost always were the same in identical twins, and only rarely so in fraternal twins. Any new set of twins could then be compared with respect to a list of such traits (e.g., hair, eye, and skin color). The probability that fraternal twins would by chance be alike with respect to all the traits, and thus misclassified as identical twins, was quite small if a sufficiently large list was employed. This, of course, involved a bit of circular reasoning, for it was necessary first to identify a group of identical twins in order to determine in what traits they were alike and to develop criteria for classifying identical twins.

The ideal was to find good "Mendelian" traits, practically unaffected by environmental differences, which were segregating in the family of the twin pair. Then, if the twins were identical with respect to all of these, they would undoubtedly be identical twins; if unlike in any, they would be fraternals.

Unfortunately, most of the human single-locus conditions then known were of rare occurrence and could therefore be used only in exceptional cases. Nevertheless, the criteria of physical similarity which were gradually evolved allowed reasonably unambiguous classification of most twin pairs. (Later, a more definite set of criteria was provided by the discovery of the Mendelian basis for human blood groups, characters which are present in all humans and are essentially unmodifiable by environmental factors.)

One of the major studies to come after the establishment of reasonably adequate criteria for identifying twin types was that of Newman, Freeman, and Holzinger (1937), who were able to apply ten criteria of physical similarity in obtaining a group of fifty pairs of identical twins and another of fifty pairs of fraternal twins. The fraternal pairs selected were all like-sexed, because the identicals are necessarily so, and the authors wanted to avoid any complications due to within-pair sex differences. In addition to physical measurements and various questionnaire data on school history, interest, etc., each twin was tested with an extensive battery of tests, including the Stanford-Binet, Otis Self-Administering Test, Downey Will-Temperament Test, and the Woodworth-Mathews Questionnaire.

Salient features of the conclusions from this large study are as follows:

> In most of the traits measured the identical twins are much more alike than the fraternal twins, as indicated by higher correlations. This is true of physical dimensions, of intelligence, and of educational achievement. The only group of traits in which identical twins are not much more alike consists of those commonly classed under the head of personality. For the rest it is obvious that the twins who have the same inheritance are the more alike. By and large, this indicates, since the environment is similar for both groups, that genetic constitution is a large factor in physical dimensions (as well as appearance and qualitative differences), mental ability, and educational achievement. This conclusion seems clearly warranted.
>
> The difference in resemblance of the two classes of twins, however, is not the same in the different groups of traits. In general, the contrast is greater in physical traits, next in tests of general ability (intelligence), less in achievement tests, and least in tests of personality or temperament.[6]

VALIDITY OF ASSUMPTIONS UNDERLYING TWIN STUDIES. As we found to be the case in the correlational approach, certain shortcomings

[6] From H. H. Newman, F. N. Freeman, and K. J. Holzinger, *Twins: A Study of Heredity and Environment,* p. 352. Copyright 1937 by the University of Chicago. Extracts here and following reprinted by permission of the University of Chicago Press.

of the twin method gradually came to light. In the first place, there was some uneasiness regarding the very fundamental assumption that environment is no more and no less effective in producing differences between fraternal twins than between identical twins. Certainly, for example, it could be argued that parents tended to emphasize the similarities of their identical-twin offspring by having them dress alike, etc., whereas this tendency might be much less marked with respect to fraternal twins. In addition, persons of different genotypes might well seek out different aspects of a common environment.

In 1934 Wilson presented a direct investigation of the assumption of equal environmental effects, by asking twins about the extent to which their home, school, and play activities and preferences were shared by their co-twins. The conclusion was that both types of twins had more similar environments than ordinary siblings, and that the environment of identical twins was much more similar than that of fraternal twins.

The findings of greater similarity of environments for fraternal twins than for siblings were supported by Herrman and Hogben (1932–1933), who found sibling correlation in intelligence measures to equal .32, whereas the like-sexed fraternal value was .47 and the unlike-sexed fraternal value was .51. It appears that the difference between fraternal twin pairs is an inadequate reflection of environmental influence. For that matter, the environmental range to which siblings are usually exposed is relatively restricted, so that comparisons of identical twins and siblings could hardly give an indication of the contribution of environment to intelligence differences *in the population at large*.

Other evidence has since been provided to show that prenatal environment must also be considered in assessing twin data. Both types of twins are exposed to such factors as differences in position *in utero* and site of implantation. Only identical twins, however, are susceptible to a phenomenon called lateral inversion, which is presumably due to differences in the cytoplasmic material received by each twin. (See Price, 1950, for a thorough discussion of this phenomenon.) Fraternal twins, on the other hand, are sometimes affected by mutual circulation when their placentae happen to fuse. Generally, these effects are regarded as making identical twins less alike than would be expected on the basis of the postnatal environments, and fraternal twins more alike than would be expected on the basis of their genetic similarity.

With these complicating features of the role of environment, the apparent ease of weighing the relative effects of nature and nurture by twin study vanishes. A greater disparity observed between fraternals than between identicals may be interpreted as due to heredity or environment or to some indeterminable combination of the two, depending upon the predilections of the person making the interpretation.

TWINS REARED APART. An alternative approach had been developing since 1922, when Popenoe gave an anecdotal account of a pair of female identical twins who had been separated in infancy. Over the years they had visited each other occasionally and had corresponded, but on the whole had been subjected to quite different environments. One, for example, had had scant formal schooling, but the other had completed high school and had done some university work. From the account of one of the twins, they were not only very similar physically, but had also shown remarkable similarities in interests and intellectual abilities. Muller (1925) administered a battery of formal tests to the girls when they were thirty years old. Despite the large difference in education, the twins were remarkably alike on the intelligence tests. On the tests of association and reaction time and on temperament and emotions, however, the twins differed strikingly. Muller urged more research of this kind, but identical twins reared apart are quite rare, and the accumulation of cases was slow. Newman (1930) reported three more cases, in two of which the twins had not even known of each other's existence until adulthood. In two of the cases, intelligence-test scores showed no greater similarity than that of fraternal twins reared together, but temperament and personality were judged to be rather similar. In the third case, the intellectual resemblance was a bit better, but personalities were stated to differ substantially.

By 1937 Newman, Freeman, and Holzinger could report on nineteen cases, including Newman's original three. An extensive battery of tests was employed, consisting of the Stanford-Binet, Otis Self-Administering Test of Mental Ability, Thurstone Psychological Examination, International Test, Stanford Achievement Test, Woodworth-Mathews Personal Data Sheet, Kent-Rosanoff Free Association Test, Pressey Test of the Emotions, and the Downey Will-Temperament Test. A large reference group of fifty identical pairs reared together and fifty fraternal pairs reared together was also tested.

We have already seen (p. 195) the conclusions which stemmed from the comparison of identicals with fraternals. The following was found when the average differences between separated identical pairs were compared with the average differences between identical pairs reared together:

> In one of the physical traits, weight, and in intelligence and school achievement the differences are significantly greater, demonstrating the effect of environment on these traits. In height, head measures, and the score on the Woodworth-Mathews test, on the other hand, no significantly greater difference is found. This is important since it indicates, as does the comparison of identical and fraternal twins, that some characteristics are more susceptible to environmental influences than are others [Newman *et al.*, 1937, p. 356].

This study, therefore, demonstrated that environmental factors could affect performance on intelligence tests. The magnitude of the environmental effect is, however, difficult to assess. One of the major difficulties is that of determining just how large the *relevant* environmental differences between the separated identical twins actually were. This was attempted by ratings of various aspects of the environment by several judges. These ratings proved to be quite reliable, in that inter-judge correlation was high. By the criteria used in these judgments, most of the separated twins were not, in fact, subjected to grossly different environments, so the greater difference obtained between separated and unseparated twins provides a modest estimate of the environment's capabilities—not minimal, perhaps, but certainly not the maximal effect which could be expected from the greatest conceivable environmental differences. On the other hand, in those cases judged to have the greater environmental disparity, the phenotypic differences were greater. As Woodworth (1941, pp. 26f.) has pointed out, two of the three authors, when writing elsewhere, have concluded that relatively large differences in environment are required to produce substantial changes in the intelligence quotient.

Perhaps some of the difficulty stems from the basic problem of determining how big is big. For example, the average difference in the Binet IQ scores of all the separated twins was 8.21. For the unseparated twins, this difference was 5.35. The difference between the differences is only 2.86 points, which might be regarded as almost trivial. On the other hand, the Binet-score differences of the separated twins correlated +.79 with the ratings of differences in excellence of educational aspects of the environment, and by most standards this would be regarded as a sizable relationship.

CO-TWIN CONTROL.   The difficulty of adequate specification of environmental differences has been directly attacked in the co-twin control method which was introduced by Gesell and Thompson in 1929. In this procedure the identical twins are kept in environments as similar as possible, except for one particular feature which is under the control of the experimenter. Therefore, any differences which are found between the twins can be reasonably attributed to the known, specific environmental difference. In the Gesell and Thompson (1929) study, for example, one twin was given extensive early training in certain motor tasks. The other twin was given a shorter period of training later. The general conclusion was that special training administrered prior to the attainment of a requisite level of maturation did not confer long-term advantages in proficiency. Several other studies have appeared, dealing with memory and motor performance (Hilgard, 1933), perceptual motor tasks (Luria and Mirenova, 1936), vocabulary learning (Strayer, 1930), and language learning (Price, *et al.*, 1944).

One of the major efforts in co-twin control studies (McGraw, 1935) provides an object lesson in the importance of having adequate techniques for determining whether twins are identical or fraternal. After this study was well under way, it was discovered that the twin pair involved was actually fraternal, thus rendering the study essentially null and void from the point of view of genetic interpretation.

OTHER TWIN STUDIES. It has been convenient to outline the development of the methodology of twin studies with primary reference to studies on intelligence. This should not be taken to indicate that other areas have been neglected.

In personality traits, emotionality, and attitudes, the correlations for both types of twins have been generally found to be lower than those obtained for IQ. Nevertheless, identical twins have been found to resemble each other more closely in personality characteristics than do fraternal twins (Carter, 1933). McNemar (1933) applied the twin technique to a study of motor skills and obtained identical-twin correlations ranging from .73 for card-sorting to .95 for pursuit rotor performance. The fraternal twin-correlations were .50 for both of these tests. Jones and Morgan (1942) showed that the similarity in eye-movement pattern of identicals greatly exceeded that of fraternals. Lennox and co-workers (e.g., Lennox, Gibbs, and Gibbs, 1945; Lennox, 1951) explored the inheritance of epilepsy and brain-wave patterns by the twin method. In EEG pattern, identical-twin and fraternal-twin records were judged identical in 85 per cent and 5 per cent of the cases respectively. In epileptic patients who had twins, both were epileptic in 84 per cent of the identical-twin cases and in 10 per cent of the fraternal-twin cases. Jost and Sontag (1944) found identical twins to resemble each other more than siblings on measures of autonomic nervous-system function such as respiration and skin resistance.

A wide variety of anthropometric, biochemical, and psychological measurements has been taken on twins by Vandenberg and collaborators (Vandenberg, 1956). The importance of the genotype in determining individual differences in each characteristic was assessed by the extent to which the differences between fraternal pairs exceeded the differences between identical pairs. In general the genetic contribution was greater (i.e., the identical twins were relatively more similar) in the anthropometric than in the biochemical or psychological variables. It was also shown that, within each of these general categories, some traits were more "under genetic control" than others.

In this research, contrary to most earlier reports, some measures of personality (e.g., the Thurstone Temperament Test: Vigorous) showed as large a genetic influence as many of the intellectual measures (e.g., the WISC Vocabulary, the Standard Spelling Test, and Raven's Progressive Matrices).

A particularly large literature has grown up regarding psychoses (see Slater, 1953a and 1953b, for review). One of the most extensive programs has been that of Kallmann, who has used twin comparisons in conjunction with studies of other family members. Some of Kallmann's principal findings with respect to schizophrenia, manic-depressive psychosis, and involutional melancholia are shown in Table 3. These results are in excellent accord with a general hypothesis of genetic determination, but, of course, are not exempt from the difficulties arising

TABLE 3

EXPECTANCY RATES FOR RELATIVES OF AFFECTED INDIVIDUALS *

PSYCHOTIC CONDITION	Half sibs	Full sibs	Fraternal twins	Identical twins
Schizophrenia	7.1	14.2	14.5	86.2
Manic-depressive psychosis	16.7	23.0	26.3	95.7
Involutional psychosis	4.5	6.9	6.9	60.9

* Table entries refer to percentage of relatives of given degree of genetic relationship to affected individuals which also have condition during their lifetimes.

Data taken from Franz J. Kallmann, *Heredity in Health and Mental Disorder*, Fig. 36, p. 124. Published in 1953 by W. W. Norton and used with their permission.

from the confounding of environmental similarities with genetic similarities. Kallmann has made specific interpretations regarding the mode of inheritance of these psychotic conditions. Schizophrenia, for example, is regarded as a single-locus autosomal recessive condition. The evidence for this view is somewhat contradictory, however (see Slater, 1953a), so these simple Mendelian hypotheses must be regarded as tentative. Slater (1953a) has provided another large twin study, based upon case histories, in which various behavioral abnormalities were investigated. Both twins were schizophrenic in 76 per cent of the identical-twin pairs, and in 14 per cent of the fraternal-twin pairs. In a relatively smaller sample of psychopathic and neurotic cases, the percentage of cases in which both twins were affected was low for identical twins, and not appreciably greater than for the fraternal twins. This suggests that environmental forces play a predominant role in the last named conditions. Eysenck and Prell (1951), however, determined the scores of twins on a "neuroticism" factor, extracted from a test battery by factor analysis, and found the identical-twin correlation to be .85, whereas the fraternal-twin correlation was .22.

This sampling of twin studies is far from complete, but will perhaps serve to illustrate the tremendous effort which has gone into this particular method in the study of human behavioral genetics.

Adopted Children [7]

We may now turn to a consideration of the last general method of study of nature and nurture in humans.

In studying family resemblances of "real" parents and children, the hereditary and environmental factors are complexly interwoven—siblings, for example, share a genetic background and environmental circumstances. An adopted child, however, while sharing environment, has no genetic relationship to its family. Comparing the relative magnitudes of parent-offspring and sibling resemblance with parent-adopted offspring and adopted-sibling resemblances, therefore, offers an apparent means of separating the variables.

Following some early studies, two major investigations appeared simultaneously in 1928. One of these (Freeman *et al.*, 1928) was conducted at the University of Chicago, and the other (Burks, 1928a) at Stanford University.

THE CHICAGO STUDY.   The Chicago study used Stanford-Binet and International Group Mental Test scores for children and the Otis Self-Administering Test and a vocabulary test for adults. One group of seventy-four children had been tested prior to adoption and again several years after adoption. The average IQ of the group rose from 91.2 to 93.7, and examination of individual cases showed that those adopted into "better" homes (as judged by the ratings of field workers) gained as much as five IQ points. Children in the less adequate foster homes showed no gain. This result was taken to demonstrate the positive effects of environment.

Another group consisted of 125 pairs of siblings who had been adopted into different foster homes. The sibling correlation obtained was .25 or .34 (depending on the method of computing the correlations) —less than the frequently encountered values of .50 for siblings reared together. Of thirty-eight pairs separated after living together for five years or more, the correlation was .49, while for forty-six pairs separated before either had reached six years of age, the value dropped to .32. Evidently the commonly shared environment had increased the re-

---

[7] In the literature of this area, "foster-child" and "adopted-child" are frequently treated as synonymous, although contemporary usage would distinguish between full legal adoption and the more temporary fostering arrangement.

semblance of those who had lived together for a substantial period of time.

In thirty homes there was at least one own child and one adopted child. The correlation of adopted children's IQ scores with the own children's scores was .34. There were also seventy-two homes in which unrelated children had been adopted. The correlation between IQ's of these children was .37.

THE STANFORD STUDY.   In the study by Burks (1928a), the Stanford-Binet test was given to 214 adopted children and their foster parents, and to a control group of 105 children and their real parents. The control group was closely equated to the adopted group in terms of age of children, educational and occupational level of parents, etc. The children were tested between five and fourteen years of age and, to reduce the effect of pre-adoption environment, only children adopted before the age of twelve months were studied.

The main results are shown in Table 4.

TABLE 4

CORRELATIONS OBTAINED IN BURKS' FOSTER CHILD STUDY

CORRELATION BETWEEN IQ OF CHILDREN AND	Foster children	Control children
Father's mental age	.07	.45
Mother's mental age	.19	.46
Midparent mental age	.20	.52

The control correlations are in accord with the previous parent-child studies and the differences between control and adopted correlations argue for the important influence of hereditary factors.

By applying Wright's mathematical techniques, Burks concluded that "*Home environment contributes about 17 percent of the variance in I.Q. . . . The total contribution of heredity . . . is probably not far from 75 or 80 per cent*" (1928a, p. 308).
As a general summary statement,

> *Home environment in the most favorable circumstances may suffice to bring a child just under the borderline of dullness up over the threshold of normality, and to make a slightly superior child out of a normal one; but it cannot account for the enormous mental differences to be found among human beings* [Burks, 1928a, p. 308].

The disagreement in the general tone of the conclusions, as well as in the specific results of these two studies of adopted children, was examined by Burks (1928b), and she concluded that the factor of selective placement, whereby adoption agencies strive to place children of "good parentage" in the better homes, can account for at least part of the differences. Other authors (e.g., Anastasi and Foley, 1949, pp. 356f.) have also pointed out the subtle ways in which such selection can take place, even when specific knowledge of the child's IQ, or of that of its parents, is unknown.

SUBSEQUENT RESEARCH.   Leahy's (1935) study on adopted children was inspired by the discrepancies between the conclusions of Burks and those of Freeman *et al.* The correlations obtained by Leahy for IQ scores were: adopted children–foster fathers, .19; adopted children–foster mothers, .24; true children–true mothers, .51; true children– true fathers, .51. These results on intelligence are in striking accord with Burks'. There is also an agreement that personality and character traits are more influenced by environment than is intellectual level.

Another long-term study of adopted children was conducted by Skodak and Skeels (1949). These investigators concluded that the mean IQ of the adopted children was substantially higher than would be expected in view of the intellectual level of their true parents, and suggested that this represented a beneficial effect of environment. There was, however, a substantial correlation between the adopted child's IQ and that of the true mother. The magnitude of the correlation was found to increase with age, being very low at two years, and rising until, at about six years, the correlation was approximately .35. Honzik (1957) has compared the Skodak and Skeels results on adopted children with her results on "own" children. Figure 23 shows the comparison when educational level is used as an index of the mental ability of the mother or foster mother. The striking feature of these data is that the IQ's of the adopted children correlated as highly with their own mother's education as did the own children's IQ's with their own mother's education, in spite of the fact that the latter had been reared by their own mothers and the former had not. The correlation of the child's IQ with the foster mother's education is seen to be low at all age levels. Honzik concludes:

> The finding that the parent-child resemblance in ability follows the same age changes in the two studies, even though the true parents did not rear the children in the Skodak-Skeels group, suggests that the existing relationship is largely due to genetic factors which tend to become manifest in the child during the later preschool years [1957, p. 227].

POSSIBLE BIASES IN STUDIES OF ADOPTED CHILDREN.   In the interpretation of studies of adopted children, many of the reservations discussed with reference to other methods must be applied. Some specific problems have also been identified.

We may note, for example, a basic difficulty in drawing conclusions on the evidence of gain in IQ after adoption. The circumstances surrounding the pre-adoption intelligence testing might well have a depressing effect on the child's performance. In like manner, the IQ scores of true mothers of adopted children are frequently obtained during the

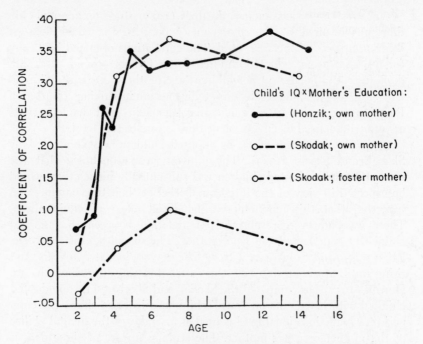

FIGURE 23. Coefficients of correlation at different ages between child's IQ and educational level of own or of foster mother. (After Marjorie P. Honzik, "Developmental studies of Parent-Child Resemblance in Intelligence," *Child Development*, 1957, 28, Figure 2. Used with permission of the Society for Research in Child Development.)

stressful period prior to delivery of an illegitimate child, and may therefore be depressed.

We have already seen the possibility of selective placement, whereby placement agencies may employ whatever information is available in placing children of superior genotype in superior home environments. The degree to which this factor influences the results has been debated, and it is likely that its effect varies from study to study. Insofar as selective placement exists, of course, there is a genotype-environment correlation which makes the accurate assessment of the relative contributions of heredity and environment impossible.

Woodworth has provided the following interesting summary of studies of adopted children:

We have thought of them as studies of environment, but they are also tests of the foster child's heredity. When we say, as we are apt to do, that children of "poor heredity," placed in good foster homes, turn out fairly well in spite of their heredity, are we not asserting the impossible? No one can achieve anything that is beyond his potentiality. If a child, from whatever parentage, develops superior intelligence, we know for certain that his heredity was good enough to make that achievement possible. We have simply been misjudging his heredity. The low economic and cultural level of his parentage has misled us. We have forgotten that the offspring of any given parents may differ widely in genetic constitution, and we have forgotten that these particular parents because of their own early environmental handicaps are probably functioning below the level of their hereditary potentialities. The more we stress the importance of environment, the less are we justified in inferring a child's heredity from the social status of his parents, and the less are we entitled to speak of a child as having "poor heredity" just because his parents are poor, uneducated, shiftless and immoral. Placement of the child in a good home gives him a chance to show how good his heredity really is. What the foster child studies are doing when seen from this angle, is to check up on the heredity of the offspring of certain classes of parents.[8]

Combined Approaches

In terms of logic and historical development, it is possible to distinguish among the various methods discussed above: pedigree, correlational, twin study, foster-child study, etc. Yet, to a considerable extent, the methods may overlap. Thus, a "foster-child" study may compare the correlation of true mothers and children with that of foster mothers and children; a "twin study" may involve the comparison of sibs, half sibs, and foster children, as well as identical and fraternal twins.

Insofar as each general approach can provide a unique source of information, the advantages of a multiple approach to any particular problem is apparent. Cattell (1953) has proposed a "multiple-variance" method in which the variability of a number of different groups, of differing genetic and environmental similarities, are simultaneously assessed in one analytic framework. For example, the variances of (1) identical twins reared together, (2) fraternal twins reared together, (3) sibs reared together, (4) sibs reared apart, (5) unrelated individuals reared together, and (6) general population, on various personality test factors, were utilized in an analysis of components of variance to de-

[8] From Robert S. Woodworth, *Heredity and Environment*, pp. 68–9. Published in 1941 by the Social Science Research Council, Bulletin 47.

termine relative contributions of heredity and environment (Cattell *et al.*, 1955, 1957). These authors have discussed a number of other groups which would provide relevant information (e.g., half-sibs reared apart) and have considered the assumptions, similar to those already described for correlational studies, twin studies, and foster-child studies, which are essential to multiple-variance analysis.

Chromosome Numbers, Sexual Abnormalities, and Mongolism

Mongolism.   This section will be chiefly concerned with Mongolism, which is one of the more frequent conditions of feeble-mindedness. It has been singled out for separate consideration because of the variety of procedures which have been employed in the attempt to understand its etiology, and also because of the new techniques which have been recently brought to bear in its study. The account of the research on Mongolism also provides a clear demonstration of the interplay among seemingly diverse discoveries in the advancement of science.

A distinctive condition, Mongolism (or Mongolian idiocy), presents a complex of symptoms, in addition to the mental deficiency, of protruding, furrowed tongue, presence of epicanthal fold of the eyes, depressed nose, short stature, and a number of other physical characteristics, including a certain configuration of creases in the palm of the hand. The brain of Mongoloids has been shown (Davidoff, 1928) to be of small size, with relatively fewer cells than normal, and with an "embryonic" convolutional pattern.

The name of the condition derives from a superficially oriental appearance of the affected individuals, and has no racial significance. (Asiatics, in fact, regard them as Caucasian in appearance [Penrose, 1959, p. 99]).[9]

Since the initial description of Mongolism in the middle of the nineteenth century, an enormous effort has been made to determine the genetic and/or environmental causal factors. Twin studies (Jenkins, 1933; Macklin, 1929) have generally shown concordance among identical twins and discordance among fraternals. However, some cases of discordance in putative identicals (e.g., van Beukering and Vervoorn, 1956) complicate the picture. In examinations of the families of Mongoloid individuals, cases have been found (Macklin, 1929; Penrose, 1934) of two, three, and even four affected sibs in the same family. In

---

[9] The inappropriateness of the terms "Mongolian idiocy" or "Mongolism" has often been mentioned. A proposal has recently been made (Allen *et al.*, communication to *Lancet*, 1961, Vol. 1, p. 775) that "Langdon-Down anomaly," "congenital acromicria," "trisomy 21 anomaly," or some other term be used to replace the older designation.

assessing the over-all evidence on familial incidence, however, Penrose concluded that

> . . . it is difficult to produce convincing evidence that the familial cases are due to familial concentration and not to chance sampling. Moreover, in some of the familial instances the diagnoses are open to doubt. . . . Furthermore, the occurrence of more than one case in a sibship might not be genetical but due to a consistent peculiarity of maternal environment [1949, p. 189].

A number of such maternal environmental factors, many of them rather vague and unspecific, have been proposed: endocrine deficiencies, "reproductive exhaustion," mental or physical strain during pregnancy, etc. (for reviews see Allen, 1958; Gates, 1946; Penrose, 1949). Whatever the relevant variable or variables, it became clear that they must change with the age of the mother, for Penrose (1941, 1949) demonstrated a striking increase in the incidence of Mongolism in the children of older mothers. The risk of a mother forty-five to forty-nine years of age is, in fact, about fifty-five times as great as that of a twenty to twenty-four-year-old mother. The genotype, and therefore the genetic constitution of the gametes produced, is basically set at conception, and does not change with age, whereas any number of environmental factors, such as those mentioned above, could easily be visualized as doing so. This seemed to indicate that environmental factors are responsible. There is some evidence, however, obtained from research on the fruit fly, that the frequency of crossing over does increase with age. Crossing over "releases" new combinations of genes, and in this sense a change in the nature of the gametes that a fly can produce does, in fact, occur with age. This may or may not be true in human beings, so the relevance to Mongolism is not known. Chromosomal abnormalities were also considered. Polyploidy (duplication of chromosomes) is known to be more frequent in some somatic cells with increasing age. It is conceivable that chromosomal alterations may also occur in reproductive cells more frequently with increasing age. Penrose (1941) and Waardenburg (1932) both, in fact, suggested that chromosomal abnormalities might underlie Mongolism.

It is clear from the foregoing that the demonstration of the effect of maternal age in Mongolism does not absolutely rule out hereditary mechanisms as important in the etiology. But the evidence from which conclusions might be drawn has been confusing. There is little consanguinity (mating of related individuals, such as cousins) among the parents of Mongoloids (Penrose, 1949). This is an indication against a recessive gene. On the other hand, the parents of Mongoloids do not themselves show the condition. This observation rules out dominance. Yet a single gene might be transmitted according to a simple Mendelian system, but not express itself in each person who received the "abnormal" genotype, owing either to environmental factors or to the effects of other genes present. On the other hand, a polygenic system could easily account for the facts.

A most interesting observation was made concerning the patterns of creases and ridges on the palms of the hands of Mongolian idiots. One special pattern, common to Mongoloids, is present only in a small percentage of the population at large. In relatives of Mongoloids, however, the incidence is greatly increased, suggesting that they are heterozygotes, or are homozygotes who by good environmental fortune have failed to develop the more severe symptoms.

KLINEFELTER'S SYNDROME, TURNER'S SYNDROME, AND CYTOLOGY. Before continuing with genetic findings regarding Mongolism, we must turn to some cytological considerations. In 1949 a cytological difference was discovered between the neurons of male and female cats (Barr and Bertram, 1949). This distinction was also found in man, and it proved possible to determine "nuclear sex" by examination of the blood (Davidson and Smith, 1954) and skin (Moore and Barr, 1955). These new techniques were quickly applied to the study of certain human sexual abnormalities which suggested intersexuality. One of these conditions is Turner's syndrome, in which the individuals, always apparent females, show sexual infantilism, dwarfism, and some other anomalies. Suggesting that some failure of sexual development was at fault, Polani *et al.* (1954) tested for nuclear sex of three Turner's individuals, and found them all to have characteristic male cell nuclei. Shortly thereafter Riis *et al.* (1956) examined skin cells of two patients showing Klinefelter's syndrome. This condition occurs in apparent males, who have small testes, failure of spermatogenesis, feminine distribution of fat, and development of the breasts. The two "males" examined showed typical female nuclei. These dramatic findings naturally gave rise to speculation about the sex-chromosome constitution of the affected individuals. With the nuclear-sexing technique it was not possible to examine the chromosomes directly, so the evidence brought forward was genetic. By examining the incidence of color-blindness, a sex-linked recessive condition in affected individuals, it was possible to infer that Turner's "women" actually had a chromosome constitution of XO or XY (Polani *et al.*, 1956), and that Klinefelter's "men" were XX (Polani *et al.*, 1958). Plunkett and Barr (1956) had previously suggested an XX complement in Klinefelter's syndrome, but also mentioned the possibility of XXY.

The direct examination of human chromosomes to test these suggestions was not feasible until the introduction of new and improved techniques by Tjio and Levan in 1956. With the improved procedure it was shown that the normal number of human chromosomes was forty-six, and not forty-eight, as had long been thought to be the case (Tjio and Levan, 1956; Ford and Hamerton, 1956; see also Ford, Jacobs, and Lajtha, 1958, for a review). Results from Klinefelter's patients showed forty-seven chromosomes, however, and detailed examination showed the Y chromosome to be present, along with an extra chromosome belonging to the size range in which the X chromosome is to be found. In all likelihood, then, some, at least, of Klinefelter's "males" are XXY (Jacobs and Strong, 1959). Ford *et al.* (1959b) and Fraccaro *et al.* (1959) found only forty-five chromosomes in Turner's patients, and provided evidence that the sex-chromosome constitution was XO.

CYTOLOGY AND MONGOLISM.　Returning now to considerations of Mongolism, it may be remembered that Waardenburg and Penrose had both suggested at one time that a chromosomal abnormality of some kind might underlie the condition. Mittwoch (1952), working before the advent of the improved cytological techniques, examined tissue from a Mongoloid individual, and reported ". . . the chromosomes were not sufficiently distinct from one another to make an exact count possible; nevertheless, the approximate diploid number of 48 chromosomes could be made out in several cells" (p. 37). Penrose (1954), in a review of the literature, accepted this evidence as ruling out gross chromosomal abnormality at least.

After the dramatic findings on abnormalities of sexual development, the issue was reopened by two groups of investigators, Lejeune *et al.* (1959) and Jacobs *et al.* (1959). Nine Mongoloid individuals were examined in these studies, and in each case, forty-seven chromosomes were found. The evidence strongly suggested that the extra chromosome was an autosome.

The crowning confirmation of the whole approach was presented almost immediately by Ford *et al.* (1959a) who found forty-eight chromosomes in the cells of an individual showing both Klinefelter's syndrome and Mongolism—the basic forty-six plus one extra autosome plus one extra sex chromosome.

These fast-breaking developments have not, of course, provided an "explanation" of Mongolism. They do clarify the irregularities and confusions of the preceding genetic data, but still to be explained are the increased incidence in the Mongoloid pattern of palm ridges in relatives, the reason that the non-disjunction which results in the extra autosome occurs more frequently in older mothers, and perhaps most basic of all, the physiological events whereby the extra chromosome, with the surplus genetic material it provides, causes the Mongoloid condition. There can be absolutely no doubt, however, but that the cytological work has opened up many new exploratory avenues, and thus tremendously enhanced the likelihood of an ultimate thorough understanding, which will carry with it the implications of remedial and preventive therapy.

It may be confidently predicted that in the future the cytological approach will be applied vigorously to a great variety of human pathological conditions. Whether the implications for behavioral genetics will be great or small cannot even be guessed at the present time.

Summary of Human Studies

One of the principal problems of human behavioral genetics has been that of definition and measurement of the phenotypes under investigation. It is generally acknowledged that any measurable attribute of an individual is a legitimate phenotype, so there can be no complaint, for example, about studying the rate of crossing out A's on a printed page, or reading comprehension, or ability to deal with verbal analogies. The difficulty arises when a common term is used to describe the trait being assessed by the various tests. Thus, different studies on the inheritance of intelligence, say, may be dealing with quite different phenotypes, and consequently may not be at all comparable. This problem is, of course, a central problem of psychometrics, and, as we have seen, the improvements in test design and standardization have at the same time improved precision of identifying phenotypes for genetic studies. In like manner, improvement in diagnostic criteria and systems of classification have led to greater clarity in research on the inheritance of feeble-mindedness and neurotic and psychotic conditions. It is to be anticipated that further progress in psychometrics and clinical classification will be profitably utilized by students of the genetics of human behavior in the future.

Another likely trend in future investigations is the greater use of factor analysis, in which the factors common to a group of tests, rather than a single test score, can be examined. This approach has been urged recently by Thompson (1957) and R. B. Cattell (1953). The latter author has provided concrete examples of such an approach to the genetics of personality (Cattell et al., 1955, 1957).

These problems are, however, subordinate to the critical difficulty of arriving at clear-cut, unambiguous determinations of the relative influences of genetic differences and environmental differences in determining the individual variability in phenotypes. These difficulties result primarily from the failure of human circumstances to comply with the assumptions of the logic underlying the methodological procedures, and this situation is basically attributable to the fact that man is not an experimental animal. It is not possible to assign various genotypes randomly to various designated environments. Siblings cannot be separated deliberately and assigned to different types of homes for rearing. Random mating cannot be guaranteed by assigning marriage partners on a random basis.

This is a fundamental consideration. In a discussion of the interpretation of correlation coefficients, Falconer (1960, p. 164) considers the problems introduced by assortative mating and by covariance due to common environments, and says, "For these reasons human correlations cannot easily be used to partition the variation into its components." Neel and Schull have asserted, "In its present context, the twin method has not vindicated the time spent in the collection of such data."[1] Woodworth (1941, pp. 45f.) concluded, "On the whole we may expect results of considerable practical value, but of no great scientific precision, from the study of foster children."

These judgments are indeed sobering, and indicate the necessity for methodological advances in the study of the inheritance of human behavior. The only satisfactory way of dealing with the problem would appear to be the precise evaluation of the extent to which the basic assumptions are not met, with proper compensation then being made in interpretation of results. This will require much more extensive knowledge concerning the important social, economic, educational, and cultural determinants than is now available. Progress in understanding the genetic basis of human behavior can occur only with concomitant progress in understanding the environmental bases.

ANIMAL RESEARCH

Selection

SELECTION FOR LEARNING PERFORMANCE. The animal researcher is able to make use of techniques not available to those working with humans. One of the most important of these is artificial selection.

Selection by natural agencies was, of course, the central theme of Darwin's theory, and "artificial" selection by man, as we have seen, has been a practical art for centuries. The Mendelian discoveries and later developments permitted a more rational approach to the practical aspects of plant and animal breeding, and allowed the development of selection procedures as scientific devices for elucidating genetic mechanisms. If the phenotypic differences shown in a population are determined to any appreciable extent by genotypic differences, a selection program in which animals from one extreme are mated together and animals from the other extreme are likewise mated together, may be expected over a number of generations to result in the establishment of two distinct lines, differing substantially in the characteristic. On the

[1] From J. V. Neel and W. J. Schull, *Human Heredity*, p. 281. Copyright 1954 by the University of Chicago. Used by Permission of The University of Chicago Press.

other hand, as Johanssen had shown with his beans, if the differences in the original population are due solely to environmental differences, such a selection procedure would have no effect. Thus the success of a selective breeding program demonstrates that at least some of the phenotypic variance in the original population was due to genotypic differences.

TOLMAN'S INITIAL STUDY.   The application of selective breeding to problems of the inheritance of behavior was reported in 1924 by E. C. Tolman. We may reasonably infer the indirect influence of J. McK. Cattell in this work, since Tolman credited Professor Warner Brown, who had been one of Cattell's doctoral students, with providing the original impetus for the study. It is also of interest that Barbara Burks was involved in the statistical evaluation of the results.

Tolman saw the genetic approach, and selective breeding particularly, as a tool for "dissecting" behavioral characteristics:

> The problem of this investigation might appear to be a matter of concern primarily for the geneticist. Nonetheless, it is also one of very great interest to the psychologist. For could we, as geneticists, discover the complete genetic mechanism of a character such as maze-learning ability—i.e., how many genes it involves, how these segregate, what their linkages are, etc.—we would necessarily, at the same time, be discovering what psychologically, or behavioristically, maze-learning ability may be said to be made up of, what component abilities it contains, whether these vary independently of one another, what their relations are to other measurable abilities, as, say, sensory discrimination, nervousness, etc. The answers to the genetic problem require the answers to the psychological, while at the same time, the answers to the former point the way to those of the latter [1924, p. 1].

As his own contribution toward this end, Tolman began with a diverse group of eighty-two rats, which were assessed for learning ability in an enclosed maze. Using as a criterion for selection "a rough pooling of the results as to errors, time, and number of perfect runs," nine male and nine female "bright" rats were selected and mated with each other. Similarly, nine male and nine female "dull" rats were selected to begin the "dull" line. The offspring of these groups comprised the first selected generation. These animals were then tested in the maze and selection was made of the brightest of the bright and the dullest of the dull. These selected animals were mated brother by sister to provide the second selected generation of "brights" and "dulls."

The results were quite clear in the first generation, with the bright parents having bright progeny, and the dull parents dull progeny. The difference between "brights" and "dulls" decreased, however, in the next generation, primarily because of a drop in efficiency of performance of the bright strain. These second-generation results were, of course, disappointing, and Tolman examined several possible explanations. In the first place, the particular maze used turned out to be a not particularly reliable measuring instrument. Secondly, it was suggested that the mating of brother with sister might have led to what was known as inbreeding degeneration—a phenomenon quite commonly encountered in genetic work.

To facilitate further investigation, an automatic, self-recording maze was developed by Tolman in collaboration with Jeffress and Tryon (1929). With the new maze, which provided superior control of environmental variables and which proved to be highly reliable, Tryon began the selection procedure again, starting with a large and highly heterogeneous "foundation stock" of rats. The energies of Tolman himself were taken up in the development of his theory of learning, and he did no further actual experimentation on behavioral genetics. Nevertheless, he made a continuing contribution to the field by insisting on the importance of heredity in his well-known H.A.T.E. (Heredity, Age, Training, Endocrine, drug, vitamin conditions) list of individual-difference variables.

TRYON'S AND HERON'S STUDIES.   Tryon's (1940) results are shown in Figure 24. It is clear that two different lines were established, one clearly superior to the other in terms of errors made in learning the maze. In fact, by generation 7 there was practically no overlap between the distributions for the two groups. The dullest bright rats were about equal to the brightest dull rats.

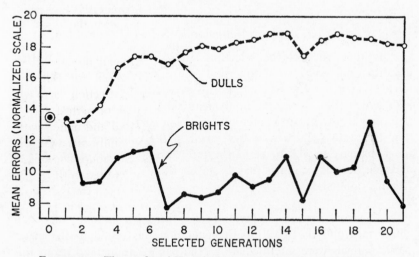

FIGURE 24.   The results of Tryon's selective breeding for maze-brightness and maze-dullness. (From data provided through the courtesy of R. C. Tryon.)

Heron (1935, 1941), at about the same time, was also selectively breeding for maze performance, beginning with a different foundation population and using a different (but also automatic) maze. This study also yielded two clearly distinct strains. Yet another successful program of selection for maze ability has been reported by Thompson (1954). In this study the rats were presented with the Hebb-Williams set of tasks, which increase systematically in complexity, thus providing a closer analogue to human intelligence tests than did the previous studies using only one maze pattern.

SELECTION FOR OTHER BEHAVIORAL CHARACTERISTICS.   Selection has also been applied to phenotypes other than maze performance. Rundquist (1933) selected for active and inactive strains of rats, using the number of revolutions in a rotating cage as the selection criterion. Hall (1938) used selection to derive an "emotional" and a "nonemotional" strain of rats, where emotionality was defined in terms of defecation and urination in a brightly illuminated open-field test. More recently, Broadhurst (1958a) has reported another successful selection program for these behaviors. Frings and Frings (1953) have successfully developed several strains of mice which differ in susceptibility to sound-induced convulsive seizures and also in the pattern of the seizure, and Nachman (1959) has selectively bred for saccharin preference in rats.

In a different phylum, Hirsch and Boudreau (1958) have developed two strains of Drosophila, characterized by different intensities of light-approaching tendencies.

Further Research on Behaviorally Selected Strains

By their success, the selection studies have demonstrated that hereditary differences were important contributors to the individual differences in behavioral phenotypes displayed in the foundation stocks with which the studies began. By reasonable inference, these conclusions may be extended to heterogeneous populations in general. In addition, the strains which were developed in the course of the breeding programs have proved to be of the greatest importance to subsequent research. Several examples may be taken from work with Tryon's and Heron's animals.

TRYON'S STRAINS.   Tryon (1940) bred his "bright" rats with "dull" rats, and the resulting F_1 generation was tested in the maze. These animals were intermediate to the parent strains and, from this and other evidence, Tryon concluded that a multiple factor genetic system determined rat maze-learning ability. Krechevsky (1933) tested

Tryon "brights" and "dulls" in a situation which offered both visual and spatial cues, and found that animals of the bright strain tended to respond to spatial cues, whereas the dull rats responded to visual cues. This outcome is in accord with the fact that the selection measure employed by Tryon was spatial maze performance. The question remained as to whether the "brights" were generally superior, or superior only in this specific type of situation. Searle (1949) examined this point directly by subjecting "brights" and "dulls" to a battery of tests which measured learning under hunger motivation, learning under escape-from-water motivation, activity, and emotionality. The "brights" learned better than the "dulls" in the hunger-motivation problems, whereas the "dulls" were superior to the "brights" in the escape-from-water situations. Furthermore, "brights" were more active in the maze but less active in rotating wheels. Other differences were found with respect to emotionality. "Brights" were more "emotional" in open spaces, while "dulls" displayed emotional behavior with respect to certain of the mechanical features of the maze. The selection program had quite obviously resulted in strains which differed from each other in complex ways—not simply in ability to learn a pattern of responses in the maze. In selective breeding, characteristics other than those deliberately sought may fortuitously become associated in the developing lines. It is not possible, therefore, without further research, to determine which of the constellation of behavior differences between strains are fundamental to the principal behavior difference, and which are only incidental.

GENES, ENZYMES, AND LEARNING. Krech, Rosenzweig, Bennett, and collaborators (Krech *et al.*, 1954, 1956; Rosenzweig *et al.*, 1955, 1958a, 1958b) have systematically investigated the relationship among genes, brain biochemistry, and behavior in descendants of the original Tryon strains, which have been maintained without selection from the twenty-first generation to the present. In a number of learning situations the descendants of the "brights" have proved to be less stereotyped and more flexible in behavior than the "dull" descendants. It has also been shown that the "brights" have a higher level of cholinesterase (ChE) activity in the cerebral cortex. This enzyme, ChE, determines the rate of breakdown of acetylcholine (ACh), which is involved in neural transmission. Krech *et al.* (1956) proposed that the greater ChE activity in the "brights" reflected greater ACh activity, and that this was related to greater efficiency of neural transmission. However, these authors recognized the possibility of fortuitous association, and undertook to determine if in the present case the relationship between the characters was only a matter of chance.

One approach was to mate animals from the separate strains to obtain an F_1, and then to mate the F_1 animals *inter se* to obtain an F_2. In the F_2 there will be genetic reassortment. If there is no genetic communality underlying the two traits, then the correlation between them should be zero. If the traits have common genetic bases, in whole or in part (or if there is linkage among relevant genes), there should be a correlation in the F_2. With reference to the present problem, there should be a negative correlation between ChE activity and the number of errors made. The actual outcome of this test, however, was a *positive* correlation in F_2—the animals with the greater ChE activity tended to make more errors (Rosenzweig *et al.*, 1958b).

Another approach was to breed selectively for cholinesterase activity, without regard to any behavioral characteristics. Again, the results were contrary to the initial hypothesis. The animals selected for high ChE activity performed more poorly, on the whole, than did those selected for low ChE activity. These results have suggested that

> . . . among strains or individuals the levels of ACh and ChE are determined by independent genetic mechanisms. In this case, raising the level of ChE activity and leaving ACh unaltered may cause too rapid a breakdown of ACh for efficient synaptic transmission. Behavioral selection, as in Tryon's case, may have been made for both ACh and ChE. To be certain about the level of ACh metabolism at the synapse will require measurement of both ACh and ChE in the same subjects [Rosenzweig *et al.*, 1958b].

Recently reported results are congruent with this hypothesis (Rosenzweig *et al.*, 1960).

HERON'S STRAINS.   Heron's strains were also subjected to further investigation. Harris, for example (1940), showed that the learning curve of the Heron "dulls" dropped from an initially high error score to about the chance level of 50 per cent correct responses. This was shown to be due to a decreasing tendency to make repeated entries into the same incorrect alley. The "dulls" never did learn to select the correct alley of the two alternatives at each choice point, but simply learned not to repeat errors. The "brights," on the other hand, showed a systematic increase in percentage of correct choices of the proper alleys. The Heron "brights" were also found to show a higher rate of bar-pressing in a Skinner box (Heron and Skinner, 1940), and a faster speed of running the maze than the "dulls" (Harris, 1940).

Comparisons of Strains Not Behaviorally Selected

In addition to the study of strains deliberately selected for behavioral differences, a very substantial number of researches have taken advantage of the existence of other strains, derived in the most part without regard to their behavioral characteristics. These studies have differed from each other in several ways. Some have consisted solely of comparisons between two, or among several, strains. For such studies, the logic has been as follows. If two strains of animals of different origins have been maintained separately, with no matings between the strains having occurred, one may safely presume that the strains differ genetically. (Indeed, under such circumstances, it would not be possible for the strains to retain genetic identity). Therefore, if the compared strains differ in behavior, and the environmental circumstances are similar, one may presume that the genetic differences account for the behavioral differences. Nothing whatever is revealed concerning the nature of the genetic differences. In other cases, the strains have been mated to provide F_1 and further generations, sometimes with the purpose of determining the presence of segregating Mendelian genes, but more often to examine the means and variances of the derived generations with respect to the parent strains. From the study of derived generations, it is frequently possible to determine something about the nature of the genetic mechanism.

In the earlier work, particularly, it was possible to make only rather vague distinctions between the strains. Thus "tame" laboratory rats were compared to "wild" rats, and many of the mouse strains compared were simply stocks from different pet shops, different laboratories, or even different trapping sites. Gradually, however, the maintenance and breeding of laboratory animals became more systematic. In the case of mice, for example, a vigorous program of selection, largely for tumor characteristics, provided a number of discrete identifiable strains. In many cases, furthermore, the selected strains were subjected to intense inbreeding, which has the effect of greatly reducing genetic variability within the strains. The obtained (relative) genetic uniformity enormously facilitates genetic interpretation of results. The gradual adoption of these inbred strains has been one of the principal advances of methodology in strain-comparison studies.

EARLIER RODENT RESEARCH: RODENT "TEMPERAMENT." One of the earliest studies on strain differences was that of Yerkes (1913), who compared tame and wild rats for savageness, wildness, and timidity. These characteristics were inferred from the observable behaviors of biting, gnashing of teeth, squeaking, jumping, hiding, excited running, urination, defecation, cowering, and trembling, exhibited when the animals were taken from the cage. Rating scales from o to 5 were established to describe the degree of the trait exhibited by each rat, and Yerkes claimed high reliability for the observations. The observations were made on wild and tame rats, on the F_1 obtained from mating tame female with wild male rats, and F_2 descendants. The wild rats received ratings of 3, 4, or 5, indicating high expressions of all three characteristics. The tame rats received ratings of 0 or 1. Most of the F_1 animals obtained high ratings, but there was a moderate spread, with some F_1 animals being found in almost every category. In the F_2, the average rating was lower and the variability was greater than in the F_1. In this study, Mendelian-like categories, such as timid vs. non-timid, or savage vs. non-savage, were not used. The use of rating scales acknowledged the quantitative variation of the traits being investigated, but with the work of Fisher and Wright still some years in the future, Yerkes had to content himself with the assertion, "The results . . . prove conclusively that savageness, wildness, and timidity are heritable behavior-complexes. It is hoped that the further study of these characteristics in the third generation hybrids, and in special matings from the first and second generation hybrids, may yield more definite results concerning the modes of transmission" (1913, p. 296).

A closely related study on mice, undertaken by Coburn (1922) at the suggestion of Yerkes, was completed in 1914, although it was not published for a number of years. Utilizing behavioral indices very much like those used by Yerkes with rats, Coburn examined wildness and savageness of wild mice, tame mice, and the subsequent F_1 and F_2 generations. For both wildness and savageness, the F_2 generation had a greater variability than the F_1. The tame mice all scored 0 on a Yerkes-type scale, and the wild mice all scored 4 or 5. The restriction of each character to 5 grades, which imposes a perhaps artificial upper and lower limit, makes comparison of the parental and F_1 variabilities difficult, but the greater variability of the F_2 generation was taken by Coburn to support a multiple-factor interpretation of the inheritance of both wildness and savageness.

Yerkes, in obtaining his F_1, had mated tame females with wild males, and the possibility existed that the outcome would have been different had wild females been mated with tame males. In the first place, the behavior of the tame mother might have provided quite different environmental stimulation to the young during their development than would a wild mother. In the second place, the relevant genes might be located on the X chromosomes, in which case the male offspring would receive all the determining genes from their mother. Obviously, in this case, the "reciprocal crosses" would be expected to differ. Coburn tested these possibilities in his mice by obtaining F_1's from both crosses: wild males with tame females and tame males with wild females. No differences were found in the behavior of the offspring of these reciprocal crosses. The factors determining wildness, savageness, and tameness thus are evidently not located on the sex chromosomes, and the behavior of the mothers of different strains (or the quality of their milk, etc.) does not provide environmental stimulation which differentially affects the phenotype.

THE WISTAR RATS.   Over a period of years, the Wistar Institute had developed an inbred strain of rats with brains of somewhat less than normal weight, and J. H. Donaldson of the Institute had suggested to J. B. Watson, of Johns Hopkins University, that the strain might be deficient in ability to acquire habits. Watson encouraged Basset to investigate the matter. Two learning problems were used. The first was the Watson circular maze, and the second was a problem box in which a treadle had to be pressed to give access to food. These problems were presented to animals of the low brain weight group, and also to a control group of "normal" brain weight, and it was concluded that the rats with less than normal brain weight were slightly inferior to the normal controls (Basset, 1914).

While Basset's work was in progress, the Wistar Institute also suggested a cooperative research program to R. M. Yerkes of Harvard. Yerkes undertook some preliminary studies, and then turned the problem over to a colleague, Mrs. Yerkes. In a footnote to the paper, R. M. Yerkes describes his interest in the research (and incidentally anticipated the later findings of Searle in regard to the Tryon strains).

> In suggesting to Mrs. Yerkes a comparative study of stock and inbred rats, I expressed especial interest in the attempt to analyze "the temperament" of the animals, for certain previous observations in comparison with those reported by Basset had convinced me that crude measurements of modifiability, if directly compared, might lead to seriously misleading conclusions because of differences in timidity, savageness, aggressiveness, sensibility, etc., in the two groups of organisms under observation [A. W. Yerkes, 1916, p. 267].

The Watson circular maze was again employed, along with the Yerkes brightness discrimination box. On the basis of the small number of animals available, it was concluded that the Wistar animals were somewhat inferior to normal control animals. The former were generally slower than the latter, and this was believed to be due to timidity.

Utsurikawa (1917) at Harvard, presumably under the influence of Yerkes, compared the Wistar rats with a control group, some of which were obtained from a Miss Lathrop, and some of which were from a second Wistar stock. A number of differences were described, with the Wistar animals being less active than the control animals, more prone to bite, more responsive to auditory stimulation, and more "timid," in that they retreated to the back of the cage as the experimenter approached. These results, in general, confirmed the work of A. W. Yerkes, who had used a control group of similar constitution with which to compare her Wistar rats.

In 1929 Crozier and Pincus presented the first of a series of studies on the inheritance of geotropic orientation in rats. It was found that three strains of rats differed in the angle of orientation adopted in climbing an inclined plane. It was shown, furthermore, that the relationship of orientation angle to steepness of the incline differed among the strains. In various F_1 and backcross-generation tests, it was concluded that variability of response, as well as magnitude of response, was inherited (Crozier and Pincus, 1932).

LEARNING BY MICE.   Meanwhile, Bagg had made a study of strain differences in learning by mice. The influence of Cattell is acknowledged by Bagg: "In the work here described an attempt has been made to apply the methods of genetics to the study of conduct. Such work was begun by Professor J. McKeen Cattell some fifteen years ago, but the results obtained by him and his students were not published and the problem was given to me" (1916, p. 222). The initial report of this study was made in 1916, and a later report, on an increased number of subjects, was presented in 1920. Albino and colored mice (mainly yellow) were presented with two learning situations, a two-choice position discrimination problem and a multiple-choice problem. A considerable strain difference was found, with the yellow mice being poorer learners. In analyzing the records of mice within the same families, Bagg was unable to find any particular resemblance. However, it was noted that the quick learners exhibited a high degree of flexibility of behavior, as reflected in their quick mastery of the discrimination problem when the situation was reversed, and the formerly incorrect response was made correct. This relatively greater flexibility was later found in "bright" rats, as noted above (p. 215).

It should also be noted that Bagg, in a limited way, had applied some artificial selective breeding in his research. Two exceptionally poor learners of the yellow strain were mated, and their offspring proved to be greatly inferior to the white mice.

Another study on mouse learning was soon presented by Vicari (1921). The maze was an adaptation of the Cattell-designed maze used by Bagg, and two different strains of mice were employed—the Japanese Waltzer and the Bagg albino. Both of these strains had been inbred for nine or more years, and consequently could be expected to be relatively uniform genetically.

Several measures of performance were used—the number of errorless trials, the number of consecutive errorless trials, and the running time. With respect to the first two measures the strains were quite similar, but the Japanese waltzers showed much longer running times than the Bagg albinos.

Turning to the F_1 hybrids, a surprising result is found: 10 percent of the mice in this generation made more perfect trials than any parent in either parent race; some individuals excel all those in the parent races in the number of consecutive perfect trials; and the time averages, instead of being intermediate between those of the parent races, are considerably lower, lower even than the averages for the albinos [Vicari, 1921, p. 132].

Thus, hybrid vigor was identified in a behavioral characteristic.

A subsequent report (Vicari, 1929) gave the results for four highly inbred mouse strains, their F_1's and F_2's. In addition to the Japanese waltzing mice and the Bagg albino strain, this study included a dark brown strain and a brown strain with abnormal eyes (the eye abnormality being due to a mutation experimentally induced by X-rays and involving defects ranging from reduction in size to absence of one or both eyes).

In examining the learning curves for reaction time, Vicari found it possible to identify three types of curves: Type I, a flat curve, e.g., the dark brown animals' curve in Figure 25; Type II, a gradually descending curve, e.g., the Bagg albino curve in Figure 25; and Type III, a descending-ascending curve which was displayed only by the Japanese waltzers. When waltzers were mated with Bagg albinos, the Type II curve characteristic of the albinos was found for the F_1 and F_2. The F_1 animals were faster than either parent, and the F_2 animals were inter-

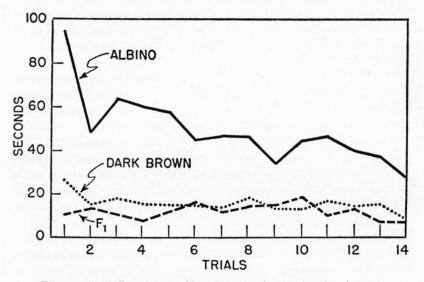

FIGURE 25. Different types of learning curve for running time for two mouse strains and their F_1. (After Vicari, 1929).

mediate to the parents. When albinos were mated with dark brown, the dark browns' Type I curve appeared in F_1. This outcome is shown in Figure 25. The average F_2 curve also resembled a Type I, but was irregular. Closer inspection led to the conclusion that thirty-five F_2 animals showed Type I and eleven showed Type II—very nearly a 3 : 1 Mendelian ratio!

Finally, crossing abnormal-eyed mice, characterized by a Type I curve but with generally high reaction time, with a dark brown, also with a Type I curve but much lower reaction time, gave an F_1 which was faster than either parent during the last half of the testing period —once again Vicari had found hybrid vigor. The F_2 resembled the dark brown parental strain.

In all three crosses the F_1 curve fell closest to the curve of the fastest parent, suggesting dominance of fast reaction time over slow reaction time. The hybrid vigor in the waltzer albino F_1, followed by intermediacy of the F_2, and the greater variance of F_2 relative to F_1, suggested that these two strains differed in respect to multiple factors. For the albino × dark brown cross, where a 35 : 11 F_2 ratio was found, Vicari proposed that the parent strains differed with respect to only one gene.

Generally speaking, the examination of individual family pedigrees gave results in accord with these interpretations.

THE DAWSON STUDY.   In 1932 Dawson reported another mouse study, dealing with what was termed wildness and tameness. Two parental strains were obtained: one, the wild strain, consisted of laboratory-reared descendants of wild trapped mice which were easily excited, resisted handling, and were prone to bite. The other, tame stock consisted of relatively placid, easily handled mice obtained from various sources. From these strains, reciprocal F_1, F_2, and backcross generations were obtained.

The behavior measured was the time required for a mouse to traverse an enclosed runway approximately twenty-five feet long. Wild animals ran the runway much more quickly than did the tame animals. No difference was found between reciprocal F_1's, and the F_1 mean speed was nearly equal to that of the wild parents. The F_2 mean speed was slightly less than that of the F_1, but closer to the wild mean than to the tame mean, and F_2 variability was greater than F_1 variability. The backcross of F_1 to wild produced animals which ran as rapidly as the wild parents, and the backcross to tame gave animals which ran almost as slowly as the tame parents.

Dawson concluded from these results that the genes for "wildness" (as defined) were almost completely dominant, and that no maternal effect existed. Examination of the results for the sexes separately gave no evidence of sex linkage. Two to three gene pairs were estimated to account for the difference between tame and wild.

Dawson also applied selective breeding within strains for four generations. The fastest of the wild were mated, and the slowest of the tame were mated. This selection had no effect on the wild line, but produced progressively slower animals in the tame line. This result amply demonstrates that considerable genetic variability existed in the original tame stock, a fact which renders interpretation of the results somewhat ambiguous.

RECENT MOUSE RESEARCH.   Thus far, we have seen the procedure of strain comparison utilized in studies on learning and various attributes of "wildness" of rats and mice. In subsequent years there was a marked increase in the types of behavior pattern investigated and also some improvement in the breadth of coverage of other species. The large number of researches which have been performed makes it impossible to do more than briefly list some representative examples.

AGGRESSIVENESS.   Scott (1942) found a strain of mice designated C3H to be more likely to initiate aggression than were C57BL mice. Ginsburg and Allee (1942), however, showed that males of the C57BL strain were superior to C3H in ability to win fights. The role of environment was also considered in this study, and it was found possible to make a given mouse either more or less aggressive by subjecting it to a systematic series of victories or defeats. Fredericson (1952) then showed that foster rearing of C57BL and BALB/c animals did not affect their aggressive behavior. Ecological implications of strain differences in aggressiveness were pointed out by Calhoun (1956), who placed small samples of mice in rooms containing food and a water supply and numerous nesting boxes. C57BL mice were placed in one room and DBA/2 mice in another. The DBA/2 mice were much less successful than the C57BL in reproducing themselves under these conditions. At least part of the difference was attributed to the fact that DBA/2 animals fought more often and more intensely than the C57BL animals. Occasionally, an aggressive DBA/2 was even found to attack a female, something which was never observed in the C57BL colony. Generally, the C57BL's appeared more adaptable to the environment, making quicker use of new food and nesting material, and, in respect to fighting behavior, the C57BL pattern tended to become one of threats and retreats, or relatively mild pushing about. Among the DBA/2's, on the other hand, the dominant male vigorously attacked subordinate males at every opportunity.

The mouse has also been featured in studies on exploratory or locomotor activity. Fredericson (1953) showed that, in an enclosed area,

C57BL mice were more prone than C3H or C Bagg albino mice to leave the area adjacent to the wall and to go to the center of the field. Thompson (1953) tested a number of inbred strains on several behavior traits, including the amount of locomotor activity displayed in an apparatus which contained numerous barriers. C57BL and C57BR sublines were very active, while BALB/c mice and mice of an A strain were very inactive. Other strains were more or less intermediate. The same general ranking of strain activity was later found (Thompson, 1956) in a Y maze, and in several other types of apparatus (McClearn, 1959), showing that the behavioral differences were not an idiosyncratic result due to the peculiarities of any one apparatus situation.

LEARNING.   Relatively few of the more recent studies have been concerned with learning in mice. King and Mavromatis (1956) found C57BL mice to condition more rapidly than BALB/c mice in a shock-avoidance situation, but the BALB/c mice relearned more rapidly. Other studies (McClearn, unpublished data) have shown C57BL to be about equal to BALB/c mice in maze and discrimination learning, and both of these strains are superior to C3H animals. Denenberg (1959) has reported a difference between the conditioning rates of two C57 sublines which had been separated for approximately thirty generations. The genetic changes which have occurred during this interval are probably quite small relative to the total genotype, and the results appear to indicate, therefore, that changes in a relatively small number of genetic factors may appreciably influence learning ability.

ALCOHOL PREFERENCE.   Strain differences have also been shown in alcohol preference when animals were given a choice between plain water and a 10 per cent alcohol solution (McClearn and Rodgers, 1959). C57BL mice gradually come to drink most of their daily consumption from the alcohol bottle, while animals from the A, DBA, and BALB/c strains almost completely abstain. F_1's between C57BL and the non-preferring strains show a mean preference higher than that of the non-preferring parent strain, but considerably lower than that of the C57BL strain (McClearn and Rodgers, 1961).

AUDIOGENIC SEIZURES.   Another area in which mouse studies have made important contributions is that of the genetics of audiogenic seizures. Hall (1947) reported that DBA mice were much more prone to convulsive seizures than were C57BL mice, when presented with a loud auditory stimulus. In analyzing the responses of F_1, F_2, and back-cross animals, derived from these parent strains, Witt and Hall (1949) concluded that susceptibility to seizure was determined by a single autosomal dominant gene. Ginsburg, Miller, and Zamis (1950) mated a different C57BL subline to DBA and found that the seizure incidence of the F_1 was intermediate. In the F_2, seizure incidence was about three-fourths of that in F_1. These authors took these data to indicate the presence of two or more non-dominant alleles. It was further found that different sublines of DBA had different degrees of susceptibility, and that the F_1's and F_2's derived from crossing these sublines with C57BL mice also differed. Ginsburg (1954) has emphasized, on the basis of differential response to various metabolites, that different genotypes underlie the seizure proneness of several susceptible strains which he has investigated. Fuller, Easler, and Smith (1950) also rejected the single-gene explanation in favor of a multiple-factor hypothesis.

RECENT RAT RESEARCH: HOARDING, ACTIVITY, AND EMOTIONALITY. In an investigation of rats, Stamm (1954) demonstrated large differences among three strains in food-hoarding behavior. The F_1 between a high-hoarding and low-hoarding strain hoarded as much as the high-hoarding parent strain, and a backcross of F_1 to the low-hoarding strain was intermediate between these two groups (Stamm, 1956). Broadhurst (1958b) studied five rat strains, including the three used by Stamm, in respect to locomotor activity and emotionality, as defined by defecation. Clear strain differences were found in both types of behavior, which were not, however, significantly correlated with each other. In comparing the strain characteristics with Stamm's results, a correlation between hoarding tendency and defecation was found.

Carr and Williams (1957) have also reported differences in locomotor (exploratory) behavior in an investigation of three rat strains.

DOMESTICATION, HORMONES, AND BEHAVIOR. A number of studies have compared the inbred Wistar albino rats with wild rats, in attempts to identify endocrine changes associated with the process of domestication. Hatai (1914) showed that wild Norway rats had heavier adrenals and gonads, but smaller hypophyses than the Wistar. No strain differences, however, were found in thyroid weight. King and Donaldson (1929) compared a group of gray rats, which had been in captivity for ten generations, with both wild animals and with the Wistar strain. Behaviorally, the gray line had become somewhat less savage, but were still less tame than the Wistars. Relative to the wild rats, the hypophyses, adrenals, and gonads of the gray rats were heavier, lighter, and equal, respectively. Relative to the Wistar strain animals, these glands were lighter, heavier, and heavier, respectively. In general, the results suggested a change in endocrine pattern of the gray rats toward that of the Wistars. Farris and Yeakel (1945) utilized the criteria of tendency to defecate and/or urinate in an illuminated field in an effort to objectify the behavioral differences between wild and Wistar rats, and found the latter group to display much less emotional elimination.

Richter (1952) compared a line descendant from the original Wistar strain with rats trapped in the wild, and reported smaller adrenals, larger hypophyses, and more quickly developing gonads in the domesticated animals. Richter regards the changes as due to natural and artificial selection in the laboratory setting, where there is protection against predators, and an advantage given to the more fertile, milder, and "better-adjusted" rats. The argument is extrapolated to man, and evidence of similar changes during human "domestication" is presented (Richter, 1952, p. 283).

The general impression from the above studies is that laboratory selection, acting upon polygenic systems, has gradually altered the endocrinic basis of behavior described as indicating tameness. Keeler and King (1942), however, have summarized "character sketches" of various mutant stocks, and concluded that tameness may be accomplished by a mutant coat-color gene. Reservations concerning this interpretation have been expressed by Scott and Fredericson (1951).

AUDIOGENIC SEIZURES.   Rats have also been employed in the study of susceptibility to audiogenic seizure. Strain differences have been found (Farris and Yeakel, 1943; Maier, 1943), and various experiments were oriented toward the problem of determining the number of genes involved. As was true in the case of the mouse research on this topic, the interpretation changed from a simple dominant hypothesis (Maier and Glaser, 1940) to a multiple-factor hypothesis (Maier, 1943; Finger, 1943). Hall (1951), in reviewing these researches, has taken the view that ambiguity in this case was due to the lack of genetic homogeneity within the strains employed.

MYERS' STUDY.   We may close the consideration of studies comparing strains of rats with the remarkable investigation of Myers (1959). In this experiment, which dealt with shock-avoidance learning, there were five variables: type of stimulus (CS) (buzzer vs. tone); type of response (pressing a bar vs. rotating a wheel); time of testing (day vs. night); shock condition (floor and three walls shocked vs. floor and all four walls including manipulandum [bar or wheel] shocked); strain of animal (Sprague-Dawley vs. Wistar). When the data were analyzed in terms of the relative increase in responses, above operant level, during the period between CS and shock, a bewildering array of interactions emerged. When the manipulandum was not shocked, Sprague-Dawley rats were superior to Wistar rats when a tone CS was employed, but were inferior when a buzzer was used. Furthermore, under this condition, both strains performed better during the day testing when tone CS was used, but more poorly when buzzer CS was used. However, when the manipulandum was shocked, differences between day and night testing were greatly reduced. The Wistars' performance to tone CS was better than the Sprague-Dawleys', but for buzzer CS conditions, strain differences were very small. Myers presented an ingenious explanation, based on an assumed strain difference in emotional startle responses to the manipulandum, with the level of such responses increasing at night in both strains. Whether or not this explanation proves ultimately to be correct, the empirical data have provided an admirable demonstration of the subtle ways in which genotypic differences may interact with environmental variables.

RESEARCH ON OTHER SPECIES.   Sex drive was found to differ among males of different guinea-pig strains (Valenstein *et al.*, 1954), and it was demonstrated that the administration of sex hormones to previously castrated animals did not eliminate the strain differences (Riss *et al.*, 1955). Furthermore, the effectiveness of various conditions of social experience upon subsequent sexual behavior was found to vary from strain to strain (Valenstein *et al.*, 1955).

In rabbits, strain differences have been reported in nest-building behavior (Sawin and Crary, 1953), and in aggression (Denenberg *et al.*, 1958).

In mice of the genus *Peromyscus*, the study of various species and subspecies has revealed differences in climbing and jumping ability (Horner, 1954), in maternal behavior (King, 1958), in activity on an elevated maze (King and Shea, 1959), and in habitat selection (Harritt, 1952). In some instances the various subspecies or races are interfertile, and F_1 animals can be obtained for study. For example, Harritt (1952) mated *Peromyscus maniculatus bairdi*, which selected an artificial grass environment rather than an artificial tree-trunk environment, with *Peromyscus maniculatus gracilis*, which preferred the tree-trunk habitat. The F_1 results suggested dominance of the genetic factors determining grass preference, for the F_1 showed a strong preference for this type of habitat.

The well-established dog breeds have also provided valuable research material. James (1941) studied the behavior of dogs of a number of breeds in classical Pavlovian conditioning situations. Many animals were found to fall in one of two extreme behavior types: excitable or lethargic. Many others were intermediate. Some breeds were almost exclusively of one behavior type. For example, Basset hounds were all lethargic and German shepherds were all excitable. Five Basset hound-shepherd F_1's were also studied, and were found to be intermediate. In seven F_2 animals the entire range from one extreme type to the other was displayed.

In other dog studies, breed differences have been shown in the development of dominance hierarchies (Pawlowski and Scott, 1956), response to different modes of rearing (Freedman, 1958), spontaneous activity (Anderson, 1939), "emotional behavior" (Mahut, 1958), trainability (Fuller, 1955), specific behavior characteristics such as trail-barking propensity (Whitney, 1932), and aggression (Fuller, 1953).

Whereas research on mammals has been predominant, some investigations have been made of other taxonomic groups. Hinde (1956), for example, investigated various threat, submission, and courtship behavior patterns in canaries, goldfinches, and green finches, and in F_1's derived from these species. In those instances where both parents possessed the behavior pattern, it was found to be unchanged in the F_1. When only one parent showed the behavior, or when it was shown in different degrees in the two parents, expression was intermediate in the F_1.

Differences in behavior among several Drosophila species have been intensively investigated from the point of view of the reproductive isolation of one species from another (see Spieth, 1958; Santibañez and Waddington, 1958; Manning, 1958). Another example of insect research is provided by Rothenbuhler (1958), who found one inbred line of honey bees which quickly removed diseased brood from the comb, and another line which did not. The F_1 resembled the last-named line, indicating that the "hygienic" behavior pattern is recessive.

The above must be regarded as only a sample of the literature available, but will perhaps serve to illustrate that clear evidence of genetic influence has been obtained in a wide variety of behavior patterns and at various phylogenetic levels.

THE SEARCH FOR SINGLE GENE EFFECTS.   In view of the history of genetics it is understandable that in many of the pioneer behavioral studies rather persistent attempts were made to interpret the results in accord with simple Mendelian hypotheses. It is, of course, legitimate, and, indeed, obligatory, to examine any results to determine if they are susceptible to a single-locus interpretation. In the earlier discussion of genetic principles, however, it was pointed out that the dependence of most behavior patterns upon many integrated organ systems makes a polygenic hypothesis *a priori* more likely. In fact, we have seen that many of the simple interpretations had to give way later to polygenic ones. On the other hand, the success of the human researches in establishing the simple genetic basis of some mental-deficiency syndromes provides a reminder that single genes, strategically located in the causal paths leading to a phenotype, may produce large effects. Similar reminders are available in the mouse literature, particularly in the studies on neurological and labyrinthine disorders.

WALTZING AND OTHER "NEUROLOGICAL MUTANTS." As a matter of fact, some of the very earliest behavioral genetics studies dealt with one of these conditions, which is known as "waltzing." Waltzing is a periodic, extremely rapid whirling movement, and was characteristic of a strain of mice called "Japanese waltzing" or "Japanese dancing" mice. The syndrome also includes head-shaking and deafness.

Von Guaita reported (1898, 1900) that mating waltzers with normal albino mice yielded offspring which did not show the waltzing characteristic. Darbishire (1904) also mated waltzers with normal albinos in a study aimed at determining if coat color and waltzing were inherited in a Mendelian manner. Two hundred and three F_1 offspring were obtained, none of which waltzed. When the F_1 animals were mated to other F_1 animals, the resulting F_2 consisted of 458 non-waltzers and 97 waltzers. Darbishire concluded that, while waltzing was recessive in good Mendelian fashion in the F_1, the F_2 results were too discrepant from the expected 3 : 1 ratio to support the notion of Mendelian segregation. In general, from the waltzing and coat-color data, Darbishire upheld the biometrical insistence on a form of blending inheritance, and denied the "purity of gametes."

In 1907 R. M. Yerkes published a book devoted to a description of the behavior and capabilities of the Japanese waltzing mouse. With respect to waltzing behavior, Yerkes noted that one line of waltzers tended to whirl to the left while another line consisted of left-whirlers, right-whirlers, and mixed-direction whirlers. He suggested that the "pure" waltzer inherited a tendency to whirl to the left, and that this tendency was obscured in the one line because its ancestry included some non-waltzing mice. No attempt was made to relate this suggestion to Mendelian genetics, although Darbishire's results and Bateson's Mendelian interpretation of them had been considered earlier in the book.

Later research (summarized in Grüneberg, 1952) has made it clear that waltzing is a Mendelian recessive condition, and that the discrepancies in F_2 ratio, such as were noted by Darbishire, are due to reduced viability of the homozygous animals, which results in the death of some of this group before they can be classified.

A number of other mutants have been found which give rise to waltzer-like symptoms (e.g., jerker, fidget, shaker), thus illustrating that similar phenotypes can result from the action of different genes.

Other "neurological" conditions, involving, variously, muscular tremor, incoordination, abnormal posture, head-shaking, and deafness or auditory hypersensitivity have also been described as single-gene effects.

DROSOPHILA MATING.   Insect research has provided more examples of single-gene effects. Several studies (e.g., Reed and Reed, 1950; Merrell, 1953) have shown that some conditions determined by a single gene lower mating activity in Drosophila. Bastock's (1956) research provides an illustration of this type of experiment. It had long been known that mutant yellow males were less successful in mating than were normal males. Bastock's aim was to determine if this fact was due to a behavioral difference which resulted from the presence of the yellow gene, which is a sex-linked recessive. Thus it was important to obtain normal and yellow males which were highly similar in other genetic respects. To accomplish this, heterozygous females were mated to yellow brothers. The male offspring of this cross were yellow and normal in equal numbers, and other genetic differences could be expected to be randomly distributed between the two color groups.

The normal courtship pattern of the male Drosophila includes a bout of wing vibration, which evidently provides important stimuli which are detected by the female antennae. It was found that the duration of the wing vibration bouts by yellow males is shorter than normal, and this behavioral difference reduces the effectiveness of the courtship of the yellows.

The Lamarckian Issue

In general, the researches on behavioral genetics have not been particularly involved in the development of concepts within the field of genetics itself. The over-all picture is rather one of the application of already demonstrated principles and techniques to the particular subject matter of behavior. With respect to the question of the inheritance of acquired characteristics, however, the behavioral studies formed an important part of the evidence, and were centrally involved in the controversy which took place. We have seen that the Mendelian theory posited a "purity of the gametes" which was incompatible with the idea that acquired traits could be transmitted. Nonetheless, "Lamarckism" persisted obstinately and was repeatedly put forward in spite of much contradictory evidence. The first negative study in behavior was provided by Yerkes (1907) in his work, *The Dancing Mouse*. One male and one female from each of two lines was taught a black-white discrimination, and they were then mated. From their litters, one male and one female were chosen for training, and were then mated, and so on for a total of four generations. There was no indication that the offspring benefited in learning ability by having parents, grandparents, and even great-grandparents who had learned the problem. "There is absolutely no evidence of the inheritance of this particular individually acquired form of behavior in the dancer" (p. 283).

Griffith (1922) reported an experiment in which white rats were rotated day and night in revolving cages for several months. When the animals were released from the cages, they showed marked changes in posture and a characteristic circling movement. When these affected animals were mated with normal rats, some offspring were found who displayed disequilibration. Detlefson (1923, 1925) soon reported similar results. A number of defects of these studies were pointed out by later workers, the most compelling of which was the possibility that the animals had contracted a middle ear disease, affecting the labyrinthine mechanism. The accumulation of animal waste during the uninterrupted rotation of the cages would be favorable to the spread of a disease organism. In the matings the infection could be transmitted by parents to offspring, and a superficial appearance of "inheritance" would be given.

In the face of these and other objections (see Munn, 1950, p. 40), the Griffith and Detlefson studies came to be regarded generally as inconclusive.

PAVLOV'S ANNOUNCEMENT. A new round in the controversy was dramatically begun by Pavlov, who stated in 1923 during a lecture tour in the United States:

> The latest experiments (which are not yet finished) show that the conditioned reflexes, *i.e.*, the highest nervous activity, are inherited. At present some experiments on white mice have been completed. Conditioned reflexes to electric bells are formed, so that the animals are trained to run to their feeding place on the ringing of the bell. The following results have been obtained.
>
> The first generation of white mice required 300 lessons. Three hundred times was it necessary to combine the feeding of the mice with the ringing of the bell in order to accustom them to run to the feeding place on hearing the bell ring. The second generation required, for the same result, only 100 lessons. The third generation learned to do it after 30 lessons. The fourth generation required only 10 lessons. The last generation which I saw before leaving Petrograd learned the lesson after 5 repetitions. The sixth generation will be tested after my return. I think it very probable that after some time a new generation of mice will run to the feeding place on hearing the bell with no previous lesson [1923, pp. 360–1].

Thus could conditioned reflexes, through a Lamarckian mechanism, be converted into unconditioned reflexes!

CONTRADICTORY EVIDENCE.   Just a few months later, two reports contradictory to Pavlov's results were announced. Vicari (1924),
using mice, and MacDowell (1924), using rats, found no evidence that
offspring of maze-trained ancestors learned the maze with any more
facility than did their ancestors. Another negative report came from
Sadovnikova-Koltzova, who examined her data on rats' maze performance and concluded that ". . . we see that the teaching of parents did
not increase the abilities of the offspring" (1926, p. 316).

McDougall felt that Darwinian natural selection was not sufficient
to account for the evolutionary process, and that the Lamarckian principle had to be invoked. Pavlov's results were a bit too good to be true,
so McDougall had attempted to replicate them, with no success. He
had therefore written Pavlov concerning the matter, and Pavlov had replied, ". . . briefly stating that he no longer held his deductions from
his experiments to be valid" (McDougall, 1927, p. 271). Anrep, who
translated Pavlov's works into English, also told McDougall that Pavlov
had authorized him to make a retraction in the forthcoming *Conditioned Reflexes*. This was duly made in a footnote as follows:

> Experiments . . . upon hereditary facilitation of the development of
> some conditioned reflexes in mice have been found to be very com-
> plicated, uncertain and moreover extremely difficult to control. They
> are at present being subjected to further investigation under more
> stringent conditions. At present the question of hereditary transmis-
> sion of conditioned reflexes and of the hereditary facilitation of their
> acquirement must be left entirely open [Pavlov, 1927, p. 285].

Razran (1958) informs us that there is no evidence that Pavlov
carried out his announced intention to repeat the experiment, and the
whole topic is conspicuously absent from Pavlov's later publications.

McDOUGALL'S RESEARCH.   McDougall persevered, however,
and undertook a long-term investigation with Wistar strain rats. The
learning situation employed consisted of three parallel alleys in a water
tank. The animals were placed in the center alley, and upon swimming
its length could choose to turn either right or left into one of the side
alleys. Each side alley contained an escape platform and could be illuminated or left dim. The dim alley was the correct path. The platform in the illuminated alley was electrified so that the rat would receive
an electric shock if it attempted to escape the water by that route. Each
generation was obtained by supposedly random selection from the
preceding generation. The principal results were a decrease in the number of errors made in the thirty-four successive generations, and the
gradual development of "photophobia." The results were interpreted

as demonstrating the inheritance of characteristics acquired by the experience of the ancestors (McDougall, 1927, 1930, 1938; Rhine and McDougall, 1933).

Criticisms appeared at once (Hazlitt, 1927; Crew, 1930), directed primarily to procedural matters. One of these criticisms suggested that there had been non-deliberate selection of faster learning animals as parents. Furthermore, McDougall had unfortunately failed to maintain an untrained control group from the same initial stock as the trained group, but had relied upon animals newly imported to his laboratory for control observations. McDougall challenged some of the criticisms, and undertook to select for *poorer* learning ability. There was still improvement over a number of generations.

ATTEMPTS TO REPLICATE McDOUGALL'S RESULTS.   The issue was of such importance that two repetitions of the costly experiment were attempted. Crew (1936) also began with Wistar strain rats, and used an apparatus similar to McDougall's. In this study, however, a control line was maintained from the outset. Some of the control animals were tested in each generation to provide data for comparison with the trained line, and other control line animals were retained, untrained, to provide the next generation. In the trained line, of course, all animals were trained. Over eighteen generations, Crew (1936) found no convincing evidence of a decrease in errors among the trained line, and they were, in fact, not different from the untrained controls. In both groups there were wide fluctuations from generation to generation.

Agar and collaborators (1948) likewise started with Wistar rats, used an apparatus similar to McDougall's, and maintained a control line. In this experiment a progressive improvement did occur over twenty-eight generations in the trained group, but this was followed by a worsening in performance from the twenty-eighth to the thirty-sixth generation. More important, the results were remarkably paralleled by the control group, in which the parents of each successive generation *had never been trained.*

It is not possible to establish definitely exactly what accounts for McDougall's results, but the failure of Crew's and Agar's attempts to replicate them casts serious doubt on the validity of the Lamarckian explanation, and various alternative explanations have been advanced. The small size of the breeding population, for example, could lead to inbreeding depression, and all the cited researches agree that less vigorous animals learn more quickly in this particular situation. Small breeding populations are also susceptible to genetic drift, so that over a period of time a line could change quite considerably in genetic constitution, even in the absence of any selection. The possibility of gradual

and systematic change in environmental conditions of rearing and testing during the many years involved in such an experiment is another
important possibility.

Failures to demonstrate unambiguously the Lamarckian phenomenon, and the great successes of the genetical theory which pre-
supposes absence of Lamarckian effects, have brought Lamarckism
into general disrepute in modern genetics. The only notable exception is
provided by Russian Lysenkoism. One very recent line of research, moreover, has shown how apparent transmission of acquired characters may
be due to subtle selection for modifying genes (Waddington, 1957).

Summary of Animal Research

The general picture presented by animal behavioral genetics is of a
discipline which has established a base of operations by the demonstration of genetic influence in a wide variety of behaviors and in diverse
animal species. Over and above the establishment of the simple fact of
genetic contribution, some progress has been made in determining the
mode of gene action. In some cases it has been possible to demonstrate single-gene effects. In some polygenic characters, descriptions of
additive effects or of partial average dominance are available. There
have also been advances in describing the causal processes between genes
and behavioral characters.

In terms of application of current genetic theory and procedure,
behavioral genetics lags behind. For example, one of the central concepts of modern genetics is that of *heritability*, which is defined as the
ratio of the variance attributable to additive gene effects to the total
phenotypic variance. This quantity represents the genetic contribution
which is "useful" in the sense that it provides for firm prediction of the
outcome of various matings (e.g., in a selection program). Effects due
to dominance and epistasis, which are, to be sure, genetic, are dependent
upon the vagaries of combinations of genes, and consequently are less
predictable. As yet, only a few studies have attempted to estimate
heritabilities of behavioral traits (Hirsch and Boudreau, 1958; Broadhurst, 1959). Further development of behavioral genetics will require
the precise estimation of the heritabilities of a broad range of behavior
patterns.

Again, it is rather remarkable that in animal work, where the technique could be most appropriately applied, there has been so little work
on correlations among relatives. Only one study in which correlations
were the chief concern (Burlingame and Stone, 1928) has come to
the author's attention. Other techniques have also remained untried.
For example, a very recent publication by Broadhurst (1959) provides
the first example of the use of diallele crossing in studying behavioral

traits. In this procedure F_1's are obtained among a number of inbred strains, and the results provide estimates of heritability and description of the relative contributions of additive, dominance, and epistatic effects.

Another technique only recently introduced to behavioral genetics is that of chromosome analysis in Drosophila (Hirsch, 1961). In this technique specific chromosomes may be combined in desired combinations, and the contributions of each chromosome to a particular type of behavior can be assessed.

It seems reasonable to judge that the foundation of behavioral genetics is now sufficiently stable to permit the future course of research to be more detailed and refined explorations of the dynamics of genetic determination of behavior.

BEHAVIORAL GENETICS AND PSYCHOLOGY

To THIS POINT, little has been said of the relationship which studies in behavioral genetics have had to psychology in general. To a considerable extent, of course, developments in behavioral genetics were directed by contemporary trends in psychology. The great concern with the inheritance of learning ability in animals, for example, reflects the dominant role which learning theory has played in psychology. Furthermore, the techniques which could be utilized in the study of the genetics of behavior have depended upon the refinements and improvements in psychological procedures. The Watson circular maze gave way to the multiple T-maze; assessment of intelligence in humans was made ever more precise as new instruments were developed, and so on.

The reciprocal influence, that of behavioral genetics upon developments within psychology as a whole, has been limited by the predominantly environmentalistic orientation which has characterized psychological theory.

From the beginning, there have been vigorous opponents to any suggestion that the composition of a man's chromosomes could have any determining effect upon his intelligence, personality, emotional stability, or any other "mental or moral" characteristic. There ensued an intense debate, which has come to be known as the nature-nurture controversy.

In all controversies of this type, apparently, the motivations of the opposing teams are diverse and various, and this is clearly true of the nature-nurture debate. For some, religious convictions may have played a predominant role in shaping opinions. Political attitudes were also undoubtedly involved. Are not all men created equal? This was a self-evident truth to the signers of the Declaration of Independence. Arguments that some men are inherently wiser than others have appeared to some to be inimical to the democratic ideal, and to imply the rightness of a rule by the elite. The dominant political philosophy of a large part of Western culture during much of the nature-nurture controversy has insisted, on the contrary, that education and socioeconomic reform can improve the lot of individuals and thereby the stature of a culture. Pastore (1949) has presented a detailed defense of the thesis that sociopolitical allegiances have played a major role in determining opinion on this issue. In the late 1930's and the 1940's, particularly, the horror at the results of the Nazis' perverted application of their pseudogenetics of race differences led to a strong bias against any suggestion of inheritance of mental characteristics.

Another factor which presumably acted to reduce interest in psychological genetics was the dampening of the ardor of eugenicists. As newly discovered genetic principles were brought to bear on the proposals of eugenics, it became clear that some of the early hopes for quick improvement in human welfare through genetic alteration were overly optimistic. Since eugenic considerations had directly or indirectly motivated much of the human research, it was inevitable that the disenchantment would have an adverse effect on the vigor with which studies on behavioral genetics were conducted. (See Scheinfeld, 1958, for a discussion of changing views in eugenics.) Furthermore, as we have seen, there is considerable room for differences in interpretation of the evidence, especially in the case of the human data.

But the most important factor was no doubt the development of the "behavioristic" point of view which assumed a dominating role in the developing discipline of psychology, particularly in America. With J. B. Watson as the prime mover, behaviorism developed as a protest against all forms of introspective psychology. Mental states, consciousness, mind, will, imagery—all became taboo. Stimulus and response were the only acceptable explanatory terms.

The instinct doctrine, which had been brought to its culmination by McDougall (1908), was also attacked by behaviorists as being redundant and circular. Instincts had been thought of as inherited patterns of behavior in contrast to learned behavior, and with the rejection of instincts, the whole notion of heredity influencing behavior was cast into discard. The burden of explaining individual differences fell completely to environmental factors.

> So let us hasten to admit—yes, there are heritable differences in form, in structure . . . These differences are in the germ plasm and are handed down from parent to child. . . . But do not let these undoubted facts of inheritance lead us astray as they have some of the biologists. The mere presence of these structures tells us not one thing about function. . . . Our hereditary structure lies ready to be shaped in a thousand different ways—the same structure—depending on the way in which the child is brought up [Watson, 1930, p. 97].
> Objectors will probably say that the behaviorist is flying in the face

of the known facts of eugenics and experimental evolution—that the geneticists have proven that many of the behavior characteristics of the parents are handed down to the offspring. . . . Our reply is that the geneticists are working under the banner of the old "faculty" psychology. One need not give very much weight to any of their present conclusions. We no longer believe in faculties nor in any stereotyped patterns of behavior which go under the names of "talent" and inherited capacities" [p. 99].

Our conclusion, then, is that we have no real evidence of the inheritance of traits. I would feel perfectly confident in the ultimately favorable outcome of careful upbringing of a *healthy, well-formed* baby born of a long line of crooks, murderers and thieves, and prostitutes. Who has any evidence to the contrary? [p. 103].

Then came the familiar and frequently quoted challenge:

I should like to go one step further now and say, "Give me a dozen healthy infants, well-formed, and my own specified world to bring them up in and I'll guarantee to take any one at random and train him to become any type of specialist I might select—doctor, lawyer, artist, merchant-chief and, yes, even beggar-man and thief, regardless of his talents, penchants, tendencies, abilities, vocations, and race of his ancestors." I am going beyond my facts and I admit it, but so have the advocates of the contrary and they have been doing it for many thousands of years [p. 104].

Woodworth (1948) has pointed out that this extreme environmentalism was not a necessary consequence of the behavioristic philosophical position, and suggests that Watson's stand was taken, in part at least, "to shake people out of their complacent acceptance of traditional views" [2] (1948, p. 92). For whatever reason Watson sought to exorcise genetics from psychology, he succeeded to a remarkable degree, and the position taken in his *Behaviorism* soon became the "traditional view" which was "complacently accepted" by the majority of psychologists.

It is quite apparent from the account given above that this majority view was not without opposition. In fact, since Watson's pronouncement, no single year has passed without publication of some evidence showing it to be wrong. Collectively, these researches have demonstrated the important role of the genotype in many kinds of organism and in many varieties of behavior pattern. From the accumulated evidence, it is obvious that genetic differences are fundamental to individuality, in behavior as well as in physical characteristics.

It would be rash to predict in any detail the effect which the implications of this generalization will have upon psychology in the future. It does appear, however, from a striking increase in the rate of publications

[2] From Robert S. Woodworth, *Contemporary Schools of Psychology*, Revised Edition: Copyright 1948, The Ronald Press Company.

in the past decade, that a growth of interest is under way. The hope might be expressed that this growing interest presages a general understanding of the fallacy of the nature-nurture dichotomy, and an acknowledgment of the mutual, interacting, and co-operative roles played by the genes and by environmental agencies in shaping psychological characteristics.

REFERENCES

AGAR, W. E., DRUMMOND, R. H., AND TIEGS, O. W. Third report on a test of McDougall's Lamarckian experiment on the training of rats. *J. exp. Biol.*, 1948, 25, 103–22.

ALLEN, G. Patterns of discovery in the genetics of mental deficiency. *Amer. J. Ment. Defic.*, 1958, 62, 840–9.

ANASTASI, A., AND FOLEY, J. P. *Differential psychology*, rev. ed. New York: The Macmillan Company, 1949.

ANDERSON, O. D. The spontaneous neuromuscular activity of various pure breeds of dog and of inter-breed hybrids of the first and second generation. *Amer. J. Physiol.*, 1939, 126, 422–3.

————. The role of the glands of internal secretion in the production of behavioral types in the dog. In C. R. Stockard, *The genetic and endocrinic basis for differences in form and behavior.* Philadelphia: Wistar Institute, 1941. Pp. 647–753.

BAGG, H. J. Individual differences and family resemblances in animal behavior. *Amer. Nat.*, 1916, 50, 222–36.

————. Individual differences and family resemblances in animal behavior. *Arch. Psychol.*, 1920, 6, 1–58.

BARR, M. L., AND BERTRAM, E. G. A morphological distinction between neurones of the male and female, and the behaviour of the nucleolar satellite during accelerated nucleoprotein synthesis. *Nature*, 1949, 163, 676–7.

BASSET, G. C. Habit formation in a strain of albino rats of less than normal brain weight. *Behav. Monogr.*, 1914, 2, 1–46.

BASTOCK, M. A gene mutation which changes a behavior pattern. *Evolution*, 1956, 10, 421–39.

BATESON, W. *Mendel's principles of heredity.* Cambridge: University Press, 1909.

BICKEL, H., GERRARD, J., AND HICKMANS, E. M. The influence of phenylalanine intake on the chemistry and behavior of a phenylketonuric child. *Acta Paediat.*, Upps., 1954, 43, 64–77.

BÖÖK, J. A. Oligophrenia. In A. Sorsby (Ed.), *Clinical genetics.* London: Butterworth, 1953.

BORING, E. G. A *history of experimental psychology,* 2nd ed. New York: Appleton, 1950.

BRIDGES, C. B. Non-disjunction of the sex chromosomes of *Drosophila. J. exp. Zool.,* 1913, *15,* 587–606.

BROADHURST, P. L. Studies in psychogenetics: The quantitative inheritance of behaviour in rats investigated by selective and cross-breeding. *Bull. Brit. psychol. Soc.,* 1958a, *34,* 2A (Abst.)

———. Determinants of emotionality in the rat: III. Strain differences. *J. comp. physiol. Psychol.,* 1958b, *51,* 55–9.

———. Application of biometrical genetics to behaviour in rats. *Nature,* 1959, *184,* 1517–18.

BURKS, B. S. The relative influence of nature and nurture upon mental development; a comparative study of foster parent–foster child resemblance and true parent–true child resemblance. *Yearb. Nat. Soc. Stud. Educ.,* 1928a, 27 (I), 219–316.

———. Comments on the Chicago and Stanford studies of foster children. *Yearb. Nat. Soc. Stud. Educ.,* 1928b, 27 (I), 317–21.

———. Statistical hazards in nature-nurture investigations. *Yearb. Nat. Soc. Stud. Educ.,* 1928c, (I), 9–33.

BURLINGAME, M., AND STONE, C. P. Family resemblance in maze-learning ability in white rats. *Yearb. Nat. Soc. Stud. Educ.,* 1928, 27 (I), 89–99.

CALHOUN, J. B. A comparative study of the social behavior of two inbred strains of house mice. *Ecol. Monogr.,* 1956, *26,* 81–103.

CARR, R. M., AND WILLIAMS, C. D. Exploratory behavior of three strains of rats. *J. comp. physiol. Psychol.,* 1957, *50,* 621–3.

CARTER, H. D. Family resemblances in verbal and numerical abilities. *Genet. Psychol. Monogr.,* 1932, *12,* 1–104.

———. Twin-similarities in personality traits. *J. genet. Psychol.,* 1933, *43,* 312–21.

———. Ten years of research on twins: contributions to the nature-nurture problem. *Yearb. Nat. Soc. Stud. Educ.,* 1940, 39 (I), 235–55.

CATTELL, R. B. Research designs in psychological genetics with special reference to the multiple variance method. *Amer. J. hum. Genet.,* 1953, *5,* 76–93.

CATTELL, R. B., BLEWETT, D. B., AND BELOFF, J. R. The inheritance of personality: a multiple variance analysis determination of approximate nature-nurture ratios for primary personality factors in Q-data. *Amer. J. hum. Genet.,* 1955, *7,* 122–46.

CATTELL, R. B., STICE, GLEN F., AND KRISTY, N. F. A first approximation to nature-nurture ratios for eleven primary personality factors in objective tests. *J. abnorm. soc. Psychol.,* 1957, *54,* 143–59.

CATTELL, R. B., AND WILLSON, J. L.   Contributions concerning mental inheritance: I. Of intelligence. *Brit. J. educ. Psychol.*, 1938, 8, 129–49.

COBURN, C. A.   Heredity of wildness and savageness in mice. *Behav. Monogr.*, 1922, 4, 1–71.

CONRAD, H. S., AND JONES, H. E.   A second study of familial resemblance in intelligence. *Yearb. Nat. Soc. Stud. Educ.*, 1940, 39 (II), 97–141.

CREW, F. A. E.   Lamarckism. *Eugen. Rev.*, 1930, 22, 55–9.

———.   Mental deficiency. *Eugen. Rev.*, 1932, 23, 299–303.

———.   A repetition of McDougall's Lamarckian experiment. *J. Genet.*, 1936, 33, 61–101.

CROOK, M. N.   Intra-family relationships in personality test performance. *Psychol. Rec.*, 1937, 1, 479–502.

CROZIER, W. J., AND PINCUS, G.   Analysis of the geotropic orientation of young rats. *J. gen. Physiol.*, 1929, 13, 57–119.

———.   Certain principles of physiological genetics. *Proc. 6th Int. Congr. Genetics*, 1932, 2, 31–2.

DARBISHIRE, A. D.   On the result of crossing Japanese waltzing with albino mice. *Biometrika*, 1904, 3, 1–51.

DARWIN, C.   *The variation of animals and plants under domestication.* New York: Orange Judd, 1868.

———.   *On the origin of species by means of natural selection or the preservation of favoured races in the struggle for life.* New York: Appleton, 1869.

———.   *The expression of the emotions in man and animals.* London: Murray, 1872.

———.   *The descent of man, and selection in relation to sex.* New York: Appleton, 1873.

DAVENPORT, C. B.   *Heredity in relation to eugenics.* London: Williams and Norgate, 1912.

DAVIDOFF, L. M.   The brain in Mongolian idiocy. *Arch. Neurol. Psychiat.*, 1928, 20, 1229–57.

DAVIDSON, W. M., AND SMITH, D. R.   Sex diagnosis of blood. *Brit. Med. J.*, 1954, 1, 1379.

DAVIS, B. D.   Genetic and environmental control of enzyme formation. *Proc. Ass. Res. Nerv. Ment. Dis.*, 1954, 33, 23–38.

DAVIS, H.   *The works of Plato.* Vol. II. London: Bohn, 1849.

DAWSON, W. M.   Inheritance of wildness and tameness in mice. *Genetics*, 1932, 17, 296–326.

DENENBERG, V. H.   Learning differences in two separated lines of mice. *Science*, 1959, 130, 451–2.

DENENBERG, V. H., SAWIN, P. B., FROMMER, G. P., AND ROSS, S.   Genetic, physiological and behavioral background of reproduction in the rabbit. IV. An analysis of maternal behavior at successive parturitions. *Behaviour*, 1958, 13, 131–42.

DETLEFSEN, J. A.   Are the effects of long-continued rotation in rats inherited? *Proc. Amer. Phil. Soc.*, 1923, 62, 292–300.

————.   Inheritance of acquired characters. *Physiol. Rev.*, 1925, 5, 244–78.

DUGDALE, R. L.   *The Jukes*. New York: G. P. Putnam's Sons, 1877.

EAST, E. M., AND HAYES, H. K.   Inheritance in maize. *Conn. Agr. Exp. Sta. Bull.* 167, 1911, 1–142.

ELLIS, W.   *The politics of Aristotle*. London: Dent, 1912.

EMERSON, R. A., AND EAST, E. M.   The inheritance of quantitative characters in maize. *Univ. Neb. Res. Bull.* 2, 1913, 5–120.

ESTABROOK, A. H.   *The Jukes in 1915*. Washington, D. C.: Carnegie Institution, 1916.

EYSENCK, H. J., AND PRELL, D. B.   The inheritance of neuroticism: an experimental study. *J. Ment. Sci.*, 1951, 97, 441–65.

FALCONER, D. S.   *Introduction to quantitative genetics*. Edinburgh: Oliver and Boyd, 1960.

FARRIS, E. J., AND YEAKEL, E. H.   The susceptibility of albino and gray Norway rats to audiogenic seizures. *J. comp. Psychol.*, 1943, 35, 73–80.

————.   Emotional behavior of gray Norway and Wistar albino rats. *J. comp. Psychol.*, 1945, 38, 109–18.

FINGER, F. W.   Factors influencing audiogenic seizures in the rat. II. Heredity and age. *J. comp. Psychol.*, 1943, 35, 227–32.

FISHER, R. A.   The correlation between relatives on the supposition of Mendelian inheritance. *Trans. Roy. Soc. Edinburgh*, 1918, 52, 399–433.

————.   *The genetical theory of natural selection*, 2nd ed. New York: Dover, 1958.

FÖLLING, A.   Über Ausscheidung von Phenylbrenztraubensäure in den Harn als Stoffweckselanomalie in Verbindung mit Imbezillität. *Ztschr. f. physiol. Chem.*, 1934, 227, 169–76.

FORD, C. E., AND HAMERTON, J. L.   The chromosomes of man. *Acta genet.*, 1956, 6, 264–6.

FORD, C. E., JACOBS, P. A., AND LAJTHA, L. G.   Human somatic chromosomes. *Nature*, 1958, 181, 1565–8.

FORD, C. E., JONES, K. W., MILLER, O. J., MITTWOCH, U., PENROSE, L. S., RIDLER, M., AND SHAPIRO, A.   The chromosomes in a patient showing both Mongolism and the Klinefelter syndrome. *Lancet*, 1959a, 1, 709–10.

FORD, C. E., JONES, K. W., POLANI, P. E., DE ALMEIDA, J. C., AND BRIGGS, J. H.   A sex-chromosome anomaly in a case of gonadal dysgenesis (Turner's syndrome). *Lancet*, 1959b, 1, 711–13.

FRACCARO, M., KAIJSER, K., AND LINDSTEN, J. Chromosome complement in gonadal dysgenesis (Turner's syndrome). *Lancet*, 1959, 1, 886.

FREDERICSON, E. Reciprocal fostering of two inbred mouse strains and its effects on the modification of inherited aggressive behavior. *Amer. Psychologist*, 1952, 7, 241–2 (Abst.)

―――. The wall-seeking tendency in three inbred mouse strains (*Mus musculus*). *J. genet. Psychol.*, 1953, 82, 143–6.

FREEDMAN, D. G. Constitutional and environmental interactions in rearing of four breeds of dogs. *Science*, 1958, 127, 585–6.

FREEMAN, F. N., HOLZINGER, K. J., AND MITCHELL, B. C. The influence of environment on the intelligence, school achievement, and conduct of foster children. *Yearb. Nat. Soc. Stud. Educ.*, 1928, 27 (I), 103–217.

FRINGS, H., AND FRINGS, M. The production of stocks of albino mice with predictable susceptibilities to audiogenic seizures. *Behaviour*, 1953, 5, 305–19.

FULLER, J. L. Cross-sectional and longitudinal studies of adjustive behavior in dogs. *Ann. N. Y. Acad. Sci.*, 1953, 56, 214–24.

―――. Hereditary differences in trainability of purebred dogs. *J. genet. Psychol.*, 1955, 87, 229–38.

FULLER, J. L., EASLER, C., AND SMITH, M. E. Inheritance of audiogenic seizure susceptibility in the mouse. *Genetics*, 1950, 35, 622–32.

GALTON, F. *Hereditary genius*. London: MacMillan, 1869.

―――. *Inquiries into human faculty and its development*. London: MacMillan, 1883.

GATES, R. R. The inheritance of mental defect. *Brit. J. Med. Psychol.*, 1933, 13, 254–67.

―――. *Human Genetics*. New York: The Macmillan Company, 1946.

GESELL, A., AND THOMPSON, H. Learning and growth in identical infant twins: an experimental study by the method of co-twin control. *Genet. Psychol. Monogr.*, 1929, 6, 1–124.

GINSBURG, B. E. Genetics and the physiology of the nervous system. *Proc. Ass. Res. Nerv. Ment. Dis.*, 1954, 33, 39–56.

GINSBURG, B. E., AND ALLEE, W. C. Some effects of conditioning on social dominance and subordination in inbred strains of mice. *Physiol. Zool.*, 1942, 15, 485–506.

GINSBURG, B. E., MILLER, D. S., AND ZAMIS, M. J. On the mode of inheritance of susceptibility to sound-induced seizures in the house mouse (*Mus musculus*). *Genetics*, 1950, 35, 109 (Abst.)

GODDARD, H. H. *The Kallikak family*. New York: The Macmillan Company, 1912.

―――. *Feeblemindedness: its causes and consequences*. New York: The Macmillan Company, 1914.

————. In defense of the Kallikak study. *Science*, 1942, 95, 574–6.

GRAY, J. L., AND MOSHINSKY, P. Studies in genetic psychology. The intellectual resemblance of collateral relatives. *Proc. Roy. Soc. Edinburgh*, 1932–3, 53, 188–207.

GRIFFITH, C. R. Are permanent disturbances of equilibration inherited? *Science*, 1922, 56, 676–8.

GRÜNEBERG, H. *The genetics of the mouse*, 2nd ed. The Hague: Martinus Nijhoff, 1952.

GUN, W. T. J. The heredity of the Tudors. *Eugen. Rev.*, 1930a, 22, 111–16.

————. The heredity of the Stewarts. *Eugen. Rev.*, 1930b, 22, 195–201.

HALL, C. S. The inheritance of emotionality. *Sigma Xi Quart.*, 1938, 26, 17–27.

————. Genetic differences in fatal audiogenic seizures between two inbred strains of house mice. *J. Hered.*, 1947, 38, 3–6.

————. The genetics of behavior. In S. S. Stevens (ed.), *Handbook of experimental psychology*. New York: John Wiley and Sons, 1951, 304–29.

HARRIS, R. E. An analysis of the maze-learning scores of bright and dull rats with reference to motivational factors. *Psychol. Rec.*, 1940, 4, 130–6.

HARRITT, T. V. An experimental study of habitat selection by prairie and forest races of the deer mouse *Peromyscus maniculatus*. *Contr. Lab. Vert. Biol.*, University of Michigan, 1952, 56, 53.

HATAI, S. On the weight of some of the ductless glands of the Norway and of the albino rat according to sex and variety. *Anat. Rec.*, 1914, 8, 511–23.

HAZLITT, V. Professor McDougall and the Lamarckian hypothesis. *Brit. J. Psychol.*, 1927, 18, 77–86.

HERON, W. T. The inheritance of maze learning ability in rats. *J. comp. Psychol.*, 1935, 19, 77–89.

————. The inheritance of brightness and dullness in maze learning ability in the rat. *J. genet. Psychol.*, 1941, 59, 41–9.

HERON, W. T., AND SKINNER, B. F. The rate of extinction in maze-bright and maze-dull rats. *Psychol. Rec.*, 1940, 4, 11–18.

HERRMAN, L., AND HOGBEN, L. The intellectual resemblance of twins. *Proc. Roy. Soc. Edinburgh*, 1932–3, 53, 105–29.

HILGARD, J. R. The effect of early and delayed practice on memory and motor performances studied by the method of co-twin control. *Genet. Psychol. Monogr.*, 1933, 14, 493–567.

HINDE, R. A. Breeding success in cardueline interspecies pairs and an examination of the hybrids' plumage. *J. Genet.*, 1956, 54, 304–10.

HIRSCH, J.   Individual differences in behavior and their genetic basis. In Bliss, E. (Ed.), *Roots of behavior.* New York: Harper & Brothers, 1962.

HIRSCH, J., AND BOUDREAU, J. C.   Studies in experimental behavior genetics: I. The heritability of phototaxis in a population of *Drosophila melanogaster. J. comp. physiol. Psychol.,* 1958, *51,* 647–51.

HOGBEN, L.   *Nature and nurture.* London: Allen and Unwin, 1933.

HOLMES, S. J.   *The trend of the race.* New York: Harcourt, Brace, and Co., 1921.

HONZIK, M. P.   Developmental studies of parent-child resemblance in intelligence. *Child Develop.,* 1957, *28,* 215–28.

HORNER, B. E.   Arboreal adaptations of *Peromyscus,* with special reference to use of the tail. *Contr. Lab. Vert. Biol.,* University of Michigan, 1954, *61,* 1–85.

HSIA, D. Y., DRISCOLL, K. W., TROLL, W., AND KNOX, W. E.   Detection by phenylalanine tolerance tests of heterozygous carriers of phenylketonuria. *Nature,* 1956, *178,* 1239–40.

JACOBS, P. A., BAIKIE, A. G., COURT BROWN, W. M., AND STRONG, J. A.   The somatic chromosomes in Mongolism. *Lancet,* 1959, *1,* 710.

JACOBS, P. A., AND STRONG, J. A.   A case of human intersexuality having a possible XXY sex-determining mechanism. *Nature,* 1959, *183,* 302–3.

JAMES, W. T.   Morphological form and its relation to behavior. In C. R. Stockard, *The genetic and endocrinic basis for differences in form and behavior.* Philadelphia: Wistar Institute, 1941, 525–643.

JENKINS, R. L.   Etiology of Mongolism. *Amer. J. Dis. Child.,* 1933, *45,* 506–19.

JERVIS, G. A.   Introductory study of fifty cases of mental deficiency associated with excretion of phenylpyruvic acid. *Arch. Neurol. Psychiat.,* 1937, *38,* 944–63.

————.   Studies of phenylpyruvic oligophrenia. The position of the metabolic error. *J. Biol. Chem.,* 1947, *169,* 651–6.

————.   Genetic factors in mental deficiency. *Amer. J. hum. Genet.,* 1952, *4,* 260–71.

————.   Phenylpyruvic oligophrenia: deficiency of phenylalanine oxidizing system. *Proc. Soc. exp. Biol., N. Y.,* 1953, *82,* 514–15.

————.   Phenylpyruvic oligophrenia (phenylketonuria). *Proc. Ass. Res. Nerv. Ment. Dis.,* 1954, *33,* 259–82.

JONES, H. E.   A first study of parent-child resemblance in intelligence. *Yearb. Nat. Soc. Stud. Educ.,* 1928, *27* (I), 61–72.

JONES, H. E., AND MORGAN, D. H.   Twin similarities in eye movement pattern. *J. Hered.,* 1942, *33,* 167–72.

JOST, H., AND SONTAG, L. W. The genetic factor in autonomic nervous system function. *Psychosom. Med.*, 1944, 6, 308–10.

KALLMANN, F. J. *Heredity in health and mental disorder*. New York: Norton and Co., 1953.

KEELER, C. E., AND KING, H. D. Multiple effects of coat color genes in the Norway rat with special reference to temperament and domestication. *J. comp. Psychol.*, 1942, 34, 241–50.

KING, H. D. AND DONALDSON, H. H. Life processes and size of the body and organs of the gray Norway rat during ten generations in captivity. *Amer. Anat. Mem.*, 1929, 14, 106.

KING, J. A. Maternal behavior and behavioral development in two subspecies of *Peromyscus maniculatus*. *J. Mammal.*, 1958, 39, 177–90.

KING, J. A., AND MAVROMATIS, A. The effect of a conflict situation on learning ability in two strains of mice. *J. comp. physiol. Psychol.*, 1956, 49, 465–8.

KING, J. A., AND SHEA, N. J. Subspecific differences in the responses of young deermice on an elevated maze. *J. Hered.*, 1959, 50, 14–18.

KRECH, D., ROSENZWEIG, M. R., BENNETT, E. L., AND KRUECKEL, B. Enzyme concentrations in the brain and adjustive behavior-patterns. *Science*, 1954, 120, 994–6.

KRECH, D., ROSENZWEIG, M. R., AND BENNETT, E. L. Dimensions of discrimination and level of cholinesterase activity in the cerebral cortex of the rat. *J. comp. physiol. Psychol.*, 1956, 261–8.

KRECHEVSKY, I. Hereditary nature of "hypotheses." *J. comp. Psychol.*, 1933, 16, 99–116.

LAUTERBACH, C. E. Studies in twin resemblance. *Genetics*, 1925, 10, 525–68.

LEAHY, A. M. Nature-nurture and intelligence. *Genet. Psychol. Monogr.*, 1935, 17, 236–308.

LEJEUNE, J., GAUTHIER, M., AND TURPIN, R. Etude des chromosomes somatiques de neuf enfants mongoliens. *C. R. Acad. Sci. Paris*, 1959, 248, 1721–2.

LENNOX, W. G. The heredity of epilepsy as told by relatives and twins. *J. Amer. Med. Ass.*, 1951, 146, 529–36.

LENNOX, W. G., GIBBS, E. L., AND GIBBS, F. A. The brain-wave pattern, an hereditary trait; evidence from 74 "normal" pairs of twins. *J. Hered.*, 1945, 36, 233–43.

LERNER, I. M. *The genetic basis of selection*. New York: John Wiley and Sons, 1958.

LI, C. C. *Population genetics*. Chicago: University of Chicago, 1955.

LURIA, A. R., AND MIRENOVA, A. N. Experimental development of constructive activity (differential training of identical twins). Communication III. Stability of the effect of training. *Proc. Maxim Gorky Medico-Genetical Res. Inst.*, 1936, 4, 487–505.

LUSH, J. L. Genetics and animal breeding. In L. C. Dunn (Ed.), *Genetics in the 20th century.* New York: The Macmillan Company, 1951.

MCCLEARN, G. E. The genetics of mouse behavior in novel situations. *J. comp. physiol. Psychol.*, 1959, 52, 62–7.

MCCLEARN, G. E., AND RODGERS, D. A. Differences in alcohol preference among inbred strains of mice. *Quart. J. Stud. Alcohol*, 1959, 20, 691–5.

MCCLEARN, G. E., AND RODGERS, D. A. Genetic factors in alcohol preference of laboratory mice. *J. comp. physiol. Psychol.*, 1961, 54, 116–19.

MCDOUGALL, W. *An introduction to social psychology.* London: Methuen, 1908.

————. An experiment for the testing of the hypothesis of Lamarck. *Brit. J. Psychol. (Gen. Section)*, 1927, 17, 267–304.

MCDOUGALL, W. Second report on a Lamarckian experiment. *Brit. J. Psychol., (Gen. Section)*, 1930, 20, 201–18.

————. Fourth report on a Lamarckian experiment. *Brit. J. Psychol.*, 1938, 28, 321–45, 365–95.

MACDOWELL, E. C. Experiments with rats on the inheritance of training. *Science*, 1924, 59, 302–3.

MCGRAW, M. B. *Growth: a study of Johnny and Jimmy.* New York: Appleton-Century, 1935.

MACKLIN, M. T. Mongolian idiocy: the manner of its inheritance. *Amer. J. Med. Sci.*, 1929, 178, 315–37.

MCNEMAR, Q. Twin resemblances in motor skills, and the effect of practice thereon. *J. genet. Psychol.*, 1933, 42, 70–97.

MAHUT, H. Breed differences in the dog's emotional behaviour. *Canad. J. Psychol.*, 1958, 12, 35–44.

MAIER, N. R. F. Studies of abnormal behavior in the rat: XIV. Strain differences in the inheritance of susceptibility to convulsions. *J. comp. Psychol.*, 1943, 35, 327–35.

MAIER, N. R. F., AND GLASER, N. M. Studies of abnormal behavior in the rat: V. The inheritance of the "neurotic pattern." *J. comp. Psychol.*, 1940, 30, 413–18.

MANNING, A. An evolutionary approach to the study of behaviour. *Proc. Roy. phys. Soc. Edinburgh*, 1958, 27, 1–5.

MATHER, K. *Biometrical genetics.* New York: Dover, 1949.

————. The progress and prospect of biometrical genetics. In L. C. Dunn (Ed.), *Genetics in the 20th century.* New York: The Macmillan Company, 1951.

MAY, M. A., AND HARTSHORNE, H. Sibling resemblance in deception. *Yearb. Nat. Soc. Stud. Educ.*, 1928, 27 (II), 161–77.

MENDEL, G. J. Versuche über Pflanzen-Hybriden. *Verh. Naturf. Ver. in Brunn*, 1865, 4, 3–47. English translation made by Royal

Horticultural Society of London. Conveniently available in recent texts, including: Dodson, E. O., *Genetics*, Phila., Saunders, 1956; and Sinnott, E. W., Dunn, L. C., and Dobzhansky, Th., *Principles of genetics*, New York, McGraw-Hill Book Co., 1950.

MERRELL, D. J.   Selective mating as a cause of gene frequency changes in laboratory populations of *Drosophila melanogaster*. *Evolution*, 1953, 7, 287–96.

MERRIMAN, C.   The intellectual resemblance of twins. *Psychol. Monogr.*, 1924, 33, 1–58. Whole No. 152.

MITTWOCH, U.   The chromosome complement in a Mongolian imbecile. *Ann. Eugen.*, 1952, 17, 37.

MOORE, K. L., AND BARR, M. L.   Smears from the oral mucosa in the detection of chromosomal sex. *Lancet*, 1955, 2, 57–8.

MULLER, H. J.   Mental traits and heredity. *J. Hered.*, 1925, 16, 432–48.

———.   The production of mutations by X-rays. *Proc. Nat. Acad. Sci.*, 1928, 14, 714–26.

MUNN, N. L.   *Handbook of psychological research on the rat.* Boston: Houghton Mifflin Co., 1950.

MYERS, A. K.   Avoidance learning as a function of several training conditions and strain differences in rats. *J. comp. physiol. Psychol.*, 1959, 52, 381–6.

NACHMAN, M.   The inheritance of saccharin preference. *J. comp. physiol. Psychol.*, 1959, 52, 451–7.

NEEL, J. V., AND SCHULL, W. J.   *Human heredity.* Chicago: University of Chicago, 1954.

NEWMAN, H. H.   Identical twins. *Eugen. Rev.*, 1930, 22, 29–34.

NEWMAN, H. H., FREEMAN, F. N., AND HOLZINGER, K. J.   *Twins: a study of heredity and environment.* Chicago: University of Chicago, 1937.

NILSSON-EHLE, H.   Einige Ergebnisse von Kreuzungen bei Hafer und Weisen. *Bot. Notiser*, 1908–9, 257–94.

PACKARD, A. S., *Lamarck, the founder of evolution.* New York: Longmans, Green, and Co., 1901.

PASTORE, N.   *The nature-nurture controversy.* New York: Kings Crown, 1949.

PAVLOV, I. P.   New researches on conditioned reflexes. *Science*, 1923, 58, 359–61.

———.   *Conditioned reflexes.* Trans. G. V. Anrep. New York: Oxford University Press, 1927.

PAWLOWSKI, A. A., AND SCOTT, J. P.   Hereditary differences in the development of dominance in litters of puppies. *J. comp. physiol. Psychol.*, 1956, 49, 353–8.

PEARSON, K.   On the laws of inheritance of man. II. On the inheritance of the mental and moral characters in man, and its comparison with the inheritance of the physical characters. *Biometrika*, 1904, 3, 131–90.

————.   *The life, letters and labours of Francis Galton.* London: Cambridge University, 1924.

————.   On the inheritance of mental disease. *Ann. Eugen.*, 1930–1, 4, 362–80.

PENROSE, L. S.   *The influence of heredity on disease.* London: H. K. Lewis, 1934.

————.   Two cases of phenylpyruvic amentia. *Lancet*, 1935a, 1, 23–4.

————.   Inheritance of phenylpyruvic amentia (phenylketonuria). *Lancet*, 1935b, 2, 192–4.

————.   Maternal age, order of birth and developmental abnormalities. *Proc. 7th Internat. Genetical Congr.*, 1941, 235.

————.   *The biology of mental defect.* London: Sidgwick and Jackson, 1949.

————.   Observations on the aetiology of Mongolism. *Lancet*, 1954, 2, 505–9.

————.   *Outline of human genetics.* London: Heinemann, 1959.

PLUNKETT, E. R., AND BARR, M. L.   Congenital testicular hypoplasia. *Anat. Rec.*, 1956, 124, 348.

POLANI, P. E., BISHOP, P. M. F., LENNOX, B., FERGUSON-SMITH, M. I., STEWART, J. S. S., AND PRADER, A.   Colour vision studies and the X-chromosome constitution of patients with Klinefelter's syndrome. *Nature*, 1958, 182, 1092–3.

POLANI, P. E., HUNTER, W. F., AND LENNOX, B.   Chromosomal sex in Turner's syndrome with coarctation of the aorta. *Lancet*, 1954, 2, 120–1.

POLANI, P. E., LESSOF, M. H., AND BISHOP, P. M. F.   Colour-blindness in "ovarian agenesis" (gonadal dysplasia). *Lancet*, 1956, 2, 118–20.

POPENOE, P.   Twins reared apart. *J. Hered.*, 1922, 13, 142–4.

PRICE, B.   Primary biases in twin studies. *Amer. J. hum. Genet.*, 1950, 2, 293–352.

PRICE, B., KOSTIR, W. J., AND TAYLOR, W. M.   A twin-controlled experiment on the learning of auxiliary languages. *Genet. Psychol. Monogr.*, 1944, 29, 117–54.

RAZRAN, G.   Pavlov and Lamarck. *Science*, 1958, 128, 758–60.

REED, S. C., AND REED, E. W.   Natural selection in laboratory populations of *Drosophila*. II. Competition between a white-eye gene and its wild type allele. *Evolution*, 1950, 4, 34–42.

RHINE, J. B., AND MCDOUGALL, W.   Third report on a Lamarckian experiment. *Brit. J. Psychol.*, 1933, 24, 213–35.

RICHTER, C. P.   Domestication of the Norway rat and its implication for the study of genetics in man. *Amer. J. hum. Genet.*, 1952, 4, 273–85.

RIIS, P., JOHNSEN, S. G., AND MOSBECH, J.   Nuclear sex in Klinefelter's syndrome. *Lancet*, 1956, 1, 962–3.

RISS, W., VALENSTEIN, E. S., SINKS, J., AND YOUNG, W. C.   Development of sexual behavior in male guinea pigs from genetically different stocks under controlled conditions of androgen treatment and caging. *Endocrinology*, 1955, 57, 139–46.

ROBERTS, J. A. F.   Resemblances in intelligence between sibs selected from a complete sample of an urban population. *Proc. 7th Int. Congr. Genetics*, 1941, 252.

ROPER, A. G.   *Ancient eugenics.* Oxford: Blackwell, 1913.

ROSENZWEIG, M. R., KRECH, D., AND BENNETT, E. L.   Effects of pentobarbital sodium on adaptive behavior patterns in the rat. *Science*, 1956, 123, 371–2.

————.   Brain enzymes and adaptive behaviour. *Ciba Foundation Symposium* on the *Neurological basis of behaviour*, 1958a, 337–55.

————.   A search for relations between brain chemistry and behavior. *Psychol. Bull.*, 1960, 57, 476–92.

ROSENZWEIG, M. R., KRECH, D., BENNETT, E. L., AND LONGUEIL, C.   Strain differences of rats in behavior and brain chemistry. Paper delivered at APA, Washington, Sept., 1958b.

ROTHENBUHLER, W. C.   Genetics of a behavior difference in honey bees. *Proc. 10th Internat. Congr. Genetics*, 1958, 2, 242.

RUNDQUIST, E. A.   Inheritance of spontaneous activity in rats. *J. comp. Psychol.*, 1933, 16, 415–38.

SADOVNIKOVA-KOLTZOVA, M. P.   Genetic analysis of temperament in rats. *J. exp. Zool.*, 1926, 45, 301–18.

SANTIBAÑEZ, S. K., AND WADDINGTON, C. H.   The origin of sexual isolation between different lines within a species. *Evolution*, 1958, 12, 485–93.

SAWIN, P. B., AND CRARY, D. D.   Genetic and physiological background of reproduction in the rabbit. II. Some racial differences in the pattern of maternal behavior. *Behaviour*, 1953, 6, 128–46.

SCHEINFELD, A.   The Kallikaks after thirty years. *J. Hered.*, 1944, 35, 259–64.

————.   Changing attitudes toward human genetics and eugenics. *Eugenics Quart.*, 1958, 5, 145–53.

SCOTT, J. P.   Genetic differences in the social behavior of inbred strains of mice. *J. Hered.*, 1942, 33, 11–15.

SCOTT, J. P., AND FREDERICSON, E.   The causes of fighting in mice and rats. *Physiol. Zool.*, 1951, 24, 273–309.

SEARLE, L. V.   The organization of hereditary maze-brightness and maze-dullness. *Genet. Psychol. Monogr.*, 1949, 39, 279–325.

SIEMENS, H. W.   *Die Zwillingspathologie.* Berlin: Springer, 1924.

————.   The diagnosis of identity in twins. *J. Hered.*, 1927, 18, 201–9.

SKODAK, M., AND SKEELS, H. M.   A final follow-up of one hundred adopted children. *J. genet. Psychol.*, 1949, 75, 85–125.

SLATER, E.   *Psychotic and neurotic illnesses in twins.* London: H. M. Stationery Office, 1953a.

————.   Psychiatry. In A. Sorsby (Ed.), *Clinical genetics.* London: Butterworth, 1953b.

SPENCER, H.   *The principles of psychology.* Vol. I. New York: Appleton, 1897.

SPIETH, H. T.   Behavior and isolating mechanisms. In A. Roe and G. G. Simpson (Eds.), *Behavior and evolution.* New Haven: Yale University, 1958, 363–89.

STAMM, J. S.   Genetics of hoarding: I. Hoarding differences between homozygous strains of rats. *J. comp. physiol. Psychol.*, 1954, 47, 157–61.

————.   Genetics of hoarding: II. Hoarding behavior of hybrid and backcrossed strains of rats. *J. comp. physiol. Psychol.*, 1956, 49, 349–52.

STARCH, D.   The similarity of brothers and sisters in mental traits. *Psychol. Rev.*, 1917, 24, 235–8.

STERN, C.   *Principles of human genetics,* 2nd ed. San Francisco: Freeman, 1960.

STRAYER, L. C.   Language and growth: The relative efficacy of early and deferred vocabulary training, studied by the method of co-twin control. *Genet. Psychol. Monogr.*, 1930, 8, 209–319.

TALLMAN, G. G.   A comparative study of identical and non-identical twins with respect to intelligence resemblances. *Yearb. Nat. Soc. Stud. Educ.*, 1928, 27 (I), 83–6.

THOMPSON, W. R.   The inheritance of behaviour: behavioural differences in fifteen mouse strains. *Canad. J. Psychol.*, 1953, 7, 145–55.

————.   The inheritance and development of intelligence. *Proc. Ass. Res. Nerv. Ment. Dis.*, 1954, 33, 209–31.

————.   The inheritance of behavior: activity differences in five inbred mouse strains. *J. Hered.*, 1956, 47, 147–8.

————.   Traits, factors, and genes. *Eugen. Quart.*, 1957, 4, 8–16.

THORNDIKE, E. L.   Measurements of twins. *Columbia Univ. Contr. Phil. Psychol.*, 1905, 13, 1–64.

———. The resemblance of siblings in intelligence. *Yearb. Nat. Soc. Stud. Educ.*, 1928, 27, (I), 41–53.

———. The resemblance of siblings in intelligence-test scores. *J. genet. Psychol.*, 1944, 64, 265–7.

TJIO, J. H., AND LEVAN, A.   The chromosome number of man. *Hereditas*, 1956, 42, 1–6.

TOLMAN, E. C.   The inheritance of maze-learning ability in rats. *J. comp. Psychol.*, 1924, 4, 1–18.

TOLMAN, E. C., TRYON, R. C., AND JEFFRESS, L. A.   A self-recording maze with an automatic delivery table. *Univ. California Publ. Psychol.*, 1929, 4, 99–112.

TREDGOLD, A. F.   *Mental deficiency (amentia)*. London: Bailliere, Tindall and Cox, 1908; 6th rev. ed., 1937.

TRYON, R. C.   Genetic differences in maze-learning ability in rats. *Yearb. Nat. Soc. Stud. Educ.*, 1940, 39 (I), 111–19.

UDENFRIEND, S., AND COOPER, J. R.   The enzymatic conversion of phenylalanine to tyrosine. *J. biol. Chem.*, 1952, 194, 503–11.

UTSURIKAWA, N.   Temperamental differences between outbred and inbred strains of the albino rat. *J. Anim. Behav.*, 1917, 7, 111–29.

VALENSTEIN, E. S., RISS, W., AND YOUNG, W. C.   Sex drive in genetically heterogeneous and highly inbred strains of male guinea pigs. *J. comp. physiol. Psychol.*, 1954, 47, 162–5.

———. Experiential and genetic factors in the organization of sexual behavior in male guinea pigs. *J. comp. physiol. Psychol.*, 1955, 48, 397–403.

VAN BEUKERING, J. A., AND VERVOORN, J. D.   A case of uniovular twins of which one child was normal and the other had the syndrome of Mongolism. *Acta Genet. Med. Gemellol., Roma*, 1956, 5, 113–14.

VANDENBERG, S. G.   The hereditary abilities study. *Eugen. Quart.*, 1956, 3, 94–9.

VICARI, E. M.   Heredity of behavior in mice. *Yearb. Carnegie Inst. Washington*, 1921, 132–3.

———. The non-inheritance of the effects of training. *Science*, 1924, 59, 303.

———. Mode of inheritance of reaction time and degrees of learning in mice. *J. exp. Zool.*, 1929, 54, 31–88.

VON GUAITA, G.   Versuche mit Kreuzungen von verschiedenen Rassen der Hausmaus. *Ber. Nat. Ges.*, Freiburg, 1898, 10, 317–32.

———. Zweite Mitteilung über Versuche mit Kreuzungen mit verschiedenen Rassen der Hausmaus. *Ber. Nat. Ges.*, Freiburg, 1900, 11, 131–8.

WAARDENBURG, P. J.   Das Menschliche Auge und seine Erbanlagen. *Bibliogr. genet.*, 1932, 7, 1–631.

WADDINGTON, C. H.   *The strategy of the genes*. New York: The Macmillan Company, 1957.

WAGNER, R. P., AND MITCHELL, H. K.   *Genetics and metabolism*. New York: John Wiley and Sons, 1955.

WATSON, J. B.   *Behaviorism*. New York: Norton and Co., 1924. Rev. ed. 1930.

WHITE, R. W.   *The abnormal personality*. New York: Ronald Press, 1948.

WHITNEY, L. F.   Inheritance of mental aptitudes in dogs. *Proc. 6th Internat. Congr. Genet.*, 1932, 2, 211–12 (Abst.).

WILLOUGHBY, R. R.   Family similarities in mental-test abilities. *Yearb. Nat. Soc. Stud. Educ.*, 1928, 27 (I), 55–9.

WILSON, P. T.   A study of twins with special reference to heredity as a factor determining differences in environment. *Hum. Biol.*, 1934, 6, 324–54.

WINGFIELD, A. N.   *Twins and orphans*. London: Dent, 1928.

WITT, G., and HALL, C. S.   The genetics of audiogenic seizures in the house mouse. *J. comp. physiol. Psychol.*, 1949, 42, 58–63.

WOODS, F. A.   *Mental and moral heredity in royalty*. New York: Henry Holt and Co., 1906.

WOODWORTH, R. S.   *Heredity and environment*. New York: Social Science Research Council, Bull. 47, 1941.

————.   *Contemporary schools of psychology*, rev. ed. New York: Ronald Press, 1948.

WRIGHT, S.   Systems of mating. *Genetics*, 1921, 6, 111–78.

————.   The genetics of quantitative variability. In E. C. R. Reeve and C. H. Waddington (Eds.), *Quantitative inheritance*. London: H. M. Stationery Office, 1952.

YERKES, A. W.   Comparison of the behavior of stock and inbred albino rats. *J. Anim. Behav.*, 1916, 6, 267–96.

YERKES, R. M.   *The dancing mouse*. New York: The Macmillan Company, 1907.

————.   The heredity of savageness and wildness in rats. *J. Anim. Behav.*, 1913, 3, 286–96.

ZIRKLE, C.   The knowledge of heredity before 1900. In L. C. Dunn (Ed.), *Genetics in the 20th century*. New York: The Macmillan Company, 1951.

PART II

Perception, Learning, and Memory

CHAPTER 5

Nativism and Empiricism
in Perception

JULIAN E. HOCHBERG

INTRODUCTION

Perception IS THE NAME for the inferred psychological processes which underlie our awareness of the world around us. Its study occupies an old and influential place in psychology. In fact, a great deal of the initial thinking in this area was done first by philosophers and theologians, and later by physiologists, long before psychology was a separate science.

Psychology is concerned with the responses one makes to one's world or environment (which includes other people). Accordingly, thinking about psychology frequently starts with some assumptions about perception, and when these are not explicit, the psychologist may inadvertently base his theories (and even his research methods) on invalid or outmoded ideas about perception. For in the study of perception, as in all science, both knowledge and opinion change, owing to the interactions between new facts, techniques, and fashion. Even the problems which comprise the subject-matter change, although the old names may move up to cover new problems, and old assumptions may blind us to new possibilities.

In this paper we will follow the career of one of the major traditional problems of visual perception: the question of whether our abilities to perceive the spatial aspects of our environment must be learned, or whether some or all of them may be innate. This issue dominated the psychology of perception from the beginning, and remains a challenge today, after some 300 years of dispute.

255

It should be made clear at the outset that we are not initially concerned with the issue of whether or not *practice* affects perception—only with the question of whether some irreducible ability to perceive space is part of our equipment at birth, or whether it is completely learned.

At first glance one might think that the question is simply settled, and that quite different consequences would follow from these two alternative points of view: if we are born with certain ideas, we would seem to be stuck with our innate endowments; if, on the contrary, our minds and ideas are built up through the experiences we have, anyone can be "improved," and all ideas and laws, institutions, etc., as well as space perception, must be relative, must be products of the particular experiences we have had in our individual lifetimes. Actually we will see that these conclusions do not follow necessarily at all. Moreover, the conceptual conflict between environment and heredity, between "nature" and "nurture" continues undecided (but somewhat altered) to this day.

We will follow the problem of "nature vs. nurture" through five main stages in its history: (1) the formative years were spent in the hands of philosophers and "armchair" psychologists, and then (2) sensory physiologists and "physiological psychologists" set the problems and devised the methods of the early years of experimental psychology. During these first two stages, the predominant belief was that our ability to perceive space had to be acquired by learning from our experiences with the things and people around us, i.e., that we see space by "nurture" (the things that happen to us as we are growing up) rather than by "nature" (the structure with which we are endowed at birth). This approach is known as *empiricism*. Traditionally, those who held this viewpoint are called *empiricists*, as distinguished from the *nativists*, who held the opposite opinion. More-or-less casual self-observation provided the major research method for investigating the nature-nurture question in both of these stages. (3) The first systematic experimentation on this issue coincided with the advent of *Gestalt* theory, which was also the first major nativistic "school," as far as our problem was concerned. Gestalt psychologists were still interested in the philosophical and physiological preoccupations of the preceding two stages. In all three stages, psychological research findings were frequently used as the bases for systems of philosophy and of speculative physiology. (4) The present period is still emerging, in which technological applications have brought the study of perception "down to earth" (it is probably the second most important field in psychology—after test-construction—as far as practical application is concerned), and in which its own characteristic interests, independent of both philosophy and physiology, finally begin to emerge. (5) Direct experimental investigation of the nature-nurture question in space perception only begins at this stage.

As we will see, the importance and purpose of the nature-nurture question were quite different in each of these stages. Each period will be introduced with a brief description of background or "setting," followed by a series of the investigations which shaped the decisions for each, and, finally, we will summarize the consequences of each stage.

THE FIRST STAGE: EMPIRICIST PHILOSOPHERS AND ASSOCIATIONIST PSYCHOLOGISTS

A FEW CENTURIES AGO various philosophers were sure they understood the fundamental principles of how men acquire knowledge, and of the nature of thought, and they based upon their diverse beliefs quite varied social and religious prescriptions for man's life and for his government. Their assumptions are to be found, even today, firmly rooted in the language of common sense, and hidden away in the most unexpected corners of modern scientific thought. Our "nature-nurture" question makes its formal entrance on stage in this period; [1] let us see briefly why it was considered so important at the time, and the means by which men tried to answer it.

The Philosophers: the Deductive and Introspective Methods

It was the age of reason. To the enlightened man, the universe appeared as an immense clockwork mechanism, started at creation and running mechanically ever since. The motions and positions of all things in the universe—including animals, which Descartes explained as mere reflex-machines—were inexorably predestined by mechanical causation (or by natural law, as opposed to continuing divine supervision). The next step was obvious: to reduce man and his thoughts to nothing more than a part of the mechanical universe, with all his apparently creative

---

[1] Actually, we can trace this question to earliest history: *cf.* Heraclites (Boring, 1942, p. 4); consider, too, the dialogue between Socrates and Theaetetus from Plato's *Theaetetus* (Dyde, 1899, pp. 12, 26). The conversation starts out with this exchange: "*Soc.* . . . Knowledge is perception, you say? *Theaet.* Yes . . . *Soc.* And perception of reality . . . since it is knowledge, can never be false? *Theaet.* So it appears." By the end of this discourse, those familiar with Socrates' manner will not be surprised to find this apparent conclusion completely refuted: "*Soc.* . . . Does the soul not perceive the hardness of a hard object through the touch, and in the same way the softness of a soft object? . . . But the essence and existence of these, and the opposition of each to the other, . . . the soul itself judges, bringing them all together and passing them in review. . . . Men and animals from their very birth perceive by nature those feelings . . . which reach the soul through the body; but reflections . . . on the essence of these . . . come only after effort and . . . a wide experience. . . . Then, Theaetetus, sensible perception and knowledge will never be the same. *Theaet.* Clearly not, Socrates; indeed, it is now quite evident that knowledge and sensation are different."

and spontaneous activity simply explained as *passive* mechanical response to his environment. There was hope for the eventual understanding of the entire universe, with no exceptions and no mysteries—
not even man's soul. It is within this setting, but with other initial purposes, that we pick up the philosophical investigation of thought and
perception.

DESCARTES.   Our present story will start with Descartes (seventeenth century), and his prescription of how to recognize the Truth.
(This philosophical inquiry is part of "epistemology": how shall we
know what is true in our conflicting ideas about the world and the things
in it?) This question was very important in an age when reason was still
being called upon to support the power of kings, on the one hand
(Hobbes, 1651), and the rights of man, on the other (Locke, 1690).
Descartes held that what is clear, compelling, and consistent among our
ideas must be true, for certain knowledge is born into our souls, i.e.,
is innate. Descartes was a nativist; therefore, our knowledge about the
size, form, motion, and position of objects was, he thought, a set of ideas
which are innately correct. A series of contrapuntal arguments and investigations by Hobbes and Locke, Berkeley and Hume, quickly reached
the opposite conclusion.

HOBBES AND LOCKE.   Locke (and, essentially, Hobbes before
him) maintained that *all* ideas must derive from something previously
experienced. This philosophical position is empiricism: all our knowledge comes through our senses.

> . . . It is past doubt that men have in their mind several ideas, such
> as are those expressed by the words, whiteness, hardness, sweetness,
> thinking, motion, man, elephant, army, drunkenness, and others: it is
> . . . then to be inquired, How he comes by them? . . . for which I
> shall appeal to every one's own observation and experience. . . . *All
> ideas come from sensation or reflection.* . . . Our observation, em-
> ployed either about external sensible objects, or about the internal op-
> erations of our mind, perceived and reflected on by ourselves, is that
> which supplies our understandings with all the materials of thinking.
> These two are the fountains of knowledge, from whence all the ideas
> we have, or can naturally have, do spring. . . . Let any one examine
> his own thoughts, and thoroughly search into his understanding, and
> then let him tell me, whether all the original ideas he has there, are
> any other than of the objects of his senses, or of the operations of his
> mind considered as objects of his reflection. . . . [Locke, 1690, pp.
> 75f.]

In short, the human mind contains only two kinds of mental in-
gredients: First, there are the present sensory experiences (e.g., *sensa-*

tions: red, cold, etc.). Second, there are the residues they leave behind— what we would now call *images* (e.g., the thoughts of red, cold, etc., which may come to mind even when there is no real red object before our eyes, or cold object to touch).

The combinations in which sensations and images occur together in our mind are governed by the *laws of association:* briefly, if the sensation "red" occurs frequently together with that of "sweet" (as in strawberry jam), eventually a red sensation or image will bring to mind an image of sweetness, and vice versa.

If this reasoning is valid, there are very serious limits on the ideas which we can trust; only material objects affect our senses, and all our ideas must derive from these (Locke, 1690, pp. 110f.):

> As simple ideas are observed to exist in several combinations united together, so the mind has a power to consider several of them united together as one idea; . . . Ideas thus made up of several simple ones put together, I call *complex*; such as are beauty, gratitude, a man, an army, the universe; which, though complicated of various simple ideas, or complex ideas made up of simple ones, yet are, when the mind pleases, considered each by itself as one entire thing, and signified by one name. . . . I believe we shall find, if we warily observe the originals of our notions, that even *the most abstruse* ideas, how remote soever they may seem from sense, or from any operations of our own minds, are yet only such as the understanding frames to itself, by repeating and joining together ideas, that it had either from objects of sense, or from its own operations about them. . . .

It was as an attempt to answer this materialistic philosophy that Berkeley took the next step, maintaining that we cannot have any trustworthy ideas about even the material objects of the physical world. The nature-nurture problem first appears as a specific systematic perceptual issue in the course of this attempt.

BERKELEY: THE EMPIRICIST THEORY OF SPACE PERCEPTION. Specifically, Berkeley undertook to prove that we cannot sense directly the characteristics of the physical world, such as spatial distance.[2] Berkeley's analysis was extremely influential. We will follow four stages of this fundamental investigation, considering first the abstract idea of distance;

[2] He undertook this to prove an epistemological point—as one step in what was essentially a brilliant attempt to prove the existence of God, even without invoking innate ideas of Him. (Briefly, everything we know comes through our senses; therefore nothing can be said to exist if we do not perceive it; we cannot directly perceive the "real world" of physics, i.e., size, distance, etc.; therefore, the real world doesn't "exist," so far as any of our perceptions of it are concerned; how then do we account for the consistency of our sensations, which are arranged *as though* there were a real world? Because the real world exists by virtue of God's perception of it.)

second, the idea of the distance of a far-off object; third, the idea of the distance of a near object, and finally, after having demolished the idea of space as a direct or immediate perception (i.e., as a sensation), we will see what happened to our ideas of all the other characteristics of the familiar world of things and people.

Case 1: Abstract distance. "Distance of itself [i.e., empty space without objects] cannot be immediately seen. For, distance being a line directed endwise to the eye, it projects only one point in . . . the eye, which point remains . . . the same, whether the distance be longer or shorter" (Berkeley, 1709, p. 174). When we think we *"see"* distance, consequently, it must be only indirectly thought of, being brought to mind by some other idea. So much for the idea of *abstract distance,* or *space.*

Before we continue Berkeley's investigation, we must consider briefly an earlier examination of the problem of visual space perception, undertaken against an artistic rather than a philosophical background. When an artist wants to draw a recognizable scene—say, a landscape or a countryside—his intention is as follows (though he doesn't usually phrase it this way): to create a stimulus pattern to which people will respond in more or less the same way as they would have responded to the countryside itself. But the artist cannot duplicate the countryside with real bark or real trees, real clouds in real distance, etc.—he must *extract* those aspects which are necessary in order to obtain the desired responses, yet which can be arrayed on a flat surface of canvas or paper. The great Leonardo daVinci is responsible for the formal discovery of most of these aspects, or depth "cues" (Boring, 1942, pp. 303f.). Like the artist's canvas, the retina of the eye (the light-sensitive surface at the back of the eye) may be considered bidimensional. The stimulus patterns which are necessary for us to perceive depth when we look at a picture on a flat surface are, at the same time, the stimulus patterns which must be on the retinae of our eyes if we are to perceive distance and solidity when we look at the objects in the world around us (so long as we use only one eye, and remain stationary). The most familiar of these factors—now known as "secondary depth cues," for reasons we will soon see—are illustrated and named in Figure 26, together with drawings which show why some of them *are* "cues" (indications) of depth. The reader should acquaint himself with these—especially *size perspective*—before proceeding with Berkeley's analysis.

Now, as to the distance of specific objects far away in space:
Case 2: The perception of far objects' distances.

   . . . the estimate we make of the distance of objects *considerably remote* is rather an act of judgment grounded on experience than of sense . . . when an object appears faint and small which at a near distance I have experienced to make a vigorous and large appearance, I

. . . conclude it to be far off.—And this . . . is the result of experience; without which, from the faintness and littleness, I should not have inferred anything concerning the distance of objects. . . . [This must be true, since there is] . . . no apparent *necessary* connexion between small distance and a large and strong appearance, or between great distance and a little and faint appearance. [Berkeley, 1709, p. 176f.]

That is, a "large and strong appearance" *might* result from a far-off object (and sometimes does: cf. Figure 26). Thus Berkeley maintained we cannot directly sense the distance of far objects. But what about near objects? Can we see their distance directly? After all, our two eyes make a smaller angle as they converge on far-off objects (Figure 27), and isn't there a very necessary and *innate* connection between an obtuse angle and near distance, and an acute angle and farther distance?

Case 3: Convergence and near objects. In answer, Berkeley (1709) notes: "I appeal to any one's experience, whether, upon sight of an object, he computes its distance by the bigness of the angle made by the meeting of the two optic axes" (p. 179). Such angles exist only in the mathematical analysis which one can make on paper, or can observe by watching someone else's eyes while they converge. However, Berkeley proposed that when we converge our own eyes, we do receive a sensation from the muscular contractions, which, because of previous experiences, eventually comes to suggest the idea of greater or lesser distance:

Not that there is any natural or necessary connexion between the sensation we perceive by the turn of the eyes and greater or lesser distance. But—because the mind has, by constant experience, found the different sensations corresponding to the different dispositions of the eyes to be attended each with a different degree of distance in the object—there has grown an habitual . . . connexion between these two sorts of ideas . . . From all of which it follows, that the judgment we make of the distance of an object . . . is entirely the result of experience . . . a man born blind, being made to see, would at first have no idea of Distance by sight: the sun and stars, the remotest objects as well as the nearer, would all seem to be in his eye, or rather in his mind . . . . each . . . as near to him as the perceptions of pain or pleasure, or the most inward passions of his soul. [p. 187] . . . Having a long time experienced certain ideas perceivable by *touch*—as distance . . . and solidity—to have been connected with certain ideas of sight, I do, upon perceiving these ideas of sight, forthwith conclude what tangible ideas are, by the . . . ordinary course of nature [likely] to follow [p. 191].

What is true concerning distance is true for all the other characteristics of the objects around us as well. Size, for example—is this a charac-

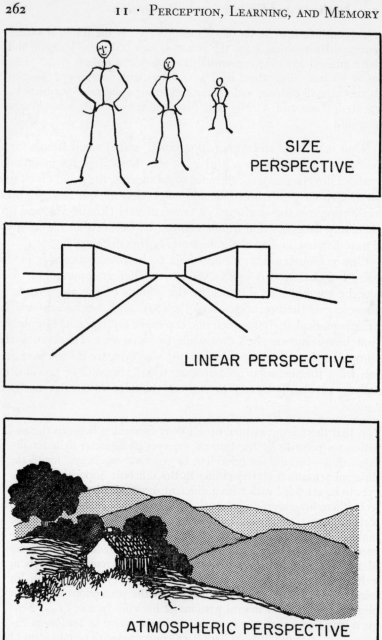

FIGURE 26a. Monocular secondary depth cues. Illustrations of size perspective, linear perspective, and atmospheric perspective.

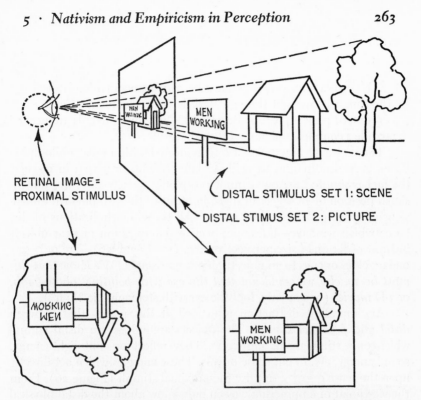

RETINAL IMAGE =
PROXIMAL STIMULUS

DISTAL STIMULUS SET 1: SCENE

DISTAL STIMUS SET 2: PICTURE

FIGURE 26b. Illustration of interposition. As this diagram shows, the "cues" of interposition may be projected as retinal images by at least two different sets of distal stimuli—the actual scene and a picture of the scene. In fact, an infinite number of sets of distal stimuli will do so. This is also true for size perspective and linear perspective.

teristic of the object itself, rather than a built-up idea in the mind of the observer? No, Berkeley maintained, for the following reasons:

Case 4: The perception of size.

The magnitude of the object which exists [outside] the mind . . . continues always invariably the same: but, the visible object still changing as you approach to or recede . . . hath no fixed and determinate greatness. Whenever therefore we speak of the magnitude of any thing, for instance, a tree or a house, we must mean the tangible magnitude [e.g., the idea of size as given by the sense of touch]. . . . Moreover, . . . the very same quantity of visible extension which in the figure of a tower doth suggest the idea of great magnitude shall in the figure of a man suggest the idea of much smaller magnitude . . . owing to the experience we have had of the usual bigness of a tower and a man. . . . [pp. 197–8].

As we see distance so we see magnitude. And we see both in the same way that we see shame or anger in the looks of a man . . .

Without . . . experience we should no more have taken blushing for a sign of shame than of gladness [pp. 202f.].

EXAMINATION AND SUMMARY OF THE EMPIRICIST CONTRIBUTION. By the time we have got through Berkeley's development (Cases 1–4), the *empiricist* position is fully developed. Only minor details are needed to provide a complete "picture of the mind."

These elegant arguments are rediscovered with a great philosophic flurry, every so often, as we will see later (cf. pp. 309–10); in essence, the fact is simply this: one cannot completely specify the three-dimensional position of an object in space in terms of the two physical dimensions of a flat (static) retinal image.[3] All the visual indications of distance which we have—linear perspective, interposition of near objects in front of far ones, size-perspective, etc. (see Figure 26)—are only secondary clues or cues to an object's depth or distance. *We know that this must be so, else we could not fool the eye with painting, photograph, or 3-D movies* (or similarly, fool the ear with stereophonic "hi-fi").

An important distinction is needed at this point—that between *distal* and *proximal stimuli*. The objects around us are distal stimuli which only stimulate us indirectly. They reflect or emit light-energy, sound-energy, etc. to our sense organs. These energies which act directly upon the sense organs comprise the proximal stimuli (Figure 26). From the viewpoint of empiricism, we can only know about the distal physical world—about space and the objects which are at rest or in motion within it—through these proximal stimuli. Figure 26b shows two quite different, alternate possible distal spatial arrangements which could give rise to the same proximal stimuli.

The methods employed in these arguments were not merely logical exercises by philosophers. An essential ingredient was the observation of the facts of vision and of thought—i.e., psychological investigation (although of a highly restricted type). Thus Berkeley's method of proof actually involves a considerable amount of self-observation:

And I believe whoever will look narrowly into his own thoughts, and examine what he means by saying that he sees this or that thing at a distance, will agree with me, that what he sees only *suggests* to his understanding that, after having passed a certain distance, *to be measured by the motion of the body, which is perceivable by touch,* he shall come to perceive such and such tangible ideas . . . there are two sorts of objects apprehended by the eye—the one primarily and immediately, the other secondarily and by intervention of the former . . . the first sort . . . may, indeed, grow greater or smaller, more

[3] Similarly, a moving object would seem to require four sets of dimensions, including the dimension of time, and, even with the latter, the image on our retina contains only three dimensions—at least this is true, *geometrically* speaking.

confused, . . . or more faint. But they do not, cannot approach or recede from us. Whenever we say an object is at a distance, . . . we must always mean it of the latter sort, which properly belong to the touch, and are not so truly perceived as *suggested* by the eye, in like manner as thoughts by the ear. . . . No sooner do we hear the words of a familiar language . . . but the ideas corresponding thereto present themselves to our minds: . . . so closely are they united that it is not in our power to keep out the one except we conclude the other also. We even act in all respects as if we heard the very thoughts themselves. . . . Hence it is we find it so difficult to discriminate between the immediate and mediate objects of sight, and are so prone to attribute to the former what belongs only to the latter [1709, pp. 191, 194f.].

In fact, both Berkeley and Locke employed, in a sense, one real experiment. Locke quoted a letter, which Berkeley in turn quoted from Locke, and both of them rested arguments on the findings of this "experiment":

> . . . I shall here insert a problem of . . . the learned and worthy Mr. Molineaux, which he was pleased to send me in a letter some months since; and it is this: "Suppose a man *born* blind, and now adult, and taught by his *touch* to distinguish between a cube and a sphere of the same metal, and nighly of the same bigness, so as to tell, when he felt one and the other, which is the cube, which the sphere. Suppose then the cube and the sphere placed on a table, and the blind man be made to see; . . . [could he] now distinguish and tell which is the globe, which the cube?" [No.] "For though he has obtained the experience of how a globe, how a cube, affects his touch; yet he has not yet obtained the experience, that what affects his touch so or so, must affect his sight so or so; or that a protuberant angle in the cube, that pressed his hand unequally, shall appear to his eye as it does in the cube" [Locke, 1690, p. 100].

The reader should notice, however, that even though this experiment and its conclusion were quite convincing to Locke and Berkeley, it was quite imaginary. We will return to Mr. Molineaux' experiment later (p. 317), in somewhat more solid (but modified) form.

The use of psychological methods to support philosophical theory led to a first division of interest. Philosophers continued to inquire what these new assumptions implied about the nature of our ideas of truth, causation, etc.,[4] but a certain amount of interest was also turned to the

---

[4] Much that is characteristic of contemporary philosophy or theory of science, as well as the very hardy metaphysical weed of *solipsism*, originated in these assumptions as to how we perceive and how the mind works—untested assumptions (cf. Michotte, 1946). These led without pause into our most familiar philosophy of science; consider Hume's two definitions of *cause*. (1) " . . . an object precedent and contiguous to another, and where all the objects resembling the former are placed in

new problems raised about the nature of mind, and to the new approach to these problems. Those philosophers most concerned with such matters (and that must include Locke, Berkeley, and Hume) were the first systematic psychologists.

The Case for Nurture Continued: the Associationists

The goal of these early armchair psychologists was nothing less than the complete understanding of the human mind: to discover the elements of which all of our ideas and thoughts were, in various combinations, supposed to be composed. Just as the chemist can explain the millions of different substances around us in terms of a vastly smaller number of elements which, in various combinations, will account for all the properties of these substances, the associationists hoped to reduce the apparently infinite diversity of thoughts and ideas—the myriad objects and their relationships which we may perceive or think about—to the combinations of a limited number of mental elements. Hartley and Mill best typify the program: ". . . the *ideas of sensation* are the elements of which all the rest are compounded" (Hartley, p. 314), and ". . . the task which was proposed . . . [by Mill] is an attempt to reach the simplest elements which by their combination generate the manifold complexity of our mental states, and to assign the laws of those elements, and . . . of their combination" (Mill, 1869, p. x).

This purpose logically imposes certain limitations on subject-matter and method; in order for any set of elements to be scientifically useful, they should meet certain requirements: (1) they must, of course, be fewer than the objects one wishes to explain, or nothing has been gained by their use; (2) the rules for their use must be specified, so that the appropriate conditions of analysis are known and the results can be communicated; (3) they must be predictable and stable, so that what any given element contributes to the result of one combination of elements, it will also contribute in any other combination (or at least, if the effect of that element changes, it does so in a predictable manner: see pp. 296–300); (4) finally, the qualities of the elements must be such that, when properly combined, all the important properties of each object we wish to analyze will be explained, with nothing left over to necessitate additional factors for each case which arises.

ASSOCIATIONIST ASSUMPTIONS AND METHODS.   The methods of the associationists (and of the empiricist philosophers) were those of

---

a like relation of priority and contiguity to those objects that resemble the latter," and (2) ". . . An object precedent and contiguous to another, and so united with it in the imagination, that the idea of the one determines the mind to form a more lively idea of the other" (Hume, 1739, p. 172).

introspective observation (i.e., self-observation) and *logical analysis*, both of which we have already seen exemplified in Berkeley's arguments. Their assumptions about how the mind works determined the nature both of their problems and their methods:

First, it was assumed that the mind can in some fashion step back and observe its own functioning (*reflection*), and that such self-observation does not affect that which is being observed.

> By reflection, . . . I . . . mean that notice which the mind takes of its own operations, and the manner of them, by reason whereof there come to be ideas of these operations in the understanding [Locke, 1690, p. 76].

Second, it was assumed that the elements of consciousness (sensations and images) are stable, independent units into which experience can be analyzed. That is, these elements must survive unchanged the various combinations into which they may enter, otherwise the task cannot be performed:

> Though the qualities that affect our senses are, in the things themselves, so united and binded that there is no separation, . . . yet it is plain the ideas they produce in the mind enter by the senses simple and unmixed. . . . and there is nothing can be plainer to a man than the clear and distinct perception he has of these simple ideas; which, being each in itself uncompounded, contains in it nothing but one uniform appearance or conception in the mind, and is not distinguishable into different ideas [Locke, 1690, p. 83].

Third, there must be some lawful method, which we can discover, by which these elements come to be combined; if they got stuck together in some undiscoverable fashion, merely knowing what the elements are would get us no closer to explaining the thoughts which are supposedly composed of them. In the words of Hume (1739):

> As all simple ideas may be separated by the imagination, and may be united again in what form it pleases, nothing wou'd be more unaccountable than the operations of that faculty, were it not guided by some universal principles . . . Were ideas entirely loose and unconnected, chance alone wou'd join them; and 't is impossible the same simple ideas should fall regularly into complex ones (as they commonly do) without some bond of union among them, some associating quality, by which one idea naturally introduces another [p. 10].

As Hartley (1740), the first of the associationist psychologists (see p. 266), formulated this process of association:

> *Sensations, by being often repeated, leave certain Vestiges, Types, or Images, of themselves, which may be called, Simple Ideas of Sensation* . . . it seems reasonable to expect, that, if a single sensation can

leave a perceptible effect, trace, or vestige, for a short time, a sufficient repetition of a sensation may leave a perceptible effect of the same kind, but of a more permanent nature [pp. 56f.] . . . *Any Sensations, A, B, C, etc., by being associated with one another a sufficient Number of Times, get such a Power over the corresponding Ideas a, b, c, etc. that any one of the Sensations A, when impressed alone, shall be able to excite in the Mind, b, c, etc. the Ideas of the Rest* [p. 65].

Lastly, what are the combining laws by which associations form? Will just any sensation stick to any other sensation? At first it was held that sensations which were related to each other in certain ways, would tend to be associated more easily and more strongly than others:

The qualities, from which this association arises, and by which the mind is after this manner convey'd from one idea to another, are three, *viz*. RESEMBLANCE, CONTIGUITY in time or place, and CAUSE and EFFECT [Hume, 1739, p. 11].

But these special laws for combining the psychological elements (i.e., "resemblance" and "cause and effect") have certain drawbacks, which are particularly important to a thoroughgoing empiricist: (1) It is uneconomical to have several laws, if it turns out that one will do. (2) "Resemblances" etc. are difficult to measure—can we always decide whether sensation A is more similar to sensation B than it is to sensation C? (3) Most important of all: a relationship is not a *thing*, although it depends upon things.

This last point is subtle, but important. "Smaller than" cannot be seen, but one object may appear smaller than another. No idea of a relationship can exist in the mind, by the empiricist doctrine, only the ideas compounded of sensations and images arising from specific objects (cf. p. 259). How, then, can relationships affect the laws of association? Let us see the basic tools of associationism at work in the hands of James Mill, the most thoroughgoing of the associationists, as he tackles this psychological problem.

ASSOCIATIONIST CONTENT: THE DISSECTION OF PERCEIVED OBJECTS AND THEIR RELATIONSHIPS.   James Mill undertook to analyze these ideas of relationship by careful self-observation. The *law of frequency of repetition* was long considered to be one of the rules by which ideas become associated with each other; to Mill (1869) it became the basic principle:

The causes of strength in association seem all to be resolvable into two; the vividness of the associated feelings; and the frequency of the association . . . we convey not a very precise meaning, when we speak of the vividness of sensations and ideas [pp. 83f.]. . . . Next, we have to consider frequency of repetition; which is the most . . . important cause of the strength of our associations. . . . The process becomes very perceptible to us, when . . . we proceed to learn a . . . foreign language. At the first lesson, we are told . . . the meaning of perhaps twenty words. But it is not joining the word and its meaning once, that will make the word suggest its meaning to us another time. We repeat the two in conjunction, till we think the meaning so well associated with the word, that whenever the word occurs to us, the meaning will occur along with it. . . . By force of repetition the meaning is associated, at last, with every word of the language, and so perfectly, that the one never occurs to us without the other [pp. 87–9].

As to what a perceived (or thought-of) object consists of, consider a tree or a house (Mill, 1869).

Case 5: Analysis of an object.

In using the names . . . of what I call objects, I am referring . . . only to my own sensations . . . in a particular state of . . . concomitance. Particular sensations of sight, of touch, of the muscles, are the sensations, to the ideas of which, colour, extension . . . taste, smell, so coalescing as to appear one idea, I give the name, idea of a tree [p. 93]. [These components are not always observable, since] . . . simple ideas, by strong association, run together and form complex ideas . . . two complex ideas may be united . . . in the same manner as two or more simple ideas coalesce into one. . . . Some of the most familiar objects with which we are acquainted furnish instances of these. . . . Brick is one complex idea, mortar is another . . . these . . . with ideas of position and quantity, compose my idea of a wall. . . . In the same manner my complex idea of glass, and wood, and others, compose my . . . idea of a window; and these . . . ideas, united together, compose my idea of a house . . . [pp. 114ff.].

In short, we do not *sense* a house, nor can we have any abstract idea of one—only the sum of all the simple ideas ("red," "hard," etc.) which originated in simple frequency of sensory association. Why do we not normally notice these complexities? Presumably, because of the strength of the associations between the sensations. Note this well: *in order to carry his empiricism through consistently, Mill was forced to assume the existence of components which he could not observe,* as the next example shows.

Case 6: Unnoticeable elements.

Where two or more ideas have been often repeated together, and the association has become very strong, they sometimes spring up in such close combination as not to be distinguishable. Some cases of sensation are analogous. For example: when a wheel, on the seven parts of which the seven prismatic colors are respectively painted, is made to revolve rapidly, it appears . . . white. By the rapidity of the succession, the several sensations cease to be distinguishable. . . . Ideas, also, which have been so often conjoined, that whenever one exists in the mind, the others immediately exist along with it, seem to run into one another, to coalesce, as it were, and out of many to form one idea; which idea, however in reality complex, appears to be no less simple than any of those of which it is compounded. . . . It is to this great law of association, that we trace the formation of our ideas of what we call external objects; that is, the ideas of a certain number of sensations, received together so frequently that they coalesce [Mill, 1869, pp. 91–3].

In fact, shortly thereafter, Mill presents an analysis which does two things at once: (1) It accounts for the fact that certain ideas or perceptions seem to be *innately* connected to each other, even though they really are not. (2) As we will see, *it really argues implicitly that we cannot observe any of the fundamental elements!*

Case 7: The origin of apparently necessary connections between ideas.

Some ideas are by frequency and strength of association so closely combined, that they cannot be separated. If one exists, the others exist along with it, in spite of whatever effort we make to disjoin them . . . it is not in our power to think of colour, without thinking of extension. . . . We have seen colour constantly in combination with extension, spread as it were, upon a surface. We have never seen it except in this connection . . . . and so close is the association, that it is not in our power to dissolve it. . . . Of all the cases of this important law of association, there is none more extraordinary than . . . the acquired perceptions of sight. . . . I see, from my window, trees, and meadows, and horses . . . each of its proper size, of its proper form, and at its proper distance; and these particulars appear as immediate informations of the eye, as the colours which I see . . . Yet . . . the sight . . . of distance . . . is in reality a complex state of consciousness; . . . a number of ideas, . . . so closely combined by association, that they appear not one idea, but one sensation [Mill, 1869, pp. 93–6].

What Mill has said really implies that we cannot, after all, observe the basic mental elements of which the world we perceive is composed. We will meet this difficulty again in the expositions of thoroughgoing empiricism (i.e., of discovering, by use of the method of introspective analysis, that the method of introspective analysis—and its assumptions —is in fact inadequate).

RELATIONSHIPS.   But what about relationships between objects; how do we come to perceive these? Since the mind can contain nothing which does not derive from the sensations, any abstract ideas of *relation-*

ship—such as greater, or smaller, more (or less) similar, x-causes-it to-do-so-and-so, etc.—must really not be directly experienced, but must instead be built up out of other elements. The most important of these was, as we have seen, *resemblance* or *similarity*, and Mill easily reduces it to a special case of the law of frequency.

Case 8: Similarity. Consider the concept of "similarity" (or "resemblance"): ". . . we are accustomed to see like things together. When we see a tree, we generally see more trees than one; when we see an ox, we generally see more oxen than one . . . we may refer resemblance to the law of frequency, of which it seems to form only a particular case" (Mill, 1869, p. 111). We have already seen the relationship of cause and effect to be similarly analyzable (see footnote 4).[5]

EXAMINATION AND SUMMARY OF THE ASSOCIATIONIST POSITION. Most of these associationist assumptions are still current in one form or another, although each has been repeatedly attacked, abandoned, or revised. The armchair methods do not lend themselves to experimental use; they involve no controlled changes of situation, they offer no statement of how much or how little reliance can be put on a given observation, nor of how to reproduce the observation. The conclusions that were reached had weight only to the extent that they were congenial to those to whom they were described.

Nevertheless, the approach was a convincing one, and many of its assumptions can be found, in various combinations, scattered widely through today's psychology and philosophy, and through other sciences which must occasionally draw upon either of these disciplines. Today associationism's survival is astonishing, in the face of logical attack and in view of the inconsistency between its assumptions and its own findings (see Cases 6 and 7). It would seem that its greatest virtue is the absence of any really plausible, specific, systematic alternative.

So far we have sampled the investigations themselves, which consisted of discussion and dissertation, methods congenial to philosophers; for most of the cases which follow, we will have to present brief descriptions of each case, rather than present excerpts, because our story con-

[5] An even more thoroughgoing reduction of "similarity" to sheer *frequency of association* appears in a recent extension of Mill's treatment: "In the first instance, it is on the whole more likely that receptor organs sensitive to physically similar stimuli will be excited at the same time, and it is therefore to be expected that especially close connections will be formed. . . . Where the physical stimuli can vary continuously in one or more dimensions, as in the case of light or sound, mixtures or bands of various frequencies of light or sound waves usually occur together and those which are more closely similar in a physical sense probably occur more frequently together." From Friedrich Hayek, *The Sensory Order,* pp. 62, 63, published by the University of Chicago Press. Copyright 1952 by the University of Chicago. Reprinted by permission of the publisher.

tinues with the development of experimental psychology and its laboratory research.

EXPERIMENTAL PSYCHOLOGY: SENSORY PHYSIOLOGISTS AND PHYSIOLOGICAL PSYCHOLOGISTS

THE EARLIEST experimental psychologists did not come from the ranks of the philosophers via associationism; instead, they started as physiologists. The division between sensory physiology and early experimental psychology is not easy to draw. Frequently major work was performed in one discipline by an investigator who considered that he was working in the other. A brief word about this background may be in order.

THE PHYSIOLOGICAL PSYCHOLOGISTS: BACKGROUND.   This second line of development may also be picked up with Descartes. In the Age of Reason, one readily believed that all matter in motion, which includes living creatures, can be understood in terms of cause and effect. Descartes showed that animals could be considered as complex reflexmachines, whose behavior is merely the intricate outcome of physical cause and effect in the following schema:

Purely physical energies (light, sound, etc.) excite motions in the sensory nerves, and these change the distribution of fluid pressures at the brain, and thence in the motor nerves; these changes in pressure move the muscles—and hence the whole organism. That is, the animal acts or behaves completely as a function of external and internal physical events, all of which are (in principle) subject to mechanical analysis. Descartes provided for man to be activated by a soul, in addition to regulation by these reflex mechanics. However, it was neither necessary nor helpful to retain the concept of the soul, if one sought to discover (and/ or speculate about) the detailed physical operation of the human body as a machine, i.e., if one assumed that it was possible to account for all human activity by physiological chains of cause and effect.

Behavior, from this viewpoint, is initiated by the effects of the physical world on the physical state of the brain, i.e., upon our "knowledge" of the world. Consequently, the job of tracking down the mechanisms by which knowledge about the physical world was gained through each individual's senses became a very important one. This job was the task of sensory physiology.

SENSORY PHYSIOLOGY: THE ELEMENTS OF VISION—LIGHT, COLOR AND SHADE.   Very simple observation shows us that our knowledge about the world is of several kinds: if we cover our ears, the speaker's lips move visibly, but no words are heard; if we close our eyes, his speech is audible, but no speaker can be seen. We have different senses through which we perceive the world, as a result of stimulation by different kinds of physical energies (or combinations of them).

For example, the retinae in our eyes are altered by the action of light (i.e., they are "sensitive" to light), and that is how we see whether light is present upon our retinae. Our knowledge of the world of sight however, is very much more detailed than this simple distinction of light vs. dark—we can tell a near man from a far one, a happy from a sad one, a man from an apple, a ripe apple from an unripe one, and so on, without apparent end. The world we see seems infinitely rich in distinctions and diversity. What mechanisms make this possible?

This problem is the counterpart of the one which faced the associationists. The latter had to find the elements of experience, the sensations; the sensory physiologists looked for the bodily processes underlying those sensations.[6]

THE DOCTRINE OF SPECIFIC NERVE ENERGIES.   Descartes had proposed that physical stimulation of the sense organs set in train a nervous process proceeding inward to the central portions of the nervous system, then outward to the musculature; physiologists later discovered this to be true. That is, there are at least two different classes of nerves: those which bring sensory information into the central nervous system, and those which carry orders out to the muscles.

Within this gross division of function, why not assume that each individual sensation we experience arises through the stimulation of a definite nerve fiber or group of fibers? This was formulated as the Law of Specific Nerve Energies by Johannes Müller, as follows:

> . . . *external agencies can give rise to no kind of sensation which cannot also be produced by internal causes, exciting changes in the condition of our nerves. . . . The same external cause also gives rise to different sensations in each sense, according to the special endowments of its nerve.* The mechanical influence of a blow, concussion, or pressure excites, for example, in the eye the sensation of light and colours . . . by exerting pressure upon the eye, when the eyelids are closed, we can give rise to the appearance of a luminous circle; by more gentle pressure the appearance of colours may be produced, and one colour may be made to change to another. . . . *Sensation consists in the sensorium receiving through the medium of the nerves, and as the result of the action of an external cause, a knowledge of certain qualities or conditions, not of external bodies, but of the nerves of sense themselves. . . . The immediate objects of the perception of our senses*

[6] At this point, we run into another problem handed on to psychology by philosophy—that of the relationship between *mind and body*. Except for one brief glance later on (p. 296), we will not concern ourselves with that issue here.

are merely particular states induced in the nerves, and felt as sensa-
tions . . . by the sensorium; but inasmuch as the nerves of the senses
are material bodies, and therefore participate in the properties of mat-
ter generally occupying space, being susceptible of vibratory motion,
and capable of being changed chemically as well as by the action of
heat and electricity, they make known to the sensorium, by . . . the
changes thus produced in them by external causes, not merely their
own condition, but also properties and changes of condition of external
bodies . . . [1843, pp. 707–14].

It soon became evident that it was not the individual nerves which are different for the different sensations, but rather the place in the brain to which each is connected. In short, the brain was supposed to be somewhat like a modern telephone center, with each incoming line servicing one, and only one, point on the switchboard. Presumably, if the sensory nerve coming to that point on the switchboard tagged "red-point-dead-ahead" is stimulated, that is what the individual sees.

The job then became one of identifying the receptors and end-organs responsible for each sensation we experience. For any two sensations which can be distinguished as different, there must exist at least two specific nerve energies. This, then, delineated the task of the sensory physiologist.

A DIGRESSION: THE ELEMENTS OF COLOR.   Let us turn tempo-rarily from the nature-nurture issue to an example which will illustrate the aim and procedures of the sensory physiologist—the study of the "basic elements" of color.

First, consider that we can see not only light and darkness—we actually can distinguish among a very great number of colors of light—reds, oranges, yellows, fuchsia, magenta, purple, maize, citron, violet, turquoise, etc., etc. People trained to notice and name color differences have listed some ten dozen distinguishable hues.

We know, since Newton's first experiments with the prismatic spectrum, that different wave-lengths (or "undulations") of light have something to do with the sensations of color or hue. Shall we assume that the retina contains ". . . an infinite number of particles, each capable of vibrating in perfect unison with every possible undulation?" Young stated:

From three simple sensations, with their combinations, we obtain seven primitive distinctions of colours; but the different proportions, in which they may be combined, afford a variety of traits beyond all calculation. The three simple sensations being red, green, and violet, the three binary combinations are yellow, consisting of red and green; crimson, of red and violet; and blue of green and violet; and the seventh in order is white light, composed of all three united [1807, p. 440].

It was found that (with certain qualifications) we can choose a set of three wave-lengths, such as 650 mμ (red), 530 mμ (green), and 460 mμ (blue), with which, when mixed in different proportions, we will be able to match any color we can see. Therefore, it seemed to be unnecessary to discover the mechanisms whereby we distinguish 128 different hues—all we need do is to discover how we see these primary hues, and then all of the rest can be explained as combinations of these elements.

The greatest of sensory physiologists, Hermann von Helmholtz, systematized Young's theory as follows:

1. There are three kinds of nerve fibers in the eye. The excitation of one kind produces the sensation of red; of the second, green; of the third, violet.

2. Light excites all three kinds of fibers, with an intensity which varies according to the wave-length of the light. The fibers which are sensitive to red, are excited most by light of the longest wave-length; those which are sensitive to violet are excited most by light of the smallest wave-length.

> Three kinds of photochemically decomposible substances are deposited in the end organs of the visual nerve fibres. . . . The three color values of the colors of the spectrum depend essentially upon the photochemical reaction of these three substances to the light. . . . By the disintegration of all the substances sensitive to light, the nerve fibre laden therewith, is set into a state of excitation. . . . [These three systems of fibres probably] act differently in the brain only for the reason that they are united to different functioning parts of the brain [1896, p. 581].

Thus we have come a long way toward solving the problem—at least for *color*. What explanation can we now offer from this viewpoint for the rest of the qualities of the world we see?

Light is reflected from an object in front of the eye (this object is called the *distal stimulus*), and this light is focused by the lens of the eye to fall upon the light-sensitive cells on the retina at the back of the eye (this projected image on the retina is called the *proximal stimulus*).

If the object reflects light predominantly in the neighborhood of 650 mμ, the red-sensitive retinal cells respond, and we see red; if the object reflects a nearly equal mixture of all the wave-lengths, all three types of cells are stimulated about equally and we see white (at least, according to the Young-Helmholtz theory discussed above). If the object reflects much light, many retinal cells will be excited in the stimulated region and they will discharge nerve impulses frequently; the object will then appear bright. If the object reflects little light, few fibers will be excited, with infrequent discharges, and the object will appear dark. If there is no light reaching the corresponding part of the retina, the object will appear black. We see that we now have a set of elements out of which to construct all the colors and shades which we can perceive through vision.

But what about the rest of what we see? The things we perceive are not only a collection of points of varying color and shade—they are objects in space, with characteristics of size, of position, of distance, of shape. What are the elements and underlying mechanisms for these? Quite simply: no new ones. *No receptor cells or specific nerve energies could be found for these spatial characteristics.* Therefore, in order to explain how we see size, position, distance, and shape, the sensory physiologist seemed pressed to leave behind his observations of actual bodily structure, and he had to turn instead to methods in which the only observations made were of psychological phenomena. This is the point at which sensory physiology ran up against the nature-nurture issue, and the stage at which the discipline of experimental psychology appeared.

EARLY EXPERIMENTAL PSYCHOLOGY: THE PHYSIOLOGICAL PSYCHOLOGISTS.   The work of sensory physiologist and associationist philosopher had converged in the attempt to give a complete picture of man, of his behavior, and of his conscious experience. As could be expected, a definite group of workers began to bring the experimental method to bear upon this potential science of mind. In the earliest stages it was impossible to distinguish closely between physiology and psychology. When Helmholtz studied retinal receptors, he was a sensory physiologist; when he attempted to explain how we see size, position, motion, shape, and distance, he was a psychologist.

It is only by its unified interest in psychology for its own sake, and by its self-conscious use of experimental procedures, that early experimental psychology is to be distinguished from its predecessors. As we shall see, these very differences soon forced the old conceptual system apart at the seams. However, despite its inadequacies, and despite repeated attacks from widely divergent sources, that conceptual system remains as a picture of man which has never been completely replaced. We have seen this picture in somewhat fragmentary form. Let us review again this general standpoint, inherited from the empiricists, associationists, and sensory physiologists.

From the point of view of the physiological psychologist we do not directly *see* things, people, or the space in which they move. An object reflects light to the retina of our eye, this light stimulates the receptor cells upon which it falls, and it is always the aggregate of specific nerve energies thus aroused, not the object, nor the light from it, that causes the group of sensations we experience.

Envision a flat mosaic like a tile floor, built of sensitive elements, at the back of the eye: the *retina*. Each element, or receptor cell, is sensitive to light. These receptors, their sensitivities, and their specific nerve energies come in at least four different kinds: the *rods*, which are sensitive only to different degrees of light ("white," "gray," or "black"); and three kinds of *cones*, which are maximally sensitive to the wave-lengths of 650, 530, and 460 mμ, respectively.[7]

Equal stimulation of all the cones gives rise to white or gray; uniform lack of stimulation, to black; unequal stimulation, to the appropriate intermediate hues.

Out of this mosaic of light and shade and color, the world of space as we perceive it was thought to be constructed (via past experience) as we will describe in some detail for the qualities of *size, position, shape,* and *motion* of an *object*.

SIZE.   If the object is large (or near; see Figure 26), the proximal stimulus will cover a larger area of sensitive retinal cells than if the object is small (or far away).

> The same object seen at different distances will be depicted on the retina by images of different sizes and will subtend different visual angles. The farther it is away, the less its apparent size will be. Thus, . . . knowing the size of an object, a human being, for instance, we can estimate the distance from us . . . by means of the size of the image on the retina . . . similarly, artists arrange figures of persons and animals in landscapes to enable them to form some idea of the dimensions of other objects in the scene . . . this relation between distance and size . . . can only be acquired by long experience, and so it is not surprising that children are . . . apt to make big mistakes. I can recall when I was a boy going past the . . . chapel . . . where some people were standing in the belfry. I mistook them for dolls and asked my mother to reach up and get them for me, which I thought she could do [Helmholtz, 1910, pp. 282f.].

POSITION OR LOCALITY.   As Wundt stated in 1907,

---

[7] This theory of color vision—the Young-Helmholtz theory—held sway for so many years that many psychologists, physiologists, physicists, and medical men today believe it to be fact, as opposed to the long "discredited" Hering "four-color" theory, which was based instead on four primary hues: red, green, yellow, and blue. Within the decade, however, new data have been obtained which make some variations of the four-color theory much more acceptable (Hurvich and Jameson, 1955). The history of the methods by which the primary color elements were decided upon, and the recent work suggesting that the decision was in error, provides a valuable case history of concept and research in psychology and its related biological sciences.

All spacial ideas are arrangements either of *tactual* or of *visual sensations* [p. 115]. . . . With regard to its spatial attributes, every visual idea may be resolved into *two* factors: 1) the location of the single elements in relation to one another, and 2) their location in relation to the ideating subject [p. 128] . . . we immediately connect with the simplest possible impression of a point the idea of its *place* [p. 129]. Retinal impressions [like] . . . Tactual impressions can gain spacial qualities only through . . . local signs [p. 141; "local signs" being attributes of the sensation which indicate the position of its proximal stimulus on the retina, when coupled with sensations of strain which arise from the eye muscles].

SHAPE.   A shape, or two-dimensional form, is also, of course, a product of learning.

. . . [It] is an extent which is bounded . . . in a certain way. . . . As the eye follows different boundary lines, it traverses different distances and rests at points of different position. Different names have been given to the impressions which call forth in this way different complexes of sensation in and about the eye: circle, square, cross, etc. . . . After a time, these movements become unnecessary. The practiced retina is able to distinguish shape at a glance [Titchener, 1902, pp. 173f.].

MOTION.

Movement is a continuous change of position. The materials for the idea of movement are, therefore, in part the same as those for the idea of locality. Our idea of movement is made up, in part, of the ideas of an object in different position. The other factor in the idea of movement is the persistence of sensation after the cessation of stimulus. By the help of an after-image or of memory we are able to perceive an object, as it were, in two places at once: in the place which it has just left, and in the place to which it has just come [Titchener, 1902, pp. 178f.].

THE PERCEPTION OF AN OBJECT.   In short, the *size, position,* and *shape* of a perceived object depend upon the number and pattern of retinal receptors which are stimulated; the perceived *motion* of an object depends upon how these variables change in time; and the perceived *color* and *brightness* depend upon what kind of receptors are excited, and how rapidly they fire nerve impulses to the brain.

The fundamental thesis of the empiricist theory is:

The sensations of the senses are tokens for our consciousness, it being left to our intelligence to learn how to comprehend their meaning. The tokens which we get by the sense of sight may vary in intensity and . . . in colour. There may also be some other differences between them depending on the place of the retina that is stimulated, a so-called *local sign*. . . . We also feel the *degree of innervation* which we cause to be communicated to the nerves of the ocular muscles . . . any other sensations, not only of sight, but of the other senses also, produced by a visible object when we move our eyes or our body so as to look at the object from different sides or to touch it, etc., may be learned by experience. The content of all these possible sensations united in a total *idea* forms our idea of the body; and we call it perception when it is reinforced by actual sensations; . . . This is the actual . . . content of any such idea of a definite object. It has no other; . . . The only psychic activity required for this purpose is the regularly recurrent association between two ideas which have often been connected before. The oftener this association occurs, the more firm and obligatory it becomes [Helmholtz, 1910, pp. 533*f*.].

We see that, in the main, the explanation of our perception of the world remained pretty much the same, some 200 years after Berkeley:

It is only by experience that we ever could have learned about the laws of illumination, shading, atmospheric haze, geometrical concealment of one body by another, the sizes of men and animals, etc. At any rate, no advocate of the intuition theory has yet ventured to maintain that the origin of these apperceptions was intuitive [Helmholtz, 1910, p. 292].

However, something important had now changed: the purpose for which the nature-nurture problem was being considered was now quite different, as we will see.

Evolution of the Empiricist Movement

The empiricist philosophers had investigated the nature-nurture issue for religious and philosophical purposes (pp. 257–9). The question was whether there is any necessary connection between our perceptions of the world and the world itself, and the empiricist answer was *no*. Closely related to this problem, however, was a psychological question, viz., how do we perceive the world? This is the question which the associationists and the physiological psychologists undertook to answer —not in order to prove a religious point nor to settle an epistemological issue, but in order to understand how man's mind works. This purpose is a very different one, and it changed both the nature-nurture issue and the methods used to answer it (even though the people who tackled the problem were usually too close to the change to see that it had occurred).

As a philosophical problem it had been important to show that a particular physical distance would not *necessarily* be perceived as being that distance, and vice versa. As a psychological problem the question is merely whether (or to what extent) a particular physical distance *is* perceived as such. To the philosopher the issue was important because it underlay all fields of knowledge, and affected our tests of truth and certainty. To psychologists the issue has only two proper reasons for importance: (1) if it furthers our understanding of some specific, testable psychological problems; (2) it if contributes to our general picture of mental processes.

The early sensory physiologist, with the neurological techniques then available, could find no anatomical structures which might be sensitive to depth, distance, objects, form, etc. The choice then seemed simple: either (1) we deny that there are any structures which are sensitive to the distance of objects, and adopt the empiricist position, or (2) we continue to search for sensory mechanisms which *can* respond to distance. In other words, empiricism offered a means of filling the vast gap between the existing knowledge about sensations and about the peripheral sense organs, on the one hand, and the world of things and people in which we live and act, on the other hand. The latter were presumed to be built up out of the former, and it was this belief which made the study of the sensations important—and which resulted in the failure to experiment on any of the so-called secondary cues (Figure 26, p. 263), even though they turn out to be in fact stronger than the so-called primary cues (as we will see in Case 14). The empiricist philosophers' conclusions had biased the psychologists' imagination.

But the empiricist philosophers were not completely alone in influencing the development of the psychological problem of nature vs. nurture in perception. Let us now turn, very briefly, to the *nativist philosophers.*

The Nativist Philosophers and Psychologists

Descartes, with whom we started this story, held that we are born with certain innate and valid ideas of size, form, position, motion, etc. We have seen how an opposed line of philosophical empiricism developed into a tradition of psychological investigation, culminating in Helmholtz.

Immanuel Kant restored authority to the nativist viewpoint in philosophy. His argument, simplified to bear on our present issue, is that the categories into which we organize our sensations must themselves be determined by the nature of our minds, not by the world in itself (which of course we can never know except as our minds categorize it); hence the concept of space must be innate.

There were really two points involved in Kant's nativism. One was the philosophical one, which need not concern us further. The other was a psychological question: even if one grants that the abstract idea of space may be an innate characteristic of our thoughts, we still have a concrete set of problems—what are the relationships between specific stimulus arrangements and specific perceptions of spatial arrangements of objects, and to what extent are these specific relationships learned or innate?

Kant may or may not "refute" Berkeley in philosophy, but it was still necessary to find the receptor organs and specific nerve energies for the sensations of depth, even if one wished to accept depth perception as being innate. How was this to be done? One answer was provided by a revised theory of binocular disparity (i.e., of the role played by the somewhat different images received by the two eyes [see Figure 27]), as discussed in the next two cases. This "depth cue" had been brought

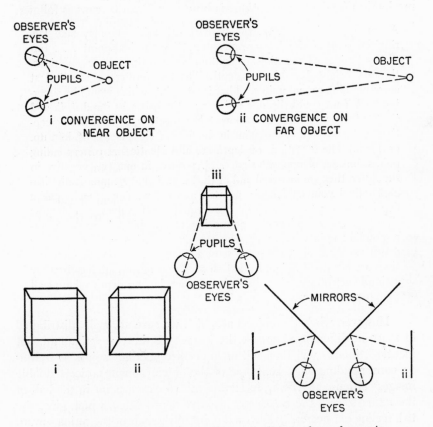

FIGURE 27. Binocular depth cues. The upper diagram shows changes in binocular convergence as a function of distance. The lower diagram shows how binocular disparity serves as a cue to depth: i and ii are the images received by the left eye and the right eye, respectively, when the observer fixates cube iii. If image i is presented to the left eye, and ii to the right eye, by a device such as the stereoscope (on right), the observer will also perceive the cube iii.

under experimental investigation by Charles Wheatstone (1838), who noted that ". . . the same object in relief is, when viewed by a different eye, seen from two points of sight at a distance from each other equal to the line joining the two eyes. What would be the visual effect of simultaneously presenting to each eye, instead of the object itself, its projection on a plane surface as it appears to that eye? . . . the most complex figures of three dimensions may be accurately represented to the mind, by presenting their two perspective projections to the two retinae" (pp. 10–13).

THE THEORY OF INNATE SIGNS OF DISTANCE.   A somewhat simplified version of Hering's theory, which presents a possible receptor mechanism for depth perception via binocular disparity, runs as follows:

> As an illustration of . . . the nativistic theories, we may take Hering's account of visual space-perception. Every retinal point . . . furnishes, besides its sensations of light and colour, three space-sensations, those of height, breadth and depth. The two former are identical at corresponding retinal points. [That is, at points which would be superimposed if we could slip one retina over the other, as i and i', iii and iii' in Figure 28. These sensations, taken together, furnish the perception of the position of the point in the field of view, i.e., right, left, up, or down.] The sensations of depth are also identical at corresponding points, but are of opposite sign, . . . positive in one eye, negative in the other; they are identical and of the same sign at symmetrically situated retinal points. [That is, points i and i' have equal and opposite depth values, points i and iii' have equal depth values of the same sign.] . . . Every binocular perception of an object imaged on corresponding points has, then, the average direction and the average depth value of all these space sensations. But . . . the depth-sensations are of opposite sign; so that all such perceptions are localized, by a simple act of sensation, in a plane which has no depth-value at all [Titchener, 1926, pp. 337f.].

However, when the objects at which we gaze are really distributed in space at different distances, the images on the two retinae are not identical; images will then fall on non-corresponding points as well as on corresponding ones, i.e., some of the object(s) will project "double images" (Figure 28). Now, in Hering's theory, each point in the half of the retina toward the ears has a negative depth value, which gives rise to a feeling of "nearer," while each point in the half of the retina toward the nose has a positive depth value, which gives rise to a feeling of "farther." Consider points at some distance from the observer, along the direction of the line-of-sight.

> Each such point presents a . . . double-image which falls on symmetrical halves of the retina, which, for example, . . . fall on the

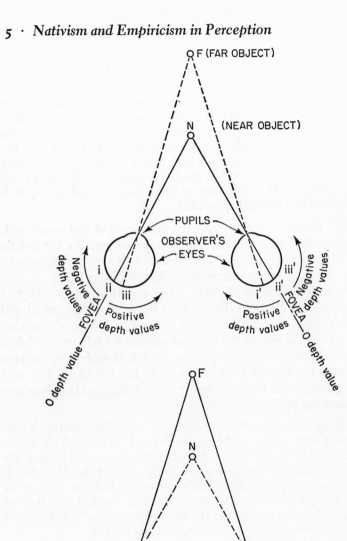

FIGURE 28. Double images in Hering's theory. When the eyes are fixed on the near point, N, its image falls on the fovea of each eye (ii and ii′); the images of the far point fall on iii and i′. Since both of these have positive depth values, F appears farther than N. Similarly, when the eyes are fixed on the far point, F, images of N fall at i and iii′, both of which have negative depth values; again N appears nearer than F.

outer half of the retina when the stimulus-point lies nearer than the fixation-point. [That is, nearer than the point of intersection of the lines-of-sight of the two eyes.] Since the outer half of the retina pertains to the negative depth-value or nearness-value, it follows that a double-image lying on this half of the retina must appear nearer than the fixation point . . . [Hering, 1861, pp. 305f.].[8] [Thus, when the two eyes fixate the farther of the two points, F (in Figure 28), the images of N (at points i and iii') both have a negative sign, indicating that N is nearer than F. When the two eyes fixate N, the images cast by F will fall at iii and i', both of which have a positive sign, indicating again that F is farther than N.]

If this theory were true, then the experience of distance would be just as immediate a sensation as that of red. And here, for the first time, we will discuss an *experiment* (as opposed to a simple unmanipulated self-observation) brought to bear on the nature-nurture issue:

Case 9: Retinal signs of depth. Place a vertical wire a little to the left of a pin, and closer to the eye than the head of the pin, at which you gaze (Figure 29). This will give rise to two images of the wire: ii (to the left of the pin, as the observer will see it) falls on the left eye, for which the depth value is positive, and it should therefore appear farther than the pin; iii (which appears to the left of ii) falls on the right eye, and should have a negative depth value, and therefore appear nearer than the pin.

> . . . if my eyes stay perfectly steady, and my entire attention is concentrated with all my might on the focused [pin], suddenly the illusive image in the left eye recedes *behind* the pin. . . . However, the slightest faltering of the gaze or simply *the thought* that the other illusive image is nearer will instantly restore the first one again to its place *in front of* the [neutral plane]; for then the fact that the two images are related to one and the same object comes in and disturbs the pure sensory impression [Helmholtz, 1910, p. 553].

There are three things we should notice about this: (1) It is the first real experiment we have encountered in the history of the nature-nurture issue, except for the imaginary one suggested by Mr. Molineaux and quoted by Locke and Berkeley (p. 265). (2) The nativist side of the argument here is that a given degree of binocular disparity should result in a fixed perception of distance—we will shortly see the nativist and empiricist viewpoints apparently changing sides on the question! (3) The experiment is only related to the question very indirectly (unlike the one of Mr. Molineaux). If the results remained uncontested, one still had to think hard about why this comprises evidence for the nativist position, or why this might be advanced as a refutation of Berkeley. But the results were *not* uncontested:

[8] Translated by the author.

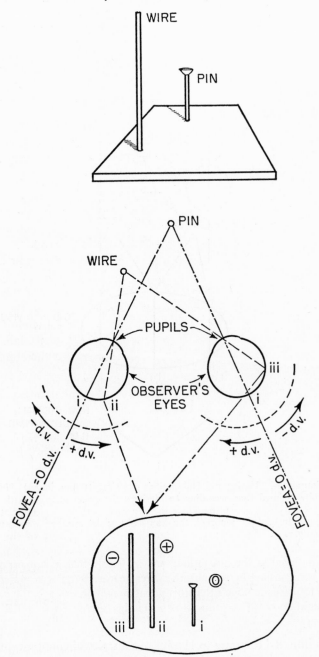

FIGURE 29. Hering and Helmholtz's experiments (Case 9). If one fixates the head of the pin, careful observation will reveal two images of the wire, *ii* corresponding to the proximal stimulus on the inner half of the left eye, and *iii* corresponding to the proximal stimulus on the outer half of the right eye. (Remember that retinal images are reversed right for left from what we see.)

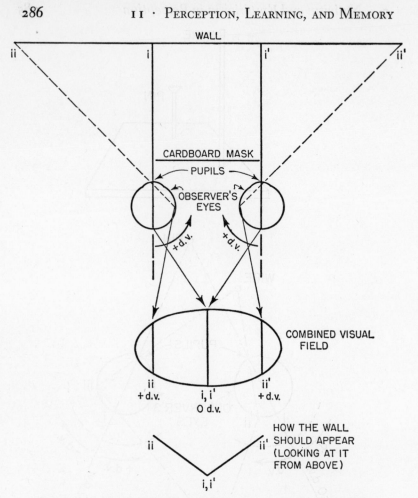

FIGURE 30. Hering and Helmholtz's experiments (continued). Helmholtz claimed that according to Hering's theory an observer with his eyes masked as shown should see the two parts of the wall meeting at an angle. Instead, he reported, the wall looks as flat as when viewed normally.

I have gazed at the pin so long and so fixedly that at last everything was extinguished by the negative after-images. But I have never been able to persuade myself that this phenomenon occurred in the main as it ought to occur according to the Hering theory [Helmholtz, 1910, p. 554].

Helmholtz' response to Hering was a series of counter-explanations and counter-experiments, for example:

Case 10: Against retinal signs of depth.

Cut a strip of black paper of the same width as the interpupillary distance, and hold it in front of the face, so that each eye can see only those objects that are on the same side as the eye. Thus, except for a small central portion . . . the entire field of view will be seen monocularly . . . all the conditions . . . seem . . . favourable for bringing out . . . Mr. Hering's hypothetical depth-feelings; and we should expect now to see the two parts of the wall on the border between the two visual fields meeting . . . at . . . a small acute angle [see Figure 30]. . . . But there is no sign of this to be seen, and the wall looks just as flat as it does when it is viewed by both eyes [Helmholtz, 1910, p. 555].

But the empiricist rebuttal rested on more than an individual refutation of an individual experiment. Nativist arguments (like Hering's) held that the perceptions of space are as dependent upon specific, fixed physiological receptors (or connections between receptors) as the sensations of color or brightness. Since this does not appear to be true on more occasions than it does appear to be (as we have seen in the last sentence of Case 9, and as we will see in the next three cases), the nativists had to assume that effects of past experience had overcome the innate experiences of space in each of these many cases. To the empiricist this was a grossly uneconomical explanation:

. . . if the factors derived from experience are able to give the correct information as to . . . space even in spite of opposing direct space-sensations, they must be still better . . . able to give the correct information . . . when there are no such obstacles to be overcome. . . . I think it is always advisable to explain natural processes on the *least* possible number of hypotheses . . . [Helmholtz, 1910, p. 557].

However, we should notice that this argument involves not only a question of nativism vs. empiricism; there also appears to be *an assumption that nativism must involve fixed connections, and that any departure from this argues for empiricism,* and here we have a large number of relevant experiments.

Two artificial but intriguing classes of stimulus situations took on special importance because of this controversy: (1) The *illusions* refer to situations in which what we perceive by vision does not fit the physical world as we measure it (see Figure 35, p. 292); these were challenges which the empiricist had to meet, since one would think that our perceptions would fit the physical world if they arose completely as a reflection of that world. (2) *Ambiguous stimuli* are patterns which give rise to two or more different experiences, such as the reversible perspective patterns of Figures 36, 37, and 39 (pp. 298, 301, and 304, respectively). Here the challenge faced the nativist, according to Helmholtz, since a fixed receptor mechanism would seem to be irreconcilable with such variability of perception.

THE EVIDENCE AGAINST FIXED CONNECTIONS. We have a great deal of experimental research which bears *indirectly* on the nature-nurture question via the question of fixed connections. In each and every aspect of space perception which we have been considering (i.e., position, two-dimension shape, distance, or position in the third dimension, size, and motion—see p. 278), we can show cases in which simple fixed relations do not exist between the proximal stimulus (i.e., the retinal image), and what observers appear to perceive.

TWO-DIMENSIONAL POSITION.   In order for us to be able to recognize position on the basis of innate physiological connections, each receptor element must have a specific nerve energy of position—a local sign (see p. 278)—so that we can know *where* on the retina the proximal stimulus falls. (In fact, empiricist theories also required some kind of local sign, but they did not have to assume that these signs would be cues to the perceived position of objects.) Problem: Can we identify the position of a solitary spot of light on the retina?

Case 11: The autokinetic effect. If we place a subject in a room which is completely darkened except for one spot of light, the spot cannot be localized—in fact, it appears to wander about in a lively and erratic manner, unless more of a spatial reference framework is provided; that is, sometimes the observer is sure of seeing motions when no motions are objectively present, or, on the other hand, he may not be aware of very considerable objective motions (Helmholtz, 1910, p. 273).

SHAPE.   Little explicit attention had been given to shape as such. In general, it was treated as a matter of position; for example, if we have stimulated positions *a*, *b*, *c*, and *d* in Figure 31, we should see a straight line; if we stimulate positions *e–h* in addition, we should see a longer straight line, whereas if we stimulated positions *i–l*, instead of

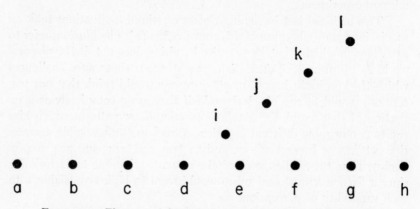

FIGURE 31.   Elements of shape. Is the experience of a straight line simply the sum of the sensations of position of the points stimulated at *a* through *h*? Is a bent line simply the positions *a* through *l*?

e–h, we should see a bent line. Problem: is perceived shape determined by the retinal positions which are stimulated?

Case 12: Successive shape contrast. If a subject wears spectacles consisting of prisms which distort vertical lines, so that they appear bent to the left, the lines eventually appear straight (even though their retinal images have not changed); if we now remove the spectacles, lines which are objectively straight will appear bent to the right (Wooster, 1923; Gibson, 1933; Kohler, 1951).

SIZE.   As for size, no one seriously proposed any mechanism for perceiving size which was not based on position (see p. 277); i.e., if we stimulate the positions indicated by the shaded area in Figure 32,

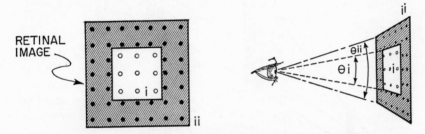

FIGURE 32. Apparent size. Is apparent size simply a matter of the number of retinal elements stimulated? Note that the large square (ii) at right subtends a larger visual angle (θ_{11}) and projects a larger retinal image, i.e., stimulates more retinal elements, than does the smaller square (i).

the size of the square which we perceive should increase accordingly. Nevertheless:

Case 13: Size constancy. Rods 20, 50, and 100 cm. long were shown, one at a time, at a distance of 50 cm., to an observer, who had to choose rods of equal length from among groups of rods which were placed at distances of 300 and 375 cm. Figure 33 summarizes the observations of Martius, who performed the experiment: the dotted lines show the judgments of size which *would* have been made if perceived size were dependent upon the size of the retinal image. The solid lines show the judgments which *were* made: notice how they remain practically constant even though the distance (and therefore the retinal image) changed size (Boring, 1942, p. 293).

We will see shortly that the same kinds of objections which may be offered to the idea of fixed connections for the perception of position, shape, and size also arise with respect to the perception of motion. However, we must first consider some of the further implications of the last experiment.

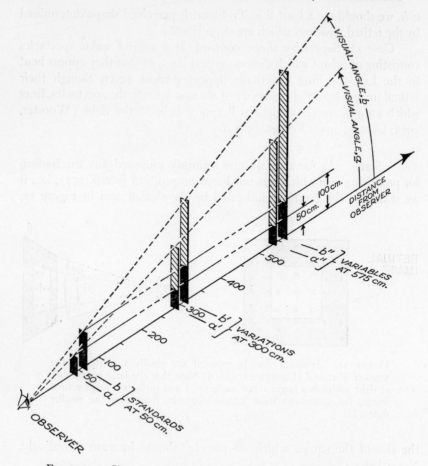

FIGURE 33. Size constancy (Case 13). The two solid bars, *a* and *b*, are standard rods at 50 centimeters' distance from the observer, and the horizontal dotted lines mark their physical heights. The shaded areas at *a′*, *b′* and *a′′*, *b′′*, show the sizes to which rods of variable height would have to be set when placed at 300 and 575 centimeter distances from the observer, respectively, in order to subtend equal visual angles and to produce retinal images equal to those of the standards, *a*, *b* at 50 centimeters. The heights of the variables which actually did appear equal, to the observer, are symbolized by the solid black bars at *a′b′*, and *a′ ′b′ ′*. Note how much closer these settings are to the physical heights of the standards than they are to the shaded areas which mark the equal visual angles. (After data gathered by Martius, 1889, abstracted from a diagram in Boring, p. 293.)

The Constancies and the Illusions

The size-constancy experiment of Case 13 is not an isolated phenomenon. Our perceptions of most of the apparently objective characteristics of an object, such as its size or its shape, are not usually simply determined by the size, shape, etc. of its retinal image.

Thus, if in an otherwise perfectly dark room, we view either a large and a small circle at the same distance from us, or two circles of the same size, one near and one far, what we see in *both* cases is determined by the proximal stimulus—a large circle and a small one. If, under the same circumstances (called *reduced* or *impoverished*), one views, either an upright circle and an upright ellipse, or an upright circle and one at a slant, again what one sees is appropriate to the proximal stimulus—a circle and an ellipse. This seems simple enough. However, if we allow other surrounding objects to be visible, the situation changes radically, and what are known as the *perceptual constancies* appear. A near circle and a far one of equal radius appear to be of almost the same size, despite quite different proximal stimulus sizes; an upright circle and a slanted one both appear almost equally circular, even though their proximal stimuli are quite different in shape (Figure 34).

In other words, under normal circumstances and for normal observers, even if the retinal image is changed because of a variation in the

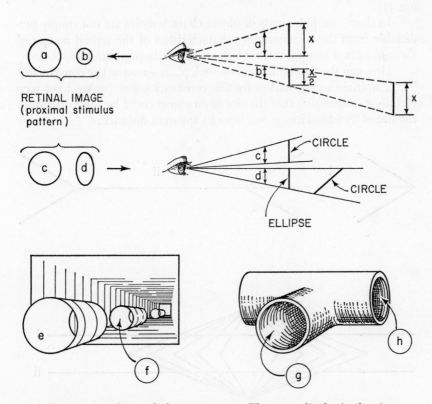

FIGURE 34. Size and shape constancy. The same distal stimulus (a disk) may produce proximal stimuli of different sizes (*a, b; e, f*) and of different shapes (*c, d; g, h*); despite such changes in proximal stimulation, the object normally will be perceived in accordance with its distal (and constant) characteristics.

viewing conditions (e.g., distance from the object), the perception of that object remains relatively constant (and correct). Such constancy is found in almost every case in which discrepancies are frequently found between proximal and distal stimulation. What we actually see is normally in better agreement with the characteristics of distal stimulation than with proximal stimulation. Thus, in addition to *shape constancy* and *size constancy*, which were just described, we can readily demonstrate *brightness constancy* (if a piece of coal in sunlight reflects more light to the eye than does a sheet of white paper in the shade, the coal still appears black, the paper white), *color constancy, motion constancy,* etc.

The *geometric optical illusions* also provide spectacular demonstrations of the fact that the same stimuli can give rise to different experiences. In these, the stimulus pattern which gives rise to one sensation of length (or straightness, or angle, or size, or the like) when it stands alone, appears quite different in the context of other lines (see Figure 35).

In short, our judgments of object characteristics are not simply predictable from the corresponding characteristics of the retinal images of those objects. This appears to reject a simple nativist position.

How can the empiricist explain such phenomena as the constancies? The empiricist's explanation for the constancies was (as we have seen Helmholtz maintain) that the size of an object could be computed from the size of its retinal image and from its apparent distance:

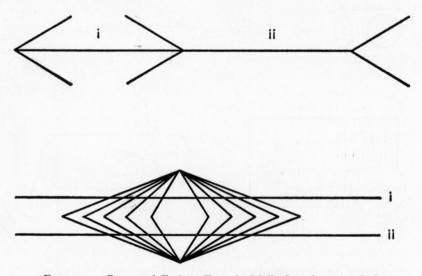

FIGURE 35.   Perceptual illusions. Top: the Müller-Lyer figure in which i and ii are of equal physical length. Bottom: lines i and ii are straight and parallel.

An astronomer . . . comes to real conscious conclusions . . . when he computes the positions of the stars in space, their distances, etc., from the perspective images he has had of them at various times. . . . His conclusions are based on a conscious knowledge of the laws of optics. In the ordinary acts of vision this knowledge of optics is lacking. Still, it may be permissible to speak of the psychic acts of ordinary perception as *unconscious conclusions*, thereby making a distinction of some sort between them and the common so-called conscious conclusions. And while it is true that there . . . [is] doubt as to the similarity of the psychic activity in the two cases, there can be no doubt as to the similarity between the results of such unconscious conclusions and those of conscious conclusions [Helmholtz, 1910, p. 4].

The reader should note the reintroduction of *unconscious processes*, not amenable to introspective observation (cf. Mill, Case 6). This introduces with it a considerable lack of economy—a point we will take up shortly.

EXAMINATION AND SUMMARY OF NATURE AND NURTURE IN EARLY EXPERIMENTAL PSYCHOLOGY. At this stage the nature-nurture issue looks as follows:

The empiricists held that all our ideas of the world come through our senses and that we could not sense such properties as distance and size of objects directly—we had to learn to do so. The evidence for this position was mainly introspection and logical analysis.

The associationists sought the sensory elements of which all mental content was composed; their methods were the same as those of the empiricists.

The sensory physiologists looked for the receptor organ and the specific nerve energies corresponding to every sensation. Since neither of these appeared to exist for shape, size, or distance, they were assumed (by empiricist psychologists) to be combinations of more basic sensations, built up through past experience as originally suggested by the empiricist philosophers. Experimental psychology (or physiological psychology) emerged as the systematic study of these elements and their combinations.

Nativistic psychologists, who maintained that the experience of distance or space was just as immediate as any other sensation, attempted to find physiological receptor mechanisms (and specific nerve energies) which could be sensitive to space; Hering proposed such a mechanism based on binocular disparity. The evidence against such fixed connections seemed overwhelming, however, unless we also assume that learning processes modify whatever the fixed connections would (on innate grounds alone) lead us to see. That is, we would have to assume that a certain amount of space perception is learned, even if there are innate components as well. Extreme (or strong) nativism seems, at this stage, to be untenable.

Helmholtz pointed out that it is uneconomical to assume that our perceptions are innate, if we are then to explain them almost entirely in terms of learning through experience. Now, this argument epitomizes a very important change in the nature of the nature-nurture problem: to the original philosophical empiricist, even a very little bit of nativism is damaging, since a basic problem is at stake.

To appeal to "economy," on the other hand, is the act of a scientist or technologist, rather than of a philosopher; it appeals to the relative convenience or utility of an idea (or theory) for predicting or explaining things that are observed to happen (or which are made to happen), rather than to the absolute truth or falsity of the idea.

Moreover, the economy of the extreme empiricist position was itself no longer very impressive (Koffka, 1935, p. 86; Köhler, 1913). In order to explain our perceptions, it had, at one and the same time, to appeal to self-observation (introspection) as its main source of data, and to maintain the following three points to be true (which would throw the introspective method under a considerable shadow of suspicion): (1) that there are sensations (which were normally treated as the elements of experience) which cannot be experienced—the unnoticed sensations; (2) that there are experiences which seem to be elements, and which no amount of observation will show to be compounds, but which really are compounds instead of elements; (3) that we construct most of the world that we perceive by processes like reasoning, and that these processes are unconscious and cannot be observed, no matter how hard we examine our perceptions. This certainly seems like a cumbersome position to defend, and the inevitable conflict continued for a decade or so. The actual questions under dispute got more and more technical, and their relationship to the nature-nurture issue got increasingly more indirect.

We will not follow this up here, because, just about this time, another series of major changes in purpose and method occurred. The form of the next major rebuttal from the nativists came, not as an attempt to defend nativism by showing that there *are* fixed connections after all, but quite the reverse. The radically new approach was *Gestalt* theory, which proposed that (1) the ability to perceive spatial characteristics *is* inborn, and that (2) spatial experiences are indeed as immediate as any of the so-called sensations, but that (3) fixed relationships between proximal stimulus and perceptual experience or response do not exist, and are not necessary for either (1) or (2) to be true. Gestaltists conceded that individual receptor organs could not be found for the experience of distance, true enough, but that, for that matter, they could not really be found for, say, red, either, *or for any other experience*. This radical proposition was the only course left open to nativism, as we have seen, as a consequence of the preceding experiments.[9] The reason for this unorthodox proposal is mainly to be found in the failure of the entire previous attempt to find stable sensation-elements. Psychology had learned a lot about sensory experience, and had gathered a respectable quantity of perceptual facts, but the general theoretical framework collapsed and carried its problems and methods with it, for a number of reasons.

This collapse, although real enough, was by no means complete. The course upon which the study of perception continues today is closely related in many respects to the earlier concepts, problems, and methods. The field is, however, now more sophisticated by several stages. It has had to undergo considerable change through contact with the technological needs of war and industry and, above all, by passing through a sometimes astonishing and always excited period of theoretical (and to some extent experimental) conflict between antithetical schools of general psychological thought. Much of this conflict was over what the very subject matter and the problems of psychology should be.

GESTALT NATIVISM

Schools of Psychology

The empiricism of Helmholtz is quite representative of what became officially *Psychology* in the hands of Wundt, Titchener, and Külpe. The introspective search for the elements of conscious experience became involved in increasingly more cumbersome qualifications and restrictions, and controversies broke out between equally well-trained observers as to what the facts were, controversies which could not be resolved. Basic differences of opinion in a systematic field of thought give rise to the voluble phenomenon of *schools*, which are consistent and mutually opposed viewpoints and systems of explanation of subject-matter and of method. Psychology was torn into four major divisions—Functionalism, Behaviorism, *Gestalttheorie*, and Psychoanalysis. All four schools have contributed to the present status of the study of perception, but we will consider only two of them: Behaviorism very briefly, and the *Gestalt* movement in somewhat greater detail.

Behaviorism appeared to reject the entire area of psychology as it was previously conceived. It maintained that *introspection* is subjective,

[9] The Gestaltists declared, on several occasions, that they were neither nativists nor empiricists, but that they were "beyond" this issue. However, as we have seen, for our purposes empiricism does not consist in saying that the perception of space can be affected by or improved by learning, but in the "strong" position that space comes *only* through learning. We will see that, with respect to *all* the spatial dimensions we have been considering (pp. 277–8), the Gestaltists were nativists.

while the data of science must be objective, and consequently most of what had been the field of perception was (among others) decreed out of existence. The subject matter of scientific psychology was to be restricted to the observation of physical stimuli, and of the physical responses to those stimuli by physical organisms. But defining away a field of inquiry on such tenuous philosophical grounds [1] does not really do away with it, and declaring a method to be out of bounds can only be done successfully if the method has no use anyway.

On the positive side of the ledger, behaviorism professed a healthy disrespect for pure theory and for the shackles of philosophical orthodoxy; a tolerance and even admiration for the applied and practical (a goal which frequently got submerged in the course of behaviorism's own theoretical squabbles between its subschools); an impatience with concepts and explanations which are not rooted in observation; and a demand for the quantitative and readily observable, rather than for the tricky, exclusive, and qualitative introspective observations which had previously dominated psychology.

BACKGROUND OF GESTALT NATIVISM.   The Gestalt revolution was in some ways extremely radical, while in other respects it was in close continuity with the earlier aims and methods of experimental psychology. Gestaltists' interests were the traditional ones: research was oriented toward the laboratory, and the main problems were those involved in the perception of objects, of their qualities, of their spatial position and their motion. The Gestaltist methods—with certain important changes in the method of introspection—were also traditional. The main differences comprise (1) a set of criticisms of other approaches, (2) a set of positive assertions, and (3) a program of research investigation.

GESTALTIST CRITICISMS.   Gestaltists asserted that:

(1) Forms, shapes, and space are not built up out of elementary sensations as a result of past experience.

(2) The elements which were revealed by analytic introspection (Cases 1–8) were *not* typical of the workings of the mind; they do not compose the fabric of perceived things, nor are they normally present in conscious experience (except in the highly artificial trained attitudes of traditional associationists and experimental psychologists; contrast this with assumption [3], p. 266).

---

[1] One cannot quarrel with the behaviorist's demand for "*objective*" data if, by objective, we understand "reliable," "repeatable," etc. (see Brunswik, 1952). However, a distinction between "subjective" and "objective" based on distinguishing "mind" from "body" is not factual nor methodological; it may be the province of metaphysics or religion, but it is not a legitimate tool of science.

(3) The physiological units which were employed by orthodox psychology and sensory physiology—the specific nerve energies—are neither representative of the real organism, nor adequate as explanations of human experience. The nervous system is not anything like a telephone switchboard, nor are the workings of the mind like the functioning of one.

(4) The process of *association of ideas* is too gross, too mechanistic, and a completely unrealistic picture of the learning process.

(5) Likewise, the philosophical setting, empiricism, is obsolete philosophically, and was based, in the first place, on poor (and too analytic) introspection.

POSITIVE ASSERTIONS OF GESTALTISTS. (1) Forms and shapes are themselves the natural units of experience; they are as immediately perceived as is the sensation of "red"—in fact, more so—and they are *not* composed of such apparently simpler elements.

(2) Accordingly, introspection should be naïve and "whole-perceiving," instead of being analytic and directed toward breaking down these natural units.

(3) Corresponding to these whole units of experience are processes in the nervous system having the same characteristics of extended, bounded wholes—this is in contrast to the discrete, separate, all-or-none nerve impulses and specific nerve energies which were taken to be the elements of the classical viewpoint. Such extended physiological processes (or "fields") are dynamically self-contained, organized systems, rather than mere added-together collections of specific nerve energies. Illustratively, the Gestalt model for the nervous system is more like a flow of electrolytic current or the interactions in a lather of soap bubbles than like the structuralist's picture of individual messages in a telegraph switchboard.

(4) The philosophy of Kant is a more valid starting point than that of Berkeley and Hume. The space, objects, and motion we apprehend are as much due to the inborn characteristics of our mental processes as they are to the characteristics of the world around us.

THE GESTALT PROGRAM AND METHODS. Instead of trying to isolate the elements of experience and then to cement them together again with the process of association, Gestaltists attempted to discover the *laws of organization* of perception and therefore of the nervous system. Their program involved three sorts of methods: (1) *demonstrations*, (2) *phenomenological introspection*, (3) *psychophysics*, and one major polemical technique, (4) *outflanking* or *absorption*. It is worth discussing these methods briefly, because the nature-nurture issue becomes the subject of more general experimental investigation at this time, and the *method* of investigating the issue itself becomes part of the controversy.

Demonstrations. The most frequent Gestalt method was the crucial experiment. This phrase describes, for the most part, the use of an immediate demonstration to support or attack a given theoretical position. See Figure 36, which illustrates a number of the Gestalt laws of organization by the use of such demonstrations. The demonstration as a

FIGURE 36. "Laws of organization."

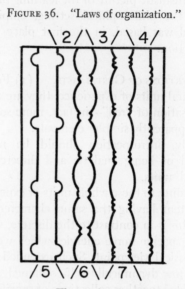

This illustrates *symmetry.* The enclosed areas, 5, 6, and 7, rather than the less symmetrical areas, 2, 3, and 4, tend to be seen as distinctive forms.

This illustrates *proximity.* The dots are much more likely to be seen as groups *ab, cd, ef,* and *gh,* rather than as alternative groupings such as *bc, de, fg,* and *hi.*

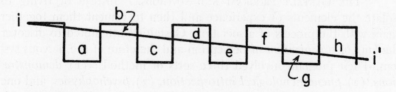

This illustrates *good continuation.* It is much easier to see a straight unbroken line (i-i') and a crenelated zigzag line than an assemblage of independent adjacent trapezoids (*a-h*).

method is at least one step better than the armchair method (see p. 266), and is understandably important in a science where more systematic quantitative investigation can absorb innumerable lifetimes without achieving any striking accomplishment, fame, or advancement. It flourishes best where there are universal assertions to be punctured by one negative case, and we should remember that *Gestalttheorie* faced, in effect, the universal assertion that the perceptions of forms and relationships must be learned. Demonstrations of simple geometric groupings were also used to discover the *laws of organization;* these laws presumably determine which figure we will see when the proximal stimulus actually permits more than one alternative organization to appear readily. (Cf. Figure 36.)

There is one unfortunate aspect of demonstrations as a method of investigation: unless the alternatives which the demonstration is to test are derived from clearly opposed theories, usable information is not likely to be provided. What is perhaps worse, the demonstration can deal with only one case at a time, yet its propaganda effects extend to other parts of the opposing system which it appears to disprove, and tend to set up straw men (i.e., to make one ignore alternative options which could legitimately be taken by the viewpoint under attack). The reader can best illustrate this for himself by attempting an easy task: to rebut the demonstrations of Figures 36 and 41 from the viewpoints of Berkeley (see pp. 259–66) or Mill (see pp. 268–70).

The demonstration method is suited to a qualitative, tight, logical, predominantly rational system—in short, to philosophical argument rather than to scientific investigation. Consequently, the nature-nurture issue tended to be treated as a black-and-white, all-or-none question (see p. 295).

Phenomenological introspection. Here "phenomenological observation" means the unanalytical, qualitative observation of what is immediately given in experience. It is an auxiliary tool, not an end in itself, and ideally supplements more quantitative methods. Quantitative measurement is always narrow and abstractive, and some nonquantitative observation is always necessary to round out the picture and to suggest what needs to be measured next.

With this variety of introspection (which is far less restricted than that of empiricists and associationists), a great many more attributes of the world of things and people began to be mentioned, even if they were not systematically investigated. Phenomenological introspection revealed that colors are not only red, green, and blue, or combinations thereof—they are warm and cool, active and recessive, bulky or filmlike as well (Katz, 1935, pp. 7–38). Objects are not only solid shapes which can be specified in terms of a three-dimensional coordinate system— they are also threatening, happy, soft, etc. (Katz, 1950, pp. 81–5). Psychologists began really to acknowledge that these are aspects of the perceived world to be studied in addition to the dimensions of space, time, color, and brightness. A "smile" may, it is true, be reduced to simple spatial dimensions, in the sense that it can be plotted point by point on a graph of spatial positions (see p. 277) but, perceptually speaking, it remains something more than its positional plot for all that. However, the Gestaltists' *primary* concern was still with the traditional physical qualities of experience—size, distance, shape, and so forth—and with the discrepancies between the real world and the perceived world (i.e., with illusions; see p. 292).

Psychophysics. This refers to the various procedures by which we determine the measured, quantitative relationships between physical variables and psychological variables; as a set of methods it was little used by Gestaltists, but, where it was used, there appeared the germ of a change in both method and subject matter.

This last point is an important one, and we will take it up again shortly.

First we will consider the nature-nurture issue in terms of a new technique that Gestalt theory brought to the problem; specifically, the technique of *absorption*.

GESTALT THEORY ASSIMILATES THE EMPIRICIST'S ARGUMENTS INTO A NATIVIST VIEWPOINT. Let us take up the specific problem with which we last left the issue of nature vs. nurture. Hering, on the nativist side, had proposed that there *were* inborn (but unknown) native physiological (retinal) mechanisms for sensing distance, based upon the binocular disparity between local signs (see Case 9). In answer, Helmholtz mounted a five-point counteroffensive: he had (1) contested the observations, (2) deplored the appeal to unknown physiological structures, (3) pointed to the evidence that the relationship between stimulation and response was highly variable, instead of being nativistically fixed, and argued that—since it could be shown that (4) the so-called empirical or secondary factors outweighed binocular disparity, and that these were "obviously" learned—(5) it was uneconomical, in the face of all this, to appeal to additional unknown nativistic factors when learning would account for all the phenomena. The Gestaltists accepted most of Helmholtz' points, but appropriated them as arguments in favor of nativism.

PHYSIOLOGY. Gestaltists boldly declared that far from being too unorthodox, Hering had stayed too close to a picture of sensory physiology which was simply completely wrong:

An example from the psychophysiology of space perception will illustrate this: when a number of stimuli act on different points of the sense organ at the same time, it has been the custom to interpret the action of each stimulus separately, and the total process has been considered a summation of the elementary processes which each stimulus would have aroused [p. 19]. . . . The facts of vision require that we treat them as properties of a *single* physical system in which the totality of stimulus conditions both individually and collectively is determined by the whole which they comprise [Köhler, 1920, p. 20].

VARIABILITY OF THE PSYCHOPHYSICAL RELATIONSHIP. Gestalt theory rejected fixed connections as a basis for sensation—or as a basis for anything else, for that matter:

> If . . . things look as they do because the proximal stimuli are what they are . . . two propositions should hold: (1) changes in the proximal stimulation unaccompanied by changes of the distant stimulus-object should produce corresponding changes in the *looks* of the [perceived] . . . object, and (2) any change in the distant object which produces no effect in the proximal stimulation should leave the looks of the [perceived] . . . object unchanged . . . [Koffka, 1935, p. 82].

From proposition (2) in the quotation above, no change could occur in the appearance of things without some changes in the pattern of proximal stimuli. However, this is not true: Figure 37 changes its appearance while you look at it; reversible perspective figures display the same alternations (see Figure 39).

Thus, we cannot say that what we perceive is determined simply by the proximal stimulation. As to whether point (1) holds, Case 13 (and all the *constancy* phenomena discussed on p. 291) show that it does not. Things do not look as one would expect on the basis of the proximal stimulation; they look more like the distal stimuli with which we must actually deal. Therefore the empiricists assumed that we acquire experience by dealing with things, and this experience determines our

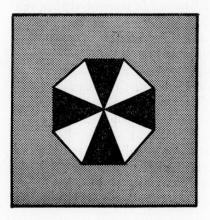

FIGURE 37. Figure-ground reversal. The white cross and the black cross alternate in perception.

perceptions. And this has led the empiricists (as we have seen—p. 293) to explanations in terms of unconscious inferences made about unnoticed sensations.

But will this explain anything? It is easy to understand how a judgment which is based upon a sensory experience might in turn influence the interpretation of the sensory experience; for example, if we see smoke, we might judge that the smoke must come from a fire. However, ". . . we do not understand how a non-sensory process produces out of an unnoticed sensory process a noticed datum which has all the direct characteristics of a sensory process and is different from the non-noticed one. . . ." (Koffka, 1935, p. 87.)

REVERSIBLE-PERSPECTIVE FIGURES.　Gestaltists had not completely abandoned an innate binocular mechanism for sensing depth; the new version, however, did not depend on fixed connections, as had Hering's:

> . . . which pairs of points . . . on the two retinae will cooperate in determining the perceptual organization depends upon the two . . . patterns. . . . the *processes* started in the two optical tracts . . . will interact according to their structural properties; i.e., figure will interact with figure and ground with ground and not *vice versa* . . . [Koffka, 1935, p. 269].

However, Gestaltists did not attempt to deny that the so-called empirical factors (or secondary factors) could influence and overpower the binocular factor; in fact, a most elegant experiment was designed to show just that.

Case 14: Organization vs. "primary" cues. Kopfermann (1930) placed the three glass plates (*a, b,* and *c,* in Figure 38) in a box, each two cm. farther away from the observer, so that the line segments marked 2 and 3 were at the greatest distance, 5 was nearest, and 1 and 4 were between the extremes. Despite the differences in accommodation, convergence, and so on which must accompany the three sets of line segments, 4 and 5 appeared to be in contact and to be at the same distance, etc., since these lines were always seen as the base of a cube (i, ii, iii, iv) as shown in *d.* The effect is particularly striking when the slight parallax due to eye motions starts to disrupt the figure. Instead of separating into the three separate planes which actually comprise the distal stimulus, the lines seem to stretch and bend in order to maintain their (quite illusory) contact.

Kopfermann was here investigating the conditions for perceiving *solidity,* and this stands at the heart of the nature-nurture issue as it was originally formulated, e.g., about our perception of objects.

Was Kopfermann's experiment (which seems to refute Hering's nativistic doctrine of innate binocular depth) to be taken to support Helm-holtz' empiricist argument? By no means, for two reasons: first, the so-called secondary cues which were provided by visual stimulation alone have here readily overcome the presumably more primary ones of accom-modation, convergence, etc. which should be much more powerful fac-tors on the basis of frequency of association, if nothing else. Secondly, an empiricist explanation does not really predict anything about these presumably empirical factors; in fact, as Kopfermann proposed (see below), they may be more readily explained as innate organizational factors.

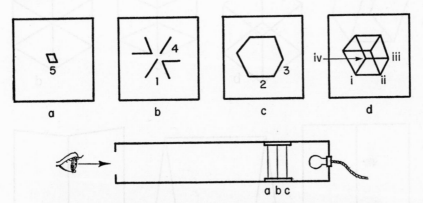

FIGURE 38. Organization vs. "primary" cues (Case 14). The stimuli are presented on three glass plates arranged as shown in the lower dia-gram, *a* being nearest, *b*, 2 cm. farther away, *c*, 4 cm. farther away. Despite the cues of accommodation and convergence, observers see the cube *d*. (After Kopfermann, 1930, and used by permission of Springer-Verlag.)

Case 15: Goodness and apparent depth. In Figure 39, *d* and *e* appear to be simple, flat, two-dimensional patterns; *a* and *h* appear quite tridimensional and solid, while the intervening figures can appear as either flat or tridimensional (Kopfermann, 1930). In terms of what the Gestaltists called the laws of organization, *d* is a perfectly simple and symmetrical plane figure, whereas, in order for it to be perceived as a cube, the straight lines would have to be separated into parts. In *a* the plane figure would be the more irregular, with the greater amount of interference with good continuation (see Figure 36 for Wertheimer's laws of organization).

Here Kopfermann has explained *which* of the reversible-perspective figures would appear most three-dimensional, by referring to (presum-ably) *innate* organizational factors. Can the empiricist do as well, treat-ing them as empirical factors (see pp. 311–13)? Perhaps eventually he will, by studying how things that are really solid are likely to have pro-duced retinal images associated with tactual experiences of solidity, in the life of any given individual (see Brunswik's ecological study of proximity, Case 20); he certainly cannot do so at present.

However, here it is nativism which encouraged the discovery of specific psychophysical relationships. This is the first systematic and specific attempt to displace the empirical explanation of the *secondary* cues since Berkeley, more than two hundred years before, and anticipates the gradient theory of Gibson (Case 22) in that respect.

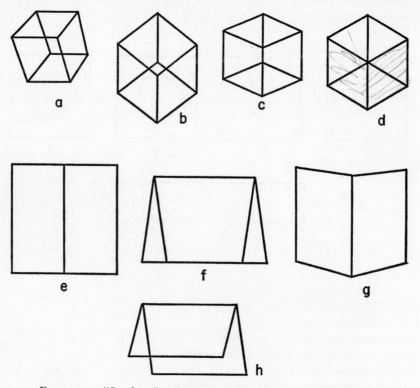

FIGURE 39. "Goodness" and the apparent depth of reversible-perspective figures. Note that *d* and *e* are "good" two-dimensional forms, whereas *a* and *h* are not. (After Kopfermann, 1930.)

EMPIRICIST ASSOCIATIONISM IS UNECONOMICAL. Helmholtz had argued that nativism was uneconomical. Gestaltists showed that this conclusion was due to the assumptions which both nativists and empiricists had made about the nature of the psychological and physiological elements, and not to nativism itself (Koffka, 1935, p. 86; Köhler, 1913). Having seen that the Gestaltists adopted many of the empiricists' arguments against the earlier nativists, let us survey the Gestalt objections to empiricism as such.

Case 16: Size constancy in chicks. Three-month-old chicks (which peck at large grains spontaneously) were trained by Götz (1926) to peck only at the larger of a pair of grains; each grain was then placed at a different distance from a doorway through which the chick was released. The smaller grain was at 15 cm., the larger one at various greater distances; up to 73 cm., chicks chose the larger one—even though, at this distance, the retinal image of the larger one was about $\frac{1}{30}$ the area of the smaller one. In short, the chicks were displaying the same kind of *perceptual constancy* we noted in Case 13, and which the empiricist explained in terms of "unconscious inferences."

We *could* say that—in three months—the chicks learned that what-looks-larger-is-really-smaller-but-nearer, and that an inference or computation (see p. 293) was really involved here. However, we will see later (Cases 24 and 27) that similar behaviors in space can be obtained with chicks and other animals after *no* previous visual experience. Furthermore, it seems very unlikely that chicks are capable of such computation. In fact, human adults who are quite capable of making the appropriate size and distance judgments may be unable to perform the computation (Brunswik, 1948). The distinction between sensation and perception (see p. 279) appears to be entirely unwarranted in the case of the chick. Now, we will see that it is quite likely that there are differences between species (pp. 323-4), but remember the origin of this controversy (p. 259): Berkeley's initial attempt was to prove that innate perception of space is impossible, and we see that that appears to be untrue—for the chick, at least.

THE PERCEPTION OF MOTION.   Empiricists assumed that perception of an object's motion is built up out of the association of successive groups of sensations from each position on the retina and from eye-motions, as the distal object moves in space and the proximal stimulus moves across the retina (Figure 40, top). This theory suggests the following obvious questions: Can we detect the successive component sensations in the perception of motion? Is motion of proximal stimulation on the retina necessary for the experience of motion? The answer is *no* to both these queries. Consider the so-called *phi phenomenon* of Wertheimer:

Case 17: Apparent motion. If a light is turned on and then off at A (Figure 40, bottom) and, after a suitable interval, another light is turned on at B, motion is perceived to occur between A and B. There is no real motion across the retina, neither are there any successive component sensations from intermediate positions on the retina, so we can conclude that such sensations are not *necessary* to the perception of motion. Moreover, under optimal conditions such illusory apparent motion appears more real and convincing, even to trained observers, than actual motion from A to B.

In short, motion must be considered as much a direct experience as any other visual experience, rather than being built up out of more elementary sensations of position.

FORM.   We have seen that earlier psychologists had considered *form* or *shape* to be learned by the habitual association of neighboring

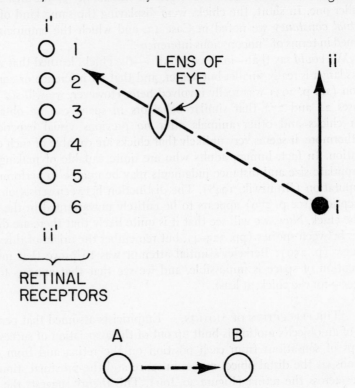

FIGURE 40. Apparent motion. Top: when the object moves from *i* to *ii*, is our experience of motion composed of the sensations from the successively stimulated retinal receptors (1–6)? Bottom: if a light is turned on and then off at A and another light is turned on at B after a suitable interval, motion is perceived as indicated by the arrow.

sensations of light and shade together with the muscle sensations that arise from eye movements and the like. This empiricist theory of form perception suggests the following question:

Can we perceive forms which were not previously learned? We have to be very cautious here, because the question has not really been subjected to direct test. However, we can answer a closely related question:

Case 18: Familiarity and form. Gottschaldt (1926) showed subjects simple patterns (*a* figures), like *a* in Figure 41, 520 times, with instructions to learn them. They were then shown new unfamiliar *b* patterns, which contained a repetition of one of the *a* figures. After all this practice, the subjects predominantly failed to recognize the *a* figures within the *b* patterns.

Apparently, shapes which were quite unfamiliar could be made to mask shapes which subjects had practiced hundreds of times.[2]

The interpretation of such experiments requires considerable caution, since the factors (such as proximity, similarity, and good continua-

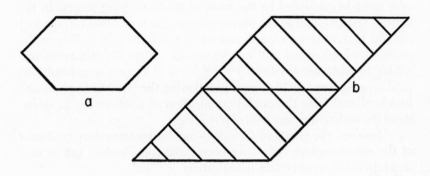

FIGURE 41. Concealment of familiar forms. Top: subjects were shown simple forms like *a* more than 500 times with instructions to learn them but usually failed to recognize them when they were embedded in more complex patterns like *b* (Case 18). Bottom: for explanation see footnote 2 to Case 18, below. (*a* and *b* from Gottschaldt, 1926; *c* from Wertheimer, 1923; used by permission of Springer-Verlag.)

tion—Figure 36) which had overpowered the experience of a few hundred practice trials might themselves be due to many thousands or millions of experiences during early life (see Case 20). However, we should notice that for the first time the factor of perceptual practice or experience was being directly *manipulated* in a nature-nurture experiment.

[2] In fact, we can perform a simplified investigation of this point right now (adapted from Wertheimer, 1923): look very briefly at *c* in Figure 41, then write down a brief description of what you saw: ten words will suffice. Now turn to footnote 2* on p. 3?9.

Review of the Gestalt Contribution

After several decades, the laws of organization remain largely mere demonstrations, not followed up by systematic investigation; this is also true of most of the new dimensions hinted at by phenomenological introspection. Practical application, although potentially vast, consisted of a few demonstrations of camouflage. Many controversies were devoted to discourses about the philosophy of science, to the law of isomorphism (i.e., the statement that the forms which we consciously experience must be paralleled by the form of the underlying process in the nervous system), and to the nature-nurture question. However, the fact remains that what we see still cannot be predicted very well from the proximal stimuli which fall on our retinae.[3] Most Gestaltists seemed willing to postpone any further application of the organizational laws until investigators [4] could succeed in following the "law of isomorphism" backward, and from the careful examination of what we see, to understand the underlying principles of physiology.

However, the effects of Gestalt theory on contemporary treatment of the nature-nurture issue have been quite considerable. Let us now step into the scene of current investigation.

CONTEMPORARY INVESTIGATIONS

THERE HAVE BEEN no clear developments (nor victories) of any of the schools. No new, self-consciously *systematic* over-all positions

[3] In part, it should be admitted, the dearth of progress can be blamed on the Nazi destruction of the scientific community in Germany; in America, behaviorism offered the most unsympathetic of receptions to the new doctrine carried by the refugees to America's soil and schools. I believe, however, that the main ailment lay in the approach itself and in the tradition which preceded it: the tendency to talk of "brain fields" without specifying ways in which they can be tested, to stress *phenomenology* over *psychophysics*, is a far from revolutionary one, and behaviorists had considerable justification when they suspiciously classed Gestalt theory as just another aspect of structuralism (i.e., of the approaches of Wundt and Titchener).

[4] The foremost of these is W. Köhler, and the most celebrated of such attempts was the study of the *figural after-effects*. On the basis of a long series of demonstrations Köhler and Wallach (1944) proposed that certain distortions of apparent position, which occur as the effects of protracted viewing, might be interpreted as a "satiation" of the tissues in the optic area of the cortex. Köhler considers this as evidence for the existence of extended Gestalt brain processes, and it is true that none of the attempts to explain these phenomena in terms of orthodox physiology have succeeded completely. However, after almost two decades of investigation, (1) it is doubtful that research in this area has contributed anything to our knowledge of physiology, (2) no suitable elaboration of "Gestalt physiology" has suitably explained the figural after-effects without vagueness, and (3) no knowledge has yet been gained here that is of clear use either to theoretical or practical psychology. It is also clear that Gestaltists are not free from the classical tendency to refer (and defer) the problems of behavior to speculative underlying physiological mechanisms.

have taken hold, and so we might close with the picture of the field given in the preceding section (pp. 295–308)—but, if we did so, we would miss some important lessons which were only implicit in what has gone before.

Empiricism Revisited

One recent and famous series of investigations instituted by Ames (Lawrence, 1949) consisted largely of a number of very ingenious demonstrations. These showed (as had previous studies; see Case 15) that the secondary depth cues of interposition, perspective, etc. could, under certain conditions, overpower the so-called primary cues of accommodation and sometimes of convergence and binocular disparity as well. Also, in the absence of other determining factors, the known size of an object could affect a subject's judgment of its distance.

For example, the large card in Figure 42 is demonstrated as *appearing* nearer than the small one, although the reverse is really the case. The distorted room of Figure 43 is a famous view, occurring in almost every introductory psychology textbook.

These demonstrations, it was held, proved all our perceptions of the spatial world to be determined by our past experiences:

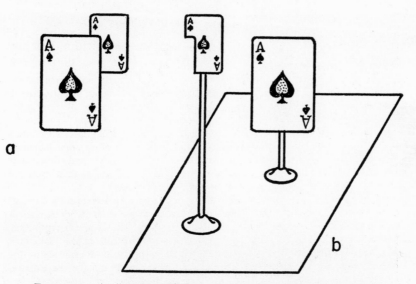

FIGURE 42. An "empiricistic" demonstration. In a darkened room two playing cards (*b*) are exposed to an observer who views them with one eye. When the two cards are arranged so that the cutout of the small card is in line with the corner of the large card (*a*), the latter is seen in front.

---

[2]* Pattern *c* in Figure 41 is made up of M and W; these symbols are very familiar, yet the odds are good that they did not appear in your written description.

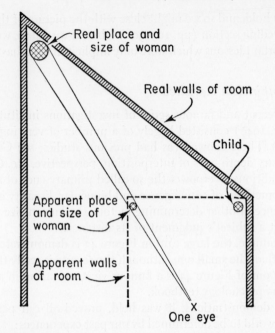

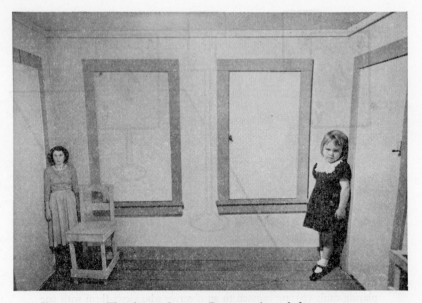

FIGURE 43. The distorted room. Bottom: view of the room as seen monocularly through a peephole. Top: diagram showing the objective stimulus situation giving rise to the illusion of size. Note that the room is very asymmetrical. One corner is three times as far away as the other from the observer's eye. All dimensions are chosen so as to be exact geometrical projections of a normal rectangular room as seen by the observer. (From D. Krech and R. S. Crutchfield, *Elements of Psychology*, pp. 144–5. Published in 1958 by Alfred A. Knopf, and used with their permission.)

[These demonstrations] . . . have resulted in a new conception in the nature of knowing and of observation. This theory neither denies the existence of objects nor proposes that they exist . . . apart from the perceiving organism. Instead, it suggests that the world each of us knows is a world created in large measure from our experience in dealing with the environment [p. 50]. . . . These phenomena cannot be explained by . . . reference to the pattern in the retina of the eye, because for any given retinal pattern, . . . the organism apparently calls upon its previous experiences and assumes that what has been most probable in the past is most probable in the immediate occasion [p. 52]. . . . According to the new theory of perception developed from the demonstrations we have described, perception is . . . based on action, experience and probability. . . . This view differs from the old rival theories: the thing perceived is neither just a figment of the mind nor an innately determined revelation of reality [p. 55] . . .[5]

This is not a particularly novel thesis, as we have seen in previous pages. It is what has been called "the strong empiricistic position" (Slack, 1959). Ingenious as these demonstrations were, it should be evident that they display in wood and paint the anecdotal observations made by every empiricist from Berkeley (see p. 260) to Helmholtz (see p. 277). At most, such indirect investigations could prove (subject to the reservation discussed in the next paragraph) that our past experiences can affect our perception of space. Few nativists proposed otherwise (see Case 9). What such demonstrations cannot do, no matter what their ingenuity,[6] is prove that we can perceive space *only* because of what we have learned by experience.

THE NECESSITY OF ECOLOGICAL SAMPLING. Most of the empiricist arguments point to a phenomenon and say, "Obviously, we see it thus-and-so because we have seen such-and-such most frequently in the past"; this is not enough. First it must be shown that "we *have* indeed seen such-and-such most frequently in the past." In order for this to be the case, a really enormous gap in the empiricist position must be filled. The argument is, that what we see is determined by what stimuli have confronted us, in what combinations, with what frequency. Now, so far, all the empiricist arguments have rested on some more-or-less casual assumptions about what we "must" have seen. However, (1) we cannot be sure of this without actual evidence, and (2) even if we were to accept the empiricist position in principle (as this writer does to a limited extent), we could not hope to predict what people will perceive until we knew in detail the frequencies of associations between stimuli to which

[5] From W. Ittelson and F. Kilpatrick, "Experiments in Perception," *Sci. Amer.,* 1952, 185, pp. 50–5. Used by permission of the *Scientific American.*
[6] It is doubtful that these demonstrations have shown even that much in any unequivocal fashion (Pratt, 1950).

they had been exposed in the past. The precise nature of what the environment offers (to inscribe upon the *tabula rasa*, according to the empiricist's assumptions; see p. 258) is known as the *ecological distribution of stimuli*, i.e., the make-up of our visual environment. This is not an easy concept to grasp, but is essential to any evaluation of the nature-nurture controversy. The classical example of an ecological investigation of space perception is Egon Brunswik's study of size constancy.

Case 19: An ecological survey of size constancy. In Case 13, the two stimulus variables, proximal size and distal size, were systematically varied. In Brunswik's investigation,

> . . . they were not systematically varied in accordance with a preconceived plan of an experimenter, but randomly sampled from the normal environment of a university student, stopped in her daily routine by . . . a passive . . . "recorder" of the objective situation. The subject then [wrote] her estimates of the . . . [size] which happened to be most prominently attended to by her . . . , as well as of other elements of the situation. . . . The coefficient [between distal size and perceived size] is about .99 for the total sample of 93 situations.[7]

Can we really predict what people will see, after a study of *ecological distributions*, by employing the empiricist assumptions? Brunswik has attempted to demonstrate that the Gestalt law of proximity (see p. 298) is really an empirical factor after all, that it is a perceptual habit learned because of the ecological distribution of stimuli.

Case 20: Proximity as an ecological variable. Brunswik and Kamiya (1953) chose a sample of seven shots from a motion picture, reproduced in a magazine. A search of these found about 900 pairs of parallel lines, which were classified: (1) as to proximal separation (e.g., 0.5–1.0 mm., 1.0–2.0 mm., etc.), and (2) as to whether they arose from a single relatively permanent object, or were more accidental alignments between unconnected objects. A low correlation was found between connectedness and closeness ($r = .12$), which was statistically significant. "The proof, just reported, . . . opens up the possibility of viewing the stimulus configuration involved in this factor, proximity, as a cue acquired by generalized probability learning" (Brunswik, 1956, p. 122).

Three important points are raised by this experiment: (1) There is a definite change of posture here. Empiricism is on the defensive, trying to do as well at predicting as does the nativist Gestalt law of proximity (and, to the reader who understands statistics, not doing very well while borrowing that law). (2) The experimental procedure is defective. We

---

[7] From Egon Brunswik, *Perception and the Representative Design of Psychological Experiments*, pp. 44ff., published 1956 by the University of California Press. Here and throughout excerpts used with their permission.

would *expect* that pictures which are made specifically to be easy to interpret would use the Gestalt factors appropriately, to avoid confusion (even the beginning photographer learns to avoid aligning subjects with telephone poles): a representative survey is needed, as in Case 19. (3) Perhaps most important, the simple discovery and use of the law of proximity preceded by many years Brunswik's attempt to derive it as an empiricistic consequence of the ecological distribution of stimulation. It is clear that, at least for certain aspects of spatial perception, one can understand and predict what people perceive while side-stepping completely the nature-nurture problem. We do not have to know the innate physiological mechanisms nor must we have a thorough knowledge of past associations in order to know what people will see. This last point must be examined here in greater detail, since on it depends the future status of our problem.

Side-stepping the Nature-Nurture Issue

It will be recalled that Helmholtz opposed the nativist proposals of innate binocular-distance sensations on the grounds that so-called empirical factors can and do overcome binocular disparity in determining how we see space (see p. 287). Kopfermann reversed the argument by showing that such so-called empirical factors could be predicted better in terms of the so-called Gestalt laws (which presumably rest on innate physiological laws of organization) than by any empiricism. But must we really invoke innate physiological mechanisms (i.e., nativism) as our only alternative to that of past association (i.e., empiricism)?

SOLIDITY OF OBJECTS.   Let us look once more to the ambiguous (reversible) figures, whose appearance the Gestalt theory appeared to predict so well.

Case 21: The psychophysics of ambiguous tridimensionality. A set of reversible-perspective figures adapted from those of Kopfermann (Case 15) were judged as to relative degree of apparent flatness vs. apparent depth by large numbers of observers. Hypothesis: the greater the geometrical complexity in two dimensions, the greater the tendency to see the figure as three-dimensional. Figure 44 graphs the two-dimensional complexity within each "family" of figures (the various projections of a cube, of a pyramid, etc.) against the observers' judgments of solidity (Hochberg and Brooks, 1960).

We see that it is possible to predict the degree of apparent spatiality or tridimensionality of ambiguous shapes quite well, without knowing anything about either (1) the effects of past experience, or (2) the physiological laws of organization. We can find psychophysical correspondence (i.e., we can predict what people will see with different stimuli)

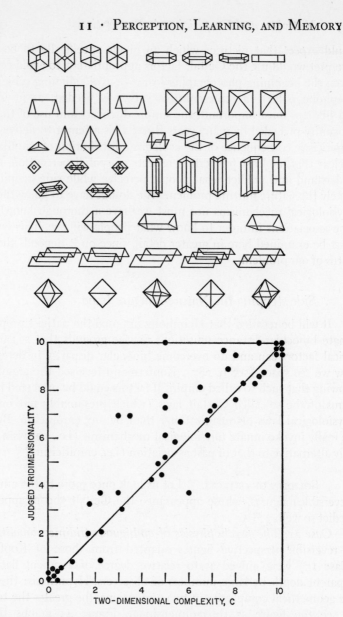

FIGURE 44. Psychophysics of ambiguous tridimensionality (Case 21). Top: ambiguous depth figures. Bottom: fit of judged tridimensionality of above patterns to measured two-dimensional complexity, C. $C = \dfrac{(T_1 + T_2 + 2T_3)}{N_T}$, where C is two-dimensional complexity, T_1 is number of angles, T_2 is number of different angles divided by number of angles, T_3 is number of separate continuous line segments, and N_T is number of such tests which apply to a given set of figures.

without taking a stand or having any opinion about (and even without ever having heard of) the nature-nurture issue.

SPACE PERCEPTION: THE EMPIRICAL FACTORS.   What about the perception of pure space or distance, the point at which the nature-nurture problem formally took its start (see Case 1)? The most important distance cues were found to be the so-called empirical factors, but there was very little study of them until recently. The most striking and comprehensive treatment is to be found in the work of J. J. Gibson (1950a). Gibson has, on occasion, expressed empiricist sentiments and, on other occasions, nativist leanings, but both are equally irrelevant to his actual concern which is, quite simply, to rebuild the analysis of space perception without drawing upon either Berkeley's introspection or his philosophical bias (see p. 259).

Largely under the pressure of aviation's need to have some applicable theory of space, Gibson (1946, pp. 181–95) started with the basic phenomenon that adults *do* after all perceive space and distance (regardless of whether this be learned, innate, or both). He discovered an impressive array of proximal physical stimulus dimensions which *could*—despite all tradition to the contrary—be correlated with the experience of space, surface, and depth. For example, the rate of change (technically called the *gradient*) of the density of texture in the retinal image of a surface is nicely correlated with the physical slant of that surface with respect to the observer (Figures 45 and 46).

Case 22: Stimuli for distance: gradients (Gibson, 1950b). Observers were shown flat surfaces in the frontal plane (i.e., upright and perpendicular to the line of sight, as in Figure 45); each surface had a distribution of texture on it, which was more dense at one edge than at the other, and which varied smoothly—in other words, there was a *texture-density-gradient* across the surface. The texture-density-gradients varied in their steepness, and the slant at which observers judged the surface to be was found to vary with the steepness of the texture-density-gradient (Figure 46). The gradient of texture density is only one of a number of physical variables in the retinal image which could conceivably act as simple, direct stimuli for a simple, direct experience of "surface-at-a-slant."

Gibson has shown that many of the traditional distance cues can be viewed as simply local expressions of over-all gradients (cf. Figure 47). These are stationary cues, i.e., they occur in the absence of motion, either of the observer or of any parts of the environment. Even more striking are Gibson's analyses of the *optical expansion pattern* (Gibson, 1950a; Gibson, Olum, and Rosenblatt, 1955): this is a possible cue about the distance and motion of seen objects based upon changes in the visual image which are caused by the relative motion between the observer and his environment. Figure 48 shows diagrams representing the motion of each point in the visual image which is projected to the eye from the elements of a plane surface, with respect to which an observer is moving. As long as we assume that the observer is viewing a

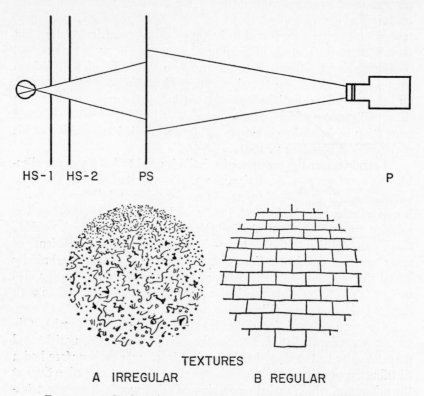

TEXTURES

A IRREGULAR   B REGULAR

FIGURE 45.   Gradients as possible depth cues (Case 22). Top: apparatus for presenting gradients. The subject looks monocularly through two hole-screens (HS-1 and HS-2) at a translucent projection screen (PS). A photographic image is projected on the screen. The angle subtended by this image at the eye is equal to the angle of the scene subtended at the lens of the camera which made the photograph. Bottom: examples of irregular and regular textures. Regularity refers to the degree to which the distribution of stimulus elements is uniform and cyclical. (From J. J. Gibson, "The Perception of Visual Surfaces," Amer. J. Psychol., 1950, 63, pp. 376–7. Reprinted by permission of The American Journal of Psychology.)

rigid surface, each pattern is a precise index of the specific distance, direction, and speed of the observer relative to the surface. It is instructive to compare the sets of stimuli for space perception shown in Figure 48 with the traditional ambiguous depth cues of Figure 26.

Gibson has taken a much larger view of normal visual proximal stimulus-patterns than the slices with which Berkeley had started, and

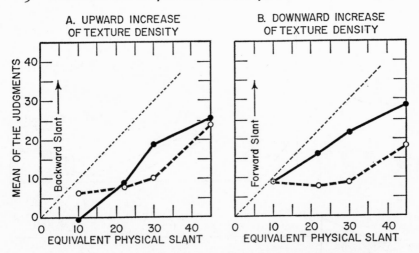

FIGURE 46. Judged slant as a function of the "physical slant equivalent to texture density." "Equivalent physical slant" is a measure of the density of the texture gradients. The 45-degree lines indicate judgments to be expected if there were a one-to-one correspondence between equivalent physical slant and judged slant. The obtained judgments for regular texture are shown by the solid lines, and for irregular texture by the broken lines. (From J. J. Gibson, "The Perception of Visual Surfaces," *Amer. J. Psychol.*, 1950, 63, p. 380. Reprinted by permission of *The American Journal of Psychology*.)

found in them simple over-all physical variables (which, if they had been noticed at all, were previously ignored as "learned" or "secondary" factors). Note that those variables are what Gibson calls *higher-order variables*: they do not exist as local stimuli at all—they are *Gestalt* factors in the sense that they extend over the retinal image as a whole, they are not *Gestalt-ish* in that they are defined completely in terms of physical stimulation, with no attempt to refer to unknown, inner laws of organization or to equally unknown physiological processes.

Thus we see that we *can* study the perception of space quite well, without recourse to either pole of the nature-nurture issue. A gradient may be the stimulus which will result in a specific spatial experience through the operation of some innate mechanism of retina or brain, or it may be learned, or it may be a result of the interaction of both nature and nurture—but regardless of which of these be true it can be used equally well to predict and control what people will perceive.

Epilogue: Molineaux' Experiment and Related Studies

WE CAN NOW RETURN to the question of whether (and how much) the perception of space depends on learning, as a problem in its own right, without philosophical, religious, political, physiological, or

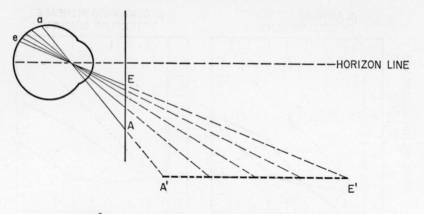

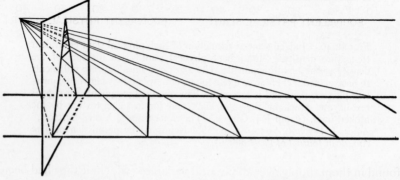

FIGURE 47. How spatial distance generates gradients. Top: a picture-gradient, the corresponding retinal gradient and the projected longitudinal surface corresponding to both. Middle: method of drawing gradients. The projection of a longitudinal surface on a picture plane is obtained according to the rules of projective geometry. Bottom: gradients of vertical spacing. (From J. J. Gibson, *The Perception of the Visual World*, Figures 28, 30, and 37, on pages 79, 82, and 89. Copyright 1950 by James J. Gibson. Reproduced by permission of Houghton Mifflin Company.)

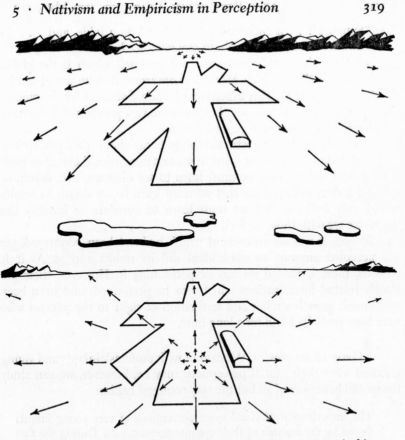

FIGURE 48. Gradients due to motion. As the observer moves in his environment, the proximal stimulus-pattern changes. The patterns of change in the retinal image projected by a surface—the motion gradients of the pattern—are quite different for different distances and motions between the observer and the surfaces around him, and provide the observer with a *possible* source of very precise information about his spatial environment. The upper diagram displays the gradients resulting from a motion *parallel* to a surface. The lower diagram shows motion at an *angle* to a surface. (From J. J. Gibson, *The Perception of the Visual World*, Figures 53 and 58 on pp. 121 and 128. Published in 1950 by Houghton Mifflin Company, and used with their permission.)

even systematic psychological controversies hanging on the issue. The indirect arguments pretty much cancel each other out, as we have seen. Not surprisingly, we will find the direct evidence to be too sparse, too equivocal, and too complex to provide any simple answers to the original questions.

Research with Humans

In the original setting of the problem, both Locke and Berkeley had considerable faith in an imaginary experiment by Molineaux. This was: "Suppose . . . a cube and sphere placed on a table, and . . . (a man blind from birth) be made to see; whether *by his sight, before he touched them,* he could now distinguish and tell which is the globe, which the cube?" To which Molineaux answered that he would not be able to do so (p. 265). This experiment is indeed support for the empiricist theory of space perception, but there are two points which decrease its value as a basis for much generalization.

First, it has only very restricted things to say about space perception. It does *not* say that we must learn to see two-dimensional extent or position; it does *not* say that we must learn to see distance, size, depth, or solidity; it does not even say that we must learn to see shape; its results would only indicate that we must learn to correlate or identify the shapes we see with those we feel.

Second, it was an experiment *which had not been performed,* yet was accepted anyway, so self-evident did its results appear. As it is phrased, there is indeed no way of performing it. However, there are closely related investigations which *can* be performed, and have been performed: growth studies and restoration of sight to the persons who have been partially blind for a long time.

GROWTH STUDIES.   We cannot with profit ask infants and young children what their spatial perceptions may be; however, we can study the spatial behaviors of all but the very youngest babies:

> The imperfection of visual space perceptions of very young infants is shown by the manner of their eye-movements. . . . During the first days of life, the absence of coordination between the movements of the two eyes . . . is very evident . . . one must conclude that the new-born infant is incapable of perceiving the positions (and distances) of objects . . . with any precision. . . . In consequence, . . . unable to perceive depth, he must see objects shrink when they move away, and expand when they come closer . . . [Translated by the author from Bourdon, 1902, pp. 359–61.]

This conclusion about size perception in children has been the subject of many anecdotes, as we have seen (see p. 277), and of some actual experimental research.

Case 23: The growth of size constancy. Beyrl (1926) performed a size-constancy experiment (using boxes and dishes) with subjects who ranged upward from two years of age. The youngest children did not obtain the complete size constancy which characterized the adults, but neither did they make their judgments purely in terms of the retinal image.

The fact that size constancy is not as good with two-year olds as it is with adults suggests (1) that improvement and learning do occur, which supports an empiricist view, and (2) that the fact that size constancy is as good as it is, even with two-year olds, might be taken to support a nativist explanation. Against the first point we have the following argument: the difference found between children and adults may be due to the method of testing, and disappears with other procedures (Koffka, 1935, pp. 288f.). A striking display of visual depth perception at a very early age appears in Case 24.

Case 24: Depth perception in the human infant: the visual cliff. E. J. Gibson and R. D. Walk (1960) performed the only direct experiment we have in this area:

> [The visual cliff] consists of a board laid across a large sheet of heavy glass which is supported a foot or more above the floor. On one side of the board a sheet of patterned material is placed flush against the undersurface of the glass, giving the glass the appearance as well as the substance of solidity. On the other side a sheet of the same material is laid upon the floor. . . . [Each of] 36 infants ranging in age from six months to 14 months . . . was placed upon the center board, and his mother called him to her from the cliff side and the shallow side successively. All of the 27 infants who moved off the board crawled out on the shallow side at least once; only three of them crept . . . onto the glass suspended above the pattern on the floor. . . . The experiment thus demonstrated that most human infants can discriminate depth as soon as they can crawl [p. 64].

The empiricist would say that any size constancy which we find in the two-year old, and depth perception in the one-half to one and one-half-year old, is simply the acquisition of one-half to two years of experience. This may be, but, as regards the age range to which the issue has any relevance, we have pushed the problem into a very small age-bracket indeed. Both of these arguments could be settled, if only we could ask questions of a newborn infant. Obviously, we can neither ask questions about the experiences of newborn infants nor can we use indirect measures which depend on muscular coordination (like reaching) before the muscular coordination has been achieved. For this reason it would be desirable to experiment with children or with adults who have matured normally in all other respects, but have been deprived of visual experiences (as in Molineaux' experiment).

RESTORED SIGHT.   While we cannot restore vision to the completely blind, there have been a number of studies in which congenital and other long-term cataracts (a condition of clouded vision in which only vague patches of light and shade can be seen) were removed. The questioning procedures employed in these cases and the reports of the findings have not really been good enough for us to draw very confident conclusions.

Case 25: Restored sight. The most comprehensive review of such cases is by von Senden (1932).

Most of the patients studied were suffering from cataracts which either developed rapidly after birth or developed . . . over a period of years. A number of these patients could not be considered as totally blind. . . . But their impression of the outer world consisted of a vague gray mass with changing intensity, which did, however, not really provide a conception of space and depth for them [p. i]. [This is the closest approach to Molineaux' experiment.] . . . It has shown unambiguously in all cases . . . that the operated patients fail completely to recognize visual objects on the basis of a tactual form image. . . . When he is requested to say something about the form of an object the patient interprets this task as . . . if it were a purely tactual task [p. 147] . . . the true state of affairs would seem to be that the patients had no real apprehension of space at all before the operation and that everything spatial is completely new to them [p. 149] . . . [as far as distance and depth are concerned; however] . . . it is erroneous to draw the conclusion . . . that the patient . . . has no impression of depth at all at the first visual experiences [p. 116]. . . . He sees all the colored surfaces at a certain distance from himself. The distance . . . is fairly stable [p. 157]. . . . For a long time all judgments are based on color alone, while absolutely no attention is paid to contour. The same form in a different color is not recognized as the same object. . . . Even when he seriously concerns himself with the aspect of form . . . the form as such has no noticeable effect. . . . This . . . is prolonged . . . because the patient does not use his peripheral vision, and because of this must successively bring all the parts of the contour into the small region of optimum clearness of vision [p. 164].

Many difficulties are inherent in such observations, especially important being the difficulty of repeating them. For this reason we must turn to research with animals for supplementary information.

Studies with Animals

Recent years have seen an increasing amount of research performed with animals, trying to determine the extent to which various aspects of spatial perception are dependent on learning. One series has provided an especially close parallel to von Senden's (and Molineaux') idealized situation:

Case 26: Visual deprivation in the chimpanzee. Riesen (1950) pointed out that:

But such cases of congenital cataract do not give us very satisfactory evidence on the elementary problem of how disease affects the development of visual behavior. There are too many other variables; we must take into account: (1) the degree of the patient's previous blind-

ness, since he was not in total darkness, (2) the limit . . . imposed
. . . by the fact that the eye . . . lacks a lens, and (3) . . . in all
these cases there [is] . . . another visual handicap—jerky movements of the eyeballs known as spontaneous nystagmus . . . it is
highly desirable to eliminate these variables by setting up a controlled experiment that will determine the effects of disuse on normal
eyes. Obviously such an experiment cannot be risked in human beings; . . . The most logical subject . . . is another higher primate.
The chimpanzee was chosen, because its behavior, like man's, is dominated by vision, and . . . is intelligent . . . two newborn . . . infants . . . were housed in a completely darkened room. During the
first 16 months the only light . . . was an electric lamp . . . for intervals of 45 seconds several times daily for . . . care and feeding.
When they were first tested . . . at . . . 16 months, both . . .
showed extreme incompetence . . . their eyes were sensitive to light
. . . but . . . both failed to show any visual responses to complex
patterns of light until after . . . many hours in illuminated surround-
ings . . . they did not blink at a threatening motion toward the face.
When an object was advanced slowly toward the face, there was no reaction until the object actually touched the face, and then the animal
gave a startled jump [p. 17]. [There are clearly deteriorative processes involved:] Faik was raised in . . . normal light . . . until the
age of seven months . . . he had excellent use of vision. Then from
the age of eight to 24 months he was kept in the darkroom. . . .
When Faik was returned to daylight living quarters . . . he had lost
all ability to utilize vision. . . . His recovery of vision has been slow
and is still only partial [p. 19].[8]

This evidence of visual deficiences caused by disuse makes the
Molineaux experiment almost impossible to perform at present—impossible, that is, for the purposes for which it was proposed.[9] The vision of
the blind adult, to whom sight is given for the first time, does *not* provide any indication of the innate visual ability of the infant, not only
because of the deteriorative changes which have probably occurred
during the years, but also because of different, compensating processes
which such adults may have developed. We must attempt to study the
infant itself.

However, the human infant displays insufficient behavior coordination to permit its study to give us very much useful information. If we
turn to the chick, a very different picture emerges:

[8] From A. H. Riesen, "Arrested Vision," *Sci. Amer.*, 1950, 183, pp. 16–19.
Used by permission of *Scientific American*.

[9] Although it is possible to raise animals with translucent eyecoverings, so that
they receive diffused light but no sharp contours, the procedure does not bypass the
possibility of deteriorative changes: the possible existence of contour-sensitive receptors
and, indeed, of *any* set of innate mechanisms which could suffer from disuse presents
an almost insuperable obstacle.

. . . the perfection of vision in chicks immediately after birth is something astonishing, compared to its imperfection in the newborn human. If one keeps them blindfolded for the first two or three days of life, one sees them, often [only] two minutes after removing the blindfold, follow the motions of an insect creeping on the ground, with all of the precision of an adult fowl [Translated by the author from Bourdon, 1902, p. 359.].

Experimental research supports such anecdotes:
Case 27: Localization in the chick. Hess (1956)

. . . sought a method that would prevent normal visual experience and yet would not interfere with the normal physiological development of the eye. . . . Suppose that a chick first sees the light of day wearing prisms which cause a displacement of the visual image seven degrees to the right. If the exact . . . localization of objects in space is a totally learned ability . . . performance should be unaffected by . . . [the] prisms . . . it should start pecking . . . in a random fashion until, after trial and error, the object is eaten. Gradually, as sensory-motor associations are built up . . . accuracy should improve. . . . [Prisms were placed on chicks at hatching, and records were kept of where chicks pecked at a brass nail embedded in modeling clay] . . . We must conclude that the prisms clustered its pecks about the spot where the object was seen (i.e., 7° to the right). It did not simply peck at random until it struck the target . . . [and it] appeared unable to learn through experience to correct its aim. Its only improvement was to increase the consistency of the distance by which it missed the target.[1]

In fact, birds seem to have certain innate visual abilities to get around in space, which are completely unknown to the human:
Case 28: Innate celestial navigation by birds.

. . . The lesser white throat [a migratory warbler] normally first travels southeastward across the Balkans and then turns due south, flying along the Nile to its winter home . . . as long as the planetarium sky (which was visible to birds in glass-topped cages) was adjusted to the approximate latitude of Germany. . . . Johnny (a bird subject whom we will describe in a moment) took up the expected flight position facing southeast. But as we . . . [simulated] more southerly latitudes, . . . at the latitude of 15 degrees, it set its course due south! . . . [Thus] Johnny, a bird which had spent all its life in a cage and never traveled under a natural sky, let alone migrated to Africa, still displayed an inborn ability to use the guidance of the stars to follow the usual route of its species, adjusting its direction nicely at each given latitude.[2]

[1] From E. H. Hess, "Space Perception in the Chick," Sci. Amer., 1956, 195, pp. 71–80. Used by permission of the Scientific American.

[2] From E. G. F. Sauer, "Celestial Navigation by Birds," Sci. Amer., 1958, 199, p. 45. Used by permission of the Scientific American.

Although Case 24 could not prove the innate basis of human depth perception, the same investigators (Gibson and Walk, 1960) investigated a number of other species of animals, with striking results.

Case 29: Other animals on the visual cliff. As in Case 24, infants were placed on a board with two sheets of glass on either side, with a pattern placed flush against the glass on one side, and the same pattern placed down on the floor below, on the other side. In this series of investigations, Gibson and Walk

> . . . observed the behavior of chicks, turtles, rats, lambs, kids, pigs, kittens and dogs. . . . In the chick . . . depth perception manifests itself with special rapidity. At an age of less than 24 hours [and with no visual experience] the chick can be tested on the visual cliff. It never makes a mistake and always hops off the board on the shallow side. [Rats reared in darkness also appear to be capable of the visual cliff discrimination (apparently using a motion-dependent cue—see p. 315 and Figure 48). For the species which have been studied so far] . . . a seeing animal will be able to discriminate depth when its locomotion is adequate, even when locomotion begins at birth [pp. 64–71].

Summary of Cases 23 to 29

Actual research with humans and animals does not support either a nativist or an empiricist position. Processes of maturation, deterioration, and learning all interact to form a very complex picture. There appear to be great differences in the innate abilities of different species, but these may be complicated by the even greater differences in the age at which effectively coordinated behavior appears. Certainly, most of what we mean by space perception appears to be innate in the chick and in many other animals. It seems unwise to generalize to the human for the preceding reasons. However, if we remember that the early statement of the nature-nurture issue (and much of the following two hundred years of controversy) rested upon the logical demonstration that it was impossible for *any* creature to have innate spatial abilities, we see that the pecking of a chick comprises a serious refutation of the original argument.

THE NATURE-NURTURE QUESTION AND ITS EVOLUTION AND EFFECTS

LET US NOW REVIEW the ways in which the purposes, the methods, and the effects of this inquiry have changed (and changed each other) through the course of two centuries of investigation:

Purposes

In the hands of the empiricists (and Berkeley, most specifically) the problem was whether we can have any idea of space at all which is not learned through experience. This is what we may call the strong form of the question, and was in keeping with the purpose for which the question was asked. Since generalization was to be made to all of human knowledge, even a little innate space perception would destroy the point to be established.

The associationists' (p. 266) purpose was to determine the composition of our thoughts and consciousness; now the strong form of the problem was no longer required in order for the question to be of psychological interest in the following sense.

As far as the epistemological purpose of the empiricist philosophers was concerned, the point had been made, and the issue had moved on; there was no longer any way in which even the most striking proof of the innate perception of space could have anything to say about the truth or falsity of our ideas. Philosophers had realized that all men could be born into the world with perfectly uniform, thoroughly innate ideas —and those ideas might still be false. As far as the psychological purpose of the associationists was concerned, there was really no *a priori* reason to have much attachment to either position. Since the subjects of investigation were always full-grown and well-educated adults, it would not have mattered very much one way or the other, in their analysis of the structure of ideas in those adults, whether some of the more primitive aspects of space perception were innate.

For the sensory physiologist the purpose was again different: it seemed quite easy to find the structures of the eye which were sensitive to light, shade, and color, but it seemed impossible to find any structures sensitive to space or distance. If the sensory physiologist was to discuss space perception at all, it had to be either in terms of some specific physiological mechanism (such as the one proposed by Hering), *or* in terms of its being built up somehow out of light, shade, and color (as Helmholtz proposed).

The experimental psychologists' purpose breaks up into two parts. First, both nativist and empiricist answers had been presented as being important to psychologists because they presumably enable us to predict what people will see. However, as we have just noted, we really can study the perception of space quite well without ever getting involved in the question of nature and nurture. This part of the initial purpose has now become obsolete. Second, the question of whether space perception is learned and, if so, *how much, when,* and *in what manner,* remains as a separate set of problems in which we may be interested for their own sake, as we have seen in the last section of this paper.

Methods

Just as the purposes of attempting to answer the nature-nurture question have changed, so have the methods used. The empiricist philosophers sought to examine any ideas which seemed to be of crucial philosophical importance, and (by introspection and logical analysis) to show how they originated. The associationist psychologists continued to rely upon these tools, which they used to catalogue the elements out of which all thought was presumably composed. The sensory physiologists introduced more objective measures, wherever there were physiological mechanisms to which to refer, but saw no reason to go beyond the methods of the associationists where no such physiological mechanisms were in evidence. The Gestaltists began the first systematic experiments on the non-physiological factors in space perception, mostly by use of demonstrations (and a few sporadic quantitative psychophysical studies). Only in the last decade or so has full-fledged psychophysical research in human (and animal) space perceptions finally begun.

Effects of Changes in Purpose and Method

The effects of the various changes in purpose and method are easy to recognize. To the empiricists and associationists, there was clearly no reason to attempt a psychophysical study of space perceptions, since these were presumed to be built up by the highly individual and accidental experiences of each person; consequently, introspection or individual self-observation was the primary method employed and only qualitative reports could be obtained. Self-observation, on the other hand, could hardly suffice to give us any detailed and unequivocal information of the sort we have seen resulting from the later experiments, and we can expect that the increasing demand for precise prediction of spatial abilities and performance will result in continued and increasing reliance on psychophysical measurement.

We are not yet finished with the nature-nurture problem, but we have reached the end of the original line. From this point forward no real vestige of the original purpose remains. Both problem and method have become completely transformed (although tradition is strong, and frequently investigators seem not to notice that the old names conceal new problems).

REFERENCES

BERKELEY, G.   Essay towards a new theory of vision, 1709. In *Selections from Berkeley*, Alexander Campbell Fraser, 6th ed. Oxford: Clarendon Press, 1910.

BEYRL, F.　Über die grossen Auffassung bei Kindern. *Z. f. Psychol.*, 1926, 100, pp. 34–371.

BORING, E. G.　*Sensation and perception in the history of experimental psychology.* New York: Appleton-Century-Crofts, 1942.

BOURDON, B.　*La perception visuelle de l'espace.* Paris: C. Reinwald, 1902.

BRUNSWIK, E.　Statistical separation of perception, thinking and attitudes (Abstract). *Amer. Psychologist*, 1948, 3: 342.

――――.　*The conceptual framework of psychology (Int. Encycl. of Unif. Sci.*, ed. by R. Carnap and C. Morris, Vol. 1, No. 10). Chicago: University of Chicago, 1952.

――――.　*Perception and the representative design of psychological experiments.* Berkeley: University of California, 1956.

BRUNSWIK, E., AND KAMIYA, J.　Ecological cue-validity of "proximity" and of other Gestalt factors. *Amer. J. Psychol.*, 1953, 66, 20–32.

GIBSON, E. J., AND WALK, R. D.　The "visual cliff." *Sci. Amer.*, 1960, 202, 64–71.

GIBSON, J. J.　Adaptation, after-effect and contrast in the perception of curved lines. *J. exp. Psychol.*, 1933, 16, 1–31.

――――.　*The perception of the visual world.* Cambridge: Houghton Mifflin Co., 1950.

――――.　The perception of visual surfaces. *Amer. J. Psychol.*, 1950, 63, 367–84.

GIBSON, J. J. (Ed.).　*Motion picture testing and research.* AAF program, Report no. 7, 1946.

GIBSON, J. J., OLUM, P., AND ROSENBLATT, F.　Parallax and perspective during aircraft landings. *Amer. J. Psychol.*, 1955, 68, 372–85.

GOTTSCHALDT, K.　Über der Einfluss der Erfahrung auf die Wahrnehmung von Figuren. *Psychol. Forsch.*, 1926, 8, 261–317.

GÖTZ, W.　Experimentelle Untersuchungen zum Problem der Sehgrössenkonstanz beim Haushuhn. *Zts. f. Psych.*, 1926, 99, 247–60.

HARTLEY, D.　*Observations on man, his frame, his duty and his expectations*, 4th ed. London: J. Johnson, 1801.

HAYEK, F.　*The sensory order.* Chicago: University of Chicago, 1952.

HELMHOLTZ, H. V.　*Physiologic-optics*, 2nd ed., 1896. Transl. by B. Rand, pub. in *The Classical Psychologists.* Houghton Mifflin Co., 1912.

――――.　*Handbook of physiological optics.* Transl. from 3rd German ed., 1910, by J. P. C. Southall, ed. Vol. III, Optical Soc. Am., 1925.

HERING, E.　*Beitrage zur Physiologie*, Heft 1. Leipzig: Engelmann, 1861.

HESS, E. H.　Space perception in the chick. *Sci. Amer.*, 1956, 195, 71–80.

HOBBES, T. *Leviathan.* Ed. by W. Molesworth: Vol. III. London, 1839.

HOCHBERG, J., AND BROOKS, V. The psychophysics of form: reversible-perspective drawings of spatial objects. *Amer. J. Psychol.*, 73, 1960, 337–54.

HUME, D. *A treatise of human nature.* 1739. Ed. by L. A. Selby-Bigge. Oxford: Clarendon Press, 1888.

HURVICH, L., AND JAMESON, D. A. Quantitative theoretical account of color vision. *Trans. N. Y. Acad. Sci.*, Ser. II, 1955, Vol. 18, 1, 33–8.

ITTELSON, W., AND KILPATRICK, F. Experiments in perception. *Sci. Amer.*, 1952, 185, 50–5.

KATZ, D. *The world of color.* London: Paul, Trench, and Trubman, 1935.

———. *Gestalt psychology, its nature and significance.* New York: Ronald Press, 1950.

KOFFKA, K. *Principles of Gestalt psychology.* New York: Harcourt, Brace, and Co., 1935.

KOHLER, I. *Über aufbau und Wandlungen der Wahrnehmungswelt. Oesterr. Akad. Wiss. Philos. Histor. Kl. Switz-Ber.*, 1951, 227, 1–118.

KÖHLER, W. Über unbemerkte Empfindungen und Urteilstäuschungen. *Zts. f. Psych.*, 1913, 66, 51–80.

———. *Gestalt psychology.* New York: Liveright, 1929.

———. *Die physischen Gestalten in Ruhe und im stationären Zustand.* Erlangen, 1920. Transl. and abridged in Ellis, W. A *sourcebook of Gestalt psychology.* New York: Harcourt, Brace and Co., 1938.

KÖHLER, W., AND WALLACH, H. Figural after-effect, an investigation of visual processes. *Proc. Amer. Philos. Soc.*, 1944, 88, 269–357.

KOPFERMANN, H. Psychologische Untersuchungen über die Wirkung zweidimensionaler Darstellungen körperlicher Gebilde. *Psych. Forsch.*, 1930, 13, 293–364.

LAWRENCE, M. *Studies in human behavior.* Princeton: Princeton University, 1949.

LOCKE, J. *Essay concerning human understanding.* 1690. Philadelphia: Troutman and Hays, 1853.

MICHOTTE, A. *La perception de la causalité.* Louvain Inst. Superieur de Phil., 1946.

MILL, J. *Analysis of the phenomena of the human mind,* Vol. I. Ed. by J. S. Mill, London: Longmans, Green, Reader, and Dyer, 1869.

MULLER, J. *Elements of physiology.* Transl. by W. Bally. Philadelphia: Lea and Blanchard, 1843.

PLATO. *Theaetetus*. Transl. by S. Dyde, reprinted in Rand, B.: *The classical psychologists*. New York: Houghton Mifflin Co., 1912.

PRATT, C. C. The role of past experience in visual perception. *J. Psychol.*, 1950, 30, 85–107.

RIESEN, A. H. Arrested vision. *Sci. Amer.*, 1950, 183, 6–19.

SAUER, E. G. F. Celestial navigation by birds. *Sci. Amer.*, 1958, 199, 42–47.

SLACK, C. W. Critique on the interpretation of cultural differences in the perception of motion in Ames' trapezoidal window. *Amer. J. Psychol.*, 1959, 72, 127–31.

TITCHENER, E. B. *An outline of psychology*. New York: The Macmillan Co., 1902.

———. *A textbook of psychology*. New York: The Macmillan Co., 1926.

VON SENDEN, M. *Raum-und Gestaltauffassung bei Operierten Blindgeborenen vor und nach der Operation*. Leipzig: Barth, 1932. Transl. by members of the Laboratory of Psychology, Cornell University, AFC–AF411 (128), 42, 1950.

WERTHEIMER, M. Untersuchungen zur Lehre von der Gestalt, II. *Psychol. Forsch.*, 1923, 4, 301–50.

WHEATSTONE, C. Contributions to the physiology of vision. *Phil. Trans. Royal Soc. Lon.*, 1838; reprinted in Dennis, W. *Readings in general psychology*. New York: Prentice-Hall, 1949.

WOOSTER, M. Certain factors in the development of new spatial coordination. *Psychol. Monogr.*, 1923, 32, No. 4.

WUNDT, W. *Outlines of psychology* (4th German ed.). Transl. by C. H. Judd. Leipzig: Engelmann, 1902.

YOUNG, T. *A course of lectures on natural philosophy*. London: 1807, I, 440.

CHAPTER 6

Rewards and Punishments
in Human Learning

LEO POSTMAN

MANY OF OUR EDUCATIONAL, social, and legal practices are based on the assumption that rewards and punishments are effective and reliable tools for the modification of behavior. The general belief is that actions which are followed by rewards are strengthened, while actions which are followed by punishments are weakened or eliminated. These assumptions of common sense have not received undivided support from the experimental study of behavior. In fact, the role played by rewards and punishments has become one of the most controversial issues in contemporary learning theory.

Philosophical discussions of rewards and punishments as regulators of human conduct have a long and time-honored history. The experimental investigation of the problem is, however, of fairly recent origin. It is only since the turn of the century that empirical answers have been sought to these basic questions: (1) Are stimulus-response associations strengthened when a reward follows the response? (2) Are stimulus-response associations weakened when a punishment follows the response? (3) What is the relative effectiveness of rewards and punishments in modifying behavior? (4) Are rewards and punishments necessary as well as sufficient conditions for the acquisition and elimination of habits?

The search for empirical answers to these questions began with the pioneer investigations of Edward Lee Thorndike (1898, 1911). Thorn-

331

dike's experiments constituted the first systematic investigation of the influence of rewards and punishments on learning and problem-solving. His theoretical interpretations set the stage for a searching and productive debate concerning the fundamental nature of the learning process. For half a century filled with unceasing experimental labor, he continued his investigations of the basic laws of learning. For much of this time he continued to occupy the center of the stage, attracting both strong support and vigorous criticism. For supporters and critics alike, Thorndike's formulations of the laws of learning were a basic point of departure.

Thorndike's early work was concerned with the nature of animal learning. In his later work he applied the concepts and principles derived from the studies of animals to problems of human learning. It was his conviction that the fundamental laws of learning hold true regardless of wide differences among species in structure and native endowment. Although our own concern will be primarily with the role of rewards and punishments in human learning, we shall begin with a brief discussion of Thorndike's studies of animal behavior.

THORNDIKE'S STUDY OF ANIMAL INTELLIGENCE

THE PUZZLE BOX.   Thorndike's first major series of experiments was published in 1898 under the title, *Animal Intelligence: An Experimental Study of the Associative Processes in Animals*. The subjects of the investigation were cats, dogs, and chicks. To study the course of learning in these animals, Thorndike developed an apparatus which has become known as the puzzle box. The puzzle box consists of an enclosure in which the animal is confined and from which it can escape "by some simple act, such as pulling at a loop or cord, pressing a lever, or stepping on a platform." Thorndike's customary procedure was to confine the animal in the box, put a piece of food outside in full sight of the animal, and then to observe the subject's behavior. He was interested both in the sequence and quality of the animal's actions, and the speed with which it performed the correct response. Training was usually continued until the animal had fully mastered the correct response and performed it almost immediately after being put into the box.

The character of the animals' behavior and Thorndike's general interpretation of the learning process are well illustrated in his description of the cats' performance in the puzzle box.

> When put into the box the cat would show evident signs of discomfort and an impulse to escape from confinement. It tries to squeeze through any opening; it claws and bites at the bars or wire; it thrusts its paws out through any opening and claws at everything it reaches; it continues its efforts when it strikes anything loose and shaky; it may

claw at things within the box. It does not pay very much attention to the food outside, but seems simply to strive instinctively to escape from confinement. The vigor with which it struggles is extraordinary. For eight or ten minutes it will claw and bite and squeeze incessantly. . . . Whether the impulse to struggle be due to an instinctive reaction to confinement or to an association, it is likely to succeed in letting the cat out of the box. The cat that is clawing all over the box in her impulsive struggle will probably claw the string or loop or button so as to open the door. And gradually all the other non-successful impulses will be stamped out and the particular impulse leading to the successful act will be stamped in by the resulting pleasure, until, after many trials, the cat will, when put in the box, immediately claw the loop or button in a definite way [1898, p. 13*f.*].

LEARNING BY TRIAL AND ERROR.   The basic outlines of a theory of animal learning emerge in this quotation. When an animal faces a new problem situation, its initial responses are determined by its "instinctive" tendencies. Thus, the cat reacts to confinement by squeezing, clawing, biting, etc. By "instinct" Thorndike meant in this context "any reaction which an animal makes to a situation *without experience*" (1898, p. 14). If the animal has been in a similar problem situation before, its initial reactions will, of course, be conditioned by its earlier experiences. If it has escaped from other confinements by clawing rather than biting, its initial response to the new confinement is more likely to be clawing than biting. From among the animal's initial reactions one is selected by success, i.e., the association between the situation and the successful response is strengthened by the satisfying consequences of the response. As learning continues, the successful response becomes stronger and stronger while the unsuccessful responses become weaker and weaker. This is the doctrine of "learning by trial and error with accidental success" (1898, p. 105), or, as it has become more generally known, *trial-and-error learning*.

The speed with which successful responses are learned selectively varies widely from situation to situation and from individual to individual. Figure 49 shows the learning curves for a group of cats which learned to escape from a puzzle box by moving a wire loop suspended in the box. The time which elapsed before performance of the successful response is plotted for successive trials. The individual curves are marked by considerable irregularity and there are wide differences among the individual animals. Nevertheless, all curves show a rapid reduction in time scores, i.e., a speedy acquisition of the correct response. The speed with which a new problem is solved depends on the difficulty of the task and on the amount of experience which the animal has had with similar problems in the past. The effects of prior experience are well illustrated in the two sets of curves in Figure 50. These curves show the progress of learning for a puzzle box from which the cat could escape by pressing a lever projecting into the box. Cats 1 through 5 came to this problem after considerable experience with puzzle boxes. Cats 10 through 12 had had experience with only one box. The experienced cats learned the new problem very rapidly. Their time scores either dropped precipitously, or started low and remained low (except for one atypical trial of Cat 2).

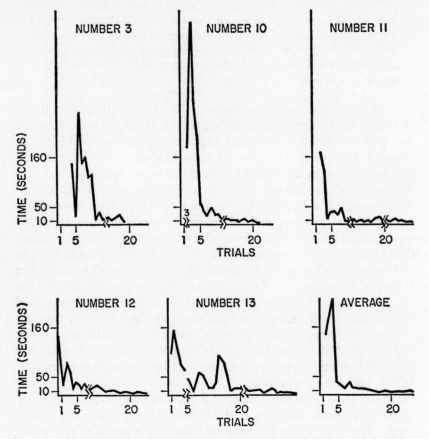

FIGURE 49.   Learning curves of cats in a puzzle box.
(After Thorndike, 1898, p. 18.)

The inexperienced animals, especially Nos. 10 and 12, showed slower progress.

Some of the learning curves, such as those of Cats 1 and 3 in Figure 50, show such an abrupt change of behavior that one might be tempted to ascribe a sudden "insight" into the problem to the animal. Thorndike emphatically denied such an interpretation. Sudden drops in the time curve were largely restricted to simple acts; they did not appear when a complex act or a series of responses were required for the solu-

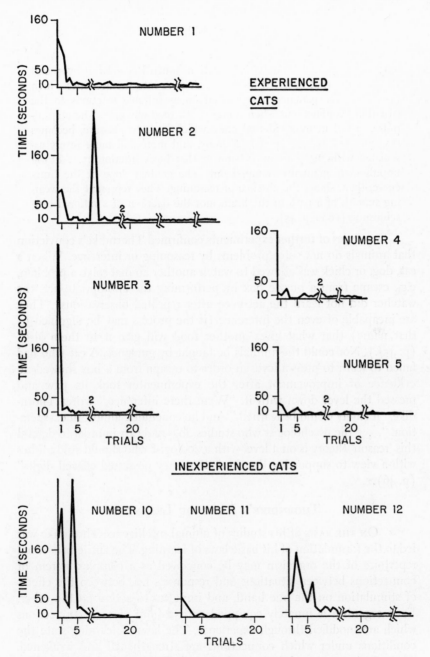

FIGURE 50. Learning curves of cats with different amounts of prior experience in a puzzle box. (After Thorndike, 1898, p. 22.)

tion. In all such cases, the learning curve was much more likely to be gradual. There was little in the animals' behavior to suggest the solution of problems by inference or reasoning.

> The cat does not look over the situation, much less *think* it over, and then decide what to do. It bursts out at once into the activities which instinct and experience have settled on as suitable reactions to the situation "confinement when hungry with food outside." The one impulse, out of many accidental ones, which leads to pleasure, becomes strengthened and stamped in thereby, and more and more firmly associated with the sense-impression of that box's interior. . . . Futile impulses are gradually stamped out. The gradual slope of the time-curve, then, shows the absence of reasoning. They represent the wearing smooth of a path in the brain, not the decision of a rational consciousness [1898, p. 45].

Two series of further experiments confirmed Thorndike's conviction that animals do not solve problems by reasoning or inference. When a cat, dog, or chick was allowed to watch another animal solve a problem, e.g., escape from a puzzle box by performing the appropriate act, the watcher did not learn the act even after repeated observations. "They are incapable of even the inference (if the process may be dignified by that name) that what gives another food will give it to them also" (p. 45f.). Nor could the animals be taught by guidance. A cat who had failed to learn to press a lever in order to escape from a box showed no evidence of improvement after the experimenter took its paw and pressed the lever down with it. "Were there inference," writes Thorndike, "it surely would be learned." And he concludes, almost in exasperation, ". . . the psychologist who studies dogs and cats in order to defend this 'reason' theory is on a level with a zoologist who should study fishes with a view to supporting the thesis that they possessed clawed digits" (p. 46).

THORNDIKE'S LAWS OF LEARNING

ON THE BASIS of his studies of animal intelligence Throndike was led to the formulation of his basic laws of learning. The entire behavioral repertoire of the organism may be conceived as a complex system of connections between situations and responses, i.e., between the effects of stimulation on the one hand, and impulses to action on the other. Each organism is innately equipped with a fund of such connections which are modified through experience. The laws of learning state the conditions under which connections are strengthened and weakened. The most important of these are the law of effect and the law of exercise.

THE LAW OF EFFECT.   The original statement of the law of effect read as follows:

Of several responses made to the same situation, those which are accompanied or closely followed by satisfaction to the animal will, other things being equal, be more firmly connected with the situation, so that, when it recurs, they will be more likely to recur; those which are accompanied or closely followed by discomfort to the animal will, other things being equal, have their connection with the situation weakened, so that, when it recurs, they will be less likely to occur. The greater the satisfaction or discomfort, the greater the strengthening or weakening of the bond [p. 244].[1]

In short, satisfaction stamps in connections between situations and responses, and discomfort stamps them out, and the effectiveness of these consequences depends on the degree of satisfaction and annoyance.

The key words requiring definition are "satisfaction" and "discomfort." What is the nature of the consequences which serve to strengthen and weaken connections between situations and responses? Thorndike offered the following general definitions:

By a satisfying state of affairs is meant one which the animal does nothing to avoid, often doing such things as attain and preserve it. By a discomforting or annoying state of affairs is meant one which the animal commonly avoids and abandons [p. 245].

Food when hungry and water when thirsty are examples of satisfiers; pain and confinement are examples of annoyers. It is important to note that satisfaction and discomfort are not defined in terms of subjective pleasure or annoyance; rather they are identified in terms of the reactions which a given consequence evokes from the animal—approach to satisfiers and avoidance of annoyers. It is true that in early discussions of the law of effect, satisfaction and discomfort often seem to be identified with subjective pleasure and annoyance. The basic definitions of satisfaction and discomfort do not, however, refer to subjective feelings. Rather, after-effects are classified in terms of the organism's reactions of approach and avoidance. Satisfiers often are favorable to the survival of the individual or the species and annoyers are often harmful, but the correlation is not perfect. There are satisfiers, such as certain foods and drinks, which are biologically harmful. What is satisfying and annoying depends on the momentary state of the nervous system.

Whatever the exact nature of satisfiers and annoyers, they exert their effects *directly* on the connections which they follow. The action of satisfiers and annoyers is independent of ideas or intellectual understanding. The only necessary condition for the operation of the law of effect is that a connection between situation and response be followed by a satisfier or annoyer. As Thorndike emphasized, the law of effect

[1] This and other excerpts below from Thorndike's *Animal Intelligence*, copyright 1911, are used with permission of The Macmillan Company, New York.

does *not* assert that responses which are *in themselves* satisfying are learned and responses which are in themselves annoying are weakened. Rather, it is the *after-effects* of a response to a situation which are the critical determinants of learning. "There is no pleasure along with the association of situation and response. The pleasure does not come until after the association is done and gone" (1911, p. 148).

Given the basic condition of satisfaction or discomfort, there are a number of variables which regulate the action of the law of effect. It is to these variables that the phrase, "other things being equal," refers. Thus the frequency with which the connection has occurred is important. This is the action of the law of exercise to which we shall return presently. Frequency of occurrence may compensate for weakness of satisfaction or discomfort. "A slightly satisfying or indifferent response made often may win a closer connection than a more satisfying response made only rarely" (1911, p. 248). The potency of after-effects also depends on the "closeness with which the satisfaction is associated with the response." Thus the longer the delay between the response and the after-effect, the less effective will be the consequence in strengthening the connection. Attention to the response is also favorable to the operation of the law of effect. "The successful response is as a rule only a part of all that the animal is doing at the time. In proportion as it is an eminent, emphatic part of it, learning is aided. Similarly, discomfort eliminates most the eminent, emphatic features of the total response which it accompanies or shortly follows" (p. 249).

THE LAW OF EXERCISE.   The second basic law of learning is the law of exercise which states: "Any response to a situation will, other things being equal, be more strongly connected with the situation in proportion to the number of times it has been connected with that situation and to the average vigor and duration of the connections" (p. 244). In this law Thorndike states the traditional doctrine that frequency of occurrence strengthens associations. The principle of frequency had earlier been applied by empiricist philosophers to the association of ideas: the more frequently two ideas follow each other the more strongly they become linked. Thorndike now extends the principle to the strengthening of connections between situations and responses.

Some time later, in his *Educational Psychology* (1914), Thorndike extended and refined the law of exercise by distinguishing two component principles, the *law of use* and the *law of disuse*. The law of use is essentially synonymous with the original law of exercise and asserts that the connections between situations and responses are strengthened by exercise. The law of disuse states: "When a modifiable connection is not made between a situation and a response during a length of time, the connection's strength is decreased" (1914, p. 4). Connections between situations and responses grow weaker with time unless they are renewed by exercise.

SUMMARY OF EARLY CONNECTIONISM. We have now stated the basic principles of learning which had their origin in Thorndike's study of animal intelligence. Let us briefly summarize the key concepts and hypotheses. The basic units in the analysis of behavior are connections between situations and responses. "Situation" denotes the state of the individual determined both by external stimulation and by internal conditions. "Response" is a disposition to *action* determined by both the original nature of the organism and the effects of past learning. Learning consists of changes in the strength of connections between situations and responses. The strength of a connection is measured in terms of the probability that a situation will evoke a given response; the higher the probability the stronger is the connection. The characteristic course of learning is trial and error, with accidental success. When the organism faces a problem, its initial responses are determined by its instinctive dispositions and by habits acquired in similar situations. Some of these responses will not be successful and will be weakened. Responses that are successful are strengthened; the more frequently an unsuccessful response occurs, the weaker becomes its connection with the situation; the more frequently a successful response occurs, the stronger becomes its connection with the situation. Reward and frequency, effect and exercise, are the keys to the modification of behavior.

CONNECTIONISM IN HUMAN LEARNING

IT WAS THORNDIKE's firm belief that his fundamental principles applied with equal force to human learning and to animal learning.

> These simple, semi-mechanical phenomena . . . which animal learning discloses are the fundamentals of human learning also. They are, of course, much complicated in the more advanced stages of human learning, such as the acquisition of skill with the violin, or of knowledge of the calculus, or of inventiveness in engineering. But it is impossible to understand the subtler and more planful learning of cultivated men without clear ideas of the forces which make learning possible in its first form of directly connecting some gross bodily response with a situation immediately present to the senses.[2]

He concludes that the principles governing such simple learning will "still be the main and perhaps the only facts" needed to explain the most subtle and complex forms of human learning.

[2] From E. L. Thorndike, *Educational Psychology*, 1914, p. 16, and used by permission of Teachers College, Columbia University, New York.

Guided by this conviction, Thorndike embarked on a research program devoted to the experimental analysis of exercise, reward, and punishment in human learning. This work came to full fruition about thirty years after the original study of animal intelligence. The results of a truly monumental body of experiments on human learning were summarized by Thorndike in a series of books which appeared in the 1930's and which represent the most complete exposition of connectionist theory. These books are *Human Learning* (1931), *The Fundamentals of Learning* (1932), and *The Psychology of Wants, Interests and Attitudes* (1935). They do not set forth a well-integrated and formalized theory supported by internally consistent evidence. Rather they present to us the picture of a theoretical system in a state of change and transition, an honest struggle to make sense of empirical data which often ran counter to theoretical expectations and, indeed, to well-established beliefs. Over the years the experimental evidence forced Thorndike to make drastic revisions in his original theory. The fundamental principles announced in *Animal Intelligence*—the law of exercise and the law of effect—underwent profound changes as a result of the evidence obtained from human subjects. Thus the connectionism of the 1930's was a far cry from the exuberant connectionism of the turn of the century.

We shall now present a series of representative experiments which bring to the fore the main features of Thorndike's analysis of human learning. Each of the experiments highlights a basic proposition of the new connectionism which subsequently became a focus of much theoretical debate and experimental inquiry.

Tests of the Law of Exercise

THE EFFECTS OF FREQUENCY.   The law of exercise had stated that stimulus-response connections are strengthened by exercise, but experiments with human subjects served to throw doubt on the significance of sheer frequency as a condition of learning. The principle of exercise gave rise to two specific experimental questions: (1) What is the consequence of repeated exposures to the same situation? (2) What is the consequence of repetitions of the same stimulus-response sequence?

(1) Let us first consider the influence of frequency of exposure to the same situation. Suppose there is a situation, S, to which an individual is exposed repeatedly and to which he can make variable responses, $R_1, R_2, R_3 \ldots R_n$. Assume further that his initial tendency is to favor some of these responses over the others. For example, R_1 might have a higher initial frequency than any of the other responses. If the strength of S-R connections varies directly with the sheer frequency of past occurrences, it follows that the initially more frequent responses should gain more and more in strength relative to the less frequent ones. Thus the

initial advantage of R_1 should be enhanced at the expense of the other responses with repeated exposures to the situation. This deduction was put to an experimental test in the following experiment (1931, pp. 3–15):

A subject is provided with a pad of paper and a pencil and is instructed to close his eyes and to draw a four-inch line with one quick movement. The procedure is repeated over and over again until the subject has drawn more than 2,000 lines none of which he has ever seen. Distributions of responses were obtained in twelve successive sittings at each of which the subject drew close to 200 lines. The results clearly supported two major conclusions. First, under constant external conditions there was considerable variability of response. The length of the lines varied all the way from 3.7 in. to 6.2 in. Second, the large number of repetitions failed to strengthen the initially more frequent responses. For example, lines of 5.1 and 5.3 in. were the most frequent in the initial sitting, accounting respectively for 14 and 16 per cent of all responses. During the twelfth sitting these percentages had declined to 11 and 6, respectively. If anything, the initially weak responses gained somewhat at the expense of the stronger. There was no consistent increase in the accuracy of the responses. The sheer repetition of the situation, no matter how frequent, produced no learning.

These conclusions were confirmed by Thorndike in a variety of situations and with large numbers of subjects (1932, pp. 6–63). The common feature of all these experiments was that (a) the same situation or group of situations was repeated a large number of times, and (b) the subjects received no information about the accuracy of their responses, and they were neither rewarded nor punished. Simple tasks which could be conveniently repeated a large number of times were used, such as judging the lengths of a series of objects, writing a digit between 0 and 9 in response to each of a series of words, completing a series of letters so as to form one of several possible words, etc. In each of these cases, the initially frequent responses showed no gain with repetition. Occasionally there was a reduction in the variability of the responses and the subjects' behavior showed shifts toward stereotypy, but the direction of such shifts could not be predicted from the initially dominant responses.

(2) We consider next the effects produced by the frequency of occurrence of a stimulus-response sequence. Is exercise more effective when a fixed stimulus-response sequence is repeated, i.e., when a prescribed connection is practiced? The experimental investigation of this question presents some serious difficulties. In ordinary learning experiments, the ability to retain or anticipate the correct response may be a source of satisfaction to the subject even in the absence of external reward; hence, exercise and effect combine to produce improvement

with practice. In order to evaluate the contribution of repetition as such, Thorndike used situations in which the subject was repeatedly exposed to stimulus-response sequences but was not motivated to learn these sequences. Such conditions of training are usually described as "incidental learning." The influence of sheer frequency, with the influence of rewards and punishments minimized, can be assessed most unequivocally under incidental conditions.

In one experiment (1932, pp. 80–90), for example, 254 word-number pairs were the learning materials. Each pair consisted of an English word followed by a two-digit number. The frequency with which individual pairs occurred in the total series was varied widely. There were also some critical pairs which were so placed in the series that each of them always *followed* a particular number. Thus there was an opportunity for exercise to strengthen not only connections between words and numbers but also to establish associations between certain numbers and those words which followed them invariably.

The total series was read to 200 students at the rate of 2 sec. per pair. The instructions made no reference to a future memory test. An attempt was made, however, to manipulate the degree of attention with which the subjects listened to the reading of the materials. One half the subjects received instructions which stated: "Do not give any closer attention than is required for you to keep awake and to hear the words and numbers." The instructions given to the other half of the subjects, on the other hand, requested them "to pay as close attention as you would in an average class."

After the entire series had been read, the subjects were given two tests: (a) they were presented with the words and asked to supply the numbers which had gone with each word; (b) they were presented with the numbers which had always preceded one of the recurrent critical pairs and asked to supply the *word* which always followed a given number.

The effect of exercise on the strength of word-number associations is shown in Figure 51. The latter presents the percentage of correct number responses as a function of the frequency with which the pairs had occurred in the series. Separate curves are presented for the groups receiving different instructions. Although there are some irregularities, the percentage of correct responses increases substantially as a function of exercise. The subjects instructed to pay relatively close attention consistently surpassed those who had been told to remain passive during the reading of the materials. This difference illustrates the important effects which the subject's set at the time of learning may have on the amount of retention. By contrast, exercise failed to strengthen the connections between particular numbers and the words which invariably followed them as part of another pair. The percentage of correct words given in response to the preceding numbers was less than one, which can easily be attributed to random guessing.

THE PRINCIPLE OF BELONGING.   The difference between the two tests—that for word-number associations and that for number-word associations—exemplifies a principle which, according to Thorndike, modifies the action of the laws of learning. This is the principle of *belonging*. The basic condition for the establishment of a connection is the temporal contiguity of two events, e.g., of a stimulus and a response. Such a sequence may or may not carry with it a "sense that the second

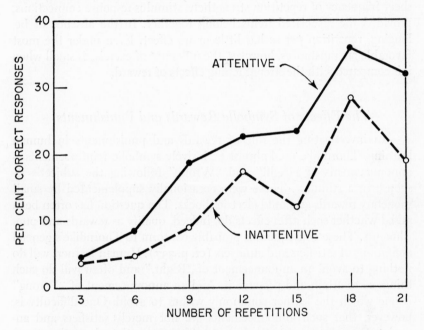

FIGURE 51.   The effects of frequency of exposure on the repetition of stimulus-response sequences. (Data from Thorndike, 1932, p. 118, and used by permission of the Bureau of Publications, Teachers College, Columbia University, New York.)

thing belongs with the first," e.g., that the response belongs with the stimulus. To the extent that a sequence of events is perceived as going together, they have the property of belongingness. Although Thorndike did not define belongingness precisely, he appears to have meant by it little more than the subject's disposition to divide the learning materials into a succession of units.

The belonging which is always or nearly always necessary in order that the repeated occurrence of a sequence may strengthen the connection between the first term of the sequence and the second need not

be more than the least which the word implies. There need be nothing logical, or essential, or inherent, or unifying in it. Any "this goes
with that" will suffice. Each nonsense syllable in a series which is read
as a series "belongs" to the one before it in the series. 1492 belongs to
Mr. Jones as his telephone number as truly as to Christopher Columbus as an auspicious year. In an experiment, 1492 may truly belong to
65 or 7843 or sig nop.[3]

In the present experiment, the word and number making up a pair belonged together; on the other hand, the number in one pair and the
word in the next pair did not. As the results of the experiment show,
sheer frequency of repetition strengthens stimulus-response connections,
provided the associated items belong together. In the absence of belonging, repetition *per se* has little or no effect. Even under the most
favorable circumstances, however, the influence of exercise is small when
it is compared with the strengthening effects of reward.

The Effects of Symbolic Rewards and Punishments

In investigating the role of rewards and punishments in human
learning, Thorndike used almost exclusively symbolic reinforcements—
announcements of "Right" and "Wrong" following the subject's response to a stimulus. These were occasionally supplemented by small
monetary rewards and mild electric shocks. The question has often been
raised whether such after-effects do, indeed, qualify as rewards and punishments. These consequences probably conform to Thorndike's general
definitions of satisfiers and annoyers (cf. p. 337). Human learners will do
nothing to avoid an announcement of "Right," and often will do such
things as to attain and preserve it. And an announcement of "Wrong"
is one which the learner commonly wishes to avoid. One difficulty is,
however, that such announcements are not merely satisfiers and annoyers; they also provide the learner with *information* about the stimulus-response sequences which are correct and incorrect in a given situation. When symbolic after-effects are found to have a significant
influence on learning, it is not certain whether their effectiveness is due
to their rewarding and punishing characteristics or to the information
which they impart to the subject. This problem could not be resolved
by *a priori* arguments concerning the nature of symbolic after-effects.
The answer was therefore sought in experiments which pitted the rewarding and informative characteristics of after-effects against each
other. Before considering such critical experiments, however, let us il-

[3] From E. L. Thorndike, *The Fundamentals of Learning*, 1932, p. 72. Excerpts
here and following used by permission of the Bureau of Publications, Teachers College, Columbia University, New York.

lustrate Thorndike's basic empirical findings concerning the action of symbolic after-effects.

     ᶜ   THE STRENGTHENING EFFECTS OF SYMBOLIC REWARDS.   The influence of rewards can be investigated conveniently in situations in which the subject's initial responses to the situation are variable but are likely to include correct responses which can be strengthened selectively. An example of such a situation is provided by the following experiment in which a group of subjects was trained to increase the precision of their judgments of length (1932, pp. 177–81).

The series of stimuli consisted of fifty strips of paper of uniform appearance but varying in length, in 1-cm steps, between 3 and 27 cm. Thus there were twenty-five different lengths, and each length was represented by two identical strips. The strips were presented in random order against a fixed background, and the subject estimated the length of each strip in integral numbers. A standard of comparison was provided by a 10-cm strip the length of which was known to the subject and which was kept in full view throughout the experiment. The initial accuracy of the judgments was determined in a pretest in which the subject judged the entire series without receiving any knowledge of results. There followed seven training series during which each correct judgment was fol-lowed by an announcement of "Right," and each incorrect judgment by an announcement of "Wrong." No information was given, however, about the direction or magnitude of the error. A final test, again without knowledge of results, was used to evaluate the total effects of the train-ing. As Figure 52 shows, the average error (measured in terms of devia-tion from the correct value) declined steadily throughout training. Com-parison of the final test and pretest shows a reduction in error of 61 per cent. These results are in striking contrast with those of a control group which went through the same procedure but was neither rewarded nor punished. There is no evidence of improvement in the performance of the control group, and on the final test the mean error is slightly higher than on the initial test. In the absence of rewards and punishments, sheer frequency of exposure to a situation did not lead to improvement.

The experiment which we have just described is one of a great many which firmly established the effectiveness of symbolic after-effects in modifying behavior. Results such as these, however, leave open the question of the extent to which the net improvement reflects the strengthening of correct associations by reward and the weakening of incorrect associations by punishment. To answer this question, it is necessary to use situations in which the effects of rewards and punish-ments can be measured separately and compared.

In one well-known experiment by Thorndike (1932, pp. 278–80), the subjects were presented with a series of 200 Spanish words, and for

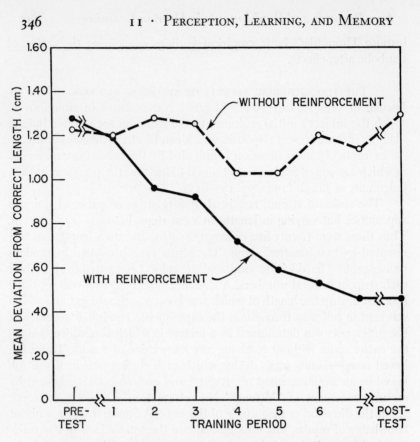

FIGURE 52.   The effects of practice with and without reinforcement on judgments of length. (Data from Thorndike, 1932, pp. 179f., and used by permission of the Bureau of Publications, Teachers College, Columbia University, New York.)

each word had to choose the correct meaning from a set of five alternatives. For example, the first few items of the test read as follows:

1. abedul   ameer.....birch.....couch.....carry.....punch
2. abrasar   oaf.....walk.....fill.....alienate.....burn
3. aceite   oil.....copper.....acerbity.....crab.....ferment

Whenever the subject chose the correct alternative, the experimenter rewarded him by an announcement of "Right," and whenever he chose one of the incorrect alternatives, the experimenter punished him by an announcement of "Wrong." Nine subjects served in the experiment. The series was repeated on successive days until twelve or more repetitions had been completed. As a result of the training, the subjects showed considerable increases in the number of correct choices. Was this improvement due to the strengthening effects of "Right," the weakening effects of "Wrong," or both?

In order to arrive at a conservative estimate of the relative effects of rewards and punishments, Thorndike made the following analysis. He considered (1) all those cases in which the response was rewarded on the second trial but not on the first, and (2) all those cases in which the response was punished on the second trial but was not the same wrong response that had been given on the first trial. (Exclusion of all responses which had been given on the first trial served to minimize the number of cases in which the subject's choice was influenced by experiences prior to the experiment or by initial biases in favor of a particular alternative.) The frequencies with which these particular responses were repeated on the third trial provide a measure of the effects of the rewards and punishments. The average percentages of repetition were forty for rewarded responses and twenty-five for punished responses. In evaluating these results, Thorndike made the assumption that but for the rewards and punishments each of the five alternatives would have had an equal probability of being chosen. Thus he estimated the chance level of repetition at 20 per cent. Measured against this chance baseline, the reward had increased the probability of repetition by 20 per cent. As for the punishment, it had not decreased the probability of repetition at all; in fact, the stimulus-response connection appeared to be slightly strengthened by the punishment!

THE ROLE OF PUNISHMENT.   The failure of punishment to weaken stimulus-response connections contradicted not only the expectations of common sense but Thorndike's original theory of effect as well. The experimental results, however, stubbornly refused to produce evidence for the weakening effects of punishment. Thorndike and his associates performed a large number of experiments which were designed along the same lines as the study which we have just described. Typically, the subject was presented with a series of discrete stimuli to each of which he could make one of a set of alternative responses. Some of the responses were rewarded and the others were punished. A variety of stimulus materials were used; motor as well as verbal responses were studied (1931, 1932, 1935). With impressive uniformity, stimulus-response connections were strengthened by rewards and failed to be weakened by punishments. Frequently punishments had a strengthening effect which, however, was never as great as that of reward. Further analysis showed the influences of both rewards and punishments to be cumulative. Several successive rewards or several successive punishments accentuated the results produced by single after-effects (Rock, 1935; Tuckman, 1933).

On the basis of the experimental evidence Thorndike was forced to conclude that his original conception of the effects of punishment had been in error. Punishment does not have effects which are opposite to those of reward, i.e., it does not weaken connections in the direct and automatic way in which reward strengthens them. Nevertheless, Thorndike was not prepared to deny altogether the effectiveness of punishment in the elimination of errors and the modification of behavior. Whatever effects punishment does have, he suggested, are indirect rather than direct. Punishment, even though it may not weaken the connection which it follows, favors variability of behavior and thus provides an opportunity for the correct response to be made and to be strengthened by reward. In his own words:

> Rewards and punishments alike will teach by virtue of the conditions and activities which they produce in the animal. Rewards in general tend to maintain and strengthen any connection which leads to them. Punishments often but not always tend to shift from it to something else, and their educative value depends on what this something else is. They weaken the connection which produced them, when they do weaken it, by strengthening some competing connection [1932, p. 277].

At first glance, this analysis may appear to contain a contradiction. It is asserted (1) that punishment per se does not weaken stimulus-response connections, and (2) that punishment produces variability of behavior. But an increase in the variability of behavior seems to imply a weakening of the punished connection; if behavior becomes more variable after a punishment, then the punished connection itself must be less likely to occur after the punishment than before. The contradiction is resolved if we interpret Thorndike's analysis to mean that punishment fails to weaken connections in an *absolute sense* but does weaken them in a *relative sense*. A numerical example may make the point clear. Let us assume that the initial probability of a response is .20. The response occurs, and if it is neither rewarded nor punished, the probability of its recurrence on the next trial is .30. If the response is punished, however, behavior becomes more variable and the probability of recurrence is only .24. Now .24 is greater than the initial probability of .20. Thus punishment has *not* reduced the absolute strength of the response but has reduced it relative to a neutral baseline (cf. Stone, 1953).

By now it will be clear that we have made use of the law of exercise in order to give a consistent account of the effects of punishment. That is, we have assumed that sheer occurrence strengthens a stimulus-response connection (in the example above, it raised the probability of occurrence from .20 to .30). Thus we must invoke the law of exercise in order to explain the fact that punishments frequently *appear* to strengthen stimulus-response connections. Such apparent strengthening effects of punishment represent the residual effects of exercise which prevail in spite of the variability induced by punishment. As Thorndike himself put it, "There is more gain in strength from the occurrence of a response than there is weakening by the attachment of 'Wrong' to it" (1931, p. 45).

Thorndike was always open to persuasion by experimental fact and ready to revise his theoretical position in the light of new evidence. We have already seen that the results of his own researches led him to abandon the "punishment clause" of the law of effect. The weight which he ascribed to sheer repetition similarly reflected the unfolding experimental evidence. In the original statement of the laws of learning, exercise was treated as one of the principal conditions of behavior change. The investigations concerned with the effects of sheer frequency (cf. pp. 340–4) caused Thorndike to deprecate the power of repetition per se, although he conceded that "frequency plus belonging" did produce at least some learning. The analysis of the effects of punishment served to produce new evidence for the effectiveness of repetition—sheer occurrence of a connection strengthens it more than punishment weakens it. In one of his last books, *Man and His Works*, Thorndike explicitly reaffirmed the effectiveness of exercise when he wrote, "In a great majority of cases . . . every occurrence of a response to a situation increases the probability that the situation will, if it recurs, evoke that response" (1943, p. 26).

CONNECTIONISM—THE FINAL VERSION

WE ARE NOW READY to summarize the major changes in connectionist theory which resulted from the experiments on human learning.

(1) *The law of exercise* is, after all, retained as a basic principle of learning. Sheer frequency, however, remains of minor significance as compared with the powerful selective influence of reward.

(2) *The law of effect*, which originally had been a principle of selective learning by both reward and punishment, has become a law of reward only. Rewards strengthen connections, but punishments do not weaken them in comparable ways. The effects of punishments are erratic and unreliable and may be offset by the positive influence of exercise. When punishment does lead to the modification of behavior, its action is indirect; by inducing variability of behavior it may help to produce the responses which can be strengthened by reward.

(3) *Auxiliary principles* are introduced to take account of some of the complexities introduced by the perceptual and verbal dispositions of the human learner (1932). Foremost among these is the principle of *belonging*, which we encountered in connection with the analysis of exercise. Other auxiliary principles may be briefly mentioned here. According to the principle of *impressiveness*, the perceptual vividness of stimuli favors learning; the principle of *polarity* states that stimulus-response connections function most readily in the order in which they

have been practiced; according to the principle of *identifiability*, the more easily the correct stimuli and responses can be discriminated, the more rapidly will they be associated; finally, the principle of *availability* asserts that the ease with which a response can be connected with a stimulus depends on the learner's initial readiness to perform the response. We shall not elaborate these auxiliary principles further because they are peripheral to the main connectionist thesis; they merely recognize the existence of factors, largely rooted in the learner's past experience, which serve to modify the action of the laws of exercise and effect.

While Thorndike made major revisions in his laws of learning, he never wavered in his conception of learning as the strengthening of connections between stimuli and responses. Both "stimulus" and "response" were defined broadly and flexibly. The term "stimulus" was used to refer to events widely varying in scope and complexity, ranging all the way from specific sensory events to the general features of a learning situation. Similarly, the term "response" designated a variety of reactions, from specific muscular movement to integrated series of actions. In any given instance, stimulus and response are defined in terms of units which yield stable functional relationships and serve the interests of the investigator. Connections between stimuli and responses account for the sum total of the organism's behavior, and changes in the strengths of connections determine the modification of behavior.

> Any given person is what he will think and feel and do in various circumstances. He is the probabilities that each of the R's that he can produce will be evoked by each of the total S's that can evoke anything from him. He is the total of his S-R probabilities. It is by adding to these S-R connections, and by changing the probability of one or another of them up or down, that the environment changes him.[4]

The strengthening effects of reward are inevitable and automatic, i.e., do not depend on the learner's understanding of the relationship between his action and the occurrence of the reward. Such "cognitive" factors as sets and expectancies serve to limit and to modify the operation of the laws of learning, but they are secondary to exercise and reward which modify behavior directly and automatically. In fact, sets and expectancies may themselves be regarded as stimulus-response connections acquired in accordance with the basic laws of learning.

In the application of the law of effect to human learning, the operational definition of reward and punishment as distinct from "information" remained a difficult and persistent problem. A closely related problem was the specification of the mechanism by which after-effects strengthen stimulus-response connections. Thorndike's original definitions of "satisfiers" and "annoyers" were in terms of responses of ap-

[4] From E. L. Thorndike, *Man and His Works*, pp. 23–4, copyright 1943 by Harvard University Press and used with their permission.

proach and avoidance and made no reference to sensory pleasure and pain. The mechanism of strengthening was referred to changes of conductivity in the neurons (1911, pp. 246–50). Extension of the theory to the action of symbolic after-effects in human learning compounded the difficulty of these problems. Since announcements of "Right" and "Wrong" were used almost exclusively as after-effects, rewards and punishments typically conveyed information to the subject. The schematic theory of neural conductivity was of little value in the explanation of the action of symbolic after-effects.

In the face of these difficulties, Thorndike's theoretical analysis of the mechanism of effect in human learning became less and less specific. In his later writings he came to identify the strengthening effects of reward with the occurrence of a *confirming reaction* or *O.K. reaction* of the nervous system (1933b). The confirming reaction is the "unknown reaction of the neurones" which are aroused by a satisfier and which serves to strengthen the connection which it follows. While Thorndike was unwilling to speculate about the precise physiological basis of the confirming reaction, he did specify some of its functional properties. First of all, the confirming reaction is independent of sensory pleasure, and thus symbolic satisfiers, such as the announcement of "Right," may arouse it. Second, the confirming reaction is highly selective with respect to the classes of connections on which it will act at any given time. For example, it may act on verbal responses to a situation without at the same time influencing postural reactions and gross bodily movements. Third, the confirming reaction may exert its effects on behavioral units of different magnitudes and complexities; "anything which may be connected with anything in the mind may be more strongly connected therewith by the confirming reaction" (1943, p. 36). Fourth, the confirming reaction often issues from some "overhead control" in the brain, i.e., it may be contingent upon the relevance of the behavior to the prevailing wants and purposes of the organism. Last but not least, the confirming reaction is a biological force which is largely independent of the intellectual understanding of the learner.

It does not act logically or teleologically. . . . Its influence does not pick out the "right" or "essential" or "useful" connection by any mystical or logical potency. It is, on the contrary, as natural in its action as a falling stone, a ray of light, a line of force, a discharge of buckshot, a stream of water, or a hormone in the blood. It will strengthen . . . to some extent connections which are wrong, irrelevant or useless, provided they are close enough to the satisfier in the succession of connections.[5]

[5] From E. L. Thorndike, *The Psychology of Wants, Interests and Attitudes*, pp. 39f., copyright 1935 by D. Appleton-Century Co., Inc., and used by permission of Appleton-Century-Crofts, Inc.

Elsewhere, Thorndike sums up his position whimsically when he says, "The confirming reaction is more like the knee jerk than like either a syllogism or a cash register" (1943, p. 35). This is the doctrine of the automatic action of after-effects.

CONNECTIONISM AND REINFORCEMENT THEORY

SOME OF THE BASIC concepts of Thorndike's connectionism have become part and parcel of modern behavior theory. Specifically, Thorndike's views have had an important influence on the development of Hull's system, which is one of the most influential contemporary theories of learning. One of Hull's contributions was the attempt at integration, in a unified conceptual scheme, of the basic laws of classical conditioning and of Thorndike's principles of trial-and-error learning. The law of effect, reformulated as the *law of primary reinforcement*, occupies a central position in Hull's theory (1943, 1952). Like the law of effect, the law of primary reinforcement asserts that rewards strengthen stimulus-response connections. There are, however, important differences between Hull's and Thorndike's formulations. Thorndike defined a reward or satisfier as a state of affairs which the organism is disposed to approach, i.e., he defined rewards in terms of behavioral criteria, and treated symbolic rewards on a par with other satisfiers. Hull, on the other hand, identified a reward or reinforcing state of affairs with the reduction of a biological need (hence the phrase "primary reinforcement"). The law of primary reinforcement is supplemented by the principle of secondary reinforcement. Any stimulus which has been repeatedly associated with primary reinforcement (drive reduction), acquires reinforcing properties and can serve to strengthen stimulus-response associations. Thus the symbolic rewards and punishments used by Thorndike would be regarded as secondary reinforcers. In general, the influence of such secondary reinforcements is weaker and less lasting than that of primary reinforcement.

Hull regarded reinforcement as a necessary condition of learning, and the strength of a habit was entirely a function of the number of reinforcements (Hull, 1952). Whereas Thorndike considered reward as the most reliable and significant determinant of learning, he conceded some small independent influence to sheer exercise. Thus the principle of effect occupies an even more central position in Hull's theory than in Thorndike's.

There was also a systematic difference between Thorndike's and Hull's approaches to the problem of punishment. Thorndike treated punishment as a class of after-effects. His concern was with the difference between rewards and punishments *as after-effects*. Hull regarded punishing states of affairs as *instigators* of behavior and the cessation of punishment as a reinforcement. Hence the administration of a noxious stimulus gives rise to trial-and-error behavior, and the response terminating the punishment is reinforced. When Thorndike spoke of punishment as a condition of variability, he argued along similar lines but his major concern remained with the effects of punishment on preceding connections.

Thorndike's formulation of the law of effect did not make it possible to distinguish between the effects of reward on learning and on performance. The strength of a connection was inferred directly from its probability of occurrence. The probability of a particular response to a stimulus depends, however, not only on the strength of the association between the stimulus and the response, but also on the conditions under which the reaction to the stimulus is determined, particularly the motivational state of the organism. Thus it becomes necessary to distinguish between the determinants of habit strength (strength of stimulus-response connections) and other variables influencing performance. In Hull's analysis, reinforcement is a determinant of *habit strength*. Reinforcement is a necessary but not a sufficient condition for increasing the probability of a response. The effects of past reinforcements become manifest only if such variables as the intensity of the organism's drive satisfy the requirements for performance. In Hull's analysis of the conditions of learning and performance, the principle of effect gained in conceptual precision and predictive value. In spite of the many modifications introduced by Hull (1943, 1951, 1952), the continuity between the law of effect and the principle of reinforcement is apparent.

CENTRAL CONTROVERSIAL ISSUES

HULL'S THEORY ABSORBED and modified the connectionist model and the law of effect. On the other hand, opposition to Thorndike's views served as a major catalyst in the development of other theories of learning. Objections to the connectionist model came primarily (1) from those who emphasized the importance of perceptual organization in learning, and (2) from those who preferred to look upon learning as the acquisition of new information or knowledge rather than the modification of *stimulus-response* associations. Thus both Gestalt psychologists, whose analysis of learning was rooted in principles of perception, and cognitive theorists such as Tolman were fundamentally opposed to the connectionist model.

Gestalt Criticisms of Connectionism

The basic thesis of Gestalt psychology is that the laws of perceptual organization are also the laws of learning. Every experience, it is assumed, leaves a neural *trace* which preserves the organized properties of the original perception. Perceptual organization depends on the *relations* among stimuli; thus proximity, similarity, and a common spatial orientation favor the perceptual grouping of objects. Sheer contiguity, therefore, cannot account for learning and retention; the relations among the events to be associated are of critical importance; it is these relations which determine the amount of perceptual organization and hence the coherence of the memory trace. The observed fact of association should be regarded not as an inevitable result of contiguity but as an outcome of perceptual organization. Köhler summarizes the argument as follows:

> Suppose . . . that items appear as parts of a unitary experience. . . . Under such circumstances the unitary process will be followed by a neural trace which has the same unitary character. What will happen if at a later time a part of the unitary trace is once more thrown into action, for example, by presenting the first member of a pair? Because of the unitary character of the trace, this excitation will spread more easily within the trace than to other regions of the tissue. Thus the parts of the trace which are not directly excited will be indirectly excited. But this is just the physiological event which we suppose to happen in recall "by contiguity," i.e., when two items A and B are associated. . . . From the present point of view association is therefore simply coherence within the unitary trace of a unitary experience.[6]

Since Gestalt psychologists regard learning as a function of perceptual organization, they reject exercise and effect as basic conditions of learning. Frequency, they argue, is effective only insofar as repeated exposures provide an opportunity for perceptual organization to be achieved, especially when such organization is difficult because of a lack of intrinsic relationships between the items to be associated. (Recall, in this connection, that by belongingness Thorndike explicitly did not mean such an intrinsic relationship between the items in a sequence.) Similarly, rewards and punishments are effective because they serve to "restructure" the problem situation. The attainment of a reward may give rise to an experience of "closure" and thus serves to establish meaningful relationships among the component features of the task.

It is not surprising that Gestalt psychologists were among the most determined critics of Thorndike's analysis of learning. The connectionist model was rejected because it represented learning as "blind" and "mechanical" rather than based on the perception of meaningful relationships. A double-barreled attack was leveled against Thorndike's experimental findings. First of all, Thorndike was criticized for having put

[6] From W. Köhler, "On the Nature of Associations," *Proc. Amer. Philos. Soc.*, 1941, pp. 492f. Used by permission of Prof. Köhler and the American Philosophical Society.

his subjects into problem situations in which the solution was purely arbitrary, so that learning based on the perception of meaningful relationships was impossible in principle. Thus, commenting on the puzzle boxes which Thorndike used in his study of animal intelligence, Koffka wrote:

> Without possessing some technical experience, even a man placed inside of such a box would be unable to comprehend these mechanisms of release. . . . Accordingly, the connection between the movement made and its effect upon the animal must necessarily be of a purely arbitrary sort.[7]

Such strictures are, of course, easily extended to the experiments with human subjects in which arbitrary associations between words and numbers were learned. In short, the contention was that Thorndike's experimental situations denied the subjects the opportunity to respond to meaningful relationships. Thus the essential role of perceptual organization was said to have been obscured.

At the same time, however, Gestalt critics went to some pains to show that even in difficult and arbitrary situations the subjects' behavior was not altogether stupid. For instance, Koffka pointed to the sharp drops in some of the learning curves of Thorndike's cats (cf. Figure 50) as possible evidence for the occurrence of insight. (Thorndike attributed such sudden drops in the time curves to a high degree of transfer from earlier learning.) The fact that animals frequently vary their specific movements in performing a given task was also cited against the connectionist interpretation of learning. "The art of learning simply cannot be explained by the mere repetition of a movement which leads to pleasure" (Koffka, 1928, p. 177). Similar criticisms were voiced by Adams (1929) who repeated some of Thorndike's experiments on problem-solving in animals. Adams reported that his cats, unlike Thorndike's, often gave evidence of insightful approaches to the solution of the problems.

It is interesting to note that self-contradictory arguments were used in these criticisms. It cannot be the case that in Thorndike's situations the associations are "necessarily of a purely arbitrary sort" *and* that sharp drops in the learning curves obtained in these very situations are a sign of insight into a relationship. Thorndike's choice of experimental situations was undoubtedly influenced by his theoretical preconceptions. These procedures for studying problem-solving were in principle unacceptable to Koffka, whose preconceptions were altogether different. Nevertheless, he accepted and reinterpreted the data when they appeared to conform to his own theoretical views.

[7] K. Koffka, *The Growth of the Mind*, 1928, p. 185, and used by permission of Humanities Press, New York.

Gestalt psychologists coupled their criticisms of connectionist theory with attempts to show that insightful learning is the rule when organisms are faced with problems in which the perception of means-end relationships is possible. Köhler's experiments with anthropoids, described in *The Mentality of Apes* (1927), provide probably the best known examples of "intelligent" problem-solving in animals. Among the most familiar situations are those in which the animals were required to construct and use tools in order to obtain a reward—to fit two sticks together to rake in a piece of fruit or to build a "ladder" from orange crates in order to reach a lure suspended from the ceiling. Köhler's apes apparently were often able to attain their goals without a period of trial and error with accidental success.

The difference between the conclusions reached by Thorndike and Köhler illustrates an important general point about the course of theoretical controversy. The choice of experimental situations necessarily reflects the theoretical convictions of the investigator. In designing his apparatus and experimental procedures, the investigator seeks to create conditions in which the predictions derived from his theory can be tested; more likely than not his experiments fail to meet the conditions required by an alternative theory, and evidence supporting the latter cannot come to light. It is fair to say that Thorndike used puzzle boxes because he conceived of problem-solving as a process of trial and error; Köhler required his subjects to invent tools because he believed that the solution of a problem depended on the animal's ability to perceive the relationships among the critical features of the situation. Thorndike found no evidence for the perception of relationships, and Köhler rarely observed trial and error with accidental success. Both investigators found what they set out to discover, and their choice of experimental situations made it unlikely that they would find anything else. The theoretical issue was joined because each considered his own situation as the prototype of problem-solving in general. Such single-minded investigations represent an essential step in the development of clearly defined theoretical alternatives. Once the alternative interpretations have been sharply distinguished, they can be pitted against each other, and the conflict resolved by new evidence.

The main force of Gestalt criticism was directed against the failure of the connectionist model to recognize the role of perceptual organization in learning. Gestalt psychologists have not devoted much effort to the analysis of the effects of rewards and punishments in human learning, although one of the most challenging experimental attacks on Thorndike's hypothesis of effect was made by investigators with a Gestalt background (see pp. 393–5 below). The general opposition of Gestalt psychology to stimulus-response analysis and to the theory of after-effects has, however, helped to sustain the controversy aroused by Thorndike's experiments and theoretical interpretations.

Cognitive Theory vs. Connectionism

Opposition to Thorndike's views was by no means limited to Gestalt theorists. Rejection of the connectionist model was equally urged by the cognitive learning theorists of whom Edward Chace Tolman was the pre-eminent exponent. For the cognitive theorist, learning consists essentially of changes in the organism's knowledge about the environment. As a result of experiencing sequences of environmental events, the organism learns what leads to what, and particularly what responses will lead to rewards or punishments in a particular situation. The acquisition of such *expectancies* is not, however, dependent on rewards or punishments. What an organism learns in any given situation depends on its capacity to differentiate the features of the environment and the relationships among them. Thus certain stimuli in the environment come to function as *signs*; the organism knows that in the presence of these signs, certain behaviors will lead to such and such consequences or significates, e.g., rewards or punishments. The more easily discriminable the environmental features and the more frequently the organism has been exposed to them, the stronger will be its expectancy concerning the relationship between sign, behavior, and significate. At any given moment, the organism's response to sign stimuli will depend on its prevailing motivation. It will perform the responses which it expects to lead to a particular consequence if and when that consequence will serve to satisfy its needs (Tolman, 1932).

Tolman's analysis, like Hull's, makes a sharp distinction between learning and performance. Learning is cognitive change—the acquisition of knowledge about contingent sequences of sign, response, and significate. Performance is the utilization of this knowledge in accordance with the needs of the moment. In advancing toward an expected goal, the organism may use a variety of different responses. The particular movements which are used in locomotion toward a goal, and in the manipulation of means and ends, depend both on the physical features of the environment and on motor capacities and skills. The important point is that the organism learns "behavior routes," and not specific effector responses.

The basic approach of cognitive theory is well illustrated in the following quotation from Tolman in which he describes what happens when a rat learns the true path through a maze:

> We believe that in the course of learning, something like a field map of the environment gets established in the rat's brain. We agree

with the other stimulus-response school that the rat in running a maze is exposed to stimuli and finally led as a result of these stimuli to the responses which actually occur. We feel, however, that the intervening brain processes are more complicated, more patterned and often, pragmatically speaking, more autonomous than do the stimulus-response psychologists. Although we admit that the rat is bombarded by stimuli, we hold that his nervous system is surprisingly selective as to which of these stimuli it will let in at any given time. . . . The stimuli, which are allowed in, are not connected by just simple one-to-one switches to the outgoing responses. Rather, the incoming impulses are usually worked over and elaborated . . . into a tentative, cognitive-like map of the environment. And it is this tentative map, indicating routes and paths and environmental relationships, which finally determines what responses, if any, the animal will finally release.[8]

This analysis applies to human learning as well, except that man's cognitive maps are vastly more differentiated and complex than those of the rat. And similarly, the patterns of motives which govern the utilization of knowledge and the release of appropriate behaviors are infinitely more complicated in man than in the rat. Nevertheless, the formal model used in the analysis of behavior transcends differences among species in capacities and skills. In thus searching for a universal model of learning, cognitive theorists and connectionist theorists are of one mind.

Cognitive theory rejects the law of effect as a principle of *learning*. Rewards and punishments are not necessary for the development of cognitive maps. Expectations concerning rewards and punishments do, however, govern *performance*. In a choice situation, the organism will perform that response whose expected consequence is most rewarding in terms of its momentary motivational state. By the same token, responses whose expected consequences would be punishing are avoided. Thus, rewarded responses are repeated, and punished responses are avoided, *provided* the organism's motivation with respect to the rewards and punishments remains more or less constant from occasion to occasion.

From the point of view of cognitive theory, rewards and punishments may serve still another function because they are sources of strong sensory stimulation for the organism. A piece of food placed in the mouth of a hungry subject or a strong electric shock applied to one of his limbs are both examples of such sensory effects. Sensory intensity or vividness favors perceptual differentiation. Hence rewards and punishments can function as perceptual *emphasizers* which influence the speed with which environmental events can be discriminated and retained (Tolman, 1932, p. 387). They exert such an influence on the acquisition of expectancies, however, by virtue of their sensory characteristics and

[8] From E. C. Tolman, "Cognitive Maps in Rats and Men," *Psychol. Rev.*, 1948, Vol. 55, p. 192, and used by permission of the American Psychological Association.

not because they produce momentary decreases or increases in the organism's needs.

It is clear that there was little disposition to quarrel with Thorndike's generalization that responses rewarded in a given situation tend to be repeated when that situation recurs. This generalization, which may be described as the *empirical law of effect*, has been accepted by theorists of widely different persuasions (cf. McGeoch, 1942, pp. 572–613; Postman, 1947). Thorndike's conclusions concerning the effects of punishment—that punished connections are not reliably weakened and may, indeed, be strengthened by virtue of their sheer occurrence—met, however, with considerable doubt and resistance. From the point of view of cognitive theory, the repetition of a punished response represents a failure on the part of the organism to make use of information gained through past experience. When such failure occurs, it may be ascribed to the equivocal implications of a "Wrong" as compared with a "Right." In contrasting the informational value of "Right" and "Wrong," Hilgard writes as follows:

> The intelligent response to *Right* is to do again what was last done.
> . . . The intelligent response to *Wrong* is to do something different,
> but what to do is less clear. It is necessary both to remember what not
> to do and to form some sort of hypothesis as to what to do. Under
> time pressure this vagueness might well produce an asymmetry be-
> tween responses following *Right* and *Wrong*.[9]

Above all, the assertion that punishments do not weaken stimulus-response connections ran counter to common sense and social practice. When experimental results violate common sense, there is of course a strong disposition to doubt the validity of the experiments and to look for methodological flaws and artifacts which can account for the empirical findings without overturning the common-sense beliefs.

There was equally stubborn resistance to the hypothesis that after-effects, whether rewarding or punishing, modify stimulus-response connections *automatically*. The contention that after-effects may change behavior independently of the subject's perception of the problem situation or his understanding of the significance of the rewards and punishments is clearly at variance with both the Gestalt and cognitive conceptions of the learning process. Such a conception again runs counter to the common-sense view of the ways in which rewards and punishments modify behavior.

We shall now review some of the specific experimental issues which grew out of the disagreements about the role of rewards and punishments in human learning. We shall concentrate on the two issues which

[9] From E. R. Hilgard, *Theories of Learning*, 2nd. ed., copyright 1956 by Appleton-Century-Crofts, Inc., New York, and used by their permission.

have remained the focus of theoretical controversy and which for a long time have eluded definitive experimental solutions. These two questions concern (1) the effects of punishment and (2) the automatic action of after-effects.

Do Punishments Weaken Stimulus-Response Connections?

According to Thorndike, a punishment does not *directly* weaken the connection which it follows. To test this hypothesis, it is necessary to use situations which minimize the opportunity for the correct response to be performed and reinforced following the punishment. The multiple-choice situations used by Thorndike were designed to satisfy this requirement. When the subject guesses numbers in response to a series of words, for example, the items follow each other in rapid succession, and there is little chance to substitute a correct response for one called wrong. Such a procedure has been called a "vanishing situation" because the stimulus situation changes before a punished response can be changed or corrected. It is only in such "vanishing situations" that the effects of punishment per se can be assessed, independently of competition from successful substitute responses to the situation. At the same time, it must be recognized that such situations are unusual. The results obtained in "vanishing situations" cannot be generalized to the effects of punishment in general. Even as restricted to "vanishing situations," however, Thorndike's conclusions concerning the effects of punishment were widely questioned.

The Need for an Empirical Baseline

The problem of a priori chance.   In his multiple-choice experiments Thorndike used deviation from *a priori* chance to assess the effects of rewards and punishments. Suppose, for example, that subjects are required to guess a number between 1 and 10 to each of a series of words. When the series is presented for the first time, the probability of any one number being chosen was assumed to be .10. When the series was presented for a second time, the probability of repetition of the first response was again taken to be .10, unless the connection between the stimulus and the response was strengthened, say, by a reward during the first presentation. In short, Thorndike assumed that all the alternative responses to a given stimulus are equally likely, and that deviation from this chance expectancy provides a measure of learning. It was this method of measurement which revealed the asymmetry between the effects of rewards and punishments. The use of *a priori* chance as a baseline for the measurement of the effects of training has proved to be an error. It cannot be assumed that the subject's initial choices are truly haphazard. Rather, they are likely to reflect at least to some extent habits and predispositions with which he enters the experimental situation. Thus there may be pre-experimental associations between certain words and numbers or habits governing the order in which different numbers are guessed. Hence repetitions above *a priori* chance would be expected on successive trials even in the absence of learning, because the dispositions which favored the initial choices would persist from trial to trial (Hull, 1935). The assumption of a chance baseline would result in a systematic overestimation of the effects of reward, i.e., some of the repetitions which were the result of the subject's initial response dispositions would be credited to reward. By the same token, possible weakening effects of punishment would be underestimated. Punished responses may be repeated with a higher than chance frequency, not because the punishment had no weakening effect, but because such weakening effects were not sufficient to overcome the response biases of the subject. Similarly, what Thorndike considered the strengthening effects of sheer occurrence may have been due to non-random selection of responses.

Thorndike and his associates recognized the possibility of error in their definition of chance expectancy and took a number of steps to make their measures of learning as free of bias as possible. As we have already seen, Thorndike often used responses which made their first appearance on the second trial for purposes of measuring the strengthening and weakening effects of punishments. Such responses, he assumed, did not have strong initial associations with the stimulus items (cf. p. 347). In the experiments on word-number association, empirical corrections for the subjects' "number favoritism" were introduced, i.e., an estimate was made of the amount of repetition to be expected from the subjects' consistent preferences for some number responses rather than others. The initial probability of a correct response was also varied systematically (Lorge, 1933a, 1933b). The introduction of these corrections did not change the conclusions concerning the effects of rewards and punishments.

Empirical corrections for response favoritism undoubtedly reduce the bias introduced by the use of a chance baseline in the measurement of the effects of rewards and punishments. Such a procedure, however, still does not permit a precise evaluation of the influence of punishment. Specifically, it remains impossible to determine whether punishment has any weakening effect at all which is masked by the strengthening effect of sheer occurrence of the response. This question can be answered only by obtaining an empirical baseline of repetition for responses which are *neither rewarded nor punished*. The effect of punishment per se can then be evaluated against this baseline.

The determination of an empirical baseline offers serious methodological difficulties, especially when the effects of symbolic rewards and punishments on human subjects are to be measured. The lack of any after-effect, i.e., the failure to give either a reward or a punishment, does not necessarily create a strictly neutral situation. The subject may interpret the lack of response by the experimenter as tacit approval or disapproval. In addition, the context of an experimental situation may create a set to repeat the first response when the situation recurs. In the presence of such a set, a repetition, which the learner recognizes as such, may serve as a reinforcement favoring further repetition (Stone, 1953).

ATTEMPTS AT CONSTRUCTION OF AN EMPIRICAL BASELINE.   Several attempts have been made to construct empirical baselines of repetition which would permit the unequivocal evaluation of the effects of punishment. Some of these studies appeared to yield definitive conclusions and were accepted widely, but upon further analysis were found subject to error. A much cited experiment by Tilton (1939) is a case in point.

The learning materials used by Tilton were nonsense syllables. A multiple-choice test was constructed in which each item consisted of a stimulus syllable and four response syllables. Prior to the administration of the test the experimenter read aloud the entire list of stimulus syllables, and along with each stimulus syllable read *one* of the responses which would later appear in the multiple-choice test. Half the subjects were informed that the particular responses that had been read would be correct on the test. The other half of the subjects were told to consider these items as incorrect. These preliminary instructions were used to make the procedure meaningful to the subjects and to discourage them from using some arbitrary sequence of positions in making their choices. The multiple-choice test was then administered for six successive trials during which the subjects were not informed whether their choices were right and wrong. The frequencies of repetitions during these unreinforced trials were used to estimate the empirical baseline of repetition in the absence of rewards and punishments. Tilton found such repetitions to be considerably higher than chance—of the order of 35 rather than 25 per cent. Measured against this empirical baseline, rewards were found to have strengthening effects and punishments had definite weakening effects. Tilton concluded that Thorndike's measurements of the effects of punishment had been made against an improper baseline and thus were invalid.

Tilton's results have been frequently cited as a serious challenge to Thorndike's interpretation of the effects of punishment. Analysis of Tilton's experimental procedure (cf. Stone, 1950) shows, however, that there is very serious doubt about the validity of this empirical baseline. The subjects were informed in advance which responses would later be correct or incorrect. Even if *retention* for these items was low and could not account for the high level of repetition, the instructions undoubtedly caused subjects to repeat those items which they believed, correctly or incorrectly, to be right according to the experimenter's instructions. This assumption is strengthened by the fact that the very same subjects who provided the data for the empirical baseline had previously served in an experiment in which the conventional procedure of rewarding and punishing responses was used. It is reasonable to conclude that Tilton's baseline was systematically too high and did not provide an appropriate level of reference for evaluation of the effects of punishment per se. In spite of these major flaws the results of this study were widely accepted, probably because they seemed to support the established common-sense views of punishment that had been challenged by Thorndike's experiments.

For purposes of constructing an empirical baseline of repetition, two features of punishment have to be taken into account: (1) a punishment provides an after-effect, i.e., there is some environmental reaction to the response, as contrasted with a situation in which there is no after-effect at all, and (2) the punishing after-effect is assumed to be annoying to the organism (or to provide information about the incorrectness of the response). It is possible that the apparent failure of punishment to weaken stimulus-response connections is due to the opposed effects of these two aspects of punishment: (1) the occurrence of an after-effect per se, the sheer something happening after the response, may strengthen the connection, but at the same time, (2) the annoying or informative characteristic of the punishment may weaken it. The net effect on repetition would depend on the relative strength of these two influences. Evidence which seemed to support this interpretation was presented in an experiment by Stephens (1934a).

Stephens' subjects had the task of hitting an invisible target with a stylus. Two lights—one signaling a hit and the other signaling a miss—were used to administer rewards and punishments. On some trials, however, neither light was flashed, and on other trials both the "correct" light and the "incorrect" light were flashed simultaneously. The difference between these two last conditions was used to measure the effect of "something happening," since absence of lights and the simultaneous presence of both lights were alike in being neither rewarding nor punishing. Responses followed by *both* lights were repeated more often than those which had no after-effect at all. The sheer occurrence of an after-effect, even though it was neither rewarding nor punishing, seemed to strengthen stimulus-response connections. When the two-light situation was used as an empirical baseline of repetition for evaluating the influence of unequivocal after-effects, it was found that rewards *increased* and punishments *decreased* the frequency of repetitions.[1] Stephens concluded that when the influence of an after-effect per se is taken into account, rewards and punishments may have opposite effects on repetition.

Again, however, the validity of the empirical baseline on which Stephens based his conclusion was questioned. Is it really safe to assume that a "neutral" after-effect, such as the flashing of both lights in Stephens' experiment, is completely uninformative and devoid of incentive value? If the influence of "something happening" is to be properly evaluated, it is necessary to guard against possible informative or rewarding effects of the neutral signal. Using the same task as Stephens (hitting an invisible target), Courts and Waggoner (1938) attempted to provide the necessary control. Six types of after-effects were used: (a) announcement of "Right"; (b) announcement of "Right" accompanied by a light; (c) announcement of "Wrong"; (d) announcement of "Wrong" accompanied by a light; (e) a light alone; and (f) control trials on which there were no after-effects whatsoever. Note that in the critical conditions—(b) and (d)—the possible informative or rewarding effects of light have been ruled out. When a light appears, it accompanies a verbal announcement and thus does not add any reward or information. The announcement of "Right" with and without light yielded almost identical levels of repetitions, and so did the announcement of "Wrong" with and without light. As usual, "Right" resulted in higher levels of repetition than did "Wrong." Thus the addition of a light to an informative announcement had no effect. Interestingly enough, however, the light alone led to a higher level of repetition than the absence of any after-effect whatsoever. Courts and Waggoner interpreted this finding as consistent with their view that "neutral" after-effects by themselves function as signals of approval. This last conclusion is, of course, purely speculative. The experiment does show that the *addition* of neutral signals to informative after-effects does not change the level of repetition. Whether "something happening" after a response is strengthening in and of itself, or only if it is misinterpreted as a reward, remains an open question. In experiments of this kind, the verbal reports of the subjects cannot be used to settle the question since their interpretations of the situation are often inadequately verbalized and quickly forgotten.

It would seem that Stephens' hypothesis is not capable of a rigorous experimental test and has not led to the determination of an acceptable

---

[1] In a related experiment with verbal tasks Stephens (1934b) used a nonsense symbol as a neutral after-effect to control for the influence of "something happening." Again there was some evidence for weakening effects of punishment, but it was limited to initially strong associations. In this situation there was, however, considerable opportunity for rehearsal and correction. In a further study in which the possibility of rehearsal and correction was minimized, the effectiveness of punishment was greatly reduced if not eliminated (Stephens and Baer, 1937).

empirical baseline. So far at least it has not been possible to make a sharp and clear operational distinction between the two characteristics of after-effects proposed in his analysis—that of "something happening" and that of creating a rewarding or punishing state of affairs. Nor does it seem defensible to assume that such characteristics of after-effects, even if they can be distinguished analytically, summate in a simple algebraic fashion to produce their net effect on behavior.

REFINEMENT OF EMPIRICAL CONTROLS.   A shortcoming common to the early attempts at establishing an empirical baseline was the failure to isolate the effects of punishment from other influences. When punished connections are compared with rewarded or unreinforced connections *in the same series,* such factors as serial position (cf. Tilton, 1945) and delayed effects of other rewards and punishments have not been fully controlled. A simpler and more elegant procedure consists of using two groups of subjects who respond to the same series and are treated alike in all respects except that a critical response or set of responses is punished in one group and not in the other. The difference between the groups in the repetition of the critical responses can then be ascribed directly to the effects of punishment. This procedure was first used in a series of experiments by Stone and his associates (1948, 1950, 1951a, 1951b, 1953). These experiments did not produce any evidence for the weakening effects of punishment and often showed significant strengthening effects. The method and results of Stone's experiments are well illustrated in the following study (1953).

A series of forty three-letter words were exposed to the subjects at a 3-sec. rate. The subjects were instructed to respond to each of the words with a number between 1 and 10. Some responses were followed by an announcement of "Right," other responses by an announcement of "Wrong," while for some responses there were no after-effects. The experimenter made his announcements in a fixed order, regardless of the numbers chosen by the subject. The three types of after-effects followed each other in random order for the first sixteen responses of the series. A random sequence of announcements was also used for the last sixteen items in the series. The eight central items provided the critical responses used in the evaluation of the effects of punishment. For the control group, none of these central responses was followed by an after-effect; for the experimental group the two midmost responses were followed by an announcement of "Wrong," whereas the three responses on either side were not followed by an after-effect. Thus, in the case of the eight central items, the sequence of events for the control group was NNNNNNNN, and for the experimental group, NNNWWNNN. This arrangement isolates the critical responses from the remote effects of other rewards and punishments, and differences between the experimental and control group can be attributed directly to the effects of punishment. The series was repeated six times so that the cumulative action of punishments could be determined.

Figure 53 shows the percentages of repetition of the two critical responses as a function of practice. Note first of all that on Trial 2, i.e., after one presentation of the series, the punished items are repeated *more frequently* than the responses to corresponding control items. For both groups the level of repetition exceeds *a priori* chance, probably as a

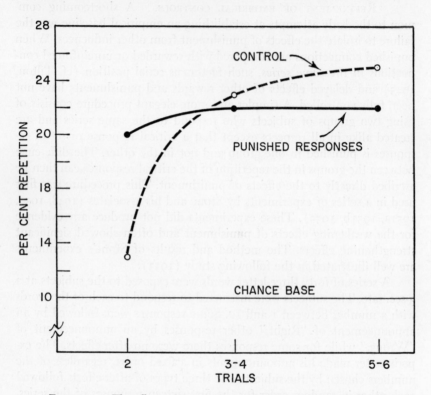

FIGURE 53. The effects of successive punishments on the repetition of responses. There were no after-effects under the control condition. (After Stone, 1953, p. 146.)

result of guessing habits and pre-experimental associations between words and numbers. Thereafter the control group increases its frequency of repetition at a faster rate than the experimental group. There is, however, no absolute decrease in the repetition of punished responses; instead, there is a slow increase. It is quite possible that the curves of the experimental and control group rise for different reasons. For the experimental subjects, responses may be fixated by punishment. As for the control subjects, they may have a set to reproduce their previous responses which favors repetition. This interpretation is supported by additional control data reported by Stone. With materials and instructions carefully designed to eliminate the motive to repeat—the subjects were instructed that their responses to a series of nonsense syllables would be used to test the law of chance—there was no increase in unreinforced repetitions after the second trial. At the very least, Stone's experiment shows that the weakening effects of punishment emerge extremely slowly. In conjunction with the additional control data just mentioned, the results strongly suggest that punishment has positive fixative effects. Results consistent with this interpretation were reported by Stone in several of the other experiments in his series.

Thorndike's findings concerning the effects of punishment cannot be simply dismissed by reference to a faulty baseline of repetition. Careful determinations of an empirical baseline of repetition which appropriately isolate the effects of punishment in a "vanishing situation" yield results consistent with Thorndike's interpretation.

The Law of Emphasis

Quite apart from the direction and magnitude of the effects of punishment, the mechanism of its action has remained a focus of controversy. Whatever the net effects of punishment, Thorndike believed its action to be fundamentally automatic. Cognitive theorists, on the other hand, have stressed the perceptual impact of punishment as a determinant of learning. To the extent that punishment modifies the organism's perception of environmental events, it necessarily influences learning. In addition, punishment as a negative incentive influences performance. This approach to punishment is illustrated in the well-known experiment by Tolman, Hall, and Bretnall (1932) which was offered as a "disproof of the law of effect" and proposed a set of alternative principles consonant with cognitive theory.

The basic hypothesis of the experiment was that punishment, particularly when it involves intense sensory stimulation, serves to give perceptual *emphasis* to the events which it accompanies or follows. If that assumption is valid, punishment for correct responses as well as for errors should facilitate learning. The subjects' task was to learn the correct path through a punchboard maze. This maze consisted of thirty pairs of holes distributed in an irregular pattern over the surface of a large board. One hole in each pair was arbitrarily designated as correct. The subjects responded to each pair by punching one of the holes with a stylus. Four conditions of reward and punishment were used. For the Bell-Wrong Group each error was followed by the sound of a bell. For the Bell-Right Group each correct response was followed by the sound of a bell. In the case of the Bell-Shock-Wrong Group, each error was followed by the sound of a bell *and* an electric shock. Finally, for the Bell-Shock-Right Group, each correct response was followed by the sound of a bell *and* an electric shock. The mean numbers of errors made by the different groups during twenty runs through the maze are shown in Table 1.

We compare first the influence of each type of after-effect on correct responses with its influence on incorrect responses. Bell for correct responses results in faster learning than bell for incorrect responses. This is in agreement with Thorndike's repeated finding that rewards are more effective than punishments. The next finding is more unexpected. Bell *plus* shock for correct responses results in faster learning than bell *plus* shock for errors. At first glance it appears that punishment for correct responses is more effective than punishment for errors. We must recall, however, that the subjects were instructed explicitly that a shock signified

TABLE 1

MEAN NUMBERS OF ERRORS IN TWENTY TRIALS UNDER
DIFFERENT CONDITIONS OF REINFORCEMENT FOR
RIGHT AND WRONG RESPONSES (FROM TOLMAN,
HALL, AND BRETNALL, 1932, P. 607)

Condition	Mean number of errors
Bell-Wrong	117.22
Bell-Right	103.81
Bell-Shock-Wrong	128.82
Bell-Shock-Right	105.71

a correct choice. The electric shocks, though painful, were therefore unequivocal signals of success. The results can be fairly interpreted to mean that a symbolic reward is more effective than a symbolic punishment even when both are accompanied by sensory discomfort.

Let us assume, however, that the shock does function as an annoyer. Do the results constitute critical evidence against the law of effect? There is little difference between the Bell-Right and Bell-Shock-Right Groups, i.e., the addition of shock does not detract from the effectiveness of a signal for correct responses. The Bell-Shock-Wrong Group, on the other hand, makes a larger number of errors than does the Bell-Wrong Group, i.e., the addition of shock increases the repetition of wrong responses. The results would, in fact, be damaging to the law of effect in its original form (see p. 337), which ascribed significant weakening effects to punishment. The revised law of effect states, of course, that punishment has variable effects and may, indeed, strengthen stimulus-response connections. The addition of shock to reward should not, therefore, reduce the repetition of rewarded responses, nor should shock for errors necessarily reduce the repetition of wrong responses. The results appear not to be inconsistent with Thorndike's revised theory of effect.

It is clear from the discussion of Tolman, Hall, and Bretnall that their theoretical argument is directed against the original version of the law of effect (Thorndike's revised views on punishment were still quite new). On the basis of their findings, Tolman and his associates proposed three principles which they regarded as substitutes for the law of effect within the general framework of a cognitive approach to learning. These were the law of motivation, the law of emphasis, and the law of disruption.

The law of motivation states that the "ultimate reason" for learning is the attainment of final success or the avoidance of final failure. The organism uses its knowledge so as to maximize rewards and minimize punishments. This principle refers to the conditions which maintain the activity of learning and govern performance once learning has taken place.

The law of emphasis describes the role played by rewards and punishments in learning proper, i.e., in the acquisition of the knowledge which is utilized in performance. In a trial-and-error situation, learning is conceived as the establishment of cognitive patterns or expectations in which correct and incorrect responses are differentiated from each other. Rewards and punishments serve as sources of perceptual emphasis and thus influence the differentiation of the correct and incorrect choices. The results of the experiment are said to show that emphasis on correct responses favors learning, whereas emphasis on incorrect responses does not.

Finally, the law of disruption asserts that any intense emotional stimulus such as an electric shock will tend to disrupt learning. This additional principle would account for the relatively small effect which the addition of shock to bell had in the case of right responses. The disruption caused by the shock detracted from the emphasis given to the correct response by the shock. This analysis illustrates well the cognitive approach to reward and punishment, particularly the distinction between the conditions of learning which are essentially perceptual and the motivational determinants of performance.

Of the three principles proposed by Tolman, Hall, and Bretnall, it was primarily the law of emphasis which received attention in subsequent experiments. The conclusion that emphasis on correct responses is more beneficial to learning than is emphasis on errors was confirmed by several investigators (Hulin and Katz, 1935; Porter and Hall, 1938; Silleck and Lapha, 1937). There have also been contradictory findings. In the experiments by Courts, emphasis had no effect when the informational value of the signals was controlled (Courts, 1937; Courts and

Waggoner, 1938). In any event, Tolman's analysis served to focus attention on the perceptual and informational characteristics or rewards and punishments as contrasted with their satisfying and annoying properties. Thus the issue of the mechanism of after-effects was again highlighted even though the empirical results of Tolman's study are essentially consistent with those of Thorndike.

The Spread of Effect

Many of the experimental results concerning the effects of symbolic rewards and punishments are equally consistent with a connectionist and a cognitive interpretation. The theoretical stalemate created an urgent need for crucial experiments which would make it possible to arbitrate between the conflicting interpretations. Such crucial evidence seemed to be provided by the discovery of the *spread of effect* which in turn quickly became a focus of experimental and theoretical controversy.

Discovery of the Spread of Effect

The gradient of repetition of errors.   To repeat what has been called "Right" is reasonable, intelligent behavior, and the fact of such repetition does not in and of itself prove that the action of after-effects is automatic. If, however, symbolic rewards strengthen connections which are wrong and irrelevant, the assumption of automatic action becomes more compelling. It is because the spread of effect concerns the strengthening of *wrong* connections by reward that it was considered of crucial theoretical significance by both Thorndike and his critics.

In 1933 Thorndike published a monograph entitled *An Experimental Study of Rewards,* in which he presented a considerable amount of evidence showing that a reward strengthens not only the connection which it immediately follows but also *punished connections which precede and follow the rewarded one.* The closer in a series of items a punished connection is to the rewarded one, the more it benefits from this spread of effect. Thus there is a double gradient of repetition of wrong responses around a rewarded response—a *fore-gradient* and an *after-gradient.*

The phenomenon was first demonstrated in a study in which the subjects' task was to supply the missing words in a series of statements, such as: Bill is..... The ship brought..... Dogs like to....., etc. There were 108 such statements. Responses were called "Right" and "Wrong" according to a key specifying the acceptable responses. The series was repeated two or three times in succession. As usual, punishment did not appear to weaken responses, and the closer a punished response was to a rewarded response the more likely it was to be repeated. Encouraged by this result, Thorndike reanalyzed some of his earlier experiments on multiple-choice learning and found considerable evidence for spread of effect which had been overlooked in previous treatments of the data. The bulk of the monograph presents new experiments which were designed explicitly to measure the spread of effect. Several of the experiments used the familiar procedure of having the subject guess a number between 1 and 10 to each of a long series of words and to call his guesses right or wrong according to a prearranged key. In addition, the responses to some words were called "Right" regardless of the subject's response. The series were repeated several times. The pooled results of three experiments using this general procedure are presented in Figure 54.

The values plotted in Figure 54 represent the degrees to which punished connections at various distances from a rewarded response were strengthened. These values were obtained as follows. The frequency of repetition was determined for punished responses which were so remote from a rewarded response that the spread of effect was for all practical purposes nil. Responses five or more steps removed appeared to satisfy

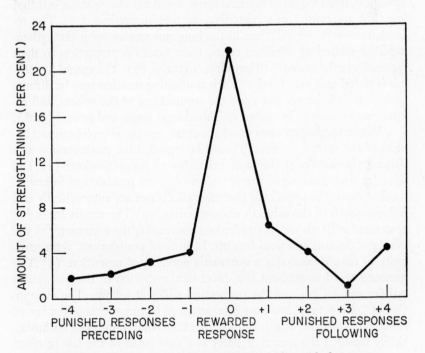

FIGURE 54. The spread of effect: amounts by which punished responses were strengthened as a function of distance from reward. (From Thorndike, 1933, p. 55, and used by permission of the Bureau of Publications, Teachers College, Columbia University, New York.)

this requirement. The percentages of repetition for punished responses one, two, three, and four steps removed from a reward were then expressed as deviations from this empirical point of reference. Note that all the values were larger than zero, i.e., all the punished responses which were fewer than five steps removed from a reward were strengthened relative to the empirical point of reference. And the closer a punished connection was to the reward the more it was strengthened. Brandt (1935) obtained similar results and also supported Thorndike's conclusion that the degree of spread depends on the number of serial steps rather than the amount of time separating a punished response from the rewarded connection.

THORNDIKE'S EXPLANATION OF THE SPREAD OF EFFECT.   Thorndike offered two alternative explanations of the spread of effect—the *scatter hypothesis* and the *spread hypothesis*. According to the scatter hypothesis, the confirming reaction which is the agent of reinforcement by reward will, as it were, occasionally miss its aim and strengthen a connection to which it does not belong. In general, the confirming reaction will influence the connection which it immediately follows, but "being a biological, not a logical or mystical force, it will not always strike just that one, but sometimes one preceding, or one succeeding. . . . The rewarded connections will then in the long run receive many strengthenings, the neutral or punished connections some, in proportion to their proximity to the reward" (Thorndike, 1933a, p. 67). The spread hypothesis is stated only very briefly. "Each confirming reaction may be diffuse, spreading its influence out upon the connections of the system, and influencing one most, its nearest neighbors next most, and so on" (*ibid.*).

While keeping an open mind about the specific neurological mechanism of the spread of effect, Thorndike regarded the phenomenon as a striking vindication of the basic principles of connectionism: (1) The selective strengthening of wrong responses which precede and follow reward supports the hypothesis that after-effects can act automatically and independently of the subject's understanding. (2) The results are in full agreement with his earlier conclusions concerning the asymmetry of the effects of rewards and punishments. In spite of punishment, sheer proximity to reward generates a systematic gradient of repetition. (3) The presence of a fore-gradient is a direct demonstration of the fact that a satisfier can act back on the connection which it follows. The assumption of "retroaction" had long been attacked by opponents of the law of effect (cf. Postman, 1947). No wonder, then, that Thorndike enthusiastically reported the spread of effect as a new proof of the law of effect (1933c) and that his findings stimulated a long series of critical analyses and new experiments.

Methodological Issues

The experimental and quantitative procedures which Thorndike used to demonstrate the spread of effect came in for considerable criticism. Serious questions were raised about (1) the method used in determining the frequency of repetition as a function of distance from reward, and (2) the appropriateness of the baseline against which the gradient was plotted.

ARTIFACTS OF MEASUREMENTS.   In tabulating the frequencies of repetition for a given point on the gradient, Thorndike included all responses which occurred at a given distance from a reward except those which were at the same distance from two rewards. Assume that the experimental protocol included the following sequence:

$$R_1 \ W_1 \ W_2 \ W_3 \ R_2$$

W_2 is midway between two rewards, *following* R_1 by two steps and *preceding* R_2 by two steps; it would therefore not be included in the computation of the fore- and after-gradients. W_1 and W_3 would, however, be included twice each. W_1 would be counted as (1) following R_1 by one step and (2) as preceding R_2 by three steps. Similarly, W_3 would appear both in Position -1 and Position $+3$ (cf. Figure 54). In short, except for the special case of items equidistant from two rewards, punished responses between two rewards contribute to both the fore- and after-gradients. This procedure necessarily favors a symmetrical gradient. If only the after-gradient is reliable (as later studies have indicated) the method of scoring would produce a spurious fore-gradient (Tilton, 1945).

As Hilgard has pointed out, the use of data from several successive repetitions of the same series introduces a bias in favor of a gradient of effect. Successive practice series reduce the number of wrong responses relative to the number of correct responses. As a result, the average distance of the punished responses from the nearest reward also decreases. The punished responses that do remain are likely to be stereotyped errors which are resistant to modification. As training continues, these persistent errors necessarily occur near correct responses and inflate the number of repetitions close to a reward (1956, 41f.).

The baseline used by Thorndike in plotting the gradient of effect has also been questioned. It will be recalled that the values shown in Figure 54 are deviations from the frequency with which punished responses remote from a reward (five or more steps away) are repeated. Such a baseline, however, may neglect the influence of serial position. For example, responses at the beginning and end of a series are favored in repetition, and this fact must be considered in measuring the spread of the influence of reward. This difficulty would be avoided if at each serial position the frequency of repetition of rewarded or punished responses were expressed as deviations from the values obtained without reinforcement. We have already seen in the earlier discussion of punishment that the determination of such a baseline faces serious difficulties. When Tilton plotted repetitions of rewarded and punished responses against his empirical baseline he (1) confirmed the existence of a symmetrical gradient, but (2) found that all punished responses were weakened relative to the baseline, even those immediately adjacent to a reward (Tilton, 1945). The inadequacy of Tilton's baseline has already been pointed out (p. 362f.). It does not, however, detract from his independent confirmation of the spread of effect.

These are some of the searching criticisms which were raised against Thorndike's procedure and his treatment of the experimental results. Some of the methodological deficiencies were removed by later investigators, but the basic phenomenon of the spread of effect has been confirmed repeatedly under well-controlled experimental conditions and with rigorous methods of quantitative analysis. It is true, however, that the after-gradient has survived critical experimental analysis better than has the fore-gradient. Only rarely has an investigator (e.g., Duncan, 1950) failed to find evidence for an after-gradient; experiments showing a reliable fore-gradient have been few and far between (Duncan, 1950; Martens, 1946).

The methodological improvements introduced into the original procedure for measuring spread are illustrated by a study of Martens, 1946 (also reported by Taylor, 1947). The stimulus items used in this experiment were twenty-five adjectives exposed on a memory drum. The subject responded to each of the items with a number between 1 and 10. Responses to two of the items were arbitrarily called "Right," and the others were called "Wrong." The serial positions of the rewards were determined in advance and were varied systematically from subject to subject. The rewards were so placed that there were equal numbers of points on the fore-gradient and on the after-gradient with each position classified unequivocally. Following one training trial on which announcements of "Right" and "Wrong" were made, there was *one* test trial on which repetition of rewarded and punished responses was measured. To determine an empirical baseline of repetition, the same series was presented to another group of subjects which was instructed to indicate a number suggested by each of the words, in the manner of a free-association experiment. This group was neither rewarded nor punished. We note the following improvements as compared with Thorndike's original procedure: (1) the rate of exposure is controlled by use of a memory drum; (2) the number of rewards and punishments is fixed and thus made uniform for all subjects; (3) positions preceding and following the reward are equally represented; (4) each response is scored only once in accordance with its position; (5) use of only one training and test trial avoids the complications introduced by successive repetitions of the same list. Under these highly controlled conditions both a fore- and after-gradient were found. As compared with the empirical baseline, punishment significantly decreased the frequency of repetition. This last finding is, however, difficult to interpret since free-association instructions may have established an effective set to repeat earlier responses.

Thus, however faulty some of the features of the original experiment may have been, the spread of effect may be regarded as an established fact, at least as far as the after-gradient is concerned. But while the fact has been accepted, further analysis has continued to throw doubt on Thorndike's original interpretation. The developments in the interpretation of the spread of effect are, indeed, an excellent example of the productive give and take in the experimental analysis of an empirical finding.

Alternative Interpretations of the Spread of Effect

THE ISOLATION HYPOTHESIS.   One of the early attempts at reinterpretation of the spread of effect suffered from serious logical errors and need be discussed only briefly. That was an attempt to view the spread of effect as a matter of perceptual organization during learning. In Thorndike's experiments a few rewards were typically scattered through a long series of punishments. There was evidence in the experimental literature that the perceptual isolation of an item in a homogeneous series favors the learning of that item. For example, when a few numbers are scattered through a series of nonsense syllables, the numbers are learned better than if they are surrounded by other numbers (Von Restorff, 1933). This finding has been used by Gestalt psychologists to support their contention that the laws of perceptual organization —in this case the principle of figure-ground segregation—are also the laws of learning and memory (Koffka, 1935). Proceeding from the same theoretical assumption, Zirkle published a series of experiments (1946a, 1946b) in which he argued that the spread of effect results from the isolation of a few rewards in a homogeneous series of punishments rather than from the action of reward per se. The following experiment (1946b) was offered in support of his thesis.

The stimuli were sixty words, to each of which the subjects guessed a number between 1 and 10. The majority of the stimuli were eight-letter words printed in lower-case black letters, and most of the responses to these words were called "Wrong." To obtain different degrees of isolation of reward, responses to the following stimulus items were called "Right": (1) a nonsense syllable printed in red capital letters which appeared about two-thirds of the way through the series; (2) two eight-letter words printed in black capital letters, one of which appeared early, and the other late, in the series; (3) five typical stimuli, i.e., eight-letter words printed in black lower-case letters. These three cases were assumed to represent high, medium, and low degrees of perceptual isolation respectively. In the first two, perceptual isolation was presumably produced both by the change in the appearance of the stimulus and the occurrence of a reward in the midst of a series of punishments; in the third, there was only the usual shift from a series of punishments to a reward. Figure 55 shows the gradients of repetition of errors as a function of the degree of isolation of the rewarded response. The higher the degree of isolation, the more frequent is the repetition of the rewarded response itself, and also the steeper is the after-gradient of error repetition. The differences in the fore-gradient are only slight. According to Zirkle, these results support two conclusions: (1) the more isolated an item is, the better it is

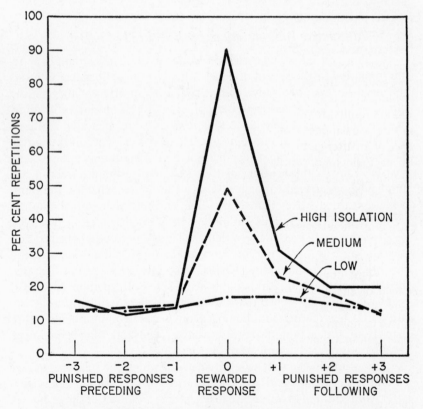

FIGURE 55. Spread of effect as a function of the degree of "isolation" of the rewarded response. For full explanation see text. (Data from Zirkle, 1946, pp. 305f., and used by permission of the American Psychological Association.)

retained; (2) "responses neighboring upon a key response which has become isolated *tend to become isolated themselves* because of their association with the key response. . . . In general, the degree of isolation would tend to decrease with decreasing proximity to the key isolated response" (1946b, p. 313). Thus the gradient of effect is reduced to a gradient of isolation.

This explanation of the spread of effect cannot stand careful scrutiny. Let us grant the assumption that isolation of an item favors acquisition. The perceptual theory of memory, on which Zirkle bases his analysis, does not in any sense imply that items close to the isolated one should be favored in retention. Thus the assumption of a spread of isolation is purely *ad hoc*. What is more serious, however, if we do postulate a spread of isolation, is that results exactly opposite to those obtained by Zirkle would have to be predicted. Items neighboring upon an isolated reward should be differentially recalled as *errors*; hence the beneficial effects of isolation should lead to a gradient of *decreased* rather than increased repetition of wrong responses. Thus Zirkle's theory leads to the highly implausible conclusion that proximity to an isolated reward favors the retention of stimulus-response associations but systematically distorts memory for after-effects. The fact that isolation does not influence the fore-gradient further adds to the inconsistency of the argument. There appears to be only one conclusion which can legitimately be drawn from Zirkle's results: frequency of repetition of the rewarded response (which in this case happens to be brought about by isolation) favors the appearance of an after-gradient. The next section will discuss an explanation of this fact which has greater power and generality than the *ad hoc* assumption of a spread of isolation. Zirkle's abortive theory illustrates what we may call the error of "partial fit." On the face of it, spread of effect did appear to be systematically related to perceptual isolation. The precise nature of the relationship was not, however, correctly deduced from the theory. Thus confirmation of the hypothesis was claimed prematurely.

THE GUESSING-SEQUENCE HYPOTHESIS. In his analysis of the spread of effect, Thorndike concerned himself exclusively with the effects of rewards and punishments on *stimulus-response connections*. There is, however, another way of looking at the conditions of response repetition in a typical experiment on the spread of effect. The responses which the subject makes to successive stimuli may not be entirely independent of each other; e.g., he may have a disposition to guess numbers in a non-random sequence. Having guessed a 7, he may be more likely to guess a 6 or an 8 rather than a 1 or another 7. Suppose now that a subject has, indeed, given a non-random sequence of numbers in response to a series of stimulus words and has been rewarded for some and punished for the others. If the rewarded number is repeated on the following trial, the subject's bias will make it probable that the number which followed the rewarded response on the preceding trial will follow it again. The reward serves to insure the repetition of a key response which initiates a sequence of succeeding responses. Such linkages among successive responses are, however, probable rather than certain. Given the repetition of the rewarded response, some subjects will repeat the number in the position immediately following the reward while others will not. Those subjects who repeat their responses in the first position after the reward are likely to repeat, in turn, their responses in the second position. Again, however, the linkage is probable rather than certain. The larger the number of steps by which a response follows the reward, the less becomes the probability that all the intermediate responses have been repeated. Thus the non-random sequence initiated by the rewarded response becomes less and less effective and a gradient of repetitions is generated. The gradient of effect may, therefore, not be due to the spread of influence of the reward but may reflect pre-existing linkages among responses.

This interpretation of the spread of effect was first suggested by Tolman (1936) in a critical review of one of Thorndike's books. Experimental evidence supporting this view did not, however, appear until ten years later, and it came to light in a study which had been designed for a quite different purpose. That study was conducted by Jenkins and Sheffield in 1946 in order to test the hypothesis that the spread of effect is produced by the selective rehearsal of rewarded responses. According to that hypothesis, an announcement of "Right" causes subjects to rehearse the correct response and distracts them from attending to the adjacent wrong responses. The closer an error is to the reward, the more damaging should be the effects of such distraction on the elimination of that error, i.e., there should be a gradient of repetition of wrong responses. In order to assess the validity of this interpretation, Jenkins and Sheffield compared the standard procedure used in measuring spread with an experimental condition. In the experimental condition, subjects guessed a number to each stimulus word, heard an announcement of "Right" or "Wrong," and immediately thereafter performed an additional task— calling out the opposite of a word provided by the experimenter. The interpolated task, which was omitted in the standard condition, was expected to provide equal amounts of distraction after reward and punished responses and thus eliminate the gradient. The results did not bear out this expectation. The interpolated task served to reduce the number of correct repetitions and raised the general level of repetition of errors, but comparable after-gradients were obtained under both conditions. In analyzing their results, Jenkins and Sheffield found, however, that the after-gradient was limited to those cases in which the rewarded response was repeated. When the rewarded response was not repeated, a gradient failed to appear. This finding suggested that the after-gradient was produced by the subjects' guessing-habits. The presence of the rewarded response was essential for reinstating the non-random sequence of responses which had occurred on the training trial. Here is an example of "serendipity"—the successful exploitation of an accidental finding.

TESTS OF THE GUESSING-SEQUENCE HYPOTHESIS.   There is still some question whether or not the after-gradient is, indeed, dependent upon repetition of the rewarded response. Some investigators have reported such a dependent relationship (Jenkins and Cunningham, 1949; Martens, 1946; Marx, 1957), whereas others have failed to find it (Duncan, 1951; Postman, 1961). Negative results are, of course, damaging to the guessing-sequence hypothesis since the non-random series of guesses responsible for the gradient is assumed to be anchored to the rewarded response. In addition, the comparison between gradients around rewarded and non-rewarded responses raises a serious methodological problem, viz., that of subject selection. In any given experimental sample, speed of learning, and hence the number of repetitions of rewarded responses, will vary from subject to subject. Fast learners will contribute a larger proportion of the responses following repetition of the rewarded response than will slow learners; the converse will be true for responses following non-repetition of the rewarded response. Thus any comparison between the two gradients is complicated by the fact that all subjects do not have an equal opportunity to contribute to each. If speed of learning reflects the effectiveness of the reinforcement administered during training, there may be corresponding differences in the spread of effect which are not a matter of guessing sequences.

An unbiased test of the dependence of the after-gradient on repetition of the rewarded response requires that the frequency of such repetitions be varied without recourse to selection of subjects. In order to meet this requirement, Postman (1961) measured the spread of effect for different groups immediately after the end of training and after an interval of twenty minutes. A typical after-gradient was found on the immediate test. This gradient persisted on the delayed test in spite of a substantial drop in the repetition of rewarded responses after the retention interval. In fact, the large majority of the response sequences which contributed to the gradient on the delayed test followed non-repetition of the rewarded response. Thus, when subject selection is avoided, there appears to be little evidence for dependence of the after-gradient on repetition of the rewarded response. In this connection it is also useful to recall that in the study of Jenkins and Sheffield, the introduction of a distracting task decreased the repetitions of the rewarded response without reducing the after-gradient. Dependence of the after-gradient on repetition of the rewarded response is clearly implied by the guessing-sequence hypothesis, but the empirical evidence on this question remains at best equivocal.

The complexity of these facts was not generally recognized, however, and the guessing-sequence hypothesis received wide acceptance as an explanation of the spread of effect, especially since other experiments appeared to support it directly.

According to the guessing-sequence hypothesis, the spread of effect reflects linkages between successive responses rather than differences in the strength of stimulus-response associations. It follows that an after-gradient should be found even if the positions of the stimuli which led to punished responses are shifted between the training and test trials, i.e., there should be a gradient as a function of the step-positions following reward regardless of the identity of the specific stimuli. The procedure of shifting stimuli between training and test was first introduced by Zirkle (1946a) in a paper which appeared at about the same time as the study by Jenkins and Sheffield. Zirkle used a series of sixty words to each of which subjects responded with a number between 1 and 10. Six rewarded responses were scattered through the series so that each reward was preceded and followed by six punishments. The critical new feature of Zirkle's design was that the serial order of the punished connections was changed from trial to trial. Thus a punished connection which was immediately adjacent to a reward on one trial might be four steps removed from it on the next trial, and so on. Two gradients of repetition were then determined (1) for punished stimulus-response connections which were at various distances from the reward during a training trial and appeared in new positions during the test trial, and (2) for successive step-positions before and after the reward which were occupied by different stimulus items during the training and test trials. The repetitions of wrong responses to specific stimulus words which had shifted their serial positions failed to show a gradient. On the other hand, a clearcut after-gradient and a somewhat less pronounced fore-gradient were obtained when repetitions were plotted for successive *step-positions* without regard to the stimulus words. Although Zirkle pointed out that these findings were inconsistent with Thorndike's views, he did not give an explanation in terms of guessing sequences. The systematic development of this hypothesis must be credited primarily to Jenkins and Sheffield.

Using a procedure similar to Zirkle's, i.e., shifting the serial positions of stimulus items from trial to trial, Jenkins and Cunningham (1949) again obtained results favoring the guessing-sequence interpretation. (One feature of the procedure used by Jenkins and Cunningham should be noted especially. The subjects were run in groups, and instead of making announcements of "Right" and "Wrong," the experimenter gave the instruction "Repeat" at the "reward" positions. Thus the method of reinforcement was quite different from that used by Thorndike.) Figure 56 shows the gradients for (1) the "Thorndike analysis" in

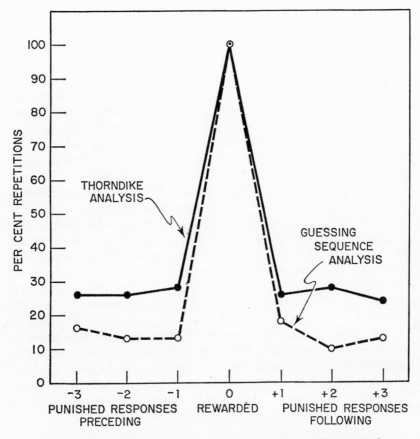

FIGURE 56. Gradients of effect as a function of distance from reward during training ("Thorndikian" analysis) and distance from repeated rewarded response during test ("guessing-sequence analysis"). (From Jenkins and Cunningham, 1949, p. 160, and used by permission of the American Psychological Association.)

which repetitions are plotted for specific stimulus-response associations, and (2) the "guessing-sequence analysis" in which repetitions are plotted against serial positions without regard to the identity of the stimulus items. Only sequences following repetition of the rewarded response are included. The "Thorndike analysis" yields no evidence for a significant gradient. By the "guessing-sequence analysis," there is no fore-gradient but a significant after-gradient for the first two steps following reward.[2]

[2] Jenkins and Cunningham conducted a supplementary experiment in order to obtain direct evidence for the number-guessing habits which were assumed to generate the spread of effect. When subjects were instructed to write down random series of numbers as rapidly as possible, it was found that (1) there was a pronounced tendency to avoid giving the same number twice in succession, although that would have been entirely appropriate in a random series, and that (2) there was a strong

Neither analysis produced a gradient around non-repeated rewarded responses. It is interesting to note that the over-all level of repetition is higher for the "Thorndike analysis." It is probable that pre-existing associations between specific words and numbers contribute to the level of repetition of specific stimulus-response associations.

The procedure of shifting the positions of the stimuli is designed to assess the strength of sequential dependencies which are independent of specific stimulus-response associations. To the extent that this objective is achieved, the procedure may not provide a fair test of the spread of effect as originally conceived by Thorndike. According to Thorndike, the effects of reward spread to neighboring stimulus-response connections. For purposes of testing this hypothesis, the term "stimulus" should denote not only the identity of an item but also the context established by the preceding items and the temporal order of the series. Shifts in the positions of the stimuli cause each item to appear in a new context. Thus the "Thorndike analysis" shown in Figure 56 measures not repetitions of responses to recurrent stimuli but rather generalization of responses to substantially changed stimuli. For this reason the negative results of the analysis cannot be considered as crucial evidence against Thorndike's hypothesis.

The implications of the guessing-sequence hypothesis were tested in several further experiments. The hypothesis implies that a gradient of repetition should be obtained even in the *absence of reward*, provided only that certain key items, corresponding to the rewarded responses in Thorndike's experiments, are repeated. In an experiment designed to test this prediction, Sheffield (1947) instructed his subjects to guess four series of numbers, ostensibly to check on their ability to "divine by clairvoyance" the sequence of digits in a standard table of random numbers. The four columns of fifty guesses each were treated as though they were responses on successive trials in a standard experiment on the spread of effect. Each repetition of a number in the same serial position in two successive columns was scored as a "repeat" and considered analogous to the repetition of a rewarded response. The number of repetitions in the five positions following such a chance repeat was then determined. The results are presented in Table 2, and show a typical after-gradient diminishing to a chance level at the fifth position. Note, however, that the level of repetition is considerably lower than that typical of Thorndike's experiments (about 20 per cent in the first position after reward). Shef-

_____

bias in favor of numbers close to the one given just before, e.g., to follow a 5 by a 4 or a 6. The tendency to avoid immediate repetition of a number has also been noted by Smith (1949). Such preferences shared by subjects may contribute to the gradient following repeated rewarded responses. Idiosyncratic biases can, however, add to the total effect. What is critical is the repetition of sequences, regardless of whether a subject's sequence is unique or shared by other subjects.

field suggested several factors to account for this discrepancy. In the absence of stimulus words, pre-experimental word-number associations could not contribute to the over-all level of repetition. The instructions emphasized the randomness of the number sequence, whereas no reference to the sequence of responses was made in Thorndike's instructions. Finally, the subjects were not distracted by a learning task. Preoccupation with the recall of numbers may encourage the use of well-established guessing sequences. The hypothesis that the distraction provided by a learning task maximizes the influence of sequential response biases was tested in a subsequent experiment by Sheffield and Jenkins

TABLE 2

GRADIENT OF REPETITION FOLLOWING CHANCE
REPETITION OF A KEY RESPONSE (FROM
SHEFFIELD, 1949, P. 576)

Position after chance repetition	Per cent of repetition
1	13.3
2	11.4
3	11.2
4	10.6
5	10.2

(1952). The procedure for obtaining sequences of number guesses was essentially the same as in Sheffield's study. Under the experimental condition, however, the subjects were given the additional task of learning a list of paired associates. Under the control condition they simply guessed numbers. The introduction of a learning task raised the level of repetition of number sequences only under highly circumscribed conditions. A fixed order of presentation had to be used for the paired associates, and the increased repetition occurred only on trials on which the subjects attempted to recall the response terms of the paired associates. These results offer only weak support to the distraction hypothesis. It is entirely possible that associations were formed between specific numbers and individual response terms in the list of paired associates (cf. Marx, 1956, 145f.). The fact that a fixed order of word pairs favored the recurrence of guessing sequences again points to the importance of stimulus context in determining repetition of responses.

It appeared, then, that under certain very special conditions guessing sequences could generate gradients of the same order of magnitude as had been obtained in studies of the spread of effect. Sheffield and Jenkins were ready to conclude that wherever the spread of effect had been observed, guessing sequences were responsible for it. That conclusion did not, of course, follow logically from their results. The possibility remained open that gradients of repetition of errors can be produced both by the spread of the effects of reward and by the operation of guessing sequences. That possibility had to be taken seriously because of two important limitations of the evidence supporting the guessing-sequence hypothesis. First, some of the experiments demonstrating the operation of response biases did not use rewards and therefore did not meet the conditions of Thorndike's theory. Second, the guessing-sequence hypothesis could not explain the occurrence of fore-gradients which had been obtained with sufficient frequency to represent an unanswered challenge to the hypothesis. Thus demonstration of the fact that guessing sequences can generate gradients did not constitute a refutation of the spread of effect. The critical next step was to measure the spread of effect under conditions in which the influences of guessing sequences are controlled without preventing the effects of rewards from manifesting themselves.

Some recent experiments by Marx and his associates (Marx, 1957; Marx and Goodson, 1956) have done precisely that. Marx introduced some new features into the analysis of the spread of effect: (1) Instead of simply counting frequencies of repetition and non-repetition, he measured the *degree* of change in responses on successive trials. By this means, more subtle effects of reward could be detected than by an all-or-none analysis of repetitions. (2) Careful attempts were made to hold guessing habits constant and to test for a residual gradient of repetition attributable to reward per se. The study of Marx and Goodson illustrates these procedures.

A multiple-choice learning task was used. The stimuli, exposed on the top of a box, were twenty-seven rows of twelve holes each. The subjects (school children) chose one hole in each row and attempted to insert a stylus into it. When the stylus went in to the hilt the response was a success; on other trials the insertion of the stylus was blocked and the response was a failure. Each row was labeled with a stimulus word. Thus the formal features of the typical Thorndikian experiment were translated into a situation in which the responses were motor movements rather than verbal responses. Only a small number of responses (from one to three per subject) were successful, and these were scattered at predetermined positions through the series. A control group performed the same series of responses but was never successful. For purposes of analysis, both the experimental and the control group were divided into repeaters and non-repeaters, i.e., those who did and those who did not repeat their responses in the key positions on the training and test trials. For experimental subjects, responses in the key positions had been rewarded and for control subjects they had not. Some control subjects, however, had repeated their responses in the key positions by chance.

To measure the tendency to repeat errors, the difference between the positions chosen on the first and second trials was used. The smaller the difference score the more similar were the choices on the two trials. Figure 57 presents the after-gradients of error repetition for experimental and control subjects who repeated their responses in the key positions (there were no fore-gradients). The gradient for the experimental (rewarded) group is regular and pronounced, that for the control group is only slight. Both groups had repeated the key response, and *the influence of guessing sequences therefore had been held constant*. The steeper gradient of the experimental group must be attributed to the direct action of reward.[3] The conclusion that guessing sequences may

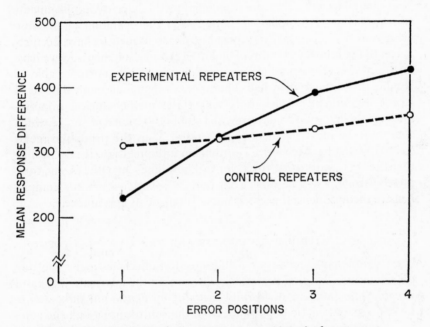

FIGURE 57. Gradients of effect following repetition of a key response. Experimental repeaters were rewarded after key response during training, whereas control repeaters were not. (After Marx and Goodson, 1956, p. 423, and used by permission of the American Psychological Association.)

account for all of the spread of effect may, indeed, have been premature. We appear to have come full cycle, and the hypothesis that the spread of effect reflects the automatic action of rewards must remain on the books.

As we look back on the vicissitudes which have marked the develop-

[3] In his interpretation Marx stresses the strengthening effect which the reinforcement of a key response has on the total sequence of responses which is anchored to that key response. He prefers to speak of "serial response-response reinforcement" rather than of the spread of effect from one discrete stimulus-response association to another (1956, 149f.).

ment of ideas about the spread of effect, we recognize a familiar phenomenon—the cyclical rise and fall of an explanatory hypothesis in response to changes in experimental method and empirical evidence.
When Thorndike first found the gradients of repetition of errors, he accepted them enthusiastically as proof for a proposition of his theory
which was most urgently in need of support, the automatic action of
after-effects. It is interesting that he did not recognize the role of guessing sequences, although he was clearly concerned about the possibility of
artifacts. His thinking was focused on the conditions determining the
strength of stimulus-response associations; the consideration of response-
response linkages was not part of his customary methods of analysis. Opposition to Thorndike's theory stimulated methodological improvements
and reanalyses of the phenomenon. When the operation of response
biases was demonstrated, the spread of effect seemed to have been reduced to the innocuous status of an artifact of measurement. As we have
seen, however, the guessing-sequence hypothesis was no more able to
handle all the facts than had Thorndike's original account. The most
recent experiments, which fully reflect the methodological improvements since Thorndike's days, reveal a stubborn residual of spread which
appears to be indeed a function of reward. Thus the pendulum seems
to be swinging back toward a Thorndikian interpretation. It may well be
that the cycle will repeat itself, for if Thorndike's hypothesis was completely wrong it will be driven out only by a better and more comprehensive theory. Such a theory has not as yet made its appearance.

LEARNING WITHOUT AWARENESS AND THE LAW OF EFFECT

THORNDIKE'S STUDIES.   The spread of effect has major theoretical significance because it appears to exemplify the automatic action of
reward. The problem of *learning without awareness* similarly derives
much of its systematic importance from the controversy about the automatic action of after-effects. In the argument of "information vs. effect"
the effect interpretation would be strongly supported if it could be
shown that rewards and punishments can influence stimulus-response
connections even while the subject remains unaware of what it is he is
learning. Thorndike recognized the systematic importance of such a
demonstration and performed a number of experiments showing that
the influence of after-effects does not depend on the subject's understanding of the situation (1932, pp. 207–75).

In one typical experiment the subjects were shown a series of cards
on each of which four lines of equal length had been drawn. The subjects' task was to judge which of the four lines was longest. Since the
lines were actually equal, the responses were necessarily guesses. Different cards in the series had, however, certain distinctive features, such as

a small ink blot, two white crossbars on one of the lines, a number marked in the middle of the card, etc. The subjects' "judgments" were differently rewarded so as to reinforce associations between the identifying features of the cards and particular responses. Thus a judgment of the second line as the longest might be rewarded if the card had an ink blot, a judgment of the third line as longest if one of the lines was broken by crossbars, etc. At the end of the experiment the subjects were asked to state whether they had recognized the rule according to which the judgments had been called right. Ability to verbalize the principle governing the administration of rewards was, therefore, used as the criterion of awareness. When only those subjects who showed no evidence of awareness were considered, it was found that the rewards had, indeed, produced an increase in the number of "correct" responses. Understanding of the stimulus-response contingency governing the administration of rewards was not essential for learning.

The success of such experiments depends, of course, on the validity of the criterion of awareness. The subject's ability to verbalize the conditions of reward provides a criterion which has face validity, although it is obviously not foolproof. The errors of interpretation which can be introduced by the use of an inappropriate criterion of awareness are illustrated by a well-known experiment of Thorndike and Rock (1934).

The experiment was conducted as a study of free association. A series of 320 (in some cases 640) words was read to the subjects, and they were instructed to respond to each word with the first association that came to mind. At the beginning of the experiment subjects were informed that for each stimulus word some associations had been arbitrarily designated as right and others as wrong. Actually, announcements of "Right" and "Wrong" were made according to a rule, viz., sequential or rote associations such as "yours—truly" were called right, and denotative associations such as "yours—mine" were called wrong. In some cases in which the association could not be readily classified, no announcement was made. There was a gradual increase in the number of "correct" associations, i.e., subjects learned to give the class of associations for which they were rewarded. From the fact that the improvement was gradual, Thorndike and Rock concluded that the subjects had not been aware of what they were learning. Presumably insight into the correct principle would have led to a sudden increase in correct responses. Inspection of individual records produced little evidence of sudden shifts in responses. Although there was considerable variability in the amount learned, gradual improvement was the rule.

Thorndike and Rock regarded the gradual rise of the learning curve as evidence for the lack of awareness. The validity of this criterion was questioned in a critique of the experiment by Irwin, Kaufman, Prior, and Weaver (1934). These investigators pointed out that the slope of the learning curve does not necessarily reflect the presence or absence of insight. Even after a subject has understood the principle according to which responses are called correct, he must learn to apply it. If the responses prescribed by the principle are complex or unfamiliar, the acquisition of the necessary skills may take time and the curve of performance may show a gradual rise. Irwin and his associates demonstrated the validity of their criticism by means of a supplementary experiment. The same materials and procedure were used as in the experiment of Thorndike and Rock, except for the addition of one critical feature: some time during the experiment each subject was explicitly taught the distinction between right and wrong responses. The subject's understanding of the rule was checked with the aid of examples. Their results show that even after the principle had been fully understood, improvement usually continued to follow a gradual course. No valid inferences concerning the presence or absence of awareness can be drawn from the slope of the learning curve.

VERBALIZATION AS A CRITERION OF AWARENESS.   This critical analysis by Irwin and his associates left indeterminate the problem to which Thorndike and Rock had originally addressed themselves, viz., whether differential reward and punishment can strengthen a *class* of responses without the learner's becoming aware of the principle governing the after-effects. The experiment was therefore repeated by Postman and Jarrett (1952), who used, as Thorndike had in other studies, the subject's ability to verbalize the principle governing rewards as the criterion of awareness. In order to determine the relationship between the course of learning and the point at which verbalization occurred, they required their subjects to state their hypotheses about the class of rewarded responses at the end of every block of twenty trials. Consider first those subjects who succeeded in stating the principle. Figure 58 shows the number of correct responses (out of twenty) plotted against the distance (in blocks of trials) from the point at which the principle was verbalized. There is a small but steady improvement prior to statement of the principle. Verbalization is accompanied by a pronounced increase in the number of correct responses, which is, in turn, followed by a further period of gradual improvement. Performance remains, however, far from perfect. Another group of subjects which was informed of the correct principle at the beginning of the experiment showed gradual improvement similar to that on the post-verbalization trials in Figure 58. These results show that (1) improvement is possible prior to verbalization of the principle; (2) ability to verbalize the rule is correlated with a substantial acceleration of improvement; and (3) ability to verbalize the rule is not necessarily followed by errorless performance.

The level of performance reached after verbalization depends on the skill required for application of the rule.

Subjects who never succeeded in verbalizing the principle showed little evidence of improvement. The subjects may be considered learners of relatively low ability. Their initial rate of improvement is also lower than that of the verbalizers *prior to* statement of the principle. This finding suggests that learning without awareness and the ability eventually to verbalize the principle may be a function of the same variables.

A principle which could be stated and applied more readily than that of sequential association was used by Philbrick and Postman (1955).

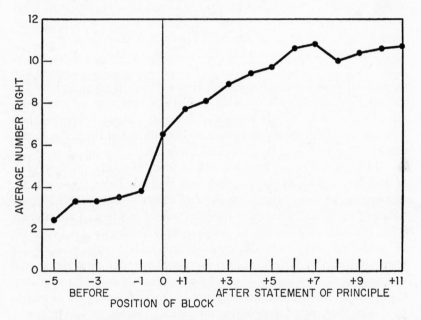

FIGURE 58. Mean numbers of correct responses as a function of distance from point of verbalization of the principle according to which reinforcements were administered. (From Postman and Jarrett, 1952, p. 250, and used by permission of the *American Journal of Psychology*.)

In this study subjects were required to respond with a number to each of a series of words. Reinforcement was given for numbers equal to the number of letters in the word minus one. There was significant improvement prior to the point at which the rule could be verbalized. The amount of such improvement was greater for subjects who were eventually able to state the rule than for those who were not. The same procedure was used by Di Vesta and Blake (1959), who found that improvement in the absence of verbalization occurs regardless of whether subjects are instructed to look for a principle or are discouraged from doing so. A set to find a principle did, however, have a beneficial effect on performance. The same principle of reinforcement was used successfully to produce improvement prior to verbalization in the experiment of Hirsch (1957).

There seems to be no sharp dividing line between learning without awareness and learning with awareness. Rather, awareness as reflected in verbalization represents an advanced stage in the development of a habit under conditions of differential reinforcement. Thus verbalization of a principle may be considered at the same time a result of past improvement and a condition of further improvement (cf. Hirsch, 1957; Postman and Sassenrath, 1961). To the extent that awareness of what is being learned is not a necessary condition of the effectiveness of reward, the results are consistent with Thorndike's position.

The *amount* of learning without awareness seems to depend on the readiness with which the general rule governing correct responses can be applied to specific instances. This conclusion is suggested by the fact that recent experiments using relatively simple principles have obtained considerably higher degrees of learning without awareness than have the studies using the procedure of Thorndike and Rock. An experiment by Cohen *et al.* (1954) is a case in point.

The subjects were presented with a series of eighty cards on each of which a common English verb was printed. Below the verb six pronouns—"I," "we," "you," "he," "she," "they"—were listed. As each card was exposed, the subjects had the task of making up a sentence, using the verb and one of the six pronouns. Whenever the pronouns "I" and "we" were used, the experimenter said "Good" in a casual, unemotional tone. Whenever the other pronouns were used, the experimenter made no comment. There was also a control group to which the experimenter never made any response. As the left-hand part of Figure 59 shows, there was a progressive increase in the use of the rewarded pronouns for the experimental group but not for the control group. The right-hand side of Figure 59 shows the effects of procedures which are analogous to the operations of extinction in conditioning. The group for which rewards were discontinued (Straight Extinction) failed to show a decline in the use of the critical responses; in fact, it does not differ from the group for which the rewards were continued. The influence of the symbolic after-effects appears to be quite persistent in this situation. The group for which the rewards were shifted from "I" and "we" to "he" and "they" (Reinforcement of Competing Responses) shows the expected change in responses. Inquiry at the end of the experiment indicated that the subjects had not become aware of, i.e., could not verbalize, the rule governing the experimenter's responses. As a matter of fact, many subjects could not recall the fact that the experimenter had occasionally made an encouraging remark. Other experiments using this procedure yielded similar results (e.g., Taffel, 1955).

Changes in verbal response patterns of which the subject remained unaware have also been obtained in experiments using the technique of operant conditioning. In such situations there is not a series of discrete trials on each of which the subject responds to a specific stimulus. Rather, the subject emits responses, e.g., pronounces words at his own rate. It has been possible to enhance substantially the use of a particular class of responses, e.g., plural nouns, by differential reinforcement

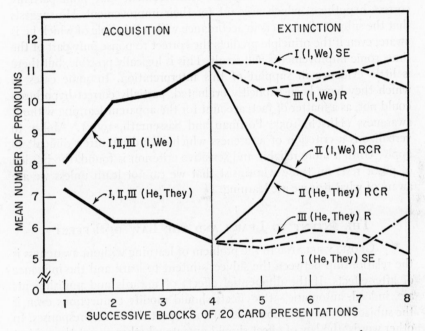

FIGURE 59. Acquisition and extinction of a verbal response as a function of the conditions of reinforcement. SE = straight extinction; RCR = reinforcement of competing response; R = continued reinforcement. (From Cohen *et al.*, 1954, p. 108, and used by permission of the American Psychological Association.)

(Greenspoon, 1955; Sidowski, 1954). Again, such results were often obtained with subjects who remained unaware of the principle of reinforcement or, indeed, of the fact of reinforcement itself. (For reviews of such experiments see Krasner, 1958, and Verplanck, 1956.)

There is by now ample empirical evidence to support the conclusion that after-effects can significantly modify behavior even when the subject is unable to verbalize the principle according to which the after-effects are administered. These results support Thorndike's contention that the influence of after-effects may be automatic, i.e., that the operation of the law of effect is independent of the learner's awareness. As we have stated before, the validity of this conclusion rests on the adequacy of the definition of awareness in terms of the learner's ability to verbalize the relationship between his responses and the occurrence of after-effects.

This definition has been questioned, especially by those who doubt the possibility of learning without awareness. Adams (1957), for example, insists that subjects who learn under reward without being able to verbalize the conditions of reinforcement may hold partially correct hypotheses which account for their improvement. He suggests that the subject always acts in accordance with a principle of which he is aware; even if the principle predicts the correct response only part of the time, some improvements will result. This is logically possible, but there is little evidence in support of this interpretation. In some cases in which they have been explicitly evaluated, partially correct hypotheses could not, as a matter of fact, account for the apparent learning without awareness (Hirsch, 1957; Postman and Sassenrath, 1961).[4] Ability to verbalize is a criterion of awareness which is, indeed, often difficult to apply. Until a more reliable and sensitive criterion is found, the burden of proof rests on those who insist that we cannot learn unless we are aware of what it is we are learning.

THE INTENT TO LEARN AND THE LAW OF EFFECT

CLOSELY RELATED to the problem of learning without awareness is the relationship between the subject's intent to learn and the influence of after-effects. If the differential effects of rewards and punishments are, indeed, automatic, after-effects should modify connections even if the subject has no intention to learn and repeat the correct responses. In other words, the law of effect should operate whether or not the subject understands the relevance of the rewards and punishments to the subse-

---

[4] Tatz (1960) recently reported data obtained in a study of verbal conditioning which he interprets as evidence for the dependence of "learning without awareness" on the presence of partially correct hypotheses. His procedure, data, and conclusions are open to serious doubt: (1) Evidence concerning the subjects' hypotheses was obtained after the experiment in a lengthy interview which proceeded "from general to specific." Under these circumstances there is a possibility that subjects' reports were biased by suggestive questions. (2) In two of the four conditions of the experiment there were no subjects who failed to report either a successful or partially successful system so that the relationship between partially correct hypotheses and performance could not be evaluated at all. (3) The performance of subjects who verbalized the principle used by the experimenter was poorer than that of subjects who devised a system of their own. In spite of some *ad hoc* explanations offered by Tatz, this finding throws serious doubt on the validity of the information obtained in the post-experimental inquiry.

quent repetition or avoidance of particular responses. In order to test this implication of the theory of effect, Wallach and Henle (1941, 1942) designed an experiment in which "the instructions were so framed that no sensible reason for the repetition of correct responses was given to the subject. Only the satisfying after-effect of these responses could then be responsible if successful reactions should be repeated more frequently than by chance" (1941, p. 341).

Specifically, the subjects in the experiment of Wallach and Henle were told that they were taking part in a study of extrasensory perception and were required to guess the number between 1 and 10 which had allegedly been paired with each of a series of words. After each guess the experimenter would make an announcement of "Right" or "Wrong." The subjects were informed, however, that the numbers paired with the words were changed in a random fashion from presentation to presentation. Thus a number called "Right" on one trial might or might not be right again on subsequent trials. These instructions were assumed to eliminate the motivation to learn and repeat the rewarded responses. The series was repeated twenty times in succession, with the position of the rewarded responses varied systematically from trial to trial. In a subsidiary experiment another group of subjects was interrupted after six presentations of the list and asked to recall their last response to each of the stimulus words. Thus measures of repetition and recall were used to evaluate the differential effectiveness of rewards and punishments when there was no intent to learn.

Rewarded responses were not repeated more frequently than punished ones. For both types of responses the level of repetition was about 11 per cent, i.e., very close to chance. This level of repetition is, of course, considerably lower than that typically obtained in Thorndike's experiments, and the usual difference in favor of rewarded responses is completely absent. The percentages of recall were somewhat higher—about 18 per cent—but again there was no difference between rewarded and punished responses. Wallach and Henle concluded that the law of effect fails to operate in the absence of a motive to learn. They considered their results as evidence for the view that rewards are effective only to the extent that (1) they provide the learner with information about the correctness or incorrectness of a response, and (2) the learner is motivated to use this information on later occasions.

At first glance, the results of Wallach and Henle do, indeed, appear to cast serious doubts on Thorndike's theory of after-effects and to support a cognitive interpretation of the role of reward on learning. Unfortunately, however, the experiment suffered from a serious methodological flaw which makes the findings inconclusive. Repetition of responses was measured on twenty successive presentations of the list, with different responses to the same stimuli rewarded on each trial.

The continuous shift of rewards from one set of responses to another probably produced a considerable amount of associative interference which would obscure the effects of reward. The same difficulty applies to the test of recall which was given after a series of repetition tests. In view of these considerations, Postman and Adams (1954) repeated the procedure of Wallach and Henle with two modifications: (1) only one learning trial was used, followed by a test of repetition during which no reinforcements were given; (2) separate groups of subjects were given a test of recall for their responses immediately after training without prior tests of recognition. The results of this experiment are compared with those of Wallach and Henle in Figure 60. The percentages of both repetition and recall were considerably higher in the experiment of Postman and Adams, in agreement with the assumption that the negative findings of Wallach and Henle were vitiated by substantial amounts of associative interference. When this source of

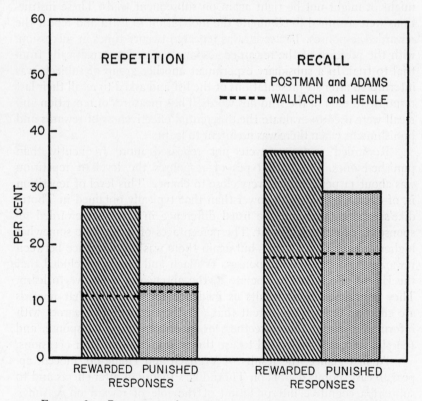

FIGURE 60. Percentages of repetition and recall of rewarded and punished responses in two studies of the law of effect in incidental learning. For a description of the two studies see text. (Data from Wallach and Henle, 1941, pp. 344 and 347, and Postman and Adams, 1954, pp. 616, 618, and 621f.)

error is removed, rewarded responses are repeated and recalled significantly more often than punished ones. In a similar study using the ESP procedure, Porter (1957) also obtained a higher proportion of repetitions of rewarded than of punished responses. Rewards are more effective than punishments even when learning is incidental rather than intentional. It is important to note that these results remain substantially the same whether the proportion of rewarded responses in the series is high or low. Thus, rewarded responses are repeated more often than punished ones, not only when there are a few "Rights" scattered through a series of "Wrongs," but also when the relative frequencies of the two announcements are reversed (Postman and Adams, 1955). Clearly, the differential effects of rewards and punishments on incidental learning are not a matter of the perceptual "isolation" of the rewarded connections.

Bitterman (1954) explored still another variation of the ESP procedure. In addition to an experimental group receiving the usual announcements of "Right" and "Wrong," there was a second group which was informed after each guess what the correct number was. The results for the first group were in substantial agreement with those of Postman and Adams, although the differential effects of reward were smaller in Bitterman's study. The second group, which was corrected after each wrong guess, showed a significant shift from punished to corrected responses. Thus the information about the correct responses was effective even though it was offered "in the context of punishment" (1954, p. 415). Bitterman interprets this finding as evidence against the law of effect and in favor of a cognitive interpretation. This interpretation is untenable for two major reasons. First, the effectiveness of a correction after punishment is in full accord with Thorndike's revised law of effect. In a non-vanishing situation, such as that used by Bitterman, punishment produces variability of response and thus favors the substitution of the correct response for the incorrect one.

Second, a cognitive interpretation cannot account for the difference between a simple announcement of "Right" and a correction, both of which give exactly the same information to the subject.[5] The reason for this discrepancy is not clear, but the finding lends little support to the equation of after-effect and information. In any event,

---

[5] A recent experiment by Hillix and Marx (1960) shows that different after-effects do not necessarily produce the same results when the amount of information conveyed by them is equated. In a multiple-choice learning situation subjects who merely observed the experimenter performed better than subjects who were rewarded for their own correct responses. Since the amount of information given to the two groups was the same, the difference must be attributed to other factors, possibly the greater distraction by errors when the subject rather than the experimenter makes the overt responses.

the fact that both direct reward and correction favor incidental learning is contrary to the hypothesis of Wallach and Henle that after-effects influence acquisition only when the subject is motivated to learn. Intent to learn is not a necessary condition for the positive action of after-effects. The apparently crucial evidence against the law of effect presented by Wallach and Henle has failed to withstand subsequent critical analysis.

Conclusion

WE HAVE DISCUSSED some of the major problems in the experimental analysis of rewards and punishments in human learning. As our account clearly shows, this work has been dominated by the theories and investigations of Edward L. Thorndike. His laws of learning have been the focus of attack and defense; his experimental procedures and analyses set the stage for later investigations.

The generalizations to which Thorndike was led by his experimental work have remained controversial. His basic conclusions were: (1) Sheer frequency of repetition produces only small amounts of learning. (2) Reward reliably strengthens stimulus-response connections and is the single most powerful determinant of learning. (3) Punishment does not weaken connections directly; whatever beneficial effects punishment does have must be attributed to the variability of behavior produced by annoyers, which in turn leads to the substitution and reinforcement of correct responses. (4) The action of after-effects upon connections is direct, automatic, and inevitable.

Both the connectionist model and the doctrine of effect have been the target of prolonged and vigorous criticism. The debate has been very productive indeed. The weaknesses in Thorndike's original experimental designs and quantitative analyses have stimulated the development of more rigorous and refined methods in the study of rewards and punishments. The empirical correction of *a priori* estimates of chance and the investigation of guessing habits are just two examples of such methodological improvements. Opposition to the connectionist doctrine has sustained the critical examination of the basic concepts of learning theory. The development of the distinction between learning and performance, which represents an essential advance over the original connectionist model, is a case in point. Ever since the original formulation of the law of effect, adherents of Thorndike and his opponents have sought to devise crucial experiments which would put some of the basic propositions of the theory to experimental test. Here we recall, above all, the studies of punishment, the spread of effect, and learning without awareness. The central assumption of Thorndike's system—that the influence of after-effects upon connections is automatic and inevitable, "biological rather than logical"—has remained a focus of fundamental disagreement.

In spite of the many empirical and conceptual problems which still await solution, the basic propositions of Thorndike's theory have weathered with considerable success both theoretical critiques and attempts at experimental refutation. Time and again, as in his views on punishment and the spread of effect, he appeared to have been proven wrong but eventually found new support from still further experimental analyses of these problems. The picture of the learning process which Thorndike sketched more than fifty years ago is still very much on the books. No comprehensive theory of human learning can afford to ignore the heritage left to us by Thorndike.

REFERENCES

ADAMS, D. K. Experimental studies of adaptive behavior in cats. *Comp. Psychol. Monogr.*, 1929, 6, No. 27.

ADAMS, J. K. Laboratory studies of behavior without awareness. *Psychol. Bull.*, 1957, 54, 383–405.

BITTERMAN, M. E. Information and effect in incidental learning. *Amer. J. Psychol.*, 1954, 67, 612–31.

BRANDT, H. The spread of the influence of reward to bonds remote in sequence and time. *Arch. Psychol.*, 1935, 27, No. 180.

COHEN, B. D., KALISH, H. I., THURSTON, J. R., AND COHEN, E. Experimental manipulation of verbal behavior. *J. exp. Psychol.*, 1954, 47, 106–10.

COURTS, F. A. The alleged retroactive effect of visual stimuli subsequent to a given response. *J. exp. Psychol.*, 1937, 20, 144–54.

COURTS, F. A., AND WAGGONER, D. The effect of "something happening" after a response. *J. exp. Psychol.*, 1938, 22, 383–7.

DI VESTA, F. J., AND BLAKE, K. The effects of instructional "sets" on learning and transfer. *Amer. J. Psychol.*, 1959, 72, 57–67.

DUNCAN, C. P. The action of various after-effects on response repetition. *J. exp. Psychol.*, 1950, 40, 380–9.

———. Stimulus-generalization and spread of effect. *Amer. J. Psychol.*, 1951, 64, 585–90.

GREENSPOON, J. The reinforcing effect of two spoken sounds on the frequency of two responses. *Amer. J. Psychol.*, 1955, 68, 409–16.

HILGARD, E. R. *Theories of learning*, 2nd ed. New York: Appleton-Century-Crofts, Inc., 1956.

HILLIX, W. A., AND MARX, M. H. Response strengthening by information and effect on human learning. *J. exp. Psychol.*, 1960, 60, 97–102.

HIRSCH, J. Learning without awareness and extinction following awareness as a function of reinforcement. *J. exp. Psychol.*, 1957, 54, 218–24.

HULIN, W. S., AND KATZ, D. A comparison of emphasis upon right and upon wrong responses in learning. *J. exp. Psychol.*, 1935, 18, 638–42.

HULL, C. L. Special review of Thorndike's *The Fundamentals of Learning. Psychol. Bull.*, 1935, 32, 807–23.

———. *Principles of behavior.* New York: Appleton-Century, 1943.

———. *Essentials of behavior.* New Haven: Yale University Press, 1951.

———. *A behavior system.* New Haven: Yale University Press, 1952.

IRWIN, F. W., KAUFMAN, K., PRIOR, G., AND WEAVER, H. B. On "learning without awareness of what is being learned." *J. exp. Psychol.*, 1934, 17, 823–7.

JENKINS, W. O., AND CUNNINGHAM, L. M. The guessing-sequence hypothesis, the "spread of effect," and number-guessing habits. *J. exp. Psychol.*, 1949, 39, 158–68.

JENKINS, W. O., AND SHEFFIELD, F. D. Rehearsal and guessing habits as sources of the "spread of effect." *J. exp. Psychol.*, 1946, 36, 316–30.

KOFFKA, K. *The growth of the mind.* New York: Harcourt, Brace, and Co., 1928.

———. *Principles of Gestalt psychology.* New York: Harcourt, Brace, and Co., 1935.

KÖHLER, W. *The mentality of apes.* New York: Harcourt, Brace, and Co., 1927.

———. On the nature of associations. *Proc. Amer. Philos. Soc.*, 1941, 84, 489–502.

KRASNER, L. Studies of conditioning of verbal behavior. *Psychol. Bull.*, 1958, 55, 148–70.

LORGE, I. The efficacy of intensified reward and intensified punishment. *J. exp. Psychol.*, 1933, 16, 177–207. (a)

———. The effect of the initial chances for right responses upon the efficacy of intensified reward and intensified punishment. *J. exp. Psychol.*, 1933, 16, 362–73. (b)

MCGEOCH, J. A. *The psychology of human learning.* New York: Longmans, Green, and Co., 1942.

MARTENS, D. Spread of effect in verbal serial learning. *Amer. Psychologist*, 1946, 1, 448 (abstract).

MARX, M. H. Spread of effect: A critical review. *Genet. Psychol. Monogr.*, 1956, 53, 119–86.

————. Gradients of error-reinforcement in a serial perceptual-motor task. *Psychol. Monogr.*, 1957, 71, No. 437.

MARX, M. H., AND GOODSON, F. E. Further gradients of error reinforcement following repeated reinforced responses. *J. exp. Psychol.*, 1956, 51, 421–8.

PHILBRICK, E. B., AND POSTMAN, L. A further analysis of "learning without awareness." *Amer. J. Psychol.*, 1955, 68, 417–24.

PORTER, E. H., JR., AND HALL, C. S. A further investigation of the role of emphasis in learning. *J. exp. Psychol.*, 1938, 22, 377–82.

PORTER, L. W. The effect of "right" in a modified Thorndikian situation. *Amer. J. Psychol.*, 1957, 70, 219–26.

POSTMAN, L. The history and present status of the law of effect. *Psychol. Bull.*, 1947, 44, 489–563.

————. Spread of effect as a function of time and intraserial similarity. *Amer. J. Psychol.*, 1961, 74, 493–505.

POSTMAN, L., AND ADAMS, P. A. Performance variables in the experimental analysis of the law of effect. *Amer. J. Psychol.*, 1954, 67, 612–31.

————. "Isolation" and the law of effect. *Amer. J. Psychol.*, 1955, 68, 96–105.

POSTMAN, L., AND JARRETT, R. F. An experimental analysis of "learning without awareness." *Amer. J. Psychol.*, 1952, 65, 244–55.

POSTMAN, L., AND SASSENRATH, J. The automatic action of verbal rewards and punishments. *J. gen. Psychol.*, 1961, 65, 109–36.

ROCK, R. T., JR. *The influence upon learning of the quantitative variation of after-effect. Teach. Coll. Contr. Educ.*, No. 650. New York: Teachers College, Columbia University, 1935.

SHEFFIELD, F. D. "Spread of effect" without reward or learning. *J. exp. Psychol.*, 1949, 39, 575–9.

SHEFFIELD, F. D., AND JENKINS, W. O. Level of repetition in the "spread of effect." *J. exp. Psychol.*, 1952, 44, 101–7.

SIDOWSKI, J. B. Influence of awareness of reinforcement on verbal conditioning. *J. exp. Psychol.*, 1954, 48, 355–60.

SILLECK, S. B., JR., AND LAPHA, C. W. The relative effectiveness of emphasis upon right and wrong responses in human maze learning. *J. exp. Psychol.*, 1937, 20, 195–201.

SMITH, M. H. Spread of effect is the spurious result of non-random response tendencies. *J. exp. Psychol.*, 1949, 39, 355–68.

STEPHENS, J. M. The influence of punishment on learning. *J. exp. Psychol.*, 1934, 17, 536–55. (a)

————. Further notes on punishment and reward. *J. genet. Psychol.*, 1934, 44, 464–72. (b)

STEPHENS, J. M., AND BAER, J. A. The influence of punishment on learning when the opportunity for inner rehearsal is reduced. *J. genet. Psychol.*, 1937, 51, 209–17.

STONE, G. R. The effect of negative incentive in serial learning: III. Fixation due to an isolated verbal punishment. *J. gen. Psychol.*, 1948, 38, 207–16.

———. The effect of negative incentives in serial learning: II. Incentive intensity and response variability. *J. gen. Psychol.*, 1950, 42, 179–224.

———. The effect of negative incentives in serial learning: V. Response repetition as a function of successive serial verbal punishments. *J. exp. Psychol.*, 1951, 42, 20–4. (a)

———. The effect of negative incentives in serial learning: VII. Theory of punishment. *J. gen. Psychol.*, 1953, 48, 133–61.

STONE, G. R., AND WALTER, N. The effect of negative incentives in serial learning: VI. Response repetition as a function of an isolated electric shock punishment. *J. exp. Psychol.*, 1951, 41, 411–18. (b)

TAFFEL, C. Anxiety and the conditioning of verbal behavior. *J. abn. soc. Psychol.*, 1955, 51, 495–501.

TATZ, S. J. Symbolic activity in "learning without awareness." *Amer. J. Psychol.*, 1960, 73, 239–47.

TAYLOR, D. W. Spread of effect in one-trial learning in relation to the guessing sequence hypothesis. *Amer. Psychologist*, 1947, 2, 313 (abstract).

THORNDIKE, E. L. Animal intelligence: an experimental study of the associative process in animals. *Psychol. Monogr.*, 1898, 2, No. 8.

———. *Animal intelligence: experimental studies.* New York: The Macmillan Company, 1911.

———. *Educational psychology, Vol. II. The psychology of learning.* New York: Teachers College, Columbia University, 1914 (reissued 1921).

———. *Human learning.* New York: Century, 1931.

———. *The fundamentals of learning.* New York: Teachers College, Columbia University, 1932.

———. An experimental study of rewards. *Teach. Coll. Contr. Educ.*, No. 580. New York: Teachers College, Columbia University 1933. (a)

———. A theory of the action of the after-effects of a connection upon it. *Psychol. Rev.*, 1933, 40, 434–9. (b)

———. A proof of the law of effect. *Science*, 1933, 77, 173–5. (c)

———. *The psychology of wants, interests and attitudes.* New York: Appleton-Century, 1935.

————. *Man and his works*. Cambridge: Harvard University Press, 1943.

THORNDIKE, E. L., AND ROCK, R. T., JR. Learning without awareness of what is being learned or intent to learn it. *J. exp. Psychol.*, 1934, 17, 1–19.

TILTON, J. W. The effect of "right" and "wrong" upon the learning of nonsense syllables in multiple-choice arrangement. *J. educ. Psychol.*, 1939, 30, 95–115.

————. Gradients of effect. *J. genet. Psychol.*, 1945, 66, 3–19.

TOLMAN, E. C. *Purposive behavior in animals and men*. New York: Century, 1932.

————. Connectionism; wants, interests, and attitudes. *Char. and Personal.*, 1936, 4, 245–53.

————. Cognitive maps in rats and men. *Psychol. Rev.*, 1948, 55, 189–208.

TOLMAN, E. C., HALL, C. S., AND BRETNALL, E. P. A disproof of the law of effect and a substitution of the laws of emphasis, motivation, and disruption. *J. exp. Psychol.*, 1932, 15, 601–14.

TUCKMAN, J. The influence of varying amounts of punishment on mental connections. *Teach. Coll. Contr. Educ.*, No. 590. New York: Teachers College, Columbia University, 1933.

VERPLANCK, W. S. The operant conditioning of human motor behavior. *Psychol. Bull.*, 1956, 53, 70–83.

VON RESTORFF, H. Über die Wirkung von Bereichsbildungen im Spurenfeld. (In W. Köhler and H. von Restorff, Analyse von Vorgängen im Spurenfeld.) *Psychol. Forsch.*, 1933, 18, 299–342.

WALLACH, H., AND HENLE, M. An experimental analysis of the law of effect. *J. exp. Psychol.*, 1941, 28, 340–9.

————. A further study of the functions of reward. *J. exp. Psychol.*, 1942, 30, 147–60.

ZIRKLE, G. A. Success and failure in serial learning: I. The Thorndike effect. *J. exp. Psychol.*, 1946, 36, 230–6. (a)

————. Success and failure in serial learning: II. Isolation and the Thorndike effect. *J. exp. Psychol.*, 1946, 36, 302–12. (b)

C H A P T E R 7

Memory for Form

D O N A L D   A.   R I L E Y

LIKE RESEARCH WORKERS in other areas, those interested in memory search for principles or factors common to seemingly diverse events. Superficially, memories of past occurrences seem to change in different ways. Sometimes the memory of a previous event seems to fade and disappear; sometimes old memories seem to be supplanted by new ones; at other times, memory seems to be qualitatively modified, so that the change is not a weakening, but a distortion. Can such seemingly different types of memory change be explained by the same set of assumptions, or must we invoke principles of response competition to account for one and principles of perceptual organization to account for another?

In this chapter we will consider one particular class of memory experiment which has been extensively used as a tool to investigate this problem. The experiment closely resembles a situation we frequently encounter in our daily experience. The observer sees some form, or object, or design, and is later tested for his memory of what he has seen. In the memory test the subject may be asked to describe the form or object, or to pick it out from a group of similar items, or perhaps to draw it from memory. Regardless of the method of measuring retention, the memory may well be faulty either in the sense that there has been loss or in the sense that the memory is somehow distorted or inaccurate. It is with attempts to understand such changes that we will be concerned.

HISTORICAL BACKGROUND

THE SERIES OF EXPERIMENTS to be described are concerned with a particular interpretation of memory change that was first advanced by the German psychologist, Friedrich Wulf, in 1922. In tracing the history of research on Wulf's interpretation, we will try to show how the difficulties in testing his hypothesis became increasingly apparent as one experiment followed another. Also, we will show how later experimenters were able to improve on the efforts of their predecessors. Finally, the emergence of a competing hypothesis will be described.

Wulf was not the first person to attempt systematic investigations of memory change, nor was he the first to advance explanations to account for the changes. Prior to Wulf, investigators had tested for memory by showing a subject a simple geometric form, and then at a later time requiring the subject to draw the form from memory. This early work has been summarized by Woodworth (1938). As a result of their studies, these early investigators had concluded that with the passage of time there was a fading of the trace, or image, of the originally perceived stimulus figure. This weakening alone might account for some errors in memory. Other factors, however, were assumed to become more and more important in determining memory changes as the memory of the figure became weaker. These other factors may be briefly enumerated.

(1) The subject may recall the verbal description of the stimulus that he made at the time of original viewing. Since this verbal description may only approximate the figure, distortions in a drawn reproduction conforming to the verbal description will probably occur.

(2) Closely related to this is the possibility that in memory the observer exaggerates details that were particularly noticed at the time of original perception.

(3) The memory of similar forms experienced at other times or at the time of original viewing may partially determine the memory.

(4) Finally, in the case of reproduction, the subject's limitations as an artist may result in an inaccurate representation of the original figure.

Presumably, any or all of these factors may influence the subject's performance in memory.

THE GESTALT HYPOTHESIS

BECAUSE WULF INTRODUCED a new interpretation of these memory changes and because our main concern is with the examination of his hypothesis, our detailed history begins with his work.

Wulf's interest in changes in the memory for simple geometrical forms grew out of his adherence to *Gestalt* psychology, then a new and vigorous intellectual movement. Gestalt psychologists had been interested primarily in problems of visual perception. This was partly because they believed that an understanding of perception would throw light on general principles of psychological functioning and on general principles of brain functioning. The Gestalt psychologists emphasized the fact that the perceived shape of a stimulus object frequently does not agree perfectly with the pattern of stimulation that strikes the retina. Examples of this fact are to be found in optical illusions and reversible figures. The Gestalt psychologists agreed that the incoming sense event was an important determiner of the perception. But they argued that the difference between the pattern of retinal stimulation and the object as perceived indicates that events in the central nervous system are also partial modifiers of perception. They further asserted that their evidence indicated that the modifications in perception which arise from cortical activity result in perceived figures being "better" than the figures cast upon the retina by external stimulation. Now, a better figure never was defined precisely, but their examples indicated that the general meaning included changes toward regularity, symmetry, and simplicity of figures. Illustrative of this tendency toward "good form" were findings of Lindemann and Granit (in Koffka, 1935, pp. 141f.), who showed a subject irregular figures under conditions of reduced stimulation. An immediate reproduction of the figure by the subject was more regular and simpler than the original. According to Gestalt theory, this change resulted from forces in the cortex acting to simplify the perception. These hypothetical forces were called *autochthonous forces*, a term which implies they are inherent in the nature of the brain. In this particular study the relative effect of these forces was presumably enhanced by reducing the strength of the incoming stimulation.

If one were interested in demonstrating the plausibility of the assumption that perception is partly determined by such forces, one might try to reduce the restraining effect of the external stimulation to a minimum. Wulf saw that while reducing the incoming stimulation might partially accomplish this, stimulating the subject and then waiting a while before testing the subject's memory would be even more effective. During the interval the autochthonous forces could act to modify the trace [1] of the perception in the direction of a better figure with no relevant incoming stimulation acting to check the modification.

[1] *Trace* is used by some psychologists as a shorthand for the nervous-system change that remains after perception of a stimulus has occurred. Associationist psychologists have been neutral on the nature of the trace or else have assumed that it was a change in the excitability of some unspecified fibers. Gestaltists have assumed that the trace is distributed in the brain in a way that is related to the original geometric representation on the retina. Even more important, the shape of the trace in the brain is assumed to determine the form of the remembered object.

Wulf's Study

To test his hypothesis, Wulf simply presented a group of line drawings of geometrical figures to his subjects, and then after varying periods of time had them draw the figures from memory. He claimed that the results of his experiment demonstrated memory changes that were consistent with the Gestalt position, and inconsistent with the associationist position held by the earlier investigators. It should be emphasized that he claimed the discovery of a hitherto unknown factor in the determination of memory. It is not surprising that his work provoked further research.

To understand clearly why so many other persons were stimulated to research on this problem, it is necessary first to describe in some detail Wulf's analysis of the problem, his experiment, and his interpretation of his results.

THE EXPERIMENT. In his experiment Wulf showed the six subjects twenty-six line drawings of abstract forms, no more than four forms being shown in any single sitting. These forms are shown in Figure 61. Thirty seconds after the subject had seen a form he drew the figure as he recalled it. A second reproduction was made after twenty-four hours, a third after one week, and in a few cases a fourth reproduction was made two months later. At the one-week reproduction, a small part of the original figure was shown as a cue, but the subject was not told that the piece shown was correct.

WULF'S INTERPRETATION. In his analysis of the results Wulf compared the subjects' reproductions with the original figures, and by inspection determined whether the characteristics of the original figure had been exaggerated in reproduction (called sharpening), minimized in reproduction (called leveling), or reproduced unchanged. Wulf's results seemed clear-cut. From a total of 400 reproductions, 394 usable records were obtained. Of these, 392 showed either sharpening or leveling, according to Wulf. Furthermore, the changes that the subjects made in the first reproductions were judged by Wulf to be more pronounced in later reproductions. That is, later reproductions exaggerated the errors of the first reproductions of a figure. These exaggerations tended to be progressive.

Wulf carried his classification further in his attempt to specify the causal factors underlying the changes he observed. On the basis of the reproductions and on the basis of what the subjects said about their reproductions, he identified three ways in which, he believed, either leveling or sharpening was achieved. These classes he called *normalizing*, *pointing*, and *autonomous* change (see Koffa, 1935, p. 498).

Normalizing changes were changes in which the reproduction more closely resembled some well-known or conventional figure. Apparently the subjects' statements of what they remembered were an important source of information in categorizing the change. For example, a change in Figure 61s was called normalizing because the subject said the figure

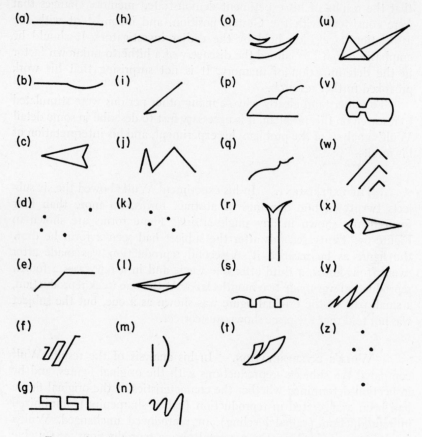

FIGURE 61. Figures by F. Wulf, "Uber die Veränderung von Vorstellungen," *Psych. Forsch.*, 1922, 1, 333–73. Used by permission of Springer-Verlag, Berlin.

he remembered looked like a bridge, *and* because in Wulf's estimation the figure he drew looked more and more like a bridge. Pointing designated changes that occurred when the subject emphasized in reproduction a feature of the stimulus noted at the time of original perception. These factors of normalizing and pointing seem to have much in common with the earlier associationist interpretation.

More important for the position Wulf was attempting to establish was the third kind of change. This he called autonomous change because he thought he had found changes that were determined by the form of the specific trace under consideration, rather than by extraneous factors such as the effects of previous experiences. The physiological trace of the original neural event was assumed to be gradually modified by the cortical (autochthonous) forces into a simpler and more regular pattern. Then, when the now changed trace was reactivated by the memory test, the figure reproduced would be better than the original, in accord with Gestalt laws of perceptual organization. The evidence for this third class of changes came from cases in which, in Wulf's judgment, the trend of the reproductions was opposed to the trend that would be expected from normalizing, and in which pointing was not evident. For example, according to Wulf, the normal "apprehension" of Figure 61v is "medicine flask." Since the usual medicine flask has a smaller top relative to the bottle than does this figure, any trend toward normalizing should increase the difference between the two parts of the figure. However, the reproductions of one of the subjects moved toward equality of the two sides. Thus, Wulf argued, the change in this case was toward increasing symmetry, but was not consonant with past experience.

WULF'S REJECTION OF ALTERNATIVE INTERPRETATIONS. In considering possible alternative interpretations, Wulf gave close attention to the position of G. E. Müller (see Woodworth, 1938), who had assumed that with the passage of time images become weaker and less definite, and hence resemble each other more and more. Wulf argued that this hypothesis could not account for leveling, because, according to Müller's ideas, all parts of a figure should come to resemble each other more and more. Wulf said this was not the case. In many cases of leveling, one part of the figure will change, but not another. In addition to this difficulty with an associative theory, Wulf pointed out that if leveling were due to a weakening process, then leveling should be accompanied by uncertainty on the part of the subject; but this change did not occur.

Turning to the problem of sharpening, Wulf disposed of the *attention* hypothesis, which he considered the major alternative to the Gestalt hypothesis. He said that while special attention to one part of the figure might result in exaggeration of the figure in reproduction, it could not account for progressive change on successive reproductions. So Wulf had worked his way into a truly enviable position. He was convinced that Gestalt theory could account for a change in any direction and that the most reasonable alternatives could not account for any of the changes. Whether a change was attributable to pointing, normalizing, or autonomous change, it was a manifestation of movement toward good Gestalt.

THE EFFECT OF WULF'S EXPERIMENT.   Was Wulf's experiment a satisfactory one? In one sense, the answer is a strong no. As we will see, the relation between theory and fact is impossible to determine both because of the obscurity of his own theory and because of the many methodological weaknesses in his experiment. In another sense, however, it was just as emphatically successful. The study not only suggested that a theory originally devised to account for facts of perception is relevant to problems of memory, but it pointed to the sorts of facts that are necessary to test the theory. A large amount of research was thereby stimulated. Investigators who doubted Wulf's interpretation of his own data and who felt that Wulf had misinterpreted the associationist position were anxious to perform a better experiment that they hoped would refute him. Researchers who were sympathetic to Wulf's position also tried to set up more adequate experiments. In any case, many people realized the systematic importance of Wulf's paper, and were concerned with getting a clearer picture of the facts regardless of what theoretical position they happened to support. In this connection it is well worth asking just what it is that makes a piece of pioneering research fruitful in the sense that it leads to new efforts and findings from a number of other investigators. Certainly one of the requirements is that the research deal with a problem that has recognizable implications for the current problems in the field. Another possibility that is suggested by the Wulf experiment is that its very ambiguity might have been one of the reasons that it stimulated so much further research. This sort of speculation is, of course, difficult to test because of the absence of facts. It is worth noting, however, that in the thirty-five years following Wulf's paper many attempts were made to clarify theoretical issues, to develop adequate methods for testing these clarified propositions, and to establish some relevant facts. It is the history of these efforts that we will now consider.

Gibson's Experiment

J. J. Gibson (1929), in an experimental reply to Wulf, argued that Wulf had not conclusively demonstrated the case for cortical forces in memory change. Rather, he asserted, the sort of change described by Wulf could be accounted for on the basis of the subject's verbal habits and the way the subject originally understood, or responded to, any given figure. For example, if Figure 62a was interpreted on original inspection by the subject as a mortar and pestle, then the reproduction of this figure would appear more like 61b. If, on the other hand, it was interpreted as a light bulb, then the reproduction might appear like 62c.

In setting up his own experiment, Gibson raised three methodological points. First, Gibson asked why it was that Wulf was able to classify virtually all the reproductions he examined as instances of either leveling or sharpening. Gibson's answer was that Wulf's selection of figures precluded any other sorts of change. That is, all the figures were asymmetrical. Gibson attempted to correct for this peculiarity by systematically changing the nature of his figures. One group of subjects saw only straight line figures, while another group saw only curved line figures. Half the figures for each group had gaps in them; half did not. A second criticism raised by Gibson was based on the observation that in order to measure the change in memory, one must be sure that

(a)   (b)   (c)

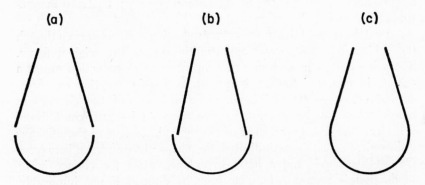

FIGURE 62. Figures illustrating Gibson's interpretation of memory change (see text). (From J. J. Gibson, "The Reproduction of Visually Perceived Forms," *J. exp. Psychol.*, 1929, 12, 1–39. Used by permission of the American Psychological Association.)

the subject has accurately perceived the forms. To insure that his subject would accurately perceive the forms, Gibson gave them repeated training with the figures prior to the memory tests. This procedure of repeated training was quite revealing, for in some cases subjects made errors in drawing the figures in trial after trial, even though the correct stimulus figures were shown before each reproduction. Finally, Gibson questioned whether each subject should reproduce only a small number of figures—one or two, for example—or whether the number should be larger. He argued that in order to keep the situation as close to real life as possible a large number of figures should be used. Consequently, different groups of subjects were tested on between ten and twenty-five different figures.

After the subjects had been exposed to the forms and had attempted to reproduce them from memory, Gibson classified the response changes, much as Wulf had done. The categories he used were: (1) object assimilation, i.e., change toward a known object; (2) verbal analysis, i.e., change influenced by statements made during learning; (3) figure assimilation, i.e., change toward another geometrical figure in the series; (4) completion and disintegration, i.e., closing of gaps or falling apart of figures; (5) correct linearity, i.e., straightening out of curved lines. In view of the fact that all his changes fell into these categories, Gibson concluded that the changes in reproduction could be accounted for by perceptual habits and that it was unnecessary to assume the action of field forces modifying the nature of the trace over a period of time.

Toward the end of his article Gibson asked whether his data provided a test of the hypothesis that autochthonous forces operating in the direction opposed to the original perception can occur. He concluded that his data did not test for this possibility because of the shape of his original figures. What, then, did the Gibson experiment actually demonstrate that was not already known?

First, he showed that incorrect reproductions will occur even though the subject has had several opportunities to see the original figure. There is a danger in assuming that an incorrect reproduction means a change in memory. Rather, it may mean a misperception or an inaccurate drawing habit. Second, since so many of the changes in reproductions can be accounted for in the ways indicated by Gibson, it is clear that a demonstration of change independent of these factors is difficult. Further, as he indicated, the test of the difference between a Gestalt hypothesis and a habit hypothesis, when the change in reproduction is toward a familiar form, is difficult if not impossible. Gibson, of course, would have liked to have figures which tested for the presence of autonomous change, but he did not achieve this goal. Third, Gibson pointed out that the sort of change that is found depends frequently upon the nature of the figure selected.

New Evidence for Gestalt Theory

The next two investigators to report on this problem were G. W. Allport (1930) and F. T. Perkins (1932). Both presented evidence that they believed supported the hypothesis of autonomous change.

ALLPORT'S STUDY.   Allport used only two forms which he showed to a large number of school children. These forms are shown in Figures 63a and 63b. He argued that since these forms are unfamiliar to the subjects, object assimilation should not occur. Further, since these forms are too complex for verbal conceptualization, no verbal analysis should occur. Thus in Allport's opinion the situation is one which should test for the sort of change Wulf had claimed is most clearly outside the assumptions of association theory. In his experiment the subjects were shown the figures and then required to reproduce them by drawing

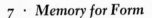

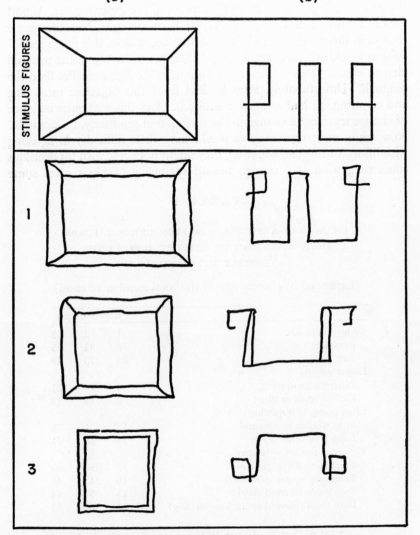

FIGURE 63. Figures used by Allport (top, and two series of reproductions described as typical by the author). (From G. Allport, "Change and Decay in the Visual Memory Image," *Brit. J. Psychol.*, 1930, 21, 142. Used by permission of Cambridge University Press.)

them immediately, again after two weeks, and again after four months. In general, Allport interpreted the changes he observed as being in the direction of greater symmetry, greater simplicity, and smaller size.

ADVANCES INTRODUCED BY ALLPORT.   In some respects Allport's paper represented a clear methodological advance over the experiments of his predecessors. First, rather than using a classification scheme which depends to a large extent on the judgment of the experimenter, Allport merely measured and counted. Rather than asking, "Does this figure change in the direction of object assimilation, or does this figure level?" Allport would ask questions such as, "Does the wide strip in the pyramid change in size? Does it change in location? Is the figure smaller than the original?" Unfortunately, after he had done this objective measuring and counting, he had to make a decision. Does this particular instance of change represent a change in the direction of symmetry, for example? Now while most psychologists would have little difficulty in agreeing with his measuring and counting, they might not agree with his decisions concerning what is a change toward symmetry. Table 1 gives some

TABLE 1

CHANGES OF REPRODUCTIONS FROM ORIGINAL FORMS
THAT, ACCORDING TO ALLPORT, SUPPORT THE
GESTALT HYPOTHESIS *

(Expressed in percentages of the total number of cases)

	Reproduction		
	1	2	3
Reduction in size			
Pyramid	78	92	95
Key	66	73	78
Displacements			
Interchange of parts	4	14	21
Key inverted or tilted	9	15	19
Chief points of instability			
Strip trouble in pyramid	54	71	76
Loop trouble in key	54	68	71
Tendency toward symmetry			
Equalizing strips (pyramid)	39	52	56
Becoming square (pyramid)	10	13	40
Both loops reversed (key)	18	37	44
Both loops reversed or unchanged (key)	64	69	73

* Taken from G. Allport, "Change and Decay in the Visual Memory Image," *Brit. J. Psychol.*, 1930, *21*, 142. Used by permission of Cambridge University Press.

striking examples of progressive change that Allport considered changes toward symmetry that supported Gestalt theory. It would seem clear enough to most people that equalization of strip sizes and a change from rectangularity toward squareness are both examples of change toward symmetry. It is probably less clear that reversal of the loops in the Greek key or no change at all in the loops is also a change toward symmetry. Yet they were so regarded by Allport. For, he argued, if changes occur that *maintain* symmetry, this may be considered evidence for the Gestalt position. And generally speaking, it was true that if one loop was reversed in orientation, the other loop was also reversed. Allport also interpreted the progressive reduction in size as evidence for the Gestalt hypothesis, primarily because the effects were progressive. These facts of progressive change did not fit in well with Gibson's hypothesis concerning habits of perception. No other associationist interpretation was considered by Allport.

A second methodological advance that was introduced by Allport was the deliberate selection of figures which were intended to test the Gestalt theory of autonomous change. It is important to note, however, that while he attempted to select figures that would not be subject to object assimilation or verbal formulation, he presented no evidence that he had been successful in his selection. Now, while he might have believed he had succeeded in this, it is quite likely that others would disagree. Clearly, objective evidence on these assumptions would have been desirable.

A third important change in method was the reduction in the number of figures on which the subjects were tested. Both Wulf and Gibson had used a considerable number of figures, but Allport used only two. Gibson had argued that a number of figures should be used in the experiment because this more closely approximated the conditions of everyday life than would the use of a small number of figures. By such an argument the conclusions of Gibson's experiment would seem to have more generality and more validity than the conclusions of Allport's experiment. But if Gibson's experiment was intended to reproduce the conditions of everyday life, why were the conditions controlled as they were? Why, for instance, were all the figures the same size? Why were the figures shown on an apparatus that controlled the time of exposure of the individual items? Surely these conditions do not approximate real life, nor did Gibson intend them to. Rather, he wanted to say something about the causes of memory change independent of variations in inspection time and figure size. The point is an important one. In general, laboratory experiments are not set up to imitate the most typical case found in nature. Instead, they are intended to answer some specific question of interest to the experimenter.

In retrospect, we can point out that Gibson's use of a large number of figures had an effect that has since been well established in other learning situations. If the subject is exposed to many figures in the course of a short period of time, it is almost inevitable that there will be assimilation from one figure to another. Now, the hypothesis of autonomous change asserts that there are forces *not* dependent on past experience which under certain circumstances will change the memory of a given form. If one is to test for the presence of such autonomous change, one would try to eliminate as much as possible the other factors which might influence this change. One way to do this would be to restrict the number of figures that the subject sees in a test situation. From this standpoint Allport's experiment must be considered a significant advance over Gibson's and Wulf's.

To summarize Allport's paper, he introduced three distinct methodological advances. The first was the attempt to specify the nature of the form which might produce autonomous change. The second was his counting technique, which eliminated a great deal of the subjectivity of classification. And the third was the use of a restricted number of figures. On the substantive side, perhaps Allport's major contribution is the reemphasis of Wulf's observation of continuous change in the memory for form. Allport had strengthened Wulf's position by his paper.

PERKINS' STUDY.   Perkins' paper (1932), appearing some time after Allport's, made much the same point. He said that if the figure as originally perceived is unbalanced or lacking in symmetry, then the progressive changes in memory will be in the direction of a better figure; i.e., the reproductions will become more symmetrical. Perkins' procedure was substantially the same as Wulf's. Each subject saw five figures. Subjects reproduced the figures immediately and then again on days two, three, nine, sixteen, thirty, and forty-nine. The figures were deliberately selected to be simple and asymmetrical. In his report Perkins stated that all observed changes were in the direction of symmetry and better balance, and the changes in successive reproductions were progressive. Figure 64 gives several examples presented by Perkins of progressive change in the direction of greater symmetry. Careful examination of these figures will indicate to the reader some of the difficulties in testing the assumption of progressive change toward symmetry, even with relatively simple figures. Although all figures show general changes, and in this writer's opinion all end up more symmetrical than they started, the evidence for regular progression is questionable. Figure 64b, for example, shows only one discrete change from drawing 4 to drawing 5. Figure 64c shows a decrease in symmetry from drawing 3 to drawing 4. In Figure 64d, judgments about increasing symmetry are extremely difficult until the last three drawings, where the trend seems clear. Figure 64e presents similar ambiguities.

Perkins' classification method is open to the same criticism as Wulf's. The method for deciding whether a drawing was more or less symmetrical than its predecessor was subjective, and the only judge of this change was the experimenter. We cannot conclude that Perkins' subjects did not change their drawings in the direction of greater symmetry. We can only conclude that the limitations of his method leave the question where it was. Again, it should be mentioned that Allport's procedures were superior to Perkins'. Objective scoring makes the bases of classification clear, so that other investigators can state the grounds for their agreement or disagreement. Secondly, and just as important, objective scoring reduces the temptation to argue from a selected example that happens to support the beliefs of the experimenter.

What do we know thus far? We know that of four different studies that we have examined, three have reported changes that the investi-

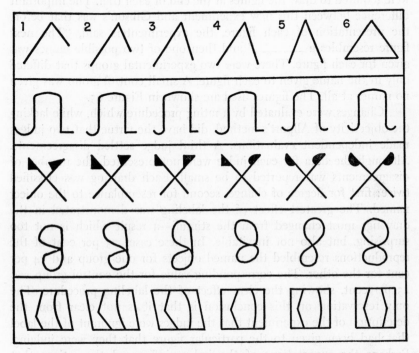

FIGURE 64. Examples of successive reproductions from Perkins's work. (From F. T. Perkins, "Symmetry in Visual Recall," *Amer. J. Psychol.*, 1932, 44, 473–90, and used by permission.)

gators believed were in accord with the Gestalt hypothesis. More specifically, the investigators reported changes that they believed could not be explained on the basis of previous experiences influencing the direction of change. But it was pointed out earlier, in the discussion of Allport's paper, that evidence about the effects of past experience had not actually been presented. Rather, an explanation based on past experience had been ruled out on the basis of *argument*. Clearly, it would be desirable to rule out by *experimental means* the effects of past experience in a test for autonomous change, but this seems difficult to achieve with adult human beings. Alternatively, one might manipulate the past experiences of subjects to see how different sorts of previous training influence changes in reproduction.

The Effect of Suggestion on Drawn Reproductions

Carmichael, Hogan, and Walter (1932) conducted an experiment quite similar to Gibson's in that the subjects saw a series of figures and were required to draw the figures at the end of each trial. The important difference between this new experiment and Gibson's was that before the presentation of each figure, the experimenters said, "The next figure resembles a _____," and then one of two possible names was given for each figure. There were two experimental groups that differed only in the name given to each figure. A small control group was given no names at all. The figures used are shown in Figure 65.

Changes were evaluated by a rating procedure which, while lacking the objectivity of Allport's method, did have the virtue that two judges made independent evaluations. A third judge settled disagreements. Although the data for each judge were not presented, the number of disagreements was reported to be small. Each drawing was classified twice: first for degree of change, second for resemblance to the object named. The greatest effect of the labeling was demonstrated in the drawings most changed from the stimuli—a result which is not too surprising, but also not inevitable. In these cases 73 per cent of the reproductions resembled the named objects for one group and 74 per cent for the other. The corresponding value for the control group was 45 per cent, showing the clear effect of the labeling procedure. The only reservation on this conclusion is that it is not clear from the description of the experiment that the judges were ignorant of the label that had been given to the particular figure that they were judging. Perhaps the expectations of the judges influenced the ratings that they assigned to drawings.

The important point of this study is that it provided strong support for Gibson's conclusion that the way in which the subject interprets the stimulus will determine the nature of his reproduction. The experiment advanced over the previous ones in one sense—an important variable determining the nature of the reproduction was brought under control and manipulated. Although previous writers had asserted that such factors as verbal habits and memories of familiar objects determined changes in response tendencies, they had done so on the basis of the statements of the subject. That is, they demonstrated a relationship between one response—drawing—and another response, a verbal statement. What is cause and what is effect in such a situation is indeed difficult to determine. Carmichael, Hogan, and Walter, by changing the

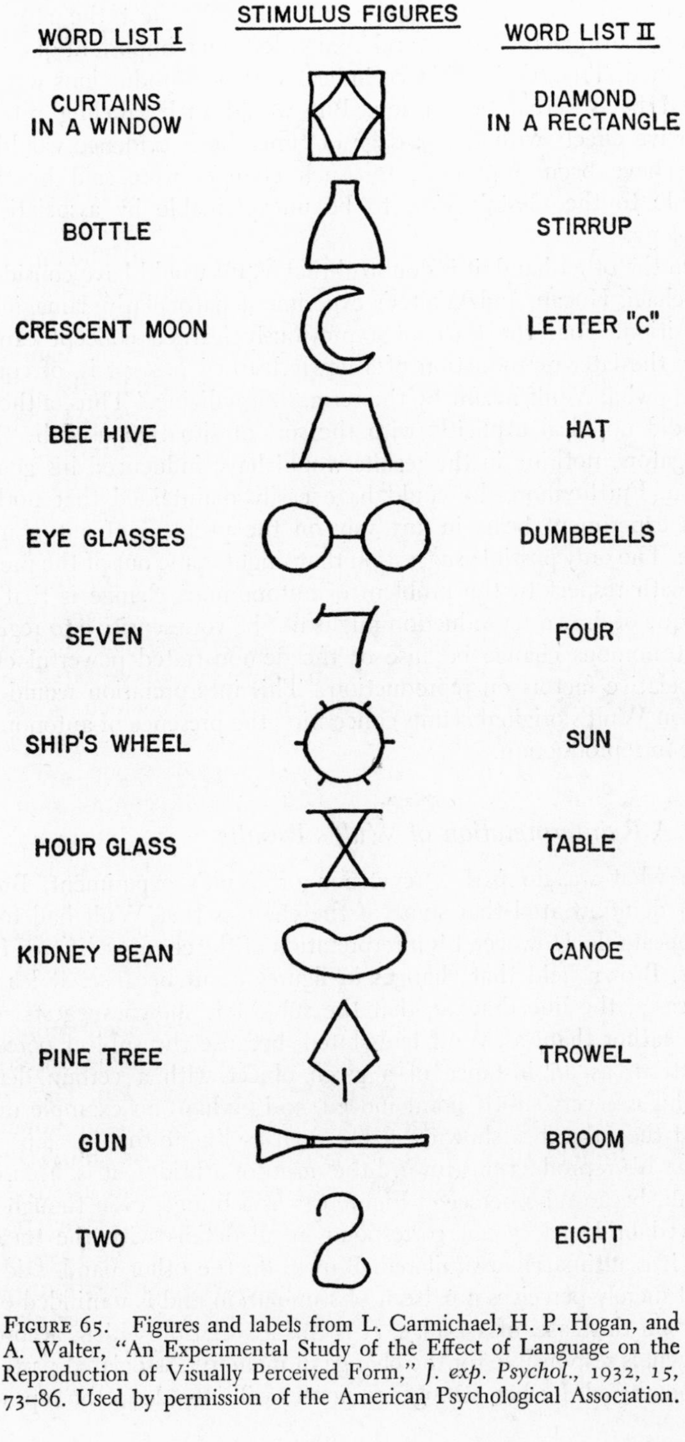

STIMULUS FIGURES

WORD LIST I		WORD LIST II
CURTAINS IN A WINDOW		DIAMOND IN A RECTANGLE
BOTTLE		STIRRUP
CRESCENT MOON		LETTER "C"
BEE HIVE		HAT
EYE GLASSES		DUMBBELLS
SEVEN		FOUR
SHIP'S WHEEL		SUN
HOUR GLASS		TABLE
KIDNEY BEAN		CANOE
PINE TREE		TROWEL
GUN		BROOM
TWO		EIGHT

FIGURE 65. Figures and labels from L. Carmichael, H. P. Hogan, and A. Walter, "An Experimental Study of the Effect of Language on the Reproduction of Visually Perceived Form," *J. exp. Psychol.*, 1932, 15, 73–86. Used by permission of the American Psychological Association.

label, showed that such a change could indeed affect the response. However, Carmichael, Hogan, and Walter left some important questions unanswered. True, their evidence indicated that reproductions were influenced by a verbal description. But would such labeling produce progressive effects with the passage of time? Such evidence would, of course, have been important, for such changes were said by those favorable to the Gestalt view to be unexplainable by associationist psychology.

On the other hand, it is doubtful that Wulf would have considered Carmichael, Hogan, and Walter's experiment particularly damaging to his position. That the trace of a previously learned concept can influence the later reproduction of a newly learned percept is, of course, precisely what Wulf meant by the term "normalizing." Thus, although Wulf did not deal explicitly with the sort of situation used by these investigators, nothing in the results would have influenced his general position. Furthermore, he could have easily maintained that nothing in this experiment bears in any way on the problem of autonomous change. The only possible suggestion that might come out of the present study with respect to the problem of autonomous change is that the technique of drawn reproduction might not be very sensitive to registering autonomous change because of the demonstrated powerful effect of associative factors on reproductions. This interpretation would cast doubt on Wulf's original claims concerning the presence of autonomous change in reproduction.

A Reinterpretation of Wulf's Results

In what was in part a repetition of Wulf's experiment, Brown (1935) demonstrated that some of the changes that Wulf had found were repeatable. However, his interpretation of the changes differed from Wulf's. Brown held that changes in figures occur because, at least in some cases, the line drawing that the subject is shown suggests some object, rather than, as Wulf had stated, because the subject perceives the pattern as an instance of a given object with a certain design. Now this is a very subtle point indeed, and perhaps an example might help. If the subject is shown a figure such as Figure 61s (p. 406) and modifies his reproductions toward the norm of a bridge, it is, according to Wulf, because he perceives Figure 61s as a bridge, even though this perceived bridge does not correspond in all details with the trace to which it is ultimately assimilated. Brown, on the other hand, said the subject merely perceives a pattern of stimulation and is reminded of an object—in this case, of a bridge. It is this association which, according to Brown, is responsible for the change in memory. Associated parts will be remembered. Earlier, stronger responses will intrude in the reproduction by virtue of the association, and non-associated details will be forgotten. Now, the important point of this is not that Brown refuted Wulf's interpretation of normalizing, but rather that he pointed out that it is perfectly possible for an associationist theorist to give an interpretation of normalizing that takes account of the known facts. What this does, of course, is to place the test of the Gestalt hypothesis more squarely on the issue as to whether or not autonomous changes in memory can be demonstrated. In connection with the Gestalt claims concerning symmetry and regularity, Brown pointed out that although a large number of changes did tend toward more regular figures, a large number also tended to become less regular. One important feature of Brown's general procedure should be mentioned: his subjects reproduced the figures only twice, once immediately after viewing the figures and again after two weeks. There were no repeated reproductions, as Wulf, Gibson, Allport, and Perkins had used. This, of course, made it impossible to measure progressive changes in the reproductions, but it did have some other virtues, as we shall soon see.

FURTHER IMPROVEMENTS ON WULF'S PROCEDURES

BROWN'S PAPER APPEARED in 1935. Two years later work published by three separate writers radically changed the approach to the problem of memory change and at the same time considerably increased understanding of the problem.

A COMPARISON OF REPRODUCTION MEMORY AND RECOGNITION MEMORY.   Let us first consider a study by O. L. Zangwill (1937). He pointed out that Gestalt theory had assumed that the subject's reproduction memory was a valid index of the changing memory trace. He argued that on this assumption a subject presented with an improved version of one of his own reproductions and with the original figure, should identify a cleaned-up version of his own reproduction as the one he had originally seen. "Improved" and "cleaned up" here merely mean that the reproduction is straightened out so that it looks like a professional drawing, as does the original, rather than a crude hand-drawing. This implication that Zangwill tested had been discussed and predicted by Koffka (1935).

In analyzing his subjects' drawings, Zangwill identified two types of persistent errors which he called "stereotyped errors" and "progressive errors." Stereotyped errors were those that deviated from the standard to about the same extent and in the same direction in each reproduction. Progressive errors increased in magnitude of deviation from the standard and in a constant direction. Zangwill tested for recognition of the standard by showing drawings that included for each subject the errors characterizing his own performance and, of course, the standard itself. If the error of recognition was in the same direction as the reproductive error, Zangwill considered that it would be evidence for the interpretation that changes in reproduction do reflect corresponding changes in the physiological trace. If, however, the changes in the two measures did not agree in direction, then he considered it evidence against the hypothesis that changes in reproduction are a valid index of changes in the trace. In the cases where a progressive reproductive error was found, only 50 per cent of the tests also showed recognition error in the same direction. In the case of the stereotyped reproductive errors, about 71 per cent showed recognition errors in the same direction. Zangwill's conclusion was that the presence of a reliable reproductive error alone could not be taken as evidence that a modification of the trace had also occurred. Zangwill also pointed out that of all the errors made, the number of persistent reproductive errors that were continuous in direction and in which the recognition error was in the same direction was only 21 per cent. Zangwill considered this fact evidence against the Gestalt concept of good configuration.

Zangwill concluded that to construct a system of hypothetical neural dynamics to account for memory change was premature. His conclusion was really based on two aspects of his evidence. The first, which we have already mentioned, was that persistent reproductive errors are not necessarily matched by errors in recognition. The second was that the reproductive deviations clearly arise from specific verbal formulations or mnemonic cues that the subject uses in memorizing the figures. Both of these arguments must be briefly considered.

The conclusion that the subjects used verbal formulations was based on the subjects' reports of how they reproduced the figures. As we have pointed out before, this argument has some of the same characteristics as the chicken-and-egg argument. One might conclude that a subject's memory is not determined by a changing brain state, because when asked to introspect, the subject says he used certain verbal cues or props in reconstruction. But perhaps it is just as reasonable to say that the same cortical change that led to the reproductive change also led to a change in the verbal formulation.

The critical information that Zangwill was the first to obtain was that recognition and reproduction do not necessarily agree with each other. Clearly, if the persistent reproductive error reflects a change in the memory trace, then this should show up in recognition. So far as the Gestalt hypothesis goes, then, these facts have one of two implications: either one of these methods of measuring memory is inadequate to test the Gestalt hypothesis, or these facts refute that hypothesis. As we shall see, both of these interpretations have been made.

There is another aspect of these findings, which merits comment before turning to the next experiment. Even if we accept Zangwill's interpretation that an erroneous verbal formulation leads to erroneous reproductions and, indeed, to persistent erroneous reproductions, why does it not also influence recognition? Why, that is, should not the erroneous verbal formulation lead to a faulty recognition? If it does not, then why does not the subject on completion of his own drawings reject them as inadequate representations of what he had originally seen? Zangwill did not suggest an answer to these questions.

SINGLE VS. SUCCESSIVE MEMORY TESTS. The second study to appear in this same year was one by Hanawalt (1937). Like Zangwill, Hanawalt was dissatisfied with the method of successive reproductions as a technique for studying memory change. Beside noting the possibilities of discrepancies between the method of reproduction and the method of recognition, Hanawalt also identified an additional problem in the method of successive reproductions—the complications introduced by repeated testing of the same subject. He questioned the implicit assumption that successive reproductions allow the tapping or measuring of a memory trace without in any way affecting the trace. The major part of his paper is an examination and a rejection of this particular notion. The principal condition in his main experiment is an improved repetition of Wulf's experiment. Perhaps the most important change was that the first two reproductions of each figure by a subject were copies made while the figure was present. Each subject copied eight figures. Then the subject reproduced the figures from memory immediately, again after one week, then after four weeks, and finally after eight weeks. To test the effect of these successive reproductions on each other, other groups of subjects who originally copied a set of the Wulf figures, as in the main condition, reproduced the figures from memory only one time. For each time interval represented in the standard condition, a different group of subjects was used in this new experimental variation—the method of single reproductions. Thus one group of subjects copied the figures twice while the figures were present and then reproduced them from memory immediately. Another group reproduced them from memory after one week, another group of subjects reproduced them for the first time from memory after four weeks, and still another after eight weeks. In addition to these groups which mirrored those in the original condition, another group of subjects was tested one day after copying. These new groups supplied information on the validity of the assumption that the method of successive reproductions provides a satisfactory way of measuring changes in this hypothetical memory trace. Table 2 shows the number of figures reproduced at each time interval under the two different methods. The greater retention by the subjects using the method of successive re-

productions indicates that earlier reproductions increase the likelihood
that the subject will be able to remember the figure at a later time.
The act of reproducing the figures from memory does not merely measure the trace and leave it undisturbed. Rather, it is a response which
partially determines the character of the next response.

TABLE 2

COMPARISON OF THE NUMBER OF FIGURES REMEMBERED UNDER CONDITION I
(SUCCESSIVE) AND CONDITION II (SINGLE) *

(Average number of figures remembered)

	Imm.	1 day	1 wk.	4 wks.	8 wks.	Number of subjects
Cond. I	6.9	...	6.6	6.6	6.5	49
Cond. II	6.9	6.3	5.7	4.8	4.4	249

* From Nelson G. Hanawalt, "Memory Trace for Figures in Recall and Recognition," *Arch. Psychol.*, 1937, No. 216, p. 24. Used by permission of the author.

ERRORS OF COPYING.   Additional information was obtained by
having the subjects copy the figures during the inspection trials. This
procedure allowed Hanawalt to determine how much of the difference
between the subjects' drawings and the standard figure is attributable
to misperception or to faulty drawing. It also allowed him to measure
further change or change in memory, from the copy rather than from the
initial inspection figure. Under conditions of successive reproduction,
Hanawalt found that 18 per cent of all the observed changes occurred
during the copying of the figures. Since some of the previous investigators had assumed that any change reflected a distortion in memory,
it is clear that an experimental error of substantial size had been uncovered. Furthermore, out of all the errors that could have formed part
of a series of progressive changes in memory, only 16 per cent did so,
and only 8 per cent actually gave support to the Gestalt theory of
change in the memory trace. These cases were drawn correctly on the
two copies, but were changed on the first reproduction, and on successive reproductions were changed progressively, or in a regular direction.

As Hanawalt pointed out, this evidence contained little to comfort
a Gestalt theorist. It will be recalled that both Wulf and Perkins had
found most or all their records characterized by progressive change.
How can we account for the differences between these studies and
Hanawalt's? Probably the main difference resides in the difficulty of
deciding when a progressive change has or has not occurred. To digress
for a moment, something of this difficulty is illustrated in a report of

Woodworth's. He made an independent analysis of the examples of progressive change given by Wulf and reached radically different conclusions from those reached by Wulf. To quote Woodworth, "In the present writer's opinion, only one of these twenty series shows an unequivocal progression, ten show progression in some respect along with unprogressive change in other respects, while the remaining nine are unequivocally nonprogressive" (1938, p. 89). Certainly the evidence for progressive change, at least under the conditions described by Wulf, seems very dubious.

But Hanawalt had much more to say. He wanted to see if progressive memory change might appear in records of subjects who reproduced the figures from memory only once. The responses of such subjects should be uncontaminated by previous attempts to reproduce the figures, and consequently should give a purer measure of the change in memory than the method of successive reproductions. Unfortunately, the advantage gained by this purer method is partly offset by a difficulty. In this new condition progressive change for any individual subject cannot be measured, since each subject draws from memory only once. Hanawalt's solution was to measure certain characteristics of each figure and to look for changes in the average value of the measured characteristic from one retention interval to the next. For example, in one of the figures (Wulf's Figure n), the sharpness of the zigzags was measured on a 5-point scale, where 2 on the scale is a figure of the same sharpness as the original figure. *One* is flatter than the original, and 3, 4, and 5 represent increasingly acute peaks—i.e., sharpening. Similar procedures were used in assessing reproductions of two other figures. For the remainder of the figures that could not be indexed on a sharpening-leveling dimension, other indices were used. For example, for Figure 61o the ratio of the lengths of the two horns was used; for Figure 61v, the ratio of the sum of the two major dimensions on each side was used, and so on. Table 3 shows for each figure the measure used, the number of usable reproductions, and the mean index for the reproduction following each time interval. Simple inspection of the table reveals two facts: first, forgetting as measured by the number of usable reproductions is great; second, some figures show no progressive change in the mean index while others do. Hanawalt, in interpreting these facts, regarded the large amount of forgetting as the salient feature of the change in memory. He believed that the progressive changes that were observed could be accounted for by object assimilation and verbal formulation; in short, the same sort of assumptions that had been made by Gibson; Carmichael, Hogan, and Walter; Brown; and Zangwill.

This latter conclusion was based primarily on the statements that the subjects made after they had drawn a figure from memory. They

TABLE 3

CHANGES IN MEMORY FOR FORM

HANAWALT'S EXPERIMENT—METHOD OF SINGLE REPRODUCTION *

Fig.	Stimulus Value	CI	CII	Imm.	1 day	1 wk.	4 wks.	8 wks.	Measure
h		x̄ 2.28	2.45	2.58	2.86	3.00	3.18	3.20	Angle size
	2.00	n 68	68	12	15	8	11	15	
b		x̄ 2.83	2.79	2.96	....	3.08	2.71	3.76	Not clearly stated but includes deepness of bowl
	2.00	n 55	55	24	....	15	9	9	
c		x̄ 3.34	3.11	3.16	....	3.44	4.03	4.06	Angle size
	2.00	n 77	77	25	....	11	8	12	
i		x̄ 31.50°	...	25.50°	....	32.30°	....	40.20°	Angle size
	30°	n 32	...	9	....	18	2	5	
o		x̄ 42	...	41.50	....	....	49.90	58.10	Short point as percentage of long point
	26	n 36	...	....	....	....	....	....	
u		x̄ 44.40	...	44.00	39.30	40.00	56.90	70.30	Height of small triangle as percentage of ht. of large
	33	n 22	...	11	10	14	15	14	
v		x̄ 51.80	...	47.80	....	54.20	47.10	70.50	Sum of two small end dimensions as percentage of sum of two large end dimensions
	56	n 56	...	22	....	17	7	4	
w		x̄ 31.40	...	33.40	31.40	54.10	57.40	69.50	Top short line as a percentage of top long line
	35	n 32	...	9	13	10	14	17	
x		x̄ 22.80	...	29.40	....	34.80	....	40	Short end length as percentage of long end length
		n 25	...	7	....	27	2	12	
s		x̄ 13.10	...	17.70	15.90	16.90	17.40	14.00	Height as percentage of length
	17	n 25	...	12	12	10	10	4	
z		x̄ 47.10	...	54.20	....	60.20	57.00	....	Horizontal as percentage of vertical distance
		n 50	...	12	....	15	8	2	

x̄ = mean score
n = number of observations

* From Nelson G. Hanawalt, "Memory Trace for Figures in Recall and Recognition," *Arch. Psychol.*, 1937, No. 216, from tables 6, 7, and 9–16, pp. 48–56. Used by permission of the author.

were asked to ". . . state that feature or anything that you believe was responsible for your remembering of the design" (1937, p. 21). To take an example, if a subject's reproduction of Figure b showed sharpening and if he said "like pyramids" or "hills" or "house tops" (p. 50), Hanawalt concluded that the sharpening was caused by object assimilation. According to such an account, when the subject first sees the figure, he might say to himself "flat pyramids." The next day the subject remembers his response of "flat pyramids" and draws the figure correctly. If, after eight weeks, the subject remembers anything at all, he may remember "pyramids" rather than "flat pyramids," and as a consequence, sharpen the figure. Such an account would explain the sharpening, while saying nothing about a modification in the form of the perceptual memory trace. This is the interpretation that Hannawalt chose to make.

The objection to this interpretation is by now obvious. One could just as easily argue that the change in reproduction is caused by a modification of the trace and that in this particular case the modification is such that the trace elicits a verbal response of pyramid and a sharpened reproduction. The underlying forces determining the change might be either normalizing forces or autochthonous forces. What is important to recognize is that theoretical positions, such as the Gestalt position, are frequently difficult to test. They may be difficult to test because the position has not been stated with sufficient clarity to allow the various investigators to see all possible implications. It is difficult to say that these results of Hanawalt's refute the Gestalt position, because it is still possible to make a Gestalt interpretation of the changes that he did in fact observe.

HANAWALT'S COMPARISON OF REPRODUCTION AND RECOGNITION. Hanawalt was interested not only in the effects on memory of repeated reproduction, but also in the relation between reproduction and recognition. Consequently, in both the successive- and single-reproduction conditions the final reproduction from memory for each subject was followed by a recognition test. Unlike Zangwill and Wulf, who had tested each subject individually, Hanawalt had presented his figures to groups of subjects. Thus he could not follow Zangwill's technique of including in the material on the recognition test improved copies of the subject's own reproductions, since these would necessarily be different for each subject. Instead, each subject saw the same recognition set. These sets were composed of ten variations of each figure selected partly from previous records and partly designed to allow variation along a single leveling-sharpening dimension for each figure. Some examples are given in Figure 66.

The recognition test turned out to be a more sensitive test of

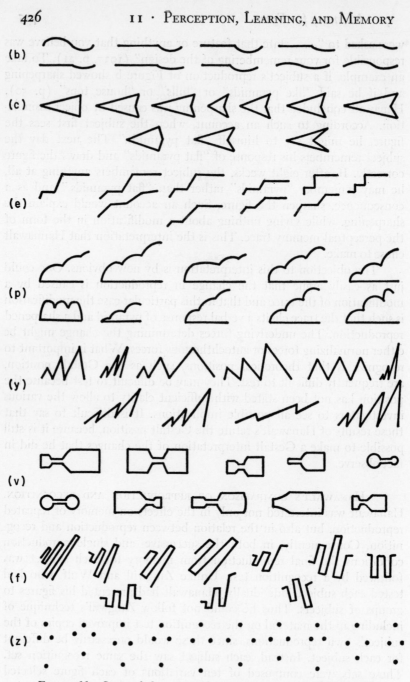

FIGURE 66. Some of the sets used in recognition tests by Hanawalt. (From Nelson G. Hanawalt, "Memory Trace for Figures in Recall and Recognition," *Arch. Psychol.*, 1937, No. 216, p. 60. Used by permission of the author.)

memory than the reproduction test, as was true in Zangwill's experiment. Even when reproduction had completely deteriorated, recognition of the correct figure still occurred. Another, and perhaps more surprising, finding is that successive reproduction which has marked effects on reproductions has no appreciable effect on recognition—a fact that Hanawalt showed in several ways. Since subjects tested by successive reproductions had a recognition test only at eight weeks after original inspection of the figures, the comparison between the two conditions was made at this point. In both conditions more than 250 subjects were tested. For those subjects who made successive reproductions, the correct or almost correct recognitions totaled 56 per cent; for those who made but a single reproduction, the corresponding value was 59 per cent. The percentage of recognitions differing from the correct ones in the same direction as the reproductions was 25 per cent for the successive condition and 23 per cent for the single condition. Furthermore, neither the presence nor absence of progressive errors in the successive drawings resulted in a difference between the two recognition conditions. In short, no analysis revealed a difference between the two conditions.

One advantage of the recognition method over the reproduction method is that the former eliminates errors attributable to the drawing skills of the subjects. By showing that the errors which occurred in reproduction were not mirrored by similar errors in recognition, Hanawalt threw considerable doubt on the adequacy of the reproduction method as a technique for measuring changes in memory. Nonetheless, Hanawalt felt he had refuted the Gestalt hypothesis of a changing memory trace. Three main reasons for his conclusion may be indicated. First, the large amount of forgetting, as measured by the single reproduction method, showed the importance of each reproduction for the later ones. Second, the subjects' apparent reliance on verbal formulation and object assimilation suggested the importance of associative factors. Finally, frequent lack of correspondence between reproduction and recognition led him to assert that changes do not occur as a result of a trace that is gradually modifying over a period of time.

HANAWALT'S INTERPRETATION OF MEMORY CHANGE. Hanawalt's interpretation was that the changes occur at the time of reproduction when the subject attempts to reconstruct a figure that he has almost forgotten. What is remembered, said Hanawalt, following Woodworth (1938), is not the previous experience in its totality but the reaction that the subject made while having the experience. However, this interpretation does not deny the possibility of a memory trace nor of a visual memory image which the subject attains introspectively, and which for Woodworth seems to have some equivalence to the trace.

Rather, this interpretation assumes that with the passage of time this trace becomes a less and less important determiner of the reproduction while the reactions made at the time of original learning become more and more important. These reactions would be primarily verbal, although there is no reason why they could not involve other response systems as well.

TESTS FOR PROGRESSIVE CHANGE IN RECOGNITION.   There are some other bits of evidence that Hanawalt believed further damaged the Gestalt hypothesis. There is, for example, the question of whether the trend either in recognition or in reproduction was toward a "better" or more *prägnant* figure. Since the reproduction procedures patently did not test the Gestalt hypothesis, Hanawalt restricted this part of the inquiry to a consideration of recognition results only. A new group of subjects who knew nothing of the other aspects of Hanawalt's study was given the task of judging the "goodness" of figures. "Good" was illustrated to the subjects by such terms as "balanced," "symmetrical," "simple," or "a figure with good continuity." As might be expected, there was considerable disagreement among judges, but for some figures the agreement was high. There was no evidence of a relationship between what subjects chose as a good figure and what another group of subjects chose in the memory tests as being the figure they had originally seen. That is, there was no evidence that the trends in recognition memory proceeded in the direction of superior recall of better figures—"better" being those figures so judged by these independent judges.

Because all of Hanawalt's recognition tests had been preceded by reproduction tests, he felt he did not have a pure test of progressive change in recognition. Consequently, he ran yet another experiment, using the recognition materials from the previous experiment. Ninety subjects were shown all twenty-four of his experimental figures in one session. As they saw each of the figures on a screen, they would circle on a recognition sheet the figure that they thought was its duplicate. As one might suspect from examination of the samples in Figure 66, this task was not easy. For ninety subjects there were a total of 624 errors. Hanawalt argued that if these errors of recognition represent the operation of Gestalt factors, then with the passage of time there should be an increase in whatever tendency was expressed by the original error. Twelve weeks later the subjects were tested again, but this time they were to mark the test figures from memory alone. Only 16 per cent of the cases showed a progressive change in the direction of original error, whereas *46 per cent showed a reversal in direction.* Twenty-four per cent were marked the same on both occasions, and 14 per cent were not scored for a variety of reasons. Not only was the progressive trend the exception, but the greatest change was in the correction during the memory test of errors made in direct copying of the test figure. Even if one were interested in disproving the Gestalt hypothesis, this seems like too much of a good thing. It suggests the operation of some previously unrecognized factor operating in the test, something preventing the appearance of a progressive effect if it happened to be there.

Hanawalt recognized this problem and suggested that the effect was a statistical one caused by the fact that if the subject originally marked a figure one or two steps removed from the correct one and after twelve weeks had only a vague memory of the figure, chance alone will favor marking one closer to the correct one because of the scarcity of test figures that increase the error in the same direction as the original error. However, he stated his belief that "if the trace has been gradually transformed due to the internal stresses, the test allows plenty of leeway for marking a figure in a positive relation with the original response" (p. 69, 1937). That is, the test allows room for subjects to show progressive errors.

While this statement appears to be justified for some of the recognition sets, it is open to question in others. For example, suppose in the examples given in Figure 66, Set v, the subject had for the first test chosen the first figure in the top row. The only possible figures that are more extreme in the same direction are the fourth figures in both rows. Both these figures have lost the left end. The question that must be asked is whether this particular experimental arrangement really gives the Gestalt hypothesis a chance. Other illustrations of the same point can be made. For example, in Set c, where the third figure in the upper row is correct, a subject marking the second figure can only continue in the same direction by marking the triangle shown first. On the other hand, Set y does seem to allow a reasonable opportunity for Gestalt factors to operate. Thus it may be concluded that while Hanawalt's work clearly showed the inadequacies of the method of successive reproductions and indeed of the reproduction method in general, it is not clear that he disproved the Gestalt hypothesis of autonomous change. This rather surprising conclusion is based on the fact that he demonstrated the inadequacy of the reproduction method and, that in his use of the recognition test, there are methodological difficulties which allow the conclusion that the Gestalt position has not been fairly tested.

A final word about Hanawalt's experiments. Both Hanawalt and Zangwill demonstrated in one way or another that memory as measured by reproduction, and memory as measured by recognition, are not necessarily the same. Now, it is frequently assumed that memory is a unitary process which can be measured by any of a number of different responses the subject might make. By this assumption, recognition and reproduction differ from each other not because they represent different processes, but rather because the particular method used is a partial determiner of the obtained result. For example, reproduction may differ from recognition because of errors introduced into reproduction by the inability to draw adequately or because of other factors such as the fact that in reproduction tests, in contrasts to recognition tests, the stimulus figure is not present at the time of the test of memory. On the other hand, errors or variations may be introduced into the recognition test by the selection of the various incorrect test items that are presented at the same time correct items are presented. If these items are quite similar to the correct figure, the subject will tend to make errors that would not otherwise appear. If the distribution of test stimuli in a recognition test is skewed in some direction, there may be a displacement of errors.

It should also be mentioned that an additional factor may cause a difference between these two methods. Quite possibly, subjects in a re-production situation frequently misinterpret the instructions of the experimenter. Rather than try to make a perfect reproduction, which they may regard as impossible, they may merely sketch what they consider to be a satisfactory approximation. Thus if they are presented with their final reproduction and the original figure, they will unhesitantly point to the original figure as the correct one, even though they have made a regular and systematic error. These three factors—variations in stimulus conditions, differences in the required response, and differences in interpretation of instructions—may all work together to create discrepancies between reproduction and recognition. While it may be reasonable to assume that these differences in results arise from the differences in method, that this is indeed the case has yet to be demonstrated.

The Introduction of a Psychophysical Method into the Analysis of the Problem

THE NEW METHOD.   As we said before, 1937 was an important year in the history of our problem. Three new attacks on the problem of memory change were introduced in that year. Zangwill had introduced the procedure of using the subject's own reproductions to test for recognition. Hanawalt showed the inadequacies of the reproduction methods and also indicated the possibilities of recognition tests. In a third paper Irwin and Seidenfeld (1937) introduced yet another procedure designed to avoid the difficulties of the reproduction method. Quite simply, they showed the subject six figures, and then as soon as all figures had been exposed they showed him the identical figures again. However, the instructions led the subjects to believe that the second figure was similar, but not identical, to the first figure. On the second exposure, the subject was asked a series of questions about each figure. For example, one of the figures was a ring with an eighteen-degree gap centered at twelve o'clock. The subjects were asked two questions. First, was the gap in the second figure wider or narrower than in the first? Second, was the area of the circle larger or smaller? The same procedure was repeated again after a pause of a few minutes, and again after seven days.

This beautifully simple method is well worth considering in detail. Note that the subject is given no opportunity to call the second stimulus the same as the first stimulus, but instead must judge "more" or "less" along some specified dimension. The assumption underlying this procedure is that if there is no change in memory that would appear in subjects in general, then a large group of subjects should approximate a fifty-fifty split on any judgment. If, on the other hand, there is a systematic change in memory, then more subjects should give one response than the other. There is a further assumption that if any particular progressive change in memory is characteristic of subjects in general, then this change will be manifested by a progressively greater percentage of the subjects making one response at the expense of the other. Such an assumption seems reasonable. Two advantages of this method over the recognition method used by Hanawalt should be noted. First, it does not force the subject to identify any figure as the one that was originally shown. With Hanawalt's procedure, a subject's memory might change in such a way that none of the test figures look correct, yet he must choose one. Second, Irwin and Seidenfeld's procedure eliminates one source of error that might have been present in Hanawalt's test. When a subject is presented with a set of figures and is asked to select the one he has seen before, the examination of each test figure presumably leaves a trace somewhat like, and therefore interfering with, the trace of the correct figure. The most likely effect of such interferences would be to increase the error of measurement and make detection of changes more difficult. The use of only one test figure certainly reduces this possibility to a minimum.

Irwin and Seidenfeld's experiment was an innovation not only in method but also in taking explicit cognizance of the fact that memory change in recognition may be stated as a problem in psychophysics and, as such, is capable of treatment by the classical psychophysical methods. Indeed, the particular method they have used is the simplest case of the method of constant stimulus differences developed by Fechner in 1860.

In the case of three of the figures, Irwin and Seidenfeld saw a clear prediction from Gestalt theory. One of the figures was an open circle, one an open triangle, and one four dots that formed an imperfect square. The predictions were that the open figures should be recalled as more closed than they had actually been and that the four dots should be remembered as forming a better square than they did. In all cases the predictions were borne out by the results of the first recognition test. The later tests did not provide convincing evidence of progressive trends. On the basis of Hanawalt's work, however, any inference concerning progressive effects must be mistrusted if it is collected by a method involving repeated tests on the same individuals. In view of this, Irwin and Seidenfeld's study should only be taken as evidence that there are some results from the first recognition test that support the Gestalt hypothesis.

SUPPORTING EVIDENCE.   Seidenfeld (1938) used much the same general procedure and figures but employed a measurement technique that allowed him to estimate the magnitude of the change in memory for the individual subject. He presented on a single card five of the six figures previously used by Irwin and Seidenfeld. Then, after intervals of three minutes, ten minutes, seven days, and twenty-eight days, he presented sheets that contained each original figure in a set of nine figures varying only in one specific characteristic. For example, the circle with the gap varied only in the size of the gap. For each set of drawings the subject was asked to select the figure that he had originally seen. Since the same subjects were used at each time interval, Hanawalt's criticism of this procedure holds here, as it does in Irwin and Seidenfeld's experiment. Two results from the first recognition test merit comment.

First, as in Irwin and Seidenfeld's experiment, more than 50 per cent of the subjects showed closure of the gap in the circle in the memory test. But the per cent deviation from 50 per cent was about half as great as it was for Irwin and Seidenfeld. This reduction in the frequency of the effect again suggests the possibility that testing for recognition by using a set of similar figures produces interference that obscures qualitative changes in memory. Second, like Hanawalt, Seidenfeld used a control group whose task was to identify the correct stimulus on the test form while the correct stimulus was present for inspection. For all figures except an obtuse angle, the judgments were correct by large percentages. This finding suggests that Irwin and Seidenfeld's failure to include this control does not necessarily invalidate their conclusions.

In a follow-up of Irwin and Seidenfeld's experiment, Irwin and Rovner (1937) were able partly to confirm their original observations. Each subject was tested only once—three minutes after the original inspection. This should have made the results directly comparable to the first results from the earlier study, but they introduced two modifications in procedure. First, each subject saw only one stimulus, and in the recognition test was asked only one question about the figure (e.g., whether the gap in the circle was larger or smaller than before). This procedure avoids the difficulties involved in showing a subject several figures, and asking more than one question about many of them. Unfortunately, the meaning of the results was obscured, for during the interval between the original showing of the figure and the test, each subject was required to write out a description of the figure that he had seen. These data are hard to interpret, and it is difficult to assess the reasons for changes from the results of the first experiment when such changes did occur. For example, one of the most striking findings of the first experiment was that 72.5 per cent of the subjects reported the gap in the circle as appearing larger in the recognition test than it had appeared in the original inspection. That is, closure occurred. In this new experiment, however, only 52 per cent responded similarly. Irwin and Rovner pointed out that in every case the judgments in their experiment differed from 50 per cent in the same direction as the judgments in the Irwin and Seidenfeld experiment, and that this sort of occurrence would not be expected by chance. While this certainly suggests that some of the discrepancies from 50 per cent represent real trends, the wide variation in scores from one experiment to the next makes it difficult to decide in which values to have faith.

FAILURE TO CONFIRM IRWIN AND SEIDENFELD'S ORIGINAL OBSERVATION. Fifteen years after Irwin and Seidenfeld's experiment, Hanawalt (1952) repeated it except that he used a different group of subjects at each retention interval. He failed to repeat Irwin and Seidenfeld's results with the stimuli that they considered most relevant to the Gestalt hypothesis. Since, at the briefest time interval, both experiments followed essentially the same procedure, this lack of repeatability suggests that Irwin and Seidenfeld's method may be unreliable. Perhaps unreliability with this method is not surprising, for each of the figures was shown only once prior to testing, and all six figures were shown before any test was made. Under such conditions, any systematic trends might well be masked.

MEMORY CHANGE IN BLIND SUBJECTS. Tennies (1942), using the same general procedure and materials as Irwin and Seidenfeld, compared changes in the tactual memory of blind and sighted individuals. Since he also repeatedly tested the same subjects, the repetitions after the first recognition test must be discounted, but certain facts are of considerable interest. For the circle with the gap, almost all the blind subjects remembered the original gap as smaller than the identical gap when the same figure was used as a test stimulus, and almost all remembered the circle itself as smaller. For none of the other figures was such shrinking consistently found, but in some cases there were suggestions concerning the possible reasons. For example, in the case of the obtuse angle the subjects remembered the original angle as greater or smaller, depending on whether they felt the angle with the apex toward or away from them. The sighted subjects were less consistent in their behavior but did show a similar trend for the circle.

Taken as a group, these four experiments plus Hanawalt's repetition of Irwin and Seidenfeld's experiment seemed to reopen the question that Hanawalt's earlier work appeared to have settled. Yet the method used by these experimenters was not adequate to determine whether memory for figures shows progressive change. The further question of whether the change is in some specifiable direction, i.e., toward good Gestalt, and what the proper explanation of such a change would be is still more remote. The most important contribution is the use of the single identical stimulus in testing.

A TEST OF THE "VERBAL-LABEL" THEORY OF PROGRESSIVE CHANGE. A short time later Hanawalt and Demarest (1939) published another paper that was designed to determine whether a verbal label given to a subject at the time of a delayed reproduction could determine the nature of the reproduction. The method was substantially the same as that originally used by Carmichael, Hogan, and Walter. The main difference is that the suggestions to the subjects were given at the time of the reproduction test rather than at the time of original inspection. One hundred and forty-eight subjects were shown twelve figures—one at a time—from Carmichael, Hogan, and Walter's experiment. They were then divided into nine different groups. Three were control conditions that were given no suggestion at the time of reproduction. Three groups received one word for each of the items shown, and the last three groups were given another word for each of the items shown. The words were the same as those which Carmichael, Hogan, and Walter had originally used. Within the control groups and within each of the two different suggestion groups the subjects were divided into three different reproduction conditions. One group of subjects in each set reproduced the figures immediately after seeing them. Another group in each set reproduced the figures after two days, and a third group after seven days. Table 4 summarizes the results of the experiment and gives a code that explains the columns. The results in this table are based on ratings of two independent judges; a third judge served as a referee. One of the independent judges had no theoretical expectations concerning the outcome.

The table presents several quite interesting facts. First, in the control conditions reproductions made at progressively longer time intervals after original inspection show an increasingly large proportion of the total reproductions associated with a response that the subject said he had made at the time of original inspection. They suggest quite reasonably that Carmichael, Hogan, and Walter probably would have

TABLE 4

CLASSIFICATION OF REPRODUCTIONS IN THE VARIOUS CONDITIONS IN
HANAWALT AND DEMAREST'S EXPERIMENT *

Classification of Reproduction

Recall Period	No. of Subjects	Like Learning Assn. %	Learning Assn. and Sugg. Same %	Like Sugg. in Recall %	No Change Noted %	Change Unaccounted for %	No. of Drawings	Av. No. per Subj.
Control Group—No Suggestion								
Immediate.....14		63	..	..	18	18	164	11.7
2-days.........14		75	..	..	11	13	126	9.0
7-days.........18		93	..	..	1	6	107	5.9
Suggestion in Recall Period—List I								
Immediate.....14		24	36	12	13	16	158	11.3
2-days.........17		34	30	19	6	11	193	11.3
7-days.........21		18	38	33	2	10	200	9.5
Suggestion in Recall Period—List II								
Immediate.....15		33	13	23	22	10	172	11.5
2-days.........17		40	18	29	8	5	170	10.0
7-days.........18		25	23	45	1	5	158	8.8

* "Like Learning Association" means that the judges were able to detect a change in reproduction which seemed to be due to the learning association, reported by the subject after testing to have been present in the learning period.

"Learning Association and Suggestion Same" means that the same word was suggested in the test period as was reported by the subject to have been present in the learning period. In these cases it was not possible to separate the two factors.

"Like Suggestion in Recall" means that the judges were able to detect in the reproduction some evidence which they believed to be due to the verbal suggestion given in the test period.

"No Change Noted" means that the reproduction looked so much like the stimulus figure that it was considered a correct reproduction.

"Change Unaccounted for" means that the change was of such a nature that it could be attributed neither to the learning association nor to the suggestion given in the test period.

From N. G. Hanawalt and I. H. Demarest, "The Effect of Verbal Suggestion in the Recall Period Upon the Reproduction of Visually Perceived Forms," *J. Experimental Psychology*, 1939, *25*, p. 164. Used by permission.

found progressive trends in their data had they tested after varying lengths of time. Secondly, the two suggestion conditions clearly bear out Hanawalt and Demarest's hypothesis that the response will be determined in part by a suggestion given to the subject. The longer the time since the original inspection, the greater is the importance of a suggestion made at the time of reproduction.

Hanawalt and Demarest were also able to show that by some objective indices the results were consistent with the results from ratings in Table 4. Take, for example, the figure called either "a curtain in the window" or "a diamond in a rectangle" (figure 1 in Figure 65 on p. 417). The percentage of subjects closing the bottom two lines to form a diamond-shaped object was greater for the group given the word "diamond" than for the group given the word "curtains." Furthermore the discrepancy between the two groups increased from the immediate reproduction to the seven-day reproduction. Similar results were obtained for other figures. The writers interpreted their results in terms of a reaction theory of memory. They assumed that the reproduction could be determined either by a reaction following the suggestion of the experimenter or by a verbal response that the subject makes himself. As time passes and the reaction made at the time of original inspection becomes weaker, the suggestion of the experimenter at the time of reproduction would be more and more important in determining the reproduction that the subject makes.

Clearly, as Hanawalt and Demarest suggested, this evidence that a reaction at the time of original inspection and a reaction at the time of reproduction can both determine changes in the reproduction from the original figure more emphatically than ever calls into question the necessity of assuming an autonomously changing trace. It is interesting, however, that the results from the control groups definitely suggest that even without suggestion from the experimenter at the time of reproduction, there are progressive changes in reproduction which seem to be determined by the subject's implicit original reaction.

An experimental critique of Hanawalt's work.   A reply to Hanawalt and Demarest was not long in coming. Goldmeier (1941), in a paper defending the Gestalt position, criticized Hanawalt's general procedures, not on the grounds that he had failed to demonstrate the effects of past experience and suggestion on reproduction, but rather on the ground that his technique did not allow for the appearance of autonomous change. Specifically, he referred to the investigations of Köhler and Von Restorff on a Gestalt theory of learning, in which they enumerated three factors which, they said, reduced the availability of the trace for use by the subject. These three factors were (1) a long series of designs, (2) uniformity or similarity of designs, and (3) the use of designs which have no firm structure, i.e., which are not good Gestalten. He argued that Hanawalt's experimental materials suffered from all three defects, namely, the subject was exposed to too many designs and there was too much similarity or interference among the designs.

Further, he said that the designs were not of the sort that would demonstrate progressive autonomous change.

Goldmeier's experiment was a repetition of Hanawalt's first study in which subjects were first shown a series of forms. While seeing these forms, they copied them twice, and then different groups reproduced the forms from memory at differing lengths of time after original exposure. His procedure differed from Hanawalt's in that subjects saw six rather than eight forms, and the forms were designed, so Goldmeier said, to allow autonomous change. His forms are shown in Figure 67. In analyzing his results, Goldmeier found changes that increased in frequency as time went by for most of the figures. For instance, the number of subjects who reproduced Figure 67-A1 by changing the curves increased

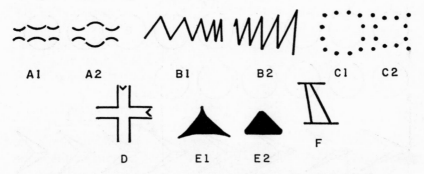

FIGURE 67. Figures by E. Goldmeier, "Progressive Changes in Memory Traces," *Amer. J. Psychol.*, 1941, 54, 490–503, and used by permission.

with each succeeding test interval. In Figure 67-A2, there was an increase in the number of subjects who changed the gaps in the figures. In 67-B1, there was a slight tendency toward increasing sharpness; in 67-B2, greater frequency of changes in the angles; in 67-C, changes in the roundness of the figures; in 67-D, changes in the locations of the small arrows; in 67-E, changes in the pointedness or roundness of the figures; and in 67-F, changes in the angle of the left-hand vertical line.

Unfortunately, Goldmeier's results are so difficult to analyze that conclusions concerning the meaning of these changes are impossible to reach. Some of the changes are small and fluctuating. In other cases the prediction that would be made by a theory of autonomous change is not clear, nor is it clear how the reproductions changed. Thus, in Figure 67-A1, while more subjects drew the figures with changes in the curves at each successive reproduction, it is not clear whether subjects drew the lines more curved or less curved. It is only known that the subjects were more likely to change after six weeks, for example, than after three days. Similarly, in 67-B2, with the passage of time, more subjects varied the angular separation from the beginning of the jagged line to the end. But it is not clear whether the subjects tended to draw the two more equal or less equal. In short, Goldmeier's general ideas were provocative, but his results are hard to interpret.

The Experiment of Hebb and Foord

ANALYSIS OF PROCEDURE.   An attempt to correct these deficiencies and allow a more clear-cut test of the Gestalt hypothesis was made by Hebb and Foord (1945). They recognized the importance of

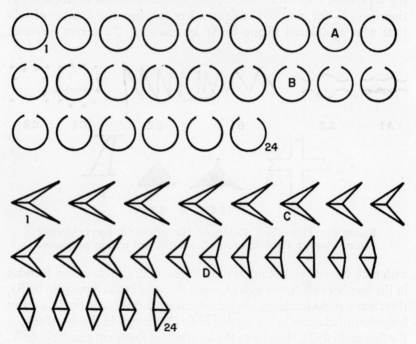

FIGURE 68.   Inspection and test figures used by D. O. Hebb and E. N. Foord, "Errors of Visual Recognition and the Nature of the Trace," *J. exp. Psychol.*, 1945, 35, 335–48. Used by permission of the American Psychological Association.

restricting the number of figures to which the subject was exposed and, furthermore, of attempting to state what sort of change might be expected from Gestalt theory. It should be noted that these are the first experimenters to deal explicitly with the problem of what sort of change would be predicted and then to develop figures specifically tied to their analysis. In their experiment each subject inspected only two figures, and each subject was tested only once by a recognition procedure. Some subjects were tested after five minutes; others after twenty-four hours. The figures were selected so as to minimize interference from one to the other, and to make difficult the labeling of the specific characters of the figures. This latter aim was accomplished by taking figures from points in a series where only quantitative variation occurs. Their inspection and test figures are shown in Figure 68.

Consider first the two circular inspection figures, A and B. Some subjects saw one of these broken circles; others saw the other one. The gaps in these figures differ substantially, but they do not present identifiable points on a continuum in the sense that a circle with a gap of 180 degrees is known as a semicircle and has special properties that make identification easy. Why did they use two values of each type of inspection figure rather than one? To quote: ". . . the use of two separate diagrams in each series as original stimuli with separate groups of subjects achieves two objectives. If verbal cues affect the recognition of one of the two diagrams, they may not be as effective with the other. Also, if the particular figure chosen as original stimulus happened to be close to the 'perfect' instance of such a figure, Gestalt theory would not require that a progressive error occur. By using two diagrams from each series the probability is increased of finding for one figure, at least, conditions suitable to the demonstration of spontaneous activity within the trace" (Hebb and Foord, 1945, p. 342). All these considerations apply both to the arrowhead and to the circle. In the case of the arrowheads, the inspection figures selected are within a range of arrowheads that vary from each other only quantitatively. Presumably, if there is a progressive change, it would be toward sharpening, although Gestalt theory is sufficiently vague that the hypothesis can be disproved only if no progressive change of any sort occurs. Further, as stated above, there is no way of knowing in advance just what particular arrowhead should result in a stable trace. Clearly, both inspection arrowheads cannot if there is some one cortical representation of the arrowhead for which stress is minimized. Either one or the other must change in some direction if the Gestalt hypothesis is to be considered tenable. In the case of the circle, closure should occur. But one size of gap may be more susceptible to the action of the cortical forces than the other. Perhaps the size of the smaller gap is easier to verbalize than the larger, and consequently is more stable. Again, two different sizes of gap are a precaution.

Hebb and Foord also pointed out that a bimodal distribution of responses by the subjects might also be considered as evidence for a Gestalt position. If some subjects verbalize the design sufficiently precisely that the recognition performance is determined completely by a reinstatement of the verbal response, then responses should show no change over a period of time. Others who did not verbalize with this precision would show the expected shift.

In the recognition test the figures were presented on cards strung on rings. Different subjects started at different points on the ring of cards. Subjects merely looked until they found the card they believed to be the one they had previously seen.

RESULTS AND INTERPRETATION.   When the evidence was examined, no support for the Gestalt theory was found. The only difference between the five-minute groups and the twenty-four-hour groups was that the latter groups were more scattered in their choices. There was no evidence of any trend over a course of time in either direction for either figure, nor was there any indication of bimodality. The basic results of Hebb and Foord's experiment have been repeated by George (1952), who also extended their negative findings to longer time intervals.

These results are precisely what would be expected from a theory that asserts that the changes in memory for form result from weakening of memory rather than from change in the quality of the memory. Surely this experiment should finish the Gestalt hypothesis once and for all. The theory had originally been advanced in connection with evidence that had been collected under Wulf's poorly controlled conditions. That evidence had been refuted. The present attempt seemed to look for evidence supporting the Gestalt position under much more sensitive conditions. No such effects were found.

But Hebb and Foord's experiment did not end the discussion nor the research. One point that has been mentioned before needs re-emphasis. The Gestalt psychologist believes that progressive memory changes in the direction of a "better" figure must occur. He believes this not because a Gestalt psychologist named Wulf once did an experiment that suggested such changes; rather, he does so because he assumes that the same factors that determine how we perceive will determine the manner in which we remember. If there are tendencies to perceive objects in accord with the principle of *Prägnanz*, or good Gestalt, then surely these effects should be enhanced when the restraints imposed by the physical stimulus are absent.

The questions the Gestalt psychologist might reasonably ask, then, are, "Are there any flaws in Hebb and Foord's experiment?" "Are there any possible reasons why progressive changes did not show up?"

By now the reader should be convinced that the experiment that cannot be criticized does not exist. We have already suggested that showing several forms either in the training period or in the test period might seriously interfere with the sensitivity of the test. Hebb and Foord's experiment can be criticized on both grounds. Consequently, the experiment cannot be considered crucial against the hypothesis of autonomous change. On the other hand, there is no doubt that Hebb and Foord's experiment added considerably to the weight of evidence against Wulf's original conclusions. If autonomous changes occur, they must be small and easily disrupted.

The Effect of "Verbal Labeling" on Recognition Memory

Several years after Hebb and Foord's experiment, Prentice (1954) conducted a study which seemed to throw even more doubt on Wulf's hypothesis. Prentice argued that the sort of changes in figure reproduction found by Carmichael, Hogan, and Walter and later by Hanawalt and Demarest were probably changes that were restricted to the act of reproducing the figure and not changes in the memory of the form: the absence of such changes would presumably be shown by stability of recognition memory.

In Prentice's experiment, subjects were first given two inspection trials with the figures used by Carmichael, Hogan, and Walter. During these trials, subjects were divided into two groups which were given different labels for each figure, as in the experiment by Carmichael, Hogan, and Walter. Immediately after the two successive inspection trials subjects were given a recognition test. The stimuli for this test were all the original figures, and for each one, two progressive distortions in the direction of each label. For example, there was a dumbbell-shaped figure identical with one of the original drawings, two distortions made to look like telephones, and two distortions made to look like eye-glasses. For each variety of distortion one of the two was made to look more like the named object than the other. The results were quite conclusive. The subjects made many errors, but their errors were symmetrically distributed around the original figures. There were no significant changes in the forms of the recognized items.

Prentice's conclusion was that the use of verbal labels during learning does not modify the visual experience or the memory of this experience. Rather, it appears to influence what the subject draws if instructed to draw a figure like the one he was originally told about and which, of course, he also originally saw. But why does the subject reproduce according to the suggestion, but not recognize according to suggestion? Prentice's answer is that these comments of the experimenter may be regarded by the subject as a form of special instruction (in effect, e.g., "this is the one to be drawn like a telephone").

An alternative interpretation of Prentice's failure to find systematic changes in recognition is that the failure was due to insensitivity of the measuring procedure. In drawing figures diverging from the norm, and presenting them for recognition, the experimenter gambles. Eye-glasses can assume many forms. If the modification of the subject's memory toward eye-glasses does not agree with the particular version the experimenter has drawn, then the original figure might be chosen by the subject despite modifications in memory. Also, as was pointed out in connection with both Hanawalt's experiment and with Hebb and Foord's experiment, the use of many figures as in Prentice's recognition test may

produce so much interference and confusion between the items as to
mask progressive trends, which a more sensitive test would reveal. For
both these reasons Prentice's experiment cannot be regarded as final.
Verbal labeling may or may not influence recognition memory for
geometrical forms. We do not at present know.

Demonstration of Interference Effects When Many Test Stimuli Are Used

The plausibility of this second objection has been shown by a more
recent study by Carlson and Duncan (1955). Their interest was aroused
by the fact that in Hebb and Foord's study, although there was no evidence of any progressive change from five minutes to twenty-four hours,
there was evidence that the subjects had responded in a biased fashion
in the memory tests. For example, subjects tended to remember the
circle with the small gap as being more open than they had actually
seen it. Carlson and Duncan called attention to a weakness in Hebb and
Foord's design, namely, that in the recognition test there were more
circles with gaps larger than the original figure than there were circles
with gaps smaller than the original figure. This bias in the test figures,
they felt, might be an important determiner of the responses of the
subject.

Carlson and Duncan tested different groups of subjects after three
minutes, after one week, and after two weeks. Each subject was shown
only one figure, either a circle with a twenty-degree gap centered at 225°
or an inverted V, the right leg of which was half the length of the left
leg. Both these figures were designed to meet the requirements of asymmetry that Koffka (1935) had discussed and which Hilgard (1948) had
argued were perhaps not present in the Hebb and Foord figures. In other
words, the experiment was designed to be as favorable as possible to the
Gestalt hypothesis. The test situation was a series of nineteen figures that
were larger or smaller than the standard in progressive steps of two degrees. These were made into a book which was placed in front of the
subject in such a fashion that he could open the book at any point and
start in either direction. The critical finding in this study was that the
recognition choices of particular subjects were determined by the point
at which they opened the book. For example, in the test with the circles,
of the fifty-eight subjects who opened the book on a circle with a gap
smaller than the original figure, thirty-four chose as correct a figure with
a smaller gap. Of the fifty-nine who began the test with a card containing a circle with a larger gap, thirty-six chose as correct a figure with a
larger gap than in the original figure. The conclusion is that the results
obtained by this procedure are determined in part by interference effects
generated by the test list. Consequently, the results from experiments

using a serial-test technique cannot be regarded as crucial evidence against the Gestalt hypothesis. The finding also casts doubt on the conclusiveness of Prentice's finding that labeling does not influence recognition memory.

RECENT EXPERIMENTS USING A SINGLE FIGURE IN THE RECOGNITION TEST

CARLSON AND DUNCAN'S EXPERIMENT makes it clear that to test appropriately for a change in recognition memory, only one stimulus figure should be presented, both in the training trial and in the recognition test. In two recent experiments, the first by Crumbaugh (1954) and a later one by Karlin and Brennan (1957), these conditions have been met.

CRUMBAUGH'S USE OF PSYCHOPHYSICAL PROCEDURES.   Although Crumbaugh tested for memory change with several different figures, no subject saw more than one figure. The inspection figure and the test figure for each subject were always identical except that they appeared on opposite sides of a fixation point. In the series of presentations of the inspection and test figures, the first figure, i.e., the inspection figure, appeared half of the time on the right and half of the time on the left. The order of presentation was random. The subjects were told that there would be slight differences between the two figures and that they were to respond with "greater" or "less" or "equal" to the particular characteristic being judged. If the subject judged the figures to be equal, the response was accepted, but the trial was repeated until a response of greater or less was given. Crumbaugh's experiment differed from earlier experiments in that the time intervals between the inspection stimulus and the test stimulus were very small. The inspection stimulus would appear for five seconds. Then at varying times afterward the test stimulus would appear also for five seconds. The time intervals were varied randomly among: zero seconds, i.e., directly following the inspection figure, or 0.3 seconds, two seconds, five seconds, or twelve seconds. Typically, each subject made the comparison between inspection and test eight times with each time interval. The stimuli are shown in Figure 69. They were : (1) a broken circle with a fifteen-degree gap;

Exp. 1   Exp. 2   Exp. 3   Exp. 4   Exp. 5

FIGURE 69. Stimuli used in Crumbaugh's experiments. (From J. C. Crumbaugh, "Temporal Changes in the Memory of Visually Perceived Form," *Amer. J. Psychol.*, 1954, 67, 647–58, and used by permission.)

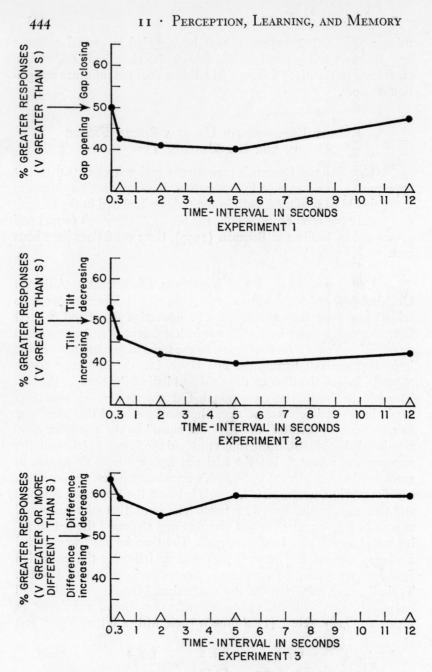

FIGURE 70. Results from the experiments by Crumbaugh. (From J. C. Crumbaugh, "Temporal Changes in the Memory of Visually Perceived Form," *Amer. J. Psychol.*, 1954, 67, 647–58, and used by permission.)

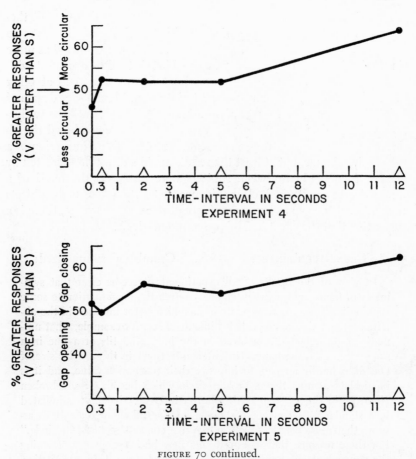

FIGURE 70 continued.

(2) a line tilted fifteen degrees; (3) two discs with a size ratio of twenty-five to thirty-one; (4) an ellipse with a ratio of diameters of seven to eight; (5) a broken circle with a ninety-degree gap. The variables to be judged for the five figures were, respectively, gap size, tilt, relative size, circularity, and gap size.

The results of Crumbaugh's experiments are shown in Figure 70. The experiments showed differences in judgment with different time intervals, but the results are difficult to interpret. For the circle with the fifteen-degree gap, the size of the gap was remembered as larger than its true size except at the shortest and longest intervals. This change in recalled gap size appeared to be statistically reliable, but it is hard to understand in terms of Gestalt theory. The recalled gap is larger, rather than smaller, as one would expect. And the trend reverses rather than being progressive. For the second figure, the tilted line, most subjects remembered the line as more tilted than it had actually been, except at the zero-second interval. For this figure, although a progressive effect was present, it was opposite to the trend toward symmetry that Gestalt theory seems to predict. The experiment with the circles of different size showed that at most time intervals the circles were remembered as more similar in size than they actually were, with this tendency greatest with zero-second delay. Accuracy was greater at five seconds than at other points, but, again, this seems difficult to interpret. Memory for degree of ellipticity shows chance fluctuations around no change, until the twelve-second interval where a preponderance of subjects remembered the ellipse as more circular than it had been. Again there is no indication of a progressive change, but at least the results are in a direction predicted by Gestalt theory. Finally, when subjects were tested on the recall of a ninety-degree gap, there is clear evidence that at twelve seconds subjects remembered the gap as less than ninety degrees. Furthermore, there is a suggestion that the effect had increased progressively.

CRUMBAUGH'S INTERPRETATION.   Crumbaugh summarized:

> In view of the results of all experiments it seems clear that symmetry of figure (autonomous change) rather than assimilation to some standardized or normative figure is the chief factor involved in the obtained progressive changes. It is difficult to see, for example, what normative figure could be involved in the increasing tilt of a line in a square. Similarly, a change (in either direction) in the relative size of two disks hardly appears to improve their normative value, and it is illogical to assume that a broken circle which becomes *more* broken (increase in the 15° gap at the shorter intervals) is being assimilated to a standardized concept of "circle." It is still more difficult to assume that most people have a normative concept of "*broken* circle." For these reasons, the present results may be interpreted as favoring the concept of autonomous change. If the changes were assimilative, we should certainly expect them to progress consistently in the direction of a particular figure, rather than to start in one direction and then to reverse.[2]

This excerpt highlights the extent to which different interpretations can be placed on facts when the criteria for testing hypotheses are not agreed upon. Crumbaugh's argument contains three assumptions which should be examined. First, it is asserted that the memory of the figures moves in the direction of symmetry rather than toward some norm. It is true that in two of the experiments, the circles of unequal size and the ellipse, there was a tendency toward symmetry. In the gap experiments the larger gap closed, but the smaller opened. If a closed circle is symmetrical, these results do not support the interpretation. The diagonal line became more tilted in memory. It is hard to understand in what

[2] From J. C. Crumbaugh, "Temporal Changes in the Memory of Visually Perceived Form," *Amer. J. Psychol.*, 1954, 67, 647–58, and used by permission.

sense this change represents an increase in symmetry. Second, it is implied that if the experimenter cannot think of a normative figure that is in the direction of the change, then the change must be considered as *prima facie* evidence for autonomous change, regardless of direction. But this is hardly a conclusive argument, for another person might think up many possible norms which may influence the memory of each figure. Perhaps the most frequently seen broken circles have gaps somewhere in between 15° and 90°, so that assimilation to this norm results in opening of the small gap and closure of the large one. There may be many such figures in everyday experience, such as the letters C and G (Karlin and Brennan, 1957). Perhaps the norm for two disks, one above the other, is a figure 8. Of course these guesses may be wrong, but it is important to recognize that the Gestalt theory of autonomous change will not be strongly buttressed by asserting that it is difficult to think of a norm. Nor will Gestalt theory be discredited because a possible norm happens to occur to a critic. The third assumption in the quoted passage is that if a trend reverses itself, assimilation is ruled out as a possible explanation, but autonomous change is not ruled out. This interpretation conflicts with that of earlier writers who had regarded *progressive* change as one of the criteria for evidence of autonomous change. Presumably, autonomous change occurs because the cortical trace is moving toward some more stable distribution of forces. Nothing in such a view suggests that reversals in change are to be expected. The fact that assimilation toward a norm does not predict a reversal does not mean that such a reversal must be considered evidence for autonomous change. Crumbaugh's finding of reversals raises a difficult problem of interpretation, but it does not offer support for a concept of autonomous change. In conclusion, some sorts of memory change have been demonstrated, but little or nothing can be said concerning the factors causing such change.

ANOTHER PSYCHOPHYSICAL STUDY.   Similarly, Karlin and Brennan's experiment does not support the Gestalt position. Their experiment, which was substantially similar to Crumbaugh's, involved only two figures, a circle with a fifteen-degree gap and an ellipse with the vertical dimension about three times the length of the horizontal dimension. The gap in the circle was centered at 90° for half of the subjects and at 270° for the rest of the subjects. Each subject saw only one of the two figures. In the experiment for memory of gap size, the circle with the gap was presented two times in each of sixty trials. On each trial, the subject was required to say whether the gap was the same size, larger, or smaller on the second exposure than on the first. The trials varied only in the length of time between the two successive exposures. On the first ten trials and the last ten trials (fifty-one to sixty), the two exposures were separated by one second. On the second ten trials and on trials forty-one through fifty, the two exposures were separated by four seconds, and on the middle twenty trials, the interval between exposures was eight seconds. The procedure with subjects who were tested with the ellipse was the same.

In the case of the circle with the gap, the shortest time interval between the two exposures produced a very slight tendency toward "closure." That is, there was a slight increase in the number of judgments of "gap greater" from the first to the second time. With the two longer time intervals there was a reversal in the relative frequencies of the judgments (i.e., opening), with the greatest frequency of judgments of the second gap as smaller than the first at the longest time interval. Thus, as was true for Crumbaugh's results, there was a progressive trend in the judgment, but it was in the direction opposite to what would be expected by the principle of closure. Karlin and Brennan's results with the ellipse were rather inconclusive. Although subjects regularly remembered the figure as more elliptical than it actually was, the results were quite irregular and showed no systematic trends as a function of time.

These two studies, the most adequate to date, show no support for Gestalt theory. Curiously, in both of the experiments with the fifteen-degree gap, the results not only fail to support the Gestalt hypothesis, but they are actually in the opposite direction, and the Karlin and Brennan study shows a progressive trend. In both experiments this opening effect is statistically reliable. How is this to be accounted for? Crumbaugh suggests that the reduction in the opening effect that he found at the longest (twelve-second) time interval might lead to closure with yet longer time intervals. But there is no evidence to support such a conjecture, and it does not explain why the opening occurs with the shorter times. Karlin and Brennan suggest that the memory of the gap as larger than it actually was may be an example of the principle of emphasis. According to this argument, the subject notices the gap as the unusual feature of the design, and hence tends to emphasize it in retention. While this interpretation sounds reasonable, it should be kept in mind that there is no direct evidence that recognition memory is influenced by selective emphasis at the time of original learning. Indeed, Prentice's evidence, while inconclusive, is negative (1954). Another fact which must be borne in mind in evaluating the change in the circle with the fifteen-degree gap is Crumbaugh's result from the experiment with the ninety-degree gap. In that experiment, increases in the time between the first and second exposures resulted in closure. Crumbaugh's interpretation of this finding was that it is an example of autonomous change; Karlin and Brennan's is that it might be due to assimilation to some letter such as C or G. Perhaps *both* the tendency to remember the fifteen-degree gap as larger than it was and the tendency to remember the ninety-degree gap as smaller may be ascribed to assimilation to some common figure such as a letter that typically has a gap between these two values. The term "assimilation" here means nothing more than an assertion that somehow the size of the gap that is remembered is influenced, not only by the most recently seen circular figure with a gap, but also previously seen circular or near-circular figures with gaps. To put it another way, recognition memory should be subject to proactive effects in the same way as other sorts of memory.

As we have previously seen, changes in reproduction do not necessarily mean that there will be corresponding changes in recognition. The changes in reproduction that were produced by Carmichael, Hogan, and Walter were not duplicated by Prentice when retention was measured by recognition rather than reproduction. The argument made by Prentice was that the verbal labeling does not modify the memory of the perceived figure, but rather serves as a special instruction that is used by the subject in drawing the figure. In the experiments by Crumbaugh and by Karlin and Brennan, the situation is reversed. For the first time clear evidence exists for modification in memory for form when the test is a recognition test. It seems likely that under similar conditions modification in memory as measured by reproduction should also be found. Throughout the history of this problem, the reproduction method has shown itself to be more sensitive than the recognition method in revealing behavorial changes. If the method less sensitive to change now reveals changes, the more sensitive one should also. Such an assertion, of course, implies that both sorts of response are in part determined by the same event, and that it is this event in common that is changing and thus producing a change in recognition memory.

Progressive Change Measured by the Method of Reproduction

That parallel changes in reproduction and recognition would be found if the proper experiment were run is strongly suggested by a recent experiment by Walker and Veroff (1956). Their experiment was essentially a repetition of Hanawalt's first main experiment in which he compared the methods of successive and single reproduction. Their general procedures were somewhat simpler than Hanawalt's, and they were able to demonstrate progressive trends in memory as measured by reproduction. Rather than using the large number of figures that each subject in Hanawalt's experiment saw, Walker and Veroff reduced the number of figures seen by each subject to three. The two sets of figures used are shown in Figure 71. One group of subjects saw the circle with a twenty-degree gap, a fifty-five-degree angle and a quadrilateral with the lengths of diagonals in the ratio of 1.25 to 1.00. For another group, the corresponding stimulus values were eighty degrees, one hundred and fifty degrees, and 2.10 to 1.00. For each drawing made by a subject, the only score taken was gap size, angle size, or the ratio of the two diagonals. Consequently, there was no need for ratings by judges as there had been for Hanawalt and most others using the reproduction method. Each subject was shown his set of figures one at a time, and was required to draw

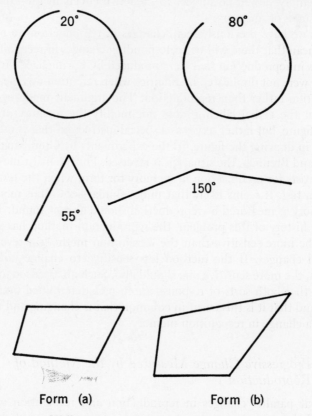

Form (a)   Form (b)

FIGURE 71. Walker and Veroff's stimuli. (From E. L. Walker and J. Veroff, "Changes in the Memory-Trace for Perceived Forms with Successive Reproductions," *Amer. J. Psychol.*, 1956, 69, 395–402, and used by permission.)

each figure from memory immediately after seeing it. Each figure was shown for five seconds, and the subject was allowed fifteen seconds to draw it. Then each of the two groups which had seen different sets of figures was divided into two groups. One group immediately made a second set of drawings from memory, and a third set two weeks later. The second group of subjects made their second set of drawings from memory, two weeks after the original viewing and drawings, and they made their third set immediately after the second set.

Walker and Veroff's results are shown in Figure 72. For all types of

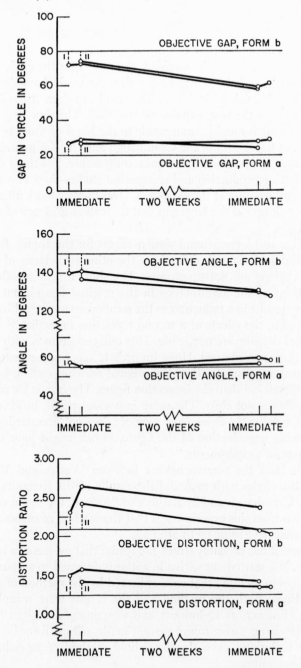

FIGURE 72. Results from Walker's and Veroff's experiment. (From E. L. Walker and J. Veroff, "Changes in the Memory-Trace for Perceived Forms with Successive Reproductions," *Amer. J. Psychol.*, 1956, 69, 395–402, and used by permission.)

figures there are changes from the original figures in the drawings made immediately after viewing, and further, though not necessarily progressive, changes in the later tests.

For our purposes of the moment, the results for the circles with the gaps are the most interesting. In the drawing made immediately after seeing the figure, subjects who saw the small gap drew it too large, and subjects who saw the large gap drew it too small. The time between viewing and drawing is roughly comparable to the range of times between inspection and test figures in the Crumbaugh and the Karlin and Brennan experiments. The results are also quite comparable. For these short time intervals both reproduction and recognition studies show closure for the large gap and opening of the small gap. Over the two-week interval there is a further closure of the large gap, but no further evidence of change in the small gap.

Walker and Veroff found similar effects for the angles. But the results for the quadrilaterals differ from the other two classes of figures in that the changes are not progressive. The short time intervals produce exaggerations of the asymmetries in the original figures, but the two-week delay results in a reduction in the recalled asymmetry. Finally, with one exception, the effects of a second repetition immediately following the original drawing are negligible. This one exception is with the more asymmetrical quadrilateral. Here, immediate repetition results in drawings of greater asymmetry than the original drawings, which in turn are more asymmetrical than the inspection figure. The reason for such a progressive effect is not clear. The more important result, however, is that the act of drawing the figure from memory does not necessarily influence the following reproduction of the figure, as one might have concluded from Hanawalt's experiments.

Aside from the correspondence between Walker and Veroff's results for the circles with gaps and the results of the recognition experiments by Crumbaugh and by Karlin and Brennan, the major conclusion to be drawn from this experiment is that the method of successive reproductions may have some merit after all.

By now it has probably struck the reader that we seem to have come full circle. We started out with a hypothesis designed to account for certain changes in memory that were collected by the method of successive reproductions. Both the method and the results were completely discredited. However, as techniques and experimental designs improved, progressive changes were found again. Finally, with still further improvements in technique, even the discredited method of reproduction appears to have value.

As a footnote to this discussion of the method of single stimulus presentation, it is of interest to note that in a recent experiment Lovibond (1958) has introduced yet another psychophysical method into the study of memory change. He used the adjustment method to study the memory for a form like the unequal-sided inverted V used by Carlson and Duncan. During training, the subject saw two inverted V's, and adjusted the short arm on one to match the length of the short arm on the other. In the test the variable figure was presented alone, with instructions to make the line the same length as the original standard figure as he remembered it. Different groups of subjects were tested after three minutes, after one week, and after two weeks. No statistically significant trends were found, but the method is of interest in its own right. It is quite likely that further use of this and similar methods will occur in the future.

THE EFFECT OF VERBAL LABELS AND TRAINING ON MEMORY FOR FORM

THE WORK OF CRUMBAUGH, and of Karlin and Brennan on one hand and of Walker and Veroff on the other, establishes that changes in the memory for form occur whether the changes are measured by reproduction or recognition. These studies do not, however, tell us what factors determine such changes. Three recent experiments have been concerned with attempts to identify factors controlling memory change. Two of these studies examine the effect of verbal labels on changes in memory. The other is concerned with the effect of memorization-training procedures on changes in memory for form.

VERBAL LABELS.   The two studies that have examined the effects of verbal labels on memory for form are extensions of Carmichael, Hogan, and Walter's experiment. The first of these by Bruner, Busiek, and Minturn (1952) demonstrated that the application of names to the figures influences immediate reproduction of the figures. The major difference between this study and the earlier one by Carmichael *et al.* is that in this study the drawn reproduction was made for each figure immediately after the figure was seen, whereas in the previous study all drawings were made only after all figures had been exposed. Bruner, Busiek, and Minturn wanted to know whether the naming of the stimulus resulted in the subject's drawing the figure to approximate his (the subject's) concept of the label. They pointed out that in order to evaluate the degree to which memory change has actually influenced the subject's drawing, three pieces of information are needed. First, how would the subject have drawn the figure if allowed to copy as exactly as possible? Second, what does the subject's concept of the figure suggested by the named verbal label look like? And third, what does the subject's concept of the label that was not used look like? Let us take as an example the pine tree drawing in Figure 65 on p. 417. During the experiment some subjects were told, "I am going to show you a figure resembling a *trowel* which I shall ask you to reproduce. . . ." For other subjects, the words "pine tree" were used. Following his reproduction of the figure each subject copied the figure as accurately as possible, and also drew a trowel and a pine tree that looked as much as possible like the figures in question. Thus each subject's own norms were used as standards against which to evaluate his responses in the test situation. While this procedure is not free of contamination, it does seem to provide more opportunity for precise evaluation of the effect of verbal labels than does the earlier technique in which the judge uses his own notion of what a particular label means. Another feature of this experiment was an attempt to show that the briefer the time of original figure exposure, the stronger would be the influence of the label. Subjects first saw each figure for a 10-millisecond duration, then at 50 msc., and finally at 100 msc. Following each exposure the subject drew the figure. Although this serial technique seems to favor the appearance of a maximum effect of the labeling at 10 msc., the slight trend that was found was not statistically significant. This failure to find a decrease in the effect of the label with increasing exposure time is rather surprising. At the briefest time interval, 10 msc., one would expect a subject to see little or nothing of the stimulus. Under this condition the label should have a very large effect. On the other hand, the longest exposure, $\frac{1}{10}$ sec., should allow some determination of the response by the visual stimulus. The absence of a reliable trend suggests the possibility that under the labeling conditions the subjects were not influenced by the visual stimulus. To conclude, as the authors wished to, that the results show an interaction between perception of the visual stimulus and past experience with a stimulus class is therefore unjustified.

The next investigators to study the effect of language on reproduction, Herman, Lawless, and Marshall (1957), showed more clearly that variation in exposure times influences the effect of verbal labeling. Using somewhat longer exposure intervals than Bruner *et al.*, they were able to show that when the stimulus is exposed for two seconds or one second, the effect of the verbal label is greater than when the figure is exposed for five seconds. Although the general procedures of this experiment are much closer to those of Carmichael *et al.* than to those of Bruner *et al.*, and hence lack some of the technical niceties of the latter study, there are three other interesting findings of the study that merit mention. First they showed that although the labeling of a figure by the experimenter changed the reproductions to conform to the label, the control group that received no labeling made almost as many changes that conformed to the labels as did the experimental groups. Apparently, the ratings of these investigators were more sensitive than those of Carmichael *et al.*, who did not find such shifts in the control conditions.

Herman, Lawless, and Marshall ran another group of subjects who were shown the figures and were merely told to write the word or phrase which came to mind. Sixty-three per cent of the responses were judged to be like the labels from the word lists of Carmichael *et al.* Even when the experimenter does not supply a label that results in the functioning of some norm, the subject may supply the label. In reproduction, the response of the subject is presumably determined in part by the reaction to the specific instance just seen, and in part by the reaction elicited by the label—including an implicit label the subject himself may give. A final finding of Herman, Lawless, and Marshall was that labels exert a greater influence on reproduction if the subjects are not told they will be expected to draw the figures than if they are. The implication is that close inspection of the figure can reduce the influence of the label.

The import of the various studies of the effects of verbal labels on reproduction memory is that the giving of the label by the experimenter results in the subject reproducing a figure that is like some sort of average figure with which he has associated the label in the past. Since the most recently seen figure with which the label has been associated is the experimenter's drawing, this figure might be expected to exert a stronger influence on the reproduction than figures or instances seen at more remote times. But with the passage of time the effects of the earlier instances exert a greater and greater influence, thus resulting in progressive changes. This assertion is very similar to the generalization known as Jost's Second Law, which has received some empirical support from studies of verbal learning. Jost's Second Law states that if two associations are now of equal strength but of different ages, the older one will lose strength more slowly with the further passage of time (see McGeoch, 1946, p. 140).

This alleged action of an associative habit resulting in the subject drawing an approximation of the typical case would certainly be more easily accepted if there were specific evidence that drawn reproductions converge on a norm with the passage of time. In a study by Postman (1954) the reasonableness of such memory changes as a result of the influence of norms has been amply demonstrated.

THE EFFECT OF TRAINING.   Postman's purpose was to investigate the way in which learning a set of rules for the construction of pairs of figures influences the memory for figures that conform to the rules and for those which violate the rules. The figures used in the experiments are shown in Figure 73. On the left are "code" items and on the right are "breakdown" items. It will be seen that all breakdown pairs are recombinations of the code pairs. The first two breakdown pairs for each design are formed by taking part of the left-hand code figure and adding it to the right-hand code figure. The other two breakdown pairs are formed

FIGURE 73. Stimuli from L. Postman's experiment, "Learned Principles of Organization in Memory," *Psychol. Monogr.*, 1954, 68, No. 374. Used by permission of the American Psychological Association.

in the opposite way. Prior to the memorizing and testing of a set of breakdown figures, different subjects were given one of four kinds of preliminary training. In Condition I (code training), subjects were given explicit instructions in how the breakdown pairs are all regroupings of the parts of the code pairs. In addition to such instruction the subjects were also given practice trials in which they were shown each breakdown pair and then required to draw both the breakdown pair and the code pair from memory. In Condition II (pair training), subjects saw and drew the same breakdown pairs as in Condition I, but they received no code training. In Condition III (code transfer training), subjects received code training on all codes as in Condition I, but the training was restricted to two of the breakdown pairs for each code. In Condition IV (figure training), subjects received training on the items, but received neither code training nor training on which pairs belonged together.

In Experiment I, following the pretraining, all subjects were given a serial learning task in which twenty-four of the breakdown items were to be committed to memory in a set serial order. After a given number of trials, subjects were asked to reproduce as many of the items as they could. In this test of memory, subjects in Condition I (code training), II (pair training), and IV (figure training) did about equally well. Subjects in Condition III (code transfer training), who learned different items from those they had practiced in pretraining, performed less well. Subjects in Condition I were less prone to commit errors that violated the rules of code construction than were the subjects in other conditions.

Experiment II investigated change in memory over a period of time. Only pretraining Conditions I and II were compared. Following the pretraining and memorization task, different groups of subjects were given reproduction tests for immediate memory, after one day, after one week, and after two weeks. The memorization task, while similar to Experiment I, differed in that some of the items which were memorized violated the rules for code construction that had been employed in the pretraining. Postman's results are shown in Figure 74. The term "normal" in the title of Figure 74 means that the results concern only the correct reproduction of figures conforming to the principles of the code. The other results were tabulated separately. Two points should be mentioned. First, there is a considerable amount of forgetting. Second, the interaction between the two curves is statistically reliable. The code condition is inferior until the two-week interval, when it first becomes superior. Apparently, this superiority of Condition II arises from the presence of the code-violating items in the memorization task. These items are more disruptive to performance and to memory in the code group than in the non-code group. However, as more and more items are forgotten with the passage of time, the code training of the subjects in Condition I aids in the reproduction of the figures, and this condition finally equals or even exceeds the other one. The other results of the experiment are consistent with such an interpretation. For example, in both conditions some errors in reproduction occurred when the subjects modified their reproduction of a code-violating figure so as to conform to the code. This sort of error was always greater in Condition I than in Condition II. Furthermore, the frequency of this type of error increased with the passage of time in Condition I, but in Condition II it reached a peak at seven days and then declined. The implication is that the memory of the specific figure is forgotten more rapidly than the memory of the code. Hence the code comes to determine the nature of the reproduction more and more as time passes.

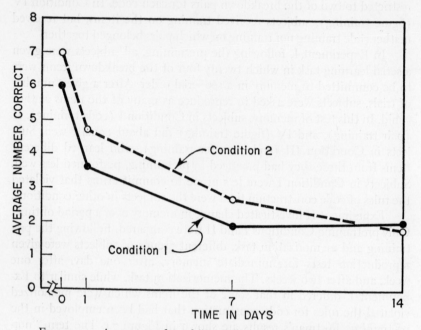

FIGURE 74. Average number of "normal" figures correctly reproduced by the two groups in Postman's Experiment 2. (From "Learned Principles of Organization in Memory," Psychol. Monogr., 1954, 68, No. 374. Used by permission of the American Psychological Association.)

Postman's conclusions in Experiment II summarize his argument:

Our findings support Woodworth's view that changes in the reproduction of designs depend both on the amount of "true forgetting" since the end of training, and on the habits and skills with which the subject enters the retention situation. The poorer the memory for the specific details of the original figures, the greater is the weight of these habits and skills in determining the reproductions. In this experiment, we have manipulated, under controlled conditions, the habits which the subject could bring to bear on the reproductions. These manipulations resulted in systematic and progressive changes in the reproductions. No appeal to the "development of the memory trace in accordance with principles of organization" is necessary to account for these findings. On the contrary, our results show that progressive memory changes can be built into the subject by giving him information concerning the nature of the stimuli and by teaching him rules for organizing these stimuli. When called upon to reproduce a form which he cannot clearly recall, S uses this information and applies these rules just as he uses whatever drawing skills he has in reproducing the figures. *The changes in performance over time can be fully accounted for in terms of learned responses without recourse to autonomous changes in a hypothetical trace field.*[3]

In a third experiment Postman demonstrated that code training also made memorized items more resistant to retroactive inhibition than the pair training without the code training. Such a result would be predicted from an associationist interpretation of the change in memory with the passage of time, for contemporary association theory regards an interval of time between learning and retention as merely a way of introducing interpolated activity into the situation and a way of permitting proactive effects to develop.

Postman's experiments do not prove that the memory changes observed by Crumbaugh, by Karlin and Brennan, and by Walker and Veroff were instances of behavior controlled by a previously established norm. What they do show is that previously established habits can determine changes in reproduction memory over a period of time. The next question is clear. Can techniques of the sort developed by Postman be applied to the problem of recognition memory? Will figures of the sort used by Crumbaugh and others show modification in memory when artificial norms have been established?

A REVIEW OF THE HISTORY OF RESEARCH ON CHANGES IN MEMORY FOR FORM

ONE MAJOR TREND characterizes the development of research on memory for form. This trend is an increasing methodological sophistication on the part of experimenters attempting to test Wulf's original hypothesis about autonomous change in the memory trace. A second trend that may be distinguished from the first is the developing emphasis on the alternative associationist accounts of such changes. Although many of the studies that have been discussed bear on both these developments, the two trends may be considered separately. We shall begin with method.

After Wulf's study the first important improvements in the test for autonomous change were to be found in Allport's experiment. His basic contributions were the reduction in the number of stimuli that the subject was shown, and the introduction of objective methods for assessing change in reproduction. It is rather surprising to note that none of the studies conducted during the following decade equaled Allport's study

[3] From L. Postman, "Learned Principles of Organization in Memory," *Psychol. Monogr.*, 1954, 68, No. 374. Used by permission of the American Psychological Association.

in reducing the number of stimulus figures used, although several of the studies explicitly tested the hypothesis of autonomous change.

The next development was Zangwill's attempt to test for both reproduction and recognition, a procedure that was stimulated by Koffka's discussion of the problem in 1935. The ingenious notion of using the subject's own reproductions in a recognition test has not been repeated in combination with other recent improvements. It seems likely, however, that such a study will be carried out in the future.

In the same year as Zangwill's study, Hanawalt demonstrated that each reproduction influences the following reproductions. This critical fact forced a reinterpretation of the previous studies of temporal changes in memory, and changed the nature of almost all the subsequent research on the problem. Hanawalt's failure to find progressive change under his single-reproduction condition cast doubt on previous findings which had found evidence for a progressive change in the trace. Another methodological contribution of considerable importance was Hanawalt's discovery of the role of drawing errors in the determination of reproductive change. Clearly, no claim of a change in memory could be made unless the magnitude of drawing errors could be assessed.

Irwin and Seidenfeld's paper, which also appeared in 1937, set the stage for much subsequent research. They were the first investigators to use simple psychophysical procedures to assess memory change. Although the method of identical stimuli has not been universally used in subsequent studies, the considerable simplification of the measures of memory change in all subsequent work undoubtedly reflects the contribution of this paper.

The next landmark in the refinement of method in the search for autonomous change was Hebb and Foord's paper which they published in 1945. Except for their failure to use the method of identical stimuli, these investigators succeeded in incorporating most of the improvements of their predecessors. Each subject saw only two figures which were deliberately selected to test the Gestalt hypothesis. Each subject was given only one recognition test, and each was required to judge only one aspect of the stimulus. The dimensions to be judged were not easily remembered by means of a verbal label. The failure to find any evidence for progressive change under what appeared to be highly favorable conditions was considered a major blow to the Gestalt theory of autonomous change. George and Carlson and Duncan extended and refined Hebb and Foord's technique but did not change the main conclusions reached by Hebb and Foord.

The next major improvement in method occurred in the experiments by Crumbaugh in which the method of identical stimuli was first fully exploited as a psychophysical technique. Each subject judged only one property of one stimulus pattern. As in a psychophysical experiment, the "standard" (the first exposure of the stimulus) and the "variable" (the second exposure of the same stimulus) were shown many times. The experimental variable was the time between the two exposures. Crumbaugh's other innovation was the use of an extremely short range of time intervals—between immediate succession and twelve seconds. His finding of reliable changes in the memory of certain properties of the figures he used is a tribute to the sensitivity of his method. Karlin and Brennan substantiated Crumbaugh's finding of change in the memory of the size of a fifteen-degree gap in a circle; the gap was remembered as wider than it had actually been.

Finally, Lovibond has recently explored the possibility of using yet another psychophysical method, the adjustment method, in studying changes in the memory for form.

It appears clear from the experiments of Crumbaugh and of Karlin and Brennan that it is possible to demonstrate changes in the memory for form, even when the experimenter does not introduce special training procedures either before or with the memory tests. As we have already indicated, however, these demonstrations cannot be taken as proof of the hypothesis of autonomous change.

The second trend in the history of research on memory for form is the increasing explicitness of an alternative interpretation of memory change. Although the general hypothesis of "true" forgetting and assimilation to other forms antedated Wulf by some time, the experimental attempts to demonstrate the action of such factors really seem to start with the work of Carmichael, Hogan, and Walter. These writers were careful to point out that their results did not disprove the hypothesis of autonomous change. But their work did indicate the possibility that changes identical in nature with those that might be expected from the theory of autonomous change might be produced by labeling. Hanawalt and Demarest, who showed that labeling introduced at the time of the memory test could influence the nature of the reproduction, extended the applicability of the hypothesis. Although such evidence hardly disproves the theory of autonomous change, in an indirect way the finding damages the changing-trace hypothesis. If a verbal label can produce such a change when introduced at the time of the retention test, there is no need to assume any change in a trace other than weakening of the memory. Changes may be assumed to occur because of the contribution of two types of response tendency to the final reproduction: that aroused by the instructions to draw the original figure, and that aroused by the assertion that the original figure looked like a "————."

The reasonableness of this interpretation is most clearly revealed in Postman's experiments. He showed that learned ways of classifying stimuli according to certain rules of organization could later influence the direction of memory change and the resistance to memory change in retention and retroactive-inhibition experiments. The learned principle of organization serves the same function as the process aroused by labeling in other experiments. Again, no claim is made that the results of these experiments refute the hypothesis of an autonomously changing trace. Rather, the results suggest that the concept is superfluous, since the types of changes predicted by the Gestalt theory can clearly be accounted for in other ways.

Is the hypothesis of autonomous change testable? Perhaps two different approaches to this question should be briefly considered. First, can further experiments of the kind conducted by Crumbaugh possibly confirm the Gestalt hypothesis? It would seem that the answer must be no. For, even when progressive changes are demonstrated, it is now clear that such a change may occur because of some previously existing norm, or a habitual mode of response. On the other hand, if autonomous change does not occur under some particular set of circumstances, one may argue that these are not the proper circumstances for producing autonomous change.

Why is it that the associative hypothesis does seem testable while the hypothesis of autonomous change does not? The answer appears to be that the factors that determine the presence or absence of the hypothesized associative dispositions determining the degree of change in the reproduced form can be manipulated by the experimenter. But there is no obvious way of manipulating the hypothesized autochthonous forces that, according to Gestalt theory, control autonomous change. To be sure, one can probably show that some figures are more susceptible to change in memory than are others. In the adult human subject, however, the lack of control over the subject's background makes a clear test of the hypothesis impossible.

The second approach would be to consider other kinds of experiments that have not yet been applied to this problem. One possibility would be to use visually naive animals in some type of one-trial learning experiment. The animal would then be expected at some later time to demonstrate by a discriminative response the change in memory. Although one might be able to spell out the details of such an experiment, the technical problems appear so formidable that one would immediately inquire about the chances of finding some effect. The decision would, of course, depend on one's theoretical persuasions. If one were convinced by the Gestalt argument, the problem of working out the technical details might be a fascinating challenge. For most associationists, pursuit of this problem might appear a questionable investment of time.

Still another possible approach to the problem of autonomous change would be to consider ways of more directly controlling or measuring the activity of the cortex in its relationship to memory. Various experiments that have attempted to interfere with the electrical field that the Gestalt psychologist assumes controls perception and memory have yielded negative results (Lashley, Chow, and Semmes, 1951; Sperry and Miner, 1955; Sperry, Miner, and Myers, 1955). Similarly, what little is known about the effect of direct electrical stimulation of the cortex on memory suggests that stimulation of very restricted locations is capable of arousing elaborate memories (Hebb, 1949, p. 15). While it is too soon to make final judgments about so complex an issue as this, findings of this sort do not appear to support Gestalt conceptions of energy distributions over substantial areas of the cortex.

We started our discussion of memory for form with a description of a new hypothesis that had developed from Gestalt theory. The confirmation of this hypothesis was announced in an experiment which in retrospect offers little support for any specific hypothesis. Nevertheless, a series of experiments was undertaken to test this hypothesis by improving on the original experiment. As we have seen, the improvements were numerous, but the experiments that were adequate from a standpoint of method did not appear for about thirty years. Now the question is whether the Gestalt hypothesis is even testable—at least by the methods that have been employed. If not, does this suggest that the experiments done were a waste of time? Should psychologists spend more time thinking and less time doing experiments? There is probably no satisfactory way of answering. But questions do seem to become clearer in the course of experimentation and fact collection. Experiments are not merely a way of testing hypotheses, but they are also a way of becoming more clear about what questions should be asked and about questions which seem to lead nowhere. The present series of experiments has served this purpose well. Perhaps we are now in a position to ask further questions about memory with a greater likelihood of getting clear answers than in the past.

REFERENCES

ALLPORT, G. W.   Change and decay in the visual memory image. *Brit. J. Psychol.*, 1930, 21, 138–48.

BROWN, W.   Growth of memory images. *Amer. J. Psychol.*, 1935, 47, 90–102.

BRUNER, J. S., BUSIEK, R. D., AND MINTURN, A. L.   Assimilation in the immediate reproduction of visually perceived forms. *J. exp. Psychol.*, 1952, 44, 151–5.

CARLSON, J. B., AND DUNCAN, C. P.   A study of autonomous change in the memory trace by the method of recognition. *Amer. J. Psychol.*, 1955, 68, 280–4.

CARMICHAEL, L., HOGAN, H. P., AND WALTER, A. A.   An experimental study of the effect of language on the reproduction of visually perceived form. *J. exp. Psychol.*, 1932, 15, 73–86.

CRUMBAUGH, J. C.   Temporal changes in the memory of visually perceived form. *Amer. J. Psychol.*, 1954, 67, 647–58.

ELLIS, W. D.   *Source book of Gestalt psychology*, New York: The Humanities Press, 1950.

GEORGE, F. H.   Errors of visual recognition. *J. exp. Psychol.*, 1952, 43, 202–6.

GIBSON, J. J.   The reproduction of visually perceived forms. *J. exp. Psychol.*, 1929, 12, 1–39.

GOLDMEIER, E.   Progressive changes in memory traces. *Amer. J. Psychol.*, 1941, 54, 490–503.

HANAWALT, N. G.   Memory trace for figures in recall and recognition. *Arch. Psychol.*, 1937, No. 216.

————.   The method of comparison applied to the problem of memory change. *J. exp. Psychol.*, 1952, 43, 37–42.

HANAWALT, N. G. AND DEMAREST, I. H.   The effect of verbal suggestion in the recall period upon the reproduction of visually perceived forms. *J. exp. Psychol.*, 1939, 25, 159–74.

HEBB, D. O.   *The organization of behavior*. New York: John Wiley and Sons, 1949.

HEBB, D. O., AND FOORD, E. N.   Errors of visual recognition and the nature of the trace. *J. exp. Psychol.*, 1945, 35, 335–48.

HERMAN, D. T., LAWLESS, R. H., AND MARSHALL, R. W.   Variables in the effect of language on the reproduction of visually perceived forms. *Perceptual and motor skills*, 1957, 7, 171–86.

HILGARD, E. R.   *Theories of learning*. New York: Appleton-Century-Crofts, 1948.

IRWIN, F. W., AND ROVNER, H.   Further study of the method of comparison applied to the problem of memory changes. *J. exp. Psychol.*, 1937, 21, 533–44.

IRWIN, F. W., AND SEIDENFELD, M. A.   The application of the method of comparison to the problem of memory change. *J. exp. Psychol.*, 1937, 21, 363–81.

KARLIN, L., AND BRENNAN, G.   Memory for visual figures by the method of identical stimuli. *Amer. J. Psychol.*, 1957, 70, 248–53.

KOFFKA, K.   *Principles of Gestalt psychology*. New York: Harcourt, Brace, and Co., 1935.

LASHLEY, K. S., CHOW, K. L., AND SEMMES, J.   An examination of the electrical field theory of cerebral integration. *Psychol. Rev.*, 1951, 58, 123–36.

LOVIBOND, S. H.   A further test of the hypothesis of autonomous memory trace change. *J. exp. Psychol.*, 1958, 55, 412–15.

MCGEOCH, J. A. *The psychology of human learning*. New York: Longmans, Green, and Co., 1946.

PERKINS, F. T. Symmetry in visual recall. *Amer. J. Psychol.*, 1932, 44, 473–90.

POSTMAN, L. Learned principles of organization in memory. *Psychol. Monogr.*, 1954, 68, No. 374.

PRENTICE, W. C. H. Visual recognition of verbally labeled figures. *Amer. J. Psychol.*, 1954, 67, 315–20.

SEIDENFELD, M. A. Time as a factor in the recognition of visually perceived figures. *Amer. J. Psychol.*, 1938, 51, 64–82.

SPERRY, R. W., MINER, N., AND MYERS, R. E. Visual pattern perception following subpial slicing and tantalum wire implantations in the visual cortex. *J. comp. physiol. Psychol.*, 1955, 48, 50–8.

SPERRY, R. W., AND MINER, N. Pattern perception following insertion of mica plates into visual cortex. *J. comp. physiol. Psychol.*, 1955, 48, 463–9.

TENNIES, L. G. Memory trace and perception in the blind. *J. exp. Psychol.*, 1942, 30, 23–39.

WALKER, E. L., AND VEROFF, J. Changes in the memory-trace for perceived forms with successive reproductions. *Amer. J. Psychol.*, 1956, 69, 395–402.

WOODWORTH, R. S. *Experimental psychology*. New York: Henry Holt, 1938.

WULF, F. Uber die Veränderung von Vorstellungen. *Psych. Forsch.*, 1922, 1, 333–73.

ZANGWILL, O. L. An investigation of the relationship between the process of reproducing and recognizing simple figures with special reference to Koffka's trace theory. *Brit. J. Psychol.*, 1937, 27, 250–76.

PART III

Individual Differences & Personality

CHAPTER 8

The Nature & Measurement
of Intelligence

READ D. TUDDENHAM

*Progress in science is governed by
the laws of repulsion; every step forward is made by
refutation of prevalent errors and false theories.*

FROM *Dr. Zhivago,* BY BORIS PASTERNAK

EBBINGHAUS [1] ONCE REMARKED that psychology has a long past but a
short history. He might have made the same comment with even greater
cogency about one of psychology's problems—the nature of intelligence.
Its past stretches back to the ancient Greeks who speculated about the
soul. Its history, as an area of scientific investigation, began less than
three quarters of a century ago, a decade or more after Wundt founded
his famous laboratory at Leipzig in 1879 and inaugurated the modern
era in psychology. The phrase "mental test" was first used in an American journal in 1890. The first crude intelligence test of the current type,
that of Binet, appeared only in 1905. The word "intelligence" is itself a
relatively recent term in psychological literature, rarely encountered before the opening of the present century. As Wechsler notes (1958, p. 3),
it did not rate a separate entry in Baldwin's encyclopedic *Dictionary of*

---

[1] Ebbinghaus (1850–1909) was a German psychologist famous for his monumental investigation of memory, published in 1885.

469

Philosophy and Psychology, published in 1901, but was given merely as an alternate to, or synonym of, intellect. Writers of textbooks seldom treated the topic, as Spearman complained.

> Right up to the present day a large number—perhaps even the majority—of the best accredited textbooks on psychology do not so much as mention the word "intelligence" from cover to cover.[2]

Considering the recency of the idea, interest in intelligence and in intelligence testing has grown at a phenomenal rate. On the basis of such tests, one and three quarters million soldiers were classified and assigned in World War I and another four million in World War II. Hardly a child has emerged from our school systems in the last twenty-five years without having his intelligence "measured," and oftentimes important educational and vocational decisions have hinged on the outcome. Business and industry have shaped their personnel policies to results of tests. The very phrase "intelligence quotient" and its symbol "IQ" have become household terms. In perhaps no other area has psychology had so much impact upon society at large, nor aroused such intense curiosity.

You, the reader, have probably had questions about it: "How intelligent am I, compared with my family, my friends, and my fellows?" "Am I intelligent enough to succeed in my vocation?" "Can I increase my intelligence?" You may have speculated as well about problems of broader social import: "Is intelligence inherited and unchangeable, or can it be modified by the environment?" "Are men more intelligent than women—or vice versa?" "Are some races inferior to others in intelligence?" "Does intelligence continue growing or does it decline in maturity?"

These are questions of the greatest importance, but the answers all depend upon a more fundamental issue: "What are we to mean by intelligence?" Psychologists have carried on a tremendous amount of research to answer such questions, but they can give no settled reply to any of them, because they have never been able to agree upon the basic meaning of the word. Writing in 1958, David Wechsler put the matter thus:

> Some psychologists have come to doubt whether these laborious analyses have contributed anything fundamental to our understanding of intelligence while others have come to the equally disturbing conclusion that the term intelligence, as now employed, is so ambiguous that it ought to be discarded altogether. Psychology now seems to find itself in the paradoxical position of devising and advocating tests for

[2] From C. Spearman, *The Nature of "Intelligence" and the Principles of Cognition,* 1923, p. 2, and used by permission of St. Martin's Press and The Macmillan Company, New York.

measuring intelligence and then disclaiming responsibility for them by asserting that "nobody knows what the word really means." [3]

Perhaps in consequence of the brief time span involved, it is harder to perceive the historical ebb and flow of alternative interpretations in the domain of intelligence than, for example, in that of brain localization (see Chap. 2). Rather, there has been a more or less continuous Donnybrook of rival views in which any number of theorists could and did join in. Meanwhile, more pragmatic psychologists have gone purposefully ahead testing millions without too much concern for the fray that raged around them, or for the charge that they were not really measuring intelligence at all.

How did these things come about? This chapter is devoted to an account of developments both in theory and in practice for the last seventy years. Since a mental test necessarily reflects the theoretical position (or lack of one) of its author, the nature and measurement of intelligence will be considered together. But first let us consider some of the antecedent developments which paved the way for intelligence testing.

Nineteenth-century Influences Which Shaped the Modern Approaches to Intelligence and Its Measurement

It is always hard to point to the source of an idea, for even the freshest of innovators is influenced by those who went before. The beginnings of our topic are lost in the mists of history, but the writings of Plato (429–348 b.c.) and Aristotle (384–322 b.c.) which have survived make it clear that elaborate theories of human nature were already worked out four centuries before Christ. Typical of the times was Aristotle, who postulated the existence of multiple souls to explain the behavior of men and animals which he observed, and to account for his own thoughts and dreams. The lowest soul presided over purely vegetative functions shared by all living things. Members of the animal kingdom possessed additionally a motive soul, responsible for movements of the body. Men alone possessed the highest soul, *nous*, or "intellect," which controlled reason.

The Greek theories did not survive long in their original form, but they profoundly influenced Christian thought. For example, *nous*, derived from the Greeks, became the theologians' soul and can be traced in one form or another down through the Medieval churchmen, through Descartes, to widely held religious beliefs of our own times. However, *nous* or intellect, thus viewed, was a *common* property of men which distinguished them from animals.

[3] From D. Wechsler, *The Measurement and Appraisal of Adult Intelligence*, 1958, p. 4, and used by permission of the author and Williams and Wilkins, Baltimore.

For more than two thousand years the focus was upon typifying *man* as a species rather than upon differentiating among particular men. Societies in which one's status and occupation were fixed by the level of one's birth had little use for the study of individual differences, and it did not occur to most men to concern themselves with the problem. The few who did sometimes came to regret it. For example, Beaumarchais' witty plays, "The Barber of Seville" and "The Marriage of Figaro" were branded subversive by Louis XVI's ministers because they implied that a low-born barber might be brighter than his noble master.

At the close of the eighteenth century, time ran out for the old order. The intellectual ferment which found expression in the American and French revolutions encouraged new interests and new ideas, some of them crucial for our topic.

Developments in France

In France, Franklin's experiments in electricity and magnetism fostered an interest in science which Mesmer exploited in his "animal magnetism" seances (see Chap. 12). Mesmer himself was later discredited, but his work focused attention on the phenomena of hypnosis, suggestibility, and abnormal psychology generally. Through the subsequent decades of the nineteenth century, European thinking on these topics was dominated by a succession of great French figures—Séguin, Bernheim, Liébault, Charcot, and Janet. Kraepelin, the German psychiatric taxonomist, and Sigmund Freud, the Austrian founder of psychoanalysis, both studied extensively in France and were influenced by French points of view.

Interest in the science of education, especially education of the defective, was stimulated by Itard, whose attempt during the first decade of the nineteenth century to train the famous Wild Boy of Aveyron (cf. Humphrey and Humphrey, 1932) was followed with great interest for its bearing upon Rousseau's doctrine that natural man is innately good until corrupted by society. Most significant for later developments was the publication in 1838 of a two-volume work, *Des Maladies mentales*, by Esquirol (1772–1840). He was the first to differentiate between the insane (i.e., dements) who had lost the wits they once possessed, and the feeble-minded (i.e., aments), who had never had many. In an age dominated by the anatomical preoccupations of the phrenologists (cf. Chap. 2), Esquirol proposed a functional, psychological criterion for classifying the feeble-minded into grades depending upon their use of language. This line of development culminated in Alfred Binet (1857–1911), the inventor of the first successful intelligence tests, of whom we shall have much to say later.

In sum, the French kept interest alive in psychopathology and mental deficiency, but they were primarily clinicians rather than experimentalists. It is doubtful whether the French tradition alone would have led to the quantitative approach and the emphasis upon controlled, standard procedures which characterize modern intelligence tests. Developments along these latter lines represent the influence of a different tradition in nineteenth-century psychology, that of the German experimentalists.

Developments in Germany

Curiously, the first experiments upon individual differences in a psychological function were made by an astronomer, Friedrich Wilhelm Bessel (1784–1846). Bessel had read of the dismissal in 1796 of an assistant at the Greenwich observatory near London for being nearly a second slower than his superior in observing the transits of stars used to check the accuracy of clocks.[4] Beginning around 1820, Bessel experimented upon himself and other astronomers, and found considerable variation among individuals in speed of response. The investigation of "reaction time" was carried forward and elaborated by German physiological psychologists during the next fifty years, and became a major concern of Wundt's laboratory at Leipzig. It was learned that reaction time is influenced by many factors, e.g., by the sensory modality concerned, by the intensity of the stimulus, and by whether the instructions set the subject to concentrate upon the stimulus or upon his own response. Wundt even went so far as to attempt to measure the time intervals required by the mind to perceive, to discriminate, and to associate, by noting differences in reaction time for tasks presumably involving different combinations of these complex activities.

Wundt's mental chronometry has long been discredited. Yet he and other German workers laid one cornerstone of the mental-test movement and of modern psychology in general by transferring the investigation of the mind from the realm of speculative philosophy to that of empirical science, and quantitative science at that! Further, their discovery that small-appearing differences in experimental conditions could lead to large differences in results sensitized the intelligence testers of a later day to the necessity of providing for their instruments the most complete specification of test materials, instructions, and scoring standards.

---

[4] The determination of longitude requires precise knowledge of the time. Hence, ships' chronometers were checked by the observatory, and the importance of their accuracy to a seafaring nation could hardly be overestimated. Exact observatory time was measured by noting to the nearest tenth second the time at which a star whose movements were known crossed the hairline in a telescope eyepiece. The human nervous system, before Bessel's work, was assumed to react instantaneously. Hence tardiness in reporting a star transit could only be a matter of careless inattention.

Nevertheless, the German tradition was fundamentally uninterested in, if not unsympathetic to the study of individual differences. In the astronomical context in which Bessel initiated reaction-time research, differences between subjects or within a single subject on different occasions were *errors* which reduced the precision with which physical events could be observed. German psychologists took the same view. They sought to learn the fundamental laws that govern the mind. Differences among particular minds were hindrances in studying the typical behavior of man as a species. Much of the ingenuity expended in providing strict control of all the situational variables in an experiment had as its goal eliminating, or at least minimizing, differences among subjects. One fundamental requisite for the modern developments in studying intelligence was still lacking—*a positive interest in individual differences for their own sake.* The British evolutionists supplied it.

Developments in England

Charles Darwin (1809–82) is known to all students as the father of the doctrine of evolution. The fundamental ideas were not all original with him, and time has altered our conceptions of some of the mechanisms involved. Nevertheless, the massive and painstaking documentation which he provided crushed rational, if not theological, opposition to the central idea.

Basic to the operation of evolution by natural selection—the "survival of the fittest"—was the occurrence of variations from which nature might select. The measurement of such variations among the individual members of a species became an absorbing pursuit of the evolutionists. The study of man was not neglected. Investigations of psychological variability under the impetus of evolutionary theory were concerned not only with pathological extremes—the feeble-minded, the psychotic, etc., which had most interested the French—but with the entire range from subnormal to supernormal.

The quantitative description of such variations received much attention from Darwin's cousin, the brilliant and versatile Francis Galton (1822–1911), best known as the founder of eugenics (see Chap. 4). Between 1884 and 1890, Galton maintained a laboratory at the South Kensington Museum where, for a three-penny fee, interested visitors could have themselves measured on a wide variety of anthropometric and simple psychological tests. Height, weight, arm span, breath volume, strength, color vision, hearing acuity, reaction time, etc. were recorded for nearly 10,000 persons. To summarize his data, Galton had recourse to the statistical methods of Quetelet, a Belgian statistician who had first applied to human beings the laws of probability derived earlier in connection with games of chance. The following quotations reflect both

Galton's enthusiasm for the study of variability and the charm which pervades his writing:

> It is difficult to understand why statisticians commonly limit their inquiries to averages, and do not revel in more comprehensive views. Their souls seem as dull to the charm of variety as that of the native of one of our flat English counties, whose retrospect of Switzerland was that, if its mountains could be thrown into its lakes, two nuisances would be got rid of at once [1889, p. 62].

Or again, on his discovery of lawfulness in frequency distributions:

> I know of scarcely anything so apt to impress the imagination as the wonderful form of cosmic order expressed by the "Law of Frequency of Error." The law would have been personified by the Greeks and deified, if they had known of it. It reigns with serenity and in complete self-effacement amidst the wildest confusion. The huger the mob and the greater the apparent anarchy, the more perfect is its sway. It is the supreme law of Unreason. Whenever a large sample of chaotic elements are taken in hand and marshalled in the order of their magnitude, an unsuspected and most beautiful form of regularity proves to have been latent all along [p. 66].

This discovery led Galton to the realization that a man's position on a variable can be specified wholly relativistically, i.e., by his position in a statistical frequency distribution of other men. Apparently, Galton was unaware of the tremendous importance of this conception. Since all his tests could be scored in physical units—inches, cubic centimeters, foot-pounds, seconds, etc.—he did not need to develop purely statistical scales such as percentile ranks or standard scores. Yet in measuring functions which lack a physical scale, for example intelligence, there is no alternative to statistical scaling. Modern mental tests from the Army Alpha of 1917 to the Wechsler Adult Intelligence Scale (WAIS) of 1956 characterize a person essentially according to his position relative to other men measured on the same test, the actual scale units being usually derived from certain features of the frequency distribution of crude scores.

There is, to be sure, another important class of intelligence tests, especially those designed for children, which evaluate an individual child not by describing his position in a distribution of his peers, but rather by determining the *age* at which the performance of the average child just equals the performance of the child in question. This procedure, exploited by Binet, may also owe something to evolutionary theory. On the anatomical evidence Darwin was led to the formulation beloved of charade-players—"ontogeny recapitulates phylogeny." This is simply to say that the evolutionary history of a species is reflected in the sequence of development of the individual members of that species; thus the gills which characterize a certain embryonic stage among air-breathing mammals are evidence for their evolution from fishlike marine ancestors. From studying embryological structure, it was a short step to seek for sequential stages in the *behavior* of infants and children, e.g., in loco-motor patterns, which could throw light on the nature of our most ancient forebears. Darwin kept a diary of such observations of his own son. By Binet's time the basic idea was well established that children vary in the age at which they acquire a particular bit of behavior, but that the *order* of acquisition of the successive stages of development is quite invariant, a fact upon which the concept of mental level is based. Thus the two fundamental patterns of statistical scaling found in modern intelligence tests, the deviation scale and the age scale, involve ideas formulated by the British evolutionists.

MENTAL TESTING IN THE UNITED STATES: THE FIRST PHASE (1890–1905)

FOR THE CONVERGENCE of German experimental methodology and British interest in individual differences, our account must now turn to the United States. The starting point is J. McKeen Cattell (1860–1944), who in 1890 published an article entitled "Mental Tests and Measurements," apparently the first use of the term.

Contributions of J. McKeen Cattell

Cattell was an American who studied in Germany as a young man, learning there the techniques of the experimentalists and absorbing their concern for precision and control. He took his degree with Wundt in 1886, but his lifelong interest in individual differences allied him much more with Galton. During the twenty-six years that he headed the laboratory at Columbia University, he influenced a generation of students in the direction of differential psychology, though the potentialities for applying it to practical affairs probably made it congenial to the American temper anyhow.

Cattell's 1890 paper described the detailed procedure for a series of ten separate tests, as follows:

    I. Dynamometric pressure
   II. Rate of movement
  III. Sensation-areas (two-point dermal discrimination)
  IV. Pressure causing pain (threshold determination)
   V. Least noticeable difference in weight
  VI. Reaction time for sound
 VII. Time for naming colors
VIII. Bisection of a 50-cm. line

IX. Estimation of a 10-second interval

X. Number of letters remembered on once hearing

These tests, for some of which Cattell noted his debt to Galton, were "made on all who presented themselves." For psychology students, there was a longer list of fifty, mostly measures of sensory discrimination and grouped according to the sense modality involved.[5]

Cattell stated a rather ambitious purpose for his tests:

> Psychology cannot attain the certainty and exactness of the physical sciences unless it rests on a foundation of experiment and measurement. A step in this direction could be made by applying a series of mental tests and measurements to a large number of individuals. The results would be of considerable scientific value in discovering the constancy of mental processes, their interdependence, and their variation under different circumstances. Individuals, besides, would find their tests interesting, and, perhaps, useful in regard to training, mode of life or indication of disease [1890, p. 373].

Cattell then urged uniformity of procedure by different workers to enhance the comparability, and hence the scientific value, of their findings. The paper was followed with a brief commentary by Francis Galton, who sounded a modern note in emphasizing the importance of independent test validation:

> One of the most important objects of measurement is hardly at all alluded to here and should be emphasized. It is to obtain a general knowledge of the capacities of a man by sinking shafts, as it were, at a few critical points. In order to ascertain the best points for the purpose, the sets of measures should be compared with an independent estimate of the man's powers. We may thus learn which of the measures are the most instructive [p. 380].

In neither Cattell nor Galton was there any clear tendency to conceptualize intelligence as an entity, though Galton did refer to securing a "general knowledge" of capacities by a sort of sampling procedure. The tests they described were simple, discrete, and specific, and presumably the "powers" they measured were likewise.

American Enthusiasm for Tests, 1890–1900

The publication of Cattell's proposals was followed by a great deal of interest in mental testing. Many of the eminent American psycholo-

---

[5] In emphasizing discrimination, Cattell was in accord with Galton, who had justified such tests by appeal to Locke's theory: "The only information that reaches us concerning outward events appears to pass through the avenue of our senses; and the more perceptive the senses are of difference, the larger is the field upon which our judgment and intelligence can act" (1883, p. 27).

gists of the day made up tests of their own and used them to collect data. Jastrow introduced tests similar to Cattell's at the Columbian Exposition in Chicago in 1893. Franz Boas, at Clark, used tests on school children in 1891, as did Münsterberg at Harvard in 1891 and Gilbert at Yale in 1893. So great was the enthusiasm that a special committee was set up by the American Psychological Association in 1895 "to consider the feasibility of cooperation among the various psychological laboratories in the collection of mental and physical statistics." Another committee was formed in 1896 by the American Association for the Advancement of Science to organize an ethnographic survey of the white race in the United States, which would include a program of psychological testing.

Yet the academic interest in testing which seemed so flourishing in 1895 was moribund by 1905. G. M. Whipple's monumental *Manual of Mental and Physical Tests,* which appeared first in 1910, preserved the remains but did not resuscitate them. What had happened?

Reaction: the Studies of Wissler and Sharp

After so great an outburst of enthusiasm, a reaction was perhaps inevitable, especially since mental tests lay far afield from the concerns of such influential men as William James, the Harvard psychologist-philosopher, or E. B. Titchener, the Cornell introspectionist whose "mental measurements" concerned sensation. However, the heaviest blows were dealt by two research studies, one by Clark Wissler, the other by Stella Sharp.

Wissler's paper (1901) was based on some of Cattell's data. Utilizing the then new Pearson correlation method, Wissler reported in quantitative terms upon the consistency of the psychological tests with one another, with anthropometric measures (e.g., height, weight) and with college grades.

The results were disappointing. Physical measures showed a general tendency to correlate with one another, and the correlations among grades earned in different courses were also positive, ranging from .11 to .75. However, correlations between physical tests and college grades were low, and neither category showed much relation to Cattell's psychological tests. Most dismaying, the latter group failed even to correlate with each other, r's between different pairs ranging from −.28 to +.39—"little more than a mere chance relation." In the absence of correlations among them, Wissler could only conclude that each psychological test measured an independent ability. It followed that such tests had very limited value for predicting the useful capacities of the individual.

Sharp's study (1899) had a somewhat different orientation. It will be recalled that Cattell's tests were mostly of simple sensory functions which could be scored in precise physical units, e.g., seconds, centimeters, etc. Nevertheless, they were expected, on the basis of Locke's reasoning, to provide a sound basis for predicting the higher mental powers of individuals. There were other mental testers of the period, notably Münsterberg in this country and Oehrn, Kraepelin, Ebbinghaus, and Binet in Europe, who favored and actually invented tests to measure directly complex mental functions, such as judgment, reasoning, memory, imagination, and the like. Generally speaking, these psychologists were the heirs not of British Associationism but of the faculty psychology of the Continent, and in most cases they were interested in applied psychology and psychiatry.

Stella Sharp, a student in Titchener's laboratory at Cornell, set out to evaluate the claims made for tests of complex functions, particularly a set which had been described by Binet and Henri in 1896. Following Binet and Henri, Sharp included several tests for each complex function. For example, there were five tests of memory: for letter series, for digits, for word series, for sounds (several questions asking the subject about his memory for melody) and for sentences—such as, "The Chinese regard us as strictly just and truthful, and it is only when we disabuse them of that impression that they show us any disrespect." Other functions tested included imagery, imagination (based on responses to ink-blots), attention, etc.

Not only was each function assessed by several tests, but the tests were repeated several times,

> in order that it may be observed whether the variations in the different individuals maintain a constant relation to one another at various times, and consequently, under varying subjective conditions. . . . This necessitated of course a very large extension of the time beyond the limit allowed by the French investigators. . . . Since the experiments were of this detailed character, the number of subjects was necessarily restricted. . . . The subjects consisted of seven advanced students . . . , three men and four women, all of whom had had training in introspection. . . . [Sharp, 1899, p. 349].

Sharp's conclusions were carefully framed and fair, but created a negative impression.

> The results, we believe, have shown that while a large proportion of the tests require intrinsic modification or a more rigid control of conditions, others have really given such information as the Individual Psychologist seeks. . . . In general, however, a lack of correspondences in the individual differences observed in the various tests was quite as noticeable as their presence. . . . Whether the fact indicates a relative independence of the particular mental activities under investigation, or is due simply to superficiality of testing, can hardly be decided. While, however, we do not reject the latter possibility, we incline to

the belief that the former hypothesis is in a large proportion of cases the more correct.

But little result for morphological [i.e., introspective] psychology can be obtained from studies of the nature of the above investigation. So many part-processes are involved in complex activities, and the manner of their variation is so indefinite, that it is seldom possible to tell with certainty what part of the total result is due to any particular component. It is doubtful if even the most rigorous and exhaustive analysis of test results would yield information of importance as regards the structure of the mind. At all events, there is not the slightest reason to desert the current laboratory methods [i.e., Titchenerian introspection] for the "method of tests" [p. 389].

Sharp's recommendations for repetition on several occasions and for carefully controlled procedure reflected the scientific scrupulousness of experimental psychologists, but if taken seriously could only have rendered tests unfeasible for use outside the laboratory. Worse, the disappointing lack of self-consistency which the tests revealed made their empirical utility doubtful anyway. Most damaging from the point of view of the structural psychology of the day, the "method of tests" contributed little to the introspective analysis of the mind. Experimentalists might safely go back to measuring their "pure" sensations and perceptions, and philosophers return to their speculations.

On the original issue, to be sure, Sharp supported Binet, but this aspect of her work was lost sight of.

In fine, we concur with MM. Binet and Henri in believing that individual psychical differences should be sought for in the complex rather than in the elementary processes of mind, and that the test method is the most workable one that has yet been proposed for investigating these processes. The theory of the German psychologists, who hold that the simplest mental processes are those to which the investigator should look for a clue to all psychical differences existing among individuals, we believe would be productive of small, or at any rate, of comparatively unimportant results [p. 390.]

In retrospect, it is surprising that the Wissler and Sharp studies should have counted so heavily against the "method of tests." Wissler's tests were of the simple sensory variety which have never differentiated effectively among people except, perhaps, between normals and feeble-minded. Moreover, the criterion of college grades is itself so unreliable a measure of ability (as every mediocre student knows) that high correlations were scarcely to be expected. Most important of all, the subjects in both studies were advanced university students, highly selected and probably quite homogeneous in ability—and Sharp had only seven of them altogether. Nevertheless, the conclusions were taken as a condemnation of mental measurement. When modern intelligence tests were introduced a few years later, it was under non-academic auspices. University departments were often uninterested where they were not hostile.

ALFRED BINET AND THE BINET SCALES

ALFRED BINET (1857–1911) was a brilliant and original worker whose place in the history of psychology would be secure even if he had never originated the famous tests which bear his name.[6] Originally trained in medicine, he was the leading French psychologist of his day, founding with Beaunis (1830–1921) at the Sorbonne the first French psychological laboratory (1889) and the first French psychological journal, *L'Année psychologique* (1895).

Author of many books and articles, he was above all a tireless investigator. Few topics escaped his attention—literally from the psychic life of micro-organisms (1887) and insects (1894) to that of great calculators and chess players (1894); from head measurements (1901) and anthropometrics (1910) to perceptions of ink-blots (1896) and handwriting (1906). There is scarcely an area or type of approach in modern psychometrics of which it cannot be said "Binet was first," yet his wide-ranging investigations were the antithesis of superficial. His insight and inventiveness, combined with the most scrupulous care in observing and recording, make his studies still models of their kind. As Peterson remarked,

> Through all this search, Binet has shown a master's hand in discovering realities in human nature and in *letting facts lead*, rather than being determined by prejudice and theories.[7]

Nevertheless, Binet grew up in the French tradition of psychology. His own work reflected that tradition, not only narrowly, in his interest in psychopathology (which gradually faded out in favor of experimental psychology and pedagogy), but broadly, in clinical concern with the whole individual rather than with abstracted psychological dimensions. As a result, his studies had always a somewhat more pragmatic flavor than those of his British or German contemporaries.

Binet's "Individual Psychology"

Characteristically, Binet labeled his approach "individual psychology," and argued that the most important differences among individuals

---

[6] The evolution of Binet's philosophical and psychological views is thoroughly described in the monograph of Varon (1935).

[7] From J. Peterson, *Early Conceptions and Tests of Intelligence,* 1925, p. 149. Published by World Book Company, Yonkers, New York.

are to be found precisely in those higher mental activities, reasoning, judgment, and the like, which had seldom been studied, either because they could not be measured along physical dimensions or because they inseparably merged the supposedly elementary units of mental activity in which most psychologists were interested. The correctness of his view was confirmed by Stella Sharp, as we have seen. However, his major investigation of 1896 (with Henri) which Sharp repeated, reveals in Binet another facet of the French tradition, namely, its acceptance of the categories of the faculty psychologists as a basic point of departure for psychological analysis. To cover the field of individual psychology, Binet and Henri proposed several tests to measure each of eleven mental faculties, including memory, imagery, imagination, attention, comprehension, suggestibility, aesthetic appreciation, force of will (persistence), moral sentiments, motor skill, and judgment of visual space. Yet less than ten years later, Binet was able to abandon the faculty view altogether in his famous 1905 scale for measuring intellectual level.

During the decade between the two publications, Binet conducted a long series of investigations with children, both normal and defective, trying out empirically a great variety of tests for suggestibility, attention, sensory discrimination, memory, etc., to discover which ones showed the clearest relationship to age, to school attainment, and to teachers' estimates of mental ability. This work was notably careful and thorough, and gradually led Binet from a concern with tests which *should* measure one or another of the conventional faculties, to those which in fact *did* measure differences in intellectual level.

This work came to fruition when in 1904 the Minister of Public Instruction appointed a commission to study the measures to be taken to assure the benefits of education to defective children. As Binet tells us, the Commission decided to provide special schools for the purpose, and further

decided that no child suspected of retardation be eliminated from regular schools and admitted to a special school without having undergone a pedagogical and medical examination attesting that his intellectual state renders him unable to profit in the ordinary measure from the instruction given in regular schools.

But how to conduct the examination of each child? What methods to follow? What observations to make? What questions to ask? What tests to invent? How compare the child to the normal? The Commission did not believe it ought to say; its work was administrative regulation, not science.

It seemed to us that it would be extremely useful to give a guide to future examination commissions: It is necessary that these commissions be properly oriented from the beginning. It is necessary to guard against the judges who will compose them getting into the habit of leaving decisions to luck, based on subjective and hence uncontrollable impressions, which will be sometimes good, sometimes bad, and will give too large a part to the arbitrary, the capricious. This would indeed be unfortunate, and the interests of the children demand greater circumspection. It will never be to one's credit to have attended a special school. We should at the least spare from this mark those who do not deserve it. Mistakes are excusable, especially at the beginning. But if they become too gross they could injure the good name of these new institutions [i.e., special schools]. And finally, as a principle, we are convinced, and will not cease repeating, that one must introduce into the practical procedures [of testing] the precision and the exactitude of science every time one can, and one can almost always [Binet and Simon, 1905a, pp. 163–64].

Note in the above paragraph both the concern with scientific rigor and the warmth and human sympathy which were typical of the man.

The Binet Scales

THE 1905 SCALE.   The famous 1905 scale which Binet and Simon, his collaborator, produced to aid the Commission in its work is regarded as the first successful test of general intelligence, the direct ancestor of the Stanford-Binet and most other modern intelligence scales. Yet it was a pragmatic tool intended to meet a specific, if limited, social objective—to screen from the school population those children unable to profit by regular instruction. Preconceptions and theories about the nature or indeed the existence of general intelligence entered in hardly at all. As Binet wrote,

Our goal, when a child is placed in our presence, is to make a measurement of his intellectual capacities, in order to learn whether he is normal or is retarded. To this end we must study his present state, and that state only. We need concern ourselves neither with his past nor with his future; in consequence, we will neglect the etiology, and specifically we will not make a distinction between acquired and congenital feeblemindedness; even more emphatically, we will set aside all considerations of pathological anatomy which might explain his intellectual deficit. So much for the past. Concerning the future, the same abstention; we seek not at all to establish or prepare a prognosis, and we leave unanswered the question of knowing whether his retardation is curable or not, ameliorable or not [Binet and Simon, 1905a, p. 191].
    Our goal is not at all to study, to analyze and to disclose the aptitudes of those who are inferior in intelligence. That will be the object of future work. Here we confine ourselves to evaluating, to measuring their intelligence in general; we shall establish their intellectual level; and to give an idea of this level, we shall compare it to normal children of the same age or of an analogous level . . . [p. 193].

The fundamental idea of this method is the establishment of what we shall call a *metrical scale of intelligence*; this scale is composed of a series of tests, of increasing difficulty, starting at one end from the lowest intellectual level that can be observed, and emerging at the other end at the level of average, normal intelligence, with each test corresponding to a different mental level [p. 194].

The thirty tests constituting the 1905 scale covered not only a very wide range of difficulty, but also a great diversity of content drawn from Binet's earlier work on many different topics. Included were visual co-ordination—following a lighted candle with the head and eyes (Test 1), executing simple orders and imitating gestures (Test 6), naming objects in a picture (Test 9), digit-span (Test 19), suggestibility—comparing two lines of equal length or trying to find in a picture nonexistent objects, the *patapoum* and the *nitchevo* (Test 13), defining words ranging from familiar objects (Test 14) to abstract terms (Test 30), sensory discrimination of lines (Tests 10 and 21) and of weights (Tests 12, 22, and 23), comprehension—What is the thing to do when you are sleepy? (Test 27), and many others whose value is attested by their inclusion in scales of the present day.

The standardization was grossly inadequate—about ten children at each of five age levels, 3, 5, 7, 9, and 11, selected by their teachers as possessing average ability, plus an unstated number of feeble-minded children. The scoring procedure, empirical but necessarily tentative, permitted only a rough classification of subjects according to the highest level reached; idiots could not go beyond Test 6, nor imbeciles beyond Test 15. The boundaries for morons were less definite, though they were unable to answer abstract questions passed by most normal eleven-year-olds.

The age of the subjects clearly had a bearing upon their success. Binet had as yet no good method of making allowance for age differences, but in the following passage he was clearly groping toward the concept of mental age:

It is possible . . . [that we will someday succeed in] . . . finding signs of psychological retardation, wholly independent of age. It would obviously be a great advantage to recognize such signs. But for the present, what strikes us most often are the resemblances between very young normals and older subnormals. These resemblances are so numerous and so curious that to read the description of the reactions of a child whose age has not been given, one could not say whether he is normal or subnormal [Binet and Simon, 1905c, p. 321].

INNOVATIONS.   The limitations of the 1905 scale are clear. Less apparent are the features which made it a turning point in the history of mental measurement. In this scale for the first time, tests of diverse content were *combined* to strike an average level of performance rather than to measure separately the dimensions of conventional psychological analysis—faculties, sensory thresholds, or whatever. Moreover, the inclusion or exclusion of specific test content was an empirical matter, reflecting Binet's many years of prior experimentation to discover which tests were corroborated by criterion judgments. Lastly, the tests were not precise laboratory determinations but brief, simple, and eminently practical tools for examining children in a schoolroom.

> We have desired that all our tests be simple, rapid, convenient, precise, heterogeneous, keeping the subject in continuous contact with the examiner. . . . Speed is a necessity with these sorts of examination. It is impossible to prolong them more than twenty minutes without tiring the subject, and during this time it is necessary to probe him from all angles and to carry out at least ten tests, which leaves only about two minutes for each one . . . [Binet and Simon, 1905b, p. 195].

Clearly, here speaks a man familiar with the realities of working with children and with the defective.

The publication of the 1905 scale attracted considerable attention from those working on problems of mental deficiency or of educational classification. Goddard translated it into English for use at the Vineland Training School in New Jersey. Decroly and Degand tried it out in Belgium, and other workers, including Terman, were in communication with Binet and suggested tests of their own.

THE 1908 SCALE.   In 1908 appeared a new Binet-Simon scale, drawing extensively upon the earlier instrument but embodying fundamentals of organization only dimly forecast in the 1905 test. Significantly, the new publication was titled, "The Development of Intelligence in Children." The focus of the 1908 scale shifted sharply from the subnormal to the normal, and the tests for idiots were dropped. The general plan of numerous brief tasks, diverse in content and ordered empirically by difficulty, was retained. However, for the first time tests were now classified by level, from age three to age thirteen, according to the age at which normal children should be able to pass them. The allocation of tests to age levels was rather crude, not only because of the small standardization sample, but also because of the practical complications of finding tests at precisely the levels of difficulty required. In general, the tests assigned to a given level were passed by from 50 to 90 per cent of normal children of that age. This time the standardization group consisted in all of 203 children, aged three to twelve and tested within two months of their birthdays.

The arrangement of tests by age levels permitted the examiner to express the developmental level of a given child as the *age* at which the average child achieved equivalent ability. Although no definite stand-ards of passing of failing were set on individual items, the child was assigned a basal *mental age* corresponding to the age level at which he passed all tests but one. An additional year of mental age was assigned for each five tests passed at more difficult levels.

Here is the essential pattern of an age scale, widely adopted in later, more refined instruments. Although there are serious statistical diffi-culties inherent in constructing an accurate age scale (cf. McNemar, 1942, pp. 84ff.), the method has the undoubted merit of providing an easily understood way to describe differences between children in general level of ability. Two complications remained, however, in the 1908 scale: first, the number of tests at each level varied from three to eight; second, the mental-age score was meaningful as a measure of brightness only in relation to the chronological age of the child con-cerned.

THE 1911 SCALE.   In 1911, shortly before his untimely death, Binet published a further, thorough-going revision (Binet, 1911b), re-locating many of the tests and providing five at each age level. The scale was also lengthened by the addition of five tests for fifteen-year-olds and five for adults. By equalizing the number of tests at each age level, Binet made it possible to assign fractional units of mental age—one-fifth of a year for each test passed beyond the basal level. However, he never utilized a brightness index which was independent of age. The concept of "intelligence quotient," i.e., mental age divided by chrono-logical age, was first proposed in 1912 by Stern in Germany (Stern, 1912, pp. 48ff.), and successfully exploited by Lewis M. Terman in the famous Stanford revision of 1916.

Criticisms of the Binet Method

Despite the general success of the new scales, it should not be thought that enthusiastic support greeted Binet's efforts at every hand. Teachers and psychiatrists alike were incredulous that a forty-minute examination could be more accurate and reliable a basis for judgment than long interviews or even extended acquaintance. Binet's rebuttal was characteristic. He set critics to establishing the mental level of particular children, and demonstrated that always they themselves resorted to the self-same method of tests. However, they used it awk-wardly. Their tests were over-dependent upon special knowledge, and they changed the scoring standards and even the instructions to the subject so much from child to child that their conclusions were far from accurate.

As evidence accumulated over the years, it became clear that not all the tests were properly located, those at the lower levels tending to be too easy and those at the upper too hard—but this was a matter of detail. More serious was the charge that Binet's quantitative approach neglected important differences of a qualitative sort. To be sure, his tests were deliberately constructed for quantitative screening, and they are remembered best of all of Binet's work because they served a pressing social need. However, Binet's investigation of qualitative differences in the intelligence of his two daughters (Binet, 1903) has seldom been matched for thoroughness and subtlety.[8] It refutes the charge that he was interested only in the quantitative, but it had no immediate utility and was eclipsed by his other work.

Critics have also pointed out that Binet's "metrical scale of intelligence" lacks a zero point and does not permit true measurement in the physical sense, but only an ordinal ranking among individuals. This limitation certainly exists, but Binet was the first to point it out.

> . . . I have not sought . . . to outline a method of measurement in the physical sense of the word, but only a method of classification of individuals. The procedures that I have described will make it possible, when they are perfected, to place a person before or after another such person or series of persons; but I do not think that we can *measure* one of their intellectual aptitudes in the sense that we measure a length or a volume. Thus, when the person studied can retain seven digits after one hearing, one can classify him, from the point of view of his memory for digits, after individuals who retain eight digits under the same conditions, and before those who retain six. This is a classification, it is not a measure. It is not at all the same thing to measure three wooden beams, to say that one is six meters long, one seven, and the other eight. In this latter case one really measures; one establishes, for example, that the difference between the first beam and the second is equal to the difference between the second and the third, and that that difference is equal to one meter. It is absolutely precise. But we can not know in the case of memory whether the difference between a recall of six digits and a recall of seven digits is or is not equal to the difference between the recall of seven digits and the recall of eight; moreover, we do not know the value of that difference; we do not measure, we classify! [Binet, 1898, pp. 122f.].

Another charge has been that the tests do not measure intellectual ability apart from the effects of experience, and that the resultant score is hence not a proper measure of native endowment. This objection

---

[8] The line of careful, qualitative inquiry has been brilliantly extended by Jean Piaget at the University of Geneva. Piaget and his coworkers of the Centre d'Épistemologie Génétique, notably Bärbel Inhelder, have published a series of painstaking investigations of the sequential development of perception and of logical thinking from infancy to adolescence. However, this work is normative rather than differential in emphasis, and as such falls outside the scope of this chapter.

derives from a curious misunderstanding of Binet, the historical origin of which we shall consider later. Binet, to be sure, tried to choose only content for his tests that would be familiar to all the subjects for whom they were intended. But the psychologist who had pointed out the futility of trying to measure faculties separately from one another was the last person to attempt to measure innate biological endowment apart from the matrix of learned social behavior through which it is expressed.

Binet did not live long enough to check the consistency of test performance across appreciable intervals of time, but he rejected the view held by some later workers that intelligence as measured by tests is unchangeable. Indeed, he reacted against what he called the "brutal pessimism" of those who regard intelligence as a fixed quantity which cannot be increased. To prove the contrary, he and his collaborators developed methods, called by him "mental orthopedics," for raising the intellectual level of the defective.

> Having on our hands children who did not know how to listen, to pay attention, to keep quiet, we pictured our first duty as being not to teach them the facts that we thought would be most useful, but *to teach them how to learn*. We have therefore devised . . . what we call exercises of mental orthopedics. [Examples are practice in sitting still, carrying a glass of water without spilling any, etc.] . . . In the same way that physical orthopedics straightens a crooked spine, mental orthopedics strengthens, cultivates and fortifies attention, memory, perception, judgment, and will . . . [From Binet's *Les idées modernes sur les enfants*, 1911, p. 150].

And again:

> Now if one considers that intelligence is not a single indivisible function with a particular essence of its own, but that it is formed by the combination of all the minor functions of discrimination, observation, retention, etc., all of which have proved to be plastic and subject to increase, it will seem incontestable that the same law governs the ensemble and its elements, and that consequently the intelligence of anyone is susceptible of development. With practice, enthusiasm, and especially with method one can succeed in increasing one's attention, memory, and judgment, and in becoming literally more intelligent than before; and this process will go on until one reaches one's limit [p. 143].

Binet's Conception of Intelligence

Our account of Binet's contributions should not close without a brief discussion of Binet's concept of intelligence. It is clear from what has gone before that Binet's 1905 scale was an empirical device to meet a specific social need. His later revisions, though embodying all the essential features of current tests which ambitiously purport to measure "general intelligence," assumed their final form not by deduction from a formal theory of intelligence, but grew like a mosaic by the gradual accretion of specific test ideas and procedures culled from a lifetime of research.

Curiously, Binet nowhere in his voluminous writings defined intelligence as such. At different times he emphasized one or another of its aspects. In his earlier writings he gave most weight to the power of memory and imagery. Later he stressed attention, conceived broadly as adaptation to new situations. Still later, he described judgment—the power to comprehend and to reason—as an essential component in intelligence. Although he continued to use the vocabulary of faculty psychology, the sequence of his work is evidence that he concerned himself less and less with distinguishing or measuring separate mental faculties in intelligence. For him, they were inextricably interwoven both in real-life adaptation and in tests of whatever kind. Intelligence was the sum total, or rather the resultant, of all the higher processes in complex interaction, and could be measured only by an extensive sampling of many kinds of behavior.

Regarding intelligence as a product of many abilities, Binet sought in his tests to measure not an entity or single dimension—"general intelligence"—but rather an average level—"intelligence in general." Within this broad domain, the criterion for retention or rejection of a particular type of test was empirical—whether it yielded large individual differences and whether these were congruent with age differences, teachers' estimates, or the like. Such was Binet's insight and fertility of invention that an astonishing proportion of the tests which have stood the test of time can be traced back to one or another of his early investigations.

INTELLIGENCE TESTS IN THE UNITED STATES: 1910 TO THE PRESENT

THE DISAPPOINTING OUTCOME of the American testing movement of 1890–1905 has already been described. Reports of Binet's successes in the years after 1905 aroused little interest in university centers of the United States, although Cattell, Thorndike, and others at Columbia University continued to use tests of special functions to measure fatigue, transfer of training effects, etc. Also, G. Stanley Hall at Clark University, though not a tester, created an atmosphere friendly to empirical research upon individual differences, and attracted as students L. M. Terman, F. Kuhlmann, and other leaders of the next generation of differential psychologists.

Quite different was the enthusiastic reception given Binet's papers by the clinicians and educators who were struggling with the practical problems of mental classification which had interested Binet. Foremost among the latter was H. H. Goddard (1866–1957), another distinguished student of G. S. Hall, who, from 1906 to 1918, was the psychological director of the Vineland Training School, a New Jersey institution for the feeble-minded.

The Work of H. H. Goddard

Goddard was not particularly impressed with the 1905 Binet series, but changed his mind when the 1908 revision reached him. He wrote:

> When I read Binet's *Measuring Scale*, I rejected it as too formal and exact. I thought "mind" could not be measured in that way. A second thought showed me that my impression or feeling was of no value compared to the serious declaration of a man like Binet. I accordingly set about trying out the scale on our children. The more I used it the more amazed I was at its accuracy [In K. Young, 1924, p. 35.]

Thereafter Goddard translated the Binet scales into English, and spent many years in vigorous and eloquent advocacy of Binet's approach to the measurement of intelligence. Probably no one else had so much to do with launching the Binet method in the United States. Yet it often happens that the devoted disciple transforms the ideas of the prophet in the very process of transmitting them. So it was in this case.

Accepting Binet's empirical *method*, he substituted for Binet's *idea* of intelligence as a shifting complex of inter-related functions, the concept of a single, underlying function (faculty) of intelligence. Further, he believed that this unitary function was largely determined by heredity, a view much at variance with Binet's optimistic proposals for mental orthopedics.

In retrospect, it seems inevitable that Goddard should have espoused these ideas. On the conceptual side, Goddard, like most Americans, was far more influenced than were the French by developments in Britain. The work of Galton and the evolutionists had emphasized the importance of heredity, and Spearman in 1904 had "demonstrated" the unitariness of intelligence (see below, pp. 502–4). On the practical side, Goddard was working with grossly defective children whose mental retardation was only one aspect of a general biological inadequacy, expressed from birth in anatomical and physiological abnormality as well. Nowadays we would regard some of these conditions as congenital, resulting from prenatal accident or infection, e.g., German measles. Goddard saw such defects as evidence for the prepotency of heredity. He was probably strengthened in this view by the fact that the defective are far less able to learn than the normal, and environmental manipulation, even intensive training, often produces only meager results.

Goddard, always more the social reformer than the dispassionate researcher, labored long and hard for his twin enthusiasms, eugenics and Binet testing, and soon had them indissolubly linked in the public mind. He wrote his famous genealogical study, "The Kallikak Family" (1912), to prove his hereditarian thesis, though his facts lend themselves about as well to an environmentalist interpretation (see Chap. 4). The following quotations summarize his mature views on intelligence and intelligence testing:

> Stated in its boldest form, our thesis is that the chief determiner of human conduct is a unitary mental process which we call intelligence: that this process is conditioned by a nervous mechanism which is inborn: that the degree of efficiency to be attained by that nervous mechanism and the consequent grade of intelligence or mental level for each individual is determined by the kind of chromosomes that come together with the union of the germ cells: that it is but little affected by any later influences except such serious accidents as may destroy part of the mechanism.[9]

On this base he proposes a sweeping program of social reform:

> It is no useless speculation that tries to see what would happen if society were organized so as to recognize and make use of the doctrine of mental levels . . . it is quite possible to restate practically all of our social problems in terms of mental level. . . . The great advantage of having every man doing work on his own mental level would prove fundamental. Testing intelligence is no longer an experiment or of doubted value. It is fast becoming an exact science. The facts revealed by the Army tests cannot be ignored. Greater efficiency we are always working for. Can these new facts be used to increase our efficiency? No question! We only await the Human Engineer who will undertake the work [pp. vi, vii].

Who could resist the appeal of so broad and utopian a vista? Mental testing was adopted in every training school, every teachers' college in the land, and even stormed the citadels of experimental psychology on university campuses. There were few who noticed the logical flaw behind the eloquence—that the hereditary, biological intelligence that Goddard postulated and the intelligence which the tests in fact measured were *not* the same thing. In subsequent sections of this chapter

[9] From H. H. Goddard, *Human Efficiency and Levels of Intelligence*, 1920, p. 1. Published by Princeton University Press. Excerpt here and following used with their permission.

we shall see how failure to distinguish between these two caused endless confusion and controversy.

Lewis M. Terman and the Stanford-Binet

Although Goddard was in the forefront of the Binet movement in the United States, he was not alone. Whipple and Huey both published translations of Binet's tests in 1910. Kuhlmann and Wallin issued their versions in 1911. Nevertheless, the first thoroughly revised and re-standardized test on the Binet pattern for American children was the well-known Stanford-Binet of Lewis M. Terman. This test, published in 1916, was a major landmark in the history of psychometrics, and earned enduring fame for its author.

Lewis M. Terman (1877–1956), the twelfth child in an Indiana farm family of fourteen, was originally interested in the study of individual differences by an itinerant book peddler and phrenologist who visited the Terman home when the boy was nine or ten, and predicted great things for him after feeling the bumps on his head— at least one instance when phrenology served society well. After an undergraduate education at a local teachers' college and at Indiana University, Terman went to Clark University and G. S. Hall to work for his Ph. D. His life-long interest in the gifted began with his doctoral dissertation in 1905 and culminated in his classic *Genetic Studies of Genius*, the five volumes of which were published between 1925 and 1959. His researches in psychological masculinity-femininity and in marital happiness are almost as well known. Not the least of his many achievements was his part, as departmental head (1922–42), in building at Stanford University one of America's most distinguished departments of psychology. But there is no doubt that his most significant contribution was the Stanford-Binet, and the concept of the IQ, borrowed from Stern (1912), which it embodied.

The work of constructing the 1916 version took several years and involved altogether some 2,300 subjects—a considerable increase from the fifty on whom Binet had founded his first scale eleven years earlier. Although Terman dropped certain tests, introduced others, and re-assigned many to different age levels on the basis of the American standardization, his 1916 scale resembled Binet's 1911 version closely in its adherence to the age-scale pattern.

The practice of dividing mental age earned on the test by actual chronological age yielded a brightness index, the famous "IQ" which was independent of the subject's years, and could hence be used to compare subjects differing in age. The IQ concept was simple, easy to understand, and easily applied to children, who were the main subjects of study by tests. Statistical difficulties inherent in the use of such a ratio which led to numerous misinterpretations and misunderstandings, were not fully appreciated until later.[1]

In theoretical position, Terman adopted Binet's view.

> The assumption that it is easier to measure a part or one aspect of intelligence than all of it is fallacious in that the parts are not separate parts and cannot be separated by any refinement of experiment. . . . After many vain attempts to disentangle the various intellective functions, Binet decided to test their combined functional capacity without any pretense of measuring the exact contribution of each to the total product. It is hardly too much to say that intelligence tests have been successful just to the extent to which they have been guided by this aim.[2]

And again:

> The reader will understand, of course, that no single test used alone will determine accurately the general level of intelligence. A great many tests are required; and for two reasons: (1) because intelligence has many aspects; and (2) in order to overcome the accidental influences of training or environment. If many tests are used no one of them need show more than a moderately high correlation with the scale as a whole. As stated by Binet, "Let the tests be rough, if there are only enough of them" [p. 77].

Although Terman's careful standardization of his test placed it far ahead of all rivals, Terman had only modest hopes for it.

> I was a little surprised that my publications in the test field were so favorably received. I knew that my revision of Binet's tests was superior to others then available, but I did not foresee the vogue it was to

----

[1] There was, to be sure, a problem in calculating IQ's for adults, which had to be met by a special procedure. It was known empirically that the average adult did no better on these tests than the typical sixteen-year-old youth. Hence the rule was set that adult IQ's should be calculated by dividing mental age, not by actual chronological age, but by a fictitious CA of sixteen years, regardless of actual age. To permit brighter than average adolescents to earn IQ's over 100 and to maintain the symmetry of the IQ distribution at all age levels, enough difficult tests were included and assigned to so-called "adult" levels of the scale to permit a maximum MA of nineteen years and six months. While this expedient worked reasonably well in practice for calculating adult IQ's, it involved the use of a fictitious CA, and of MA's which do not in fact correspond to the average performance level of any real age group. In later years, the whole age-scale concept was severely criticized by David Wechsler as being fundamentally misleading and inappropriate for the measurement of adult ability (1958, Chap. 2).

[2] From L. M. Terman, *The Measurement of Intelligence*, 1916, p. 43. This and the following excerpt are used by permission of the Houghton Mifflin Company, Boston.

have and imagined that it would probably be displaced by something much better within a few years.[3]

The "something much better" did not appear for another twenty-one years, and then once more from Terman's own hand—the revised Stanford-Binet of 1937, to which Merrill, McNemar, and others made important contributions (Terman and Merrill, 1937; McNemar, 1942). This version retained the basic age-scale arrangement, but provided two parallel forms and extended the possible M. A. range from two years to twenty-two years and six months. The construction and standardization were models of their kind, and based on a truly national sample. The test is currently in wide use, although the age-scale design has certain inherent weaknesses (along with unique advantages), and some clinicians prefer the excellent Wechsler tests which have appeared since 1939.[4]

Growth of the Testing Movement

As with Binet's contribution, Terman's was seized upon not only because of its intrinsic merit, but also because it met a pressing social need. Compulsory education and the burgeoning of the public-school system demanded in the United States, as in France, a simple and convenient method of screening for over-all scholastic ability. To achieve it, Terman was willing to forego more differentiated or qualitative assessments of intellectual status, and to leave in abeyance questions as to the ultimate nature of intelligence.

> I am fully aware that my researches have not contributed very greatly to the theory of mental measurement. On problems of less theoretical significance, but of importance for the usefulness of tests and for the psychology and pedagogy of individual differences, I think I have made contributions of value [1932, p. 328].

The success of the Stanford-Binet was a triumph of pragmatism, but its importance must not be underestimated, for it demonstrated the feasibility of mental measurement and led to the development of other tests for many special purposes. Equally important, it led to a public acceptance of testing which had important consequences for education and industry, for the military, and for society generally.

[3] From L. M. Terman, "Trails to Psychology," in C. Murchison, ed., A History of Psychology in Autobiography, Vol. 2, 1932, p. 324. Excerpt here and following used by permission of Clark University Press, Worcester, Mass.

[4] There has recently appeared a new revision of the Stanford-Binet (Terman and Merrill, 1960) which preserves the age-scale arrangement of subtests, but adopts a deviation IQ similar to Wechsler's to obviate the statistical difficulties inherent in the ratio IQ.

The onset of World War I in 1917 created a pressing need for a mental test to sift out from the draft men unfit for military service because of lack of intelligence, to select the more intelligent men for further training, and to provide more nearly balanced companies. Yerkes, who had produced a test in 1915 on the point-scale pattern later used by Wechsler, was made chairman of a committee including Terman, Boring, Otis, and others to produce such a device. *Army Alpha* for literates and *Army Beta* for illiterates and the non-English speaking were the result.

These instruments, unlike the Binet tests, could be given to large groups at one sitting. Between September, 1917, and January, 1919, more than 1,750,000 men were tested with Alpha. This enormous volume of data was for many years the prime source for studies of occupational, ethnic, racial, and geographic differences in ability in the United States (Yerkes, 1921).

In World War II, data were collected on some four million men, using the Army General Classification Test, AGCT-1. Numerous other tests were devised for special purposes. While the AGCT was a far more refined instrument in construction, scaling, and standardization than Army Alpha, it represents no basic break with the group tests of a generation earlier.

During the interval between wars, new mental tests, both individual and group, were devised for special groups and special needs.[5] Many group tests were prepared for different age levels and ranges of talent from kindergarteners to university students. Following Army Beta, both individual and group tests minimizing the role of language were invented for testing the illiterate, the deaf, and the foreign-speaking. Special individual tests on the Binet pattern, such as the Merrill-Palmer Scale, were published for use with infants and young children, not to mention numerous other adaptations of the Binet scales themselves, each with its special merit—e.g., the Kuhlmann-Binet for preschool testing, the Herring-Binet for brief testing, the Hayes-Binet for the blind, etc. Many such tests are now superseded and largely forgotten, but a few found an enduring place in the clinical armamentarium.

The worth of most of these tools turned ultimately on their correlation with the Stanford-Binet. During the nineteen-twenties and thirties, the Stanford-Binet came very close to constituting a sort of meter-bar standard in the domain of mental measurement. Those who defined intelligence as that quality which intelligence tests measure had the Stanford-Binet in mind.

[5] The massive *Mental Measurement Yearbooks* compiled by O. K. Buros are evidence for the growth of new test devices since Whipple's day.

The Issue of Test Validity

There was, to be sure, continuing concern about issues raised by the mental-testing movement. Central among these was the basic validity of the tests, a question which in turn hinged upon how one defined intelligence. For a 1921 symposium on the nature of intelligence, fourteen of the leading psychologists of the day submitted their respective definitions. These statements were all sound enough, though they varied in rather fundamental ways. The trouble with them was that they failed to prescribe the content appropriate to tests. As Garrett remarked, in another connection,

> Such "definition," like the time-worn shot-gun prescription, can hardly fail to hit the trouble somewhere, but just *where* is not entirely clear. Omnibus definitions are in general too broad to be wrong and too vague to be useful.[6]

Boring's suggestion was perhaps the most helpful one, that we define intelligence as that which the tests test (1923, p. 35). However, different "general intelligence" tests measure somewhat different things. Even the Stanford-Binet is a composite of many items as diverse as digit span, abstract definitions, and spatial orientation.[7]

The usual practice in industrial psychology, of validating a test by correlating it with a specific criterion variable which one is interested in predicting, failed in this instance for lack of a satisfactory criterion. Indeed, the Stanford-Binet has itself been the criterion against which many other tests were validated.

Noting that Binet and later Terman gave great weight to the relationship between success on an item and age, some critics have charged that on this basis one might as well determine intelligence by measuring stature or counting erupted teeth. This misses the point that the criteria for the selection of test content were always multiple, and the central one was the *judgment* of the psychologist. Correlations with age, with teachers' judgments, with school success, with other items, and with scale-as-a-whole were necessary empirical checks upon that judgment, not substitutes for it.

The basis of validation for mental tests might have been more acceptable had test constructors acknowledged forthrightly that their

[6] From H. E. Garrett, "A Developmental Theory of Intelligence," *Amer. Psychologist*, 1946, 1, 372. Used by permission of the author and the American Psychological Association.

[7] No single type of test content has ever been found which can be applied throughout the entire age span covered by tests, and if there were one, we should have no guarantee that it could call into play the same psychological functions at all levels.

tests rested on sampling all kinds of functions, and provided a rational scheme for doing the sampling—or had they selected, as had Thorndike in his CAVD examination, three or four types of content with the best claims and employed them at all possible levels of difficulty. For better or worse, however, Spearman (cf. pp. 502–4) had already supplied a theory that tests built from more or less accidental "hotchpotches" nevertheless could measure a *unitary, underlying* function, and Goddard had popularized the idea. That it would create new and worse problems was not evident until later, as we shall see when we return to the issue of basic test validity in the next section. Meanwhile, there arose another major issue—that of "IQ constancy." Curiously enough, it, too, derived not from Binet but from the implications of Spearman's and Goddard's theorizing.

The Issue of IQ Constancy

If, as Goddard maintained, one's total store of intelligence is fixed by one's genes, one's achievement on an intelligence test should be always the same, apart from errors of measurement and the influence of one's age and maturational status. Now "IQ" was a brightness index independent of age. It seemed to follow, at least for those who equated test intelligence with biological intelligence, that one's IQ was a constant,[8] i.e., was, within narrow limits of experimental error, a fixed personal attribute like eye color or hair texture. But those who rejected the prepotency of heredity as a determinant of intelligence, or who doubted that the tests were valid measures of intelligence, rose to attack the concept of IQ constancy defended by the hereditarians. One result was the long and acrimonious Stanford-Iowa controversy.[9]

There were facts enough to keep both sides well supplied with ammunition. The defenders of constancy acknowledged that there were sometimes appreciable discrepancies between a person's IQ's earned on different tests, but these could be at least partially explained by reference to differences in test content, in scaling techniques, and in standardization populations. Imperfections in test construction produced some variation from time to time even on the same test, but the better ones had excellent reliability over short intervals. Data for long intervals

[8] On this basis, IQ and school subject-matter tests were often contrasted as measures of "capacity" and of "achievement" respectively. A moment's reflection should, however, have sufficed to show that "capacity," i.e., potentiality, is necessarily an inferential variable. Both types of tests measure *achievement*, albeit in learning somewhat different things. When school opportunity or motivation are less than optimal, the IQ may be a better predictor of ultimate academic status under improved conditions than is the school-achievement test.

[9] See McNemar (1940) vs. Wellman et al. (1940). R. L. Thorndike (1940) supplies a review and critique of the relevant research during the decade 1930–40.

were not available until the major longitudinal studies initiated about 1930 reached fruition. Nevertheless, the impression was current that an individual would continue to maintain roughly the same IQ barring dramatic changes in physical condition or life circumstances. Also, family resemblance studies of twins, siblings, and foster children seemed on balance to accord greater importance to hereditary than to environmental determinants. (See Chap. 4.)

On the other side, there was evidence that not only direct coaching, but also general enrichment of the environment could effect significant changes in IQ. Moreover, anthropologists repeatedly warned that tests depend heavily upon familiarity with elements of middle-class urban culture, and that IQ reflects not only native endowment but also such familiarity or the lack of it (cf. Eells, 1951).[1]

The nature-nurture question could never really be stated or answered in any simple way, because heredity and environment are inevitably confounded in functional measures such as intelligence tests. Disputation has waned as facts from longitudinal studies have become available. We now know that IQ's are far from constant, even without deliberate manipulation of the environment. For example, in a brighter-than-average group of 222 tested annually during the interval from six years to eighteen years of age, the difference in IQ points between the highest and the lowest IQ earned was ten or more points for 85 per cent of the group. Nine per cent changed thirty or more points, and there were instances of fifty points of change (Honzik, Macfarlane, and Allen, 1948, p. 312). However, such changes tend to be proportional to the level of ability. A dull child generally varies less than does a bright one.

Since 1939 David Wechsler has been attacking the constancy problem from an entirely different angle (Wechsler, 1958). He has pointed out that while much attention had been given to the growth of intelligence during childhood and adolescence, the use of a fixed CA (as on the Stanford-Binet) to calculate adult IQ's involves a constancy assumption, and rests on no firmer basis than the fact that differences in average performance are very small between successive age levels during late adolescence. With test materials better adapted to adults, Wechsler has reported that ability increases at least until the mid-twenties and thereafter systematically declines, slowly at first, then faster.

To allow for this decline, Wechsler has constructed his general intelligence tests, the Wechsler-Bellevue and WAIS for adults and WISC for children on the point-scale pattern. He abandons the age scale and the concept of MA altogether. His IQ is really a kind of

---

[1] Few problems have elicited more research, with more equivocal outcome, than the relative contributions of nature and nurture to intelligence. See H. E. Jones (1954) for a lucid discussion and an extensive bibliography.

standard score which describes one's position in a frequency distribution of one's age peers.

Wechsler argues for a gradual decline in adult ability with age, on the basis of cross-sectional data collected at one time on people of different ages. However, follow-ups of some of Terman's investigations in which the same adult was tested repeatedly show not drops but gains, at least with respect to certain kinds of tests (Bayley, 1955). Also, data comparing World War I and World War II soldiers tested at the same age show large discrepancies in favor of the more recent army, suggesting that the differences between older and younger generations found by Wechsler may not necessarily reflect aging as such (Tuddenham, 1948). At present the question of the relation of age to intelligence in maturity is still an open one, complicated by conflicting evidence on whether the different aspects of intelligence grow more independent of one another in maturity than in youth (cf. Garrett, 1946; Curtis, 1949; Swineford, 1949). It seems probable that the curve of development from childhood to old age is very different for different types of items commonly lumped together in intelligence tests.

Intelligence Tests in Research

In spite of persistent concern about validity and constancy, the new tests have opened up many avenues of research. Individual and group differences have been intensively studied, with the tests used as measuring instruments. Results have often been contradictory, and even when the facts were unequivocal they have sometimes been hard to interpret. Perhaps the clearest lesson from this research endeavor is that measurements of group differences cannot transcend the measuring instrument. For example, sex differences in intelligence usually turn out in empirical studies to be small. This is a necessary consequence of using scales whose authors, from Binet to the present day, have systematically excluded test items which showed sizable sex differences. Moreover, since women excel in vocabulary and verbal skills, and men in quantitative and spatial problems, the direction of such minor differences as are found depends upon which content is emphasized by the test. Even this difference in test performance need not necessarily reflect a biological difference, but only a difference between sexes in the systems of training and reward characteristic of our culture. Hence the apparently simple question raised at the beginning of this chapter— "Are men more intelligent than women or vice versa?"—cannot be answered without specification of the measuring scale.

For analogous reasons, only a very uncritical psychologist would offer sweeping generalizations about the intellectual superiority or inferiority of particular racial or ethnic groups, despite the not very surprising fact that members of the dominant racial and cultural group in our society ordinarily score higher than others on tests of socially relevant accomplishments invented by and for members of that group.[2]

Recent Trends

Preceding paragraphs have indicated how intelligence tests have been used in research upon problems of importance to psychology and to society, even though controversy has persisted about the validity and stability of test scores. We have also seen how the success of the Stanford-Binet and the Army Alpha inspired the development of special intelligence tests for infants, adults, the nonliterate, the blind, etc. Especially in recent years there has also been a change in the organization and purpose of the tests themselves.

In the early years of testing, quantitative screening instruments were needed, and tests on the Binet pattern which yielded a single score evolved to meet the need. With the growing availability of tests, psychologists began to give more than one to a subject, and to speculate about the meaning of differences in score which were obtained. "Performance tests," i.e., non-language measures involving motor-manipulative content, were employed early in the history of testing to supplement the primarily verbal estimate supplied by the Binet.[3] Psychologists found the additional information contained in the extra scores important and suggestive for scholastic and vocational counseling.

One consequence was the development of special "aptitude" tests for particular vocations. Clerical, scientific, artistic, even medical and legal aptitude tests were invented, though it proved unexpectedly difficult to find aptitude measures which would predict success in specific lines of endeavor much better than the general intelligence tests. Another consequence, related to the burgeoning of clinical psychology during and after World War II, was the development of "diagnostic" tests which yield separate scores for different areas of cognitive functioning, and thus provide qualitative cues to the clinician. Among individual tests of this type, the Wechsler scales—WAIS, and WISC, with their separate verbal and performance IQ's, their deterioration ratios and diagnostic profiles—are well known.

The general trend toward multiple scores can be observed also in

[2] The topic is too extensive to treat here, but it should be noted that differences among racial groups, between adjacent age groups, or between sexes are ordinarily very small compared to the differences among individuals within the same group. Overlapping among groups is characteristically very large.

[3] The first well-standardized performance test was the Pintner-Paterson of 1917, though Knox had invented such tests for screening immigrants at Ellis Island and published on them as early as 1914.

the newer group tests of general intelligence. Examples are the American Council on Education Examination ACE with its quantitative and language scores, and the factor-based Differential Aptitudes Tests. This evolution from global-score to multi-score scales has been influenced, not only by changes in the way tests are used, but also by parallel developments in the theory of intelligence. To these theoretical developments we now turn.

FACTORS AND FACTORISTS

OVER NEARLY FIFTY YEARS, the Stanford-Binet and other general intelligence tests have had great value for educational classification, vocational counseling, and the like. In the preceding section we noted, however, that opinion on their basic validity has been divided to an extraordinary degree, considering their popular acceptance. In the early decades of testing, Goddard had written, "It cannot be doubted that the mental level of the individual is determined [by tests] with marvelous exactness" (1920, p. 28). At roughly the same period, Whipple, noting that to measure higher functions such as memory, numerous and repeated tests are desirable, had remarked, ". . . to try to concoct a single and final test of such a comprehensive capacity as 'general intelligence' becomes doubly absurd" (*Manual of Mental and Physical Tests*, 2nd edition, 1914, p. 12). A generation later, George D. Stoddard, one-time President of the University of Illinois, wrote scornfully, "The Iowa workers [of whom Stoddard had been one] feel that, over the years, the Stanford revisions have offered not very reliable measurements of functions not very close to intelligence" (1943, p. 116). In the same year, Prof. Henry A. Garrett of Columbia, later to become president of the American Psychological Association, voiced a more widely accepted view.

> I should like to express the opinion that the New Revision [i.e., the 1937 Stanford-Binet] is the most useful and is certainly the best constructed instrument for measuring the intelligence of children which we now possess. It represents an achievement of first rank; and one of which all psychologists, no matter what their persuasion, may well be proud.[4]

That conflicting opinions might exist when mental testing was young is perhaps understandable. That contradictory judgments could be made a generation later is evidence that the theoretical validity of intelligence tests is far less well agreed upon than their practical usefulness.

[4] From H. E. Garrett, "The Standardization of the Terman-Merrill Revision of the Stanford-Binet Scale," *Psychol. Bull.*, 1943, 40, 201. Used by permission of the author and the American Psychological Association.

In the writer's opinion the basic difficulty stems from the attempts by most workers over the years to substitute Spearman's theory of intelligence for Binet's, while continuing to use tests founded on Binet's pragmatic measuring instrument. To understand the origins of later controversies we must begin with Spearman's formulations.

Charles Spearman and the Two-Factor Theory of Intelligence

Charles Spearman (1863–1945), after a military career lasting until he was thirty-four, turned belatedly to psychology, which he studied in Germany with Wundt, Külpe, and G. E. Müller. Returning to University College, London, in 1907, he spent a long and vigorous career on new battlefields, attacking sensationism, associationism, hedonism ("an abomination"), Pavlovian reflexology ("not psychology"), Titchenerian structuralism ("distorted"), behaviorism ("a South Sea bubble"), and Gestalt psychology ("mystical and romantic"),—and advancing his own "noëgenetic laws" of the mind as a substitute for those of the associationists.[5] Curiously, he regarded his famous statistical contributions—the Spearman-Brown prophecy formula, the rank-order correlation, and even his two-factor theory of intelligence—as secondary in importance.

THE DISCOVERY OF THE TWO-FACTOR THEORY.   Spearman's theory of intelligence derived originally, he tells us, from a rather casual attempt to verify Galton's belief that differences in sensory discrimination are the basis for differences in higher abilities (see p. 477 above). Experimenting in a village school, he discovered rather high correlations among the children's school marks in various subjects, and between these and sensory discrimination as measured by a musical "dichord" of his own contrivance. Not long thereafter, he discovered the opposite findings embodied in Wissler's analyses of Cattell's data.

Since the conflicting results were there, however, they had at least to be explained. After much pondering over them, I had at last a happy thought which embodied itself in the concept of "attenuation." This means that the correlation coefficient between two abilities (or other variables) suffers a spurious decrease of apparent size from the (random) errors of measurement involved. A method was devised for determining the amount of this spurious decrease, so that allowance could be made for it [i.e., by the correction for attenuation.] The

[5] "In spite of writing, as I myself believed, in the blandest of tones, the effect upon readers has often been called provocative; so that my literary life seems to have been one long fight" (Spearman, 1930, p. 330).

upshot was to show that such decrease was quite sufficient to account for the lowness of the coefficients obtained by Cattell; and in this way the seeming contradiction between us was happily dissipated. . . .[6]

To go back to my little experiments in the village school, not only were my correlations large, but their magnitudes were noticed to have systematic interrelations. At first, this system used to be described as "hierarchical," because it was such as to allow the table of correlations to be arranged with the highest values in one corner and with the other values regularly decreasing in both horizontal and vertical directions. . . . At the present day, the most usual way of indicating this same system is by saying that the "tetrad differences" tend to be zero.[7]

I was then faced by the problem of explaining it. And here another happy thought came to the rescue. Aided by the concept of attenuation, proof could be furnished that such a system must needs occur whenever each of the abilities at issue is the compound result of *two factors*, of which one is common to all the abilities, whereas the other is specific to each different ability. Herewith was born into the world an extraordinary source of discord and labor, but also, let us hope, of progress. It has been called the "Theory of Two Factors"; or in more general terms, that of "Factors."

. . . As so far mentioned, evidence had only been brought that the analysis of each ability into the two factors was theoretically possible. There soon followed a device by which the analysis could actually be performed, and thus *the general factor could be measured*. This could be done, it was shown, simply by measuring promiscuously any large number of different abilities and pooling the results together. In such a hotchpotch of multitudinous measurements, the specific factors must necessarily—since they vary randomly from one measurement to another—tend in the average or mean to neutralize one another. Whereas the general factor, being in every measurement just the same, must in the average more or less completely dominate. Accordingly the average . . . must approximate toward being a measure of the pure general factor. In such wise this principle of making a hotchpotch, which might seem to be the most arbitrary and meaningless procedure imaginable, had really a profound theoretical basis and a supremely practical utility.[8]

The elaboration of Spearman's "happy thoughts" constituted two long papers in the *American Journal of Psychology* for 1904, and became

---

[6] Spearman does not explain why Cattell's data were presumably so much more unreliable than Spearman's own, though carefully collected and on a larger sample of subjects.

[7] For the mathematically trained reader, this simply means that determinant minors of order two drawn from the correlation matrix tend to be zero; expressed symbolically, $r_{12} r_{34} - r_{13} r_{24} = 0$, and so for all other minors.

[8] From C. Spearman, in C. Murchison, ed., A *History of Psychology in Autobiography*, Vol. 1, 1930, pp. 322–4. Used by permission of Clark University Press, Worcester, Mass.

indeed "an extraordinary source of discord and labor." Here, clearly enunciated, is the doctrine that an assortment of tests yields a measure not of "intelligence in general," but rather of "general intelligence," a *unitary, underlying, causal* factor (faculty) revealing itself in all cognitive activities, including simple sensory discrimination. To be sure, Spearman designated the common factor by a purely mathematical symbol "g"—the specifics were labeled "s's"—and speculated that it might in fact be mental energy. Nevertheless, the tests which seemed to be determined most by "g" and least by their respective specific factors involved precisely those complex "higher" functions of reasoning and judgment which accord with the common understanding of "intelligence." [9]

With the additional assumption that one's store of "g" is determined exclusively by inheritance, we have Goddard's bold thesis (see p. 491 above) and the basis for belief in "IQ constancy." In the doctrine of underlying causal variables we have the impetus for the efforts of a generation of such statistical psychologists as L. L. Thurstone, J. P. Guilford, and R. B. Cattell, and an influence upon clinical psychology so strong that David Wechsler characterized himself in 1958 as a "reformed but unchastened Spearmanite" (1958, p. vii). For the fact is that Binet, handicapped as he was by the vocabulary of faculty psychology, never adequately delineated his own evolving theory of intelligence. By default, Spearman's theory came to constitute the conceptual basis for Binet's test approach. The monarchic doctrine [1] of an underlying factor of intelligence struck a sympathetic chord among psychologists accustomed to explanations in terms of underlying "faculties," but added the simplicity and elegance of a single cause.

REACTIONS OF BINET AND TERMAN.   Although Spearman in later years blandly counted Binet a convert if not a plagiarist, Binet's reaction at the time was interested but not enthusiastic. In the same volume of *L'Année* in which he published his own 1905 scale, Binet reviewed Spearman's two papers.

[9] It should be noted that Spearman's statistical procedures permitted one to determine for a *test* the percentage of total variance associated with "g" and on this basis to select the best tests. The amount of "g" possessed by a *person* could only be estimated indirectly. On a given test, "g" and the particular "s" concerned were supposed to be involved in the same fixed proportions from person to person, although it is apparent that owing to differences in background and experience, individuals may sometimes utilize quite different knowledges and skills, yet earn the same score.

[1] It was dubbed the "monarchic" theory by this doughty ex-soldier of the Queen. Proponents of dissenting views were branded "oligarchic," e.g., Thurstone, Guilford, and R. B. Cattell, or "anarchic," e.g., Thorndike, Thomson, and Tryon (cf. Spearman, 1927).

He [Spearman] regards this conclusion [that sensory discrimination and school achievement are expressions of the same unitary factor] as *profoundly* important. It is possible. We ourselves are *profoundly* astonished at it, because of the very defective character both of the sensory experiments of the author, and of the manner in which he rated or secured ratings of total intelligence. Before pronouncing [judgment] one must wait until other investigators obtain similar results [1905, p. 624].

Terman was actively antagonized by Spearman.

I shall never forget the impression that these articles [of 1904] made on me—the dogmatic tone of the author, the finality with which he disposed of everyone else, and his one-hundred-percent faith in the verdict of his mathematical formulae. . . . The author's logic appeared to be waterproof, but the conclusion to which it led, namely, that there is a correspondence between what may provisionally be called "General Discrimination" and "General Intelligence" which works out with great approximation to *one* or *absoluteness* seemed to me as absurd then as it does now.[2]

E. L. Thorndike's Connectionist Theory

The views of Spearman's perennial antagonist, E. L. Thorndike of Columbia (1874–1949), seem to have been much closer to Binet's final position. Thorndike, influenced by the Cattell-Wissler studies in the same laboratory, developed a theory of multiple "bonds" which rejected the existence of a universal trait of intelligence in favor of a very large number of independent elementary abilities (possibly corresponding to neurons or synaptic connections) sampled in different combinations by different intelligent acts (cf. Chap. 6).

The standard orthodox view of the surface nature of intellect has been that it is divided rather sharply into a lower half, mere connection-forming or the association of ideas, which acquires information and specialized habits of thinking; and a higher half characterized by abstraction, generalization, the perception and use of relations and the selection and control of habits in inference or reasoning, and ability to manage novel or original tasks. The orthodox view of its deeper nature . . . has been that the mere connection or association of ideas depends upon the physiological mechanism whereby a nerve stimulus

[2] The underlying correspondence, via "g," between complex cognitive activities and simple sensory discrimination to which both Binet and Terman took exception, has been largely ignored in recent years by writers on factor analysis, although historically it was the foundation of Spearman's theory. The excerpt is taken from L. M. Terman, "Trails to Psychology," in C. Murchison, ed., *A History of Psychology in Autobiography*, Vol. 2.

506 I I I · INDIVIDUAL DIFFERENCES AND PERSONALITY

is conducted to and excites action in neurones A, B, C, rather than any others, but that the higher processes depend upon something quite different. There would be little agreement as to what it could be, but there would be much confidence that it was *not* the mechanism of habit formation.

The hypothesis which we present and shall defend admits the distinction in respect of surface behavior, but asserts that in their deeper nature the higher forms of intellectual operation are identical with mere association or connection-forming, depending upon the same sort of physiological connections but requiring *many more of them*. By the same argument the person whose intellect is greater or higher or better than that of another person differs from him in the last analysis in having, not a new sort of physiological process, but simply a larger number of connections of the ordinary sort.[3]

The Sampling Theory of Ability

A view somewhat similar to Thorndike's has been offered by the Scottish psychologist, G. H. Thomson (1920, 1951), and by R. C. Tryon (1935, 1959) at California. This has been called the "sampling" theory by its supporters, the "anarchic" theory by Spearman. As Thomson put it,

The alternative theory to explain the zero tetrad differences is that each test calls upon a *sample of the bonds* which the mind can form, and that some of these bonds are common to two tests and cause their correlation [1951, p. 309].

. . . Tests can differ, on this theory, in their richness or complexity, and less rich tests will tend to have low, more complex tests will tend to have high correlations, at any rate if the "bonds" tend to be *all-or-none* in their nature, as the action of neurones is known to be . . . the sampling theory would consider men also to be samples, each man possessing some, but not all, both of the inherited and the acquired neural bonds which are the physical side of thought. Like the tests, some men are rich, others poor, in these bonds. Some are richly endowed by heredity, some by opportunity and education; some by both, some by neither [pp. 315f.].[4]

Thomson was able to demonstrate that his theory fitted the facts of a hierarchical table as well as did Spearman's. With artificial "mental tests" made up by throwing dice, the correlations between throws tended toward hierarchy purely because of chance overlap.

[3] From E. L. Thorndike, *The Measurement of Intelligence*, 1925, pp. 414f. Used by permission of Teachers College, Columbia University, New York.

[4] From G. H. Thomson, *The Factorial Analysis of Human Ability*, 5th ed., copyright 1951 by University of London Press, Ltd. Excerpt here and following used with their permission.

. . . The laws of probability alone will cause a tendency to zero tetrad-differences among correlation coefficients . . .

It is, in the opinion of the present writer, this fact—a result of the laws of chance and not of any psychological laws—which has made conceivable the analysis of mental abilities into a few common factors (if not into one only as Spearman hoped) and specifics. Because of the laws of chance the mind works *as if* it were composed of these hypothetical factors. . . . The causes may be "anarchic," meaning that they are numerous and unconnected, yet the result is "monarchic," or at least "oligarchic," in the sense that it may be so described—*provided always that large specific factors are allowed* [pp. 311f.].

The psychological meaning of all this is that if, when we attack some task, some test, our ability to solve it depends upon a large number of things—genes we have inherited, pieces of information we have acquired, skills we have practiced, little habits of thought we have formed, all and sundry influences from past and present—then the correlation coefficients between performances in tests will show exactly the same relationships with one another as they would have done had our ability depended on our possession of a small number of common "factors" (plus specifics). This does not prove that we have no such "factors." But it does show that perhaps we haven't, that perhaps they are fictions [1952, p. 283].[5]

The sampling theory made little headway against Spearman's doctrine, though it was never driven from the field. One reason was that it offered not a refutation, but only an alternative explanation of the same facts. Moreover, the postulation of discrete bonds, however satisfying to connectionists, seemed to some to deny the role of global physiological variables, although as Hull (1928, p. 202) pointed out, the sampling theory provided a sounder basis for the construction of aptitude tests than the Spearman view. For those seeking general causes, "g" reigning supreme had far greater appeal than a horde of little bonds.

The overthrow of Spearman's view, when it came, was on other grounds—the tetrads sometimes failed to vanish, even within permissible limits of error! Spearman, who seems to have preferred his theory to the facts which disturbed it, felt that tetrads failed to approximate zero only when the tests (upon whose intercorrelations the tetrads were based) were improperly selected—i.e., were "unduly similar" to one another—and hence overlapped on the specific factors as well as on "g."

If such "disturbers" were found coexisting in the team of tests, the team had to be "purified" by the rejection of one or the other of the two. Later it became clear that this process involves the experimenter in great difficulty, for it subjects him to the temptation to discover

[5] Used by permission of Clark University Press.

"undue similarity" between tests *after* he has found that their correlation breaks the hierarchy. Moreover, whole groups of tests were found to fail to conform; and so group factors were admitted, though always by the experimenter trained in that school, with reluctance and in as small a number as possible [Thomson, 1951, p. 63].

These group factors were on an intermediate level of generality. Unlike specifics they were involved in more than one test, but they were less general than "g" which invests all tests.

Thurstone and the Multiple Factor Theory

Over the years, a considerable number of group factors accumulated as various test batteries were studied—a situation which destroyed both the elegance and the parsimony of the two-factor theory. Moreover, the Spearman method was extremely laborious to apply.[6] To Professor L. L. Thurstone (1887–1955) of the University of Chicago is owing a way of dealing with both the conceptual and computational shortcomings of Spearman's approach. This solution is called the *multiple factor theory* (Thurstone, 1947).

On the computational side it involves an ingenious generalization of Spearman's methods designed to discover the rank of the correlation matrix instead of proving that it is of rank one. On the conceptual side, it involves abandoning "g" in favor of as many broad group factors as necessary, each involving several but not all of the tests. As before, each test has its own specific factor, but "g" and the group factors of Spearman are reshuffled into new variables intermediate between them in generality.

> Beginning with Spearman's famous paper in 1904, there was a quarter of a century of debate about Spearman's single factor method and his postulated general intellective factor g. Throughout that debate over several decades, the orientation was to Spearman's general factor, and secondary attention was given to the group factors and specific factors which were frankly called "the disturbers of g." . . . The development of multiple factor analysis consisted essentially in asking the fundamental question in a different way. Starting with an experimentally given table of correlation coefficients for a set of variables, we did not ask whether it supported any one general factor. We asked instead how many factors must be postulated in order to account for the observed correlations. At the very start of an analysis we faced very frankly the question as to how many factors must be postulated, and it

[6] Guilford pointed out that with ten tests, there are 630 tetrads to be calculated; with twenty tests, there are 14,535 (Guilford, 1936, p. 463).

should then be left as a question of fact in each inquiry whether one of these factors should be regarded as general.[7]

Major factor systems more or less resembling Thurstone's have been developed by Hotelling, Kelley, Burt, Holzinger, and others.[8] Until now, Thurstone's methods have led in popularity by a wide margin. They are relatively less laborious than most, although the increasing availability of electronic computers may make this aspect unimportant in the future. Also, they permit one to choose, from among an infinity of mathematically equivalent solutions, that one which seems to make the most psychological sense.[9]

The process of factor analysis consists essentially of "factoring" (in a sense analogous to that in which polynomials are factored in algebra) a table composed of intercorrelations among tests, to obtain the correlations (i.e., loadings) between each one of the real tests and a new set of hypothetical variables, called "reference" factors. These last are fewer in number than the tests with which one started, provided one does not count the specific factors, which are as numerous as the original tests. The reference factors are then transformed (i.e., "rotated") into a set of final factors such that each one has very high correlations with a few tests and correlations as near zero as possible with the rest, a state of affairs, called "simple structure." [1] One may then deduce the nature of each factor, and name it by psychological analysis of the tests with which it is most highly correlated.

The computations involved are formidable, especially if the original table is a large one. Moreover, there are repeated stages in the process where the psychologist's judgment enters in. Quite apart from the subjectivity inherent in naming factors, two workers would not necessarily derive from a given table the same factors and factor loadings, though one solution can sometimes be transformed into another (cf. Wrigley, 1958). For example, Thurstone permitted his multiple group factors to be correlated with one another in order to secure better

---

[7] From L. L. Thurstone, in C. Murchison, ed., A *History of Psychology in Autobiography*, Vol. 4, 1952, p. 314. Used by permission of Clark University Press, Worcester, Mass.

[8] The history of factor analysis is a complex story in its own right, marked by numerous schisms and sects (cf. Wolfle, 1940, and Tryon, 1959).

[9] This last seems a dubious advantage to mathematicians, who prefer that a problem have a definite answer.

[1] There is an infinity of self-consistent sets of factors obtainable by rotation, which are equally "good" mathematically, in the sense that all possess the fundamental property of giving back the original test intercorrelations with which one started when the loadings are properly cross-multiplied according to the rules of the game. The "simple structure" set (provided one can be found) is preferred not on mathematical but on psychological grounds.

definition of the psychological meaning of each one; but one of the variables which must be assumed to underlie his underlying factors (i.e., the "second order factors" required to account for the correlation of the first order ones) seems to be our old friend "g." The Thurstone and Spearman conceptualizations hence are not contradictory, but merely alternative descriptions of the set of relationships appearing in the original correlation table.

> The correlations of the primary factors can be factored, just like the correlations among tests. When this is done, we find several second-order factors. One of these seems to agree very well with Spearman's general intellective factor g. The critics feature our support of Spearman's g, but they ignore the fact that this work represents at least a modest gain in unraveling the complexities of mental organization [Thurstone, 1952, p. 316].[2]

A graphic representation of the major approaches to factor analysis is shown in Figure 75.

Factor Analysis in Test Construction

The trend of mental tests over the last quarter-century from single-score devices for screening to multi-score batteries for individual guidance has already been mentioned. Multiple factor analysis has played a very important part in this development by providing a rationale for deciding what intellectual dimensions to measure and what kinds of test items to use for the measuring.

The well-known *Tests of Primary Mental Abilities* (PMA) represent the culmination of Thurstone's own work in factor analysis. The cognitive factors which Thurstone, after extensive factorial studies, regarded as best established included these seven "primary abilities": Verbal comprehension (V); Word Fluency (W); Number, i.e., computational facility (N); Space, i.e., spatial visualization (S); Associative Memory (M); Perceptual Speed (P); Reasoning (R). The PMA battery, which has been issued in several versions for different age groups, yields separate scores on most of the factors listed. This battery provides with several scores a much more differentiated description of an individual's abilities than can a single-score test, but the advantage is in part offset by the lower reliability of the necessarily briefer subscales.[3] The Differential Aptitude Tests (DAT) produced by the Psychological Corporation are another carefully constructed battery based on factor analysis.

---

[2] Used by permission of Clark University Press, Worcester, Mass.
[3] See Buros (1953, No. 716, pp. 698–710) for a critical evaluation of the PMA battery.

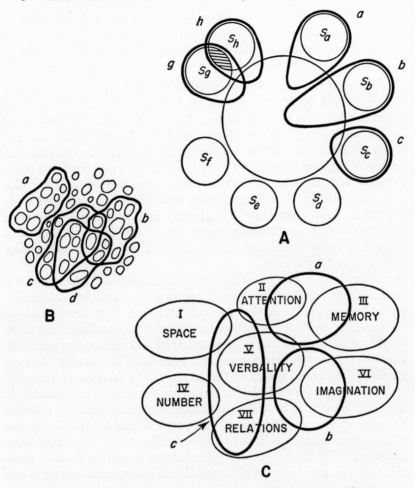

FIGURE 75. Graphic representation of Spearman's two-factor theory (A), of a sampling theory (B), and of the weighted group-factor theory (C), showing correlated tests. (By permission from J. P. Guilford, *Psychometric Methods*, 2nd ed., p. 475, Copyright, 1954. McGraw-Hill Book Co., Inc.)

The Present Status of Factor Analysis

The goal of factor analysis as conceived by its adherents is certainly a fundamental one—to discover a set of basic descriptive dimensions for psychology comparable to the variables of mass, velocity, acceleration, temperature, etc., without which classical physics would have been impossible.

The fundamental variables or dimensions of human ability are still very much within the unexplored territory reserved for psychologists.

To meet the challenge of this situation, a few of our number [the factor analysts] have stepped forward with statistical instruments . . . with which any unitary traits of personality can be isolated from the intricate web of mental life.[4]

Yet with the admission of multiple group factors, history comes full circle back to faculty psychology, in the fundamental sense that observable behavior is explained by reference to a relatively small number of "underlying" powers of the mind. To be sure, there are important differences. Factors are mathematical variables (though the process of deriving them is not free of subjectivity) and are based upon empirical test intercorrelations rather than upon philosophical speculation and tradition. Moreover, the more sophisticated factorists acknowledge that their factors are hypothetical and provisional. However, such phraseology as "primary source traits" or "basic abilities" has seemed to imply belief that factors are real and causal rather than imaginary and explanatory.

If factor analysis could demonstrate its fundamental superiority as a basis for test construction, the charge that it constitutes neo-faculty psychology would seem shallow and irrelevant. The alternative—in each specific prediction situation to construct and validate tests anew for the particular group of people concerned and against the particular criteria available—is cumbersome and inefficient. How much more attractive is the grand design of the factorists—to describe all the multiplicity of criterion variables by specifying the relative importance for each of a handful of basic human abilities derived from factor analysis; to construct a set of "factor-pure" tests, each to measure a different one of these basic human abilities; by administration of the set of tests to an individual to be able to predict by simple linear equations his most probable status on as many of all the vast array of pre-factored criteria as one wishes.

Unfortunately, this program remains mostly a program. The statistical industry of a small army of factorists over the past thirty years has not advanced us very far toward the goal. For one thing, factors, which were expected to serve us like the dimensions of classical physics, act more like the bewildering particles of the subatomic world. For example, a reasoning factor which is well defined in a heterogeneous battery of tests of many types may disintegrate into sub-factor fragments when the battery contains only rather similar types of tests.[5] Hence the

---

[4] By permission from *Psychometric Methods*, 1st ed., by J. P. Guilford. Copyright, 1936. McGraw-Hill Book Co., Inc.

[5] For Spearman it mattered not at all what one put into the "hotchpotch," provided only that "undue similarity" among tests was avoided. But the composition of a test in terms of Thurstonian factors depends very much upon what other tests are included with it in the factor analysis. Rotation toward simple structure yields somewhat more invariant factors, but does not dispose of the problem.

list of factors waxes ever longer, and the suspicion grows that we have discovered not basic dimensions of the mind, but simply more or less arbitrary classifications of tests.

The results of testing hundreds of thousands of men in the armed forces and of analyzing these data suggest to many psychologists that the number of basic mental abilities may often have been underestimated. From factorial analyses of many different matrices of intercorrelations obtained as a result of testing aviation cadets in AAF classification centers, factors that have been mathematically determined have been named as indicated in the following list. [There follows a list of twenty-nine.] [6] There is no objective method of determining whether the names attached to the factors discovered in the analyses are accurate descriptions of the mental abilities represented by the factors.[7]

And Wechsler notes rather plaintively,

. . . the profusion of factors discovered seems to contradict the intent or purpose of the factorial technique, the generally stated aim of which is to account for the major variance of a large battery of tests in terms of a minimal number of primary abilities or factors. Actually, there seem to be more factors than available tests, certainly than good tests of intelligence.[8]

Nor do the practical achievements of factor analysis thus far offer much firmer justification. As Cronbach remarked,

The best combination of two or three primary factor scores should predict grades a little better, in most subjects, than the short general mental test. The improvement of correlation is quite small, however, especially in view of the longer testing time used. All studies of prediction indicate that in its present stage of development the factorial approach has not produced tests which are superior to non-factorial diagnostic tests for practical purposes.[9]

[6] French (1951) offers 59 in the aptitude and achievement area. Guilford (1956) lists 40 factors as being well established, and in a more recent paper (1959) proposes a systematic classification which allows for 120!

[7] From F. B. Davis, *Utilizing Human Talent*, 1947, p. 59. Used by permission of author and American Council on Education, Washington, D.C.

[8] From D. Wechsler, *The Measurement and Appraisal of Adult Intelligence*, 1958, pp. 127f., and used by permission of the author and Williams and Wilkins, Baltimore.

[9] In a more recent statement, Cronbach (1960, Chap. 9) takes a less pessimistic position with respect to factor analysis, but concedes that "the number of possible factors is inexhaustible, if we are willing to make the factors sufficiently trivial" (p. 260). His discussion provides a concise and up-to-date summary of the factor-analytic point of view. The excerpt is taken from L. J. Cronbach, *Essentials of Psychological Testing*, p. 210, copyright 1949 by Harper and Brothers, New York, and used by permission of author and publisher.

Does it follow that all the effort and ingenuity of the factor-analysis movement of the last fifty years have been wasted? The writer thinks not. Factor analysis provides a systematic way of apprehending and representing geometrically the complex interrelationships latent in a large table of test intercorrelations. It may also justify itself in guiding the construction of more effective test batteries, and certainly aids us in selecting tests to minimize overlap in a team. Admittedly this is a modest achievement for a movement which has absorbed so much creative energy.

RETROSPECT AND PROSPECT

WE HAVE NOW COME rather more than full circle. In 1890 the residue of faculty psychology implicit in men's thinking shaped attempts to measure the mind. Separate faculties were postulated by such investigators as Cattell, Sharp, and Oehrn, and tests invented to measure them. Binet, and later Terman, guided more by empirical considerations than by theory, abandoned this approach to sample widely among the adjustive powers of the mind and strike an over-all average. The theories of Thorndike and Thomson, which tended to identify intelligence with the number of "connections" or "bonds" possessed by the mind, might have provided a theoretical basis for the mental tests as samplings of such connections. But the tradition of faculty psychology dies hard. The sampling view seemed almost too much on the level of common sense; and besides, no clear rules were forthcoming then or since to insure the thoroughness and representativeness of the sampling. Men preferred to explain the phenomena of intelligence by reference to underlying powers of the mind. To be sure, the first of the mathematical models of intelligence, Spearman's monarchic doctrine of a single "g" immanent in all cognitive activity, seemed a vast advance over older psychologies with their arbitrarily chosen and conflicting lists of faculties. Yet the failure of the Spearman theory to accord with the psychometric facts forced a retreat to the neo-faculty position of Thurstone, a doctrine which seems currently to be the victim of too much success in discovering distinguishable dimensions of intelligence. If the already numerous multiple group factors continue to multiply, the ironic possibility exists that Thurstonians, like the Spearmanians before them, may yet find themselves with a horde of factors almost as numerous as the sampling theorists' "bonds."

Yet it would be unjust to dismiss the research effort of the last half century as a sort of complicated ring-around-the-rosy that ends where it began. Scientific theory swings back and forth, but it also moves forward. The well-constructed, elaborately standardized, and highly reliable mental tests of today represent an enormous advance over the best efforts of Binet in psychological technics as well as in social utility. We may well be proud of them. They have, moreover, made it possible to collect a great deal of information on the nature and extent of human differences of many kinds, on interrelationships among these differences, and between them and important biological and social variables. To be sure, research has sometimes yielded contradictory results—but time and the accumulation of knowledge usually resolve matters, and it often turns out that the confusion arose not from conflicting answers but from improperly phrased questions.

Relations between Science and Society

For the thoughtful reader, the history of research upon intelligence provides an instructive example of the close link between science and the society in which it is rooted. The idea that intellectual discovery proceeds in an ivory tower is largely myth; in those instances in which scientific innovations seem to bear little relationship to the social matrix, they run a serious risk of being neglected and misunderstood until emerging human needs provide the circumstances necessary for acceptance and exploitation.

As our account has shown, early attempts to measure the mind, such as Sharp's, were laboratory exercises, and regarded as peripheral to psychology even by the academicians who invented them. Real progress began when society set the problem—to provide a feasible means of classifying persons according to ability—generated by the needs of the evolving humanitarian and educational institutions in that society. The Binet, the Army Alpha, and the other single-score tests served well the need for screening instruments; but the recent growth of clinical and counseling psychology, itself prompted by increasing public concern for the happiness and welfare of the individual members of society, is stimulating the development of multi-score diagnostic tests where formerly single score tests sufficed. This development has been paralleled by changes in factor models from Spearman to Thurstone. Indeed, the production of multi-score tests has been an important achievement of the factor analysts. But the trend toward diagnostic tools might well have taken place even without factor analysis. While most current tests are sooner or later subjected to factor analysis (e.g., the 1937 Stanford-Binet and the WAIS), it is often something of an afterthought to test construction. In short, social needs have seemed to lead, and theoretical developments to follow, the changes in mental tests over the last half century.

Moreover, as sometimes happens, the absence of an agreed-upon theoretical basis has not prevented the empirical enterprise from having reciprocally a very considerable impact upon society—witness the quasi-legal status of test results in commitment for mental deficiency, or in determining draft liability and military assignment. Tests may yet provide a more rational basis than skin color for pupil-assignment policies of the schools in areas of the United States where rapid change is producing severe strains in the structure of society.

The Need for a Theory

And what of the future? Until now, intelligence tests have proven extremely useful in the absence of a satisfactory theory or definition of intelligence. Even under these conditions, we may expect further improvement with respect to technical details. However, fundamental progress will almost surely depend upon providing our tools with a more solid theoretical foundation. Not only the psycho-technics of test construction, but also the resolution of such important questions as the relation of differences in intellectual performance to sex, age, training, etc. depend upon our success in achieving a more coherent theory.

With Spearman's two-factor model, it seemed for some years as if such a foundation had been discovered. More recently, the Thurstone group or multiple-factor theory, instigated actually by the failure of the Spearman model, was hopefully regarded as the footing upon which differential psychology might achieve a system of fundamental dimensions, with advantages as great as those conferred upon classical mechanics by the gram-centimeter-second system. Yet the very proliferation of factors has reduced them from hypothetical constructs to mere intervening variables, and robbed the factor theory of the claims to elegance and parsimony which had been its basic justification. Test constructors will continue to employ factorial procedures, provided they pay off in improving the efficiency and predictive value of our test batteries, but the hope that factor analysis can supply a short inventory of "basic abilities" is already waning.

The continuous difficulties with factor analysis over the last half century suggest that there may be something fundamentally wrong with models which conceptualize intelligence in terms of a finite number of linear dimensions. To the statistician's dictum that whatever exists can be measured, the factorist has added the assumption that whatever can be "measured" must exist. But the relation may not be reversible, and the assumption may be false. Is there an alternative?

Criteria for a Theory

First, let us consider the things which a satisfactory theory of intelligence should do. It should provide a rational basis for the construction of single-score and multi-score tests of intelligence and aptitude; it must account for the empirically known relationships among them—and between them and the usual criteria of educational and vocational success. This is to say, it must make provision both for the generality and for the specificity of individual differences in cognitive areas. It must provide an explanation of the curve of change in ability throughout the entire life span from earliest infancy to senescence, and allow for the fact that performances involving different test content wax and wane at different rates and shift in their differentiation from one another at different life stages. It must take into account the influences of brain damage and disease, sensory and motor impairment, infection, and drugs of various kinds. It must comprehend the facts on family resemblance in level and organization of abilities, accumulated in fifty years of research on the role of heredity in human differences. At the same time it must account for the demonstrated influence of education and training in altering test performance, including data on differences associated with schooling, class level, ethnic group membership, language, generation, etc. And lastly, it should be at least congruent with psychological theories of learning and motivation and theories on other levels of investigation and description, e.g., neurophysiology, biochemistry, genetics, etc. Or to put it all very briefly, our theory of intelligence must deal with empirically known facts of organization, maturation, structural and functional pathology, heredity, and environment—and fit into the total structure of science. Psychology is far from having so comprehensive a theory at present, nor is one immediately in prospect. The writer believes, perhaps overoptimistically, that there are signs of increasing agreement about some of the premises on which future theories will be built.

Basic Premises

One such premise is that intelligence is not an entity, nor even a dimension *in* a person, but rather an *evaluation* of a behavior sequence (or the average of many such), from the point of view of its adaptive adequacy. What constitutes intelligence depends upon what the situation demands, though we add precision (along with a bit of anthropocentrism) by restricting the term to evaluations of behavior involving the manipulation of symbols.[1]

[1] As I. Chein (1945) has remarked, "No psychologist has ever observed *intelligence*; many have observed intelligent behavior. This observation should be the starting point of any theory of intelligence. . . . Intelligence is an attribute of behavior, not an attribute of a person. Even though we may observe some constancy in how intelligently a person acts in different situations, we may on this basis speak of the person's characteristic behaviors and not of a genuine attribute of a person." ("On the Nature of Intelligence," *J. gen. Psychol.*, 1945, 32, pp. 111, 120). Used by permission of the author and the publisher. Cf. also Bayley (1955) and Garrett (1946).

Many psychologists would agree also upon a second premise, that in all behavior involving the manipulation of symbols (including those behavior samples we call "tests"), *content* and *process* are inextricably confounded. We inevitably sample what has been learned in the past, as well as how efficiently learning takes place in the present. In reviewing the phenomena which a good theory should explain, it is clear that some concern primarily the functional efficiency of the brain and nervous system, while others refer to the richness and organization of the mind.[2] There is hence heuristic advantage in distinguishing between content and process determinants of intelligent behavior, while recognizing that even "contents" have their physiological and anatomical representation in the brain.

The Process Aspect

At the present time, our theories do not handle the process aspect very satisfactorily.[3] Sampling theorists have little to say about it. Factorists have sometimes implied that general factors refer primarily to physiological (i.e., process) aspects of intelligence, the specifics to the content aspects, but this is only speculation. A case can be made for regarding "g" or even such factors as "fluency" and "speed" as reflecting the integrative efficiency of the nervous system; but such factors as "number," "verbal," "spatial," or the like seem actually to refer more to test *content* than to dimensions of the learning *process*.[4] Cortical conductivity and retentivity, each mediated by complex biochemical determinants, may be two dimensions of individual differences in process aspects of intelligence, or perhaps such variables take the form of differential efficiency in learning via visual, kinesthetic, or auditory

[2] Psychologists discussing this problem have often distinguished between "capacity" and "ability." The distinction has not been a particularly fruitful one. "Capacity" remains a purely inferential variable with no independent indices, and the volumetric connotations of the term seem to underemphasize the continuously changing, self-regulating aspect of a living system. "Ability," which our tests actually measure, depends both upon what has been learned in the past and upon the present efficiency of the neural mechanism, though different tasks (e.g., Wechsler's "Hold" and "Don't hold" tests) maximize sometimes one, sometimes the other.

[3] The work of Halstead (1947) is unusual in focusing primarily on this rather neglected topic. Some of his tests offer promising approaches to measuring process efficiency with relatively little content contamination. Also, Piaget (1957, 1960) who formulates the stages of cognitive development in terms of the abstract, logical operations achieved, emphasizes the process aspect, though in a genetic, normative context.

[4] Guilford's elaborate schema of mental organization classifies factors with respect to "operations," "contents," and "products" (1959, p. 470).

modes, as the animal research of Krech, Rosenzweig, *et al.* (1954) seems to suggest.[5]

Intelligence tests vary in their relative emphasis upon process vs. content; most of them tend to maximize the importance of the latter, because they are focused upon estimating the total effectiveness of the person, not the plasticity of his nervous system at the time of testing. Nevertheless, there would be great advantage, for example, in diagnosing organic pathology—brain damage, feeble-mindedness, or deteriorative states—in being able to assess directly the process aspect of intellectual functioning. Some of our tests attempt this (e.g., Wechsler's deterioration ratio) but only as a sort of by-product from tests organized primarily for other purposes. Direct physiological, chemical, or electrical indices of central nervous-system efficiency are not in principle impossible. Meanwhile, existing procedures aimed at the process level, e.g., measures of figural after-effect or of fluency and ability to shift one's set, deserve more careful exploration than they have yet received.

The Content Aspect

The adequacy (intelligence) of behavior depends not only upon the status of the neural mechanism, but also upon possession of the specific internalized experiences (i.e., learnings) which are relevant to effective action in the given situation. We assume that these determinants, too, have their representation in the form of micro-modifications of the nervous system, possibly in specific loci. These last have not been directly observed nor are they well understood. We can treat these determinants better on the psychological level, as mental contents.

With respect to such mental contents, the Thomson-Tryon sampling theory is the simplest, most elegant, and most satisfactory for explaining the facts.

Intelligence is not conceived in terms of linear dimensions. Factors have only classificatory value and reflect mostly the environmental field. The sampling theory explains phenomena of test intercorrelation on the basis that facts presented together (e.g., in arithmetic class) tend to be learned—or not learned—together. Circumstance, and the self-selection of experience in consequence of rewarding or punishing events, may lead, with increasing age, to increased differentiation and independence of abilities in different content areas. However, the richer one's total experience—conferred, for example, by a superior home or by extended schooling—the greater the likelihood that one will acquire the contents

[5] A study has been reported in which it proved possible to predict from test scores whether an individual could learn better when taught by explanation or by rote (Edgerton, 1958). Such differences may reflect basic physiological dispositions.

sampled by whatever test. On such a basis we may account for general factors, for group factors, and for the increasing differentiation of ability with age. Similarly, cognitive sex differences can be explained as a consequence of the differential training of the two sexes in our society.

The phenomena of growth and decline can also be dealt with in the framework of sampling theory. Inasmuch as learning continues throughout life, we may expect samplings of "mental contents" to show steady increase. However, the rate of acquisition may very well be a decelerating one, if only because progressively fewer situations teach anything really new. Declines which have been reported in such functions as information, vocabulary, etc. are probably artifacts of differences in education between the generations compared.[6] On the other hand, changes in rate of activity may reflect the reduced efficiency of the aging organism. Hence the relation of age to test score may depend upon whether content or process variance is maximized, either by selecting the test material or by scoring power vs. speed.

From the point of view of sampling theory, which denies that intelligence is an entity, dimension, or even a small bundle of dimensions, what is the meaning of test validity?

Generally speaking, that test is most valid which possesses the most elements in common with the criterion. Specific criteria can usually be discovered for tests of occupational or educational aptitude, and we may select our tests in accordance with their validity coefficients.

In the case of general intelligence tests, the real criterion is effectiveness in dealing with the total culture. The validity of such a test is not its correlation with some underlying dimension of general intelligence, but simply the breadth and representativeness of its sampling, and its avoidance of content relevant only to narrow kinds of adaptations. Tests of general intelligence predict many criteria with moderate success, though predicting no specific one so well as a test tailored to the purpose.[7] They thus possess very real utility and economy of application, even though they do not disclose fundamental parameters of the mind which the factorists have sought. Neither Binet, nor Terman, nor Wechsler claimed more.

Improvement in general intelligence tests, from the sampling point of view, will require better techniques for sampling the content actually required for successful adaptation to the demands of living in our culture. Brunswik's principle of ecological representativeness (1956)

---

[6] It is no accident that the more recent the study, the later the age at which intelligence is supposed to conclude its growth phase and begin to decline.

[7] Tests somewhat narrower in scope, e.g., the separate tests of a factorized battery, should predict better than general tests the criteria with which they have most in common, but by the same token, their range of predictive usefulness is necessarily curtailed.

needs to be applied to test construction. Naturally, what is relevant content will differ from age to age. We shall not be dismayed to find no tests which are equally suitable for all groups from two to eighty-two, nor shall we be surprised that "IQ constancy" declines the longer the temporal interval concerned.

The considerations outlined above are admittedly vague in some particulars, more a program than a solution for our difficulties in theory. One aspect of this approach is quite unsatisfactory—notably its failure to integrate content and process in a single formulation which can be related to theorizing on more fundamental levels.

You, the reader, are challenged to produce a better formulation.

The task is not hopeless, but will require freshness of attack and respect for empirical facts, even when they prove to be "disturbers."

REFERENCES

BAYLEY, N.   On the growth of intelligence. *Amer. Psychologist,* 1955, *10,* 805–18.

BINET, A.   La mesure en psychologie individuelle. *Rev. phil.,* 1898, 2nd sem., 113–23.

———.   *L'étude experimentale de l'intelligence.* Paris: Schleicher Frères & Cie, 1903.

———.   Review of C. Spearman: "The proof and measurement of association between two things"; "General intelligence objectively determined and measured." *Année psychol.,* 1905, *11,* 623–4.

———.   *Les idées modernes sur les enfants.* Paris: Flammarion, 1911. (a)

———.   Nouvelles recherches sur la mesure du niveau intellectuel chez les enfants de l'école. *Année psychol.,* 1911, *17,* 145–210. (b)

BINET, A., AND HENRI, V.   La Psychologie individuelle. *Année psychol.,* 1896, *2,* 411–65.

BINET, A., AND SIMON, T.   Sur la necessité d'établir un diagnostic scientifique des états inférieurs de l'intelligence. *Année psychol.,* 1905, *11,* 163–90. (a)

———.   Méthodes nouvelles pour le diagnostic du niveau intellectuel des anormaux. *Année psychol.,* 1905, *11,* 191–244. (b)

———.   Applications des méthodes nouvelles au diagnostic du niveau intellectuel chez des enfants normaux et anormaux d'hospice et d'école primaire. *Année psychol.,* 1905, *11,* 245–336. (c)

———.   Le développement de l'intelligence chez les enfants. *Année psychol.,* 1908, *14,* 1–94.

BORING, E. G.   Intelligence as the tests test it. *New Republic*, 1923, *35*, 35–7.

BRUNSWIK, E.   *Perception and the representative design of psychological experiments*, 2nd ed. Berkeley, University of California Press, 1956.

BUROS, O. K. (Ed.).   *The fourth mental measurements yearbook.* Highland Park, New Jersey: Gryphon Press, 1953.

CATTELL, J. MCK.   Mental tests and measurements. *Mind*, 1890, *15*, 373–81.

CHEIN, I.   On the nature of intelligence. *J. gen. Psychol.*, 1945, *32*, 111–26.

CRONBACH, L. J.   *Essentials of psychological testing.* New York: Harper and Brothers, 1949. Second ed., 1960.

CURTIS, H. A.   A study of the relative effects of age and of test difficulty upon factor patterns. *Genet. Psychol. Monogr.*, 1949, *40*, 99–148.

DAVIS, F. B.   *Utilizing human talent.* Washington: American Council on Education, 1947.

EDGERTON, H. A.   Adapting training methods to trainee aptitudes. *Off. Naval Res. Res. Revs.*, Oct., 1958, 17–19.

EELLS, K.   *Intelligence and cultural differences.* Chicago: University of Chicago Press, 1951.

ESQUIROL, J. E. D.   *Des maladies mentales.* 2 vols. Paris: J. B. Baillière, 1838.

FRENCH, J. W.   The description of aptitude and achievement tests in terms of rotated factors. *Psychometr. Monogr.*, 1951, No. 5.

GALTON, F.   *Inquiries into human faculty and its development.* London: Macmillan, 1883.

———.   *Natural inheritance.* New York: The Macmillan Company, 1889.

GARRETT, H. E.   The standardization of the Terman-Merrill revision of the Stanford-Binet scale. *Psychol. Bull.*, 1943, *40*, 194–201.

———.   A developmental theory of intelligence. *Amer. Psychologist*, 1946, *1*, 372–8.

GODDARD, H. H.   *The Kallikak family.* New York: The Macmillan Company, 1912.

———.   *Human efficiency and levels of intelligence.* Princeton: Princeton University Press, 1920.

GUILFORD, J. P.   *Psychometric methods.* New York: McGraw-Hill Book Co., 1936. Second ed., 1954.

———.   The structure of intellect. *Psychol. Bull.*, 1956, *53*, 267–93.

———.   Three faces of intellect. *Amer. Psychologist*, 1959, *14*, 469–79.

HALSTEAD, W. C. *Brain and intelligence.* Chicago: University of Chicago Press, 1947.

HONZIK, M. P., MACFARLANE, J. W., AND ALLEN, L. The stability of mental test performance between two and eighteen years. *J. exp. Educ.,* 1948, *18,* 309–24.

HULL, C. L. *Aptitude testing.* Yonkers-on-Hudson, New York: World Book Co., 1928.

HUMPHREY, G., AND HUMPHREY, M. *The wild boy of Aveyron.* New York: Appleton-Century-Crofts, 1932.

Intelligence and its measurement—a symposium. *J. educ. Psychol.,* 1921, *12,* 123–47, 195–216, 271–5.

JONES, H. E. The environment and mental development. In Carmichael, L. (Ed.), *Manual of child psychology,* 2nd ed. New York: John Wiley and Sons, 1954.

KRECH, D., ROSENZWEIG, M. R., BENNETT, E. L., AND KRUECKEL, B. Enzyme concentrations in the brain and adjustive behavior-patterns. *Science,* 1954, *120,* 994–6.

MCNEMAR, Q. A critical examination of the University of Iowa studies of environmental influences upon the I.Q. *Psychol. Bull.,* 1940, *37,* 63–92.

———. *The revision of the Stanford-Binet scale.* Boston: Houghton Mifflin Co., 1942.

PETERSON, J. *Early conceptions and tests of intelligence.* Yonkers-on-Hudson, New York: World Book Co., 1925.

PIAGET, J. *Logic and psychology.* New York: Basic Books Inc., 1957.

———. *Psychology of intelligence.* Paterson, N.J.: Littlefield, Adams & Co., 1960.

SHARP, S. E. Individual psychology: a study in psychological method. *Amer. J. Psychol.,* 1898–99, *10,* 329–91.

SPEARMAN, C. The proof and measurement of association between two things. *Amer. J. Psychol.,* 1904, *15,* 72–101. (a)

———. "General intelligence" objectively determined and measured. *Amer. J. Psychol.,* 1904, *15,* 201–93. (b)

———. *The nature of "intelligence" and the principles of cognition.* New York: The Macmillan Company, 1923.

———. *The abilities of man.* New York: The Macmillan Company, 1927.

———. Chapter in Murchison, C., (Ed.), *A history of psychology in autobiography.* Vol. 1. Worcester, Mass.: Clark University Press, 1930.

STERN, W. L. Über die psychologischen Methoden der Intelligenzprüfung. *Ber. V. Kongress exp. Psychol.,* 1912, *16,* 1–109.

STODDARD, G. D. *The meaning of intelligence.* New York: The Macmillan Company, 1943.

SWINEFORD, F.   General, verbal, and spatial bi-factors after three years. *J. educ. Psychol.*, 1949, 40, 353–60.

TERMAN, L. M.   *The measurement of intelligence.* Boston: Houghton Mifflin Co., 1916.

———.   Trails to psychology. In Murchison, C. (Ed.), *A history of psychology in autobiography.* Vol. 2. Worcester, Mass.: Clark University Press, 1932.

TERMAN, L. M., *et al.   Genetic studies of genius.* 5 vols. Standford, California: Stanford University Press, Vol. I, 1925; Vol. II, 1926; Vol. III, 1930; Vol. IV, 1947; Vol. V, 1959.

TERMAN, L. M., AND MERRILL, M. A.   *Measuring intelligence.* Boston: Houghton Mifflin Co., 1937.

———.   *The Stanford-Binet intelligence scale.* Boston: Houghton Mifflin Co., 1960.

THOMSON, G. H.   General versus group factors in mental activities. *Psychol. Rev.*, 1920, 27, 173–90.

———.   *The factorial analysis of human ability*, 5th ed. London: University of London Press, 1951.

———.   Chapter in Murchison, C. (Ed.). *A history of psychology in autobiography.* Vol. 4. Worcester, Mass.: Clark University Press, 1952.

THORNDIKE, E. L.   *The measurement of intelligence.* New York: *Bur. Publ.*, Teachers College, Columbia University, 1925.

THORNDIKE, R. L.   "Constancy" of the I.Q. *Psychol. Bull.*, 1940, 37, 167–86.

THURSTONE, L. L.   *Multiple factor analysis.* Chicago: University of Chicago Press, 1947.

———.   Chapter in Murchison, C. (Ed.), *A history of psychology in autobiography.* Vol. 4. Worcester, Mass.: Clark University Press, 1952.

TRYON, R. C.   A theory of psychological components—an alternative to mathematical factors. *Psychol. Rev.*, 1935, 42, 425–54.

———.   Domain formulation of cluster and factor analysis. *Psychometrika*, 1959, 24, 113–36.

TUDDENHAM, R. D.   Soldier intelligence in World Wars I and II. *Amer. Psychologist*, 1948, 3, 54–6.

VARON, E. J.   The development of Alfred Binet's psychology. *Psychol. Monogr.*, 1935, 46, No. 207.

WECHSLER, D.   *The measurement and appraisal of adult intelligence*, 4th ed. Baltimore: Williams and Wilkins, 1958.

WELLMAN, B. L., SKEELS, H. M., AND SKODAK, M.   Review of McNemar's critical examination of Iowa studies. *Psychol. Bull.*, 1940, 37, 93–111.

WHIPPLE, G. M. *Manual of mental and physical tests*. Baltimore: Warwick and York, 1910. Second ed. in 2 vols., 1914–15.

WISSLER, C. The correlation of mental and physical tests. *Psychol. Rev.*, Monograph Supplement, 1901, 3, No. 6.

WOLFLE, D. Factor analysis to 1940. *Psychometr. Monogr.*, 1940, No. 3. Chicago: University of Chicago Press, 1940.

WRIGLEY, C. Objectivity in factor analysis. *Educ. psychol. Measmt.*, 1958, 18, 463–76.

YERKES, R. M. (Ed.). *Psychological examining in the United States Army*. Washington: Mem. Nat. Acad. Sci., 1921, Vol. 15.

YOUNG, K. The history of mental testing. *Ped. Sem.*, 1924, 31, 1–48.

Clinical versus Statistical
Prediction in Psychology

H A R R I S O N G. G O U G H

INTRODUCTION

TO MANY PEOPLE the prediction problem must seem to be the basic problem of applied psychology. In schools, industry, and elsewhere the psychologist is often asked to make forecasts, for example to predict the kind of scholastic record a certain student will be able to achieve, the quality of work to be expected from a particular job applicant, the likelihood that this prisoner will do well or poorly on parole, and so on. Many of the testing techniques which psychologists have developed have arisen in direct response to such needs to predict, from Binet's endeavor to discover a method for identifying potentially slow learners among Parisian school children of the early 1900's, to E. K. Strong's efforts of the 1920's and 1930's to develop ways of measuring vocational interests and the work of S. R. Hathaway and J. C. McKinley in the 1940's in creating a valid instrument for the differential diagnosis of syndromes of psychopathology. Judgment as to the "worth" of psychological methods may well rest on the degree to which such forecasts can be made in an efficient and valid manner.

An immense body of literature now exists on a good many of the sectors of social life in which prediction might be attempted. Some examples would include predictions of personal adjustment (Horst *et al.*, 1941); scholastic performance (Crawford and Burnham, 1946; Gough, 1953; May, 1923); vocational interests and quality of work (Adkins,

1956; Strong, 1943 and 1955; Thorndike, 1934); business cycles (Mitchell, 1927); growth and change of population (Lorimer and Osborn, 1934; Pearl, 1925); length of life (Dublin and Lotka, 1936); voting behavior (Lazarsfeld, Berelson, and Gaudet, 1944); marital happiness (Burgess and Cottrell, 1939; Burgess and Wallin, 1953; Terman, 1938); crime and delinquency (Glueck and Glueck, 1930 and 1950; Hathaway and Monachesi, 1953); and recidivism on parole and probation (Monachesi, 1950; Schuessler, 1954).

In addition to the efforts concerned with such substantive problems (adjustment, criminal behavior, etc.), there has been a parallel course of development in the writings on the technical issues in prediction, including the logical (Reichenbach, 1938), the psychological (G. W. Allport, 1937; W. A. Hunt, 1959; McArthur, 1954; Meehl, 1954; Sarbin, 1944), and the psychometric (Cattell, 1937; Cronbach, 1960; Guilford, 1959; H. F. Hunt, 1950). It is one of these methodological issues—that of "clinical versus statistical prediction"—which constitutes the focus of interest of the present chapter.

The problem may be posed in a brief and simple manner: *In any given prediction situation which method is better—i.e., more accurate and more informative in a scientific way—that of the clinician or that of the actuary?* To predict a certain behavioral outcome, for example, "How well will this student do in college?" would it be better to ask for a forecast from the admissions officer who has studied the student's record, interviewed him about his goals and aspirations, and then thought about the problem in a judicious, rational, and informed way? Or would a more accurate prognostication be made if we turned the test and file data over to the statistician who would put them through his prediction equations and formulas in order to give an answer to our question?

The reader will perhaps note a certain "polarizing" effect of the above paragraph, in that his sentiments will be nudged favorably toward one of the protagonists and unfavorably away from the other. This inner preference which most people feel toward one or the other of the two modes of prediction is reflected in much of the writing on the topic. Thus by its proponents the statistical method has been described as operational, objective, reliable, sound, and verifiable, whereas by its opponents it has been called atomistic, pedantic, artificial, static, and pseudoscientific. The clinical approach, on the other hand, has been called dynamic, meaningful, deep, genuine, and sophisticated by its adherents, but by its opponents vague, hazy, subjective, unscientific, and verbalistic. Meehl (1954, p. 4) in his review of the problem of clinical vs. statistical prediction has provided a rather complete list of the strongly contrasting opinions which the issue seems to provoke.

The prediction of human behavior is so clearly an important task for psychological science that it is perhaps not surprising to find intense methodological preferences; the histories of many other significant research problems in science have shown this same strong sense of partisanship. In psychological prediction the controversy, of course, is not over the goal, but over what seem to be contrasting or even incompatible methods for attaining it. Some of the disagreement may be based on a misunderstanding of the concepts of "clinical prediction" and "statistical prediction," for it is not always easy to specify clearly where one procedure shades into the other, and the distinction itself is a matter of arbitrary definition. Perhaps our first responsibility in this chapter should be an elaboration of the two concepts so that the reader will have an adequate picture of the essential outlines of each.

Distinction between Clinical and Actuarial Prediction

In the practical context of everyday work the behavioral scientist is frequently called upon to make explicit and specific predictions about the future behavior of a given individual. He may if he chooses assign the individual to a class (or set of classes) of persons on the basis of test scores, interview data, ratings, etc., and then utilize the statistical frequency of a certain behavior in that class of persons as the foundation for his prediction about the given individual.

For example, previous tabulations of buying proclivities might have shown that in the category of persons defined by the four specifications— (1) subscribes to *The New Yorker*, (2) says "flat" instead of "apartment," (3) prefers the writings of Henry James to those of Charles Dickens, and (4) would rather have a sketch by Picasso than one of his completed pictures—the incidence of regular purchasing of bread made from "stone-ground flour" is 62 per cent. The actuarial prediction of bread-buying for a person who meets the class specifications is that he, too, will purchase the stone-ground variety. The appeal in this prediction is simply to the relative frequencies of purchasing previously observed in persons representative of this class; the prediction does *not* rest on any theory about the needs and values of such persons, nor on any other psychological inferences about them. This type of procedure, where the prediction derives solely from statistical considerations, is what is generally called the statistical (or actuarial) method of prediction.

Alternatively, prediction can be derived from a quite different set of considerations. On the basis of observations about an individual, his preferences, biases, values, etc., one could evolve a sort of psychodynamic portrait or hypothetical model, and then make a prediction based on the apparent psychological implications of the model. To illustrate, a medical-school admissions interviewer talks to an applicant, noting that he appears alert, speaks fluently, and has a well-organized fund of scientific information. From these observations the interviewer makes the induction that the applicant has superior intellectual capacity, that he can persevere constructively in the face of frustration, and that he is properly self-disciplined. These inferred attributes square 100 per cent with the interviewer's private conception of what it takes to be a good physician, and so the prediction, "Will succeed," is made and the applicant admitted. This second type of procedure is what is generally called the clinical (or case study) method of prediction.

In many situations both modes of prediction will be utilized and can be compared. For instance, in the medical school just mentioned there is very likely also a psychologist on the admissions board who is trying to make statistical predictions of the performance of students in medical school, using regression equations based on aptitude test scores, previous grade averages, and so on. Some writers (for example, Holt, 1958; Hutt, 1956; and Zubin, 1956) have urged that the clinician himself uses both modes concurrently, and that for this reason it is unwise to speak of them as opposed or alternate methods of prediction. The clinician, it is contended, should seek to formulate motivational principles and dynamic relationships pertinent to the prediction problem, but in so doing he will be guided by actuarial frequencies and by statistical analyses of the relevant data. We shall be obliged to study these views more thoroughly later, particularly in considering the differences between forecasts made in formal research settings and similar activity conducted under the concrete demands of daily practice. However, even if the clinical method seems sometimes fused with the actuarial, there is little doubt that the latter mode of prediction can be and often is used entirely independently of any clinical formulations or inductions (see Humphreys, 1956; Lundberg, 1939).

Also, in many clinical settings the exigencies (and biases) of everyday work do determine that a choice of methods will be made. Take the case of a prison inmate being considered for parole. The question is whether the man is ready for parole, i.e., whether the odds favor a successful outcome if parole is granted. Should the decision rest upon a forecast made after an intensive and prolonged clinical case study? Or should the statistical parole prediction tables elaborated by various authors (Burgess, 1928; Glueck and Glueck, 1943; Vold, 1931) be applied to determine the decision?

As another example, consider applicants for graduate training in a certain field, where the selection problem is to forecast the quality and merit of an applicant's later performance. Should the selection be based on interviews, examination of the application file, etc., by faculty members with the final decision an intuitive-clinical one made by them? Or should it be based on some specified set of test scores and biographical data combined actuarially into a predictive index? It is in the setting of concrete, on-going contexts such as these that the dichotomy of modes of prediction has tangible significance. Choices must be made, and in making these choices beliefs about the soundness and accuracy of the two approaches to prediction will find significant expression.

A Common Misconception

It should be clear from the foregoing that the distinction between clinical and actuarial methods does not rest on differences in the kind of data employed. This point is sometimes misunderstood, and the erroneous identities, *case material = clinical method* and *test scores = actuarial method*, are implicitly assumed. In fact, the clinician may derive his subjectively determined forecast from the same profile of test scores on the Strong Vocational Interest Blank used by the actuary in solving his prediction equation. On the other hand, a complex, dynamically profound series of therapeutic interviews could be analyzed either impressionistically or by means of some sort of statistical counting or tallying of signs and indices.

A second disclaimer is that the two terms do not refer to the way in which the prediction models were first derived. The actuary may be quite intuitive in the way he seeks out possible factors for use in later prediction, and the clinician may quite well have used a fully empirical method, such as factor analysis, in his evolving of a psychodynamic model of personality functioning.

The defining distinction between clinical and actuarial methods is instead to be found in the way in which the data, once specified, are combined for use in making the prediction. If the procedures, however complex mathematically, are in principle such that a clerk, or a machine, or anyone else could carry out the necessary operations and that the result would be the same in all instances, then the method is actuarial or statistical in the sense here being discussed. If the combining is done intuitively, if hypotheses and constructs are generated during the course of the analysis, and if the process is mediated by an individual's judgment and reflection, then the method is clinical. One might say, in a way, that the actuarial prediction is one *derived* from the data, whereas the clinical prediction is *created* from them.

Hart's "Experience Table"

Clinical prediction, by its nature, is as old as man; actuarial prediction, in the behavioral sciences at any rate, is a relatively recent development. Let us look briefly at some of the significant endeavors along actuarial lines. One of the first attempts to introduce an actuarial method in prediction was the "experience table" of the sociologist Hornell Hart (1923).

In early 1923 S. B. Warner had published a review of sixty life-history and background factors to determine which, if any, would be related to parole outcomes in a comparison of 300 successful with 300 unsuccessful parolees in the State of Massachusetts. His conclusion was that the items were of little or no value, and that more accurate prognoses could be made from the pre-parole criminal record and from the psychiatrist's report on those cases where the psychiatrist was willing to hazard a prediction.

Warner, however, failed to check the statistical significance of the many low-order relationships which his data revealed, and also failed to consider the possibility that a pooling of a number of weak predictors might yield a useful and valid over-all index. These deficiencies prompted Hart to a reanalysis of Warner's data, and to the conclusion that proper use of the life-history and background statistics would lead to a striking increase in the accuracy of parole prediction. It might be interjected that this sort of situation, where the more significant implications of one researcher's data are first seen by another investigator, is a frequent occurrence in the history of science.

Table 1, adapted from Hart's paper, shows how data for an experience table can be generated, and may be considered as the prototype of all later efforts of this type. The "positive" characteristics in Table 1 are the nine having a success rate of over 49.75, and the "negative" ones are the remaining twenty-one with a success rate below this figure.

Hart's own recommendation concerning the mode of application of the data presented in the table may be cited:

> In order to profit by past experience as summarized in Table 1 and as reinforced by other available data, so as in the future to parole as large a fraction as possible of the men who will succeed and as small a fraction as possible of the men who will violate their paroles, all of the information under the questions which have been proved to be significant should be combined into a prognostic score for each man coming up for parole. On the basis of such scores it would be possible to make reports to the Board in a form somewhat like the following:
>
> Jim Jones has a prognostic score of 93 points. In the past experience of the board among the men with prognostic scores in the neighborhood of 93 points, only 19 per cent have violated their paroles.
>
> Will Smith has a prognostic score of 21 points. In the past experience of the Board among men with prognostic scores close to 21 points, 80 per cent have violated their paroles.[1]

---

[1] From Hornell Hart, "Predicting Parole Success," *J. crimin. law and Criminol.*, 1923, 14, 411, and used by permission of author and publisher.

TABLE 1

CLASSIFICATIONS OF PAROLED PRISONERS FROM THE MASSACHUSETTS RE-
FORMATORY SHOWING THE PERCENTAGE OF SUCCESSFUL PAROLES AND OF
PAROLE VIOLATIONS FALLING INTO EACH GROUP, AND SHOWING WHAT PER-
CENTAGES OF THE PRISONERS PAROLED IN EACH GROUP SUCCEEDED *

| | Per cent distributions | | |
CHARACTERISTICS FOR WHICH OBSERVED CONTRASTS ARE QUITE UNLIKELY TO BE DUE TO CHANCE	Successful parolees	Parole violations	Per cent Successful
1. Men guilty of "other" crimes	11	2	85
2. Partly support unnamed persons	14	2	88
3. Men guilty of assault and battery	10	3	77
4. Occupation "none"	6	2	75
5. No criminal record	19	7	73
6. Accidental offenders	26	10	72
7. Religion of prisoner "other answers"	14	7	67
8. Extent of occupation "regular"	22	14	61
9. "Responsible" and "normal" offenders	30	22	58
10. Means of committing crime: fraud	46	59	44
11. Men using cigarettes	59	77	43
12. Character of associates "bad"	43	56	43
13. Men guilty of larceny	28	37	43
14. Men with three or more criminal records	51	68	43
15. Claim to be contributing to parents	40	55	42
16. Six or more times guilty misconduct in the reformatory	26	38	41
17. Served one or more jail sentences	43	65	40
18. Claim parents own property	22	35	39
19. Guilty of breaking and entering	24	37	39
20. Claim to attend church regularly	14	23	38
21. Evidence of disease "not answered"	10	17	37
22. Men with reformatory records	12	21	36
23. Marital relations of parents "fair," "unpleasant," or "questionable"	7	15	32
24. Serious illness "not answered"	6	15	29
25. Surgical operations "not answered"	6	16	27
26. Use drugs	2	7	22
27. Character of home "bad"	2	8	20
28. Mother drank	1	4	20
29. Father served jail sentence	1	15	6
30. Mother arrested or jailed	0	4	0

* From Hornell Hart, "Predicting Parole Success," *J. crimin. law and Criminol.*, 1923, *14*, 410. Used by permission of the publisher and the author.

The experience-table technique of forecasting has been widely extended in the years since Hart's paper, but the essentials of the method have remained the same. Even the format for reporting the prognostic score and its actuarial implications has survived, for example in the parole-prediction sheets prepared for each potential parolee in the State of Illinois Department of Corrections (see Ohlin, 1951).

Hart's proposal for prediction by means of an experience table was soon accepted by other workers. Borden (1928), for instance, studied 263 men paroled between July 1, 1923, and January 30, 1924, with success or failure on parole evaluated as of August, 1925. He correlated each factor in the experience table with the degree of success on parole, finding three factors (diagnosis of intelligence, parole prognosis made by the psychologist, and the number of previous commitments) which gave a multiple correlation of .41 with the criterion.

Work of Burgess

A more ambitious parole-prediction project, and one which won considerably wider appreciation of the method, was that of E. W. Burgess (1928). Burgess studied the institutional files of 3,000 men paroled from Illinois houses of correction. For each institution the base rate of parole violation was established, and then the experience-table factors were studied to see if significant deviations could be found. Twenty-one such pre-parole factors were identified; Table 2 gives an idea of the nature of the relationships for work-history items.

TABLE 2

PAROLE VIOLATION RATES FOR CATEGORIES OF WORK HISTORY *

| | *Violation rate by institution* | | |
SAMPLES	*Joliet*	*Menard*	*Pontiac*
All parolees	28.4%	26.5%	22.1%
No previous work record	44.4	25.0	28.0
Record of casual work	30.3	31.4	27.5
Record of irregular work	24.3	21.3	15.8
Record of regular work	12.2	5.2	8.8

* From Burgess, 1928, p. 229. Used by permission of the author and the publisher.

The figures in the first row across the table give the base rate of violation for all parolees. Scoring of an experience-table factor was achieved by assigning one point to any category with a violation rate less than this baseline, a zero weight being given to all other categories. A record of regular work would therefore receive a weighting of plus 1.

Burgess next defined nine classifications for the point totals and determined the violation-versus-non-violation rates for each class. Table 3 presents these results.

From Table 3 it can be seen that 68 of the parolees had point totals in the 16–21 range, and of these 68 men, 98.5 per cent (67 cases) were successful on parole versus 1.5 per cent (1 case) unsuccessful. At the other end of the scale, among the parolees in the 2 to 4 range of scores, 76 per cent were violators, only 24 per cent successful. These figures are quite impressive, but as so often happens in the history of research the method of analysis contains certain hidden flaws that were only later to be discovered. When we reach this later stage we will see that the deficiencies all but vitiate Burgess' findings.

TABLE 3

PAROLE EXPECTANCY RATES FOR THE BURGESS EXPERIENCE TABLE *

EXPERIENCE TABLE SCORE CLASSIFICATION	N	Expectancy rates, in percentages			
		Violators			Non-violators
		Minor	Major	Total	
16–21	68	1.5%	0.0%	1.5%	98.5%
14–15	140	0.7	1.5	2.2	97.8
13	91	5.5	3.3	8.8	91.2
12	106	7.0	8.1	15.1	84.9
11	110	13.6	9.1	22.7	77.3
10	88	19.3	14.8	34.1	65.9
7–9	287	15.0	28.9	43.9	56.1
5–6	85	23.4	43.7	67.1	32.9
2–4	25	12.0	69.0	76.0	24.0

* From Burgess, 1928, p. 248. Used by permission of the author and the publisher.

Work of the Gluecks

At the same time as Burgess, Sheldon and Eleanor Glueck (1930) were starting their studies of recidivism of 500 reformatory inmates. They used the contingency correlation to identify experience-table items bearing a significant relationship to parole outcomes. Seven highly valid factors were selected, each one weighted in scoring by assigning it the per cent figure for parole failures among persons characterized by the factor. This is a more precise use of scoring weights than the +1 or 0 weights employed by Burgess; however, it is quite unlikely, judging from modern work on test construction and item weighting, that the general level of efficiency is appreciably higher for scales having complex weighting systems than it is for those using the simpler 0 versus 1 weightings.

These early experience tables of Burgess and the Gluecks were applied by Vold (1931) to a sample of 1,192 parolees. He found the two tables about equally accurate. Vold also compared the precise scoring weights for the Gluecks' table with a simpler +1 and o weighting of experience factors, obtaining a correlation of +.92. Vold later (1935) extended his researches to prediction of inmate adjustment during incarceration, finding twenty-nine experience-table factors quite similar to those identified in the studies of Burgess and the Gluecks. Other researchers obtaining valid results with experience tables included Tibbitts (1931), who studied 3,000 Illinois parolees, Monachesi (1932), who was successful in forecasting probation outcomes, Weeks (1943), who identified fourteen social background factors predictive of juvenile delinquency, and Ohlin (1951), who found that a shortened twelve-factor version of Burgess' twenty-one-factor scale predicted as accurately as the original.

A more recent application of experience-table methodology is to be found in the researches of the Gluecks on the prediction of juvenile delinquency (1950, 1956a). To derive their table the Gluecks contrasted 500 delinquent boys with 500 non-delinquents, matched in age, education, etc. Prediction tables of three types were evolved, one covering social-history factors, one incorporating traits of character structure as rated from the Rorschach Test, and a third based on traits of temperament as evaluated by a psychiatric interviewer. The social-history table (see Table 4) is the one recommended for use (Eleanor Glueck, 1956), as it is ordinarily much easier to apply and also seems to be about as valid by itself as the combination of all three tables. The percentage of delinquents among all cases in a class is used as the "weighted score" for that class.

Case history data on 451 of the delinquents and 439 of the nondelinquents from the 1950 study were sufficiently thorough to permit application of the prediction table. Table 5 presents the results obtained (Glueck and Glueck, 1950, p. 262).

These figures are quite impressive at first inspection. However, we should keep in mind that the scores were computed on the same cases used for selecting the five component factors, and that therefore there is an unknown degree of inflation in the apparent discriminatory power of the table. In order to overcome this limitation of research design, one would need to obtain two entirely new samples of delinquents and nondelinquents and then to calculate their frequency rates for the same seven categories of scores. Until this is done it is not really possible to say how well the table will separate delinquents from non-delinquents. The figures in Table 5 also mask a very serious problem in their assumption concerning the frequency of occurrence of delinquency in the general population; we shall return to this difficulty later after having reviewed the problem of inverse probability and its relationship to the history of parole-prediction study.

TABLE 4

SOCIAL FACTOR PREDICTION TABLE AS DEVELOPED BY THE
GLUECKS *

SOCIAL FACTORS	Weighted failure score
1. Discipline of boy by father	
a. Overstrict or erratic	72.5
b. Lax	59.8
c. Firm but kindly	9.3
2. Supervision of boy by mother	
a. Unsuitable	83.2
b. Fair	57.5
c. Suitable	9.9
3. Affection of father for boy	
a. Indifferent or hostile	75.9
b. Warm (including overprotective)	33.8
4. Affection of mother for boy	
a. Indifferent or hostile	86.2
b. Warm (including overprotective)	43.1
5. Cohesiveness of family	
a. Unintegrated	96.9
b. Some elements of cohesion	61.3
c. Cohesive	20.6

* From S. Glueck and Eleanor T. Glueck, *Unraveling Juvenile Delinquency*, p. 261. Published in 1950 by The Commonwealth Fund and the Harvard University Press. Used by permission of the publisher and the authors.

TABLE 5

DIFFERENTIATING EFFICIENCY OF THE GLUECKS'
PREDICTION TABLE *

WEIGHTED FAILURE SCORE CLASS	Delinquents in category N	Delinquents in category Per cent	Non-delinquents in category N	Non-delinquents in category Per cent	Total N
Under 150	5	2.9	167	97.1	172
150–199	19	15.7	102	84.3	121
200–249	40	37.0	68	63.0	108
250–299	122	63.5	70	36.5	192
300–349	141	86.0	23	14.0	164
350–399	73	90.1	8	9.9	81
400 and over	51	98.1	1	1.9	52
Totals	451		439		890

* From S. Glueck and Eleanor T. Glueck, *Unraveling Juvenile Delinquency*, p. 261. Published in 1950 by The Commonwealth Fund and the Harvard University Press. Used by permission of the publisher and the authors.

Regression Techniques

Another method for statistical prediction, and perhaps the most widely used actuarial method, is the regression equation. For any two variables, e.g., a scholastic aptitude test (x) and first-year grade average in college (y), it is possible to write an equation of the form $y = a + bx$, for use in predicting y from x. In order to specify the parameters of the equation, i.e., to determine the correct values for a and b, these things need to be known: the average values for x and y, the standard deviations of these two variables, and the correlation between x and y. The b or beta term in the regression equation is a function of the correlation between x and y, modified by the ratio of the dispersion of scores in the two variables; it serves to indicate how many units y is increasing for every increase of one unit in x. To insure that the average of the predictions of y made from x coincides with the observed average of y, the constant a is added. Algebraically, b determines the slope of the line $y = a + bx$, whereas a determines its height or level.

The regression equation may be used with three, four, five, or more variables, the logic remaining the same as outlined here for two. For example, one might use an equation of the form $y = a + bx + cz$ to predict college grades (y) from a combination of scholastic aptitude test scores (x) and high school grades (z). A general discussion of the regression equation, its uses, assumptions, limitations, etc., can be found in most psychometric textbooks. (See, e.g., Edwards, 1958; Guilford, 1956.)

Two representative examples of the use of regression equations are presented below.

EXAMPLE 1.   Berdie and Layton (1952) studied 207 entering students in 1947 at the University of Minnesota Law School. Quantitative data were available on the following indices: Miller Analogies Test, Form G; Iowa Legal Aptitude Test; 1937 American Council on Education Test; high school percentile rank; and grade point average in prelegal courses. Grade point averages at the end of the first quarter and at the end of the first year were computed for the ninety-nine students for whom all data were available. The multiple regression equation developed to predict first-quarter grades was:

$$\hat{Y}_1 = 52.2233 + 6.3510\,X_2 + 0.1195\,X_3$$

Where: Y_1 = first-quarter grades
X_2 = prelegal grade point average
X_3 = legal information subtest from the Iowa Legal
Aptitude Test

The multiple correlation between first quarter grades and the two variables used in the prediction equation was $+.49$. The correlation between first-quarter and first-year grades was $+.56$.

EXAMPLE 2.   In a study of forty-nine University of Utah medical school sophomores, Ralph and Taylor (1950) developed a forty-five-minute testing battery using three of the eleven aptitude tests from the United States Employment Service general aptitude test series (see Dvorak, 1947, 1956) to predict cumulative grade point averages over the first five quarters of medical school. The regression equation, which gave a multiple correlation of +.55 with grades, was as follows:

$$\bar{T}_1 = 0.00704 \, X_v + 0.00848 \, X_s + 0.01135 \, X_n - 1.8728$$

Where: $\bar{T}_1$ = predicted grade average
          X_v = aptitude score in verbal ability
          X_s = aptitude score in spatial ability
          X_n = aptitude score in numerical ability

The basic form of the regression equation $(y = a + bx)$, some readers will have noted, is the equation for the straight line. It is just this property of linearity, the assumption that for every increment of x there will be a proportionate increase in y, that causes many clinicians to object. Clearly, for example, if y is "sickness" and x is "body temperature," the change in y is more significant when x moves from 98.6 to 100 than when the rise is from 101 to 102.4.

For the prediction of certain criteria, however, particularly those which are quantitative in nature, normally distributed, and demonstratively correlated with other and antecedent variables, the regression equation method has yielded excellent results. In fact, its functioning in the selection and weighting of predictor variables is sufficiently precise so that Sarbin (1941a) recommended it as a model for the sequences of thought to be followed by the clinician in diagnosing the individual case. Sarbin's classic study (1942) later showed that in attempting to predict students' college scholastic achievement, counselors did seem to use an implicit form of multiple-regression reasoning, only they used it injudiciously and inefficiently.

Sarbin's papers were followed by Chein's (1945) rebuttal and by Klein's (1948) general critique of multiple-regression technique as applied to prediction problems in clinical psychology. Klein was much less sanguine than Sarbin about the value of the regression equation as a model for all diagnostic thinking. More recently, Hoffman (1958a, 1958b, 1959) in a series of heuristic papers has proposed use of the regression method in the analysis of the predictions of the individual clinician, and as an instrument to detect the degree to which he departs from simple, linear functions in his combining of the predictive data.

An alternative to the multiple-regression equation, developed for use when the prediction problem is to place a subject in one of two or more discrete or unordered classes, e.g., "policemen versus firemen," is the discriminant function (see Garrett, 1943; Klein, 1948; and Tiedeman, Rulon, and Bryan, 1951). A comment on the history of research methodology is in order here: in spite of its apparent relevance to the kind of "A" versus "Non-A" problems so frequently faced by applied and clinical psychologists, the discriminant function has been infrequently used. A rather interesting exception was Webster's (1952) application of the multiple discriminant function to the scoring of the Thematic Apperception Test.

Other Actuarial Methods

A third category of actuarial methods of prediction might be composed of those which seek to take greater account of patterns and configurations of data and of the non-linearity thought to characterize the relationships between some predictors and some criteria. One trend in this direction is the development of indices of profile similarity (see Helmstadter, 1957; Mosel and Roberts, 1954; and Muldoon and Ray, 1958). With these methods an estimate of an individual's correspondence to a criterion classification, to another person, to his own behavior at a different time, etc. is derived from the similarity between his present profile of test scores and that of the criterion.

An interesting feature of these methods is that clinical estimates of the congruence among profiles may be included along with estimates made actuarially. Muldoon and Ray (1958) carried out such a study, using six statistical methods and eleven clinicians for estimating the similarity between a "criterion" profile on the Guilford-Zimmerman temperament scale and nineteen other profiles. A factor analysis of the seventeen similarity estimates yielded four factors, apparently involving profile attributes of shape (patterning), scatter (prominence of intra-profile variability), and elevation; the fourth factor was not designated by the authors, but seemed to involve "some subtle covariance among the statistical measures which is personified by the judgments of clinician J." Leaving aside this last-mentioned clinician, it appeared that the clinicians' judgments were predominantly influenced by the shape factor, and to a much lower degree by scatter and elevation. Meehl (1959a) also conducted a study of this type, finding that actuarial identification of profile types was more accurate than clinical judgments.

Another method which seeks to reflect some of the intra-individual patterning of traits and qualities is Stephenson's (1953) Q-sort method. In Q-sort technique one takes a set of observations (these can be single words, statements, diagnostic inferences, verbal descriptions, etc.), usually printed on small cards, and sorts them differentially according to their salience for the subject (person or thing) being appraised. For example, a Q-sort deck of 100 adjectives could be sorted into five piles by a therapist describing his patient, as follows: the ten most descriptive terms, the twenty next most descriptive, the forty most neutral or non-salient, the twenty somewhat undescriptive, and the ten least descriptive. The method lends itself well to clinical formulations of individual cases and has been widely used for such purposes. (See Block, 1961.)

Quite clearly, the method lends itself equally well to actuarial use. Meehl (1956c) has reported its employment in a provocative study of the accuracy of "cook-book" interpretations of test scores (see also Hal-bower, 1955). Four Minnesota Multiphasic Personality Inventory (MMPI) profile types were chosen to see if Q-sort "cook-book recipes" could be written for each one which would be as accurate as interpretations of individual profiles made by skilled clinicians. The "recipe" was in the form of a standardized Q-sort distribution of a 154-card Q-sort deck for patients representing each of the four profile types. The Q-sort deck contained items such as "reacts against his dependency needs with hostility," "manifests reality distortions," "utilizes intellectualization as a defense mechanism," and "shows evidence of latent hostility." These statements were sorted by the psychotherapists attending the patients, and a modal sorting then was established for each of the four profile types.

For eight new cases (two of each of the four MMPI types) the cook-book interpretation and one or more interpretations by clinicians of the same profile were correlated with a criterion Q-sort furnished by the patient's therapist. The upshot of this investigation was that the cook-book "recipes" were in fact markedly superior, in their accuracy of portrayal of individual cases, to the Q-sort interpretations of the profiles made by skilled clinicians. These results, it is obvious, hold some sobering truths for the followers of the controversy on clinical vs. actuarial prediction.

The "Sign" Approach

Another of the configural actuarial approaches to prediction brings us back to a more mundane statistical level, but to data sources which are richly complex and drawn from materials in which individual personality has presumably had ample opportunity to reveal itself. The paradigm of analysis here is the "sign" approach, in which interpretational indices of behavior are first defined and later enumerated in simple totals or other combinations for purposes of prediction. Perhaps the most frequent examples of this mode of procedure are to be found in diagnostic medicine, where some specific combination of "signs" (such as fever of a certain degree, changes in blood chemistry, alterations of mood, etc.) can be taken as indicating the presence of a particular disease entity.

This may sound more like "clinical" than "actuarial" prediction, and indeed it often is in everyday practice. However, we are referring to those instances in which the signs or symptoms can be definitely enumerated, and in which the decision as to whether the total combination constitutes a positive or a negative finding is a purely mechanical task such that anyone with a rule-book could accomplish it. This is clearly a statistical or actuarial way of proceeding, and seems to be an efficient one for dealing with data that are intrinsically complex and hard to put into usual "measurement" form.

A good example of the application of this kind of actuarial methodology in psychology can be found in the work of Bruno Klopfer (1951, 1957), a leading authority on the Rorschach ink-blot test. Clinicians who are dubious concerning any step toward statistical interpretation of test data might ponder this straightforward attempt to develop an actuarial index for the Rorschach protocol. The goal of Klopfer and his associates (1951) was to define an index of "ego strength" on the Rorschach test in such a way that scores could be assigned and from them an estimate of therapeutic prognosis made. Six facets of Rorschach response were first selected: human movement, animal movement, inanimate movement, use of shading, use of color, and use of form. Definite scoring weights were specified for different responses in each category. Then a total prognostic or ego-strength score was defined based on the sum of the six part-scores. Six total-score classifications were finally made, with tentative prognostic implications going from "a very promising case that just needs a little help" to "hopeless."

The potential uses for such an index are great, and Klopfer later (1957) sketched some interesting theoretical possibilities for relating ego strength to the incidence and course of human cancer. Studies of Cartwright (1958) on predicting psychotherapeutic outcomes and Sheehan *et al.* (1954) on the treatment of stuttering could also be mentioned.

Other examples of this "sign-tabulation" approach are to be found in the Meehl-Dahlstrom (1960) neurosis vs. psychosis indices for the MMPI, the Piatrowski (1937) Rorschach signs for organic brain damage, and the study of Gough and Pemberton (1952) on predicting success in student practice teaching.

Clinical Prediction: Level I

Having discussed various kinds and varieties of actuarial modes of prediction, let us turn now to a discussion of types of clinical procedure. In doing this a concept of "levels" will be utilized, as there seems to be a dimension involved, i.e., some methods are very "clinical," some moderately or only somewhat clinical.

The first of these levels is one dealing with frankly intuitional phenomena. It includes those instances in which the prediction to be made is not systematically thought through and reasoned, but occurs more or less spontaneously as a matter of insight. Many actuarial-minded persons tend to scoff at such phenomena, saying that they are closer to clairvoyance than to science, and that their objective value is entirely canceled by the fact that the person making the intuitive prediction can verbalize neither the cues that he has utilized as starting points nor the mental operations by which they were translated into the predictive assertion. The clinician, however, would argue that the method can be justified.

In the first place, as Meehl (1954, pp. 68–71) has demonstrated, it is quite possible to find dependable, systematic, and accurate response systems in cases where the individual is unable to specify the cue basis for these responses. A skilled outfielder notices "something" in the stance and movement of the batter and begins at once to run back for an anticipated booming fly. After his catch we ask him "Why?" and he tries to tell us. But quite likely he will not be able to say, in precise, objective language, what it was he "saw," or if he does attempt a description it will be incorrect. Why incorrect? Because if another player tries systematically to guide himself by the "stimulus rule" he finds that it does not help very much. The world of competitive sports is filled with this kind of example, where the skilled practitioner is in fact able correctly to sense ("predict") his opponent's next move, but is unable to specify the cues in such a way that the novice can learn them by rote, i.e., actuarially.

In the second place, the inability of the clinician to state the rules for the combination of stimuli and perceptions does not take his activity outside the realm of science. Reichenbach's (1938) distinction between the "context of discovery" and the "context of justification" can be mentioned here. The history of invention, including invention in the mathematical and physical sciences, is replete with instances in which the hypothesis (or prediction) was arrived at in a sudden, unanalyzed, and intuitive way. The next step, into the context of justification, of course needs to be taken with rigorously scientific precautions, in a narrower meaning of the word "scientific." The economic question that requires answering is whether the predictions made in the clinical-intuitive manner are correct more often than those made by other means, and if they are at what cost of time and money.

Berne (1949) has offered an interesting appraisal of the kind of intuitive prediction envisaged under this first category. As a matter of fact, Berne has advanced the thought-provoking assertion (1949, p. 206) that "not only is the individual unaware of how he knows something; he may not even know what it is he knows, but behaves or reacts in a specific way as if (*als ob*) his actions or reactions were based on something that he knew." Berne kept a sort of log-book or diary of his intuitive activities over a period of time as an army psychiatrist, then later tried to arrive at some formulations about cues utilized, factors related to accuracy and inaccuracy, variations in strength of the function, etc. Two of his protocols can be cited to help give a picture of the phenomenon:

Protocol No. 4.

Many years ago, after some "irrelevant" conversation with a young woman whose existence I had no reason previously to suspect, I made the following observation.

Q. I have the feeling that you are either the fourth or the seventh of eleven children.

A. I am the fourth of eleven children and I have seven brothers.

This confirmation was apparently more incredible than my observation was to the individual in question. Other sources later corroborated her statement. My remark was preceded by a feeling which might be roughly translated as follows: "If I watch this person closely for a few moments something might occur to me."

Protocol No. 5.

During the war, while talking to a young woman who was previously unknown to me, I advanced the hypothesis that she had 28 teeth. This hypothesis was based on a sudden "inspiration" which came to me at the moment without any premeditation. She had not shown her teeth and my observation, including the number 28, was irrelevant to anything we had discussed, except possibly her sadistic tendencies; nor am I in the habit of enumerating people's teeth. She herself did not think my comment was accurate, but we reviewed the situation and found that it was.[2]

From a review of protocols such as these and from his log-book Berne drew several tentative generalizations about the intuitive process: (1) the proper mood for its occurrence seems to be one of heightened alertness and receptiveness rather than a state of yoga-like withdrawal or even the kind of passive alertness characteristic of the psychotherapeutic session; (2) directed seeking of cues and specific stimuli seems to impair the accuracy of the function; (3) the intuitive function develops with practice and atrophies without it; and (4) the function is fatigable, i.e., its accuracy level falls off rapidly after a certain number of intuitions are attempted at one sitting.

[2] From E. Berne, "The Nature of Intuition," *Psychiat. Quart.*, 1949, 23, 218f., and used by permission of the publisher and the author.

Clinical Prediction: Level II

A second category of clinical prediction is that in which a somewhat greater amount of directed mental activity occurs, but the process seems nevertheless to be characterized by the discovery or postulation of a new principle rather than by the extrapolation of a previously established law. One of Meehl's cases can be cited by way of illustration:

> A patient tells a dream which begins as follows: "I was in the basement of my parents' house, back home. It seems that I was ironing, and a fellow whom I had not seen since junior high school, and whom I never went out with, and hardly knew, had brought some shirts over for me to iron for him. I felt vaguely resentful about this—oh, and by the way, he was dressed in a riding habit of all things" [grinning]. Now this patient had said in the preceding interview that it would be too easy to get into the *habit* of having sexual relations with her present boy friend, and that since she did not really care a great deal about him, she must try to avoid this. If the phrase "riding habit" is a sexual pun, we infer that the adolescent acquaintance whom she "hardly knew" represents her present friend in the dream. The remainder of the dream and her associations to it . . . confirmed this hypothesis.[3]

The therapist's interpretation (prediction) here is of the kind that is frequently made in daily practice. Yet it does not proceed in a straightforward statistical way from what the patient has said. Certain general principles seem to be involved, such as that in dreams abstract ideas are often represented by concrete images, and also in some cases through the use of the pun. Also the location of the phrase "riding habit" and the patient's emphasis upon it demand attention. Nonetheless, the clinical interpretation which is made is not derived from an experience table of patients who have had this dream or its equivalent, but from a theoretical formulation of the problem which not only is compatible with the dream's content but which, given certain other observations about the patient's hostility and dependency needs, in fact entails it.

McArthur (1956a) has also stressed this essential facet of the creation of a theory or model of the individual case as a *sine qua non* of the clinical method. He reports on a series of conferences in which clinicians were asked to make predictions of behaviors of cases in which the "facts" were known to other members of the group. McArthur summarizes the experience in this way:

> What all our clinical prophets did under these very trying validation conditions seemed to be to build from the data a clinical construct, a conceptual device, a "special theory applicable to one person," a *model*

[3] From P. E. Meehl, *Clinical Versus Statistical Prediction*, p. 71, copyright 1954 by the University of Minnesota Press, Minneapolis, and used by permission of author and publisher.

of that person, that made this statement on page 17 of the record consistent with that remarkable quotation back on page 14. Each datum became grist from which was ground a formulation of the premises governing *all* of S's behavior, the lifelong premises, the treasured self-consistencies with which the person being studied had learned to face the world. Each batch of data lent itself to hypotheses about the person, hypotheses that could be checked out against new data as the record progressed and could be revised with each successive cross-validation provided by turning another page. After conning all the data, the clinician possessed a fuzzy, but gradually sharpening, conceptualization of the man under study. "He seems to be the sort of person who . . ." Then the clinician could make his predictions by doing imaginary experiments with the model. These would be paths down which the conceptualized person could effortlessly stroll, while there were alleys into which he simply could not be made to turn. And that was how good predictions got generated.[4]

Clinical Prediction: Level III

The third category to be defined is one in which the processes of analysis and interpretation of data are carried forward still more systematically, but not fully into the realm where they can be postulated in an invariant actuarial formula. It is the kind of prediction Snygg (1949) had in mind in his notion of the "causal field" for individual behavior, and in his depiction of the process of prediction as a progression through specific stages: (1) observation of the individual's behavior leading to a reconstruction of his phenomenal field; (2) consideration of this field from a general knowledge of phenomenal fields and the laws governing their change and actualization over time; and (3) from that future field a prediction of the individual's future behavior.

Sarbin and Taft (1952) have contributed a systematic account of the ways in which clinical judgment is structured as it moves toward a specific prediction. Their analysis first distinguished five types of inference, which can be summarized briefly as follows:

(1) Deductive: The deriving of a conclusion or assertion on the basis of a previously established rule or assertion. For example, all conservatives are uninformed; Jones is a conservative; therefore, he is uninformed.

(2) Inductive: The deriving of a principle or continuum on the basis of common factors. For example, this patient shows hostility in any reminiscence concerning his father or other authority figures; he appears

---

[4] From C. McArthur, "Clinical Versus Actuarial Prediction," in *Proceedings, 1955 Invitational Conference on Testing Problems*, pp. 99–106, copyright 1956 by Educational Testing Service, Princeton, N.J. Used by permission of author and publisher.

to have an authority problem, and if I ask him about his employer he will probably again show hostility.

(3) Analogistic: The attribution of subsequent similarities to two phenomena which are similar in some initial respect. For example, the best physiology student I ever had started out to be an accountant; this new student also began as an accountant; I'll bet he turns out to be a good physiologist.

(4) Eliminative: If there is a finite series of possibilities or types, e.g., A, B, C, and D, and the instance cannot be classified as A, B, or D, then it necessarily belongs to C. For example, everyone is either for me or against me; this person is not for me, therefore he must be an enemy.

(5) Postulational (constructive): One type of event is considered *as if* it were *another* kind of event. For example, this person shows an unusual degree of bohemianism and freedom from everyday inhibitions; therefore he is probably just a bourgeois at heart.

The cues on which inferences are based are also classified by Sarbin and Taft under two headings—"classes" and "aspects." Three classes of cues are first specified: (1) analytic: readily communicable and easily identified; (2) pre-analytic: cues to which the inferring person responds but which are difficult to enumerate and locate; and (3) nonanalytic: the vague, poorly defined cognitive elements which arise from the self-perceptual field of the observer.

Under the heading of "aspects" Sarbin and Taft distinguish (1) the locus of the cue, whether internal or external to the informing person; (2) the degree of accessibility to the inferrer's self-reactions; and (3) the manner—deliberate or automatic—in which the cues are used by the inferrer.

An application of these concepts to a specific problem of prediction may be paraphrased from Sarbin and Taft in an example of a psychology professor reviewing the file of an applicant for graduate school. (See Table 6 on page 547.)

A somewhat related formulation of technique for the individual case study has been advanced by Wallin (1941). He distinguished three ways in which predictions may be made from the case study: (1) the case may be studied with reference to a series of factors known or assumed to be relevant to the prediction criterion; (2) the case may be classified typologically, and the prediction then made from the class; and (3) the case may be viewed as unique, and an attempt to identify idiosyncratic intra-individual trends and to project them into the future may be made.

As an example of Wallin's position, consider the problem of a college counselor trying to predict the scholastic achievement of an entering freshman. Using the first method, he might try to estimate (with or without tests) the student's intellectual potential and his level of need for achievement; then, using these two estimates, along with the high school grade average, he makes his forecast. In the second method he has a conceptual schema of five "types": grind, playboy, leader, hermit, and "other." On the basis of interviewing and general observation, the counselor classifies the student under the first heading, and predicts that he will achieve a B— average. With the third method the counselor might try to discover just what the student himself feels about the

TABLE 6

"PROFESSOR FLUGELHORN PICKS A NEW GRADUATE STUDENT,"
AS ANALYZED BY MEANS OF THE SARBIN-TAFT SYSTEM*

The professor's ruminations and inferences	Taxonomy of cues and inferences
1. (With irritation) I suppose this bird is going to be another of those "straight A" types.	Nonanalytic, internal, probably accessible, automatic.
2. Caesar's Ghost! It's worse than I thought; he's interested in clinical psychology.	Analytic, external, accessible (possibly) determined.
3. But let's see here, he took physiology, and a lot of mathematics.	Analytic, external, accessible, determined.
4. Oh yes, his picture . . . he looks pretty good at that, not too clean-cut.	Pre-analytic, external, accessible, determined.
5. Sort of reminds me of Rumblebottom from before the war. He started out with some funny ideas, but ended up as a good experimentalist.	Pre-analytic, external, nonaccessible, deliberate.
6. You know, I have a feeling he'll make it. I'm going to vote to accept him!	Analogistic inference (following no. 5).

* Paraphrased from Sarbin and Taft, 1952, pp. 20–1.

scholastic side of college, what his family seems to expect of him, his hopes, worries, goals, doubts, etc. From the psychological model which is evolved from this survey, an attempt is made to deduce the relevant hypotheses about grade-getting behavior.

The first method above, the reader might have noted, is not very different from what the actuary would do. He, too, would seek out the most salient factors, and then by some formal and objective method combine them in order to give the desired prediction. It is this similarity of basic operations that has led some advocates of the statistical view to say that the two approaches are really one and the same, the only difference being in the fact that the actuary is more systematic and scientific in the way he selects and weights the variables, and therefore necessarily more accurate.

Lundberg (1941) has been a leading exponent of this position. Sarbin in several of his early papers on the prediction problem (1941a, 1941b, 1942) also stressed the similarity between the clinical and statistical modes, when the clinical is considered under the first of Wallin's categories. Wallin's second method may also have some kinship with actuarial approaches of classification, but his third type would appear to be prototypically clinical.

One principle that all writers dealing with this third, more or less systematic, mode of applying clinical methods agree on is that it is a time-consuming, painstaking task. Foreman (1948) has emphasized this point, and Sanford (1956, p. 96) suggests that a minimum of six to eight hours is needed to arrive at a "dynamic formulation" of the case protocol of an entering college student. In similar vein, White (1951) contended that an attempt to cut the assessment schedule below ten to fifteen hours per subject would be tantamount to a proposal to "sabotage" a personality research project.

We have now finished our brief survey of the clinical and actuarial modes of prediction, and will be ready in a moment to consider the history of the controversy over their use in psychology. One hopes that at this juncture the reader will have developed an adequate "working notion" of the two approaches to prediction, and of some of the analytical distinctions which can be made within each category. With such an understanding we are prepared to proceed to the next stage of our discussion.

Development of the Controversy

One of the earliest interchanges in the history of the problem of clinical versus statistical prediction was that between Viteles (1925) and Freyd (1925). Viteles, writing on the clinical viewpoint in vocational psychology, insisted that test findings and test scores required the judgment and interpretation of the psychologist, in the same way that laboratory tests and findings require the interpretation of the physician before they can be used for medical diagnosis. The mental-testing movement had rapidly come into prominence following World War I, and Viteles was alarmed at the uncritical application of such tests in vocational selection and the tendency to accept test scores at face value. The task of the psychologist, said Viteles, was to weigh and balance the test results, and then to present a reasoned recommendation concerning the suitability of a job applicant. Although Viteles did not speak explicitly about the accuracy of prediction, the implication was that the clinical interpretation of test results would be more accurate than would the completely actuarial or statistical method.

Freyd quickly replied, contending that any "judgment" about the potentiality of the candidate in question had better be left to the businessman whose skills in this regard would undoubtedly be superior to those of the psychologist. Freyd then went on to the general issues in the prediction of job success and to the need for a comparative analysis of the clinical versus the statistical forecasts:

> The psychologist cannot point to the factors other than test scores upon which he based his correct judgments unless he keeps a record of his objective judgments of these factors and compares these records with the vocational success of the men judged. Thus he is forced to adopt the statistical method [1925, p. 353].

In the following year Lundberg (1926) published his paper on case work and the statistical method, a paper which has become one of the definitive landmarks in the controversy. Lundberg was impressed on the one hand by the potentiality of the experience-table method, as advanced in Hornell Hart's 1923 paper, and on the other by the apparent aversion to statistical thinking and statistical procedure characteristic of the social-case worker. Lundberg's contention was that the case method is not something opposed to or distinct from the statistical approach but rather a first step toward the statistical ideal:

> It is the thesis of this paper that the assumed opposition or incompatibility between these two methods is illusory for three principal reasons: (1) the case method is not in itself a scientific method, but merely the first step in scientific method; (2) individual cases become of scientific significance only when classified and summarized in such forms as to reveal uniformities, types, and patterns of behavior; (3) the statistical method is the best, if not the only, scientific method of classifying and summarizing large numbers of cases. The two methods are not, therefore, under any circumstances opposed to each other, nor is one a substitute for the other.[5]

This theme was reiterated by Lundberg in 1929 in an analysis of the logic of sociology and social research:

> . . . Especial attention should be called to current discussions regarding the "case" method versus the statistical method. These methods are different only in that one is largely informal, subjective, and qualitative, while the other is formal, objective, and quantitative. This being the distinction between the two, there can be little question as to their relative value for science. The so-called "case" method is

---

[5] From G. A. Lundberg, "Case Work and the Statistical Method," *Social Forces*, 1926, 5, 61. Published by Williams and Wilkins, Baltimore, and used by permission of author and publisher.

merely the informal, comparatively unsystematic, and crude form of the statistical method.[6]

Another key figure in the development of the controversy between clinical and actuarial prediction was E. W. Burgess of the University of Chicago, whose contributions to parole prediction and whose pioneering efforts in the application of the experience-table method have already been mentioned. Burgess' first systematic statement on the statistical and case-study methods appeared in 1927. His conclusion was that the two methods, properly conceived, are not in conflict with each other but are in fact complementary. Lundberg, in his 1929 book on social research, expressed agreement with this view, but insisted that case studies can become scientifically significant only when they are classified or summarized in some way so that uniformities and general trends can be detected; in other words, the case studies gain meaning only when they are viewed actuarially.

Except for Waller's disclaimer in 1934 against the statistical approach to scientific inquiry, little was written on the clinicians' side of the controversy until the appearance of G. W. Allport's book on personality in 1937. Allport distinguished three bases for predicting human behavior:

> Predictions of human conduct may be made under three conditions. First, when people are viewed *en masse*, and only the average behavior is of interest. The experienced manager of a restaurant or moving picture theater can predict remarkably well how many people of the thousands who pass his establishment every hour will turn in at his door. The insurance company predicts accurately how many people will die or be injured in a given year. Such actuarial prediction, since it has nothing whatsoever to do with the individual, has no direct bearing upon the psychology of personality. The second type of prediction, generally employed by the psychologist, comes only slightly closer. It is based upon knowledge of mind-in-general. The psychologist predicts that any man will blink his eye if the cornea is touched, or that any normal individual will show a gradual increase of proficiency while learning a motor skill. Prediction of this type is possible through the knowledge of the general properties of reflexes and habits; what is common in human nature affords the basis of the prediction.
>
> The third type of prediction, more relevant for the psychology of personality, forecasts what *one* individual man (and perhaps no one else) will do in a situation of a certain type. Such prophecies pertain to mind-in-particular, and are absolutely indispensable in ordinary life. It is only by virtue of them that we are able to select gifts that our friends will like, to bring together a congenial group at dinner, to

[6] From G. A. Lundberg, R. Bain, and N. Anderson, *Trends in American Sociology*, p. 411, copyright 1929 by Harper & Brothers, New York, and used by permission of the publisher and the author.

choose words that will have the desired effect upon an acquaintance, or to pick a satisfactory employee, tenant, or roommate.[7]

For this third type of prediction the method of choice, according to Allport, is the case method:

> The case study is the most complete and most synthetic of all methods available for the study of personality. Properly used, it has the full value both of a work of science and a work of art. It can include data drawn from tests, experiments, psychographs, depth-analysis, and statistics; it can incorporate explanations derived from the general laws of psychology: genetic, comparative, abnormal. In short, it embraces both the scientific (inferential) and the intuitive aspects of understanding [p. 395].

R. B. Cattell, also writing in 1937, took up the question of the proper roles of intuition and measurement in psychology, but came to a conclusion quite different from that of Allport:

> Intuition has an indispensable place in research, as a scaffolding under the shadow of which objective investigations may be built up; but propounded as an independent method of arriving at psychological knowledge, it would seem to be a pure illusion.[8]

G. W. Allport's contention that prediction for the individual case had to be a case-study endeavor, even if prediction *en masse* could be accomplished on a statistical basis, also came under question by F. H. Allport (1937). F. H. Allport asserted that statistical tallies and extrapolations could be readily made for the individual case, and proposed the phrase "teleonomic description" to refer to predictions for an individual case made on this basis.

Another advocate of the clinical point of view during this same period was H. A. Murray (1938), who wrote in the introduction to his *Explorations in Personality*:

> In short, then, we might say that our work is the natural child of the deep, significant, metaphorical, provocative and questionable speculations of psychoanalysis and the precise, systematic, statistical, trivial and artificial methods of academic personology.[9]

G. W. Allport reappears in our narrative in his commentary in 1939 on *The Polish Peasant in Europe and America* by Thomas and

[7] From G. W. Allport, *Personality: a Psychological Interpretation*, pp. 352f., copyright 1937 by Henry Holt and Co. This and the following excerpt are used by permission of the author and Holt, Rinehart and Winston, Inc., New York.

[8] From R. B. Cattell, "Measurement versus Intuition in Applied Psychology," *Charact. and Personal.*, 1937, 6, 131. Used by permission of author and publisher.

[9] From H. A. Murray, *Explorations in the Study of Personality*, pp. 33f., copyright 1938 by Oxford University Press, New York, and used by permission of the author and publisher.

Znaniecki (see Blumer, 1939), and in his paper in 1940 on the psychologist's frame of reference. In the former Allport specified eight criteria of a valid social theory, one of which was "predictive power," and then distinguished two kinds of prediction, actuarial prediction for populations and individual predictions for single persons. *The Polish Peasant* was a distinctive achievement, in Allport's opinion, because of its implicit recognition of this differentiation and its corresponding emphasis upon the "predictive powers of life history documents." (Blumer, 1939, p. 186.)

In his paper on the frame of reference Allport repeated this stress on the differences in prediction for a population and for a single case:

> Suppose we set out to discover the chances of John Brown to make good on parole, and use for the purpose an index of prediction based upon parole violations and parole successes of men with similar histories. We find that 72% of the men with John's antecedents make good, and many of us conclude that John, therefore, has a 72% chance of making good. There is an obvious error here. The fact that 72% of the men having the same antecedent record as John will make good is merely an actuarial statement. It tells us nothing about John. If we knew John sufficiently well, we might say not that he had a 72% chance of making good, but that he, as an individual, was almost certain to succeed or else to fail.[1]

Another important contribution to the debate between the clinical and the statistical positions came with Horst's 1941 monograph, *The Prediction of Personal Adjustment*. In this monograph Horst gave an extended reply to Allport's contention that actuarial methods, although appropriate for mass populations, are inappropriate for the individual case. Horst argued that there are two lines of response which the rebuttal might take:

> One is the view that *all* predictions are on an actuarial basis. Given more information about John Brown such as could, for example, be obtained by the case-study method, the investigator might get to know him sufficiently well to predict, as Allport says, that he "was almost certain to succeed or fail," or in other words, that his chances of making good on parole were not 72 out of 100, but higher—perhaps roughly 95 or 98 out of 100. The point is that the prediction is still made on the actuarial principle, that is, in terms of probabilities, even though the exact probabilities are not known, but can only be roughly indicated. The more that is known about a person, the more likelihood there is of reducing the size of the subclass in which he is considered to be a random member, and thus of improving the accuracy of prediction. . . .

[1] From G. W. Allport, "The Psychologist's Frame of Reference," *Psychol. Bull.*, 1940, 37, 16–17. Used by permission of the author and the American Psychological Association.

The other view holds that by a detailed intimate knowledge of John Brown, one can say not merely that John Brown *probably* or *almost surely* will make good on parole, but that he *certainly* will make good on parole. No question of actuarial prediction is involved because John Brown is a unique case unlike any other in the world and hence there are no experienced frequencies in a "subclass" with which to compare him. . . . If the position be granted, as it would not be by many analysts of the prediction process, that it is conceivable that no general classification scheme is invoked or that no repetitions or sequences of analogous behavior within the individual are involved, then there is still an actuarial problem to be solved, namely, that of distinguishing between a *feeling* of certainty and *proof* of certainty. The investigator may feel certain about each individual prediction. But the test is, what percentage of these predictions, felt certain by the investigator, turn out in practice to be correct. Again, the final answer is in actuarial terms. The predictor is correct, let us say, eighty-five times out of every 100 times when he feels certain he is correct. Thus there is no escape from an ultimate actuarial reference in the prediction with respect to John Brown [2] (pp. 27-9).

Horst *et al.* conclude their analysis by saying:

Controversies such as that traced above contribute little to the advancement of knowledge. Crucial and inescapable points on which all should agree are: (1) that the case study procedures are often a powerful method of gaining a better understanding of an individual; (2) that they are indispensable to direct prediction in the absence of known functional relationships between specified information and associated behavior which will permit a high percentage of correct judgments; (3) that they are invaluable to the process of hypothesis formation, not only in giving initial hunches about interrelationships of factors, but also in interpreting the exceptional cases after a given stage in an analysis is completed, thus leading to a new hypothesis and an improved analysis.

The year 1941 also saw publication of a symposium of six papers (Burgess, Cottrell, Lundberg, Queen, Stouffer, and Vold) on the problem of case study versus actuarial study in the journal *Sociometry*. Burgess described the development of a systematic method of case-study prediction for his work on adjustment in engagement and marriage. The case-study method can be standardized, i.e., made actuarial, up to a point by first selecting case-study judges possessing high insight and clinical discernment and, second, by explicit agreement upon the procedures to be followed in making the predictions.

[2] From P. Horst *et al.*, *The Prediction of Personal Adjustment*, Social Science Research Council, Bulletin No. 48, 1941. This and the following excerpt are used by permission of the publisher and the author.

Cottrell commented in a somewhat similar vein, but also insisted that case predictions must take account of the interaction between subject and context. Cottrell also felt it essential that the case-study worker employ an empathic mode of understanding rather than a static series of analytic categories:

> The insight and hypotheses come from the role-taking process. The categories and functional relations so discovered are then used at the syndrome classification and diagnostic level. This is as it should be, but the difficulties of the first method and the relative economy of the second make for a tendency to set up categories and types and to operate with those alone and never press exploration further. Unless insight and analytic skill are constantly kept fresh by frequent use of the role-taking process, we drift into static classification, the elements of which tend to become reified entities while our abilities to see actual dynamics of a case become correspondingly low. It is one of the tragedies of case research that the valuable insights of a skilled investigator are often taken over by followers who then proceed to apply them in a rule of thumb, symptom-tagging style—witness the history of psychiatry and psychoanalysis. It is in this manner that knowledge frequently becomes sterile and actually blind. In my opinion, it is only by frequent recourse to the empathic process of studying cases that we expand our hypotheses to cover human interaction and personality organization more completely. With these tentative formulations as guides we are then able to use fruitfully repeated observations and statistical manipulations for verification and for more efficient prediction.[3]

In other papers in the series, Stouffer delineated the similarities and differences between the two methods, and Queen and Vold commented on the general difficulties involved in making behavioral forecasts. Lundberg's contribution to the symposium was the now famous paper, "Case Studies vs. Statistical Methods—an Issue Based on Misunderstanding," already discussed above.

The statistical point of view favored by Horst in the 1941 monograph on prediction soon came under strong criticism in a 1942 article by the sociologist P. A. Sorokin, who wrote:

> As a whole the volume is typical of our age of cultivation of a misleading preciseness at the cost of an approximate validity. This cultivation is responsible, to a great extent, for a large number of predictive failures of recent social science in regard to business trends, peace and war trends, political regime trends, and many other trends. If we do not want to continue these failures and become a contemporary variety of pseudo-mathematical astrology, it is high time to replace our

[3] From L. S. Cottrell, "The Case-Study Method in Prediction," *Sociometry*, 1941, 4, 370. Used by permission of the publisher and the author.

cultivation of a misleading preciseness by a development of an approximate but valid social science.[4]

G. W. Allport's monograph in 1942 on the use of personal documents in psychological science also gave forceful expression to the case-study or idiographic point of view, coupled with a detailed criticism of the actuarial method. Deficiencies of the actuarial approach as cited by Allport included the following: (1) failure to distinguish between frequency of recurrence and the causation of recurrence; (2) assumption that the same apparent circumstances have the same meaning (and hence the same causal value) for all persons; and (3) inability to deal with latent (unmanifested) trends.

As an example of the kind of creative prediction which the tallying and counting approach of the statistician could never make, Allport cites Heine's forecasting of the Nazi state in Germany. The key difference, in Allport's judgment, is the failure of the actuarial approach to deal in underlying relationships and its consequent inability to forecast emergents:

> If predictions based on frequency were all that were possible, then a Hollerith machine worked on the basis of known frequencies by a robot could predict future behavior as well as a sensitive judge. What is missing from the code-and-frequency device is the *perceiving* of *relations*, the reasoning as from present indications to *changes* (not repetitions) that will occur in the course of time, and the variation of prediction by recognition of contingent factors (allowing, for example, for probable changes in the environment).[5]

The two necessary lines of research inquiry which arise from this formulation of the prediction controversy, added Allport, are, first, studies of the relative success of actuarial and case study predictions and, second, studies of the processes used in making predictions whether actuarial or not. With this plea for empirical knowledge there can be little dispute; the wonder is that so few of the contenders in the controversy have either looked for or requested such information.

Although not mentioned by Allport, T. R. Sarbin's Ph.D. thesis (1941b) and paper on "Clinical Psychology—Art or Science?" (1941a) bore directly on these research needs. Sarbin's thesis and subsequent paper in the *American Journal of Sociology* (1942), although preceded by studies comparing clinical and actuarial predictions (e.g., Borden,

[4] From P. A. Sorokin, "A Criticism of *The Prediction of Personal Adjustment*," *Amer. J. Sociol.*, 1942, 48, 80. Copyright 1942 by the University of Chicago and used by permission of the author and the publisher.

[5] From G. W. Allport, *The Use of Personal Documents in Psychological Science*, pp. 159–60, Social Science Research Council, Bulletin No. 49, 1942. Used by permission of the publisher and the author.

1928; Burgess, 1928; and Hamlin, 1934), were the first to focus directly and explicitly upon the comparative accuracy of each method when operating on a common pool of data.

Sarbin studied 162 entering freshmen (73 males, 89 females) in 1939 at the University of Minnesota. Predictions of first-quarter grade point averages were made for these students by a regression equation based on high school percentile rank and score on the college aptitude test, and by a clinician who had access to these data plus additional case-history and background information including a personal interview. Five counselors from the student counseling office served as the clinical forecasters. The question to be answered was, "Whose predictions are more accurate, those of the regression equation or those of the clinicians?"

The correlations between predicted and actual first-quarter grade point averages were as follows:

	Men	Women
Clinical prediction:	.35	.69
Statistical prediction:	.45	.70

The difference here is slight, but the advantage, such as it is, lies with the actuarial method. In considering this advantage, one must also recall that the investment of time, money, and professional energy in the actuarial forecast is but a small fraction of what it is in the clinical. The multiple correlation, using both the clinical and actuarial forecasts of grades, was scarcely more accurate than the prediction from the regression equation alone.

Sarbin also studied the predictions of the clinicians, finding that they overemphasized both high school grades and scholastic aptitude, and tended to overpredict the mean grade point level of the 162 students. The clinicians' formulation of the predictions, in other words, was similar to that of the equation in that the two components of previous achievement and scholastic aptitude were emphasized, but inferior in that the clinicians overstressed these factors. This finding of Sarbin is of interest in the light of the common criticism of the actuarial method as failing to take account of the complexities, interactions, and patterns sensed by the clinician and its ensuing overemphasis on tangible and perhaps trivial variables. To the extent that oversimplification occurs, the clinician may be as vulnerable as, if not more vulnerable than, the regression equation.

Another predictive study of the same period was that of Wittman (1941). She developed a prognosis scale for use with schizophrenic patients, based on thirty variables rated from their social history. The variables were all more or less judgmental (except for "marital status"), but the totaling of weights was a purely actuarial or statistical matter. This scale, called the Elgin Prognosis Scale, was scored on a sample of 343 hospital patients. For these patients the psychiatric staff made a three-step prognostic rating at a diagnostic case conference on the patient. The criterion was a five-step rating made at a therapy case conference after conclusion of shock therapy. The results of the analysis are shown in Table 7. A follow-up study by Wittman and Steinberg (1944) on 960 patients gave an essentially similar verdict, with a mean accuracy level of 68 per cent for the scale as against 41 per cent for the psychiatric staff.

On the basis of his own and Wittman's studies, Sarbin (1944) came to the conclusion that all prediction in psychology, if it is to be

TABLE 7

COMPARISON OF ELGIN PROGNOSIS SCALE
WITH CLINICAL FORECASTS*

CRITERION CATEGORIES	N	Per cent accuracy	
		Scale	Medical staff
Remission	56	90	52
Much improved	66	86	41
Improved	51	75	36
Slight improvement	31	46	34
Unimproved	139	85	49
Total	343	81	45

* From Wittman, 1941, p. 27, and used by permission of the publisher and the author.

scientific prediction and not mere guesswork, must rest on an actuarial or statistical basis. Sarbin's position encompassed the "individual case," for diagnostic and prognostic assertions here, too, must rest on statistical frequencies established for that case, or else for a class of cases of which the specific case constitutes an instance.

In spite of the theoretical importance of Sarbin's three papers of the early 1940's and the empirical relevance of his study of scholastic achievement, very little comment on them appeared in the literature with the exception of a vigorous attack by Chein (1945). Chein insisted that "probability" as used by the clinician is not a frequency concept, but rather a confidence one. Sarbin's analysis of the probabilistic nature of clinical prediction, and its necessary dependence on statistical frequencies in both pre- and post-prediction phases, would therefore go by the boards. According to Chein, the clinician has reference to his inner feelings of confidence and certainty when he speaks of "probability," not to the statistical odds of his being correct. Whether or not

Chein was correct in his portrayal of the phenomenology of the "clinician," it would seem that Allport's question of 1942 ("Who is more accurate, the clinician or the actuary?") would be in principle unanswerable if the clinician is to be exempt from probability checks.

Chein also objected strenuously to Sarbin's introduction of the prediction issue into an evaluation of the clinician's activity. Even if the individual clinician falls into the trap of attempting forecasts of patients' behavior, asserted Chein, his main concerns and responsibilities are with the control and change of behavior.

> In choosing prediction as the crucial issue Dr. Sarbin has picked his battleground with the "clinician," but this is not the ground on which the latter would stake his major claims. The "clinician" is not primarily concerned with *prediction* but with *control*. He is not content with anticipating what will happen if he does nothing, and that is only one of his minor problems; he wants to know what will happen in view of what he does or in view of his recommendations being followed.[6]

Sanford (1956, p. 96) echoed this same idea, commenting that after six to eight hours with the client the clinician will have lost interest in the relatively narrow scholastic issue of higher or lower grades in college and will have become more concerned about other and broader aspects of the student's future life.

Along this same line it is of interest to consider Symonds' (1931) definition of the case study method:

> It should be emphasized at the outset that the *case study* is not a research method. Primarily its function is to study the individual with a view toward helping him. If the case study yields evidence that is helpful in scientific investigation, this is only a by-product and not its main contribution. If the case study employs a schedule of facts to be noted, and if these facts have been obtained in a reliable, objective manner, then these data may be used in research investigations. But the case study method contains no guarantee that its observations are complete or uniform, or that scientifically valid methods were employed in getting them. The case study has the individual's interest uppermost in mind and may or may not employ a regular inquiry schedule or use consistent methods.[7]

In 1946 in his critique of methods in child psychology, Anderson attempted a summary of the issue of clinical versus statistical prediction. Anderson noted Allport's contention that most psychological

---

[6] From I. Chein, "The Logic of Prediction: Some Observations on Dr. Sarbin's Exposition," *Psychol. Rev.*, 1945, 52, 175. Used by permission of the American Psychological Association.

[7] From P. M. Symonds, *Diagnosing Personality and Conduct*, pp. 555f., copyright 1931 by the Century Co. Used by permission of Appleton-Century-Crofts Co.

laws are statistical generalizations from past experience rather than principles enabling prediction in the individual case. For example, it can be said that delinquency is five times as frequent among children from broken homes as among children from normal homes; this is a statement of probability. However, for an individual child from a particular broken home the chances of delinquency may be either zero or one hundred.

Anderson raised two criticisms of Allport's view that actuarial methods are of little help in the second instance. First, prediction in individual cases depends upon the completeness of knowledge, including knowledge of group trends, frequency rates for special subclasses, and especially for "genotypical" subclasses as opposed to "phenotypical." Second, although individual prediction is an ideal, it is not completely reached in psychology or any other science; the problem is one of successive approximations to accuracy. For some purposes a gross forecast will do ("the chances are one in five that this student will sustain an 'A' average, four in five that he will meet minimum requirements, one in twenty that he will fail"), but in other instances more precise and exact forecasts are needed. The problem in attaining the level of highly accurate prediction is more that of the kind of data available to the psychologist than of any limitation in the actuarial method.

Development of Probability Notions

An exceedingly important chapter in the history of the prediction problem is that concerned with the development of probability considerations. To begin our review of this matter, we might turn to a paper by Ohlin and Duncan (1949) in which they applied probability theory to an analysis of the experience table. Their concern was with the degree of improvement which a prediction table would yield over the base rate of violation of parole for an entire sample. If, for example, 30 per cent of all parolees became violators, then a "prediction" that all parolees would be non-violators would be correct 70 per cent of the time. To be useful, an experience table would need to surpass this base-rate accuracy of 70 per cent. Ohlin and Duncan proposed an index of predictive efficiency, defined as the percentage change in errors of prediction resulting from the use of a forecasting method other than the base rate. They applied their index to twenty-two published prediction tables, finding that most were quite inefficient. Only two showed an improvement of greater than 25 per cent, whereas others gave no improvement at all over the base rate.

Their index of predictive efficiency was followed by a later method of Duncan, Ohlin, Reiss, and Stanton (1953), modified by Duncan and Duncan (1955), called the "mean cost rating" or MCR. The MCR was designed to reflect the degree to which a classification method has succeeded in accurately assigning the cases as parole violators or non-violators (or to any such dichotomous criterion). It is defined by the expression:

$$\text{MCR} = \sum_{i=1}^{k} C_i\, U_{i-1} - \sum_{i=1}^{k} C_{i-1}\, U_i,$$

where:

> U (utility) is the proportion of total violators in the sample who could be identified if all cases in categories 1 through i were called violators;
>
> C is the proportion of total non-violators in categories 1 through $i;$ and
>
> k is the number of categories, arranged in order of decreasing violation rate.

Similar concerns over these relative probability problems in psychological studies were being voiced about this same time, particularly by Hunt (1950), Meehl (1956c), and Meehl and Rosen (1955).

We should note that researchers in the field of industrial psychology have also been sensitive to this issue, i.e., the percentage of improvement over chance (or over other defined base rates) given by a particular selection method. Taylor and Russell (1939) demonstrated that the practical utility of a selection test is a function not only of its validity (correlation with the criterion), but also of the "selection ratio"—the proportion of persons hired to those applying. If, for example, only 10 per cent of applicants are to be hired, then a selection test with a rather low validity coefficient can still be very useful; if 90 per cent of applicants are to be hired, the test would need a very high validity coefficient if it were to add practical value in selection. Jarrett (1948) extended these ideas and developed a formula for specifying the percentage of increase in output of test-selected personnel as an index of the efficiency of the test, and Brown and Ghiselli (1953) later provided convenient nomograms for use with the Jarrett statistic.

A similar approach to the problem was that of Richardson (1950) who defined the following ratio:

$$E = \frac{r(1 - P)(k - 1)}{P(k - 1) + 1} \times 100$$

where:

> E = percentage increase in effectiveness due to the selection procedure
>
> r = validity coefficient of selection technique
>
> P = proportion of applicants selected
>
> k = ratio of average effectiveness of "satisfactory" to "unsatisfactory" employees.

To illustrate Richardson's method, suppose that a "job interest questionnaire" for insurance agents has been shown to correlate +.35

with merit ratings, that 30 per cent of applicants are usually selected, and that the best 30 per cent of employed agents usually sell about 1.5 times as much insurance per year as the remaining 70 per cent of agents. Solving Richardson's formula:

$$E = \left(\frac{.35(1 - .30)(1.5 - 1)}{.30(1.5 - 1) + 1}\right) 100 = 10.65$$

we see that about an 11 per cent increase in effectiveness (as judged by sales) could be expected if the job interest test was used to pick new agents.

An interesting paper by Fisher (1959) can also be cited here. Fisher reviewed a number of prediction studies in clinical and psychometric psychology, observing in each instance that the prediction of positive status (presence of a condition or symptom) was much more likely to be accurate than the prediction of a negative one (absence of the condition or symptom). For example, if Rorschach ink-blot "signs" of organic brain damage are frequent, the diagnostic implications are quite dependable, whereas if the signs are infrequent, the odds of presence-absence are indeterminate (i.e., are reduced to those of the general base rate). Ordinarily one calculates the efficiency of a forecasting device according to its power in classifying all cases, but Fisher's analysis suggests that two probabilities might well be considered: (1) the probability of being correct when a certain critical level is reached or exceeded on the predictive instrument and (2) the probability for all other cases evaluated.

Another development of note is the "band width" concept of Cronbach and Gleser (1957). A test or estimating procedure may have great fidelity (accuracy), but only within a narrow range or band of application; for purposes of general testing the psychologist might therefore prefer to use an instrument having greater "band width," even though its maximum fidelity for any one area of prediction is less than that of other instruments. A test having great "band width" would have predictive relevance to many criteria, but perhaps only moderate accuracy for any one of them; the test having high fidelity would be very accurate with respect to a specific criterion, but would be of little value in other settings. An example of a "wide-band" device would be a general information test which might yield low positive correlations with achievement in many different college majors. A test designed specifically for mathematical aptitude which would accurately forecast grades in mathematics but not in other courses or majors would be an example of a "high-fidelity" instrument.

A related conception is that of "meaningful" versus "maximal" measurement as proposed by Wesley (see Meehl and Hathaway, 1946, p. 556). A procedure may have high consistency, large variance, and great discrimination (the case of maximal measurement), but not be associated with any of the important non-test behaviors which the researcher wishes to predict. High internal consistency of the measurement device may often—if not always—need to be sacrificed in order to attain the more fundamental aim of criterion discrimination.

Reanalysis of Parole Prediction Data

Equipped now with these views on probability, let us return to some of the earlier studies of parole and probation prediction and see how they might fare under a reanalysis. As a first example let us con-

TABLE 8

FREQUENCY TABLE OF VIOLATORS VERSUS NON-VIOLATORS,
AS DERIVED FROM TABLE 3

Burgess experience-table score category	Number of cases in each score category		
	Violators	Non-violators	Total
A. 16–21	1	67	68
B. 14–15	3	137	140
C. 13	8	83	91
D. 12	16	90	106
E. 11	25	85	110
F. 10	30	58	88
G. 7–9	126	161	287
H. 5–6	57	28	85
I. 2–4	19	6	25
Totals	285	715	1,000

sider Burgess' experience-table predictions (1928). To do this we need first to obtain actual frequencies (rather than the percentages given by Burgess) for each category. This can readily be done, using the data from Table 3: the new table (Table 8) can be generated by multiplying the total number of parolees for each score category by the frequency percentages given for that category.

The total number of violators in the sample of 1,000 parolees is 285, so the base rate of violation is obviously 28.5 per cent. If the prediction were made that all parolees would be non-violators, an error rate of 28.5 (success rate of 71.5) per cent would result. Now, how much can we improve on this by use of the experience table?

Suppose that we predict that all men with scores in the A, B, and C categories will be non-violators. We will be wrong for the twelve violators who score this high, and also for the 428 non-violators who score below the cutting point. The error rate here will be $(428 + 12) \div 1,000$ or 44 per cent, obviously too high in the light of the base rate percentage of 28.5. The next cutting point, between categories D and E, will yield 28 errors in the first column, 338 in the second. The error rate would be 36.6 per cent, again higher than the base rate. We can move down category by category, in this way, calculating error rates for each one: cutting below category E, 30.6 per cent; below F, 27.8 per cent; below G, 24.3 per cent; and below H, 30.0 per cent. (We would not cut below category I, as this would be tantamount to the over-all base rate forecast.)

At only two cutting points, levels F and G, does the Burgess table improve over the flat assertion that no one will fail, and at the *optimum* point of dichotomy (predicting parole success for all men with scores of 7 or more) the error figure (24.3 per cent) is only 4.2 percentage points under that found when one simply forecasts that everyone will succeed.

The same sort of analysis can be applied to the prediction table for juvenile delinquency developed by the Gluecks. Suppose one asks, as did Thompson (1952, p. 455), "At what point on the scale are the chances greater than 50–50 that the boy being rated will be a delinquent?" Referring back to Table 5 it can be seen that the percentage frequencies for non-delinquents are higher in the first three categories (scores below 250), but that the delinquents predominate in the remaining four categories (scores of 250 and over). Thompson's answer to the question just posed, accordingly, was that a score of 250 may be considered as a "cutting off" point between potential delinquency and non-delinquency. This cutting point could conceivably be the proper one, and Thompson's own data lend support to the contention, but unfortunately the base rate problem has not yet been considered.

The issue under emphasis here is that the efficiency of separation in Table 5 is clearly derived from the arbitrary fact that in the total of 890 subjects, 451 were delinquents and 439 non-delinquents. If, in general, about 51 per cent of all boys were delinquents, then the efficiency percentages reported in Table 5 would be approximately correct. But it seems unlikely that so high a percentage of boys should be classified as delinquents. Perhaps a more representative figure would be 10 per cent, that is to say, 10 per cent of all boys are of "delinquent temperament" whether or not arrested or otherwise legally identified.

To see how the prediction table of the Gluecks would function with this 10 per cent base rate we need to make some new calculations. In Table 5, five of the 451 delinquent boys scored below 150, giving a percentage figure of 1.1 for this category, 19 or 4.2 per cent of the 451 boys scored from 150–199, and so on; likewise, 167 or 38 per cent of the 439 non-delinquents scored below 150, 102 or 23.2 per cent scored from 150–199, etc.

Armed with these percentages for each weighted failure score class, we can proceed to construct a new experience table based on a theoretical sample of 1,000 boys. Our "given" base rate of 10 per cent will determine that 100 of these boys will be "delinquents," the remaining 900 "non-delinquents." Table 9 gives the appropriate distributions for the two groups.

From Table 9 we can see that if the true incidence of delinquent types is 10 per cent, then the prediction table will be quite wrong if boys with scores of 250 and over are called delinquent, for there will be only 86 delinquents vs. 209 non-delinquents falling above this point.

TABLE 9

MODIFIED VERSION OF THE GLUECKS' PREDICTION TABLE FOR DELINQUENCY, WITH THE BASE RATE FOR DELINQUENCY SET AT 10 PER CENT

Weighted failure score class	Delinquents in category		Non-delinquents in category		Total
	N	Per cent	N	Per cent	N
Under 150	1	0.3	343	99.7	344
150–199	4	1.9	209	98.1	213
200–249	9	6.1	139	93.9	148
250–299	27	15.8	144	84.2	171
300–349	32	40.5	47	59.5	79
350–399	16	50.0	16	50.0	32
400 and over	11	84.6	2	15.4	13
Totals	100		900		1,000

This is a far different picture than one gets from a naive reading of the table in its original form, and it leads to a different conclusion about the validity of the table from that found in most of the published literature on the Gluecks' scale for juvenile delinquency.[8] Even if the base rate for juvenile delinquency were set at 20 per cent, the cutting score of 250 would be more often wrong than right, for of the 359 boys who would score at 250 or above (in a random sample of 1,000 boys), about 52 per cent would be non-delinquents.

This base rate problem may seem to make the entire possibility of accurate prediction rather remote, but this is not really the case. The essential point is to set the cutting score on a scale in its proper place (see Cureton, 1957). The seven categories in Table 9 are too coarse to permit precise application of Cureton's method, although it is clear that for our base rate of 10 per cent the optimum cutting score would be

[8] The critical analyses of Reiss (1951) and Rubin (1951) should be cited as exceptions to this generalization.

somewhat over 350 (27 delinquents score at or above 350, vs. 18 non-delinquents). For a base rate of 20 per cent the optimum point of dichotomy would fall at 300, and would identify 118 delinquents vs. 59 non-delinquents. Incidentally, the reader should be keeping in mind that this base-rate problem does not exist only to bedevil the actuary; it is every bit as important in evaluating the accuracy of the clinician's predictions.

Before leaving these studies on the prediction of parole and probation outcomes and delinquency, we might ask about the comparative validity of clinical attempts in the same domain. An astonishing state of affairs is discovered when one looks for evidence relevant to this question: in spite of the fact that the clinical forecast of likelihood of success on parole is the standard one in nearly every prison and reformatory in the country and that literally thousands of opportunities for comparison of clinical and actuarial forecasts have occurred, such studies are extremely rare. Equally disheartening is the absence of studies comparing, on the same sample of parolees, the major actuarial methods (experience tables, personality inventory scales, special psychological tests). We were unable to discover a single study of this type. Even the best of the actuarial endeavors (e.g., the Gluecks, 1950; Hathaway and Monachesi, 1953) reported only on their own techniques, not on the comparative efficiency of their methods and those of other researchers. Here indeed is an important and open field of research for correctional psychologists and others interested in the study of social–asocial behavior.

Let us look briefly at several studies which did offer a comparison between clinical and actuarial modes of parole prediction. The first of these is the pioneering effort of Burgess (1928). Besides the forecasts for the 1,000 parolees taken from the experience table, predictions were made by two prison psychiatrists. Unfortunately for the comparative study, the psychiatrists were permitted to waive prediction on an unspecified number of cases, so that their success rates do not reflect the more doubtful and troublesome decision problems. According to Burgess, the psychiatrists were correct in 85 and 80 per cent, respectively, of the cases for which they predicted success on parole; for the experience table the figure was 76. However, when failure was predicted, the psychiatrists were correct only 30 and 51 per cent of the time, the table 69 per cent. The over-all advantage lies with the experience table in this comparison.

The next study is that of Borden (1928), also previously cited. Borden correlated twenty-eight predictive factors with a five-point criterion of parole success in a sample of 263 parolees. The highest coefficient, +.20, was for "number of previous commitments." The "psychologist's prognosis" correlated +.16. The difference, although slight, favors the statistical item. However, as a re-working of the data by Meehl

(1954, p. 104) emphasized, predictions from either source would be almost identical in accuracy with those made from the base rate.

A third study, conducted by Glaser (1955), is one of 1,324 penitentiary parolees. Prognostications were made for various subgroups of the total sample by four psychiatrists and four sociologists, and by seven actuarial items considered separately plus a total score of these items. The clinical judgments were all derived from individual case work with the parolees, the actuarial from the institutional files. Beyond its more detailed consideration of prediction sources, Glaser's study is

TABLE 10

COMPARATIVE EFFICIENCY OF DIFFERENT SOURCES OF PREDICTION
OF PAROLE OUTCOMES

PREDICTOR	Number of cases predicted	MCR index
Psychiatrist A	36	.51
Social development pattern	1,324	.32
Psychiatrist B	62	.25
Sociologist A	435	.24
Age at first leaving home for 6 mos. or more	1,324	.22
Sociologist B	48	.22
Most serious previous sentence	1,324	.21
Total criminal record	1,324	.20
Sociologist C	710	.20
Work record	1,324	.17
Schooling	1,324	.17
Use of prison time	1,324	.14
Psychiatrist C	697	.13
Psychiatrist D	426	.12
Sociologist D	131	.10

* Derived from Glaser, 1955, p. 228, and used by permission of the publisher and the author.

noteworthy for the criterion of predictive validity employed, namely, the "mean cost rating" already discussed. With the MCR, higher values indicate more accurate prediction, and a zero value a more or less chance level of accuracy.

Perhaps the best way to summarize Glaser's findings is to list the fifteen separate sources of prediction in order of validity, along with the number of cases predicted and MCR index (Table 10).

Psychiatrist A quite clearly heads the list, but the number of cases for which he predicted is very small. The variability for the number of cases predicted is quite large, and the individual differences among psychologists and sociologists are striking. A better indication of the general value of the source of prediction might be had from pooling the four psychiatrists, likewise the four sociologists, and by putting the actuarial data into a prediction table. Doing this gives the data in Table 11.

The number of cases predicted is comparable over the three sources, so a fair comparison can be made. The actuarial table is once again the most accurate. Glaser and Hangren (1955) likewise found the accuracy of a six-variable experience table in predicting success on probation was somewhat greater than that made by the probation officer in his presentence investigation report.

A fifth paper is that by Thompson (1952), previously discussed. Of 100 boys studied in 1937–1939 at a youth guidance center, twenty could be classified as delinquents on the basis of later checks up to

TABLE 11

COMPARATIVE VALIDITY OF DIFFERENT SOURCES
OF PREDICTION OF PAROLE OUTCOMES*

PREDICTOR	*Number of cases predicted*	*MCR index*
Actuarial table	1,324	.35
Four sociologists	1,324	.19
Four psychiatrists	1,221	.14

* Derived from Glaser, 1955, p. 284–6, and used by permission of the publisher and the author.

TABLE 12

COMPARATIVE ACCURACY OF DIFFERENT SOURCES
OF PREDICTION OF DELINQUENCY*

PREDICTOR	*Number of cases predicted*	*Per cent accuracy*
1. Committee member A	95	65.3
2. Committee member B	91	61.5
3. Committee member C	83	65.1
4. Glueck scale	100	91.0

* From R. E. Thompson, "A Validation of the Glueck Social Prediction Scale for Proneness to Delinquency," *J. Crim. Law, Criminol., & Pol. Sci.*, pp. 451–70. Reprinted by permission of the author and of the *Journal of Criminal Law, Criminology and Police Science* (Northwestern University School of Law), Volume 43, Number 4, 1952.

1949. The forecasts of the three members of the selection committee who had studied each boy's case in 1937–1939 were compared with those derived from the Gluecks' (1950, 1956a) social prediction table. The results are shown in Table 12 on page 567.

Not only is the Glueck scale better in this instance, but the accuracy levels of the three committeemen are actually *lower* than the worst that could have been done simply by using the base rate, i.e., by saying that no one would be a delinquent; had this been done, an 80 per cent accuracy figure would have resulted. Finally, we may not close this section without mentioning the work of Mannheim and Wilkins (1955) in England, who found that a seven-item experience table predicted parole outcomes of Borstal inmates much more accurately than did prognoses by school governors, housemasters, or psychologists.

Status of Problem in the 1940's and 1950's

From these considerations of the parole-prediction studies we should now return to our main topic and ask whether there were other significant writings of the 1940's and early 1950's meriting attention. One such is the book on psychological assessment published in 1948 by the research staff of the war-time Office of Strategic Services (O.S.S.). This volume sought to contrast "elementalistic" with "organismic" approaches to prediction, asking, "Which method has a higher predictive validity?" but adding the provocative comment that "at this moment this question cannot be answered, no adequate researches bearing on this point having been reported" (O.S.S. staff, 1948, p. 41). Nonetheless, the sentiment of the authors seemed to lie pretty clearly with the "organismic" point of view.

Super's book on appraising vocational fitness (1949) also carried a section on prediction, in which an attempt was made to distinguish between a probability statement or estimate and a prediction in Allport's sense. Because of contingency factors (war, famine, change in environment, etc.) and unknowns in the individual, most forecasts must be of the probabilistic type, whether made subjectively by counselors, interviewers, etc., or by statistical techniques. Super's conclusions are in general agreement with Sarbin's discussion of the probability issue in prediction (Sarbin, 1942).

The general status of the problem as of the early 1950's can perhaps be summarized as follows: the methodologies of clinical and actuarial prediction had been pretty well explicated, and persuasive exponents of each position had stated their cases; the need for comparative studies had been urged by Allport, and a few pioneering efforts (particularly that of Sarbin) pitting the two modes directly against each other had been made. However, in spite of claims and counterclaims there was no systematic, detailed, comprehensive review of the problem and of the research evidence relevant to it.

Meehl's Clinical vs. Statistical Prediction

This last need was met, and met in a brilliant way, in the 1954 publication of P. E. Meehl's *Clinical versus Statistical Prediction*. Meehl's book not only developed the formal and empirical analysis of the prediction problem to the fullest extent, but also succeeded in creating a general awareness of the issue and a sensitivity to its implications. Since this book the problem has come to be recognized as a central one in personological psychology, and is treated as such by most recent texts (cf., for example, Cronbach, 1960; Guilford, 1959; Holt and Luborsky, 1958).

The contributions of Meehl's book are almost too numerous to summarize, but several may nonetheless be singled out for emphasis. One of these was the clarification of the distinction between methods of prediction and kinds of data used in making the prediction. Earlier writing (e.g., Allport, 1942, p. 160) erred in classifying studies using psychometric or statistical data as actuarial, even if the predictions from these data were made intuitively or clinically. The essential question is, given any set of data, how it may best be treated so as to yield accurate and meaningful predictions.

A second major contribution is found in Meehl's analysis of the processes of clinical prediction. Even though the actuary and the clinician agree in their predictions about an individual case, or about a large number of cases, there is no need to assume that they have followed the same logical series of inductions from evidence to prognostication. The key factor lies in the invention of hypotheses by the clinician, followed by the deduction of consequences including the specific prediction to be made. To illustrate the difference, the actuary's mode of operation is first described by Meehl in this way:

> To arrive at a prediction for the case at hand we need only apply the probability calculus in a straightforward fashion and thus arrive at a number which automatically determines what we predict. While the prediction considered as a statement about the future is not a deductive consequence in the sense that it does not follow necessarily but rather in probability, the probability number *reached* is a purely deductive consequence of the initial set of probability numbers, together with the rules of the game. If we now simply add the usual decision to predict always the more probable occurrence, the arrival at the pre-

diction is obviously a matter of sheer deductive manipulation of a mathematical sort.[9]

With this summary of the actuarial mode Meehl contrasts the logical activity of the clinician:

> But if the prediction flows as a consequence of some sort of *structural-dynamic hypothesis* concerning the personality, the formal situation is different. For this hypothesis is not itself in any sense a formal consequence, i.e., it is not straightforwardly deducible from the facts which support it. When the hypothesis has been stated, the original data are seen as entailed *by* it, in conjunction with the general laws and rules of inference. But someone has to state the hypothesis in the first place. It is in the initial *formulation* of the hypothesis that there occurs a genuine creative act with which the logician, as such, has no concern. There is a stage at which someone must have thought up a hypothesis which, in the context of discovery, was, to be sure, suggested by the facts, but is not a formal consequence of them. Whereas in the actuarial case, the frequency for a subclass is a formal consequence of the application of the principles of probability to a set of data [p. 57].

Of course, in creating his new hypotheses the clinician is influenced by past experience and by his degree of familiarity with the field in general and this type of case in particular. In this sense the clinician acts "actuarially" in even his most "clinical" behavior. However, this is not the same thing as saying that his forecasts are formally actuarial, in the way in which Sarbin and Lundberg had argued. The actuarial experiences and data are, perhaps, *necessary* to the clinician functioning as clinician but not *sufficient*. That is to say, the hypothesis generated by the clinician is not something derivable as a mechanical or statistical consequence of the set of frequency statements which in fact make up his prior experience. Recently (1957, 1959b, 1960) Meehl has continued his analyses of the logical and cognitive activity of the clinician, attempting to specify those situations (if any) in which the clinical prediction would be in principle preferred to an actuarial one. He has also considered ways of determining whether or not the clinician is in fact predicting "clinically."

The third contribution which we will mention here is found in Meehl's systematic presentation and evaluation of the evidence on accuracy of prediction. Depending on the stringency of classification with respect to relevance, Meehl found from sixteen to twenty studies which pertained to the comparative validity of the two methods. The criteria being predicted were of three main types: success in some kind

[9] From P. E. Meehl, *Clinical versus Statistical Prediction*, pp. 56f., copyright 1954 by University of Minnesota Press, Minneapolis. This and the following excerpt are used by permission of author and publisher.

of training or schooling, recidivism on parole or probation, or recovery from a psychosis. The results were overwhelmingly in favor of the actuarial methods: in all but one study the predictions made actuarially were either approximately equal or superior to those made by a clinician; in half of the studies the clinician is definitely inferior, and no definitely interpretable, fully acceptable study ranked him as clearly superior.

By 1957 Meehl had added seven more titles to the list of comparative researches, and was ready to make this observation:

> Of these 27 studies, 17 show a definite superiority for the statistical method; 10 show the methods to be of about equal efficiency; none of them show the clinician predicting better. I have reservations about some of these studies; I do not believe that they are optimally designed to exhibit the clinician at his best; but I submit that it is high time that those who are so sure that the "right kind of study" will exhibit the clinician's prowess, should *do* this right kind of study and back up their claim with evidence. Furthermore, a good deal of routine clinical prediction is going on all over the country in which the data available, and the intensity of clinical contact, are not materially different from that in the published comparisons. It is highly likely that current predictive methods are costly to taxpayers and harmful to the welfare of patients.[1]

Several of the studies included in Meehl's tally have also been reviewed in the present chapter (e.g., Sarbin, 1942; Wittman, 1941; Burgess, 1928; and Borden, 1928). For the full list the reader should consult Meehl's book and later paper, but mention might be made here of the studies on predicting length of hospitalization by Dunham and Meltzer (1946) and on psychotherapeutic outcomes by Barron (1953a, 1953b), the follow-up analysis of the Elgin prognosis scale by Lorr, Wittman, and Schanberger (1951), and the reports by Kelly and Fiske (1951) and Kelly and Goldberg (1959) on the prediction of performance in clinical psychology.

A number of symposia were held following the publication of Meehl's book, in an effort to develop the significance of his findings and analyses and to give persons of either clinical or statistical persuasions opportunity to rebut. Meehl had classified himself as at the midline of the controversy—with a strong affinity for the clinician's position and an appreciation of the logic of his arguments, but with an equally strong attachment to the methods and point of view of the actuary. The weight of his findings, nonetheless, was so detrimental to the clinical position as ordinarily held that many psychologists tended to view the book as an apologia for the actuary. This is not a correct

[1] From P. E. Meehl, "When Shall We Use Our Heads Instead of the Formula?" *J. counsel. Psychol.*, 1957, 4, 272. Used by permission of the author and the publisher.

assessment, because except for reporting that the evidence from published studies favored the actuary the book is quite judicious and impartial, albeit incisive with respect to errors and false claims.

One of these symposia appeared in the fall 1956 issue of the *Journal of Counseling Psychology* (reporting a meeting held in March, 1956, of the American College Personnel Association). In this symposium Meehl introduced the phrase "the tie that binds" to refer to the imperative need for empirical validity checks of any predictive method, be it actuarial or clinical, a need which "binds together Freud and Thurstone, Cattell and Allport, Rorschach and Hathaway, Tiedeman and McArthur" (Meehl, 1956b, p. 163). Horst (1941) earlier had made this same insistent reference to the need for validity checks, as will be recalled.

Tiedeman, the second participant in the symposium, proposed a schematic representation of the "trait model," indicating the necessary correspondence between predictive dependability and accuracy on the one hand with the frequency with which observations of trait elements can be made on the other. Tiedeman's trait model can be viewed as a statistically sophisticated version of the experience table. Its relevance to the issue of clinical versus statistical prediction is that it can help to account for areas of personality or behavior in which actuarial methods will be more and less accurate, and by implication those areas in which clinical methods might equal or surpass the actuarial.

The third participant, McArthur, stressed the point that the clinician's "dynamic model" is not just an informally compiled and unreliably read experience table, but rather a functional theory of the personality or prediction problem under consideration. This contention had earlier received Meehl's support, as we have noted, and was later to be strongly advocated in his writings on the cognitive activity of the clinician (1959b, 1960).

Another symposium was held by the Educational Testing Service in 1955, and published in 1956 (see Humphreys, Meehl, McArthur, Sanford, and Zubin). This was a very interesting series of papers, but all major issues covered there have already been touched on in our previous discussion so that the individual reports need not be summarized. Most recently, the book on clinical inference by Sarbin, Taft, and Bailey (1960) has carried forward the analysis of the clinician's cognitive activities, demonstrating more fully the way in which probability notions are recognizable factors in his thinking.

CONCLUSION

ONE MIGHT WELL ASK at this point, "Well, just where do things stand now on this problem of clinical versus actuarial prediction?" "What are the trends in the problem?" "What, if any, are the unsolved issues?" "What conclusions can be drawn from the claims and counter-claims which have been made?" A definitive answer to any of these questions would be impossible, if for no other reason than that the problem itself is in a state of active development. Compared with the other topics covered in this book, the problem of clinical versus statistical prediction is a very young one, and does not have the long history of theoretical analysis and empirical research necessary to establish stable and final reference points. However, some tentative generalizations can be essayed and some provisional conclusions attempted.

(1) There is a sort of ineluctability, in two senses, to the statistical approach. First, all attempts at prediction need to be checked, and this checking necessarily leads to a tallying and counting of hits and misses. This "validating" (see Meehl, 1954, pp. 11–15) use of statistics is an unavoidable requirement if any generalizations are to be drawn about the level of accuracy of a prediction equation, a clinical method, or even an individual clinical practitioner. The second aspect to this omni-presence of the statistical approach lies not in the intrinsic logic of the problem but in the empirical situation as of today. Since 1900 (cf. Fisher, 1954, p. 277) there has been an expansion of the use of statisti-cal methods of truly striking magnitude, a trend that shows no signs whatsoever of abating. The extrapolation of this trend suggests that statistical techniques are destined for even more usage and importance than characterizes them today.

(2) Although statistical modes of prediction at the present time seem to have surpassed the clinical ones in accuracy, neither procedure has done very well. One of the problems is that for events of low probability of occurrence (the kind that both actuaries and clinicians would like to be able to predict), it is exceedingly difficult for even an apparently valid method to raise the percentage of success over that derivable from the base rates. Some of the alleged "successes" of both clinical and actuarial prediction have, on later evaluation against the base rate, been shown to be very modest achievements indeed. Thus the key issue might well be, as Humphreys argued (1956), not that of demonstrating the superiority of the actuarial over the clinical predic-tion but that of raising the actuarial method itself to a respectable level of accuracy.

(3) As yet, however, no fully adequate study of the clinician's forecasting skills has been carried out (see Holt, 1958; McArthur, 1956a). The essential limitation in all the comparative predictions so far published is that the clinician has not been given the same initial validation experiences enjoyed by the equation. The actuarial method is first developed on precisely the same kind of sample and against precisely the kind of criterion which it will meet in the competitive run. The clinician, on the other hand, has usually started the race without

such specific experiences. What is needed is a study in which the clinician takes opportunity to examine both the cases and the criterion outcomes for these cases in a preliminary sample, just as the actuary is allowed to do. The test sample would come next, then, for both protagonists. There is no assurance that the clinician would improve his position under such conditions, but there is no gainsaying the claim that in the typical comparison up to now the clinician has been unnecessarily handicapped in the manner indicated. We should also note Allport's (1961) contention that through greater emphasis on personal (individual) dispositions and their patterning, and less stress on common traits, the clinician may come to surpass the actuary in accuracy of prediction.

(4) Proper use of the clinician's skills might well be as a supplement or addition to the forecasts of the regression equation. The actuarial system may clearly excel the clinician in its general baseline accuracy rate for any prediction problem, but even this rate might be augmented by adding clinical judgment as a separate factor. Sarbin (1942) did not find such value in the judgment of his clinicians, but more recent studies (Coyle, 1956; Trankell, 1959) have suggested that the clinician can make a contribution to prediction in this way. De Groot (1960) has also commented on the formal differences between the "competitive" model discussed by Meehl and an "improvement" model which he would recommend.

There is also the possibility, as indicated in the Meehl-Dahlstrom indices (1960) and Klopfer's Rorschach prognostic scale (1951), that the complex configural judgments of the clinician can be codified and then incorporated into an actuarial scheme.

(5) Notwithstanding the importance of the prediction criteria already employed in studies comparing clinical and actuarial methods, the clinician is often more interested in other kinds of predictions. Instead of a forecast that a particular patient will "do well" in therapy, the clinician might prefer to say that during the course of therapy his patient will probably manifest dependency problems along with a tendency to project guilt feelings. Or, in the case of predicting the scholastic achievement of an entering college student, as Sanford (1956, p. 96) has indicated, after six to eight hours with the student the clinician will have lost interest in this question and will have become more concerned about broader and more far-reaching aspects of the student's future life.

This fifth category of generalizations must obviously be viewed with caution. There are matters of psychodynamic process, equivalences between phenotypically opposite behaviors, and predictions as an adjunct or tool of therapy which are outside the present realm of the actuary. At the same time, in daily practice in hundreds of centers, the clinical method is being used to forecast outcomes where actuarial methods would be in principle and in practice equally relevant. Under such conditions the clinician cannot plead a special class of "exempt" issues, but must face the question of differential accuracy.

(6) Even in accepting the finding that for behavioral prediction actuarial methods are generally superior, it may be argued that on certain occasions the clinical method should be used, and that therefore clinicians should be trained in making predictions and should stand ready to make them when called upon. The most obvious class consists of situations which have not previously occurred, and which could not have been studied actuarially. Which men shall man the first rocket to the moon? The actuary cannot today deal with this question, but the clinician can by means of his theories of personality and its functioning under conditions of stress and privation.

Another class consists of those situations which have occurred, but not frequently enough to permit the evolution of experience tables; here again the clinician, by formulating postulates and hypotheses, may be able to make predictions which will exceed the chance level of accuracy.

A third possible class is one in which some new element appears, an element in itself too infrequent to have been tallied actuarially, but of such obvious importance that it clearly alters the prediction picture. Meehl (1957) has given an example of this contingency in the problem of predicting the movie-going behavior of a certain professor. An actuarial equation incorporating age, academic specialty, and introversion score predicts with odds of 9 to 1 that the professor will go to the movies tonight. But if the family doctor announced that the professor had just broken his leg, no actuary would stick with the equation. Here is a factor, too infrequent to have appeared in the sample of behavior giving rise to the equation and its cross-validation, which nevertheless cuts across it with unequivocal significance.

This "broken leg" case, for all its verisimilitude, must be cautiously interpreted, for it differs in several important ways from the usual circumstances wherein a clinical observation is given as the reason for setting aside the actuarial prediction: (a) the "broken leg" datum is highly objective and ascertainable with a reliability approaching unity; (b) its correlation with temporary immobility is also near-perfect; (c) it has few if any "interaction" effects—it cuts across all categories such as age, introversion-extraversion, sex, etc.; and (d) the significance is inferred without use of any abstruse or doubtful theory, being either purely taxonomic or based upon a low-level theory derivable from skeletal mechanics and common sense.

(7) Finally, it has to be recognized that there is a factor of value which enters into the choice of procedures for prediction, and

which may cancel the advantage in probability that one method has in certain instances over the other. Suppose it could be shown that in a large sample of marriageable persons, matings based on "congruence of personality traits" as measured by a true-false inventory resulted in a 10 per cent lower divorce rate than marriages entered into under the usual circumstances. How many people would want to improve the odds of their future marital happiness by putting the choice of spouse in the hands of the test?

Mann has also written on this seventh point:

> If, for example, studies show that this year 3 per cent of all seven-year-old boys were going to die from polio and that if a certain vaccine were used none would die from polio but 3 per cent would die as a result of the vaccination, it seems a reasonable guess that the parents (and presumably the doctors) would oppose substituting man-made death for natural death. . . .
>
> But consider the case of the psychiatric staff learning that, if left alone, 53 per cent of all nonpsychotic patients would leave the hospital for good; on the other hand, the figures showed that application of electroshock, insulin therapy, non-directive counseling, and psychoanalysis singly or in combination produce a remission rate of 53 per cent. It is extremely unlikely in this situation that the psychiatrist would just do nothing, nor would society permit such an economic measure as replacing the present hospital and administrators with ones who would discontinue all therapy.[2]

Contingencies of this type serve to remind us that decisions made by the human judge take into account other factors than those given by the probabilities alone, and not necessarily in an irrational or illogical way. The essential point, one should add, is that the odds for prediction should still be determined with the greatest possible precision, so that when and if they are to be used as a basis of choice their magnitudes will be accurate and trustworthy.

REFERENCES

ADKINS, D. C.   Selecting public employees. *Pub. personnel Rev.*, 1956, 17, 259–67.

ALLPORT, F. H.   Teleonomic description in the study of personality. *Charact. and Personal.*, 1937, 5, 202–14.

ALLPORT, G. W.   *Pattern and growth in personality.* New York: Holt, Rinehart and Winston, 1961.

[2] From R. D. Mann, "A Critique of P. E. Meehl's Clinical versus Statistical Prediction," *Behav. Sci.*, 1956, 1, 229. Used by permission of author and Mental Health Research Institute, Ann Arbor, Michigan.

————. *Personality: A psychological interpretation.* New York: Henry Holt and Co., 1937.

————. The psychologist's frame of reference. *Psychol. Bull.*, 1940, 37, 1–28.

————. *The use of personal documents in psychological science.* New York: Social Science Research Council, Bulletin No. 49, 1942.

ANDERSON, J. E. Methods of child psychology. In L. Carmichael (Ed.), *Manual of child psychology.* New York: John Wiley and Sons, 1946, pp. 1–42.

BARRON, F. Some test correlates of response to psychotherapy. *J. consult. Psychol.*, 1953, 17, 235–41. (a)

————. An ego-strength scale which predicts response to psychotherapy. *J. consult. Psychol.*, 1953, 17, 327–33. (b)

BERDIE, R. F., AND LAYTON, W. L. Predicting success in law school. *J. appl. Psychol.*, 1952, 36, 257–60.

BERNE, E. The nature of intuition. *Psychiat. Quart.*, 1949, 23, 203–26.

BLOCK, J. *The Q-sort method in personality assessment and psychiatric research.* Springfield, Illinois: C. C. Thomas, 1961.

BLUMER, H. *Critiques of research in the social sciences: I. An appraisal of Thomas and Znaniecki's, "The Polish Peasant in Europe and America."* New York: Social Science Research Council, Bulletin No. 44, 1939.

BORDEN, H. G. Factors for predicting parole success. *J. Amer. inst. crimin. law and Criminol.*, 1928, 19, 328–36.

BROWN, C. W., AND GHISELLI, E. E. Per cent increase in proficiency resulting from use of selection devices. *J. appl. Psychol.*, 1953, 37, 341–4.

BURGESS, E. W. Statistics and case studies as methods of sociological research. *Sociol. and soc. Res.*, 1927, 12, 103–20.

————. Factors determining success or failure on parole. In A. A. Bruce (Ed.), *The workings of the indeterminate sentence law and the parole system in Illinois.* Springfield, Illinois: Illinois State Board of Parole, 1928, pp. 205–49.

————. An experiment in the standardization of the case-study method. *Sociometry*, 1941, 4, 329–48.

BURGESS, E. W., AND COTTRELL, L. S., JR. *Predicting success or failure in marriage.* New York: Prentice-Hall, 1939.

BURGESS, E. W., AND WALLIN, P. *Engagement and marriage.* Philadelphia: J. B. Lippincott Co., 1953.

CARTWRIGHT, R. D. Predicting response to client-centered therapy with the Rorschach PR scale. *J. counsel. Psychol.*, 1958, 5, 11–17.

CATTELL, R. B. Measurement versus intuition in applied psychology. *Charact. and Personal.*, 1937, 6, 114–31.

CHEIN, I. The logic of prediction: Some observations on Dr. Sarbin's exposition. *Psychol. Rev.*, 1945, 52, 175–9.

COTTRELL, L. S. The case-study method in prediction. *Sociometry*, 1941, 4, 358–70.

COYLE, E. *Counselor prediction of academic success.* New York: Columbia University Ph.D. dissertation, 1956.

CRAWFORD, A. B., AND BURNHAM, P. S. *Forecasting college achievement.* New Haven, Connecticut: Yale University Press, 1946.

CRONBACH, L. J. *Essentials of psychological testing,* 2nd ed. New York: Harper & Bros., 1960.

CRONBACH, L. J., AND GLESER, G. C. *Psychological tests and personnel decisions.* Urbana, Illinois: University of Illinois Press, 1957.

CURETON, E. E. Recipe for a cookbook. *Psychol. Bull.*, 1957, 54, 494–7.

DE GROOT, A. D. Via clinical to statistical prediction. *Amer. Psychologist*, 1960, 15, 585 (cit. only).

DUBLIN, L. I., AND LOTKA, A. J. *Length of life.* New York: Ronald Press, 1936.

DUNCAN, O. D., AND DUNCAN, B. A methodological analysis of segregation indexes. *Amer. sociol. Rev.*, 1955, 20, 210–17.

DUNCAN, O. D., OHLIN, L. E., REISS, A. J., JR., AND STANTON, H. R. Formal devices for making selection decisions. *Amer. J. Sociol.*, 1953, 48, 573–84.

DUNHAM, H. W., AND MELTZER, B. N. Predicting length of hospitalization of mental patients. *Amer. J. Sociol.*, 1946, 52, 123–31.

DVORAK, B. J. The new USES general aptitude test battery. *J. appl. Psychol.*, 1947, 31, 372–6.

———. The general aptitude test battery. *Personnel guid. J.*, 1956, 35, 145–54.

EDWARDS, A. L. *Statistical analysis,* rev. ed. New York: Rinehart, 1958.

FISHER, J. The twisted pear and the prediction of behavior. *J. consult. Psychol.*, 1959, 23, 400–5.

FISHER, R. The expansion of statistics. *Amer. Sci.*, 1954, 42, 275–93.

FOREMAN, P. B. The theory of case studies. *Soc. Forces*, 1948, 26, 408–19.

FREYD, M. The statistical viewpoint in vocational selection. *J. appl. Psychol.*, 1925, 9, 349–56.

GARRETT, H. E. The discriminant function and its use in psychology. *Psychometrika*, 1943, 8, 65–79.

GLASER, D. The efficacy of alternative approaches to parole prediction. *Amer. sociol. Rev.*, 1955, 20, 283–7.

GLASER, D., AND HANGREN, R. F. Predicting the adjustment of federal probationers. *Natl. prob. parole assoc. J.*, 1958, 4, 258–67.

GLUECK, E. T.   Spotting potential delinquents: Can it be done? *Fed. probat. Quart.*, 1956, 20(3), 7–13.

GLUECK, S., AND GLUECK, E. T.   *500 criminal careers.* New York. Alfred A. Knopf, Inc., 1930.

————.   *Criminal careers in retrospect.* New York: the Commonwealth Fund, 1943.

————.   *Unraveling juvenile delinquency.* New York: the Commonwealth Fund, 1950.

————.   Early detection of future delinquents. *J. crimin. law, criminol. and police Sci.*, 1956, 47, 174–82. (a)

————.   *Physique and delinquency.* New York: Harper & Bros., 1956. (b)

GOUGH, H. G.   What determines the academic achievement of high school students? *J. educ. Res.*, 1953, 46, 321–31.

GOUGH, H. G., AND PEMBERTON, W. H.   Personality characteristics related to success in practice teaching. *J. appl. Psychol.*, 1952, 36, 307–9.

GUILFORD, J. P.   *Fundamental statistics in psychology and education,* 3rd ed. New York: McGraw-Hill Book Co., 1956.

————.   *Personality.* New York: McGraw-Hill Book Co., 1959.

HALBOWER, C. C.   *A comparison of actuarial versus clinical prediction to classes discriminated by MMPI.* Minneapolis: University of Minnesota Ph.D. dissertation, 1955.

HAMLIN, R.   Predictability of institutional adjustment of reformatory inmates. *J. juv. Res.*, 1934, 18, 179–84.

HART, H.   Predicting parole success. *J. crimin. law and Criminol.*, 1923, 14, 405–13.

HATHAWAY, S. R., AND MONACHESI, E. D.   *Analyzing and predicting juvenile delinquency with the MMPI.* Minneapolis, Minnesota: University of Minnesota Press, 1953.

HELMSTADTER, G. C.   An empirical comparison of methods for estimating profile similarity. *Educ. and psychol. Measmt.*, 1957, 17, 71–82.

HOFFMAN, P. J.   Criteria of human judgment ability: I. The "clinical" assessment of intelligence and personality. *Amer. Psychologist*, 1958, 13, 388 (abstract). (a)

————.   Human judgment as a decision process. *Amer. Psychologist*, 1958, 13, 368 (cit. only). (b)

————.   The prediction of clinical prediction. *Amer. Psychologist*, 1959, 14, 356 (cit. only).

HOLT, R. R.   Clinical and statistical prediction: A reformulation and some new data. *J. abn. soc. Psychol.*, 1958, 56, 1–12.

HOLT, R. R., AND LUBORSKY, L.   *Personality patterns of psychiatrists.* New York: Basic Books, 1958.

HORST, P., *et al.* *The prediction of personal adjustment.* New York: Social Science Research Council Bulletin No. 48, 1941.

HUMPHREYS, L. J. Clinical versus actuarial prediction. In *Proceedings, 1955 invitational conference on testing problems.* Princeton, New Jersey: Educational Testing Service, 1956, pp. 129–35.

HUNT, H. F. Clinical methods: Psychodiagnostics. In C. P. Stone and D. W. Taylor (Eds.), *Annual review of psychology.* Vol. I. Stanford, California: Annual Reviews, Inc. 1950, pp. 207–20.

HUNT, W. A. An actuarial approach to clinical judgment. In Bass, B. M., and Berg, I. A. *Objective approaches to personality study.* Princeton, New Jersey: D. Van Nostrand, 1959, pp. 169–91.

HUTT, M. L. Actuarial and clinical approaches to psychodiagnosis. *Psychol. Rep.,* 1956, 2, 413–19.

JARRETT, R. F. Per cent increase in output of selected personnel as an index of test efficiency. *J. appl. Psychol.,* 1948, 32, 135–45.

KELLY, E. L., AND FISKE, D. W. *The prediction of performance in clinical psychology.* Ann Arbor: University of Michigan Press, 1951.

KELLY, E. L., AND GOLDBERG, L. R. Correlates of later performance and specialization in psychology. *Psychol. Monogr.,* 1959, 73, No. 12 (whole No. 482).

KLEIN, G. S. An application of the multiple regression principle of clinical prediction. *J. gen. Psychol.,* 1948, 38, 159–79.

KLOPFER, B. Psychological variables in human cancer. *J. proj. Techn.,* 1957, 21, 331–40.

KLOPFER, B., KIRCHNER, F. J., WISHAM, W., AND BAKER, G. Rorschach prognostic rating scale. *J. proj. Techn.,* 1951, 15, 425–8.

LAZARSFELD, P. F., BERELSON, B., AND GAUDET, H. *The people's choice.* New York: Duell, Sloan and Pearce, 1944.

LORIMER, F., AND OSBORN, F. *Dynamics of population.* New York: The Macmillan Company, 1934.

LORR, M., WITTMAN, P., AND SCHANBERGER, W. An analysis of the Elgin prognostic scale. *J. clin. Psychol.,* 1951, 7, 260–3.

LUNDBERG, G. A. Case work and the statistical method. *Social Forces,* 1926, 5, 61–5.

———. *Social research.* New York: Longmans, Green and Co., 1929.

———. *Foundations of sociology.* New York: The Macmillan Company, 1939.

———. Case studies vs. statistical methods—An issue based on misunderstanding. *Sociometry,* 1941, 4, 379–83.

LUNDBERG, G. A., BAIN, R., AND ANDERSON, N. (Eds.), *Trends in American sociology.* New York: Harper & Bros., 1929.

MCARTHUR, C. Analyzing the clinical process. *J. counsel. Psychol.,* 1954, 1, 203–7.

———. Clinical versus actuarial prediction. In *Proceedings, 1955 invitational conference on testing problems.* Princeton, New Jersey: Educational Testing Service, 1956, pp. 99–106. (a)

———. The dynamic model. *J. counsel. Psychol.,* 1956, 3, 168–71. (b)

MANN, R. D. A critique of P. E. Meehl's clinical versus statistical prediction. *Behav. Sci.,* 1956, 1, 224–30.

MANNHEIM, H., AND WILKINS, L. T. *Prediction methods in relation to Borstal training.* London: Her Majesty's Stationery Office, 1955.

MAY, M. A. Predicting academic success. *J. educ. Psychol.,* 1923, 14, 429–40.

MEEHL, P. E. *Clinical versus statistical prediction.* Minneapolis: University of Minnesota Press, 1954.

———. Clinical versus actuarial prediction. In *Proceedings, 1955 invitational conference on testing problems.* Princeton, New Jersey: Educational Testing Service, 1956, pp. 136–41. (a)

———. The tie that binds. *J. counsel. Psychol.,* 1956, 3, 163–4, 171–73. (b)

———. Wanted—a good cookbook. *Amer. Psychologist,* 1956, 11, 263–72. (c)

———. When shall we use our heads instead of the formula? *J. counsel. Psychol.,* 1957, 4, 268–73.

———. A comparison of clinicians with five statistical methods of identifying MMPI profiles. *J. counsel. Psychol.,* 1959, 6, 102–9. (a)

———. Some ruminations on the validation of clinical procedures. *Canad. J. Psychol.,* 1959, 13, 102–28. (b)

———. The cognitive activity of the clinician. *Amer. Psychologist,* 1960, 15, 19–27.

MEEHL, P. E., AND DAHLSTROM, W. G. Objective configural rules for discriminating psychotic from neurotic MMPI profiles. *J. consult. Psychol.,* 1960, 24, 375–87.

MEEHL, P. E., AND HATHAWAY, S. R. The K factor as a suppressor variable in the Minnesota multiphasic personality inventory. *J. appl. Psychol.,* 1946, 30, 525–64.

MEEHL, P. E., AND ROSEN, A. Antecedent probability and the efficiency of psychometric signs, patterns or cutting scores. *Psychol. Bull.,* 1955, 52, 194–216.

MITCHELL, W. C. *Business cycles.* New York: National Bureau of Economic Research, 1927.

MONACHESI, E. D. *Prediction factors in probation.* Hanover, New Hampshire: the Sociological Press, 1932.

————. American studies in the prediction of recidivism. *J. crimin. law and Criminol.*, 1950, 41, 268–89.

MOSEL, J. N., AND ROBERTS, J. B. The comparability of measures of profile similarity: An empirical study. *J. consult. Psychol.*, 1954, 18, 61–6.

MULDOON, J. F., AND RAY, O. S. A comparison of pattern similarity as measured by six statistical techniques and eleven clinicians. *Educ. and Psychol. Measmt.*, 1958, 18, 775–81.

MURRAY, H. A. *Explorations in personality.* New York: Oxford University Press, 1938.

OHLIN, L. E. *Selection for parole.* New York: Russell Sage Foundation, 1951.

OHLIN, L. E., AND DUNCAN, O. D. The efficiency of prediction in criminology. *Amer. J. Sociol.*, 1949, 54, 441–51.

OSS ASSESSMENT STAFF. *Assessment of men: Selection of personnel for the Office of Strategic Services.* New York: Rinehart and Co., Inc., 1948.

PEARL, R. *Biology of population growth.* New York: Alfred A. Knopf, Inc., 1925.

PIATROWSKI, Z. The Rorschach ink blot method in organic disturbances of the central nervous system. *J. nerv. ment. Dis.*, 1937, 86, 525–37.

QUEEN, S. A. Social prediction—development and problems. *Sociometry*, 1941, 4, 371–3.

RALPH, R., AND TAYLOR, C. W. A comparative evaluation of the professional aptitude test and the general aptitude test battery. *J. assoc. Amer. med. Coll.*, 1950, 25, 33–40.

REICHENBACH, H. *Experience and prediction.* Chicago: University of Chicago Press, 1938.

REISS, A. J., JR. Unraveling juvenile delinquency. II. An appraisal of the research methods. *Amer. J. Sociol.*, 1951, 57, 115–20.

RICHARDSON, M. W. Effectiveness of selection devices. In D. H. Fryer and E. R. Henry (Eds.), *Handbook of applied psychology.* Vol. I. New York: Rinehart and Co., 1950, pp. 192–4.

RUBIN, S. Unraveling juvenile delinquency. I. Illusions in a research project using matched pairs. *Amer. J. Sociol.*, 1951, 57, 107–14.

SANFORD, R. N. Clinical and actuarial prediction in a setting of action research. In *Proceedings, 1955 invitational conference on testing problems.* Princeton, New Jersey: Educational Testing Service, 1956, pp. 93–8.

SARBIN, T. R. Clinical psychology—art or science? *Psychometrika*, 1941, 6, 391–400. (a)

————. The relative accuracy of clinical and statistical predictions of academic success. Columbus, Ohio: Ohio State University Ph.D. thesis, 1941. (b)

————. A contribution to the study of actuarial and individual methods of prediction. *Amer. J. Sociol.*, 1942, 48, 593–602.

————. The logic of prediction in psychology. *Psychol. Rev.*, 1944, 51, 210–28.

SARBIN, T. R., AND TAFT, R. *An essay on inference in the psychological sciences.* Berkeley, California: Garden Library Press, 1952.

SARBIN, T. R., TAFT, R., AND BAILEY, D. E. *Clinical inference and cognitive theory.* New York: Holt, Rinehart, and Winston, 1960.

SCHUESSLER, K. F. Parole prediction: Its history and status. *J. crimin. law, criminol., and pol. Sci.*, 1954, 45, 425–31.

SHEEHAN, J., FREDERICK, C., ROSEVEAR, W., AND SPIEGELMAN, M. A validity study of the Rorschach prognostic rating scale. *J. proj. Techn.*, 1954, 18, 233–9.

SNYGG, D. Predicting the behavior of individuals. *Canad. J. Psychol.*, 1949, 3, 19–29.

SOROKIN, P. A. A criticism of *The Prediction of Personal Adjustment*. *Amer. J. Sociol.*, 1942, 48, 76–80.

STEPHENSON, W. *The study of Q-technique and its methodology.* Chicago: University of Chicago Press, 1953.

STOUFFER, S. A. Notes on the case study method and the unique case. *Sociometry*, 1941, 4, 349–57.

STRONG, E. K., JR. *Vocational interests of men and women.* Stanford, California: Stanford University Press, 1943.

————. *Vocational interests 18 years after college.* Minneapolis: University of Minnesota Press, 1955.

SUPER, D. E. *Appraising vocational fitness by means of psychological tests.* New York: Harper & Bros., 1949.

SYMONDS, P. M. *Diagnosing personality and conduct.* New York: the Century Co., 1931.

TAYLOR, H. C., AND RUSSELL, J. T. The relationship of validity co-efficients to the practical effectiveness of tests in selection. *J. appl. Psychol.*, 1939, 23, 565–78.

TERMAN, L. M. *Psychological factors in marital happiness.* New York: McGraw-Hill Book Co., 1938.

THOMPSON, R. E. A validation of the Glueck social prediction scale for proneness to delinquency. *J. crimin. law, criminol., and pol. Sci.*, 1952, 43, 451–70.

THORNDIKE, E. L., *et al. Prediction of vocational success.* New York: Commonwealth Fund, 1934.

TIBBITTS, C. Success or failure on parole can be predicted. *J. crimin. law and Criminol.*, 1931, 22, 11–50.

TIEDEMAN, D. The trait model. *J. counsel. Psychol.*, 1956, 3, 164–8.

TIEDEMAN, D., RULON, P. J., AND BRYAN, J. G. The multiple discriminant function—a symposium. *Harv. educ. Rev.*, 1951, 21, 71–95.

TRANKELL, A. The psychologist as an instrument of prediction. *J. appl. Psychol.*, 1959, 43, 170–5.

VITELES, M. S. The clinical viewpoint in vocational psychology. *J. appl. Psychol.*, 1925, 9, 131–8.

VOLD, G. B. *Prediction methods and parole.* Hanover, New Hampshire: the Sociological Press, 1931.

————. Prediction methods applied to problems of classification within institutions. *J. crimin. law and Criminol.*, 1935, 25, 202–9.

————. Crucial problems in methods of predicting social adjustment. *Sociometry*, 1941, 4, 374–83.

WALLER, W. Insight and scientific method. *Amer. J. Scciol.*, 1934, 40, 285–97.

WALLIN, P. The prediction of individual behavior from case studies. In P. Horst *et al.*, *The prediction of personal adjustment.* New York: Social Science Research Council Bulletin, No. 48, 1941, pp. 183–239.

WARNER, S. B. Factors determining parole from the Massachusetts reformatory. *J. crimin. law and Criminol.*, 1923, 14, 172–207.

WEBSTER, H. Rao's multiple discriminant technique applied to three TAT variables. *J. abn. soc. Psychol.*, 1952, 47, 641–8.

WEEKS, H. A. Predicting juvenile delinquency. *Amer. sociol. Rev.*, 1943, 8, 40–6.

WHITE, R. W. What is tested by psychological tests? In P. H. Hoch and J. Zubin (Eds.), *Relation of psychological tests to psychiatry.* New York: Grune and Stratton, 1951, pp. 3–14.

WITTMAN, M. P. A scale for measuring prognosis in schizophrenic patients. *Elgin Papers*, 1941, 4, 20–33.

WITTMAN, M. P., AND STEINBERG, L. Follow-up of an objective evaluation of prognosis in dementia praecox and manic-depressive psychoses. *Elgin Papers*, 1944, 5, 216–27.

ZUBIN, J. Clinical vs. actuarial prediction: a pseudo-problem. In *Proceedings, 1955 invitational conference on testing problems.* Princeton, New Jersey: Educational Testing Service, 1956, pp. 107–28.

CHAPTER 10

The Sucking Behavior of Mammals: An Illustration of the Nature-Nurture Question

JOHN P. McKEE
AND
MARJORIE P. HONZIK

IN HIS ATTEMPT to simplify and thus to understand himself, man has frequently begun with a dichotomy: Is it nature or nurture which accounts for a particular characteristic? Is it heredity or environment? Is it maturation or learning? We now know better than to ask "either-or" questions, so we rephrase and ask, "To what degree are hereditary factors responsible and to what degree are environmental factors responsible?" Or we may ask, "What degree of training or environmental manipulation is necessary to produce significant differences among groups that have identical heredities?" Sometimes we put it another way: "What sorts of genotypes are quite resistant to environmental influences and what sorts are quite readily modified?" Still another question is: "What *kinds* of variation in environment or training affect this particular genotype and what *kinds* do not?" It is with the role of nature and nurture in the development of the sucking response that we are concerned here.

We have chosen sucking as the focus of our discussion for several reasons: the response is peculiarly mammalian, though there may be analogues in other zoological classes (Levy, 1938); one form of it—thumb-sucking—has attracted much attention from mothers, orthodontists, pediatricians, psychologists, and nearly every other group interested in the development and welfare of children; and finally Freud made "orality" a very important concept in his theoretical account of the development of personality. These reasons would more than justify the inclusion of a chapter on the sucking response. But there is one aspect of the response which makes it a particularly desirable vehicle for expounding a general theme such as the nature-nurture question. This is the fact that sucking is a reasonably simple response which can be measured, or at least counted, without having to worry about the refinements of statistical theory that appear to be an essential part of the measuring sticks used in some other areas of psychology.

THEORISTS

Giants of the Past Express a Point of View

Let us begin with William Harvey (1651), the great physiologist who discovered the circulation of the blood. There is an earlier history, as he will make clear, but—as he will also make clear—the earlier history led nowhere.

How much the *Authority* of the *Ancients* is not rashly to be rejected, appears even in this: It was of old an opinion much prized (which yet many at this day disclame as *erroneous;* and *Fabricius* decryes it as a meer delusion, and fond perswasion) *that the Embryo did suck, in its mother's Womb:* and it had *Democritus, Epicurus, and Hippocrates* himself for its *Abbettors.* And *Hippocrates* doth establish his opinions chiefly upon two arguments; *For,* saith he, *unless it had sucked, how could it deposit any excrements: or how know to suck so soon as it is born.* . . .

The *Embryo* therfore *sucks,* and receives *nutriment* in at the *Mouth.* And this you shall soon discry, if so soon as ever he is borne, you put your *finger* into his *mouth.* Which according to *Hippocrates,* would not be, had he not *sucked* before in the *Womb.* For we see young Children make *essays,* and attempt upon all performances: namely, moving their *Limbs, crawling* along, and indeavouring to *speak:* all which they attain at last with dexterity, by long practice, and education. But so soon as ever they are born, nay before they are born, they will *suck.* For we have found by experience, that while they yet stick fast in the *Birth,* before they can either *cry* or *breath,* they will seize upon the *finger* extended to them, and *suck* it.

Nay, *A New-born Child* is more exact at sucking, than a grown *body,* or himself either if he discontinue it but a few days. For the *Infant* doth not compress the *Nipple,* and suck at the rate that we do by *gulping* down: but as if he would devour the Nipple, he still draws it in to his *mouth,* and by aid of his *tongue,* and *palate,* he sucks the milk, as if he chewed it; with farre more earnestness and slight, then a *grown body.* Wherefore he seems to be good at it of old, and to have practised it in the *womb*; for we see how soon he unlearns it by discontinuance [pp. 353; 360–1].

So wrote William Harvey in 1651. The question was essentially this: Is the sucking response learned *in utero*, or does it occur full-blown and ready-made without previous practice? Harvey casts his vote for learning rather than maturation. He also suggests that the infant may *un*learn (forget) how to suck. Without significant change the question is the same one that had interested Hippocrates two thousand years earlier. Harvey's remarks make clear the reason: those two thousand years were distinguished chiefly by speculation and argument—so-called rational psychology—and by appeal to authority rather than to evidence. In the absence of additional evidence there is no need for additional questions. Any reasonably intelligent person can think up most of the relevant questions about a limited number of observations—and there were plenty of "reasonably intelligent" ancient Greeks! There could be no really new questions until the old answers were examined in the light of some new facts.

All this is not to say that Harvey, who made the truly revolutionary observations of the circulation of the blood, had no new observations about sucking. Indeed, he is quite explicit about his observations of sucking during birth and during the first few days after birth. But the sucking response was no more than a peripheral interest for Harvey, and so he was content simply to answer the same ancient question rather than to ask a new one. So, like all men, a product of his times, he too cites the original authorities and the original observations.

Another 140 years passed without a new empirical question, and in 1794 Erasmus Darwin remarks, when arguing, in keeping with the British empiricism of the time, that "instincts" are learned:

> The celebrated Harvey observes, that the foetus in the womb must have sucked in a part of its nourishment, because it knows how to suck the minute it is born, as any one may experience by putting a finger between its lips, and because in a few days it forgets this art of sucking, and cannot without some difficulty again acquire it. . . . The same observation is made by Hippocrates [p. 152].

Another eighty years go by and Erasmus' grandson Charles defends the other side of the question in the *Expression of Emotions in Man and Animals* (1872):

> When there exists an inherited or instinctive tendency to the performance of an action, or an inherited taste for certain kinds of food, some degree of habit in the individual is often or generally requisite. We find this in the paces of the horse, and to a certain extent in the

pointing of dogs; although some young dogs point excellently the first time they are taken out, yet they often associate the proper inherited attitude with a wrong odor, and even with eyesight. I have heard it asserted that if a calf be allowed to suck its mother only once, it is much more difficult afterwards to rear it by hand. . . . A remark to much the same effect was made long ago by Hippocrates and by the illustrious Harvey; for both assert that a young animal forgets in the course of a few days the art of sucking, and cannot without some difficulty again acquire it. I give these assertions on the authority of Dr. Darwin [p. 30].

Even in so great an innovator as Charles Darwin we find the same appeal to the same authorities. Charles Darwin obviously did not even go to the original source, but simply took his grandfather's word. (Equally obviously we have taken Harvey's word for what Hippocrates wrote!) Darwin *does* suggest that *both* learning (habit) and an "inherited or instinctive tendency" may be necessary for sucking.

Of course, neither Hippocrates nor Harvey nor Darwin was primarily interested in sucking *per se*. For each of them sucking was illustrative of, or incidental to, something else which preoccupied him. It is perhaps not surprising that they did not trouble themselves unduly about a single particular response of the human infant. They had other more absorbing projects that kept them thoroughly busy.

But times have changed. Sucking, and particularly thumb-sucking, is a phenomenon that excites intense and widespread interest among both laymen and scientists. Bragman (1931) has pointed out that laymen (Pepys) and artists (Ghirlandajo, Il Borgognone, and Fra Lippo Lippi) of earlier periods have noted thumb-sucking, but it is hard to believe that there has ever been so intense and widespread an interest as during the last forty years. No mothers' manual is complete without a discussion of the subject; no pediatric handbook fails to mention it; preoccupation with the question is almost an occupational disease among orthodontists (Johnson, 1937; Swinehart, 1938; Picard, 1959); and personality theorists appear to feel obligated either to assert or deny the importance of early oral experience.

Modern interest in sucking is due very largely to Sigmund Freud. In 1879 Lindner, a pediatrician, had estimated the incidence and frequency of thumb-sucking and, according to Freud himself, anticipated some of Freud's views. But it is primarily to Freud and Freudianism that we owe our present interest. We are also indebted to Freud for asking a great many new questions about sucking. In particular, we owe him our interest in the *purpose of non-nutritive sucking*. Neither Harvey nor either of the Darwins was much interested in non-nutritive sucking *per se*, and none of them exploited the concept of "motivation" to a very large degree. As we shall see shortly, Freud's emphasis on the "motivation" involved in sucking has generated a tremendous amount of research during the last thirty years or so.

Freud (1905) became interested in both nutritive and non-nutritive sucking because he believed that the human being was so constituted that the course of development of sexuality was intimately related to individual differences in infantile oral behavior and gratification. In his *Three Contributions to the Theory of Sex*, in a section called the *Manifestations of Infantile Sexuality*, Freud writes as follows:

> Thumb-sucking, which manifests itself in the nursing baby and which may be continued till maturity or throughout life, consists in a rhythmic repetition of sucking contact with the mouth (the lips), wherein the purpose of taking nourishment is excluded. A part of the lip itself, the tongue, which is another preferable skin region within reach, and even the big toe—may be taken as objects for sucking. Simultaneously, there is also a desire to grasp things, which manifests itself in a rhythmical pulling of the ear lobe and which may cause the child to grasp a part of another person (generally the ear) for the same purpose. The pleasure-sucking is connected with a full absorption of attention and leads to sleep or even to a motor reaction in the form of an orgasm. Pleasure-sucking is often combined with a rubbing contact with certain sensitive parts of the body, such as the breast and external genitals. It is by this path that many children go from thumb-sucking to masturbation.
>
> Lindner himself clearly recognized the sexual nature of this activity and openly emphasized it. . . . Through thumb-sucking we can study directly the essential features of infantile sexual activities. . . .
>
> It is, moreover, clear that the action of the thumb-sucking child is determined by the fact that he seeks a pleasure which he has already experienced and now remembers. Through the rhythmic sucking on a portion of the skin or mucous membrane, he finds gratification in the simplest way. It is also easy to conjecture on what occasions the child first experienced this pleasure which he now strives to renew. The first and most important activity in the child's life, the sucking from the mother's breast (or its substitute), must have acquainted him with this pleasure. We would say that the child's lips behaved like an *erogenous zone*, and that the stimulus from the warm stream of milk was really the cause of the pleasurable sensation. To be sure, the gratification of the erogenous zone was at first united with the gratification of the need for nourishment. The sexual activity leans first on one of the self-preservative functions and only later makes itself independent of it. . . . The desire for repetition of sexual gratification is then separated from the desire for taking nourishment; a separation which becomes unavoidable with the appearance of teeth when the nourishment is no longer sucked but chewed. The child does not make use of a strange object for sucking but prefers his own skin, because it is more convenient, because it thus makes himself independent of the

outer world which he cannot control, and because in this way he creates for himself, as it were, a second, even if inferior, erogenous zone. . . .

Not all children suck their thumbs. It may be assumed that it is found only in children in whom the erogenous significance of the lip-zone is constitutionally reinforced. [Here Freud suggests genetic individual differences.] If the latter is retained in some children, they develop into kissing epicures with a tendency to perverse kissing, or as men, they show a strong desire for drinking and smoking. But should repression come into play, they then show disgust for eating and evince hysterical vomiting. By virtue of the community of the lip-zone, the repression encroaches upon the instinct of nourishment. Many of my female patients showing disturbances in eating, such as *hysterical globus*, choking sensations and vomiting, have been energetic thumb-suckers in infancy.

In thumb-sucking or pleasure-sucking, we are already able to observe the three essential characters of an infantile sexual manifestation. It has its origin in an *anaclitic* [1] relation to a physical function which is very important for life; it does not yet know any sexual object, that is, it is *auto-erotic*, and its sexual aim is under the control of an *erogenous zone*. [2]

These passages are only a small part of what Freud has to say about orality. Beside the effects on adult sexual behavior, Freud also asserted that personality characteristics are associated with the oral component of pregenital sexuality and with the way it is encouraged or restricted in development. The literature on these matters is vast. In fact, it is so extensive that it almost defies reading, and we shall not consider it. We shall examine only that literature which deals with behavior that is "oral" by definition—that is, with behavior involving the mouth. In what sense, if any, is there a "need" or "drive" or "instinct" to suck? If there is such a "motivational state," what are the conditions necessary for its development? How common is this non-nutritive sucking? What are the consequences of encouraging, permitting, ignoring, or preventing

[1] The precise meaning of the term "anaclitic" is not perfectly clear. The word does not appear in the 1909 edition of G. and C. Merriam Co.'s *Webster's International Dictionary*. The 1961 edition gives "characterized by dependence of the libido upon a non-sexual instinct (such as the hunger drive)." The 21st (1947) edition of *Dorland's American Illustrated Medical Dictionary* gives: "Leaning against or depending on something; a term applied to the first love object on account of the original dependence on such a person (the mother) for care and feeding." The sense of "depend" is not specified. By *anaclitic origin*, did Freud mean only that the pleasurable qualities of sucking are first *experienced* while nursing? Or that the pleasurable qualities *develop as a consequence* of the association of sucking with food-taking? Or that the "need" to suck develops as a consequence of this association?

[2] Taken from *The Basic Writings of Sigmund Freud*, trans. and ed. by Dr. A. A. Brill, pp. 585–7. Copyright 1938 by Random House, Inc. Reprinted by permission of the Brill Trust.

it? What kinds of conditions lead to differences in the amount of non-nutritive sucking that children and other young animals indulge in?

The Modern Controversy: Psychoanalysis vs. Behaviorism

Most psychoanalytically inclined investigators have paid little attention to Freud's assertion that thumb-sucking is a pleasure-sucking which "has its origin in an anaclitic relation to a physical function which is very important for life." In other words, most psychoanalysts have assumed the presence of a need to suck which has properties similar to the need for food. The "need" to suck is assumed to increase as a function of the time since the last sucking and to decrease whenever the child actually sucks.

During the twenty or twenty-five years after 1905, Brill's translations of Freud gradually became more and more widely known in the United States. One of the most imaginative and also one of the most empirically minded of American psychoanalysts is David Levy, who in 1928 and 1934 published two papers which have by now almost attained the status of classics.

The first of these papers is based upon Levy's (1928) interviews with mothers who were attending a "Better Babies" conference. Case histories from clinics and private practice had seemed to suggest that thumb- and finger-sucking in childhood was the consequence of too short a sucking time during nursing. It was to check this hypothesis systematically that Levy undertook the investigation. All told, he obtained information from 66 mothers who had 112 children. Twenty-eight children were thumb-suckers. From interviews with the mothers Levy concluded that the thumb-suckers had been treated differently from the non-thumb-suckers. As compared with non-thumb-suckers, thumb-suckers had fewer night feedings, were more frequently fed at four-hour intervals as opposed to three-hour intervals, were more frequently fed by schedule as opposed to demand, and were less likely to have been given pacifiers. In addition, the thumb-suckers had more frequently withdrawn spontaneously from a very rapidly flowing breast or bottle (because they were sated), and had more frequently been removed from the breast or bottle after a predetermined interval. Thumb-suckers had also been subjected at earlier ages to changes in feeding schedules which increased the intervals between feedings and decreased the duration of feeding times. Levy also reported that thumb-sucking versus non-thumb-sucking was not associated with whether the baby had been breast-fed or bottle-fed. It is not clear from psychoanalytic theory that it should be. Otherwise Levy's findings are quite in keeping with the psychoanalytic hypothesis. Ever since, they have been referred to as supporting the notion of an *innate* "need" to suck, while the hedonistic aspect of Freud's pleasure-sucking has been neglected.

A very curious bit of blindness occurred at this point. Levy noted that "in certain cases lip and tongue-sucking appeared to be related to excessive sucking of the breast." The blindness lies in the fact that this finding, which suggested an acquired or learned aspect of non-nutritive sucking went unnoticed.

Why?

Probably because personality enters into science. During the twenties the views of John B. Watson (1928), who had a genius for publicity as well as an extremely effective pen, had become very widely disseminated. His influence on middle-class mothers, magazines, and pediatric thought was tremendous. The same was true in academic circles. As is always the case, the time drew near for the pendulum to swing back. Watson, whose belief that complex adult behavior was almost entirely the result of the conditioning and patterning of reflexes—or, more generally, of learning—had very pronounced views about child rearing. His protest took the following form:

> Professor John Dewey and many other educators have been insisting for the last twenty years upon a method of training which allows the child to develop from within. This is really a doctrine of mystery. It teaches that there are hidden springs of activity, hidden possibilities of unfolding within the child which must be waited for until they appear and then be fostered and tended.
>
> The behaviorists believe that there is nothing from within to develop. If you start with a healthy body, the right number of fingers and toes, eyes, and the few elementary movements that are present at birth, you do not need anything else in the way of raw material to make a man, be that man a genius, a cultured gentleman, a rowdy or a thug.
>
> In the process of socializing your child another problem often comes up. It is thumb-sucking or hand or finger-sucking. This highly unsocial act is difficult to control if it gets a good start in early infancy. Sometimes an object is sucked such as a piece of cloth, an old blanket or other covers. When the mother is very careless the nipple of the nursing bottle is persistently sucked and later chewed after the milk has been consumed. Millions of mothers who are almost criminally careless use a pacifier to keep the child quiet. The child sucks it all during his waking hours.
>
> There is nothing to be alarmed about in early thumb-sucking [sic!]. Many infants are born almost with a finger in the mouth. This is due to their position *in utero*. If you will watch the new-born youngsters for a few months after birth you will see the result of this pre-birth position of the hands. Rarely does the infant move the hands below the waistline. Hence it is natural that the mouth should be "discovered" before any other part of the body. He discovers it by the

usual "trial and error" method. Trial movements cease when the fingers touch the mouth. Then sucking movements immediately begin. Sucking movements do not have to be learned. They are well established in most infants at birth (or shortly thereafter). *In other words, thumb-sucking is a now familiar conditioned response connected with eating.*[3]

It is somewhat startling that Watson, the arch-environmentalist, takes a maturational position about the initial appearance of sucking. For him it was only *thumb*-sucking that was learned.

As befits his role as propagandist for behaviorism, Watson speaks the language of stimulus and response. For Watson's "conditioned response" Freud wrote—in somewhat more hedonistic and motivational terms—"anaclitic pleasure-sucking." Whether the terms have different empirical meanings is not yet certain, and we shall consider the question in our Summary.

Part of Watson's own intellectual debt to Freud is apparent in his next sentence:

The lips belong to the general area of the sex field too, so that in part thumb-sucking is a sex response (using this word in its broad modern sense) closely akin to masturbation which is a habit even infants may form.

Watson continues:

If persistent thumb-sucking is in part a food habit, we should expect to find it most persisted in by children who are continually hungry or whose bodies are not kept free from irritation. You will see this view supported in every poorly run orphan or nursery home.

If persisted in for long at any early age before the bony, tendinous and muscular tissues harden, the mouth becomes misshapen and the fingers and hands are changed in their contours. There are many other bodily changes which may occur, such as interference with the proper growth and position of the teeth.

The effect of thumb-sucking upon the child's personality is the most serious aspect of all. It is an infantile type of reaction which when carried over beyond the age of infancy ends in a pernicious habit almost impossible to break. Indeed, if carried through adolescence in the modified form of nail-biting, finger-biting, cuticle-picking or finger-picking, it becomes practically impossible to break. It is then classed as a neurotic trait.

The act brings with it a kind of soothing or quieting effect like a drug. As long as the individual is allowed to engage in it he is perfectly docile in all of his reactions. Scold him about it, try to check it and he

[3] From J. B. Watson, *Psychological Care of Infant and Child*, pp. 40–1, 133–4, copyright 1928 by W. W. Norton and Co., Inc., New York. This and the following excerpt are used by permission of the publisher.

becomes irritable and uneasy. Apparently when the child has his fingers in his mouth *he is*, speaking broadly, *blocked to all other stimuli*. Hence the persistent thumb-sucker cannot be as easily made to respond to toys and other objects upon which we normally train children. The outside world doesn't get a good chance at him. He doesn't conquer his world. He becomes an "exclusive" and auto-erotic. With his fingers safely in his mouth the child may sometimes not even react to dangerous stimuli. Our own experiments at Johns Hopkins show that even when stimuli which are known to produce fright are shown to the thumb-sucking child they lose their power to arouse him.

How can we correct thumb-sucking? The answer is, *cure it during the first few days of infancy*. Watch the baby carefully the first few days. Keep the hands away from the mouth as often as you are near the baby in its waking moments. And always when you put it into its crib for sleep, see that the hands are tucked inside the covers—and if you examine the sleeping infant from time to time see when you leave it that the hands are under the covers.

If the habit develops in spite of this early scrutiny, consult your physician about the infant's diet. Tell him about the thumb-sucking. If, after changes in the diet, thumb-sucking persists, then take more drastic steps to break the habit. Sew loose, white cotton flannel mitts with no finger or thumb divisions to the sleeves of the night gown and on all the *day dresses, and leave them on for two weeks or more—day and night*. So many mothers leave them on only at night. Unless the child is watched every moment the hand will at one time or another get back to the mouth. You must be careful to see that the dress or night gown is fastened securely but not tightly at the throat—else if the infant is persistent he will learn to disrobe himself to get at his hands. If the habit still persists make . . . the mitts [of] rougher and rougher material.

I have tried many methods that will not work. Those clumsy aluminum mitts are ineffective. The child bangs himself over the head and eyes and nine times out of ten gets out of them in one way or another. Pasteboard tubes over the elbow joint are used in some good hospitals but they are cruel. The child cannot rub an irritation or scare away a fly or mosquito. Coating the fingers with bitter aloes has never worked out for me. Occasionally the infant goes right ahead without baulking at the aloes, or if he does make a wry face or two he soon goes on serenely. I've never had any success with taping the finger. Either he picks the tape off after a time (if one year of age or over) or else sucks the finger, tape and all.

I have tried punishment—sharply rapping the finger with a pencil. This is beautifully effective while the experimenter is around but at night the habit reasserts itself. Scolding and corporal punishment likewise have proved wholly ineffective [pp. 134-9].

These remarks, which were published in 1928, the same year as Levy's first paper, are quite representative of Watson's general views on the subject of child-rearing. It was also in 1928 that Watson's primitive behaviorism—the behaviorism of the merely *reacting* organism—reached its zenith. There were several challengers for its pre-eminence, but in this context we need to consider only one—psychoanalysis. Since Watson and his followers had overemphasized the learned aspects of human development, it was only natural that Freud's followers should emphasize the unlearned ones. The parts of Levy's findings which suited the Freudian purpose were the ones which Freudians noted and emphasized. But since most of us seldom pay close attention to the proponents of views which we "know" to be wrong, the arch-behaviorists failed to discover the little bit of Levy's data which would have bolstered their own cause.

It is also interesting that psychoanalysts have not called attention to the extraordinary difficulty that Watson experienced in extinguishing the so-called "conditioned response" of thumb-sucking. Extreme resistance to extinction is frequently taken as evidence that rewards and "motives" are involved in behavior, and this is exactly what psychoanalysts have argued.

In any event the star of simon-pure behaviorism began to wane and psychoanalysis grew increasingly more influential. Levy continued to study the development of non-nutritive sucking, and his next paper (1934) on the subject was even more widely noted and quoted. He separated a litter of six puppies into three pairs when they were ten days old. One pair continued to nurse the bitch while the other two pairs were fed artificially. One pair was fed a formula from very slowly flowing nipples while the other pair was fed first by tube, and then— after their thirteenth postnatal day—by very rapidly flowing nipples. The shift from tube to rapidly flowing bottle was made because the tube-fed pair lost weight. Both artificially fed pairs were on a four-hour schedule. During the twenty days that the experiment continued—the eleventh to the thirtieth postnatal days of life—the bottle-fed puppies were observed closely and also tested for their readiness (eagerness) to suck. The tests consisted of inserting a nipple-covered finger in the puppy's mouth and rating the vigor with which it sucked. If what we shall call the neo-Freudian view is correct, then, of course, the pups with rapidly flowing bottles should have sucked the proffered finger more vigorously. And they did. (Fleischl [1957], using three puppies, reports an almost exact duplication of Levy's experiment.) Furthermore, the short-time suckers appeared restless, mouthed their own bodies more, and required a greater volume of formula to make a normal weight gain. The obvious interpretation followed: that deprivation of oral-sucking gratification results not only in a greater readiness or "need" to suck but also in a general malaise which expresses itself in restlessness and interference with optimal metabolic functioning.

Marquis (1941), studying quite a different question, later provided empirical evidence that newborn human babies on a three-hour schedule were less active than those on a four-hour schedule. How to tell whether a newborn human (or puppy) is "active" or whether he is "restless" is a nice question.

During the next ten or fifteen years Levy's findings and interpretations became very widely known and, in the flood-tide of Freudian influence, accepted. Roberts (1944) confirmed them by interviewing thirty mothers of seven- and eight-month-old infants. The fifteen known thumb-suckers were reported to have spent considerably less time nursing than the fifteen known non-thumb-suckers. Abrupt shortening of nursing time also appeared to increase the likelihood of thumb-sucking. Investigators who did not subscribe to Freudian views continued to study thumb-sucking during the period, but for the most part their findings attracted much less attention. We shall examine them later in a more appropriate context.

At about this time Ribble (1943) published a very influential little book called *The Rights of Infants*. In it and other papers Ribble (1939) took an extremely nativistic position with respect to the development of sucking. Spitz (1945, 1946a, 1946b) has more recently emphasized the same point of view. In Ribble's words:

> During the first three to six months of an infant's life sucking is his most gratifying and all absorbing activity. . . . Sucking usually reaches a maximum intensity about the fourth month of life, and, if it has been freely and agreeably exercised to this time, begins to diminish spontaneously when the baby begins to vocalize, to bite, and to grasp with his hands . . . Most important to the infant himself is the pleasure value of sucking. . . . Sucking is then a part of the instinctual behavior with which the child is equipped at birth. . . . Very quickly rhythmic intervals become established in which the infant shows evidence of a "wish to suck.". . .[4]

In short, Ribble stresses the notion that the human infant "needs" sensory stimulation and especially oral stimulation. In support of her view she cites a number of individual case histories and her own observations that infants who were fed at three-hour intervals "were organized better and much less restless than those fed less often." Pinneau (1950, 1955) has subjected both Ribble and Spitz to some truly devastating criticism on the grounds of oversimplification, overgeneralization, bad neurology, and lack of scientific rigor. We quite agree with that criticism, but so far as the applied psychology of mothers and infants is concerned we agree with Ribble on one major point. Babies do seem to thrive on

[4] From M. A. Ribble, *The Rights of Infants*, pp. 22–3, copyright 1943 by Columbia University Press and used by their permission.

stimulation—particularly tactile stimulation. As a wise and affectionate mother told one of us, "Ribble says it's all right to love your baby." An antidote to Watson was needed and Ribble provided it.

Learning Theory Leads to Some Experiments

In 1948 a new series of papers, originally stimulated by R. R. Sears and his associates, began to appear. During the thirties and forties American psychology developed a tremendous interest in learning theory, and Sears is one whose training included both psychoanalytic and learning theory. One of the questions which has preoccupied such learning theorists is the following: Under what conditions, if any, does an "acquired drive" arise? Many persons have suggested that behavior which has frequently been followed by reward will gradually acquire the capacity to act as a reward itself, and further, that there develops a "need" or "drive" or "motive" to perform that behavior.[5] This notion may be very close to what Freud had in mind when he said that thumb-sucking is "anaclitic." The question which this next series of papers attempts to answer is not, "Does the average or normal baby show a sucking instinct?" but rather, "To what extent is the sucking 'drive' due to the fact that in normal infants a great deal of sucking is accompanied by the reward of food?" In the words of the experimenters (Davis, Sears, Miller, and Brodbeck, 1948):

> . . . Whether the drive that causes such behavior is inborn is difficult to determine. The fact that feeding usually accompanies sucking during the first weeks of life means there is ample opportunity for the baby to learn a sucking drive if he does not already possess it. The necessary conditions for this would be the frequent occurrence of the act (sucking) followed by satisfaction of a primary drive (hunger). To determine whether the sucking drive is inborn or learned requires a comparison of the frequency of oral activities and frustration reactions in two groups of babies, one of which has had the experience of sucking followed by feeding, and the other of which has fed without sucking.
>
> An opportunity to make this comparison was presented to us by a group of babies who were fed from birth from a cup. This method of feeding reduces nutritive sucking far below that which would occur among babies fed at the breast or from a bottle. According to the psychoanalytic theory, these babies would be expected to show more non-nutritional sucking and more emotional disturbance than babies

[5] To act as a reward is not the same as to show drive properties. In the present instance the notion is that because sucking has frequently led to reward there *develops* a drive to suck which can be reduced (only?) by sucking. Presumably the response of sucking (or the stimulation resulting from the response) is the goal of the *drive* to suck. In short, sucking becomes an end in itself.

fed from birth by bottle or breast. According to the learning theory, on the other hand, the cup-fed babies should show less indication of a sucking drive than bottle- or breast-fed babies because they had less opportunity to associate sucking and feeding.

The present report is concerned with investigations made on 60 newborn infants divided into three groups of 20 each according to the method of feeding: cup, bottle or breast. Daily measurements were made during the first 10 days of life on the strength of the sucking response, the frequency of non-nutritional oral movements, the amount of general body activity, the amount of crying and the interest in food.

A comparison of trends in the three groups . . . shows that there was an important difference between the breast-fed group and the other two groups. Neither the bottle- nor the cup-fed group showed any significant increase in median duration of response to the sucking test during the ten days. In contrast, the breast-fed group, which started lower than they, increased until it was substantially higher during the last seven days.[6]

In their discussion the authors suggest that "this more vigorous sucking among the breast-fed infants, together with the greater number of rewarded sucks they necessarily had, very likely accounts for their increased response (greater habit strength) in the last seven days." Then, following their inclinations in learning theory, they toy with the possibility that this greater "habit strength" reflects a "secondary drive." (Of course, their earlier remarks assume *some* sort of "drive.") But the fact that the bottle-fed babies, who—according to the learning theory— should have been similar to the breast-fed, were indistinguishable from the cup-fed, discouraged them from taking that plunge. Instead, they suggested that an unforeseen, uncontrolled variable be looked into first. This additional factor was the hospital nipples which were so designed that the bottle-fed babies, like the cup-fed babies, normally consumed their feedings in about half the time required by the breast-fed.

And sure enough, in 1950 Brodbeck reported that infants fed from birth by means of rapidly flowing nipples showed little increase in scores on sucking tests, while those fed from slowly flowing nipples showed larger increases. Furthermore, Brodbeck found, just as Hullian learning theorists expected, that infants who received large amounts of formula from bottles developed a greater readiness to suck than those who received only small amounts.

In the same year Sears and Wise (1950) reported a modification of Levy's original (1928) investigation. Among the improvements were the use of independent judges of the mothers' responses in the interviews and the selection of a sample that included a number of children who

[6] From H. V. Davis *et al.*, "Effects of Cup, Bottle and Breast Feeding on Oral Activities of New-born Infants," *Pediatrics*, 1948, 3, 549–50, 553–4. Courtesy of Charles C Thomas, Publisher, and of the author and *Pediatrics*.

had been weaned very early in life—in fact, five of the children had been cup-fed from birth, and five others had been weaned before they left the hospital at two weeks. All told, seventy-five mothers of eighty children ranging in age from two to eight years were interviewed about a wide variety of child-behavior and child-training procedures. The transcripts of the interviews were then rated by two other investigators for the "dependent" and "independent" variables thought to be relevant to orality.

In this paper Sears and Wise tried to distinguish between two aspects of the weaning process—the strength of the oral "drive" and the degree of interference with the "drive." As an index of "drive strength" they selected age of weaning: the older the child at the time of weaning, the greater his oral "drive." (Note that now not only is a "drive" *assumed*, but also that it is considered to be at least in part *learned*.) As an index of the severity of oral frustration, they selected abruptness of weaning: a very sudden and all-at-once weaning was presumed to involve the greatest frustration, while a very gradual weaning that permitted the child to learn to use a cup over a considerable period of time was assumed to involve the least degree of frustration. While their results are not perfectly clear-cut, there are five findings of importance: (1) the later the weaning, the more upset the children became; (2) thumb-sucking was no more common among children weaned early or after an intermediate period than in those weaned late—in fact, there was a little evidence that thumb-sucking was more severe in the late-weaned; (3) the more abrupt the weaning (presumably the greater the interference), the greater the children's objection to it; (4) abruptness of weaning showed no clear-cut relationship to thumb-sucking; and (5) there was little evidence that thumb-sucking was more common or more severe in children who reacted strongly to weaning than in those who showed little or no disturbance. Sears and Wise concluded:

> The increased frequency of frustration reactions . . . in the middle- and late-weaned groups indicates that the oral drive is strengthened by longer retention of the sucking method of feeding. This greater drive is accompanied by at least a suggestion of a greater frequency of thumb-sucking among those children weaned late than among those weaned earlier. In other words, Levy has shown that children fed by sucking have a sufficiently strong oral drive that interference with it leads to substitute sucking, and the present data suggest that the strength of that drive is in part a function of how long the child continues to feed by sucking. The data also suggest that it is the strength of the oral drive and not the amount of frustration involved in weaning that determines the occurrence of thumb-sucking. These facts support the rephrased statement of Freud's original hypothesis that securing food by sucking increases the erotogeneity of the mouth (increases oral drive).

The finding that early weaning causes less frustration reaction than late weaning does not conflict with any previously established facts. It has been commonly thought that Levy's original finding of more thumb-sucking in children who had inadequate sucking opportunity required the assumption of an inborn or primary oral (sucking) drive. This does not necessarily follow. All of Levy's subjects had been fed by sucking, and therefore they belonged in the "middle"- or "late"-weaned groups as these have been defined in the present study. Once a child has had his sucking drive strengthened by practice, the amount of substitutive sucking would be expected to increase with interference in nutritional sucking. This is what Levy found.[7]

In the excerpt above, Sears' and Wise's use of the word "strengthened" is ambiguous. If they mean strengthened from zero that is one thing—the development of an acquired drive where *no* drive had previously existed. If they mean strengthened from a value greater than zero then they have accepted the view that there is "an inborn or primary oral (sucking) drive." [8]

Ten years after Sears' and Wise's paper, Akrawi (1960) reported a very close replication with thirty middle-class Iraqi children in Baghdad. For her subjects, who were weaned considerably later than Sears and Wise's—between six and forty-two months with a mean of fourteen—age of weaning was *significantly* related to the mothers' reports of non-nutritive sucking, biting, and mouthing and also to the investigator's observations of such behavior in a brief test period. Except for her failure to find a significant correlation between age and severity of reaction to weaning, Akrawi's other results are also consonant with Sears and Wise's: abruptness of weaning was *not* related to her measures of orality, but it *was* related to the severity of reaction to the weaning.

In passing it should be mentioned that Yarrow (1954) and Bernstein (1955) *have* confirmed the positive relation between age and severity of response to weaning. All things considered, Sears and Wise's findings have stood up rather well so far—learning theory has scored a point. Yarrow and Bernstein also found the same positive association between the extent of nutritive sucking and thumb- or finger-sucking,

[7] From R. R. Sears and G. Wise, "Relation of Cup-Feeding in Infancy to Thumb-sucking and the Oral Drive," *Amer. J. Orthopsychiatry*, 1950, 20, 136f., and used by permission.

[8] Blau and Blau's (1955) account of a single male infant observed for twenty hours a day from the third to the seventh postnatal week illustrates another—sometimes forgotten—condition which contributes to thumb-sucking. The infant, who was sometimes fed from a rapidly flowing bottle and at other times from a slow bottle, engaged in significantly more non-nutritional sucking (as well as more crying and physical activity, which may perhaps have reflected malaise) during the latter regime. The authors wryly noted that "this investigation raises the suggestion that perhaps the gratification of hunger needs temporally is of more importance behaviorally than the satisfaction of a supposed sucking need. . . ."

though in neither case was the association statistically significant. Yarrow also reported a significant *negative* association between average amount of time per feeding (nursing) during the first six months and severity and persistence of thumb-sucking. This finding is, however, based on only the thirty-one children for whom appropriate data were available.

One additional finding of Bernstein's, an ingenious one, is given in the author's words:

. . . each of the 50 subjects was asked to choose between a lollipop and a piece of chocolate. . . . The function of a lollipop as a sucking device is clear.

Before each child was permitted to see the candy, he was asked to make a choice as follows. The experimenter said: "Would you like to have a piece of candy? I have some chocolate bars and some lollipops. Which would you rather have?" After the child stated his choice, he was given the candy and observed to see what he did with it.

Of the 22 children who chose lollipops, 19 sucked them, two chewed them, and one took it home. Of the 25 children who chose chocolate, 21 chewed, one sucked, and three took it home. The mean sucking time on the lollipops was between 14 and 15 minutes, while the mean time spent eating the chocolate was between one and two minutes.

TABLE 1*

RELATION OF CANDY CHOICE TO SUCKING OPPORTUNITY

| | | Sucking opportunity | |
	Index I	*Index II*	*Index III*
Mean of Lollipop Group	22.50 mos.	28.86 mos.	37.04 mos.
Mean of Chocolate Group	18.84 mos.	23.48 mos.	29.80 mos.

* Adapted from A. Bernstein, "Some Relations between Techniques of Feeding and Training during Infancy and Certain Behavior in Childhood," *Genet. Psychol. Monogr.*, 1955, *51*, p. 29. Table and excerpt used by permission of The Journal Press, Provincetown, Mass.

Table [1] shows that the children who chose lollipops averaged 5.38 more months of sucking practice (Sucking Index II) [9] than the

---

[9] Index I is the number of months the breast and bottle were the main source of food. Index II is the number of months during which, at any time, the child was ever given the breast or bottle. Index III is a composite measure based on the number of months of breast or bottle feeding, the number of sucking feedings per day, and the average duration of sucking per meal.

group that selected the chocolate. The difference is almost significant
at the .05 level of probability.

. . . When an overall measure of sucking reinforcement (Sucking
Index III) is used to compare the groups, the mean difference in sucking reinforcement is significant at the .02 level. Sucking Index I shows
a difference in the same direction, but the difference is not significant.
The differences are clearly in a direction supporting the reinforcement
hypothesis [pp. 30–1].

Some Questions About the Learning Theorists' Experiments

Several aspects of this recent series of papers need careful consideration. Bernstein notes the distressing possibility that the high resistance
to weaning in older children is due to the fact that mothers delayed
weaning *because* their children resisted. Yarrow entertains a similar
idea when he suggests, apropos of Sears' views, that perhaps "infants
already showing a strong drive in the early weeks of life were the ones
who succeeded in obtaining long periods of breast or bottle feedings."
It would be very interesting to know if infants who show good strong
sucking behavior at birth before they are ever fed are those whose
mothers later have to give in to their children and delay weaning them.
We would expect such results. They would demonstrate that later
individual differences in sucking are due in part to factors *other* than
rewarded practice.

A second difficulty is the apparent contradiction in Yarrow's data.
He reports that short nursing periods during the first six months lead
to thumb-sucking and also that thumb-sucking is associated with late
weaning rather than early weaning. Yarrow attempts to resolve the inconsistency by appealing to the psychoanalytic theory that either
over- or undergratification leads to "fixation"—excessively strong attachment to a particular means and stage of gratification. Thus short
nursing periods during the first six months involve an "undergratification" of the "constitutionally" determined "oral stage" of psychosexual
development, while very late weaning involves an "overgratification."
Why very early weaning should not be just as undergratifying as short
nursing periods is not clear. Psychoanalytic theory is not explicit about
whether different kinds of undergratification will have different consequences, but it is certainly quite possible that these specifiably different
aspects of nursing and weaning do, in fact, lead to different outcomes.

Learning theorists would assert that an "acquired drive" develops
only when there has been a fair amount of rewarded practice. Thus a
child who is weaned late will develop an oral drive while one who is
weaned early will not. Consequently the latter will not exhibit substitutive sucking when he is weaned. Learning theorists would probably explain Yarrow's negative relation between thumb-sucking and

the length of nursing periods during the first six months somewhat as follows. Children nursed for six months may have obtained enough rewarded practice to *develop* an "oral drive" but *not* enough to *gratify* the (still-developing?) drive. Or perhaps their position would be that once a "drive" is acquired it is somehow revitalized from time to time and under a variety of circumstances and on this account would need additional opportunities for gratification.

Regardless of the precise position that they might take, Davis, Sears, *et al.*, Brodbeck, Sears and Wise, and Bernstein may be said to have espoused the environmentalists' view. They have interpreted the positive relationship between rewarded practice and various measures of sucking as due to some sort of learning. Just what is learned? Bernstein is noncommittal on this point, and Yarrow's data and views are not easily categorized. Sears and Wise and Akrawi assume that a *drive* has been acquired. That is, they accept the notion that there is some sort of *motive to suck* and ask whether that *motive* is the result of learning. They conclude that it is. These authors seem not to have considered the possibility that what has been learned is not a motive but a habit. Perhaps it is better to say that they have not troubled themselves about just precisely *what* has been learned and have cared only to demonstrate that learning of some sort appears to be involved. After all, Sears and Wise were responding to the neo-Freudian view that there is an "inborn or primary oral (sucking) drive."

But to demonstrate that experience affects a response is not the same as to demonstrate that experience leads to an *acquired drive*, and this point is important. To demonstrate an acquired drive, the phenomena that reflect acquired *drive* must be distinguished from those that reflect acquired *habit*. To date this has not been done successfully for sucking. Nothing reported in these recent papers would have upset Watson's assertion that "thumb-sucking is now a familiar conditioned response connected with eating." In fact, Palermo (1956), in a recent brief discussion of thumb-sucking, adopts a reinforcement view of learning, adds the notion of stimulus generalization, and writes a perfectly plausible explanation of Sears' data without any reference whatsoever to the notion of an acquired *drive* to suck. To change the words from "conditioned response" to "acquired drive" is not to demonstrate that the terms have different empirical meanings. In this particular case of word-changing we must be especially suspicious for two reasons. The first is that the concept of motivation has had a tantalizingly seductive appeal for psychologists. Why, is anyone's guess—but it has. Somehow we are tempted to drop a matter as "explained" if we can find a plausible "drive" or "need" or "instinct" which "lies behind" the behavior. In this case we are asked to accept the notion that interference with older children's stronger acquired *drive to suck* is responsible for their greater frustration response. But why is it not just as plausible to attribute it to their stronger *habits* of sucking? (cf. Brown, 1953).

The second reason for caution in introducing motivational terms is that in the history of psychology there are already at least two instances where enthusiastic advocates of motivation have found themselves caught in a tight little bit of circular reasoning. The two instances are McDougall's "instinct" system and Murray's "need" system. In both cases the theorists who attempted to use the concepts of "instinct" or "need" found it very difficult to spell out exactly how to determine when a particular "instinct" or "need" was present or active. In practice most of these theorists ultimately resorted to using the subject's behavior as the criterion. Thus a mother actively taking care of her baby was said to be exhibiting her maternal "instinct" or her nurturant "need." Once the investigator had uttered the word "instinct" or "need" to himself he was lulled into the false sense of security that such motivational "explanations" seem to induce. The circularity can be illustrated by the following hypothetical conversation: Why did the chicken cross the road? Because he wanted to get to the other side. How do you know he wanted to get to the other side? Because he crossed the road. This amounts to saying that the chicken crossed the road because he crossed the road—a fairly silly statement! [1]

It is the fact that the motivational construct has proved so troublesome in the past that makes us a trifle uneasy about speaking of the "acquired drive to suck."

A Theory of Child Psychology from the Continent

There remains one eminent theoretical child psychologist whose views and observations need to be considered. Jean Piaget [2] is a Swiss child psychologist of the Institut Jean-Jacques Rousseau [3] in Geneva. In

[1] The importance of specifying just how an inferred construct is related to variables other than the behavior which it is supposed to help explain has been discussed at considerable length by psychologists. A very clear exposition of the question can be found in Tolman (1938).

[2] American psychologists frequently refer to Piaget's work, but until recently he has more often served as a target than a guide. There are several reasons for this fact: his methodology is unconventional and he generalizes from very small numbers of children; he is quite frankly a mentalist which many American psychologists of the post-Watsonian era abhor; his metaphysical concerns often obtrude themselves into his psychological discussions; his terminology is so idiosyncratic that even the most conscientious translator is hard put to render a perfectly clear account of his ideas.

[3] Rousseau (1712–78) was a French philosopher, born in Geneva. Interestingly enough his *Émile* (1762) expounds the view that children—or more generally mankind—are *innately* good, noble, and so on, and are corrupted only as a result of contact with an evil environment. The "nature-nurture" question has interested quite a variety of persons.

The Origins of Intelligence in Children (1936) Piaget attempts to account for—or describe—the gradual appearance of intelligent adaptive behavior from the rather limited behavioral repertoire with which the newborn infant is equipped. Partly as a vehicle for exposition and partly because he is convinced of its own intrinsic importance, Piaget gives many detailed observations of the sucking behavior of his own children. While we are unable to give a full account of Piaget's theoretical views, some of his observations are extremely interesting. He observed that the sucking response was present shortly after birth in each of his three children, that there were individual differences among them with respect to the stimuli that would evoke the response at this very early age, and that two of his children sucked their fingers within half an hour of birth while the third did not. Piaget also notes that with increased age and experience the efficiency of thumb-sucking increases as does the range of stimuli which evoke sucking and mouthing movements.

Baldwin (1955) cites four of Piaget's observations and gives a very lucid account of his views:

At 0;1 (1) [4] Laurent is held by his nurse . . . shortly before the meal. He is very hungry and tries to nurse with his mouth open and continuous rotations of the head. His arms describe big rapid movements and constantly knock against his face. Twice, when his hand was laid on his right cheek, Laurent turned his head and tried to grasp his fingers with his mouth. The first time he failed and succeeded the second. But the movements of his arms are not coordinated with those of his head; the hand escapes while the mouth tries to maintain contact. Subsequently, however, he catches his thumb; his whole body is then immobilized,[5] his right hand happens to grasp his left arm and his left hand presses against his mouth. . . .

At 0;1 (2) Laurent in his crib cries with hunger. He is lifted to an almost vertical position. . . . He begins by calming himself and tries to suck while turning his head from left to right and back again while his arms flourish without direction. Then the arms, instead of describing a movement of maximum breadth, seem to approach his mouth. Several times each hand brushes his lips; the right hand presses against the child's cheek and clasps it for a few seconds. Meanwhile the mouth is wide open and unceasingly attempts to grasp something. The left thumb is then caught and the two arms become rigid, the right arm against the chest under the left arm which is held by the mouth. [Then] the arms again wave about in space without direction, the left

[4] "0;1 (1)" means zero years; one month (first day). That is, the baby was one month and one day old.

[5] Gesell (1937), Ribble (1943), and Gentry and Aldrich (1948) have also pointed out that the human infant seems to use his mouth actively—searchingly—for tactile exploration.

thumb leaving the mouth after a few minutes. During this time the child becomes angry, his head thrown back and his cries alternating with attempts to suck. Finally . . . the hands again approach the mouth which tries to seize the fingers which touch it. These last attempts meet with no success and crying ensues.

At 0;1 (4) after the 6 P.M. meal Laurent is wide awake . . . and not completely satisfied. First he makes vigorous sucking-like movements, then his right hand may be seen approaching his mouth, touching his lower lip and finally being grasped. But as only the index finger was grasped, the hand fell out again. Shortly afterward it returned. This time the thumb was in the mouth while the index finger was placed between the gums and the upper lip. The hand then moves 5 cm. away from the mouth only to re-enter it; now the thumb is grasped and the other fingers remain outside. Laurent then is motionless and sucks vigorously, drooling. [Watson also noted, with profound disapproval, the calming effect of thumb-sucking.]

At 0;1 (5) and 0;1 (6) Laurent tries to catch his thumb as soon as he awakes but is unsuccessful while he is lying on his back. His hand taps his face without finding his mouth. When he is vertical, however (held by the waist, his arms and torso free), he quickly finds his lips. . . . At 0;1 (9), for example, Laurent sucks his thumb while lying on his back. I take it out of his mouth and, several times in succession, he puts it back into his mouth again almost immediately (having at most groped between nose and mouth) and only grasping the thumb, his other fingers remaining outside the mouth.

Baldwin comments:

This sequence of observations, which take place within a week, shows the gradual improvement of thumb-sucking. . . . At first an apparently accidental touching of the cheek stimulates more directed head motions. Later, the directed portion of the action seems to begin even before his hand hits his face. Finally, by the end of the week, Laurent initiates the entire action and can suck his thumb without much fumbling. By the end of the sequence he apparently wants to suck his thumb; sucking is no longer a mere accidental result of random activity. . . .

At first, sucking is evoked only by a posture which has been closely related to the experience of nursing. Then with further development the sucking behavior may begin in a variety of postures. . . .

Notice, thirdly, that thumb-sucking seems to be preferred to finger-sucking. From the very first observation it seemed as though finger-sucking did not provide Laurent the kind of stimulation that reduced his restlessness. Thus, on the first day the finger did not stay in the mouth. Perhaps it was not as "suckable" because it did not provide the same pattern of stimulation on the inside of the mouth as the mother's breast. Later during the same day, when the thumb rather than the finger happened to find its way into his mouth, Laurent's restlessness ceased. Since he did not move, the thumb stayed in position; this prolonged the sucking experience. The fact that thumb-sucking reduces restlessness has the effect of keeping the thumb in the mouth once it gets there and contributes to the learning of the thumb-sucking behavior.

Sucking an object makes it stimulate the inside of the mouth, which in turn is the stimulus for sucking. Thus, sucking is a circular, or self-perpetuating, action. When the child is actually nursing, the gradual ingestion of milk accompanies this circular reaction. . . . The ingestion of food reduces the intensity of stimulation from hunger . . . , so that the child goes to sleep and his sensitivity to the stimulation in the mouth disappears.

What seems to happen is that thumb-sucking itself becomes a satisfying activity. [In this passage Baldwin expresses almost the same point of view as Sears and his collaborators.] In Piaget's observations, for example, the baby sucked his thumb *after* a meal, and it is common to see babies go to sleep sucking a thumb. This finding implies that thumb-sucking has become satisfying as well as stimulating.[6]

Piaget (1936) examines the development of both nutritive and non-nutritive sucking quite explicitly from the point of view of the nature-nurture question and he is quite aware of the intricacies of the question. For while he writes, "The sucking reflex is hereditary and functions from birth, influenced either by diffuse impulsive movements or by an external excitant," he later writes:

. . . It is extremely precarious to specify when acquired adaptation actually begins in contradistinction to hereditary adaptation. . . . When the child systematically sucks his thumb, no longer due to chance contacts but through coordination between hand and mouth, this may be called acquired accommodation. Neither the reflexes of the mouth nor of the hand can be provided such coordination by heredity (there is no instinct to suck the thumb!) and experience alone explains its formation. But if this is clear with regard to that kind of behavior pattern, in how many others is it impossible to draw a clear boundary between the pure reflex and the utilization of experience? [1936, pp. 47f.].

The following remarks from Piaget are—regrettably—somewhat out of context, but they give the flavor of Piaget's thought far better than a paraphrase would:

In a general way one can say that the [sucking] reflex is consolidated and strengthened by virtue of its own functioning. . . . From the start of this primitive mechanism, a sort of circular process ac-

---

[6] From A. L. Baldwin, *Behavior and Development in Childhood*, pp. 182f., copyright 1955 by Dryden Press, New York, and used by permission of Holt, Rinehart, and Winston, Inc., New York.

companies the function, the activity of the reflex having augmented due to its own use. . . . After the first feeding one observes, in Laurent, sucking-like movements, in which it is difficult not to see a sort of auto-intoxication. Besides, the progress in the search for the breast . . . seems also to show how much the function itself strengthened the tendency to suck. The counter-proof of this is, as we have seen, the progressive decay of reflex mechanisms which are not used. . . .[7] The [sucking] reflex must be conceived as an organized totality whose nature it is to preserve itself by functioning and consequently to function sooner or later for its own sake.[8]

Putting out the tongue and finger-sucking thus constitute the first two examples of a behavior pattern which prolongs the functional use of the reflex (sucking-like movements), but with the acquisition of some element external to the hereditary mechanisms. The new use of the tongue seems to go beyond the simple play involved in sucking. With regard to the thumb, let us repeat that no instinct to suck the fingers exists. . . . In characterizing these acquisitions it must also be noted that they imply an active element. It is not a question of associations imposed by the environment, but rather of relationships discovered and even created in the course of the child's own searchings. It is this twofold aspect of acquisition and activity which characterizes what we shall henceforth call "circular reactions". . . [pp. 32f.; p. 38; pp. 47f.; p. 55].

Circular reactions are important in Piaget's theory, and thumb-sucking is a nice illustration of the way in which something external to the child's sucking gradually becomes incorporated in the sucking schema. No other theorist is concerned in quite the same way with the infant's gradual development of goal-directed behavior from what originally appears to be unknowing searching.

So far we have considered only papers that are based upon more or less explicit theories. Certainly theory-building and theory-testing are one very important path that science follows. But it is not the only path —nor necessarily the best path. Experiments designed to test a theory may be quite important in establishing the truth or falsity of the *theory*

[7] This observation is exactly the same as the one reported by Harvey (1651), but as a matter of fact we have been unable to find any really convincing *evidence* that sucking movements *do* disappear in infants who are fed by cup. In a marginal comment on an earlier version of this chapter Professor Sears wrote: "It was commonly agreed among the pediatric nurses in the Kansas University Hospital that the reflex *did* disappear with cup-feeding, but—alas—neither Fredeen nor I quoted them in a technical journal, and thus, no doubt, this is not a fact."

[8] The motivational point of view incorporated in this remark is similar to the views of other child psychologists (Jersild, 1954). Nissen (1954) takes essentially the same position in his consideration of motivation in the chimpanzee.

The excerpts are taken from J. Piaget, *The Origins of Intelligence in Children*, copyright 1952 by International Universities Press and used by their permission.

and yet tell us only a very little about the development of the particular *behavior* at hand.

For the sake of argument let us agree that Sears and others have demonstrated that the development of the sucking response is affected by learning. For those whose major interest is in learning theory this is an important accomplishment. But for those interested primarily in the sucking response or in the nature-nurture question, it is far from the end. What else affects the response? Does the work with puppies really apply to babies? If so, then would monkeys or chimpanzees yield results that are even more applicable? It is hard to imagine a more obvious way of studying the effect of variations in "nature" than to select different species. Let us then have a look at phylogenesis.

PHYLOGENESIS

RECENTLY ANIMAL PSYCHOLOGISTS and ethologists have begun to look closely at the internal states associated with sucking. Some of this work is experimental and represents another line of descent from Levy's experiment with puppies.

Levy's Experimental Successors

Ross (1951a, 1951b), James (1957, 1959), and James and Gilbert (1957) have all reported similar or related investigations with puppies. Ross, using cocker spaniels, has found that puppies fed from birth by eye dropper or rapidly flowing bottles show markedly greater vigor and persistence on tests of non-nutritive sucking than do normally nursed puppies (unlike the cup-fed infants studied by Davis, Sears, *et al.*). This difference disappeared when the puppies were returned to the mother for a few days. In Levy's puppies, "compensatory" sucking continued for quite a long period. But so did the "deprivation." Interestingly enough, Ross found it extremely difficult to keep the dropper-fed pups alive even though the amount of food taken in was known to be sufficient. The high mortality may have been due to lack of "mothering"—pervasive and persistent prodding, nuzzling, licking, cleaning, and so forth. If so, the facts are consistent with Ribble's and Spitz's position. Blauvelt (1955) speculates somewhat the same way in discussing the mother-kid relationship in goats. But we recommend caution in generalizing from such distant species to human babies.

So far as Ross's results go (many of the puppies died, and those assigned to the dropper group were those that appeared to be weakest at birth so it is difficult to be very confident), they extend Levy's findings to a different breed of *dogs*. A methodologically rigorous repetition would be extremely desirable. Meanwhile, Ross (1951a) has reported tentative evidence—again with dogs—that the effect of interfering with the normal nursing pattern seems to depend upon the age at which the interference occurs. Cockers were permitted to nurse, then separated from the mother at different ages, and compared with control puppies who remained with her. Ross found no differences between the control puppies and the experimentals who were removed from the mother at two, four, or five weeks, but "overt excess sucking on the body parts of littermates was noticed in the puppies separated at three weeks of age, similar to the behavior described by Levy in collie puppies. These results support in part the concept of sucking 'need'. . . and are also of interest in terms of the 'critical period hypothesis.'" This hypothesis is that the particular age at which varying environmental conditions are introduced is a very important determiner of the effect those conditions will have on the response. As an illustration consider the experiment of Scott, Ross, and Fisher (1959) who weaned basenji and cocker spaniel puppies at different ages. Weaning between the tenth and eighteenth postnatal days led to a marked increase in score on a test of non-nutritive sucking, while weaning between nineteen and twenty-eight days led to only a slight increase. Puppies weaned after twenty-eight days failed to suck at all on the tests.

James (1957) has begun to investigate the role of hunger as a factor in eliciting the sucking response. He too has used small numbers of dogs. While his results are still preliminary, they suggest that a full stomach (filled by pouring milk through a tube) does not inhibit sucking in puppies of such an age that normally they would be nursing. But a full stomach does appear to inhibit *eating* in puppies that have been weaned.

Rosenblatt, Turkewitz, and Schneirla (1962) have begun a somewhat different sort of analysis of the feeding behavior of the domestic cat. They point out that nursing is a distinctly social behavior and that disruption of the behavior after varying periods of isolation from the mother is sometimes due to social variables rather than to specific sensory or motor effects. They also note the very rapid progress which neonatal kittens make in adjusting to the mother's mammary surface—after the fourth day "most of the kittens adopt their own individually specific nipple regions for suckling."

Species Differences: The Naturalistic Approach

Beside the experimental work with dogs and cats there are scattered references to other species of mammals. With a few exceptions investigators have relied upon *observation* and detailed *description* of *naturally occurring* phenomena rather than upon precise experimental *manipulation* of one or two variables that are thought to have theoretical importance. Naturalistic observation serves as a very useful supplement and corrective to the overenthusiastic embrace of a popular theory; it calls attention to phenomena that theories must account for. The more complete the description, the more likely it is to suggest relevant variables that affect the behavior under observation and the more likely it is to suggest other aspects of the behavior that ought to be looked into— aspects about which a particular theory may have nothing to say. Consequently we shall reproduce these descriptions at some length.

SOME BARNYARD MAMMALS.   In the Foreword to his 1934 paper Levy remarked on

. . . Dr. A. J. Carlson's observation, that calves taken from the udder and fed "from a bucket" develop ear-licking, and similar habits analogous to finger-sucking in infants. I have made several inquiries from dairy farmers who have repeated the observation as a generally accepted fact. Although they are not the results of experiments, such observations have at least the validity of "general clinical experience." The letter that follows comes to me through the courtesy of Professor H. D. Goodale, Mount Hope Farm, Williamstown, Massachusetts:

". . . there is a very distinct difference between the behavior of the calves of our dairy cattle and beef cattle. The calves of the latter are allowed to suckle their mothers, while those of the former are raised by hand. Mr. Clevenger states that he has never seen the calves of the beef animals sucking tails or a fold of skin, but that it is such a common habit among the calves of the dairy animals that it is necessary to muzzle some of the calves after each feeding for about an hour. . . .

"There are apparently very considerable differences in the behavior of the calves of dairy cattle . . . about half of them show the tendency to suck themselves, some of them much more strongly than others. . . . The difference in strength of tendency is shown by differences in the length of time necessary to use the muzzle which runs from a few days to several months. As there is very little difference in length of feeding time at corresponding ages, there is a suggestion here of other factors than length of sucking time. Certainly lack of sucking time does not always induce further sucking or else the time necessary to satisfy the instinct is much less in some calves than others."

This is one of the few explicit recognitions of the fact that infrahuman animals show marked individual differences in non-nutritive sucking. In the section on Ontogenesis we shall examine in detail such differences among humans.

Levy then comments:

Whatever the conditions are that determine differences within the group of calves that develop sucking habits, the fact remains that such habits do not occur among calves that suckle at the udder.[9]

[9] From D. Levy, "Experiments on the Sucking Reflex and Social Behavior of Dogs," *Amer. J. Orthopsychiatry*, 1934, 4, 203f. Used by permission.

Since the dairy herd and the beef herd were probably different breeds or different strains, there is a possibility that at least part of the behavioral differences between the two is due to genetic differences.

Walker (1950) has called attention to quite a different set of variables which are relevant to sucking in new born calves:

Almost as soon as it has become used to the feel of its legs [the newborn calf] will wander about close to its mother with its head stretched out and tilted slightly upwards. Compare this with the normal positioning of the adult cow whose head is more often level or tilted downwards. When an attempt is made to feed a calf from a bucket, considerable physical force is required to force the head down into the milk, even when the calf has tasted the milk, can see it and should know where to place its mouth in order to feed. The calf is far happier to suck vigorously at a finger held at a level parallel with the height of the udder, even though there is no milk, than bend down into the bucket. I think this type of behaviour may fairly be described as instinctive.

Once the calf has found the udder it experiences little difficulty in returning to the same spot on future occasions. When it first reaches the teats it will often bump the udder vigorously with the head, presumably to stimulate the letdown of the milk. Once the milk appears, no further bumping occurs until the milk supply either lessens or fails; then the calf will bump again and if this has no effect will eventually change to another teat. . . . This behaviour is reproduced exactly when the calf is on a nipple feeder and also when the calf drinks from a bucket. In the latter case the "bumping" only takes place when the milk has been drunk. The calf seems unable to grasp the fact that all the milk has gone, and thinks that by "bumping" more will appear, even though its head is in a different position from that of natural suckling from the udder. . . . The calf likes to have a warm surface against its muzzle when it is suckling, such as the udder or a hand. It was far easier to start a calf suckling an artificial feeder if the palm of the hand was placed over the calf's muzzle, than if the rubber teat alone was forced into the calf's mouth, and the head held in position.[1]

Brownlee (1950) has made similar observations about the calf.

The nursing behavior of several other domestic animals has also been described. Gill and Thompson (1956) report on pigs:

Of all domestic animals the newly-born piglet is probably the quickest to commence suckling. . . . Almost as soon as it is born the piglet finds a place on the udder and obtains milk, in some cases even before the severance of the umbilical cord and, by the time the complete litter is farrowed, it is actively competing for its place on the udder.

Nursing and suckling then follow a consistent behaviour pattern

[1] From D. M. Walker, "Observations on Behavior in Young Calves," *Bull. Animal Behav.*, 1950, 8, 9. Used by permission.

which can be divided into three parts—initial massage, milk ejection and final massage.

Each piglet . . . massages around its respective teat with rapid upward and downward movements of the snout, . . . This initial massage stage lasts for about a minute, and ends when milk flow begins.

Towards the end of the initial massage period the mammary gland distends; concurrently the piglets get more excited and take frequent trial sucks. During the next few seconds the teats become erect; the milk begins to flow practically at once and the piglets hold the teats fully extended, appearing to swallow, at furious speed, rather than to suck. The milk flow appears to stop quite suddenly; the piglets then suck vigorously as if to draw the last drop, become quite excited, attempt to push one another away and, if a spare teat is within reach, suck it alternately with the regular one.

. . . Frequently at this stage, one of the piglets, though not always the same one, will run around to its mother's nose and grunt excitedly.

This second massage by the piglets begins immediately it is apparent that there is no more milk to be had. It is much slower in rhythm than the initial massage and may continue for perhaps fifteen minutes, though normally it lasts for less than five minutes.[2]

Gill and Thompson also point out that the actual milk flow of the sow averages only fourteen seconds per nursing period, that the final massage gradually decreases from an average of four minutes to an average of slightly more than two minutes at the end of the eighth week, and that the average interval between nursings is in the vicinity of an hour and a half for the first six weeks and somewhat greater thereafter.

SPECIES DIFFERENCES AND THE NATURE-NURTURE QUESTION. "What do calves, pigs, and cocker spaniels have to do with humans?" This question, which is more commonly asked about rats, is sometimes answered, "Nothing—and I'm not concerned about humans." There are also a variety of other answers. *Our* answer is that we are trying to understand the "nature-nurture" question. One tangential line of evidence has to do with species similarities and differences. If any phylogenetic trends can be found, they may contribute to our understanding of the rôles of heredity and environment. Consider two cases: a very stereotyped response which is present in almost every member of one species and a similar response which is less stereotyped and less universal in another species. If these two cases should be at the low and high ends of a generally recognized phyletic series, and if intermediate species showed intermediate degrees of stereotypy and universality, then we would have discovered an interesting generalization. The explanation would still be

---

[2] From J. C. Gill and W. Thompson, "Observations on the Behaviour of Suckling Pigs," *Brit. J. Animal Behaviour*, 1956, 4, 46. Used by permission.

unknown—one possibility would be that the response in question is more subject to modification by the kinds of environmental variation that normally occur to members of the higher species; another would be an increase in relevant genetic variability as the phyletic level increases. Another possible generalization might be that within the class *Mammalia* there is little or no species variation in the sucking response. If such were the case, which it obviously isn't, we might be willing to extrapolate from the infra-human data to humans. As a matter of fact, one reason for dealing at such length with the various infra-human species is to show that none of these anticipated generalizations hold. Yet one of them—that of little variability within the class *Mammalia*—is implicit in the enthusiastic application of Levy's (1934) work with puppies to the applied psychology of infancy.

SOME LESS FAMILIAR MAMMALS.　To emphasize the variety of sucking that can be found in mammals, consider the bottle-nosed dolphin which McBride and Hebb (1948) rate as somewhere between the dog and the chimpanzee in intelligence.

The infant born in 1947 started searching for her mother's teats one and a quarter hours postpartum. The object of search was found thirty-two minutes later, and nursing proceeded. Four hours elapsed before the 1948 male began to seek nourishment, but he found a nipple in fifteen minutes. The 1949 specimen started to investigate his mother's inguinal region only nine minutes after birth, but nursed for the first time four hours later. He would probably have nursed sooner were it not for the fact that the half-weaned female referred to above interfered with his progress.

When the very young dolphin suckles, the mother rolls over on one side and glides slowly during the few seconds which pass while the nursing takes place. The infant swims gently, just enough to keep pace with the parent's momentum. The extruded nipple is grasped between the palate and the extended, grooved tongue, the mouth being held slightly agape. The edges of the infant dolphin's tongue are fimbriated, the fringe apparently serving to assure a water-tight seal. Dolphin mammae pour their secretion into spacious sinuses and the contents of these are expelled by contraction of the abdominal musculature as soon as the nipple is grasped by the infant. [Matthews (1948) reports that whale mothers also expel milk for their young.] Each suckling lasts, therefore, only a few seconds. . . . During the first two weeks, nursing periods are spaced at intervals of ten to sixty minutes with an average of twenty-six minutes. During each period, the infant may suckle only once, or as many as nine times. It may either rise to the surface to breathe between sucklings, or it may try each of the two nipples before taking another breath. The mother may not necessarily roll over on her side to accommodate the very young infant as it suckles, but if she does so, this is dispensed with after the second week and the infant is forced to roll from then on.[3]

If this account is representative of the species and if by "only a few seconds" the authors mean that suckling does not exceed ten seconds, then the average baby dolphin suckles well under an hour a day.

The pattern in the Alaska fur seal is different still.

The most conspicuous feature of the suckling in this species is its periodic nature. A pup will lie at its mother's side nursing intermittently for a day or so and then the female will go to sea for several days to feed, leaving her pup ashore untended. Since a female will nurse no pup but her own, a pup necessarily goes without food while its mother is at sea.[4]

"Depriving" dolphins and seals of an adequate opportunity to suck would be quite a different procedure from depriving newborn opossums (called by their friend and student, Carl G. Hartman (1952), "perhaps the stupidest of all mammals") which immediately after birth attach themselves to the nipple in the mother's pouch and remain there twenty-four hours a day for several weeks. How much actual *sucking* occurs in the very immature marsupial is not yet known.

Burrell comments:

Where no placenta exists, as in most marsupials, the young are born in a very immature condition; they become attached to an external teat, and are nourished by milk, which they cannot suck but which is impelled into them by muscular reaction on the mammary glands of the mother.[5]

Even more primitive than the marsupials are the egg-laying monotremes—the platypus and the echidna. Burrell's as yet unsurpassed observations raise a great many interesting questions:

In the echidna the mammary areas open into the pouch, which is formed as a temporary structure during the breeding season, and the young one laps its nourishment with slender projecting tongue. The platypus has no pouch, and the milk oozes out through numerous fine apertures upon two mammary areas of the abdomen, each about half an inch in diameter. These areas are covered with fur . . . The hair covering the areas serves, apparently, in place of a teat, and the young

[3] From F. McBride and Henry Kritzler, "Observations on Pregnancy, Parturition and Postnatal Behavior in the Bottle-nose Dolphin," *J. Mammalogy*, 1951, 32, 259. Used by permission.

[4] From G. Bartholomew and P. G. Hoel, "Reproductive Behavior of the Alaska Fur Seal," *J. Mammalogy*, 1953, 34, 421. Used by permission.

[5] From H. Burrell, *The Platypus*, p. 29, copyright 1927 by Angus and Robertson, Ltd., Sydney, Australia. This and the following excerpt are used by their permission

pluck at this and suck the milk from it . . . The "lips" of the young, owing to the shortness and undeveloped form of the bill at this early stage, are adapted for sucking in conjunction with the tongue.

The most remarkable and mysterious feature about the baby platypus is that it is not suckled at all by the mother for some days after hatching, for the very good reason that the maternal mammary glands are not yet actively functional. Investigations of this extraordinary phenomenon have advanced far enough to place the matter beyond doubt. . . .

. . . Examination of a considerable series of mammary glands from nursing mothers which have been collected with their young has convinced me that during the first week, at least, after hatching there cannot be more than a very slight milk-secretion, if any at all, and I think this characteristic applies to the echidna also. . . .

It is at least a significant coincidence that the onset of obvious lactation occurs simultaneously with the completed growth of the caruncle [a protuberance on the dorsal surface of the muzzle]. It may be that the stimulus afforded by this "milk-spur" is necessary to induce the very primitive milk glands of *Ornithorhynchus* to act; and the delayed lactation which I have observed may be due to the incomplete development of the necessary stimulus in the early young. How the young platypus is nourished in the meantime I do not know [pp. 184f.; 187].

The most obvious way to summarize the infra-human material that has been cited so far is to say that specialization within the class *Mammalia* is so great as to raise grave doubts about the cross-species applicability of any research on the sucking response.

INFRA-HUMAN PRIMATES.   But there is one important group of animals that we have not yet considered—the infra-human primates. One distressing fact is clear: until very recently only a few investigators interested in orality [6] have studied them. There is good reason for this lack; the more advanced species of primates are almost as much trouble and expense to take care of as humans. They reproduce slowly and seldom have multiple births. Rats and dogs are easier. Until fairly recently the requirements for a successful primate colony were not well understood. Even when they are understood, the budgets for surgeries, medicine, caretakers, and equipment are so prohibitive that only a few laboratories can afford them. In short, practical difficulties have deprived all but a few psychologists of the opportunity to study our closest animal cousins. Even so, we have found several illuminating observations.

Robert and Ada W. Yerkes, in 1929, published *The Great Apes* and

---

[6] Harlow (1958, 1959) has demonstrated clearly—and with great charm—that "mother love" in monkeys does *not* depend simply, or even primarily, on the nursing relationship of mother and child.

included reports from various sources. Following is a report of a newborn orang-outang:

> When the keeper came on duty and made his first rounds on the morning of September 25, he found "Maggie" tenderly licking an apparently normal baby, still wet, and with cord and placenta still attached. . . . the little one was seen to move about in the mother's arms, at times reaching up toward her face. "Maggie" remained lying down the entire day, cuddling her baby close to her face, but making no attempt to get it near her breast. . . . The following morning the baby was noticed as apparently searching for something with its mouth, at one time sucking on the mother's ear. . . . At 10:00 A.M., estimated as twenty-eight hours after the birth, she took hold of the cord with her teeth, close to the baby's abdomen, severed it, and then pushed the placenta over against the bars of the cage. Immediately she took up the baby and held it against her breast. It promptly found the nipple and proceeded to nurse.

Another report of an orphaned orang-outang is also included:

> Finding it so fond of hair, I endeavoured to make an artificial mother by wrapping up a piece of buffalo skin into a bundle, and suspending it about a foot from the floor. At first this seemed to suit it admirably, as it could spread its legs about and always find some hair, which it grasped with the greatest tenacity. I was now in hopes that I had made the little orphan quite happy; and so it seemed for some time, till it began to remember its lost parent, and try to suck. It would pull itself up close to the skin, and try about everywhere for a likely place; but, as it only succeeded in getting mouthfuls of hair and wood, it would be greatly disgusted, and scream violently, and, after two or three attempts, let go altogether.[7] [Harlow (1958) has reported the anatomical details of a more successful artificial primate mother.]

Finally Yerkes cites Reichenow's comment about a young gorilla—"The coming of new teeth was always announced by the fact that Adan rubbed his gums a great deal with his thumb."

Three years after Yerkes' volume appeared, Jacobsen, Jacobsen, and Yoshioka (1932) reported in great detail on the *Development of an Infant Chimpanzee During Her First Year*. This infant was reared by humans from birth. The authors remark:

> One of the daily activities manifested very early in life was sucking; the infant adapted well to the nipple and bottle and nursed with great vigor. [Wyatt and Vevers (1935) have reported on a newborn chimpanzee who made no attempt to suckle until placed at the breast a day

[7] From R. and Ada W. Yerkes, *The Great Apes*, pp. 144–6, copyright 1929 by Yale University Press, New Haven, Conn., and used with their permission.

after birth. Clearly, individual differences are of considerable extent among primates.]

Thumb-sucking appeared as early as the second day and was indulged in frequently in the first month, and although the habit persisted throughout the year, it became relatively infrequent after the second month. [Budd, Smith, and Shelley (1943) have reported a female chimpanzee who only *began* to suck her thumb during the second month and then did so more and more. Again, individual differences are clear.]

The infant adapted readily to nursing and was eager for food even to the extent of sucking its thumb before meals.

Thumb-sucking was originally observed in association with feeding, and continued to be an habitual response to a variety of situations throughout the first year.[8]

The authors also call attention to the development of thumb-sucking "as an emotional substitute in a thwarting situation": when the infant was given a nursing bottle filled with water rather than the expected milk, sucking started briefly, but was then abandoned for the thumb.

> Other instances of thumb-sucking occurred when the infant had been left alone in her crib at the Station for the afternoon. Alpha called repeatedly, stopped when she heard someone approaching in the hall, then sat sucking her thumb as the person entered the room. Calling was immediately resumed when the observer left. This incident was repeated several times during the afternoon. . . . After the ninth month, when the infant was quartered exclusively at the Station and received much less attention, she often resorted to thumb-sucking. This was especially marked when she was returned to the cage after feeding or play [p. 69].

In 1941 Gillman, after commenting briefly that he had observed foot-sucking in honey-bears, reported on thumb- and toe-sucking in two of six young baboons which he had observed very closely. The first case is Mussler, who was removed from his mother at birth, but returned to her after two days since he failed to do well. While with his mother he thrived, but because his mother mistreated him he was removed a second time when fourteen days old.

> On the very first day after this separation the baby commenced to suck its thumb. Later in the day, the big toe of the left foot was also

---

[8] From C. F. Jacobsen, M. M. Jacobsen, and J. G. Yoshioka, "Development of an Infant Chimpanzee during Her First Year," *Comp. Psychol. Monogr.*, 1932, 9, 35, 37, 41, 68. This and the following excerpt are used by permission of University of California Press.

given considerable attention. Toe-sucking apparently proved to be more attractive and thenceforth the toe-sucking habit became established.

In the early weeks of life Mussler did not move about much in his small cage, and toe-sucking seemed to be his main preoccupation. This habit was practiced mainly between feeds and only on rare occasions did he attempt to suck his toe immediately after a meal. . . . On the twenty-seventh day his central incisors erupted, but toe-sucking was not in any way accentuated. As usual, Mussler would always be found in the early morning lying on his side or leaning against a corner in the cage sucking his toe.

. . . Before the next expected feed Mussler usually could be seen hugging his soft sleeping mat and, with eyes closed, rubbing his nose in the mat, presumably searching for the nipple in the manner in which breast-fed baboons usually search the fur of their mothers. At the end of this fruitless quest he would take up his toe, and only the presence of the milk bottle would induce him to interrupt this activity.[9]

Gillman also notes a wide variety of frustrating, teasing, and fear-producing situations that frequently provoked Mussler to suck his thumb or toes. Once it occurred after he had burned himself; it occurred frequently if his bottle was taken away before he had finished, or if a preferred food was shown but not given to him. When he was very young, toe-sucking invariably followed loud noises or being dropped suddenly and then caught just before reaching the ground. We will see in a later section that human infants frequently suck their thumbs under similar circumstances.

When Mussler was strong enough to run around and withstand changes in temperature he was taken from the warm room in which he had lived since birth to the roof where the colony is housed. For a long time the roof seemed to terrify him, and whenever he was taken outside he screamed until he saw that no attention was being paid to his complaints. He would then lie on his back and suck his toe until he was picked up and returned to his room.

When six months of age he was given a small female baboon companion. Toe-sucking became less and less frequent and now at nine months it has ceased altogether. He still bears the ill effects of his former vice in the great flattening of his left big toe, which seems to have been the favored digit. [Misshapen thumbs occasionally result from prolonged thumb-sucking in humans, too.] [P. 398.]

[9] From J. Gillman, "Toe-sucking in Baboons: A Consideration of Some Factors Responsible for This Habit," *J. Mammalogy*, 1941, 22, 396. This and the following excerpt are used by permission.

In Gillman's second case, an eighteen-month-old daughter (we are still talking about baboons) was grooming her father, but apparently not according to his taste, for "he scared her off with a threatening noise. She retired to the end of the beam close to the front of the cage, cocked her feet up against the wire and brought her face into contact with the dorsum of her feet. In this position she commenced to suck her big toe most diligently. Although this group had been under close observation for several months, she was never seen to suck her toe at any other time."

Kelsey (1936), in an orthodontic journal, describes a four-and-one-half-year-old female rhesus monkey who was apparently a true problem finger-sucker and whose dental arch was considerably malformed.

> The monkey presented no timidity or embarrassment regarding her habit, . . . and the only time I saw her without her finger in her mouth was when she was running around the cage or the runways. The moment she stopped, she would immediately stick the left fore-finger into her mouth. . . . The monkey had indulged in this habit since or even before weaning.[1]

Lorna Benjamin (1959), at Harlow's laboratory at the University of Wisconsin, has conducted a valuable series of experiments on non-nutritive sucking in the rhesus monkey. She has demonstrated that for this species, non-nutritive sucking increases significantly as a function of hunger. In babies three to six months old, the increase is very rapid during the first two and a half hours after feeding, while in subjects six to nine months old, the increase for the same period is not significant but is significant after ten hours of food deprivation. (The older subjects, of course, took more formula than the younger ones.) Benjamin has also demonstrated that *mild* emotional stimuli (tones and lights) increase non-nutritive sucking in the baby rhesus, while *intense* ones (an electric shock and a "raucous buzz of 85 db.") decrease it—presumably because they evoke strong competing responses.

In another experiment with bottle-fed and cup-fed rhesus infants, Benjamin (1961) reports, "the non-nutritive sucking exhibited by the bottle-raised group far exceeded that shown by the cup-raised group."

MAN.   So much for our non-human relatives. What about *Homo sapiens*? Once again we turn to Levy (1958) [2] who has provided us with detailed accounts of the behavior of mothers and newborn in-

[1] From H. L. Kelsey, "Class I Malocclusion, with Pronounced Open-Bite, Induced by Constant Finger Sucking, in a Monkey," *Int'l J. Orthodontia and Oral Surgery*, 1936, 22, 1119. Used by permission of C. V. Mosby Co., St. Louis, Mo.
[2] From D. Levy, *Behavioral Analysis*, 1958. Courtesy of author and Charles C Thomas, publisher, Springfield, Ill.

fants at nursing time. In the first example a five-day-old boy proves very unrewarding to his mother:

Baby slept.	Mother put on clean mask—tried to put baby to breast—rubbed nipple across baby's mouth 3 times.
Baby kept eyes closed, didn't take nipple.	Mother hit baby's hand again.
Baby waved one hand in air—eyes still closed.	Mother hit baby's hand again.
Baby started to cry.	Mother tried to put baby to breast.
Baby refused to take nipple.	Mother pushed nipple at baby.
Baby put hands in mouth, refused nipple.	Mother tried to push nipple in baby's mouth.
Baby shook head vigorously, refused nipple—tasted it but wouldn't hold it.	Mother rolled baby on bed, tried to insert nipple.
Baby cried, refused nipple.	Mother sat up, picked baby up in arms. Held arms down and head tight—tried to give baby breast.
Baby refused to take nipple.	Mother lay down, put baby beside her. Shoved nipple at baby.
Baby opened eyes, refused to take nipple.	Mother tried to insert nipple again.
Baby tasted nipple, took it, sucked 2–3 times, stopped. Baby didn't suck, released nipple.	Mother shifted around in bed, groaned, shook baby hard. Mother sat up, leaned over baby, shoved nipple at him.
Baby took nipple after a few seconds, sucked about 10 times, stopped.	Mother lay back on pillows.
Baby held nipple but didn't suck.	Mother hit baby's hand to urge him to suck [p. 345].

At the other extreme, Levy describes a three-day-old girl.

Baby brought, awake and whimpering.	Mother sitting up—took baby, put to breast immediately.
Baby took nipple, sucked, fast and strong, hardly rested (biting).	Mother winced now and then, said "Ouch!" Squeezed breast at times, right hand at breast.
Baby sucking.	Mother talked to other patients, joked, looked at me, around ward.
Baby rested longer time, sighed, sucked again of own accord.	Mother talking to other patients.
Baby sucking—rested every 30–40 sucks—rests became longer.	Mother said, "Ouch!" at times—squeezed breast—talked to patients.
Baby sucked—closed eyes.	Mother talking.
Baby released nipple a second, took it again.	Mother talking to other patients. Shifted feet under covers [p. 354].

These two examples illustrate the extremes in Levy's protocols. Careful perusal of the whole of Levy's material reveals a tremendous range and variety of response in the newborn human. Some suck vigorously and do so at practically every feeding. Others suck vigorously on some occasions and lackadaisically or not at all on others. Some are militant little rebels who refuse to suck despite their mothers' most ingenious stratagems. The variability in the sucking of human infants is enormous.

It would be premature to attempt any sweeping generalizations about phyletic differences in the sucking response. (In fact, we have tried two or three and have had to revise them out of existence!) It is not even clear how the range of individual differences varies from species to species. It *is* clear that the range is great among human infants, but there may be equally impressive differences among members of other species—most investigators of other species have not looked for individual differences. There is, however, one positive statement to make: There are at least *some* species other than man for which we have evidence that non-nutritive sucking serves to tranquilize, to compensate for social frustration, allay fears, and lessen the response to bodily discomfort.

Adler, Linn, and Moore's (1958) report suggests that this phenomenon may not be limited to primates:

If one unobtrusively enters a pasture where lactating goats unaccustomed to being approached are grazing with their offspring and where the mothers and young are distributed at random, a wave of panic passes over the young animals as soon as the presence of the human stranger is sensed. Immediately each kid runs to its own mother and begins to nurse vigorously. Apparently the return to the mother's teat has an anxiety-alleviating effect on the frightened young animal. . . . Thus the nursing pattern can be seen to serve a double function. It relates not only to the problem of nutrition but also to the emotional needs of the organism.[3]

Since Adler, Linn, and Moore do not make clear that it is sucking *per se*, as opposed to taking food or being close to mother, that alleviates the anxiety, we cannot yet be certain that the calming effect of non-nutritive sucking is found in this species.

ONTOGENESIS IN MAN

MANY OF THE PAPERS reported in the first section of this chapter come from two great traditions in psychology—psychoanalysis and learning theory. Many of those papers tried to *test* the nature-nurture question with an experiment, and the work of Sears and his associates suggests that indeed learning—nurture—does affect the sucking response. In the second section we abandoned theoretical matters and looked closely at naturalistic reports of the sucking response in a wide variety of mammals. We found tremendous inter-species differences. Many would say that species differences—almost by definition—reflect differences in nature, but it must be apparent that the environment of the opossum and the environment of the dolphin preclude their showing identical sucking responses. What, then, will we find if we limit ourselves to *one* species—man? At what stage in maturation does the sucking response first appear? What particular internal and environmental circumstances first elicit the response? Are there age differences in thumb-sucking? Are boys or girls more inclined to suck their thumbs?

As in the section on phylogenesis, most of the work reported in this section has been done by experimenters or observers—indeed, sometimes this work is based on mothers' reports—who were less interested in testing a theory than in establishing some empirical facts. As we shall see, they often speculate about how the facts should be interpreted, but in general they proceed from fact to hypothesis rather than the other way around. Since science is concerned with *all* the phenomena of nature and not merely with those which appear under the very special cir-

[3] From J. Adler, L. Linn, and A. V. Moore, "Pushing in Cattle: Its Relation to Instinctive Grasping in Humans," *Animal Behaviour*, 1958, 6, 85f. Used by permission.

cumstances that a theorist may set up to test a particular *a priori* hypothesis, we shall report the facts in some detail. For the moment we take the view that it is better to know what happens than to try to guess about nature. Furthermore, if the nature-nurture question is a good question to ask about development, then the facts of development will help lead us to the answer. If the question is poor, then the facts may lead us to a better one.

The Biological Tradition

We begin with Preyer (1885), a German embryologist who participated in the remarkable growth of biological science during the latter half of the nineteenth century. Preyer makes clear that sucking can be performed considerably before normal-term birth.

> . . . In the human fetus a sucking of the obstetrician's finger has been repeatedly observed . . . when it, while touching of women in labor, happened to get into the mouth cavity. [Recall that Harvey had observed the same fact more than two hundred years earlier.]
>
> By no means all premature and almost mature new-born ones, however, suck upon touching of the lips or upon introduction of the finger into the mouth. There is lacking here the machine-like certainty, which characterizes the pure reflex movements. . . . The sick as well as the sated suckling as a rule does not suck. In the case of the latter, one cannot very well ascribe the absence of the sucking movements to a fatigue of the muscles involved. For even when these have had time to recover from the previous sucking work, the child often decidedly refuses to suck. It is probably rather a feeling of being sated which is the determining influence here, as in the case of the grown-up, when he has to chew once again after a plentiful repast. There must therefore be a certain mood present for sucking.[4]

Preyer was quite interested in the relative "reflexiveness" and "instinctiveness" of the sucking response and we have seen that Piaget examined the same question fifty years later. Indeed, the notion of instinct, which was so prominent in Charles Darwin a little earlier and in Freud a little later, is still a matter of lively interest (Gunther, 1955; Beach, 1955). Preyer's assertion that there must be a certain mood to suck can be read as an anticipation of the notion that a general state (drive? discomfort?) of the organism is involved, and his insistence upon multiple determinants—as opposed to a single determinant—also anticipates current thought.

Preyer's intellectual descendants have collected a considerable body

[4] From W. Preyer, "Embryonic Motility and Sensitivity," *Monogr. of Soc. Res. Child Develpm.*, 1937, 2, 50. Used by permission.

of knowledge about the ontogeny of oral sensitivity and behavior in the human fetus. According to Hooker (1944), sensitivity to external oral stimulation appears at about eight weeks of menstrual age, and the response to such stimulation gradually develops and differentiates until the first sucking response occurs at about twenty-nine weeks of menstrual age. Ahlfeld (cited in Guttmacher, 1937) has reported the case of an infant *born* with a swollen thumb which he put into his mouth immediately after delivery.

Prechtl (1958) has reported a very refined experimental analysis of the feeding response of human infants. He distinguishes four aspects of the response: side-to-side turning movements or a single directed turning of the head toward a tactile stimulus, "opening of the mouth and grasping with the lips," "sucking movements produced by tactile stimuli anywhere in the mouth area, but more effective inside the mouth," and swallowing. The side-to-side movements, which Prechtl has observed in six- to seven-month prematures, and directed head turning are normally present in newborns, but the latter is sometimes a bit delayed. Perhaps some sort of special experience above and beyond maturation is necessary.

A novel aspect of Prechtl's work is his report of a very reliable correspondence between the precise part of the oral region which is stimulated and the particular response which occurs in newborn infants. Generally speaking, head turning follows stimulation which is close to the left or right of the mouth; mouth opening follows stimulation of the central parts of the lips, and various lip movements follow stimulation of the outer parts of the lips. Apparently these reponses occur despite considerable variation in the stimulus. Prechtl and Schleidt (1951) have also described similar responses in other species.

The Observational Approach: Nutritive Sucking

In the United States fact-gathering about child behavior got under way in earnest in 1897 when G. Stanley Hall launched child psychology as a separate specialty. The specialty reached maturity in the 1920's with the establishment of child study centers at a number of major universities. With Watson's help the observational method and the very simple experiment came to dominate a large part of the specialty. Indeed, from 1920 to the early 1940's much of the literature of child psychology consisted of very detailed—and sometimes rather dull—inventories of what various groups of children can do.

Kashara (1916) is an early representative of this tradition. He confirmed Preyer's earlier observation that illness interferes with sucking in the newborn and that the environmental stimulus affects the response— cool or very warm milk is taken irregularly, while at intermediate temperatures it is taken regularly. Kashara also called attention to the importance of maturation. He reports that normal infants suck regularly, but that newly born and premature infants suck irregularly, as do infants with severe organic pathology. (But note that Prechtl has reported the presence of various aspects of the feeding response in anencephalic newborns. Furthermore, several pediatricians have told us informally that infants with structural anomalies that prevent normal suckling nevertheless show marked sucking responses which sometimes persist for several months. From *birth* these infants are fed by a tube inserted through the nasal passages. Apparently the behavior is most marked during feeding as the formula reaches the stomach. These observations—assuming they can be confirmed and extended—suggest a whole new group of stimuli which must be considered.) More recently, Crump, Gore, and Horton (1958) have also noted that premature infants suck less efficiently.

INDIVIDUAL DIFFERENCES.   Still another aspect of Preyer's early work has continued up to the present. This is the study of individual differences. For pediatricians and mothers such differences can sometimes be a serious problem, as when a newborn refuses to nurse. For psychologists, they call attention to the remarkable complexity of behavior and invite a search for an explanation. We shall follow the "observers'" technique of looking at the facts first. Then we shall consider possible explanations.

In 1920 Feldman remarked upon such individual differences and commented that "it is desirable that the pressures to draw off milk from the woman's breast should correspond with the suction energy of the infant." Ribble (1943) reported that "at least 40 per cent" of her infants "had to be taught to suck." But Norval (1946) classified the sucking of fifty newborns as follows: vigorous, 20 per cent; average, 76 per cent; and poor, only 4 per cent. This distribution is not greatly different from Baliassnikowa and Model's (1931; cited by Halverson, 1938). H. M. Halverson (1938) has described in considerable detail the individual differences in a sample of ten male infants. At one extreme, he found

indolent weak sucking for short periods separated by long periods of quiet, looking around, or playing with the nipple. Infants of this type have been seen to spend more than 40 minutes without completely emptying the bottle.[5]

At the other extreme, Halverson found "deep voracious sucking, interrupted by frequent rest intervals, followed finally by strong, steady

[5] "Infant Sucking and Tensional Behavior," *J. genet. Psychol.*, 1938, 53, 389; used by permission of the Journal Press, Provincetown, Mass.

sucking." Between these extremes he noted a great variety of sucking patterns—regular sucking at approximately the same pressure for a prolonged period, irregular sucking with varying pressure, and so on.

What explains such individual differences? Halverson (1944) attempted to find an answer by describing three very poor feeders:

> A was the smallest baby of the group. Although her physical condition was good, she evidently lacked sufficient sucking power to obtain the milk easily enough to permit regular swallowing and uninterrupted breathing. Periods of strong sucking in which she appeared to put an unusual amount of effort into sucking, as indicated by frequent stiffening, abrupt bodily movements, and grunting, were followed by periods of rest or weak sucking.
>
> B was a large healthy baby of good disposition. He gained rapidly in weight, appeared always to be hungry, and became excited at feeding time. Although the milk flowed easily, he sucked with great avidity as long as the supply lasted. He frequently held his breath and sucked three, four, or five times before resuming breathing. He sucked in whatever way was advantageous for obtaining the milk rapidly and permitted breathing to occur as it could. At no time was there any indication of coordinated sucking and breathing, probably because of failure to adjust his sucking power to the pressure required to obtain the milk.
>
> C was a baby of average size. She never appeared to be hungry and was easily disturbed when she did feed. She obtained the milk easily, but sucked sporadically, and usually for short intervals only. Successive sucks differed widely in power and spacing, and her rapid respiration failed to keep pace with the quick sucking movements.[6]

In short, there appears to be a different reason for each case. A was too weak; B was too hungry; C wasn't hungry enough. It is Halverson's opinion that hunger is the major motivation for the sucking of very young infants. When infants sucked at an empty nipple, they did so only 40 per cent of the time, but when they sucked for food they ranged from 60 to 90 per cent. "Although even a hungry neonate may suck for several minutes at an empty nipple, sucking is primarily a food-getting response." Freud, Watson, Levy, Piaget, Ribble, Spitz, and others would probably disagree.

Briefly, then, we know that hunger, maturity, strength, coordination, health, and the temperature of the formula affect the vigor and effectiveness of the human infant's nutritive sucking. We leave to you the task of deciding which of these variables should be classed as nature and which should be classed as nurture.

[6] "Mechanisms of Early Infant Feeding," *J. genet. Psychol.*, 1944, 64, 220f.; used by permission of the Journal Press, Provincetown, Mass.

Observers Look at Non-nutritive Sucking

Non-nutritive sucking has been studied considerably more extensively than nutritive sucking. And it is non-nutritive sucking that alarms mothers (and fathers), grandmothers, pediatricians, and dentists.

As in the case of nutritive sucking, hunger appears to be one factor that increases non-nutritive sucking. From her sample of infants in a Chicago orphanage, Kunst (1948) reports:

> Sucking frequency increased as time elapsed after feeding, whether the infants were asleep or awake. . . . The amount of sucking correlated positively with the liquid volume of the formula taken by the infant when age and weight of the infant were controlled. This observation suggests that babies seeming to need formula in excess of adopted standards may be infants who experience the more vigorous contractions. The amount of sucking correlated negatively with the caloric value of the formula consumed. . . .[7]

AGE CHANGES.   Another variable related to non-nutritive sucking is chronological age. Halverson (1938) noticed that some of his older infants engaged in a variety of oral play:

> When infants ceased sucking for a time but retained the nipple in the mouth they frequently resorted to mouthing the nipple—an activity in which the lips and tongue engaged in licking movements. At times they gummed the nipple by successive upward thrusts of the lower jaws so that the nipple was depressed between the gums. . . . At other times they thumped the nipple vigorously with the tongue, rolled it about in the mouth or held it quietly until sucking was resumed. All of these responses may be regarded as purely playful activities. . . . Licking, gumming, thumping and rolling the nipple occurred only for the older infants. . . . None of the young infants (under six weeks) exhibited these reactions, although some of them were reported as thumb or finger suckers [p. 391].

In the following remarks about age changes in her orphanage sample, Kunst illustrates very nicely the observer's "look first, interpret later" approach to the study of behavior:

> Most infants began to suck their thumbs or fingers very soon after birth and increased the frequency of their sucking quite rapidly during the first three months of life. . . . The increase in the frequency of sucking soon after birth may be due in part to improvement in muscular strength and coordination. It is unlikely, however, that frequent accidental insertion of the thumb into the mouth would lead to a

[7] From M. S. Kunst, "A Study of Thumb- and Finger-sucking in Infants," *Psychol. Monogr.*, 1948, 62, 67. Used by permission of the American Psychological Association.

habit of thumb-sucking if the practice were not uniquely satisfying because of the internal conditions in the child. . . . It should not be surprising that sucking frequency decreases after twenty-four weeks of age—the time when manipulation and concentration improve markedly. The fact that our oldest subjects sucked more on the average than did our somewhat younger infants may have been due to (1) weaning, (2) frustration of the infants at being confined to bed for large periods of the day at a time when interest in walking was developing, and (3) selective influences making for an unrepresentative sample of subjects in the highest age groups.[8]

Traisman and Traisman (1958) also report the first three months to be peculiarly important in the development of thumb-sucking. Seventy-five per cent of their subjects who became thumb-suckers (about 45 per cent of the total) had begun to suck their thumbs during the first three postnatal months. It was frequently noted in the hospital nursery for newborns.

Brazelton (1956), whose data are based on weekly reports from mothers, is still another who has noticed that most thumb- and finger-suckers begin their careers very early in life. The start of non-nutritional sucking ranged from birth to three months, except for two infants who began at nine months. Extranutritional sucking increased until seven months, when some babies were averaging four hours a day, and then began to decrease as the babies became more accomplished in sitting, crawling, etc. By twelve months, all but four of Brazelton's seventy subjects had ceased to suck their hands except under stress.

While Brazelton's data are not in complete agreement with Kunst's, they do agree that thumb-sucking increases rapidly during the first three months and remains high until at least six months. Since Kunst's infants were living in an orphanage with all the impersonality that such circumstances entail, we are not surprised that they showed a further increase toward the end of the first year. For children in normal circumstances, however, a decrease in incidence and frequency of thumb-sucking ultimately does appear, although in some individuals the behavior is extremely persistent and may occur at least intermittently under such special circumstances as going to bed up to the early teens.

The decline with age can also be observed in the longitudinal data (Figure 76) from the University of California's Guidance Study. A similar decline was also reported at the White House Conference in 1936, except that girls showed a peak at age two.

The discrepancies between the various reports of age changes in the sucking response point up a major difficulty which besets the ob-

[8] From M. S. Kunst, "A Study of Thumb- and Finger-sucking in Infants," *Psychol. Monogr.*, 1948, 62, 67–8. Used by permission of the American Psychological Association.

server who uses natural variation rather than precise experimental control. This limitation is that the samples of subjects and the conditions of observation are seldom comparable from one study to the next. Further, reports based on mothers' recollections and casual observations leave a good deal to be desired in the way of reliability and validity. Finally, each observer is likely to use measures which are the most practicable for his particular conditions, and consequently the criteria are not the same for all investigations.

The Guidance Study criterion includes even "mild episodes of sucking thumb, not daily," while Brazelton appears to have been interested primarily in thumb-sucking that looked as if it might become a problem. But we doubt that different criteria are the entire explanation

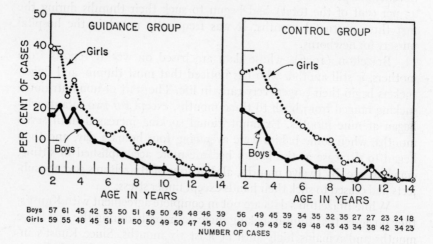

Boys 57 61 45 42 53 50 51 49 50 49 48 46 39   56 49 45 39 34 35 32 35 27 27 23 24 18
Girls 59 55 48 45 51 51 50 50 49 50 47 45 40   60 49 49 52 49 48 43 43 34 38 42 34 23
NUMBER OF CASES

FIGURE 76. Age changes and sex differences in percentage incidence of thumb-sucking. (Data from Honzik and McKee, 1962.)

for the discrepancies in the data on the effect of age. We suspect that the more Spartan the child-rearing, the longer thumb-sucking persists. Brazelton's infants were born in the 1950's after Ribble and Spock had overthrown the rigorous "treat them like young adults" doctrines of John B. Watson, but the children in the Guidance Study were born in 1928 and 1929 at the peak of Watson's influence; so were those reported at the White House Conference. It seems likely that at least some of the difference in the age trends is due to the rather different philosophies of child-rearing that were in ascendancy at the time the children were growing up. Such an interpretation would also account for the high frequency of thumb-sucking among Kunst's orphanage children at the end of the first year. This explanation of the secular trends is, of course, one based on differences in nurture.

SEX DIFFERENCES. One obvious way to obtain individuals with different "natures" is to select them on the basis of sex. We know that males and females have different heredities, and we know that some traits are sex-linked. In 1948 Balint described a quivering or quick oscillation of the tongue when some infants nursed. This phenomenon, which Balint believes to be "a form of self-indulgence, a sort of auto-erotic play, a sign of strong oral eroticism" was more common in girls than boys.

Possibly the first to report a sex difference in "oral habits" was Olson (1929). Since then, four papers have reported insignificant sex differences in the occurrence of thumb-sucking, but the difference is always in the direction of more girls than boys sucking their thumbs (Tilson, 1929; Foster and Anderson, 1930; Yarrow, 1954; and Traisman and Traisman, 1958). Four other studies find significant sex differences (Michaels and Goodman, 1934; the White House Conference, 1936; Hattwick, 1937; and Honzik and McKee, 1962). The White House Conference report comments:

> One of the most interesting aspects of [these results] is the sex difference which appears in all categories of thumb-sucking severity and at all age levels. This difference is consistently in the direction of more frequent thumb-sucking among girls than among boys. . . . [The differences] are very consistent throughout all divisions into age and severity groupings. [We have computed the critical ratio for these data and have found the sex difference to be significant.] [9]

But not all observers find a sex difference (Lindner, 1879; Levy, 1928). Further, Gesell and Ilg (1937) reported that male *infants* suck their thumbs more than female infants, and Kunst found that in her orphanage sample

> Our boy infant subjects sucked their thumbs with greater frequency than did the girls. This fact seems congruent with the hypothesis that hunger is related to sucking, since there is some evidence that boys have the higher metabolic rate and may consequently experience hunger to a greater degree than do girls . . . [p. 68].

In other words, the observers' data indicate that non-nutritive sucking may be more common in boys than in girls during the first year of life but thereafter—and especially from two to five—this addiction is more likely to occur in girls than boys (and with greater intensity). It is found whether the children are at home, at school, or at camp; it appears in first-born children and in non-first-born children (Macfarlane,

---

[9] White House Conference on Child Health and Protection, Section III, *The Young Child in the Home; A Survey of 3,000 American Families*, copyright 1936 by Appleton-Century-Crofts and used with their permission.

Allen, and Honzik, 1954). Spiro (1958) has also reported it for Israeli children living in a Kibbutz. Now that we have the fact before us, let us pursue the observers' procedure and try to interpret it.

AN INTERPRETATION OF THE SEX DIFFERENCE.   Why should sex differences occur? Possibly girls derive greater pleasure from thumb-sucking than boys do. This hypothesis suggests that the mouth is an erogenous zone which is more sensitive and pleasure-giving in the female than the male. This suggestion is essentially the same as Balint's (1948). Though not a logical necessity, it strikes us that the most plausible interpretation of this hypothesis is genetic. It can be argued that the range of environments to which boys and girls are exposed during the preschool years is about the same for the two sexes. If so, then systematic differences must be due to sex-linked genetic differences rather than to sex-associated environmental differences. Lipsitt and Levy's data (1959) suggest that the female infant is more sensitive to electro-tactual stimulation than the male. Perhaps greater oral eroticism in females is one aspect of a more general sex difference in cutaneous sensitivity. The fact that little boys are more active than girls may be another explanation of the sex differential since thumb-sucking is incompatible with vigorous play.

Another possibility is that girls identify more strongly with their mothers than boys do (Sears, Whiting, Nowlis, and Sears, 1953). If so, then, since mothers play a greater role in socializing young children than fathers do, girls' greater orality may be a response to greater frustration (though it might be as plausibly argued that girls' identification would make the maternal pressure *more effective* in eliminating the behavior).

Neither of these two hypotheses—a genetic, sex-linked difference or a cultural, sex-associated difference—asserts that *only* heredity or *only* environment affects the response. The first simply asserts that *given* a particular environment, then genetic differences between the sexes lead to a difference in response. The second asserts that even given the genetic differences between the sexes, environmental differences have an effect. Clearly the hypotheses are not mutually exclusive.

Further Findings from the Observers

So far we have dealt with a variety of isolated variables that the observers have shown to be correlated with variations in the ontogenesis of sucking—age, sex, maturity, hunger, and so on. In each case we have tried to ask whether the results give a clear-cut either-or answer to the nature-nurture question. Obviously, we think they do not. But to make our position even clearer we shall mention a few other variables that have been found to affect the sucking response as an ongoing development through time, and in a variety of ever-changing internal and external circumstances.

PRECIPITATION OF THUMB-SUCKING. In Honzik's (1959) examination of the Guidance Study files, she found that some mothers could remember and identify what seemed to start their children sucking their thumbs. Teething, illness, weaning, removal of a pacifier, malnutrition, reduction in food intake, and self-consciousness accounted for all cases but one—a six-year-old who copied a friend. These cases suggest some sort of *discomfort* or *frustration*, and it is hard not to conclude that for these children thumb-sucking somehow compensates for such unpleasantness.

CIRCUMSTANCES ASSOCIATED WITH THUMB-SUCKING. Under what conditions do children who thumb-suck actually do their sucking? The most frequent sort of occasion was when the child was tired, sleepy, or in bed. The next most frequent condition was hunger. In addition, small numbers of children sucked under a variety of miscellaneous unpleasant circumstances—after a scolding, when afraid, and so on (Honzik, 1959). Lewis (1930) had previously reported similar results, as well as the fact that sucking was more likely when children were idle than when at play. Kunst has confirmed the last observation and adds that "beginning at ages thirteen to sixteen weeks, infants tended to be distracted from sucking when attendants were in the room."

Let us mention one final observation. Tilson and Honzik have both reported that thumb-sucking does *not* appear to be related to *serious* behavior problems. Rather, it appears in reasonably happy children whose parents seem generally calm and contented. We are tempted to conclude that in American clock-oriented society—and probably Western society in general—thumb-sucking develops partly as a consequence of the general emphasis on adhering to a time-defined rather than child-defined schedule of feeding, napping, bathing, sleeping, and so on. The minor frustrations and anxieties and boredoms that result from such a regime may well encourage the development of a source of gratification which the child himself can control. But thumb-sucking does not appear to be an adequate source of gratification for disturbed children nor for severely abused ones.

A Clinician's Summary of Thumb-Sucking

Gesell (1937), who probably made very close observations of more infants than anyone else, gives a comprehensive—though somewhat unrigorous—account of the many phases in the waxing and waning of thumb-sucking:

. . . The human infant for a time uses his mouth in a snout-like manner. He seeks the breast with head-reaching movements; he frequently protrudes the lips and strains forward with his head, in the presence of a dangling object. Mouthing is a universal supplement to his manual prehension and manipulation. Even after he has learned to reach with his hands he will, with an object in each hand, grasp another by mouth—oral prehension. For that matter, Darwin himself when he was a young collector reverted to this ancient method of seizure by mouth to capture a coveted beetle at a critical moment when his two hands were already filled with other rare specimens! [p. 33.]

Finger-sucking may be prominent during the first few weeks of life, especially when the infant is hungry; but usually drops out during the period when the postural development does not permit the hands to be readily brought to the mouth. By the third month, the hands are again brought to the mouth with ease, and the fists are sucked prior to feeding and later also after feeding. During the fourth month the sucking in many cases appears throughout the day. It is at this age and indeed earlier that the lower gums appear red, swollen, and painful. Local irritation may be present weeks or even months before actual eruption. One wonders if this activity against the gums may not relieve the pain the infant may feel, especially since the infant seems to quiet when his mother rubs his gums. He probably relieves the pain and possibly aids dentition by mouthing his fist. . . .[1]

Each successive teething episode seems to exacerbate this hand-to-mouth response. With those who later become persistent thumb-suckers, the degree of the sucking may markedly lessen or even vanish between the teething periods.

Mothers often report that thumb-sucking has ceased at about a year, only to find that it returns with increased vigor at thirteen to fourteen months during the eruption of the molars.

Other inciting factors besides teething may be present. Fatigue frequently precedes thumb-sucking. The child usually goes to sleep with his thumb. A cross remark or a frustration promptly sends the thumb to his mouth. When barriers such as guards or restraints are used, the thumb-to-the-mouth urge increases markedly. During the second year when mothers are overzealous in training the child to toilet habits, they place him on the toilet many times when he has no occasion to use it. The thumb-sucking child usually does not resist this procedure but promptly begins to suck his thumb. . . .

Attempts to correct the habit before the age of two-and-a-half years are ordinarily doomed to failure. We know of a bright eighteen-month-old child who accepts and asks for "bitte aoes" (bitter aloes) and the accompanying bandages before she is put to bed. But after she is tucked in bed, her old desire returns and she does everything in her

[1] Kunst also reports a modest relationship between teething and thumb-sucking.

power to remove the bandages. If she cannot take them off, she may even climb out of bed, go to the bathroom, and wet them with water. If an aluminum mitt is used, she ingeniously contrives to put the mitt between the bars of the crib and pull it off. If all methods are unsuccessful, she may choose a substitute such as another finger. . . .

At about three years of age the child becomes susceptible to new approaches. It is interesting to note that at this same age the child who clings to feeding by bottle responds to the social pressure of shame. He may now show an elementary sense of propriety which leads him to accept a bandage or canvas finger cot as a displacement of finger-sucking. Shaming by other children in a play group often has an immediate effect and no sucking will occur as long as the child is with these children. But this change in behavior does not usually carry over into the home. . . .

In other instances the exit is dramatically abrupt. A sore mouth, an accidental wound of the preferred thumb, or even a "humorous" threat of surgical thumb removal have been known to stop the habit short. We report these observations without recommendation. . . .

There is another type of "cure" which works almost like exorcism. A child has become fetichistically attached to some object or activity which is always associated with the thumb-sucking. For example, he rubs his nose with the tail of a toy dog held in one hand while he sucks the thumb of the other hand. No other toy dog or furry object will serve as a substitute. But removal of the accessory object or interference with the accessory activity will in many cases suddenly terminate the thumb-sucking itself.[2]

In this section our purpose has been to see whether a very close examination of human ontogenesis provides a clear answer to the nature-nurture question. Gesell, Ribble, Norval, and others have pointed out that at least some infants have to be taught to suck, and normally we think that when we teach a child we are manipulating nurture. But it is the nurture of a child who has a "nature." Several observers have reported that teething is associated with thumb-sucking. In a common-sense way most people would agree that teething is "natural." But what is illness? Or hunger? Or malnourishment? Or fatigue? What is idleness? What is fear? They are certainly not easily classified as nature *or* nurture.

CULTURAL VARIATION

IN SOCIETIES where infants and young children may suck at the breast as long and frequently as they wish, the need—if such there be—to suck is met and thumb-sucking apparently occurs only infrequently.

[2] From A. Gesell and F. Ilg, *Feeding Behavior of Infants*, pp. 121–3, copyright 1937 by J. B. Lippincott Company, New York, and used by their permission.

For example, Linton (1939) reports that "the Tanala nurse their children whenever they cry" and that "thumb-sucking has never been observed . . ."; Beaglehole and Beaglehole (1946) report that thumb-sucking is rare among Maori children, and that it is "unknown" among the Pukapukans of the mid-Pacific (1941). Gladwin and Sarason (1953) state that though Truk parents have no objection to thumb-sucking on the part of their children, such behavior is nevertheless brief and intermittent.

Wallace (1948) noted that among the Mohave Indians "when a baby cries it is thought to be hungry and is suckled or the mother dips her finger in water and gives the child her finger to suck. . . . A child seldom sucks its hands or fingers while out of the cradle. Such actions are regarded as a sign of hunger and the child is offered food" [p. 26].

Probably the most complete description of orality in a preliterate society is Margaret Mead's account of the Arapesh (1935), who are extremely indulgent about nursing and weaning. Though older children engage in a great variety of oral play which they appear to be taught by other children and by their mothers and other adults, "no Arapesh child ever sucks its thumb or sucks one finger continuously" (p. 130). Mead suspects, as we do, that *thumb-sucking* "is a habit which is built up during the first few months of life, a period during which primitive children are almost always suckled whenever they cry" (p. 130). But Linton (1939) suggests, on admittedly very scanty information, that unlimited nursing is not necessarily the *only* prophylactic:

> I saw only one small infant during my entire stay in the Marquesas. It must have been about six months old, but I never saw it nurse. The feeding process was brutal. The child was laid flat on its back on the house platform while the mother stood alongside with a mixture of cocoanut milk and baked breadfruit which had been made into a thin, pasty gruel. She would take a handful of this stuff, and, holding her hand over the infant's face, pour the food on its mouth. The child would gasp and sputter, and gulp down as much as possible. Then the mother would wipe off the child's face with a sweep of her hand and pour on another handful of the mixture.[3]

Linton then remarks: "I have no data on thumb-sucking beyond the fact that I never saw any child doing it."

In *The People of Alor*, Du Bois (1944) calls attention to a somewhat similar situation—and to the fact that not all primitive children live in an oral paradise. She reports that when babies are a couple of weeks old their mothers commonly return to the fields, leaving the babies in the care of others who feed them somewhat haphazardly and unsatisfactorily. Even so, *finger*-sucking "does not seem any more prevalent, if as prevalent, as it is among ourselves. It is to be observed only occasionally for any one child and is far from common to all children" (p. 41).

In Western society thumb-sucking has been quite common, at least during the last half century. We have already referred to Klackenberg, Traisman and Traisman, and the 1936 White House Conference which give estimates of 50 to 60 per cent in Europe and the United States. Brazelton estimates 87 per cent, and Kunst's orphanage sample, which was observed very closely, reached 100 per cent. Spiro (1958) reports thumb-sucking in eleven of seventeen Kibbutz babies younger than one year and in 50 to 100 per cent of the one- to five-year-olds.

Davis and Havighurst (1946) report 51 per cent among middle-class white families and 48 per cent for middle-class Negro families. But among the lower-class families the incidence is much lower: 18 per cent in the lower-class white and 30 per cent in the lower-class Negro families. The 1936 White House Conference also reports such class differences, and Honzik has found similar class differences in the Guidance sample. This difference between the two socioeconomic groups—which Zazzo (1956) has also noted in France—illustrates the importance of culture. So far as the development of sucking is concerned, it is *presumably* the culture's oral child-training procedures that are most relevant. Mead (1954, p. 473) puts the matter this way: ". . . the question at issue is whether very early, frequent, unscheduled access to the mother's breast prevents the subsequent resort to thumb-sucking, as this seems to be the only pertinent feature common to the primitive people on whom we have reports." [4] On the other hand, the fact that thumb-sucking appears to be elicited by a variety of uncomfortable states (fatigue, fear, etc., as well as hunger) suggests that more general aspects of child care may be at least as important.

A Cross-cultural Test of Oral Fixation

A tentative answer to this possibility has been provided by Whiting and Child (1953), who analyzed data from many different cultures for which the average age of weaning ranged from less than one year up to six years. They reasoned that if weaning is very severe, it ought to evoke worry and anxiety about oral behavior and thus in premedical societies lead to explanations of disease (a universal and worrisome, anxiety-

[4] Mead probably discounts Linton's comment on the grounds that his observations are too incomplete. She also distinguishes *thumb*-sucking from finger-sucking. In the first section of this chapter Baldwin has asked whether, for very young infants, a thumb is somehow more "suckable" than a finger.

evoking characteristic of human societies) which are oral. That is, societies that use severely punitive, anxiety-evoking techniques to effect weaning ought to produce adults who blame anxiety-evoking illness on something they have eaten or drunk *or on "verbal spells and incantations performed by other people."* [5]

The procedure for testing such an hypothesis with cross-cultural data is to have the ethnographic and ethnological reports of the various societies examined by judges who rate or categorize the variables of interest—in this case severity of weaning and presence or absence of oral explanations of disease. When this was done, it was found that of the twenty-three societies that did have oral explanations of disease, seventeen were judged to wean their children more severely than average and only six weaned less severely than average. For the sixteen societies which did not have oral explanations of disease, only three were judged to wean more severely than average, while thirteen weaned less severely than average. In short, there was strong confirmation of the hypothesis.

This finding is interesting enough, but it is another finding that provides a tentative answer to the question of whether it is the culture's oral child-training procedures or something else that is responsible for oral symptoms. Whiting and Child analyzed the relationship between oral explanations of disease and a variety of *other* child-rearing practices. In no other case did they get positive findings. Furthermore, they found no cultural consistency in the anxiety-evoking qualities of child-rearing procedures. Cultures that weaned very severely were not consistently either severe or permissive in other aspects of their socializing procedures. In short, no *general* "permissive-severe" dimension of child-rearing appeared. Consequently such a trait cannot be used to account for the symptom—"oral explanation of disease." Of course, there is always the possibility that some *other* general cultural trait—one that Whiting and Child did not think to measure—is responsibile, but this sort of possibility must always be borne in mind; so far as the data go, they provide evidence for a specific or narrowly defined cultural antecedent of the symptom rather than for a general or broadly defined one. Whether any such statement applies to the "oral symptom" of *thumb-sucking* is, of

[5] The italics, which are ours, express our particular skepticism about this part of the psychoanalytically derived hypothesis. Whiting and Child argue that the "basic attitudes toward oral activity, acquired in connection with feeding and sucking in infancy, are generalized to the activity of the mouth in speaking." To readers who feel that we have violated our promise to deal only with what is obviously oral activity, our reply is simply that the reasoning is so straightforward that it can be understood and accepted or rejected quickly. This ambitious attempt to test psychological hypotheses with anthropological data obtained from many different cultures also illustrates a fairly new method of social science which has recently excited a good deal of attention. See, for instance, Orlansky (1949).

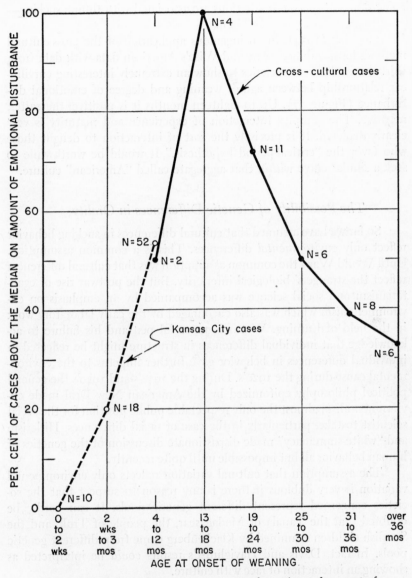

FIGURE 77. Relation between age at onset of weaning and amount of emotional disturbance shown by child. (From Gardner Lindzey, *Handbook of Social Psychology*, Vol. 1, p. 525. Published in 1954 by Addison-Wesley, Reading, Mass. Used by permission of the publisher.) Comparable data from eighty individual children from Kansas City (Sears and Wise, 1950) and from thirty-seven societies (Whiting and Child, 1953) are presented.

course, unknown. The section on Ontogenesis suggests that *a great many different specific frustrations* are associated with thumb-sucking—particularly in very young children.

Whiting (1954), in an ingenious application of the cross-cultural method, has combined Sears and Wise's American data with data from thirty-seven different societies to show an extremely interesting curvilinear relationship between age of weaning and degree of emotional disturbance (Figure 77). Up to eighteen months it is positive; thereafter, negative. The complex interaction of experience and maturity is very clearly depicted. It is precisely the sort of interaction to delight those who favor the "critical-period hypothesis." It would be worthwhile to seek a similar curve *within* that aggregate called "American" culture.

The Possibility of Genetic Differences in Orality

So far we have assumed that cultural differences in sucking behavior reflect only *environmental* differences. This is a common assumption. Until World War I the common assumption was that cultural differences reflect the strangers' biological inferiority. But the postwar rise of egalitarianism and social science was accompanied by an emphasis on environmentalism which was also encouraged by the early laboratory work in the field of learning. Watson's powerful pen and his failure to acknowledge that individual differences in structure might be reflected in individual differences in behavior gave further impetus to the environmental cause during the 1920's. During the 1930's and 1940's the general political philosophy epitomized by the American New Deal made environmentalism almost the only respectable public position for the social scientist to take, particularly in the case of racial differences. Hitlerism and "white supremacy" made dispassionate discussion of the genetics of human behavior all but impossible until quite recently.

The assumption that cultural variation reflects only environmental variation is very dubious if there is any reason to suspect that the societies concerned represent different genetic pools. It can hardly be doubted that the Tanala of Madagascar, the people of Truk, and the Swedish children examined by Klackenberg come from different genetic pools. In fact, Davis and Havighurst's results *could* be interpreted as showing an interaction of race with culture.

TONGUE TRICKS.   So far as we have been able to determine, no geneticist has yet attempted a systematic exploration of genetic factors in the development of human or animal sucking. (Such experiments with different breeds of dogs or different strains of mice should not be too difficult to carry out.) The only even remotely relevant evidence that we have been able to find concerns the ability of Chinese, Japanese, Negro, and Caucasian subjects to perform a variety of tricks with the tongue.

Sturtevant (1940) first noted individual differences of an almost all-or-none sort in the ability to fold up the lateral edges of the tongue. Though he noted that "in numerous cases the ability, at first absent, has been acquired by practice," Sturtevant concluded that "the ability to turn up the edges of the tongue, present in about 65 per cent of the persons studied, is conditioned at least in part by heredity." Sturtevant advanced two objections to the hypothesis that the familial resemblances are due to training, custom, or imitation. The first is that the association between father and child is as close as for mother and child. Environmentalists frequently take the view that similarities between mother and child should be greater than those between father and child. The argument is based on the fact that children usually have considerably more contact with their mothers than with their fathers. Such a view seems plausible, but in view of such complex phenomena as identification, remembering, and so on, it is probably naive to apply it to subjects beyond the period of infancy.

Sturtevant's second objection is that he found no subcultural differences in his heterogeneous American sample. That is, he found no differences between subjects of various (Russian, German, etc.) different national origins. This second objection is unsound. If your bias is genetic, the differences between subcultural groups can be attributed to (assumed) genetic difference. If your bias is environmental, such differences can be attributed to (assumed) environmental differences. If *no* differences are found, you can assume either no relevant genetic influence or no relevant environmental one. The facts are not complete enough to permit a sound generalization. But since Sturtevant is a geneticist he takes a genetic tack. Psychologists have made similar mistakes.

Since Sturtevant's original observations a number of geneticists have reported on the same or similar responses. Except for Gahres (1952), who reports almost no sex differences, a number of recent reports by Urbanowski and Wilson (1947), Liu and Hsu (1949), Komai (1951), and Lee (1955) have all reported that more female subjects are able to perform such stunts as tongue-rolling and tongue-folding. Even though the sex differences are not significant, the consistency is impressive. We can only speculate about whether they are related to sex differences in thumb-sucking. Komai compared his Japanese sample with Liu and Hsu's Chinese sample and Urbanowski and Wilson's Caucasian American sample and concluded that there are genetic racial differences: the frequency of subjects who could roll their tongues was highest in the

Japanese sample, lowest in the Chinese, while the American Caucasian sample was in between.

It is not clear to us why the geneticists are so convinced that they are dealing with a simple genetic characteristic. The pedigrees examined so far seldom extend over more than two generations. While we have no doubt that genetic determiners will ultimately be discovered, we cannot agree with Sturtevant's summary dismissal of the possible role of practice, though no one would quarrel with his statement that tongue-folding "is conditioned at least in part by heredity." Komai's (1951) statement seems premature:

> It seems accordingly safe to decide that the presence or absence of this ability is determined on a monogenic basis, and the gene for its presence is dominant over the gene for its absence. The penetrance of the dominant gene, however, is incomplete. This is clearly shown in the cases where both parents lack this ability. Only 65.71 per cent of the children of such parents are devoid of the ability where all of them are expected to be so.[6]

Of course, tongue gymnastics are not the same as the sucking response. But they are as close to it as any human behavior which geneticists appear to have studied so far. There is one other promising lead. In the pure-bred DBA strain of mice at the University of California, the infant mortality is very high even for young placed with foster mothers who are known to be good mothers. Possibly the sucking response of these young is inferior to that of other strains. But this is sheer speculation. A wide variety of other possibilities are equally plausible. For instance, humans show inherited deficiencies of taste sensitivity; perhaps mice do too. If so, then perhaps the DBA's fail to nurse because the stimulus supports for sucking are ineffective. So far as humans are concerned, what is needed is a very close look at the ontogenesis of orality in a wide variety of racial and cultural groups. Such material is not yet available. We do not even know whether there are racial differences in the sucking reflex of newborns.

A SUMMARY OF THE PAST AND SOME SUGGESTIONS FOR THE FUTURE

How NOW ARE WE TO ANSWER the nature-nurture question? We are inclined to think of *nature* and *nurture, heredity* and *environment,* or *maturation* and *learning* as contrasting, as opposites, as completely separate and different *things*—almost as objects that can be placed alongside each other or mixed with each other. But heredity and

---

[6] From T. Komai, "Notes on Lingual Gymnastics," *J. Heredity,* 1951, 42, 296. Used by permission of American Genetics Association.

environment are not objects—they are concepts. There is no such thing as a four-to-one mixture of heredity and environment for the very good reason that the terms refer to ideas or abstractions rather than to things. The concepts were devised to help in understanding some of the aspects of organic development that seemed not easily accounted for in the terms of early physical science. This is especially true of the term "heredity." We could of course ask about the environment of inanimate objects: does ice result from its nature (the fact that it is composed of H_2O) or from its environment (the fact that the temperature is below $0°C.$). The answer is so apparent—namely, "both"—that it has not troubled anyone in the physical sciences since Renaissance thought abandoned the ancient Greek metaphysical inquiry about "essences."

The answer "both" applies equally well to the nature-nurture question when it is asked about living creatures. Warwick and Berry (1949) successfully transplanted the fertilized ova of sheep and goats to the uteri of other females of the same species. But "all of the intergeneric transfers of goat embryos to sheep, and vice-versa, have died." Goat and sheep "natures" developed normally when growing in the species-appropriate environment. But when such "natures" were placed in the environment provided by the other species they ceased to develop altogether.

Genetics is a very young science and biochemistry is even younger. These two disciplines are the ones that will ultimately tell us about the biological nature of organisms. Already they have gained considerable insight into the intricate and delicately balanced relationships that must be maintained between the genes and their environment if normal progeny are to result. The impossibility of making any perfectly clear distinction between the terms "heredity" and "environment" is illustrated by the position effect (Srb, 1953). The complex chemical structures which make up the genes are strung along the chromosomes in such a way that one gene is part of the environment of other genes, and when this spatial arrangement is disturbed the resulting organism is quite different from normal ones. Not only are the genes part of the environment of other genes but it is also true that other environmental events—for instance, radiation and some chemicals—produce changes in the genes. In a word, "nature" is not independent of "nurture"; the first crude classification of variables, which the terms "nature" and "nurture" imply, is no longer scientifically useful.

So much for the nature-nurture question in general. What can be said about the question as it applies to the sucking response? It is only by using very inexact language that we can say anything at all. But *if* we use such language, then on the side of nature (meaning those aspects of the living organism which it is difficult or still impossible to manipulate) we might list sex (for humans), species, degree of maturity, and *some* individual differences. On the side of nurture (meaning the manipulations that we happen to have found effective in modifying the response) we might list the amount of rewarded practice, various unspecified sociocultural variables, and degree of social stimulation. This is not very much information, and it leaves quite unclassified such known-to-be-relevant variables as degree of hunger, fatigue, fear, and so on which cannot be classified as nature *or* nurture by even the loosest use of the terms.

Let us then lay the either-or question to rest and turn to new and more answerable questions.

Major Historical Sources of Research on Orality

Our more detailed knowledge of the development of the sucking response comes from a number of great intellectual traditions. The single figure who dominates the largest part of the history of scientific inquiry into the sucking response is Sigmund Freud. We have barely scratched the surface of psychoanalytic work on "orality"; even so, Freud's influence is overpowering. So far as the work reported in this chapter is concerned, probably Freud's greatest contribution was his emphasis on motivation. In pediatrics and psychiatry, Levy and Ribble are among his intellectual descendants. In child psychology, Sears and others have attempted to test Levy's formulation of Freud's hypothesis. In anthropology, Whiting and Child have tried to test modified psychoanalytic hypotheses about orality. In addition, many individual investigations might never have been conducted had not Freud raised the question of a broadly sexual and instinctive—or perhaps anaclitic—oral motivation.

A second important influence on the study of the sucking response has been the study of learning which, while it has very ancient roots (Harvey, for instance, argued that sucking was learned *in utero*), really got under way as a scientific enterprise with Ebbinghaus in 1885, only slightly before Freud's first work.

A third influence is John B. Watson who is, after Freud, perhaps the most significant figure in twentieth century psychology. Watson's environmentalism gave tremendous support to the study of learning, and his insistence that we study *behavior* radically changed the direction of American psychology.

Biological science is the fourth major source of research on the development of orality. Harvey, Preyer, Kashara, and Hooker are among the laboratory workers, while Lindner, Levy, Klackenberg, Norvall, and Traisman and Traisman represent the clinical practice of medicine; zoology and animal husbandry have many contributors; genetics is just beginning to be heard from.

Finally there is child psychology, which in the United States was strongly influenced by Watson's (1928) complaint about a

> . . . bankruptcy of facts. *No one today knows enough to raise a child.* The world would be considerably better off if we were to stop having children for twenty years (except those reared for experimental purposes) and were then to start again with enough facts to do the job with some degree of skill and accuracy.[7]

Among others, the child psychologists include Kunst, Piaget, Halverson, Sears, and Olson (and us!).

What Is Known about Orality and What to Do Next

So much for where the study of orality has come from. Where should it go? We are reasonably well convinced that the most profitable next steps will be suggested by a close look at the facts rather than by a formal theory. It is frequently said that theories suggest what new facts to seek. Perhaps. But it is also true that theories may *restrict* our search. Addiction to a theory can lead one to overlook facts that don't fit. A case in point is the failure to note Levy's early observation that prolonged nursing is sometimes associated with non-nutritive sucking.

What, then, are the facts?

The first is that within the class *Mammalia* there has been so much specialization in the course of zoological evolution that it is extremely dangerous to generalize from one species to another—especially when the species are only distantly related as, say, in the case of dogs or cattle or goats on the one hand and man on the other. A second fact is that there is not any clear parallel between the complexity of the nervous system of a species and the degree to which the sucking response of the young animal appears to depend on learning. The dolphin is a case in point. Indeed, it is not at all clear how much learning is really necessary for the early part of normal ontogenesis in *any* species. The third fact is perhaps just a tautology: the oral behaviors of closely related species are more likely to be similar than are the oral behaviors of distantly related species—consider the dolphin and the whale among the cetaceans, or the rhesus monkey, the chimpanzee, and man among the primates. The individual differences among young humans seem much more similar to those found in other primates than to those so far reported for cattle and dogs. In view of the survival value of a strong and dependable sucking reflex we would expect generally smaller individual differences in land mammals less well endowed with cortex than the primates and also in the completely aquatic mammals.

[7] From J. B. Watson, *Psychological Care of Infant and Child*, p. 12, copyright 1928 by W. W. Norton and Co., Inc., New York, and used by their permission.

SOME SPECIFIC POSSIBILITIES FOR RESEARCH.   Beside the preceding rather general observations, we can also answer a variety of specific questions. Below we have listed six groups of facts. Some are well established; others are more tentative. In almost every case the facts immediately suggest the next empirical question.

(1) In human ontogenesis the sucking reflex can first be elicited prematurely at a menstrual age of about twenty-nine weeks; that is, about six months after conception. The adequate stimulus is a light touch near the mouth (Harvey, 1651; Preyer, 1885). Before twenty-nine weeks a variety of oral responses can be elicited, but not true sucking (Hooker, 1944). Since girls generally mature more rapidly than boys, and in view of increasing evidence that Negro infants are accelerated in motor development as compared with white infants (Knobloch and Pasamanick, 1953), a search for sex and race differences in prenatal orality ought to be rewarding. Sex differences and strain and breed differences in other species would be very provocative for comparative psychologists and geneticists.

(2) The vigor of sucking in the premature human infant and neonate is directly related to maturity and to the condition of the central nervous system (Kashara, 1916; Crump et al., 1958). This fact, like those above, invites an examination of race and sex differences. A systematic inquiry into species differences in prenatal orality is badly needed.

(3) In all mammals that suck (there is some question about whether young cetaceans and marsupials actually suck as opposed to simply swallowing, and we do not know for certain about very young monotremes [Burrell, 1927]), the response is more likely to occur and is likely to be more vigorous when the infant is hungry than when it is not hungry (Halverson, 1944). Here is a place for those who are intrigued by theories to go to work. The role of thirst, as distinguished from hunger, ought surely to interest theorists interested in drive and drive stimuli. A systematic exploration of the external stimuli which will maintain the response should certainly fascinate stimulus-response psychologists. Just how much variation in taste, nutritive (drive-reducing) properties of the food, and shape and texture of the nipple (Gunther, 1955; Picard, 1959) can be tolerated? A good many years ago Davis (1928) reported that young children who are allowed to select their own diets (within certain limits) thrive, and even cure their own rickets. Would malnourished infants, as compared with normal ones, show a greater persistence in sucking on particularly nourishing bottles?

(4) In human infants who are breast- or bottle-fed, the efficiency of nutritive sucking improves with age (Kashara, 1916; Piaget, 1936), but it is not clear how large a part is played by practice. We know of no experiment in which cup-fed infants have been transferred to the breast

or bottle and compared with control infants who have always been breast- or bottle-fed. Studies of motor skills and imprinting suggest that equal amounts of practice have different effects at different ages and that the effects vary from one response system to another. Ross (1951a) and James (1957, 1959) have begun work of this kind with one breed of dogs. See also Ross, Fisher and King's 1957 summary.

(5) We have reported a modest amount of evidence that during the past thirty years or so American girls have been more likely to suck their thumbs than have American boys, at least after the first year. Will this sex difference hold up in other cultures? Will it be found in other closely related species? Does it have anything to do with the Y chromosome?

Not a great deal is actually *known* about the erotic qualities of oral behavior, but Kinsey and his associates (1953) report that, while most males are very genitally oriented in their sexual behavior, "most females prefer to be stimulated tactilely in various other parts of the body before the activity is concentrated on the genitalia" (p. 658). The apparently more diffuse eroticism of human females might very well involve oral sensitivity as well. Lipsitt and Levy (1959) have reported greater skin sensitivity in female neonates than in males. It should be easy to determine whether infants with more sensitive skin become thumb-suckers.

(6) In present-day Western society thumb-sucking appears to be more common among middle-class children than among working-class children (Davis and Havighurst, 1946; Zazzo, 1956). The precise conditions responsible are unclear. Davis and Havighurst attribute the difference to a higher level of frustration in middle-class children. But is it the general level of frustration or some specific frustration such as earlier weaning or more scheduled feeding? Miller and Swanson (1958) suggest that there may have been a recent change in this class difference, and that it is found only when more specific parental values are controlled. Parents with an "entrepreneurial" outlook appear to discourage thumb-sucking as a sign of weakness and self-indulgence, while those with a "bureaucratic" point of view are more tolerant. Even though such sociological variables are clearly relevant, the precise psychological determiners of differences in thumb-sucking remain unidentified. Is it feeding schedules? Levy's early work suggests "yes," and Roberts (1944), Fleischl (1957), and Davis (1940) all have presented confirming data. But Simsarian's findings (1947) disagree.

As an illustration that many of the psychological determiners of thumb-sucking are still unidentified, consider weaning. Ever since Freud suggested an "oral stage of libidinal development," we have been concerned about how and when to wean. Psychoanalytic theory predicts greater thumb-sucking as a consequence of both very early and very late weaning; learning theory predicts a straightforward increase in thumb-sucking as age of weaning increases; but the critical-period hypothesis warns that chronological age is a deceptively easy measure to obtain.

Sears' and Wise's data suggest that age of weaning has little or no relationship to thumb-sucking. Fredeen's clinical impression is that cup-feeding from birth is mildly prophylactic. Olson reports a curvilinear relationship, with thumb-sucking more common in children weaned early and late. Yarrow reports more thumb-sucking in children weaned very late (for American culture). Bernstein's data also suggest that thumb-sucking is more common among late-weaned children. Zazzo reports the opposite result for his French sample. In a word, the data are inconclusive so far as *thumb-sucking* is concerned. But Whiting has shown a very systematic curvilinear relationship between age of weaning and degree of *emotional upset* at the time.

The failure to obtain a consistent relation between thumb-sucking and age of weaning may be due to the development of discrimination. As infants practice nursing, they not only develop stronger sucking habits, but they may become strongly attached to particular stimuli. Many children can suck their thumbs only when holding a particular blanket, furry toy, or whatever. Perhaps children nursed in much the same way for several months cannot transfer easily from the nipple to the thumb when they are weaned, but are nevertheless upset by the frustration that weaning involves. To explore this notion, groups of infants who have always been bottle-fed with standard bottles and nipples might be tested at different ages for their willingness to nurse from *different* bottles and nipples. If our hypothesis is correct, they should show less and less willingness to switch as they grow older (up to some critical age). Control infants, nursed in a variety of ways with a variety of bottles and nipples, might show less and less *disturbance* as age of weaning increased but more and more substitutive *thumb-sucking*. The standard group ought to show the greatest *disturbance* with late weaning but the least *thumb-sucking*. At all ages, thumb-sucking should be greater in the group nursed with a variety of nipples.

Two Other Aspects of Orality That Need Study

We could multiply possibilities of this sort almost endlessly. Instead, we shall mention two quite different areas of investigation. The first has to do with the use of the mouth as an organ of sensory exploration and as an organ of prehension and manipulation. We do not mean to imply that this aspect of orality is totally distinct from sucking. Obviously, oral sensory experience is partly determined by nutritive sucking. We mean only to call attention to an aspect of orality that we have slighted. Many close observers have reported both sensory exploration and prehension (Piaget, 1936; Gesell, 1937), yet we have very little normative data or systematic knowledge of how the mouth comes to be used in these ways. We do not know what effects, if any, result from different kinds of feeding experience, thumb-sucking, or other oral history. The field is challenging and totally unexplored.

The second additional area of inquiry concerns the non-oral consequences of different oral experiences. Throughout this chapter we have limited ourselves to the *development of the sucking response*. But many persons are convinced that there is an even more interesting and socially important question involving the relation between early oral experience and the development of personality and sexual behavior. Direct measures of infantile oral experience would be extremely valuable. It is our impression that many so-called measures of, say, "the oral component of the libido" are no such thing, but are instead only assumed correlates of the assumed oral component. In passing, we suggest that if *real* oral experience in early life does have an effect on later sexual development, it may well turn out that the most relevant aspect is the development of the mouth as a sensory, exploratory, and manipulative organ. The mouth is frequently used in sexual behavior in a great variety of species including man. In any case, Kron and Stein (1961), at the Medical School of the University of Pennsylvania, appear at last to be getting such research under way more than fifty years after Freud published his *Three Contributions to the Theory of Sex*.

A Theoretical Suggestion

Still another aspect of orality which merits further thought is one which concerns general psychological theory. We refer to the question of motivation. Some human infants and some sucklings of other species engage in non-nutritive sucking when they are asleep and not hungry. "Instinct," "need," and "acquired drive" have all been used in an attempt to account for such phenomena. In our opinion none has been successful.

Recently Woodworth (1958) has stated a very interesting position on motivation:

> We're not pretending that the organic needs are derived. . . . The organic needs are autonomous. But the behavior that is enlisted in the service of our organic need *has its own rewards* [our italics] apart from the reduction of a need. The act of sucking appears to have rewards, since not only does the infant demand more of it than is necessary (Jersild, 1954) but older people take pleasure in sucking cider through a straw or smoke through a cigarette.[8]

[8] From R. S. Woodworth, *Dynamics of Behavior*, p. 128, copyright 1958 by Holt, Rinehart, and Winston, Inc., and used by their permission.

We agree with Woodworth; the rewards are what Freud and pre-Watsonian academic psychologists called "pleasure." Babies suck their thumbs because they *like* to—not because they *need* to.

The difference between "needing" and "liking" may seem trivial. It is not. This is not the place to examine in detail the concept of motivation, nor the concept of hedonism. But since we suggest that the need-drive model of motivation and the drive-reduction model of learning be supplemented by a pleasantness-unpleasantness view of behavior, we must indicate why the former seems incomplete and how the latter might be helpful.

We have three reasons for rejecting the need model of motivation as universally applicable. First, for a number of so-called biological drives purposive behavior clearly depends on a state of affairs which in itself is in no way unfavorable to the individual's survival—there is purpose but no need. The most conspicuous example is sexual behavior (Beach, 1956); another is the scratching of an itch. A third example may be pain; we know of no evidence that in and of itself a moderate degree of pain is biologically undesirable. Harlow's monkeys who seek "creature comforts" may be still another case of purpose without need. Play, curiosity, and manipulation are other possible examples. We suggest that sucking is yet another instance.

Secondly, the distinction between acquired drive and acquired habit has also proved difficult to conceptualize. In their ingenious account of the acquired fear or anxiety drive which is said to develop under escape and avoidance training, Miller (1948) and Mowrer (1939) use the acquired *habit* concept as the essential mechanism of the acquired *drive!* (Brown [1953, 1955, 1961] has examined these questions in considerably more sophisticated detail.)

The third reason for rejecting the need-drive model is that *motivation,* as an abstraction, seems to have outlived its usefulness. For the physiological psychologists, as Rosenzweig's chapter illustrates very clearly, hunger "drive," thirst "drive," and so on are gradually being supplanted by ever more precise physiological descriptions. Furthermore, "motivation" has proved extremely difficult to disentangle from "stimulus" and from "reflex." What is the "motivation" for the patellar reflex, the Moro reflex, or the Brudzinski reflex?

Perhaps reflex behavior is too molecular for the motivation concept to be useful. Many children and other young primates suck their thumbs or fingers when they are not hungry. This practice commonly begins during the first few postnatal months when most children are still nursing at the breast or bottle. Children who develop the practice learn all sorts of ways to extricate themselves from the mittens, guards, and other devices that interfering parents impose, and—as Watson makes clear—the resistance of this practice to extinction sometimes verges on the phenomenal. In these facts do we not have a clear case of the acquisition of a drive to suck and the acquiring of reward properties by the sucking act (or by the stimulation resulting from the act)?

We doubt it. The interpretation is plausible, but it is based upon a theoretically biased selection of facts. Experimentalists have failed to find evidence of acquired *drive* as distinct from acquired *habit*. Except for Calvin, Bicknell, and Sperling (1953) this failure has been reported by all rat psychologists who have used approach training (Miller, 1947; Myers and Miller, 1954; Siegel and MacDonnell, 1954). We believe that Sears and Wise have encountered the same difficulty in trying to identify an acquired sucking drive in human infants.

There is another reason for returning to pleasure: close observers have found it impossible to avoid. Beside Woodworth, Nissen (1954) and Jersild (1954) have referred to it indirectly; Freud mentions "reddened cheeks and blissful smile"; Piaget speaks of Laurent's "greed and passion"; and Kunst sees sucking as "uniquely satisfying." The clinicians, who have steadfastly refused to let logic-chopping blind them to the obvious, have inferred pleasure right along. The problem is how to make objective this "substantive, mental-presentation side of an emotion" (Tolman, 1923).

In principle, affect is objectified in exactly the same way as purpose; you find objectively different patterns of stimulation which evoke objectively different patterns of response by means of objectively different neurological patterns. (Olds' [1956] recent work suggests that the particular subcortical nuclei which participate are extremely important determiners of pleasantness and unpleasantness.) Some of these stimuli-neurology-response (S-N-R) patterns (and perhaps their associated feedbacks) are pleasant and some are unpleasant; some may be neither or neutral.

But which are which? Probably those patterns which the organism repeats and seeks are pleasant, while those which it does not repeat or avoid are unpleasant. Those which will serve as reinforcers and produce learning are more pleasant than those which will not. Obviously we have simply repeated Thorndike's criteria for the law of effect and changed the location of the satisfying state of affairs. It is our impression that many pleasant states of affairs are commonly accompanied by such verbal responses as "that feels good" or "do it again" and that unpleasant states are accompanied by "ugh" or "ouch" or "this is awful." We suspect that in many cases experimenters could elicit such classes of verbal responses with high degrees of consistency if they wished. (Nowlis [1953], for instance, has devised an Affect Check List of adjectives which shows great promise of distinguishing not merely pleasantness-unpleasantness, but even more subtle shades of affect.) The point is that if such verbal responses *are* consistently associated with the operations which define pleasantness-unpleasantness, then they can be used as tentative indicators in new circumstances for which the S-N-R and feedback pattern and the defining criteria have not yet actually been observed or for which practical difficulties are as yet insurmountable. Note that we do *not* mean that the verbal response can ever be the sole criterion of what is pleasant or unpleasant—this is the circularity from which Tolman rescued purpose, but which has continued to plague the study of human motivation.

Verbal behavior, of course, will not be helpful with lower animals or human infants. But for them there are other nonverbal responses which we know from past experience are good indicators of pleasantness-unpleasantness. That is, we have observed them in circumstances which otherwise meet the criteria of pleasantness or unpleasantness. Among them are laughing, smiling, chortling, cooing, humming, and the various cuddly noises that (as we assert) happy babies make. There is also the crying, whimpering, screaming, and thrashing about of unhappy babies. For other species there is purring, tail-wagging, whining, cowering, cringing, and so on. Once such responses are established as part of a pattern of S-N-R (and perhaps its feedback) that is pleasant or unpleasant, they, too, like verbal responses, may be used as tentative indicators.

How does this pleasantness-unpleasantness acount fit the development of sucking?

As far as the repetition and learning criteria are concerned, the relevant facts fit the need-drive, drive-reduction model as well as the hedonistic model. Other facts, however, fit the hedonistic model better.

It is clear from numerous pediatric sources that healthy—reasonably *need*less—babies suck their thumbs. It is not so clear that *happy* babies do; in fact, non-nutritive sucking is more common in bored, neglected, but physically well cared for infants (and monkeys) than in those who are engaged in pleasurable activities of other sorts. When such healthy but bored or uncomfortable babies are allowed to suck, they give unmistakable evidence of pleasure; crying and thrashing either cease or diminish, and the little contentment sounds increase. From older persons who suck their thumbs we get such verbal reports as "My thumb is my best friend" (personal communication), and

> Not all kisses equal thumb-sucking, no, no, by no means all. One cannot describe the enjoyment that goes through the entire body when one sucks one's thumb: one is far from this world; one is absolutely satisfied and supremely happy. It is a wonderful feeling. One only wishes quiet; quiet that nothing can interrupt. It is simply indescribably wonderful; one feels no pain, no sorrow, and oh! one is transported into another world.[9]

[9] Galant cited in *The Basic Writings of Sigmund Freud*, trans. and ed. by Dr. A. A. Brill, p. 585. Copyright 1938 by Random House, Inc. Reprinted by permission of the Brill Trust.

Furthermore, if we assert that sucking is pleasurable rather than acquired-drive reducing, then we are not faced with the nasty problem of accounting for the failure of the "acquired drive" to extinguish after the child is weaned. (We leave as an interesting unsettled question the kinds of unpleasantness and alternative pleasures that must be used to break the habit.)

On the basis of such observations as Piaget's we rather suspect that both the comforting qualities and the reinforcing qualities of the sucking act are present at birth and before the response is followed by food. We believe that under some conditions these properties would remain in children who were *cup*-fed from birth. If such infants were given a good deal of opportunity to suck a suitable non-nutritive stimulus, thus avoiding possible complicating structural changes in the sucking pad and masseter muscle (Gaughran, 1957; Scammon, 1919; Middlemore, 1941) as well as the total elimination of the sucking reflex by the competing increase in strength of the feeding responses, we would expect their non-nutritive sucking to be the same as that of normally nursed infants. We would expect the same proportion to be soothed by thumb-sucking, and we would expect them to be as good as normally nursed infants in learning to remove elbow splints and mitts that prevented thumb-sucking. For control infants—cup-fed but not allowed to practice non-nutritive sucking—the comforting and reward properties should be less prominent as age increases, both because of possible structural changes and also because other mouth responses would have developed to interfere with the act of sucking and thus with the pleasure it gives.

So much for another approach. It is neither original nor complete; nor will it be easy to work out the details. Our real intention is only to suggest that it is once again time to turn to our pleasures and discomforts for hypotheses about behavior. The need-drive theory—like all good theories and like the nature-nurture question itself—has led to the discovery of enough facts to show its limitations.

REFERENCES

ADLER, J., LINN, L., AND MOORE, A. V. Pushing in cattle: its relation to instinctive grasping in humans. *Animal Behaviour*, 1958, 6, 85–6.

AKRAWI, S. *The strength of the oral drive as related to age and method of weaning.* Unpublished Master's thesis, Cornell University Library, 1960.

BALIASSNIKOWA, N. J., AND MODEL, M. M. Zur neurologie des saugens. *Zsch. f. Kinderhk.*, 1931–1932, 39, 1–16.

BALINT, M. Individual differences of behavior in early infancy and an objective method of recording them. *J. genet. Psychol.*, 1948, 73, 57–117.

BALDWIN, A. L.   *Behavior and development in childhood.* New York: Dryden Press, 1955.

BARTHOLOMEW, G., AND HOEL, P. G.   Reproductive behavior of the Alaska fur seal, *Callorhinus Ursinus. J. Mammalogy*, 1953, 34, 417–36.

BEACH, F. A.   The descent of instinct. *Psychol. Rev.*, 1955, 62, 401–10.

————.   Characteristics of masculine "sex drive." In M. R. Jones (Ed.), *Nebraska symposium on motivation 1956.* Lincoln, Nebr.: University of Nebraska Press, 1956, 1–32.

BEAGLEHOLE, E. AND BEAGLEHOLE, P.   Personality development in Pukapukan children. In L. Spier *et al.* (Eds.), *Language, personality and culture.* Menasha, Wisc.: Sapir Memorial Publications Fund, 1941.

————.   *Some modern Maoris.* Wellington: New Zealand Council for Educational Research, 1946.

BENJAMIN, L. S.   Personal communication, 1959.

————.   The effect of bottle and cup feeding on the non-nutritive sucking of the infant rhesus monkey. *J. Comp. Physiol. Psychol.*, 1961, 54, 230–7.

BERNSTEIN, A.   Some relations between techniques of feeding and training during infancy and certain behavior in childhood. *Genet. Psychol. Monogr.*, 1955, 51, 3–44.

BLAU, T. H., AND BLAU, L. R.   The sucking reflex: The effects of long feeding vs. short feeding on the behavior of a human infant. *J. abn. soc. Psychol.*, 1955, 51, 1, 123–5.

BLAUVELT, H.   Dynamics of the mother-newborn relationship in goats. In Schaffner, B. (Ed.), *Group processes: Transactions of the first conference.* New York: Josiah Macy Jr. Foundation, 1955.

BRAGMAN, L. J.   Thumb-sucking and other auto-erotic tendencies in children as portrayed in art. *J. Nerv. Ment. Dis.*, 1931, 74, 708.

BRAZELTON, T. B.   Sucking in infancy, *Pediatrics*, 1956, 17, 400–4.

BRODBECK, A. J.   The effect of three feeding variables on the non-nutritive sucking of new-born infants. *Amer. Psychologist*, 1950, 5, 292–3.

BROWN, J. S.   Problems presented by the concept of acquired drives. In M. R. Jones (Ed.), *Nebraska symposium on motivation,* 1953. Lincoln: University of Nebraska Press, 1953, pp. 1–23.

————.   Pleasure-seeking behavior and the drive-reduction hypothesis. *Psychol. Rev.*, 1955, 62, 169–79.

————. *The motivation of behavior.* New York: McGraw-Hill Book Co., 1961.

BROWNLEE, A. Studies in the behaviour of domestic cattle in Britain. *Bull. Animal Behav.,* 1950, 8, 11–20.

BUDD, A., SMITH, L. G., AND SHELLEY, F. W. On the birth and upbringing of the female chimpanzee "Jacqueline." *Proc. Zool. Soc., London,* 1943, *113,* 1–20.

BURRELL, H. *The platypus.* Sydney, Australia: Angus and Robertson, Ltd., 1927.

CALVIN, J. S., BICKNELL, E. A., AND SPERLING, D. S. Establishment of a conditioned drive based on the hunger drive. *J. comp. physiol. Psychol.,* 1953, 46, 173–5.

CRUMP, E. P., GORE, P. M., AND HORTON, C. P. The sucking behavior in premature infants. *Hum. Biol.,* 1958, 30, 2, 128–41.

DARWIN, C. *On the expression of the emotions in man and animals.* London: John Murray, 1872.

DARWIN, E. [1794–1796] *Zoonomia,* printed for B. Dugdale, Dame-Street, Dublin, 1800.

DAVIS, A., AND HAVIGHURST, R. J. Social class and color differences in child training. *Am. Sociol. Rev.,* 1946, XI, 6.

DAVIS, C. M. Self-selection of diet by newly weaned infants. *Amer. J. Dis. Child.,* 1928, 36, 651–79.

DAVIS, H. V., SEARS, R. R., MILLER, H. C., AND BRODBECK, A. J. Effects of cup, bottle and breast feeding on oral activities of new-born infants. *Pediatrics,* 1948, 3, 549–58.

DAVIS, P. B. A study of thumb-sucking. *The Trained Nurse,* 1940, *104,* 422.

DU BOIS, C. *The people of Alor.* Minneapolis: Lund Press, 1944.

FELDMAN, W. M. *The principles of antenatal and postnatal child physiology pure and applied.* London: Longmans, Green and Co., 1920.

FLEISCHL, M. F. The problem of sucking. *Am. J. Psychotherapy,* 1957, *1,* 11, 86–97.

FOSTER, J. C., AND ANDERSON, J. E. *The young child and his parents.* Minneapolis: University of Minnesota Press, 1930.

FREDEEN, R. C. Personal communication, 1959.

FREUD, S. [1905]. Three contributions to the theory of sex. In *Basic writings of Sigmund Freud.* New York: Random House, 1938.

GAHRES, E. Tongue rolling and tongue folding and other hereditary movements of the tongue. *J. Heredity,* 1952, 43, 221–5.

GAUGHRAN, G. R. L. Fasciae of the masticator space. *Anat. Rec.,* 1957, 129, 383–400.

GENTRY, E. F., AND ALDRICH, C. A. Rooting reflex in the newborn infant: Incidence and effect on it of sleep. *Amer. J. Dis. Child.*, 1948, 75, 528–39.

GESELL, A., AND ILG, F. *Feeding behavior of infants.* Philadelphia: Lippincott, 1937.

GILL, J. C., AND THOMSON, W. Observations on the behaviour of suckling pigs. *Brit. J. Animal Behaviour*, 1956, 4, 46–51.

GILLMAN, J. Toe-sucking in baboons: A consideration of some factors responsible for this habit. *J. Mammalogy*, 1941, 22, 395–402.

GLADWIN, T., AND SARASON, S. B. *Truk: man in paradise.* New York: Wenner-Gren Foundation for Anthropological Research, 1953.

GUNTHER, M. Instinct and the nursing couple. *Lancet*, 1955, 268, 575–8.

GUTTMACHER, A. F. *Into this universe: the story of human birth.* New York: Viking Press, 1937.

HALVERSON, H. M. Infant sucking and tensional behavior. *J. genet. Psychol.*, 1938, 53, 365–430.

———. Mechanisms of early infant feeding. *J. genet. Psychol.*, 1944, 64, 185–223.

———. A study of feeding mechanisms in premature infants. *J. genet, Psychol.*, 1946, 68, 205–17.

HARLOW, H. The nature of love. *Amer. Psychologist*, 1958, 13, 673–85.

HARLOW, H., AND ZIMMERMAN, R. R. Affectional responses in the infant monkey. *Science*, 1959, 130, 421–32.

HARTMAN, C. G. *Possums.* Austin: University of Texas Press, 1952.

HARVEY, W. [1651]. *Anatomical exercitations concerning the generation of living creatures.* London: Printed by James Young for Octavian Pulleyn, 1653.

HATTWICK, L. Sex differences in behavior of nursery school children. *Child Develpm.*, 1937, 7, 200–26.

HONZIK, M. P. A developmental study of thumb-sucking. Unpublished ms. at University of California Institute of Human Development, 1959.

———. The patterning of mental test performance of infants suspected of suffering brain injury. Paper given at the American Psychological Association, 1960.

HONZIK, M. P., AND MC KEE, J. P. The sex difference in thumb-sucking. *J. Pediatrics*, 1962, *in press.*

HOOKER, D. *The origin of behavior.* Ann Arbor: University of Michigan Press, 1944.

HSU, T. Tongue up-folding. *J. Heredity*, 1948, 39, 187–8.

JACOBSEN, C. F., JACOBSEN, M. M., AND YOSHIOKA, J. G. Development of an infant chimpanzee during her first year. *Comp. Psychol. Monogr.*, 1932, 9, 1.

JAMES, W. T.   The effect of satiation on the sucking response in puppies. *J. comp. physiol. Psychol.*, 1957, 50, 375–8.

———.   A further analysis of satiation on the sucking response in puppies. *Psychol. Record*, 1959, 9, 1–6.

JAMES, W. T., AND GILBERT, T. F.   Elimination of eating behavior by food injection in weaned puppies. *Psychol. Reports*, 1957, 3, 167–8.

JERSILD, A. T.   *Child Psychology*, 4th ed. New York: Prentice-Hall, 1954.

JOHNSON, L. R.   Habits and their control in relation to malocclusion in children. *J. Am. Dent. Assoc.*, Sept., 1937, 24.

KASHARA, M.   The curved lines of suction. *Amer. J. Dis. Child*, 1916, 12, 73–87.

KELSEY, H. L.   Class I malocclusion, with pronounced open-bite, induced by constant finger sucking, in a monkey. *Int'l J. Orthodontia and Oral Surgery*, 1936, 22, 1119–22.

KINSEY, A., *et al.*   Sexual behavior in the human female. Philadelphia: Saunders, 1953.

KLACKENBERG, G.   Thumbsucking: frequency and etiology. *Pediatrics*, 1949, 4, 4.

KNOBLOCH, H., AND PASAMANICK, B.   Further observations on the behavioral development of Negro children. *J. genet. Psychol.*, 1953, 83, 137–58.

KOMAI, T.   Notes on lingual gymnastics. *J. Heredity*, 1951, 42, 293–7.

KRON, R., AND STEIN, M.   Report published in the *Medical Tribune*, Feb. 20, 1961, p. 24.

KUNST, M. S.   A study of thumb- and finger-sucking in infants. *Psychol. Monogr.*, 1948, 62, 3.

LEE, J. W.   Tongue-folding and tongue-rolling in an American Negro population sample. *J. Heredity*, 1955, 46, 289–91.

LEVY, D.   Finger-sucking and accessory movements in early infancy: an etiological study. *Amer. J. Psychiatry*, 1928, 7, 881–918.

———.   Experiments on the sucking reflex and social behavior of dogs. *Am. J. Orthopsychiatry*, 1934, 4, 203–24.

———.   On instinct-satiation: an experiment on the pecking behavior of chickens. *J. genet. Psychol.*, 1938, 18, 327–48.

———.   *Behavioral analysis.* Springfield, Ill.: Charles C. Thomas, 1958.

LEWIS, S. J.   Thumbsucking: a cause of malocclusion in deciduous teeth. *J. Am. Dent. Assoc.*, 1930, 1060–73.

LINDNER, S.   Das saugen an dem fingern, lippen, etc. bei den kindern (ludeln). *Jahrbuch für Kinderheilkunde und Physische Erziehung*, 1879, 14, 68–91.

LINTON, R. A., in A. Kardiner (Ed.), *The individual and his society.* New York: Columbia University Press, 1939.

LIPSITT, L. P., AND LEVY, N. Electrotactual threshold in the neonate. *Child Develpm.*, 1959, 30, 547–54.

LIU, T., AND HSU, T. Tongue-folding and tongue-rolling. *J. Heredity*, 1949, 40, 19–21.

MARQUIS, D. P. Learning in the neonate: the modification of behavior under three feeding schedules. *J. exper. Psychol.*, 1941, 29, 263–82.

MATTHEWS, L. H. *Whales.* Proceedings of Royal Philos. Soc. of Glasgow, 1948, 73, 1–13.

MCBRIDE, A. F., AND HEBB, D. O. Behavior of the captive bottle-nose dolphin, *Tursiops truncatus. J. comp. physiol. Psychol.*, 1948, 41, 111–23.

MCBRIDE, A. F., AND KRITZLER, H. Observations on pregnancy, parturition and postnatal behavior in the bottle-nose dolphin. *J. Mammalogy*, 1951, 30, 251–66.

MCDOUGALL, W. [1908]. *An introduction to social psychology*, 13th ed. Boston: J. W. Luce and Co., 1918.

MACFARLANE, J. W., ALLEN, L., AND HONZIK, M. P. A developmental study of the behavior problems of normal children between 21 months and 14 years. University of California publ. in Child Develpm., 1954, Vol. II.

MEAD, M. *Sex and temperament in three primitive societies.* New York: William Morrow and Co., 1935.

———. Some theoretical considerations on the problem of mother-child separation. *Am. J. Orthopsychiat.*, 1954, 24, 471–83.

MICHAELS, J. J., AND GOODMAN, S. E. Incidence and intercorrelations of enuresis and other neuropathic traits in so-called normal children. *Am. J. Orthopsychiat.*, 1934, 4, 79–106.

MIDDLEMORE, M. P. *The nursing couple.* London: Hamilton, 1941.

MILLER, D., AND SWANSON, G. E. *The changing American parent.* New York: John Wiley and Sons, Inc., 1958.

MILLER, N. E. Experiments on the strength of acquired drives based on hunger. *Amer. Psychologist*, 1947, 2, 303.

———. Studies of fear as an acquirable drive: I. Fear as motivation and fear-reduction as reinforcement in the learning of new responses. *J. exp. Psychol.*, 1948, 38, 89–101.

MOWRER, O. H. A stimulus-response analysis of anxiety and its role as a reinforcing agent. *Psychol. Rev.*, 1939, 46, 553–65.

MURRAY, H. A. *Explorations in personality.* New York: Oxford University Press, 1938.

MYERS, A. K., AND MILLER, N. E. Failure to find a learned drive based on hunger; evidence for learning motivated by "exploration." *J. comp. physiol. Psychol.*, 1954, 47, 428–36.

NISSEN, H. W. The nature of the drive as innate determinant of behavioral organization. In M. R. Jones (Ed.), *Nebraska sympo-*

sium on motivation, 1954. Lincoln: University of Nebraska Press, 1954, 281–321.

NORVAL, M. A. Sucking response of newborn babies at breast: 50 cases. *Am. J. Dis. Child.*, 1946, 71, 41–4.

NOWLIS, V. The development and modification of motivational systems in personality. In M. R. Jones (Ed.), *Nebraska symposium in motivation, 1953*. Lincoln: University of Nebraska Press, 1953, 114–38.

OLDS, J. E. Pleasure centers in the brain. *Scientific Amer.*, 1956, 195, 105–16.

OLSON, W. The measurement of nervous habits in normal children. Inst. Child Welfare Monogr. Ser., 1929, No. 3, Minneapolis: University of Minnesota Press.

ORLANSKY, H. Infant care and personality. *Psychol. Bull.*, 1949, 46, 1–48.

PALERMO, D. S. Thumbsucking: A learned response. *Pediatrics*, 1956, 17, 392–9.

PEPYS, S. [1669]. *Diary and correspondence.* New York: Dodd, 1887.

PIAGET, J. [1936]. *The origins of intelligence in children.* New York: International Universities Press, 1952.

PICARD, P. J. Bottle feeding as preventive orthodontics. *J. Calif. State Dent. Assoc.*, 1959, 35, No. 3.

PINNEAU, S. R. A critique on the articles by Margaret Ribble. *Child Develpm.*, 1950, 21, 203–28.

———. The infantile disorders of hospitalism and anaclitic depression. *Psychol. Bull.*, 1955, 52, 429–52.

PRECHTL, H. F. R. The head turning response and allied movements of the human baby. *Behaviour*, 1958, 13, 212–42.

PRECHTL, H. F. R. AND SCHLEIDT, W. Auslösende und steuernde Mechanismen des Saugaktes. *Zeitschr. f. Vergleich. Physiologie*, 1951, 33, 53–62.

PREYER, W. [1885]. Embryonic motility and sensitivity. *Monogr. of Soc. Res. Child Develpm.*, 1937, 2.

RIBBLE, M. A. *The rights of infants.* New York: Columbia University Press, 1943.

———. The significance of infantile sucking for the psychic development of the individual. *J. Nerv. Ment. Dis.*, 1939, 90, 455–63.

ROBERTS, E. Thumb- and finger-sucking in relation to feeding in early infancy. *Amer. J. Dis. Child.*, 1944, 68, 7–8.

ROSENBLATT, J. S., TURKEWITZ, G., AND SCHNEIRLA, T. C. Development of suckling and related behavior in neonate kittens. In E. L. Bliss (Ed.), *Roots of behavior.* New York: Harper & Row, 1962.

ROSS, S. Effects of early weaning on sucking behavior of cocker spaniel puppies. *Anat. Rec.*, 1951, 111, 492. (a)

ROSS, S.   Sucking behavior in neonate dogs. *J. abn. soc. Psychol.*, 1951, 46, 142–9. (b)

ROSS, S., FISHER, A., AND KING, D.   Sucking behavior: A review of the literature. *J. genet. Psychol.*, 1957, 91, 63–81.

SCAMMON, R. E.   On the development and finer structure of the Corpus Adiposum Buccae. *Anat. Rec.*, 1919, 15, 267–87.

SCOTT, J. P., ROSS, S. AND FISHER, A. E.   The effects of early enforced weaning on sucking behavior of puppies. *J. genet. Psychol.*, 1959, 95, 261–81.

SEARS, R. R., WHITING, J. W. M., NOWLIS, V., AND SEARS, P. S.   Some child-rearing antecedents of aggression and dependency in young children. *Genet. Psychol. Monogr.*, 1953, 47, 135–234.

SEARS, R. R., AND WISE, G.   Relation of cup-feeding in infancy to thumb-sucking and the oral drive. *Amer. J. Orthopsychiatry*, 1950, 20, 123–38.

SIEGEL, P. S., AND MACDONNELL, M. F.   A repetition of the Calvin-Bicknell-Sperling study of conditioned drive. *J. comp. physiol. Psychol.*, 1954, 47, 250–3.

SIMSARIAN, F. P.   Case histories of five thumbsucking children breast-fed on unscheduled regimes, without limitation of nursing time. *Child Develpm.*, 1947, 18, 180–4.

SPIRO, M. E.   *Children of the Kibbutz.* Cambridge: Harvard University Press, 1958.

SPITZ, R. A.   Hospitalism: An inquiry into the genesis of psychiatric conditions in early childhood. *Psychoanal. Stud. Child.*, 1945, 1, 53–74. New York: Int'l Universities Press.

———.   Hospitalism: A follow-up report. *Psychoanal. Stud. Child.*, 1946, 2, 113–17. New York: Int'l Universities Press. (a)

———.   Anaclitic depression. *Psychoanal. Stud. Child.*, 1946, 2, 313–42. New York: Int'l Universities Press. (b)

SRB, A.   *Pathways to the understanding of genetics.* Prepared for Office of Naval Research under contract Nonr-401 (2), 1953.

STURTEVANT, A. H.   A new inherited character in man. *Proc. Nat. Acad. Sci.*, 1940, 26, 100–2.

SWINEHART, E. W.   Structural and nervous effects of thumbsucking. *J. Am. Dent. Assoc.*, 1938, 25.

TILSON, M. A.   *Problems of preschool children.* New York: Teachers College, Columbia, 1929.

TOLMAN, E. C.   A behavioristic account of the emotions. *Psychol. Rev.*, 1923, 30, 217–27.

———.   The determiners of behavior at a choice point. *Psychol. Rev.*, 1938, 45, 1–41.

TRAISMAN, A. S., AND TRAISMAN, H. S.   Thumb- and finger-sucking: A study of 2,650 infants and children. *J. Pediat.*, 1958, 52, No. 5.

URBANOWSKI, A., AND WILSON, J.   Tongue curling. *J. Hered.*, 1947, 38, 365–6.

WALKER, D. M.   Observations on behavior in young calves. *Bull. Animal Behav.*, 1950, 8, 5–10.

WALLACE, W. J.   Infancy and childhood among the Mohave Indians. *Primitive man*, 1948, 21, 19–38.

WARWICK, B. L., AND BERRY, R. O.   Inter-generic and intra-specific embryo transfers in sheep and goats. *J. Hered.*, 1949, 40, 297–303.

WATSON, J. B.   *Psychological care of infant and child.* New York: W. W. Norton and Co., 1928.

White House Conference on Child Health and Protection, Section III. *The young child in the home: A survey of 3,000 American families.* Appleton-Century, 1936.

WHITING, J. W. M.   The cross-cultural method. In G. Lindzey (Ed.), *Handbook of social psychology.* Cambridge, Mass.: Addison Wesley, 1954, I.

WHITING, J. W. M., AND CHILD, I. L.   *Child training and personality.* New Haven: Yale University Press, 1953.

WOODWORTH, R. S.   *Dynamics of behavior.* New York: Henry Holt and Co., 1958.

WYATT, J. M., AND VEVERS, G. M.   On the birth of chimpanzee recently born in the Society's gardens. *Proc. Zool. Soc., London,* 1935, 195–7.

YARROW, L. J.   The relationship between nutritive sucking experiences in infancy and non-nutritive sucking in childhood. *J. genet. Psychol.*, 1954, 84, 149–62.

YERKES, R., AND YERKES, A. W.   *The great apes.* New Haven: Yale University Press, 1929.

ZAZZO, R.   Cited by Juliette Favez-Boutonier in K. Soddy (Ed.), *Mental health and infant development.* Vol. I. New York: Basic Books, 1956.

CHAPTER II

Repression

D O N A L D   W.   M A C K I N N O N
A N D   W I L L I A M   F.   D U K E S

ONE THEME in the development of psychology as a science has been that of challenge and response in which the concepts and theories, the methods and techniques, and the empirical and experimental findings in respect to a particular problem have been responses to the challenges posed by earlier formulations and reported observations. In the history of science, however, even more radical instances of challenge and response may be noted. They have been sparked by those rare geniuses, who, often quite ignorant of the history of their discipline, or unconcerned with what those who have preceded them have observed and reported, and even at times contemptuous of the claims of their peers, contribute less to the evolution of established fields of scientific inquiry than to those revolutionary movements which bring new sciences into being.

Yet one may wonder whether the fresh observations and keen insights and original formulations of such pioneers are not the prototype of scientific challenges. For these are the radical challenges which question, not the validity of a single observation or the appropriateness of a particular method or the resolving power of a given hypothetical construct, but which challenge a whole science to justify its adequacy for the observation, description, and rational correlation of the phenomena which it takes as the object of its study.

It was a challenge of this magnitude which Sigmund Freud, the founder of psychoanalysis, delivered both to psychology and to psychiatry.

REPRESSION, THE BASIC CONCEPT OF PSYCHOANALYSIS

BASIC TO THE NEW psychology which eventually was called psychoanalysis was the conceptualization of a process which Freud called repression (*Verdrängung*),[1] and of which he was in 1914 to say, "The doctrine of repression is the foundation stone on which the whole structure of psychoanalysis rests . . ." (p. 297).[2]

One of the first expositions of the concept of repression for American psychologists was made by Ernest Jones, one of Freud's earliest collaborators and later his biographer. It appeared in 1911 in the *American Journal of Psychology*. Since this particular formulation of Freud's views was to influence greatly those American psychologists who about 1930 sought to study repression in the experimental laboratory, it serves as a useful introduction to this chapter on the history of the concept of repression.

> One of Freud's most notable contributions to psychology, and a conception fundamental in his study of the present group of mental processes, was his discovery that, in addition to the other causes of forgetting, "repression" (*Verdrängung*) plays a most important part. Others before Freud had realized the existence of this, but it was reserved for him to demonstrate the extent to which it is operative in both normal and abnormal mental life.
>
> Freud regards repression as a biological defence-mechanism, the function of which is to guard the mind from painful experiences. He holds that there is in the mind of every one a tendency to forget the

---

[1] Freud was not the first to use the term "repression" in such a psychological sense. One year before Freud in his first psychoanalytical paper (1893) made reference to repression, Charles W. Page, Superintendent of the Danvers Lunatic Hospital in Massachusetts, in a paper entitled, *The Adverse Consequences of Repression* (1892–1893), described "repressed emotional sentiments" and the dynamic consequences of repression: "Auditory hallucinations are exceedingly liable to voice ideas and suggestions which the subject of them has endeavored to rule out of his mind and life, or which he has contemplated only with fear and trembling, thus linking them the more closely to his personality and rendering them the most aggressive thoughts in his mind" (H. A. Bunker, " 'Repression' in Pre-Freudian American Psychiatry," *Psychoanal. Quart.*, 1945, 14, 473).

[2] Though reference is made here and throughout this chapter to translations of Freud's works as they appeared in *Collected Papers*, these being the translations available in the period here reviewed, the reader's attention is called to the most recent authorized translation of Freud's writings, viz., *The Complete Psychological Works of Sigmund Freud*. This was translated under the general editorship of James Strachey in collaboration with Anna Freud, assisted by Alix Strachey and Alan Tyson, and published in London by the Hogarth Press.

things that the person does not like to be reminded of, in other words, painful or disagreeable memories. It is true that we often remember against our will matters that we would rather forget, but there are two explanations for this. In the first place, such disagreeable haunting memories are frequently themselves only the replacements of buried and still more disagreeable ones, with which they are associated, an occurrence allied to that concerned in the genesis of true obsessions. In the second place, the capacity to forget painful experiences is only of a certain strength, which differs greatly in different people, and is not always successful in achieving its aim. . . . Further, it must be remarked that, for reasons which cannot here be gone into, repression acts much more extensively in causing forgetfulness of internal, extremely intimate, and personal, mental processes than of what may be called external memories, known to the world, such as failure, grief, and so on.

. . . as Freud remarks, no one has so exhaustively and at the same time so incisively described both the process itself and the psychological basis of it as has Nietzsche in his *Jenseits von Gut und Böse:* "Das habe ich getan, sagt mein Gedächtnis. Das kann ich nicht getan haben, sagt mein Stolz und bleibt unerbittlich. Endlich—gibt das Gedächtnis nach." [3]

Schopenhauer, Precursor of Freud

How completely Schopenhauer foreshadowed Freud's ideas about the dynamics of motivated forgetting or repression and its consequences is revealed in the following quotation from *The World as Will and Idea* published in 1819:

The exposition of the origin of madness . . . will become more comprehensible if it is remembered how unwillingly we think of things which powerfully injure our interests, wound our pride, or interfere with our wishes; with what difficulty do we determine to lay such things before our own intellect for careful and serious investigation; how easily, on the other hand, we unconsciously break away or sneak off from them again; how on the contrary, agreeable events come into our minds of their own accord. . . . In that resistance of the will to allowing what is contrary to it to come under the examination of the intellect lies the place at which madness can break in upon the mind. Each new adverse event must be assimilated by the intellect, i.e., it must receive a place in the system of the truths connected with our will and its interests, whatever it may have to displace that is more satisfactory. Wherever this has taken place, it already pains us much

[3] " 'I did that,' says my memory. 'I could not have done that,' says my pride, and remains inexorable. Eventually—the memory yields."

The excerpt is from Ernest Jones, "The Psychopathology of Everyday Life," *Amer. J. Psychol.,* 1911, 22, 479–80, 480f. Used by permission.

less; but this operation itself is often very painful, and also, in general, only takes place slowly and with resistance. However, the health of the mind can only continue so long as this is in each case properly carried out.[4] [pp. 168f.].

AN ILLUSTRATION OF REPRESSION IN FREUD'S OWN LIFE. Concerning Schopenhauer's influence on Freud, Nancy Procter-Gregg has commented, "No one was more conscious than he [Freud] of the fact of unconscious assimilation of ideas from other men's writings, even if one has forgotten them; but in his autobiographical study, he had denied his acquaintance with these ideas of Schopenhauer until late in life . . ." "Schopenhauer and Freud," *Psychoanal. Quart.*, 1956, 25, 197. As a matter of fact, Freud (1914) disclaimed the influence of any predecessor or contemporary in formulating his ideas about repression. He asserted, "The doctrine of repression quite certainly came to me independently of any other source; I know of no outside impression which might have suggested it to me . . ." (p. 297).

Freud's Discovery of Repression

FREUD'S PREPARATION FOR THE STUDY OF PSYCHOPATHOLOGY. Sigmund Freud, born in 1856, was thirty when, after a not undistinguished career in the field of neuro-anatomy, he turned his attention for the first time to problems of psychiatry and more specifically to the study of hysteria. In preparation for his new career he had spent the months from the autumn of 1885 to the spring of 1886 in Paris observing Jean Martin Charcot, the father of modern neurology, in his clinic at La Salpêtrière. During the period of Freud's visit, Charcot was absorbed in his investigations of hysteria and hypnosis.

Later, in 1889, Freud journeyed to Nancy, France, to study the hypnotic therapeutic techniques first developed by a pharmacist, A. A. Liébault, and later extended in collaboration with Hippolyte Bernheim, a psychiatrist on the faculty of the medical school.

Freud was well acquainted with the major findings and principal tenets of both the Paris (Charcot and Janet) and Nancy (Bernheim and Liébault) schools of psychiatry, for he translated the major writings of both Charcot and Bernheim into German. Yet, when he turned his own energies to the study of hysteria, he did not follow the therapeutic practices of either Charcot or Bernheim.

FREUD'S COLLABORATION WITH BREUER. Freud's first investigations in psychopathology were undertaken in collaboration with Dr.

---

[4] From Arthur Schopenhauer, *The World as Will and Idea*, Vol. III, 1819. Translated by R. B. Haldane and J. Kemp, and used by permission of Routledge and Kegan Paul, Ltd., London.

Joseph Breuer, a Viennese practicing physician and friend of long standing. Several years prior to their joint study, Breuer in 1880 had begun to experiment with a new form of psychotherapy in his treatment of hysterical patients. It consisted of hypnotizing the patient and instructing her to recall while still in the hypnotic trance any experiences which had been intimately associated with the appearance of her symptoms. He soon discovered that his hypnotized patients would recall experiences —usually of a highly emotional and traumatic character—which they had apparently completely forgotten in the waking state. More than this, Breuer discovered that following the recall of such forgotten memories and the expression of their accompanying emotion, patients upon waking from hypnosis were cured of their symptoms.

Two Conditions under Which Repression Occurs

In their first and joint report on their researches, Breuer and Freud distinguished two groups of conditions under which the affect stirred by traumatic experience is not directly expressed, but instead at some later date finds indirect expression in the symptoms of hysteria.

TRAUMATIC EXPERIENCES.   The first group consists of "those cases in which the patient has not reacted to the psychical trauma because its nature excluded the possibility of any such reaction, as in the case of the apparently irretrievable loss of a loved person, or when social conditions made a reaction impossible, or when *the trauma concerned something which the patient wished to forget and therefore deliberately repressed* [5] *and excluded from his conscious thoughts."* [6]

HYPNOID STATES.   The second group of conditions was characterized not so much by the painful nature of the forgotten experience and the social taboo upon its expression as by the mental condition of the patient at the time the experience occurred, for example, "the half-hypnotic twilight state of daydreaming, auto-hypnosis, and the like" (p. 33).

Both groups of conditions, however, had one thing in common according to Breuer and Freud, namely,

that the psychical traumas which are not resolved by reaction will also fail of solution by means of associative absorption. [7] In the first group

[5] This is the first appearance of this term in Freud's writings.

[6] The italics are the present authors'. The excerpt is from Josef Breuer and Sigmund Freud, "On the Psychical Mechanism of Hysterical Phenomena." Translated in 1893, pp. 32f., *Collected Papers*, Vol. 1. Copyright 1924 by Hogarth Press, Ltd., London.

[7] "Associative absorption" was the term used by Breuer and Freud to refer to the working over or modifying in a normal state of consciousness of an experience or idea

the patient's intention to do so causes him to forget the painful expe-
riences and consequently to exclude them from association as far as
possible.[8] In the second group the associative absorption does not succeed because sufficient associative connection does not exist between
the normal state of consciousness and the pathological state in which
these ideas originally arose.

Thus it may be said that the ideas which have become pathogenic
are preserved with such freshness and affective force because the normal process of absorption by abreaction and by reproduction in a state
of unrestrained association is denied them [pp. 33f.].

Theoretical Differences between Freud and Breuer

Breuer and Freud did not long remain collaborators, and indeed
the seeds of their theoretical disagreements can be readily discerned in
the excerpts from their first joint paper quoted above. Later Freud
(1914) wrote of this:

> The first difference between Breuer and myself came to light in
> regard to a question concerning the finer psychical mechanism of hys-
> teria. He gave preference to a theory which was still to some extent
> physiological, as one might call it; he wished to explain the mental dis-
> sociation of hysteria by the absence of communication between vari-
> ous psychical states (states of consciousness, as we called them at that
> time), and he therefore constructed the theory of "hypnoid" states,
> the effects of which were supposed to penetrate into waking conscious-
> ness like unassimilated foreign bodies. I had taken the matter less aca-
> demically; everywhere I seemed to discern motives and tendencies
> analogous to those of everyday life, and I looked upon mental dissocia-
> tion itself as an effect of a process of rejection which at that time I
> called *defence*, and later called *repression*. I made a short-lived at-
> tempt to allow the two mechanisms a separate existence side by side,
> but as observation showed me always and only one thing, it was not
> long before my "defence" doctrine took up its stand opposite his "hyp-
> noid" theory.[9]

THE PARIS SCHOOL OF PSYCHIATRY

Dissociation Theory: Charcot and Janet

Breuer's hypnoid theory was in many respects like the etiological
theory of Charcot elaborated and extended by Pierre Janet, Charcot's co-

---

through the establishment of associative connections between it and other experiences
and ideas, in other words, the opposite of dissociation of experience and ideas.

[8] The italics are the present authors'.

[9] From Sigmund Freud, *On the History of the Psycho-analytic Movement*, 1914,
pp. 291f. Translated in *Collected Papers*, Vol. III. Copyright 1925 by Hogarth
Press, Ltd., London.

worker at La Salpêtrière. According to this view certain traumatic ideas become dissociated from the consciousness of the patient but, despite the fact that they are forgotten, continue to exert an influence and specifically determine the nature of the hysterical symptoms which subsequently develop.

But it was clear to Charcot, as it was also obvious later to Janet, that the ideas aroused in traumatic circumstances were not always dissociated. The question which they had to face and seek to answer was this: What is the factor which, when present, brings about the forgetting or dissociation of the traumatic experience, and in the absence of which traumatic episodes will be retained in consciousness?

Charcot, the neurologist, assumed, though he could not demonstrate it, that the factor which made dissociation possible and resulted in the appearance of hysterical symptoms was an hereditary organic deficiency or degeneration of the brain.

Janet, the psychologist, offered a somewhat different type of explanation, and yet one conceptually allied to Charcot's notion of deficiency or degeneration in brain function and also to Breuer's notion of hypnoid states.

Influenced in his thinking by the sensationism and elementalism of the French psychology of the 1890's, Janet assumed the building blocks of consciousness to be simple sensations, images, and ideas. Normal, integrated mental life he thought of as a flux of sensory, imaginal, and ideational elements cohering in a complex but single stream of consciousness. Abnormal mental life was the result of a dissociation or splitting of the stream of consciousness into two or more smaller streams.

Starting in his psychological systematic thinking with elements of mind, Janet was forced to assume the existence of some force or energy to synthesize and unify the mental elements which, if it existed in sufficient quantity, would result in a single consciousness, but which, if deficient, would result in a splitting of consciousness. A poverty of psychic energy (la misère psychologique) was, for Janet, the cause of anaesthesia and amnesia, the dissociation from consciousness of traumatic events.

Freud's Theory of Repression vs. Janet's Theory of Dissociation

Concerning the difference between Janet's conception of dissociation resulting from an insufficiency of psychic energy and his own notion of repression in the service of defense, Freud (1910) was later to write:

We can see now the difference between our theory and that of Janet. We do not derive the psychic fission from a congenital lack of capacity on the part of the mental apparatus to synthesize its experiences, but we explain it dynamically by the conflict of opposing mental forces, we recognize in it the result of an active striving of each mental complex against the other.[1]

DEVELOPMENT OF THE CONCEPT OF REPRESSION

Repression First Described as a Deliberate, Intended Act

In his early discussions of repression, Freud frequently described it as a conscious and intentional process. We have already seen that in the first use of the term Breuer and Freud (1893) wrote of "something which the patient wished to forget and therefore deliberately repressed and excluded from his conscious thought . . ." (pp. 32f.). Later Freud (Breuer and Freud, 1895) stated that "in the process of hysterical development, one psychic determinant is indispensable; namely, that some idea must *intentionally be repressed from consciousness* [2] and excluded from associative elaboration."

> In this intentional repression I also find the reason for the conversion of the sum of excitement, be it partial or total. The sum of excitement which is not to enter into psychic association more readily finds the wrong road to bodily innervation. The reason for the repression itself could only be a disagreeable feeling, the incompatibility of one of the repressible ideas with the ruling ideational-mass of the ego.
>
> Accordingly, the real traumatic moment [for the development of an hysterical symptom] is that in which the conflict thrusts itself upon the ego and the latter decides to banish the incompatible idea. Such banishment does not annihilate the opposing idea, but merely crowds it into the unconscious. When this process occurs for the first time, it forms a nucleus, or a point of crystallization for the formation of a new psychic group separated from the ego, around which, in the course of time, everything collects which is in accord with the opposing idea. *The splitting of consciousness in such cases of acquired hysteria is thus desired and intentional, and is often initiated by at least one arbitrary act.*[3] But as a matter of fact, something different happens than the individual expects, he would like to eliminate an idea as though it never came to pass, but he only succeeds in isolating it psychically.[4]

[1] From Sigmund Freud, "The Origin and Development of Psychoanalysis," *Amer. J. Psychol.*, 1910, 21, 194. Used by permission.

[2] The italics are Freud's.

[3] The italics are the present authors'.

[4] From J. Breuer and S. Freud, *Studies in Hysteria*, 1895 (translated). *Ner. ment. Dis. Monogr.*, New York, 1937, No. 61, pp. 83 and 88. This and the following excerpt are used by permission of Williams and Wilkins Company, Baltimore, Maryland.

Repression as a Form of Resistance

Freud (Breuer and Freud, 1895) has recorded for us a description of how in his early attempts at therapy he came to conceptualize the process of repression.

> *Through my psychic work I had to overcome a psychic force in the patient which opposed the pathogenic idea from becoming conscious (remembered).*[5] A new insight seemed to have revealed itself to me when it occurred to me that this must really be the same psychic force which assisted in the origin of the hysterical symptom, and which at that time prevented the pathogenic idea from becoming conscious. What kind of force could here be assumed as effective; and what motive could have brought it into activity? I could easily formulate an opinion, for I already had some complete analyses at my disposal, in which I found examples of pathogenic, forgotten, and repressed ideas. From these I could judge the general character of such ideas. They were altogether of a painful nature adapted to provoke the affects of shame, of reproach, of psychic pain, or the feeling of injury; they were altogether of that kind which one would not have liked to experience and preferred to forget. From all these there resulted the thought of defense, as if spontaneously. . . . An idea entered into the patient's ego which proved to be unbearable and evoked a force of repulsion on the part of the ego, the object of which was a *defense* against the unbearable idea. This defense actually succeeded, and the idea concerned was crowded out of consciousness and out of memory, so that its psychic trace could not apparently be found; yet, this trace must have existed. When I made the effort to direct attention to it, I felt the same force as a *resistance* which showed itself as a *repulsion* in the genesis of the symptom [p. 201].

Freud made much of the point that he was first led to conceive of a process of repression as a result of his experience of the resistance of his patients to the recall of painful memories. He asserted, "If anyone should seek to regard the theory of repression and of resistance as assumptions instead of as results following from psychoanalysis, I should oppose him most emphatically . . . the doctrine of repression is the outcome of psycho-analytic work, a theoretic inference legitimately drawn from innumerable observations" (1914, pp. 298f.).

Reaction of American Psychologists to the Theory of Psychoanalysis

Freud's visit to the United States and the publication in the *American Journal of Psychology* (1910) of his lectures on "The Origin and

---

[5] The italics are Freud's.

Development of Psychoanalysis," which he had given at Clark University in the preceding year, provoked among American psychologists a lively interest in psychoanalysis but no appreciable change in their theorizing or research.

This was not, however, the first time that the work of Freud was called to the attention of American psychologists. In the first volume of the *Psychological Review* William James (1894) reviewed, in addition to two books by Janet, the article by Breuer and Freud, "On the Psychical Mechanism of Hysterical Phenomena," and reported that he had found in the latter "an independent corroboration [sic] of Janet's views" (p. 199).

Some of the misunderstanding of and ambivalent attitude toward psychoanalysis on the part of American psychologists in the years which have intervened were expressed by James after hearing Freud lecture at Clark.

Ernest Jones who had accompanied Freud to Clark, has reported that "William James, who knew German well, followed the lectures with great interest. He was very friendly to us and I shall never forget his parting words, said with his arm around my shoulder: 'The future of psychology belongs to your work' " (*The Life and Work of Sigmund Freud*, Vol. 2, 1955, p. 57).

But in a letter written to Mary Whiton Calkins dated September 19, 1909, James wrote, "I strongly suspect Freud, with his dream-theory, of being a regular *hallucine*. But I hope that he and his disciples will push it to its limits, as undoubtedly it covers some facts, and will add to our understanding of 'functional' psychology, which is the real psychology." (From R. B. Perry, *The Thought and Character of William James*, 1948, p. 199.)

Freud and his disciples did "push it," but for the next twenty years (1909–29) psychoanalysis had little influence upon American psychology.[6] During this period there were frequent references to the work of Freud and his associates, but it was all seen as quite foreign to psychology—its relevance to psychiatry rather than to psychology being emphasized—and especially foreign to American psychology, which during this period was in all ways attempting to model itself after the physical sciences. It was elemental and reductive—seeking a satisfactory explanation of psychological phenomena in physiological terms. In contrast,

---

[6] William James was one of the first of American psychologists to consider seriously the claims of psychoanalysis and to discuss the work of Freud in his lectures at Harvard. For doing so, however, he was severely cirticized by Lightner Witmer, professor of psychology at the University of Pennsylvania and a pioneer in developing American clinical psychology, who in the April, 1909, issue of *Current Literature* published an article entitled, "Is the Psychology Taught at Harvard a National Peril?"

Freud had already in the 1890's become more psychological than most American psychologists were willing to be. Where they continued to have faith in the ultimate possibility of physiological explanation of psychological phenomena, Freud believed that, at least in his day, the physiological explanations that were offered were not only labored and unconfirmed but, even more seriously, a hindrance to real insight.

Psychoanalysis in American Psychological Journals

To one acquainted with the present-day character of American psychological journals, it comes as something of a shock to realize that from 1910 through the 1920's the *American Journal of Psychology* carried frequent reviews of psychoanalytic works and articles bearing such titles as "Luther's Early Development in the Light of Psychoanalysis" (Smith, 1913), "Psychoanalytic Studies of Genius" (Dooley, 1916), "A Psychoanalytic Study of Auguste Comte" (Blanchard, 1918), "Psychoanalysis of Charlotte Brontë, as a Type of the Woman of Genius" (Dooley, 1920), "A Psychoanalytic Study of Edgar Allan Poe" (Pruette, 1920), etc.[7]

But if articles of this type appeared in the pages of the *American Journal of Psychology*, they existed there more as dissociated hysterical symptoms than as ego-syntonic expressions of the *Journal's* character. One would judge that the attitude toward these psychoanalytic papers of the other contributors to the *Journal* was, like that of a hysteric toward her symptoms, one of "la belle indifference," to use Janet's phrase.

During these same years in the *Journal of Abnormal Psychology* a quite different attitude was manifest. Its pages were also open to reviews of psychoanalytic literature and to expositions of psychoanalytic theory by orthodox psychoanalysts. Indeed, from 1910 to 1921 Ernest Jones was assistant editor of the *Journal*, but almost from the beginning articles published in its pages were critical of psychoanalytic theory. Freud's ideas, though not acceptable, were at least taken seriously by contributors to this *Journal*. In 1912–13, F. L. Wells published a caustic review of psychoanalytic theory under the title, "Critique of Impure Reason." In 1914–15 Janet's articles on "Psychoanalysis" were not only critical but unfair, and provoked a heated reply from Ernest Jones (1914–15). R. S. Woodworth's "Some Criticisms of the Freudian Psychology" (1917–18) were answered by the analyst S. A. Tannenbaum (1917–18). George Humphrey contributed three articles which showed both an interest in and a critical attitude toward psychoanalysis: "The Conditioned Reflex

[7] The openness of the *American Journal of Psychology* to reviews of psychoanalytic literature and to psychoanalytic studies reflected the openness to new ideas of the mind of its editor and owner from 1887 to 1920, G. Stanley Hall, who, as President of Clark University, had invited Freud to speak there in 1909.

and the Freudian Wish" (1919–20), "Education and Freudianism" (1920–1), and "The Child's Unconscious Mind" (1920–1).

It should be noted, however, that these articles in the *Journal of Abnormal Psychology*, like those in the *American Journal of Psychology*, were armchair exercises in which the writers either sought to apply rather uncritically the concepts of psychoanalysis to biographical studies or undertook to examine critically the nature of psychoanalytic concepts and the logical structure of psychoanalysis as a system of psychology. As recently as the late 1920's it had seldom occurred to academic psychologists that the theories of psychoanalysis could, like other theories of psychology, be put to experimental test in the laboratory.

DEVELOPMENT OF AN EXPERIMENTAL PSYCHODYNAMICS

ACADEMIC EXPERIMENTAL PSYCHOLOGISTS had developed techniques for the study of sensory, perceptual, affective, imaginal, and cognitive processes and for the investigation of the simpler forms of learning and motor response, but they had no methods for the study of the more complex emotive and motivating aspects of human behavior. Already in the 1890's psychology had developed an experimental psychophysics, but as late as the 1920's it had not developed an experimental psychodynamics.

A Search for Experimental Studies with Implications for Repression

When psychologists began at last to consider seriously the possibility of submitting some of the assertions of the psychoanalysts to experimental test, they did not immediately undertake to develop new techniques expressly designed for that purpose. Instead, they searched the psychological literature to see if by chance some experiments undertaken to test other theoretical assertions might not incidentally throw light on the validity of one or another of the psychoanalytic concepts.

One of the first to make such a survey was Meltzer (1930), who reviewed the experimental literature on the relationships between feeling and memory in an attempt to discover the bearing of already established laboratory findings on that aspect of the theory of repression which posits a relationship between hedonic tone and conscious memory. Since Freud had emphasized that the purpose of repression is to avoid "unpleasure," it was easy for one not thoroughly versed in psychoanalytic writing to interpret "unpleasure" (by which Freud intended deeprooted anxiety) to mean "unpleasant" as it characterizes simple segments of the conscious experience. The studies reviewed by Meltzer were of two kinds. There were laboratory experiments in which subjects were presented with stimuli (odors, colored squares, lists of words, etc.) which, it was presumed, would evoke affective experiences. Stimuli of this nature, or the experiences of them, were categorized as "Pleasant" (P), "Indifferent" (I), or "Unpleasant" (U), either by the experimenter on an *a priori* basis, or by the subject when confronted with them. Following exposure to sets of such stimuli varying in hedonic tone, subjects attempted to recall the stimuli or symbols (numbers, nonsense syllables, words) which had been associated with them. Differences in the recall of pleasant and unpleasant items were the crucial data. In addition, there were surveys of the relative predominance of pleasant or unpleasant memories for childhood or recent events. Sixteen of the twenty-six studies reviewed by Meltzer reported a favoring of P experiences in memory, nine reported a favoring of U experiences, with indeterminate results being reported in one investigation.

Meltzer, along with other psychologists, called attention to various shortcomings in these studies—e.g., insufficient controls, small number of subjects, lack of representative sampling of stimulus situations, etc. He also recognized that most of the investigations which he reviewed had not been designed specifically to test the Freudian theory of repression. Instead, they had had their roots in the theorizing of introspectionists concerning the relation of hedonic tone to memory and in the implications of Thorndike's law of effect.

Meltzer attributed the conflicting and equivocal findings of previous studies to the fact that they had been designed to establish general laws concerning the relation of hedonic tone to memory instead of measuring individual differences in forgetting pleasant and unpleasant experiences.

Individual Differences vs. General Laws

Rosenzweig and Mason (1934) objected to Meltzer's opposing the operation of general laws to the operation of individual differences, arguing that individual differences will always be found, "but if such differences are construed in terms of the degree to which required general conditions are being satisfied, they in no way conflict with the operation of universal laws" (p. 248).

Requirements for a Test of the Repression Hypothesis

The real shortcomings of the studies reviewed by Meltzer, in so far as they might be considered to bear upon the theory of repression, were, Rosenzweig and Mason argued, two: (1) they worked with hedonic tone associated with sensory stimuli unrelated to the theory of repression rather than with conative hedonic tone associated with frustrated striving, which is the only kind of "unpleasantness" which, according to the Freudian theory, leads to repression, and (2) they "failed to develop under laboratory control the experiences which are subsequently to be tested for recall" (p. 248).

CONATIVE VS. SENSORY HEDONIC TONE. Concerning the first of these points, Rosenzweig and Mason wrote:

> Whether or not there is an ultimate difference between conative and non-conative hedonic tone, there is certainly such a difference on the phenomenal level. The pleasantness or unpleasantness associated, for example, with sensory stimulation is not the same as the hedonic tone associated with conative activity, striving to succeed. In non-conative hedonic tone the state of the total organism is less fully involved than in conative hedonic tone. There is also a difference in psychological direction of reference. Sensory pleasures and pains seem to be due to outside stimulation and not to be directly related to the individual's sense of responsibility. But conative hedonic tone derives from the success or failure of a subjective purpose and is thus more closely connected with the individual's self-esteem.
>
> If, with this distinction in mind, we turn to the Freudian theory of repression, we find that it is the *conative* type of hedonic tone which is supposed to be significantly related to memory. More specifically, repression is supposed to operate for *negative* (unpleasant) hedonic tone of the conative type and, more specifically still, for such negative hedonic tone as results when a need is frustrated because of *conflict with the individual's desire to preserve his self-respect* (super-ego). These conditions, it need scarcely be said, must be satisfied by any experiment that is to be regarded as a test of the theory of repression.[8]

LABORATORY-INDUCED EXPERIENCES. The second condition for an adequate test of the theory of repression, the developing under laboratory control of the experiences which were subsequently to be tested for recall, was met by Rosenzweig and Mason through application of an experimental technique, first developed by Zeigarnik (1927) in the laboratory of the Psychological Institute at the University of Berlin under the direction of Kurt Lewin.

Zeigarnik's Unintentional Study of Repression

Zeigarnik's (1927) experiment was the first in which, according to her claims, the essential dynamics of repression were reproduced in the laboratory, though admittedly unintentionally and not by design.

[8] From S. Rosenzweig and G. Mason, "An Experimental Study of Memory in Relation to the Theory of Repression," *Brit. J. Psychol.*, 1934, 24, 248. Used by permission of the *British Journal of Psychology*.

In this study Zeigarnik presented her subjects with a series of twenty simple tasks, such as punching holes in a sheet of paper, naming twelve cities beginning with K, putting together a jigsaw puzzle, etc. She permitted the subjects to finish half of the tasks, but interrupted them in the doing of the others. Each task, whether completed or interrupted, was immediately put away out of sight.

As soon as the series was over, each subject was asked to recall the tasks upon which he had worked. The general finding, now known as the *Zeigarnik effect*, was that the majority of the subjects (about 80 per cent) recalled more interrupted tasks than completed ones, presumably, so Zeigarnik argued, because the tension systems corresponding to completed tasks were discharged upon their completion, while the tension systems corresponding to the interrupted tasks were not discharged, and, persisting, constituted the basis for the greater recall of uncompleted tasks.

This was the general finding, but Zeigarnik (1927) also reported that there were several conditions under which uncompleted tasks were not favored in recall. One of these exceptions she labeled "repressed tasks," and wrote about them as follows.

> It often happened that a subject would be given a task which he "could not do." He felt that the task was *beyond his capacity*. The subject thought that he was being awkward and unintelligent, and was embarrassed to show his lack of intelligence before the experimenter. In short, he experienced a "feeling of inferiority." Should this task be interrupted, such a subject frequently assumed that the experimenter had detected his inferiority. The problems which in this sense could not be done, were at the time of recall extremely often forgotten. (Out of 40 problems only 13 were remembered, or 32% instead of the average recall of 68%.) [9]

Nebenhandlungen: The Technique of Incidental Tasks

Zeigarnik's research was a methodological milestone in the study of repression, for it seemed to demonstrate for the first time a feasible, inexpensive, easily administered technique for the investigation of motivated remembering and forgetting and, as Zeigarnik suggested, repression.

The technique was that of the *Nebenhandlungen*, or incidental tasks. It consisted of presenting tasks or problems, the solution of which the subject perceived as the principal objective of the experiment, while, from the standpoint of the experimenter, the real purpose of the experiment was something else, and something experienced by the subject as

---

[9] From Bluma Zeigarnik, "Uber das Behalten von erledigten und unerledigten Handlungen," *Psychol. Forsch.*, 1927, 9, 77. Used by permission of the publisher.

rather incidental and unimportant, which in Zeigarnik's experiment, was the attempt to recall the tasks which had been done.

Lewin's Contribution to Experimental Psychodynamics

Zeigarnik's experiment and her employment of the *Nebenhandlungen* technique were, however, only a specific manifestation of a new theoretical and methodological position which in the late 1920's was being formulated by Kurt Lewin. The contribution of Lewin in changing the climate of opinion about the possibility of investigating experimentally the unconscious as well as the conscious psychodynamics of behavior can hardly be overestimated.

It was in his monograph, "Die Entwicklung der experimentellen Willenpsychologie und die Psychotherapie," that Lewin (1929) most clearly expressed his confidence in, and demonstrated the possibility of, an *experimental psychodynamics* which his researches and those of his students subsequently established. There he sought to answer the then generally held prejudices against the possibility of studying experimentally the emotive and motivating processes involved in complex human behavior.

QUALITATIVE SIMILARITIES BETWEEN EXPERIMENTAL AND NORMAL BEHAVIOR. In response to the criticism that behavior observed in the laboratory is atypical because the subject, realizing that he is participating in an experiment, behaves differently from the way he would normally, Lewin noted:

1. One can so arrange the experiment that the subject, during the actual course of the experiment, is completely unaware of the fact that he is the subject: one pretends that another task is the experiment, then leaves the subject during the actual experiment and secretly observes him from another room. In the case of such task-free experiments the subject is influenced only by those forces in the situation and those factors which are also determinative of his behavior "in life." 2. . . . if one makes use of elaborate arrangements or even creates situations with strong forces, as theoretical requirements also demand shall be the case, then only a very small percentage of experimental subjects will act as though they feel themselves to be experimental subjects. Others very soon get involved in the situation and accordingly become free and natural.[1]

QUANTITATIVE SIMILARITIES BETWEEN EXPERIMENTAL AND NORMAL BEHAVIOR. Countering the objection that motivational and emo-

[1] From Kurt Lewin, *Die Entwicklung der experimentellen Willenspsychologie und die Psychotherapie*, 1929, pp. 4f., S. Hirzel, Leipzig, Germany. This and three following excerpts are used by permission of the publisher.

tional processes engendered in the laboratory are too weak and superficial to be compared with such processes in everyday life, Lewin reminded his readers that:

> One must not forget, however, that the subject still reacts to the experimental task as a *whole person* and that it is therefore completely possible through a carefully planned structuring of the situation to stir the deep levels of the person. Moreover, it is a much too microscopic understanding of behavior in the experimental situation to see it as completely dissociated from the subject's life. Behind the decision of the person "to become an experimental subject" lie for the most part very real and often very deep life forces: the ambition to pit oneself against others; the "idea of science"; the particular personage of the experimenter or of the instructor by whom the experiment will be conducted, etc. [p. 5].

EXPERIMENTATION DOES NOT REQUIRE EXACT REPLICATION OF NATURAL EVENTS.

> The emphasizing of the question of intensity reveals a misunderstanding of the *nature of experimentation.* Just as little as the establishment of the law of gravity is dependent upon the study of volcanic eruptions or of bricks blown from a roof by the wind, and just as little as the laws of hydrostatics and hydrodynamics are discovered in the observation of brooks and rivers, just so little is it necessary or even scientifically meaningful to investigate in a psychological experiment a complete replication of reality. The closeness to reality which makes an experiment a useful one from both a theoretical and a practical standpoint does not require that the same absolute intensities be realized—although particularly in psychology the transition from quantitative differences to qualitative differences is especially important— but rather that in the experiment just those dynamic properties of the system whose laws are to be investigated shall be produced [pp. 5f.].

THE CLOSENESS OF NORMAL AND ABNORMAL.   Finally, he mentioned the close relationship between normal and pathological processes.

> According to Goldstein, in the case of pathological processes it is a matter of processes which are governed by the same laws which determine normal processes, only in their case other psychophysical constellations are present and consequently other external phenomena appear. A similar relationship exists within the realm of the normal between the unusual, seldom occurring, especially intense psychological events and the usual events of everyday life [p. 6].

THE "HOMOGENIZATION" OF PSYCHOLOGY.   Lewin was interested in psychoanalytic theory and believed in the possibility of developing a rapprochement between experimental psychology and psychoanalysis, in other words, in the possibility of establishing a truly experimental psychodynamics. He thought that Freud's attitude toward the whole domain of human behavior, like his own, provided the ground upon which an all-inclusive experimental dynamic psychology could be built. In 1935 Lewin wrote:

> Freud's doctrine especially—and this is one of its greatest services— has contributed largely to the abolition of the boundary between the normal and the pathological, the ordinary and the unusual, and thereby furthered the *homogenization* of all the fields of psychology. This process is certainly still far from complete, but it is entirely comparable to that introduced in modern physics by which heavenly and earthly processes were united.[2]

To academic psychologists eager to undertake experimental analyses of psychoanalytic phenomena, Lewin's statements about scientific method became a sort of Declaration of Independence or Bill of Rights, for they proclaimed that the domain of human motivation is not the exclusive property of the clinician and the literary characterologist. Two cardinal points, one already adumbrated in the remarks just quoted, were further developed in his discussion of modes of thought in psychology (Lewin, 1931).

HISTORICAL-GENETIC VS. AHISTORICAL SYSTEMATIC QUESTIONS. The first of these stressed the necessity for distinguishing between two kinds of questions which can be asked in science: historical-genetic questions about origins of phenomena vs. ahistorical or systematic questions about the contemporaneous forces in the life space of a person which determine his behavior here and now.

With respect to the experimental study of repression, this meant for the experimental psychologist that he would not have to discover in the life history of his subjects those events which had led up to whatever repressions might now be operative in them. It would, psychologists began to argue, be sufficient to see to it that in the experimental situation the subject be made to have certain experiences, some of which would be ego-wounding and thus susceptible to repression, and others of which would be ego-enhancing and presumably not subject to repression.

Such experimental manipulation of experience here and now in the labooratory would spare the researcher the necessity of undertaking from the free associations and the verbal reports of subjects questionable reconstructions of their life histories and guesses as to what repressions had occurred earlier in their lives.

[2] By permission from *A Dynamic Theory of Personality* by K. Lewin. Copyright, 1935. McGraw-Hill Book Co., Inc., p. 22.

THE STUDY OF QUASI-NEEDS.   The second point made by Lewin was his claim that in order to study the dynamics of human motivation it was not necessary to produce real dangers to an individual or arouse his basic needs. It was sufficient, he argued, to arouse quasi-needs or intentions and study their dynamics, for their dynamics would be also the dynamics of real needs. Lewin argued that there are only quantitative differences between quasi-needs and true needs, thus making it possible to base the study of human motivation exclusively upon investigations of behavior determined by quasi-needs.

It was with such liberating methodological and theoretical ideas coming to clear expression for the first time that several younger American psychologists were emboldened to believe that an effective rapprochement between experimental psychology, with its emphasis upon the control and manipulation of variables in the laboratory, and psychoanalysis, with its concern with some of the most vital problems of human personality, was at last possible.[3]

Psychology and Psychoanalysis in the 1930's

The situation which then existed in psychology and the challenge which it offered was later vividly described by J. F. Brown (1937):

> The academic psychologist who has really studied psychoanalytical theory . . . is apt to be overwhelmed by the systematic complexity of the theory and by the importance of the problems with which psychoanalysts are concerned. . . . He must in honesty admit that his own particular school neither answers nor even poses questions of such wide systematic implication nor of such vital interest. . . . Psychoanalytical theory deals with *psychological* problems, it deals with *nearly all* psychological problems, and the problems basic to it are *vital*.
>
> The academic psychologist, however, has some advantages which psychoanalysts lack. He has been trained in the logic of science and in the experimental method. As a logician and an experimentalist, he feels, and rightly so, that many aspects of psychoanalytical theory are in need of conceptual clarification and of a somewhat more rigorous type of proof. He has been trained to accept as scientific those statements concerning experience to which competent observers give universal assent. And although he does not consider himself competent to gather the data which psychoanalysts use in making their theories, he does consider himself competent to criticize the manner in which these theories are built. He further considers himself right in demanding

[3] The role of Henry A. Murray and the Psychological Clinic of Harvard University in fostering this new movement was a vitally determining one. For the contribution of the Harvard group to experimental psychodynamics, see Murray *et al.* (1938).

from psychoanalysis that type of experimental criticism which is essential to the healthy growth of any science.[4]

Need for Clearer Grasp of Psychoanalytic Theory

With the raising of their experimental aspirations, psychologists, who would study repression in the laboratory, faced the necessity of becoming clear about the details of the psychoanalytic formulation of repression if their researches were to be adequate tests of the theory. They soon discovered, however, that to grasp clearly even a single psychoanalytic concept was an almost insurmountable task.[5] The difficulty lay in the fact that over the years Freud had repeatedly modified his theory without ever stating clearly just which of his earlier formulations were to be completely discarded, or if not discarded, how they were to be understood in the light of his more recent assertions.

Repression, Suppression, and Defense

The history of the three closely related if not synonymous terms, "repression," "suppression," and "defense," serves to illustrate the point. As was clearly revealed in the quotations from Freud's writing given in the early part of this chapter, Freud first used the terms "repression" and "suppression" to refer to a single mechanism of defense which was, however, sometimes described as though it were a quite conscious and intentional process and sometimes as a process which occurred outside of conscious awareness and control. In the course of time the term "suppression" disappeared almost entirely from Freud's writing, and increasingly his use of the term "repression" implied that the process was not a conscious, voluntary one but rather one which went on without any conscious awareness of it.

Here, as so often, when Freud was rather unclear about his concepts, or the relations among them, his collaborators sought to introduce clarity into the system. In the present instance, psychoanalysts came increasingly to restrict the term "repression" to the unconscious denial of entry into consciousness or the unconscious extrusion from consciousness of ideational representatives or associates of instinctual impulses which, if

[4] From J. F. Brown, "Psychoanalysis, Topological Psychology and Experimental Psychopathology," *Psychoanal. Quart.*, 1937, 6, 227–8. Used by permission.

[5] In his conscientious and sympathetic attempt to clarify *the* meaning of repression in Freud's writing, Madison (1956) finds at least *four* different meanings and comments that "after looking closely at the sprawling character of the repression idea, I am inclined to think that theorists have left it alone because they could not see it clearly enough to try to sharpen or develop it" (p. 76). For another attempt to trace the changing meaning of repression in Freud's treatment of the concept, see Brenner (1957).

fully recognized, would arouse anxiety. Suppression, on the other hand, came to designate this same process when it was carried out with conscious awareness.

DISTINCTION BETWEEN SUPPRESSION AND REPRESSION.   One of the clearest expositions of the distinction between repression and suppression and of the underlying dynamics of the two processes was given by Alexander (1932):

> In the exclusion from consciousness of certain tendencies there is, in addition to unconscious repression, a conscious and voluntary selective process called "suppression," which eliminates from the focus of interest everything which is even loosely connected with unconscious material [p. 113].
>
> Repression, however, is a function which excludes certain tendencies from becoming conscious. It only occurs in cases in which the mere existence of a wish, irrespective of its realization, would cause an unbearable conscious conflict. . . . Repression, in contrast to conscious rejection, is a process of inhibition which arises on a deeper level of personality—somewhere on the borderline between id and ego —and saves the conscious personality from becoming aware of a painful conflict.
>
> It is obvious that such an unconscious inhibiting process presupposes a kind of unconscious inner perception which leads to automatic, almost reflex inhibitions, similar to a conditioned reflex. This unconscious censoring function we ascribe to the super-ego. Repression is consequently based on a kind of unconscious censorship which reacts automatically to unacceptable tendencies. Although this process appears to us as a kind of unconscious selective judgment, which excludes certain definite tendencies from consciousness, nevertheless we have to assume that it operates schematically, is incapable of subtle differentiation and reacts uniformly to certain emotional factors in spite of their actual and sometimes important differences. It is comparable with a conditioned reflex rather than with a deliberate judgment.[6]

REPRESSION AND DEFENSE.   As for the changes in meaning of the concepts of repression and defense, it may be noted that in the beginning Freud wrote about defense. Reflecting upon his early works in collaboration with Breuer he wrote (1914) that "everywhere I seemed to discern motives and tendencies analogous to those of everyday life, and I looked upon mental dissociation itself as an effect of a process of rejection which at that time I called *defense*, and later called *repression*" (p. 292).

[6] From Franz Alexander, *The Medical Value of Psychoanalysis*, pp. 101–3, copyright 1932 by W. W. Norton and Co., Inc., and used by their permission.

After several years of using repression as synonymous with defense, i.e., after several years of writing about repression as the defense mechanism, Freud began to imply that repression is not the only mechanism of defense but rather one of several. By 1926 this was being explicitly stated, though the fullest and clearest relegation of repression to a position of one among many mechanisms came in Anna Freud's book, *The Ego and Mechanisms of Defence*, first published in German in 1936. Increasingly after the publication of this most influential book psychoanalysts focused their attention upon the problem of defense in all its myriad forms. Repression as a specific mechanism of defense received much less attention from this time on.

Commenting upon the change in meaning of the term "defense" in psychoanalytic thought and writing Gerö (1951) has noted that:

> The term *Abwehr*, or defense, was used first in *The Defense Neuropsychoses* . . . it was characterized as an intentional process or wish to forget (*vergessen wollen*). . . .
>
> To-day, the concept of defense is extremely complex. It refers to a set of unconscious activities of the ego which partake of all the puzzling qualities of unconscious processes, and which occur without any intentional effort. . . .
>
> Defense . . . in the main . . . is seen during the process of analysis. In this context, defense is defined as all those processes which operate toward maintaining a neurotic equilibrium, whether by opposition to an instinctual drive, by counteracting anxiety, or by avoidance of painful emotion.[7]

Summarizing these shifting trends in the usage of the terms "defense" and "repression" in psychoanalysis, defense was first thought of as a rather general process of rejection resulting in mental dissociations, then repression came to be used synonymously with defense, repression being thought of as the single and basic mechanism of defense. Later repression was assigned a more restricted role, taking its place as only one among many types of defense mechanisms. And still later defense most generally conceived came to be the emphasized concept in psychoanalytic writing instead of repression, which had earlier been emphasized as the core and basic concept of psychoanalysis.

Three Phases of Repression

For the experimental psychologist there were the questions as to what are the distinguishable stages or phases of repression and which, if any of them, can be produced in the laboratory and subjected to experimental test.

[7] From G. Gerö, "The Concept of Defense," *Psychoanal. Quart.*, 1951, 20, 565. Used by permission.

"If we examine what is spoken of as 'repression' more closely," Freud wrote in 1911, "we shall find reason to split the process up into three phases which are easily distinguishable from one another conceptually."

PRIMAL REPRESSION (FIXATION).   "(1) The first phase consists in *fixation*, which is the precursor and necessary condition of every 'repression'" (p. 453).

This first phase of repression was called *primal repression*, and elsewhere Freud (1915) wrote that it "consists in a denial of entry into consciousness to the mental (ideational) presentation of the instinct. This is accompanied by a *fixation*; the ideational presentation in question persists unaltered from then onwards and the instinct remains attached to it" (p. 86).

REPRESSION PROPER (AFTER-EXPULSION).   "(2) The second phase of repression is that of repression proper. . . . It emanates from the more highly developed systems of the ego—systems which are capable of being conscious—and may in fact be described as a process of 'after-expulsion'" (1911, p. 453).

In his paper on "Repression" Freud (1915) described this second phase of repression further:

Repression proper concerns mental derivatives of the repressed instinct-presentation, or such trains of thought as, originating elsewhere, have come into associative connection with it. On account of this association, these ideas experience the same fate as that which underwent primal repression. Repression proper, therefore, is actually an after-expulsion. Moreover, it is a mistake to emphasize only the rejection which operates from the side of consciousness upon what is to be repressed. We have to consider just as much the attraction exercised by what was originally repressed upon everything with which it can establish a connection. Probably the tendency to repression would fail of its purpose if these forces did not co-operate, if there were not something previously repressed ready to assimilate that which is rejected from consciousness.[8]

RETURN OF THE REPRESSED.   "(3) The third phase, and the most important as regards pathological phenomena, is that of miscarriage of repression, of *irruption*, of *return of the repressed*. This irruption takes its start from the point of fixation, and it involves a regression of the libidinal development to that point" (1911, p. 454).

[8] From Sigmund Freud, *Repression*, 1915, pp. 86–7. Translated in *Collected Papers*, Vol. IV. Copyright 1925 by Hogarth Press, Ltd., London.

The Three Phases of Repression and Research Possibilities

In summary, Freud (1915) wrote that ". . . the essence of repression lies simply in the function of rejecting and keeping something out of consciousness" (*Repression*, p. 86). In view of this definition "the return of the repressed" is actually not so much a third phase of repression as it is a partial failure of repression. But it was clear that Freud (1915) thought that just such failures would be especially valuable in the study of repression, for ". . . the case of unsuccessful repression will have more claim on our interest than that of repression which is eventually successful; the latter will for the most part elude our study" (p. 92).

It seemed clear to most psychologists that primal repression would also elude their study in so far as they limited their researches to the investigation of repression in adult subjects (college students). The experimental study of repression would of necessity be restricted to a study of repression proper or after-repression and to investigations of the return of the repressed.

This interpretation of repression theory was later clearly confirmed by Freud's statement in 1937 that "all repressions take place in early childhood; they are primitive defensive measures adopted by the immature, feeble ego. In later years there are no fresh repressions, but the old ones persist and are used by the ego for the purpose of further mastering instinct. New conflicts are resolved by what we call 'after-repression'" ("Analysis Terminable and Interminable," p. 328).

Three Experimental Approaches to Repression

The three phases of repression described by Freud carried implications for the psychological processes on which psychologists would have to focus their attention in their experimental approaches to repression. In primal repression ("denial of entry into consciousness") one would expect to find *inhibition of perception*, a failure to perceive anxiety-arousing stimuli presented to the subject, what eventually came to be called perceptual defense. In repression proper or after-repression ("after-expulsion from consciousness") one would expect to discover *inhibition of memory*, a failure to remember ego-wounding or anxiety-provoking experiences of which the subject was once fully aware. In failure or miscarriage of repression ("return of the repressed") one would expect to find *inhibition of response*, in other words, symptoms or compromise formations in thought and action resulting from the unresolved conflict between repressed and repressing forces.

Experimental approaches to the study of repression have indeed proceeded along these three avenues, looking for and taking as evidence of repression (1) disturbances in perception, (2) disturbances in memory, and (3) disturbances in thought and action. However, in the history of the attempts to approach repression experimentally the sequence in which these appeared on the scene is just the reverse of their listing here.

EXPERIMENTAL STUDIES OF "RETURN OF THE REPRESSED"

Studies in Word-Association

The first experimental studies of the partial "return of the repressed" were the "Studies in Word-Association" (1918) carried out by the Swiss psychiatrists C. G. Jung and F. Riklin and others, and first published in 1904. These investigations, conducted in the Burghölzli Hospital under the general supervision of Eugen Bleuler in Zürich, Switzerland, had their roots in the age-old concern of psychology with the laws of mental association, but certain results of the studies were interpreted in the light of psychoanalytic theory.

Working with both normal and psychiatric subjects, Jung and Riklin presented verbally a series of stimulus words with instructions to respond to each word with the first word which comes to mind. In addition to this standard procedure, in which the reaction time of the response was measured, Jung instituted an innovation, the *Wiederholungsversuch* (repetition experiment). This consisted of presenting the series of stimulus words on a later occasion, usually the following day, with instructions to respond to each word with the same answer which had been given the first time.[9] In the repetition experiment the subject might recall correctly his original response and without appreciable extension of reaction time, but several deviations from the normal pattern of response were noted: "(1) Memory fails at certain places, (2) the former reaction word is not given at all, (3) it is given incorrectly, (4) there is silence, (5) it is reproduced with great hesitation" (C. G. Jung, *Studies in Word-Association*, 1918, p. 396).

COMPLEXES AND COMPLEX-INDICATORS.   These and other disturbances in the associative response, even in the first presentation of the

---

[9] It is interesting to note here that the technique of the incidental task (*Nebenhandlung*) was independently "reinvented" by Lewin and his students; it was not as novel as they thought. For the subjects in Jung's experiments the one and only task of which they were aware was to respond as quickly as possible to each stimulus word with the first word that came to mind. They had no inkling that they would subsequently be asked to recall the responses they had given. The memory tested in the reproduction experiment was thus incidental memory. Jung was a forerunner of Lewin in recognizing that incidental remembering is more like the remembering of everyday life than is the remembering in laboratory-conducted memory experiments. But Jung has not been credited with the development of the "incidental-task technique." He did not take the trouble to give it a name. Lewin did, and this is important in science.

word series, e.g., lengthened reaction time, repetition of the stimulus word, perseveration of the response, etc., were, Jung concluded, indicative of a mental complex which he conceived to be a constellation of ideas with associated affects.

The complexes stirred by the stimulus words and revealed by the complex-indicators were in some cases conscious, i.e., the subject could report quite fully upon the emotional thought or memory which had been evoked, but in other instances unconscious in the sense that despite the disturbance in the associative response the subject, though he might or might not experience affect, experienced no concomitant conscious thought, or image, or memory.

In the experimental study of complexes Jung introduced yet another technique: measuring the galvanic skin response (GSR) associated with the verbal responses of subjects. He found, characteristically, that GSR's accompanying responses which were complex-indicators were on the average of greater magnitude than those which accompanied associative responses which did not indicate the stirring of complexes.

In the case of indicators of unconscious complexes Jung felt that Freud's theory of repression provided the best explanation of his findings which in turn offered, he believed, a convincing demonstration of repression. Further, Jung found that if he asked subjects to free-associate to the stimulus words which had evoked complex-indicators, the chains of association would often lead to clear associates of repressed material in a manner quite comparable to the flow of association in the psychoanalytic situation as described by Freud.

REACTIONS TO JUNG'S STUDIES. The similarities of their interests and their findings led to a close collaboration between Jung and Freud which, however, came to an end in 1914. At first Freud welcomed Jung's free-association experiments as offering a confirmation of his theory of repression. It is of interest to note that Jung's association experiments had not been undertaken to test the validity of the repression hypothesis. Instead, by chance and quite independently of the Freudian movement, Jung's experiments appeared to demonstrate repression and to offer supporting evidence for the concept. But after their break Freud (1914) wrote rather contemptuously of Jung's experimental studies and his theory of complexes which at the time appeared to be attracting more attention in some quarters than Freud's own work.

There is a third contribution . . . probably to be ascribed entirely to Jung, which I do not value so highly as others do whose concern with these matters is more remote. I mean the theory of "complexes" which grew out of the *Diagnostische Assoziationsstudien* (1906 to 1910). It has neither produced a psychological theory in itself, nor has it proved capable of easy incorporation into the context of psycho-analytical theory. The word "complex," on the other hand, has become naturalized, so to speak, in psycho-analytic language; it is a convenient and often indispensable term for summing up descriptively a psychological state. None of the other terms coined by psycho-analysis for its own needs has achieved such widespread popularity, or been so misapplied to the detriment of formulating clear concepts. Analysts began to speak among themselves of a "return of a complex" where they meant a "return of the repressed"; or got into the habit of saying, "I have a complex against him," where correctly they could only have said "a resistance against him." [1]

If Jung's experiments were destined for downgrading by the psychoanalysts, they were at first viewed with alarm by academic psychologists who felt that their previously pure association method was being prostituted in the study of psychopathology. Ziehen, one of the pioneers in the experimental study of association, protested Jung's use of the method for diagnostic purposes. In his review of Jung's *The Psychology of Dementia Praecox*, Ziehen (1908) wrote that psychologists could not be warned too strongly against such deviations from association psychology and described the attempt to apply the results of Jung's studies to dementia praecox as erroneous and dangerous.

Research Trends Stemming from Jung's Studies

Despite these first reactions to Jung's studies, this type of investigation flourished, eventuating in a bifurcation of interest in the experimental study of mental associations: (1) the utilization of complex-indicators as evidence of guilty knowledge in what came to be called the lie-detection technique, and (2) the determination of the frequency of associative responses to standardized tests of stimulus words in both normal and abnormal populations. But neither of these lines of experimental investigation, though extremely productive, bore directly upon the problem of repression.

By 1910 Jung had turned his attention to other psychological problems; the period of his interest in the experimental study of word associations was a short one (1902–9). But the work which he had initiated was carried on by others rather quietly and without controversy, but by the same token not influencing importantly either the theory of psychodynamics, including repression, or the practice of psychodiagnostics.[2]

[1] From Sigmund Freud, *On the History of the Psychoanalytic Movement*, 1914, pp. 312f. Translated in *Collected Papers*, Vol. I. Copyright 1924 by Hogarth Press, Ltd., London.

[2] For a review of this history and for the list of complex-indicators reported by various investigators, see Kohs (1914).

Luria's Theory of Behavior and the Combined Motor Method

The important subsequent events in the study of indicators of repressed complexes were extensions and technical improvements of Jung's method, which in the most important instance stemmed from a combining of technical virtuosity with a new theory of the control and disorganization of behavior (Luria, 1929, 1930, 1932).

METHOD OF THE EXTREME CASE.   If one wishes to study the dynamics of disrupted behavior, it is necessary, Luria argued, to employ the "method of the extreme case." Accordingly, in investigating the effect of emotion upon the processes of associative response, Luria conducted experiments, not with normal subjects, but with persons who had been charged with murder, the experiments being conducted immediately following their arrest. Or he suggested to hypnotized subjects prior to conducting association experiments with them that they had committed crimes which were of such a horrible nature that all memory of the experience had been repressed.[3]

In his experiments Luria had his subjects sit quietly with each hand resting lightly on the rubber surface of a tambour. This was connected pneumatically with a device which would record any movements made by the hands. In addition to the standard direction to respond to each stimulus word with the first word which came to mind, he instructed them to coordinate a slight downward pressure of the preferred hand with each verbal response, holding the non-preferred hand passive and still. Under these conditions the voluntary pressure of the preferred hand would normally be nicely coordinated with the verbal response and regular in character, but there were times when the voluntary pressure response would not occur in synchrony with the verbal response and would show irregularities, the disturbance in the response spreading in some instances to appear in involuntary movements of the non-preferred hand.

In their report of a replication of certain aspects of Luria's experiments, Huston, Shakow, and Erickson gave an exposition of Luria's basic data and of the theoretical interpretation of these data with ideal brevity:

Having trained a subject to associate a motor response of the preferred hand with every verbal response, thereby establishing a close functional relationship between them, any word occurring to the sub-

[3] The reader will note that with regard to the controversy between Lewin and the experimental dynamicists on the one side and the psychoanalysts on the other as to whether the study of less intense, normal processes (quasi-needs) will serve to reveal the dynamics of more intense, abnormal processes (needs), Luria is on the side of the psychoanalysts.

ject which he does not give as a response will appear in the voluntary movement as a partial reaction. It is assumed here that the inhibition of the verbal response is associated with affect, i.e., the subject does not respond with the first word since some complex would be revealed. Also the pressure curve may lose its smooth regular character or, to follow Luria's terminology more closely, the normal, voluntary movement is discoordinated or disorganized because stimuli which elicit responses possessing affect may also arouse larger amounts of excitation than stimuli eliciting non-affective responses. This excitation tends to discharge itself immediately via the voluntary motor pathway. Luria has referred to this tendency as the "law of the catalytic action of the stimulus." This law appears to be a corollary of another, the "law of the decreased action of the functional barrier." The functional barrier is a cortical property. It regulates by inhibition the motor activities of the organism, giving them an integrated character. Affective excitation weakens the functional barrier and hence the motor activities become disorganized. A third law is that of the "mobilization of inadequate masses of excitation." This seems to involve "neuro-dynamical perseveration." The excitation which accompanies the affect is not always discharged completely via the verbal response, hence some movements will persist in the preferred hand after the voluntary response. Under conditions of large amounts of excitation a further spread to other systems may occur, disturbing, for example, respiration and/or causing involuntary movements of the non-preferred hand.[4]

SUPPRESSION OR REPRESSION?   Luria's work was an attempt to find more sensitive and more reliable indicators of suppressed or repressed complexes. Much of his work, for example his studies with suspected and convicted criminals and with students in Russian universities just before and after harrowing examinations designed to uncover those whose thinking deviated from the Communist Party doctrine, almost certainly bear upon suppression rather than repression. But his experiment in which he hypnotized subjects and induced a complex by suggesting during the trance that they had committed a reproachable act, subsequently suggesting amnesia for the described action after waking from the trance, would appear to constitute an experimental induction of repression. Such a procedure had the merit of permitting the administration of an association test employing both neutral words and words known to be related to the suggested guilty experience both before and after the establishment of the complex.

It was this experiment which was replicated by Huston, Shakow, and Erickson (1934) with four male and eight female subjects. In

[4] From P. E. Huston et al., "A Study of Hypnotically Induced Complexes by Means of the Luria Technique," J. gen. Psychol., 1934, 11, 65f. Used by permission of the Journal Press, Provincetown, Mass.

addition to the verbal, voluntary, and involuntary reactions, respiratory responses were also studied.

The Luria studies as well as the investigation carried out by Huston, Shakow, and Erickson yielded data of extraordinary interest, but whether they succeeded in experimentally inducing and studying repression remains a moot question.

Summary

The history of experimental attempts to demonstrate the "return of the repressed" has been characterized by a diligent and not especially successful search for the broadest possible range of corroborating "complex-indicators": the GSR, respiration rate, pulse rate, involuntary movement, continuous blood pressure, and so on. But ironically, those most ingenious and competent in developing and refining such psychophysiological techniques have had little or no interest in the problem of repression.

The fact that disturbed mental associations, while suggesting the presence of repressed material, cannot reveal its nature nor distinguish between the repressed and the suppressed, thus requiring a multiplicity of cumbersome and expensive additional techniques which leave considerable to be desired by way of reliability, may explain why research in this area has in recent years been so neglected. Nor has the word-association technique found wide acceptance as a practical device. Rather, as F. Riklin has pointed out, it "enjoys a rather quiet life amid the present-day wealth of psychological diagnostic techniques" ("Jung's Association Test and Dream Interpretation," *J. Proj. Tech.*, 1955, 19, 226).

EXPERIMENTAL STUDIES OF "AFTER-EXPULSION FROM CONSCIOUSNESS"

Interruption, Frustration, Repression

Whereas Zeigarnik had rather by chance observed in the laboratory behavior which she interpreted as indicative of repression, Rosenzweig and Mason (1934) were the first to make an explicit attempt to elicit repression under conditions of laboratory control and observation.

The subjects in their experiment were forty children ranging in age from five years and six months to fourteen years and eight months. Individually, each child was given the task of solving a series of jigsaw puzzles, and the experiment was conducted as a contest with a prize to be awarded to the child who did best. A picture of each puzzle was shown to the subject for half a minute before he started to work on it. As in Zeigarnik's experiment, each subject was allowed to complete

half of the tasks but interrupted in working on the other half, the interruption being so carried out, however, as to make the child feel he had
failed. After forty-five minutes of puzzle-solving, followed by a free
interval of one minute, each subject was casually asked to name the
picture puzzles he had worked. Of the forty children, sixteen remembered more completed than "failed" tasks, thirteen recalled fewer completed than "failed" tasks, nine recalled an equal number of both, and
two recalled no tasks.

At best, only sixteen of the forty subjects could be thought of as
remembering (or forgetting) in accordance with the theory of repression, and Rosenzweig and Mason so interpreted their data, since these
sixteen subjects were on the average of a more advanced mental age
and had received a higher average rating for the trait of pride from their
teachers as compared with the other groups of subjects. As Rosenzweig
and Mason concluded, "It would seem to be that, given an individual
of sufficient intellectual maturity and a commensurate measure of pride,
experiences that are unpleasant because they wound self-respect—
perhaps it should be added in a *social* situation—are, other things being
equal, less apt to be remembered than experiences that are gratifying to
the ego. This is in keeping with the Freudian theory of repression"
("An Experimental Study of Memory in Relation to the Theory of
Repression," *Brit. J. Psychol.*, 1934, 24, 258).

One might well argue that the principal challenge to a scientist
comes from his own observations and his urge to further order and extend them. Certainly in ongoing programs of scientific research, many
of the challenges are "internal" in that they are made and responded to
by those most intimately concerned with the research project.

INDUCED FAILURE.   Such "internal stimulation" seemed to be
a major factor in Rosenzweig's programmatic study of repression. First,
he recognized a limitation in the design of his and Mason's investigation—namely, that the differences in pride, which they deemed the
principal independent variable, instead of resulting from experimental
manipulation, were dependent upon genetic differences in personalities.
Since experimenters usually have no control over such variables, Rosenzweig (1933, 1943) designed a second experiment in which he attempted to arouse feelings of pride experimentally. He presented puzzles to one group of adult subjects as an "intelligence test," and to another group in an informal manner under the guise of discovering something about the tasks, not about the ability of the subject. The latter
situation would therefore, he assumed, be less likely to pose a threat to
self-esteem.

Under the more stressful condition, seventeen remembered more finished tasks, eight recalled more unfinished, and five showed no preponderant tendency. In the neutral situation only seven recalled more finished, while nineteen remembered more unfinished tasks, four showing no difference between the two. For each individual an index of repression was computed as follows:

$$100 \left(\frac{\text{finished} - \text{unfinished tasks recalled}}{\text{finished} + \text{unfinished tasks recalled}} \right).$$

The mean index in the informal group was −7.65, and for the "intelligence test" group +2.95. These findings were interpreted as supporting those of the previous experiment and accordingly relevant to repression.

NEED-PERSISTIVE VS. EGO-DEFENSIVE REACTIONS.   Second, in appraising the results of the two experiments, Rosenzweig (1938) called attention to difficulties inherent in his method, the confounding of *incompletion* with *failure*. He warned:

> One must then be ever careful not to confuse the *unclosed need represented by the unfinished task* (perseveration) with the *unclosed need represented by the inhibited response*, say, of anger in the face of frustration. In keeping with this interpretation, evidence of repression obtained from experiments in which the criterion of failure is incompletion is particularly striking because under such conditions the repressive tendency can become manifest in terms of forgotten failures only after overcoming the competing perseverative tendency which would, by itself, make for the recall of unfinished tasks.[5]

The reactions generated by these two needs he referred to as *need-persistive* and *ego-defensive*.

TYPES OF REACTION TO FRUSTRATION.   Third, he felt challenged by the great variability in performance which occurred despite systematically imposed conditions. Not only was there frequent failure to conform to the general patterns of displaying predominantly need-persistive reactions in the neutral situation and predominantly ego-defensive reactions in the threat situation, but striking differences in immediate reaction to frustration were reported. Careful study of these individual differences in response to frustration led Rosenzweig (1934) to conclude that three types of reaction are discernible: extrapunitive, in which the world is blamed for the failure; intropunitive, in which the

[5] From S. Rosenzweig, "The Experimental Study of Repression," p. 485, in *Explorations in Personality* by H. A. Murray *et al.*, copyright 1938 by Oxford University Press, New York. This and the following excerpt are used by permission.

person blames himself; and impunitive, in which failures are glossed over and rationalized.

THE TRIADIC HYPOTHESIS.   He further speculated that these three types of reaction have a special relation to memory for successes and failures. Of special concern here is the notion that impunitiveness is correlated with the tendency to use repression as a defense. Then, because of the early demonstrated relationship between hysteria and repression (cf. Breuer and Freud's early work) and between hypnotizability and hysteria (cf. Janet), Rosenzweig (1938) postulated that ". . . hypnotizability as a personality trait is to be found in positive association with repression as a preferred mechanism of defence and with impunitiveness as a characteristic type of immediate reaction to frustration" (p. 489).

In a test of this triadic hypothesis Rosenzweig and Sarason (1942) measured repression by the index described above (p. 693), impunitiveness by an early version of the Rosenzweig *P-F Test*, and hypnotizability by the degree to which certain suggestions were followed. They reported sizable multiple correlations among these variables and their combinations.

Extension and Criticism of Interruption-Failure Technique

ALPER'S EMPHASIS ON PERSONALITY.   Not all the challenges in the after-expulsion research, however, were provided by Rosenzweig. Alper (1946) raised questions about the results of both Zeigarnik's and Rosenzweig's research on interruption and memory. She contended that personality factors—not the situational ones—were the crucial determinants of whether completed or incompleted tasks would be predominant in recall. In a sample of subjects unselected for personality factors, she hypothesized that there would be no differences in the recall of incompleted and completed tasks. Using the interruption technique with scrambled sentences, some of which were insoluble, others of which could be ordered into four meaningful arrangements, she tested ten "draft-age" males both under a relaxed condition and under one of self-esteem involvement. When she compared the average percentage scores for completed tasks recalled with those for incompleted tasks recalled in the neutral situation, she found no difference; this finding was duplicated with the "involved" situation. These results were consonant with her hypothesis. She interpreted them to mean "not that selective recall is unlawful, but rather that the direction of recall is dynamically related to the self-esteem needs of the individual . . ." (Thelma G. Alper, "Memory for Completed and Incompleted

Tasks as a Function of Personality. An Analysis of Group Data," *J. abnorm. soc. Psychol.*, 1946, 41, 417).

CONFOUNDING FACTORS IN REPRESSION SCORES. In a review of Rosenzweig and Alper's work, Glixman (1948) questioned the rationale underlying such experimental studies of repression. He contended that Rosenzweig's index of repression was inadequate because in it a change in incomplete-task recall depends not only on the increase in stress, but also on the change in the recall of completed activities. A lowered recall-difference score he indicated could occur in a number of ways: "(1) *Decrease in recall of incompleted tasks*, with either no change or an increase in recall of completed tasks; (2) *no change in recall of incompleted tasks*, but an increase in recall of completed tasks; (3) *increase in recall of incompleted tasks*, with a greater increase in recall of completed tasks" (p. 492).

When he analyzed Rosenzweig's data by comparing the recall of incompleted tasks under the two conditions (stress and nonstress), he discovered no differences, while the same comparison for completed tasks showed *more* recall in the stress situation. Glixman concluded:

> The argument that the lack of selective forgetting is attributable to strong "need-persistive tendencies" is only to admit that the experimental design or the analysis of the data is inadequate, for this is to say that there is a hopeless confounding of variables. If the recall change for incompleted tasks is considered, Rosenzweig seems to have extracted two countervalent tendencies from thin air; on the basis of no change in recall of incompleted tasks, he has suggested that there are coexistent tendencies to recall and to forget incompleted activities.
> . . . If a decrement of recall is set up as a minimum criterion for repression, then there seems to be no justification for Rosenzweig's statement that he has achieved "a closer approximation to the full concept of repression . . . than would be true if completed unpleasant tasks were in question." In fact, if Rosenzweig's data are taken into account, he seems to have achieved no approximation at all to repression.[6]

AMBIGUITY IN ALPER'S HYPOTHESIS. Looking at Alper's research, Glixman objected that her hypothesis concerning the lack of differences between the incidental recall of completed and incompleted tasks presented a major ambiguity. He argued that if emphasis were placed on recall differences *within* situations, then having *two* experimental situations (neutral and stress) was superfluous. If, on the other hand, Glixman continued, *differences* meant those between re-

[6] From A. F. Glixman, "An Analysis of the Use of the Interruption-Technique in Experimental Studies of 'Repression,'" *Psychol. Bull.*, 1948, 45, 496. Used by permission.

call of incompleted tasks under the two conditions and similar differences for completed tasks, Alper used an inappropriate statistic. Under this interpretation an inter-session measure would, of course, be indicated. When he reanalyzed Alper's data in this fashion, the recall of completed tasks under stress was significantly less than in the neutral situation, and a near-significant difference was observed for the comparable recall for incompleted tasks. On the basis of this inter-session measure, Glixman concluded that "Alper's hypothesis must be rejected. There *are* systematic changes in the recall of completed tasks as a function of stress, even when subjects have been selected randomly with respect to personality factors" (p. 500).

DEGREES OF STRESS.   Because of the apparent discrepancies in the results of experiments seemingly similar in approach, Glixman (1949) designed an experiment which he hoped would help provide a clear-cut description of the effects of stress on recall of completed and incompleted tasks. He presented twenty paper-and-pencil tasks to each of three groups who differed in the degree of stress under which the tasks were attempted (neutral, some emphasis on satisfactory performance, and great emphasis on satisfactory performance). His data indicated that as stress increases, recall of incompleted tasks decreases, but recall of completed tasks does not increase.

SEARS' APPRAISAL.   In the face of these diverse findings with the interruption procedure, Sears (1950) made the following suggestion:

> These studies emphasize the difficulties of using the "interrupted task" technique as a device for securing feelings of failure. The primary aim of the various researches by Rosenzweig, Alper, Glixman, and Sanford has been to investigate the influence of motivational strength or ego-pain on recall of the tasks with which the motivation or pain is associated. Yet this cumbersome method introduces an additional variable—the Zeigarnik effect—that is already known to influence recall, the very process that serves as the dependent variable in the experiments. Neither the logical implications nor the empirical effects of interruption are sufficiently known to permit any effective control of this extraneous but intrusive factor. Its only advantage is that it provides a means of making subjects fail. Since there are other methods of doing this, methods that do not activate any process already known to influence the dependent variable under study, there appears to be little reason for the continued use of the interruption technique. When a research operation requires as much discussion of its "psychological meaning" as interruption does, it is time to find a new operation.[7]

[7] From R. R. Sears, "Personality," *An. Rev. Psychology,* 1950, 1, 113. Used by permission.

RE-EMPHASIS ON THE SUBJECT'S EXPERIENCE. Alper (1952) vigorously defended both the general use of the interruption technique as a fruitful psychodynamic tool and her specific application of it. To Sears she retorted that since the recall pattern involved in the Zeigarnik effect is one that characterizes a person whose self-esteem needs are not readily threatened, it is not dynamically equivalent to the recall of incompleted tasks under objective stress, and hence is not an "additional" variable in stress situations. In response to Glixman she insisted that:

> Under these circumstances, S's recall of completed tasks is psychologically not independent of his recall of incompleted tasks, and vice versa. To insist on separating the two types of recall, then, as Glixman does in using an intersession measure, is to disregard the very experience which E has imposed on S experimentally.[8]

ROSENZWEIG'S RESTATEMENT. Later Rosenzweig (1952) responded to his several critics: He chided Alper for her undue stress on personality factors and pointed to what he called a basic error in Glixman's reasoning—the failure "to recognize the individual-in-his-idioverse [individual universe] as constituting the field for dynamic operations like repression" (p. 343). He accused Sears of not exercising "fitting circumspection" in his review, maintaining that his (Sears') appraisal overlooked "the essential consideration that repression is by its very nature a matter of interrupted activity. The essence of the alleged phenomenon lies in a *failure of expression or of integration* through the need for ego defense" (pp. 344–5).

In conclusion, Rosenzweig stated:

> Experimentation on repression and related concepts must invariably consider the idioverse of the subject—the balance of experimental conditions and personality variables as these are blended in the dynamic experience of the person. The "projective" variability of the "stimulus," for example, must be recognized from the start, permitted but controlled, and anticipated for the eventual analysis of the results. Research of this kind will perhaps always be approximate and partial, and will have to be supplemented by genetic studies of the individual as observed in favorable situations.[9]

EFFECTS OF PRIDE IN "REAL-LIFE" SETTING. Twenty-three per cent of the subjects in Rosenzweig's second experiment (1943) showed ego-defensive reactions in the non-stress situation, while 27 per cent

[8] From Thelma G. Alper, "The Interrupted Task Method in Studies of Selective Recall: A Re-evaluation of Some Recent Experiments," *Psychol. Rev.*, 1952, 59, 77. Used by permission.

[9] From S. Rosenzweig, "The Investigation of Repression as an Instance of Experimental Idio-dynamics," *Psychol. Rev.*, 1952, 59, 345. Used by permission.

showed need-persistent reactions under stress. This rather large number of exceptions to the general trends in his study led Sanford and Risser (1948) to attempt to improve the validity of the experimental procedure. Although they agreed with Rosenzweig on the importance of pride in self-defensive forgetting, they felt that the degree to which pride had been awakened in Rosenzweig's laboratory experiments had been definitely limited. In an effort to arouse more intense feelings of pride, and hence provide a more reliable demonstration of self-defensive forgetting, N. Sanford and J. Risser moved out of the confines of the laboratory. They claimed to have confronted subjects with an emotionally charged situation which "entailed for them more ego involvement, more threat to self-esteem, than any previous experiment on 'repression' . . ." ("What Are the Conditions of Self-Defensive Forgetting?" *J. Pers.*, 1948, 17, 245.) Specifically, twenty-five mothers were tested at their homes in the presence of their eleven-to-thirteen-year-old daughters. The tasks were of the jigsaw puzzle type, and though they were not told so, most mothers believed that they were taking an intelligence test. They were allowed to succeed on nine designs and made to fail on six. The mothers recalled 41 per cent of their successes and 27 per cent of their failures, results which, the investigators asserted, showed the self-defensive forgetting tendencies more pronouncedly than any other experiment.

Other Approaches to Repressed Memory

Concurrently with or following Rosenzweig's attempt to develop an objective method for studying the process of repression in the laboratory under conditions in which motives or needs are experimentally manipulated, several other investigators directed themselves to one or another phase of the same problem.

GUILT AS INITIATOR OF REPRESSION.   Arguing that feelings of guilt should be more potent initiators of the repression sequence than feelings of inferiority, MacKinnon (1933) devised an experiment in which each of ninety-three subjects was left alone, though observed by the experimenter through a one-way screen, to work on a series of tasks so difficult as to be impossible of solution for practically all subjects. The solutions to all problems were provided in an answer booklet, some of which they were given permission to consult, if they so wished, but looking at others was strictly prohibited.

Repression could be expected to occur only in subjects who violated the prohibition—43 per cent of the group—and then only if they felt guilty about their violations; in this instance only a small minority did.

When subsequently asked to recall the problems they had worked, violators (most of whom showed no signs of guilt) remembered most often problems whose solutions had been seen in violation of the prohibition, next most often problems whose permitted solutions had been consulted, and least often problems whose solutions had not been seen at all. The same order of frequency of recall held for non-violators, except for recall of violated tasks, there being none of these.

A small atypical group of subjects, who violated the prohibition and who both in behavior and verbal report gave evidence of guilt feelings, tended to recall problems whose solutions had been seen in violation of the prohibition less well than they recalled other problems.

Although MacKinnon stressed the congruence of his findings with deductions from psychoanalytic theory, he did not claim that they offered final proof of the repression hypothesis.

THE BEHAVIORISTIC VERSION.   Sears sought to translate repression into a behavioristic framework. A restatement of the repression hypothesis in what he called "reaction" psychology became: ". . . The fact of repression results from a conflict between mutually incompatible anticipatory goal responses when the anticipatory response to punishment or failure is dominant, i.e., overcomes the anticipatory response to reward or success. Repression itself is the *blockage of the acts*, either pure stimulus or contributory, which lead to the drive-satisfying goal" (R. R. Sears, "Initiation of the Repression Sequence by Experienced Failure," *J. exp. Psychol.*, 1937, 20, 570).

On each of three days twenty subjects learned one list of nonsense syllables before and another list after a level-of-aspiration task (card-sorting) in which half the group "succeeded" and half "failed." The failure experience produced a progressive decrement in card-sorting and adversely affected the efficiency of the syllable learning. Sears considered both of these facts as tentative verifications of one phase of the repression sequence, namely, the development of "mutually incompatible anticipatory goal responses." Later he was to repudiate experimental studies of repression as unproductive (cf. p. 701).

THE USE OF CLINICAL MATERIAL.   Sharp (1938), purporting to test Freud's doctrine of repression but belonging in the research tradition which probed for the relationship between hedonic tone and memory, focused on what she saw as three deficiencies in earlier designs —the failure to use (1) materials which would conform to *Freud's usage* of unpleasantness, (2) abnormal subjects, (3) long intervals of time. Her corrective procedures were as follows: (1) She selected, as stimulus material, phrases, common in the case histories of psychiatric patients who were subjects in the experiment (e.g., "blaming me"). These un-acceptable phrases were matched with comparable neutral (e.g., "com-

ing inside") and acceptable material (e.g., "gaining affection").
(2) She used as subjects psychiatric patients, as well as normal; and
(3) retention tests were made as long as sixteen days after original learning. In general, retention of the unacceptable material was reliably
poorer than that of the neutral or acceptable material, a finding which
she interpreted as evidence of repression.

THE INSURANCE OF PERSONAL RELEVANCE.   Gould (1942) objected to the traditional lack of personal relevance in the stimulus materials used in studies of repression. She therefore included in her
experiment operations which defined the unpleasantness or pleasantness
of stimulus items by their meaning and effect on the *subject*. Under the
guise of a personality test, subjects were required to choose one of a
pair of simple tasks (e.g., unsnarling a string or modeling an animal
from clay). No matter which task was chosen for performance, the
experimenter informed the subject, according to a prearranged schedule,
that his choice revealed some good or bad character trait (e.g., warm-
heartedness or fundamental immaturity). He then performed the task,
and upon completion made a choice from another pair of tasks until
six choices had been made. For each subject, half the traits were good,
half bad. When the last task had been performed, the subject was asked
to recall the tasks and the comments (traits) which followed his
choices. A control group repeated the procedures, except they were told
that the test was under study.

Some of her pertinent findings were: tasks associated with U comments were forgotten more than those associated with P comments; comments were forgotten relatively more often than the tasks; forgetting
was random in the control group, selective (more U that P) in the experimental subjects.

REMOVAL OF REPRESSION.   Each of these attempts to explore
the problem of repressed memory focused on some fairly specific limitation in previous studies—type of material, manner of inducing anxiety,
etc.—and sought to correct what was regarded as a deficiency. As the
concept of repression became a more common object of study, the lines
along which criticisms were directed became fairly stabilized. But Zeller
(1950a) concluded that all previous attempts to study repression were
actually abortive, asserting that "the most significant criticism has not
been specifically formulated, namely, that *no test of repression can be
considered adequate until the removal of the repression factor has resulted in the restoration to consciousness of the repressed material*"
("An Experimental Analogue of Repression. I. Historical Summary,"
Psychol. Bull., 1950, 47, 46).

Zeller (1950b) consequently added a further step to the experimental design commonly used in studying repression; this was a retention test under conditions in which the induced anxiety had supposedly been removed. In Zeller's experiment a group of subjects learned a list of paired nonsense syllables; then half the group was allowed to be successful in a block-tapping problem; the other half "failed" the task. Retention tests of the verbal material revealed significant loss for the failure group, but the loss disappeared after the rigged character of the experiment was explained and the subjects were allowed to "succeed" at the block-tapping. Zeller concluded that he had made an adequate test of repression, although he realized that alternative explanations were not excluded.

Though articles reporting experimental tests of some specific aspect of repressed memory have appeared in the psychological literature each year in the past decade, no major breakthrough seems to have occurred in the experimental study of "after-expulsion from consciousness."

A Psychodynamicist's Evaluation of Experimental Studies of After-Expulsion (Repression Proper)

In his *Survey of Objective Studies of Psychoanalytic Concepts* in 1943, Sears rendered an essentially negative judgment on the value of nonpsychoanalytic studies of repression, and predicted a rather dismal future for the experimental investigation of the concept:

> There is little to be concluded from the experimental study of repression. In general, it is possible to demonstrate that, with the required conditions crudely established, recall of either real-life or experimentally induced experiences follows the expectations suggested by repression theory. But the non-analytic data offer no refinement to the theory, no addition of relevant new variables, no streamlined techniques that promise eventual solution of the problems posed by Freud. Studies of recall of real-life experiences and efforts to tap existing repressions have been almost uniformly uninformative. Some hope may be held out for the artificial creation of repressions in the laboratory, but even these must by necessity be mild and impermanent. Indeed, the triviality of obtained differences in this field makes a most discouraging picture; and the coarseness of the experimental methods so far available for tapping the sensitive dynamics of repression does not augur well for the future.[1]

The Psychoanalyst's Evaluation of These Studies

But if experimental psychodynamicists like Sears doubted whether their colleagues had succeeded in bringing repression into the labora-

[1] From R. R. Sears, "Survey of Objective Studies of Psychoanalytic Concepts," Bull. 51, 1943, p. 120. Social Science Research Council.

Dr. Saul Rosenzweig.

64 Plympton St. Cambridge, Mass

U. S. A.

PROF. DR. FREUD   28.2.1934
WIEN IX, BERGGASSE 19

Sehr geehrter Herr

Ich habe Ihre experimentellen Arbeiten zur Prüfung psychoanalytischer Behauptungen mit Interesse zur Kenntnis genommen. Ich kann diese Bestätigungen nicht hoch einschätzen, da die Fülle zuverlässiger Beobachtungen, auf denen diese Behauptungen ruhen, macht sie von der experimentellen Prüfung unabhängig. Immerhin, sie kann nicht schaden.

Ihr ergebener
Freud

tory and often wondered whether their own procedures had been adequate to the task, the psychoanalysts were certain that they had failed. And where the psychologists had criticized each other's researches largely on the grounds that their experimental techniques and laboratory controls had not been fully adequate, the psychoanalysts rejected them on the more sweeping grounds that whatever else these researches might be they simply were not investigations of repression.

There was at first only a lack of interest on the part of psychoanalysts in the work of the experimental psychodynamicists. Upon receipt of reprints of Rosenzweig's first attempts to study repression, Freud in 1934 responded as follows:

> I have examined your experimental studies for the verification of the psychoanalytic assertions with interest. I cannot put much value on these confirmations because the wealth of reliable observations on which these assertions rest make them independent of experimental verification. Still, it (experimental verification) can do no harm.[2]

But as time went by, Freud's first rather casual opinion that experimental attempts to verify psychoanalytic concepts "can do no harm" gave way to a conviction on the part of most psychoanalysts that such studies could indeed be harmful since they misrepresented what psychoanalysts conceived repression to be.

Charges and Counter-charges

FAILURE TO TRACE REPRESSION TO EARLY LIFE EVENTS. Repression, according to psychoanalytic theory, occurs first in infancy and childhood (Freud [1937] had said *only* in infancy and childhood), and therefore all experiments in which an attempt is made to evoke repression in adult subjects does not fulfill the necessary conditions for its study.

SUFFICIENCY OF STUDYING FATE OF DERIVATIVES AND ASSOCIATES. Actually, all that most investigators had claimed was that they had studied the after-expulsion of derivatives of impulses originally repressed or of ideas and trains of thought which had found associative connections with such repressed urges.

FAILURE TO DEMONSTRATE ID-CONNECTION OF FORGOTTEN MEMORIES. This claim was, however, denied by psychoanalysts who argued that the experimentalists had failed to demonstrate that the items of experience less well recalled in the experiments were either derivations

[2] Reprinted by permission of Sigmund Freud Copyrights, Ltd., London, and Saul Rosenzweig.

or associates of primal repressions. Such proof, they insisted, could be obtained only in historical-genetic investigations which the experimental investigations obviously were not (*cf.* Rapaport's criticism [1942] of frustration experiments), but which were required since Freud had asserted that "it is not even correct to suppose that repression withholds from consciousness all the derivatives of what was primally repressed. If these derivatives are sufficiently far removed from the repressed instinct-presentation, whether owing to the process of distortion or by reason of the number of intermediate associations, they have free access to consciousness. . . . Repression acts, therefore, in a *highly specific* manner in each instance; every single derivative of the repressed may have its peculiar fate—a little more or a little less distortion alters the whole issue. . . . Not only is it [repression] . . . *variable* and *specific*, but it is also exceedingly *mobile*" (*Repression*, 1915, pp. 88f., translated in *Collected Papers*, Vol. IV, Hogarth Press, Ltd., London).

Failure to arouse id impulses.   Repression, so the psychoanalytic critics claimed, defends the ego against primarily sexual and secondarily aggressive impulses, but psychologists in attempting to study repression experimentally had been prevented by moral and ethical considerations and societal prohibitions from arousing such impulses in their subjects, most of whom had been volunteer or coöpted subjects drawn from undergraduate courses in psychology.

Id impulses not alone subject to repression.   To this, psychologists replied that it just wasn't true that according to psychoanalytic theory the only impulses subject to repression are libidinal and aggressive ones. Indeed, as early as 1896 in discussing symptom-formation in obsessional neurosis, Freud had written that "the second form of obsessional neurosis comes about if what has compelled representation for itself in conscious mental life is not the repressed memory-content *but the self-reproaches that are likewise repressed*" [3] (*Further Remarks on the Defence Neuro-Psychosis,* translated in *Collected Papers,* Vol. I, Hogarth Press, Ltd., London).

Psychologists had felt justified in assuming that the range of mental content subject to repression extends far beyond the derivatives of repressed libidinal and aggressive impulses, for Freud (1915) in his most important discussion of the concept had said that "*repression proper concerns mental derivatives of the instinct-presentation, or such trains of thought as, originating elsewhere, have come into associative connection with it. . . . these ideas experience the same fate as that which*

---

[3] The italics are the present authors'.

underwent primal repression" [4] (p. 86). It was the repression of such "ideas" and "trains of thought" that psychologists had sought to study, and they claimed no more.

FAILURE TO AROUSE SUFFICIENTLY INTENSE EXPERIENCES. Other psychoanalysts criticized the "experimental studies of repression," not on the grounds that they failed to produce the right or required kinds of experiences (the stirring of sexual or aggressive impulses), but on the ground that the experiences which they did provoke were not sufficiently intense. This criticism, directed not at the quality but at the quantity of the affect which experimentalists could evoke in the laboratory, went to the very heart of Lewin's claim that the dynamics of quasi-needs are also the dynamics of real needs and that the dynamics of the latter can be discovered by studying the dynamics of the former. In his *The Psychopathology of Everyday Life* (1901) Freud had seemed to offer a single set of principles to explain, not only symptom-formation in neurotic behavior (phenomena of great intensity), but also such everyday occurrences as slips of the tongue and pen, forgetting, errors, faulty acts, and similar mistakes (phenomena of low intensity). But when such an interpretation of Freud's work was made by academic psychologists and cited in support of their attempts to bring psychoanalytic and psychodynamic processes like repression into the laboratory for study, the psychoanalysts were quick to reject any such use of Freud's writings.

On two grounds they argued that such reasoning was in error. Kris, for example, wrote:

> Not only is it worth remembering that not all essential propositions concerning the formation of the neurotic symptom apply to parapraxes [5] (the theory of symptom formation was known to Freud when he hit upon the explanation of parapraxes, and it is doubtful whether a reversal of the sequence could have led to equally satisfactory results); but also the assumption that the conflicts that lead to parapraxes are necessarily or typically of low intensity is entirely unwarranted. Evidence to the contrary is rather suggestive. But I should like to introduce a different kind of argument. Assuming that even in some cases the intensity of the conflict that leads to parapraxes be low, the nature of the conflicts remains significant. The conflict is of the same kind as the conflict that leads to symptom formation in neurosis; it may involve libidinal and aggressive impulses, love, hate, guilt, and anxiety, and the part played by the three psychic organizations [id, ego, super-ego] may be in details comparable to that observable in symptom formation.

[4] The italics are the present authors'.

[5] A generic term for forgetting, slips of the tongue and pen, and indeed for all errors in motor adjustment which are attributed in psychoanalytic theory to unconscious wishes which deflect and distort conscious desires.

The quasi needs of the laboratory investigations are of a different kind. There is no doubt that, as Zeigarnik (1927) and a host of experimenters since the publication of her paper have shown, the need to complete an uncompleted task exists. But that need is of a very specific kind; seen from the point of view of the psychoanalyst, it is a complex desire in which, however, two elements, that of avoiding failure, or that of feeling unsatisfied because one has not complied with a task, seem to predominate—impulses in which the Ego and the Superego are predominantly involved; as a rule no Id impulses are either frustrated or gratified. Consequently, the conflict that arises when the impulse to complete is frustrated can hardly be compared to conflicts that may arise when the impulse to complete an action with aggressive or libidinal connotation is impeded. In these cases, the impediment, whether external or internal, is frequently experienced as a threat and the individual frequently reacts with anxiety.[6]

INADEQUATE TRANSLATION OF PSYCHOANALYTIC CONCEPTS.   In their attempts to bring repression into the laboratory, experimental psychologists had felt a need to translate psychoanalytic theory into the language of psychology. At first some of the translations were oversimplified and erroneous. Others were more adequate to the sense of psychoanalytic theory, but were at the same time essentially translations of the special language of psychoanalysis into the language of everyday life (e.g., Rosenzweig and Mason, 1934; MacKinnon, 1933; Sanford and Risser, 1948). Still others were more ambitious attempts to translate the terms of psychoanalysis into the language of behaviorism (Holt, 1915), Pavlovian reflexology (French, 1933), or Hullian behavior theory (Hull, 1939; Sears, 1936).

PSYCHOANALYTIC SITUATION REQUIRED FOR STUDY OF REPRESSION. Though one of the most ambitious of these attempts at translation was made by a Freudian (French), psychoanalysts were for the most part indifferent or hostile to these enterprises. Their rejection of the simpler and erroneous restatements of their theory was certainly justified, but they were hardly less critical of the much more serious attempts at a formal translation, and especially when these were made the basis for experimental studies of repression. Their argument ran as follows: the behavioral phenomena from the observation of which Freud had been led to conceptualize the process of repression were phenomena which can be elicited and observed only in the psychoanalytic therapeutic situa-

[6] From E. Kris, "The Nature of Psychoanalytic Propositions and Their Validation." In S. Hook and M. R. Kowitz (eds.), *Freedom and Experience: Essays Presented to Horace Kallen.* Used by permission of Cornell University Press, Ithaca, New York. Reprinted in M. H. Marx (ed.), *Psychological Theory: Contemporary Readings,* The Macmillan Co., New York, 1951, pp. 345–6.

tion, and will be manifest only in the interpersonal or transference relationship which develops in psychoanalytic therapy between analyst and analysand. In contrast to this, the relationship between experimenter and subject is always and of necessity transitory and superficial and consequently incapable of arousing transference phenomena of sufficient depth to permit of the study of repression. In other words, only practicing psychoanalysts are ever in a position to study repression; the investigation of repression is forever excluded from the psychological laboratory. So rigidly was this position held by some psychoanalysts that they argued that "those who advocate changes in technique, e.g., the predominance of guidance in psychoanalytic theory, are not aware of the consequences such changes will have upon the set of data to which they will be able to obtain access." (H. Hartman and E. Kris, "The Genetic Approach in Psychoanalysis," *Psychoanal. Stud. Child*, 1945, 1, 15). If change of psychoanalytic technique will bar access to the usual data of psychoanalysis, how much less can one expect to approach them by procedures so radically different from orthodox psychoanalytic therapy as is an experiment conducted in a psychological laboratory!

EXPERIMENTAL CONTROL REQUIRED FOR STUDY OF REPRESSION. But opposed to such a parochial view as this was the attitude of the experimental psychologist, which was one of mistrust of any hypothesis generated in the emotional transference relationship between analyst and patient. Just such hypotheses were, they believed, especially in need of independent verification by the accepted and long-established experimental scientific method. Always implicit and often explicit in this view was the judgment that the psychoanalytic method of research is not acceptable as scientific method.

EQUIVOCALITY OF NEGATIVE EXPERIMENTAL FINDINGS. The reply of psychoanalysts was that "the limits of current experiments in the verification of psychoanalytic hypotheses become apparent when we realize that, at the present stage of investigations, the lack of experimental verification rarely, if ever, implies invalidation of propositions. It proves rather that the ingenuity of the experimenters has not been able to master the translation from the area of life where the proposition was gained into that of the controlled situation where the experiment is performed." (H. Hartmann and E. Kris, "The Genetic Approach in Psychoanalysis," *Psychoanal. Stud. Child*, 1945, 1, 16.)

THE CONFLICT STILL UNRESOLVED. As recently as 1952 one still found charges and counter-charges being exchanged by psychologist and psychoanalyst.

The psychologist:

. . . Anyone who tries to give an honest appraisal of psychoanalysis as a science must be ready to admit that as it is stated it is mostly very bad science, that the bulk of the articles in its journals cannot be defended as research publications at all. Having said this, I am prepared to reassert that there is much to be learned from these writings. The task of making a science of the observations and relationships may, however, fall to others than the psychoanalysts themselves.[7]

The psychoanalyst speaks of

. . . the uselessness of making pallid facsimiles in the laboratory of data which are already manifest in nature, merely to get around the human reluctance to look human nature in the eye.

Many of these laboratory charades are pedestrian and limited demonstrations of things which have been proved over and over again in real life.[8]

THE VEHEMENCE OF PSYCHOANALYTIC CRITICISMS.   While it is not uncommon for scientists to be emotional in their criticism of the researches of others which call into question the validity of their own theories and reported findings, the vehemence with which psychoanalysts have criticized and rejected all attempts of psychologists to perform experimental tests of the theory of repression has been, to say the least, extreme.

It is probably fair to say that no completely adequate test of repression has yet been made; but a perfect experiment in science is rare indeed, and especially in so difficult an area of research as experimental psychodynamics. Whatever the inadequacies of the various experimental studies of repression, they hardly seem to justify the fervor of the psychoanalysts' criticism of them. It is as though their reaction (to use the psychoanalysts' own phrase) were overdetermined.

It can hardly be claimed that the psychodynamicists' experimental studies of other psychoanalytic concepts and processes such as projection, reaction formation, dream work, and the like have been characterized either by a more faithful representation of the conceptualized psychoanalytic process or by a demonstrably superior experimental design. Yet psychoanalysts, in general, have been rather favorably impressed by the attempts of non-analytical psychologists to study these other aspects of psychoanalytic theory.

The answer to this paradox may well lie in the central role which

[7] From E. R. Hilgard, "Experimental Approaches to Psychoanalysis," in E. Pumpian-Mindlin (ed.), *Psychoanalysis as Science*, 1952, p. 44, Stanford University Press, Calif. Used by permission of Basic Books, Inc., New York.

[8] From L. S. Kubie, "Problems and Techniques of Psychoanalytic Validation and Progress," in E. Pumpian-Mindlin (ed.), *Psychoanalysis as Science*, 1952, p. 64, Stanford University Press, Calif. Used by permission of Basic Books, Inc., New York.

psychoanalysts have always accorded the concept of repression in their theory. It is clearly the psychoanalysts' most highly cathected concept. And it is so because Freud (1914) wrote that "the doctrine of repression is the foundation stone on which the whole structure of psychoanalysis rests." ("On the History of the Psycho-analytic Movement," p. 297). To examine critically the concept of repression, and especially to question, as did some of the early researchers, whether there is such a process was to call into question the entire conceptual fabric of psychoanalysis.

Summary Evaluation of the Contribution of Psychodynamicists

It is ironical that it was just those psychologists who were first attracted to the theory of psychoanalysis and who sought to effect a rapprochement between it and experimental psychology who were most severely criticized by the psychoanalysts on the one side and the experimental psychologists on the other for their loose conceptual thinking and sloppy experimental technique. Their efforts to integrate the two into a broader, more comprehensive science adequate to apply some of the rigor and control and methodological refinement of traditional experimental psychology to the dynamic problems of complexly motivated behavior were appreciated by neither side and were attacked by both.

In retrospect the experimental psychodynamicists of the 1930's would appear to have achieved far less than they had hoped, and by the end of the 1940's they had largely disappeared from the psychological scene. Was their retreat from the arena of an "experimental psycho-analysis" the result of their failure to win widespread acceptance for their research program or were there other factors responsible for their defection? One cannot be certain, but by the late '40's a change in the *Zeitgeist* of psychology was everywhere apparent.

World War II took place in 1941–5, years in which few psychologists remained within the ivory towers of the university. During this period most of them had been using their psychological skills and insights in dealing with the most varied aspects of behavior under stress—a far wider range of problems "close to life" than those which the psychodynamicists had attempted to bring into the laboratory from the psychoanalyst's consulting room. Psychologists, in general, returned from war service with greatly raised sights as to what their science should be and what it could do. Psychodynamicists turned now to the far more complex problems of clinical psychology, psychodiagnostics, and personality development and assessment which were either appearing for the first time on the psychological scene or could now be approached with far more technical and statistical skill than had been possible prior to the war. And the most hard-bitten experimentalists turned to problems of emotion and motivation which before the war had seemed to be largely outside the sphere of their competence or interest.

Although the psychodynamicists failed in their specific goal of bringing repression as conceived by the psychoanalysts into the laboratory for experimental study, they achieved, even more rapidly than they had ever hoped, thanks to the facilitating effect of the war years, their broader objective, namely an enormous extension of the range and complexity of problems which psychologists would be willing to attack experimentally.

Thus it was that the kinds of problems which psychodynamicists were attempting to study experimentally before the war passed increasingly after 1945 into the hands of those who thought of themselves as "hard-headed" experimentalists and in no sense "soft-headed" clinicians and personologists. In this transition even the names of the phenomena under investigation would change; for example, the problem of repression would become the problem of perceptual defense.

EXPERIMENTAL STUDIES OF "DENIAL OF ENTRY INTO CONSCIOUSNESS"

IN THIS NEW ATMOSPHERE, interest shifted from repression as one, and perhaps the most important, form of motivated forgetting to perceptual defense as one form of motivated perceiving. There is no evidence to suggest that those who pioneered in the experimental study of perceptual defense were primarily interested in demonstrating repression. Though they saw certain aspects of their hypotheses as congruent with Freudian assertions, their theory and research had their primary roots in functionalistic psychology. Yet in the perspective of the present historical survey it can be said that this movement represents the third of the possible experimental approaches to the study of repression: the investigation of a "denial of entry into consciousness" via the demonstration of inhibition of perception or failure to perceive anxiety-arousing stimuli.

It cannot, of course, be asserted that these have been studies of primal repression, since they have used adults as subjects rather than infants and children. There is, however, a sense in which primal repression must also be thought of as after-expulsion, not of memory images but of percepts, and best studied, perhaps only available for study, in adult subjects who are able to make verbal reports on their experience.

Though he sought to distinguish between them, the close similarity of primal repression and after-repression was clearly recognized by Freud:

In general, repression of the ideational presentation of an instinct can surely only have the effect of causing it to vanish from consciousness if it had previously been in consciousness, or of holding it back if it is about to enter it. The difference, after all, is not important; it amounts to much the same thing as the difference between ordering an undesirable guest out of my drawing-room or out of my front hall, and refusing to let him cross my threshold once I have recognized him.[9]

This metaphor, *"refusing to let him cross my threshold once I have recognized him,"* highlights the paradox of the concept of "denial of entry into consciousness," for repression at the level of perception requires the assumption that "something is perceived in order not to be perceived," in other words, "perception without awareness" or "unconscious perception." All such notions seem to imply a perceiving homunculus in man and this alone would account for the violent criticism to which purported demonstrations of perceptual defense have been subjected (see below).

Motivated Perceiving

The problem as these psychologists saw it was to discover whether, and if so in what manner, perception or distortion of the perceptual process does indeed serve to shield one from anxiety-provoking events. Dissatisfied with the standard structural description of perception, including those provided by the Gestaltists as well as those framed in the tradition of Wundt and Titchener, they challenged the adequacy of theories of perception in which the only important independent variables were the characteristics of the physical stimulus and the properties of the neural system. They emphasized the adaptive role of perception in the person-environment interaction, insisting that an individual's motivational system is an important determiner of what he perceives.

GENERAL THEORY.   The basic viewpoint was expressed by Bruner (1948):

Perception, to begin with, is an activity of the total organism and, like all other activities, is an aspect of the economy of personality. It serves two general functions for the organism. Through perception we *construct* a world in which survival and adjustment are possible; through perception we also *defend* against that which is threatening, distracting, or disruptive. The two processes, construction and defense,

[9] From Sigmund Freud, *Repression*, 1915, p. 91. Translated in *Collected Papers*, Vol. IV. Copyright 1925 by Hogarth Press, Ltd., London.

serve reciprocally to maximize sensitivity to certain classes of events, and to dampen or hinder sensitivity to others. . . .

Indeed, it is possible to think of perception along a continuum from autistic wishfulness at one extreme to hypervigilance at the other. . . .

What may be called "normal" perception lies midway between these two extremes.[1]

Several complementary and partially overlapping, selective mechanisms supposedly operate to achieve these functions: *selective sensitization*, whereby perceptual thresholds are lowered for acceptable stimuli, *perceptual defense*, in which they are raised for unacceptable stimuli, *value resonance*, a readiness factor produced by one's value orientation, and *selective vigilance*, a differential sensitivity to relevant cues, positive or negative in affect (Bruner and Postman, 1947; Postman, Bruner, and McGinnies, 1948).

Perceptual Defense

Perceptual defense, then, was introduced as one in a family of constructs to account for certain systematic variations in perceptual thresholds. Such variations were observed when all the factors traditionally considered relevant to threshold determination were held constant (stimulus intensity, degree of light-dark adaptation, etc.) with only the affective meaning of the stimulus varied. The original formulation of the perceptual-defense concept was as follows: "The bulk of experimental and clinical evidence points to blockage as the process producing increase in association time to emotionally charged stimuli. Such blocking in association represents a defense against anxiety-laden stimuli. A basically similar process is at work in perception. With increase in emotionality of stimuli, recognition may lead to anxiety and is to be avoided as long as possible" (J. S. Bruner and L. Postman, "Emotional Selectivity in Perception and Reaction," *J. Pers.*, 1947, 16, 74). The impact of this idea on psychological research is easily seen in the scores of articles on perceptual defense which appeared in the psychological journals during the 1950's. The magnitude of their number inspired Blum to remark, "Probably no concept in psychology has enjoyed such dizzy popularity in a short span of time as perceptual defense" (1955, p. 24).

HISTORICAL ANTECEDENTS.   These hypotheses and constructs are certainly consonant with psychoanalytic theory, and this relationship was clearly recognized. Indeed, Postman, Bruner, and McGinnies' discussion of perceptual selectivity included this statement, "We suggest

[1] From J. S. Bruner, "IV: Perceptual Theory and the Rorschach Test," *J. Personality*, 1948, 17, 160–1. Used by permission.

that a defense mechanism similar to repression operates in perceptual behavior" ("Personal Values as Selective Factors in Perception," *J. abnorm. soc. Psychol.*, 1948, 43, 152). The general idea of perceptual defense, whereby the organism is shielded from the perception of inimical stimuli, can rather easily be subsumed under the Freudian concept of repression, Freud having specified that *"the essence of repression lies simply in the function of rejecting and keeping something out of consciousness"* (*Repression*, 1915, p. 86). This emphasis on the protective function of perception can, furthermore, appropriately be considered a mid-twentieth century revival of some of Freud's views on perception, for he had conjectured:

> *Protection* against stimuli is an almost more important function for the living organism than *reception* of stimuli. The protective shield is supplied with its own store of energy and must above all endeavor to preserve the special modes of transformation, or energy operating in it against the effects threatened by the enormous energies at work in the external world.[2]

The shift of emphasis in experimentation from the psychoanalytic concept of repression to that of defense during the late 1940's was, moreover, contrapuntal to a transition which had occurred a decade or two earlier in psychoanalysis proper. Psychoanalytic theory had moved from an id- to an ego-orientation, from a preoccupation with the repression of instinctual forces to a concern for the defense of the ego.

This conceptual similarity to psychoanalytic doctrine does not, however, guarantee that the major tenets of the later movement were necessarily an outgrowth from Freudian doctrines. Actually the same propositions regarding the adaptive functions of perception could be, and apparently in part were, as the references in the pioneer articles indicate, derived from theories and findings established in the laboratory and field, relatively independently of data from the analyst's couch. Bartlett's work (1932) on "distortion" in the cognitive processes, Brunswik's achievement approach (1934) to perception, Sanford's studies (1937) relating perceptual and ideational variables to motivation, were all logical precursors of the 1950 functionalistic theories of perceiving.

Though Bartlett's, Brunswik's, and Sanford's pertinent works were chronologically later than most of Freud's, their relationship to perceptual defense may not seem so patent as his, since each of them had been concerned primarily with the positive aspects of cognition—(e.g.,

---

[2] From Sigmund Freud, *Beyond the Pleasure Principle*, 1920, p. 27. Translated in J. Strachey (ed.), *The Standard Edition of the Complete Psychological Works of Sigmund Freud*, Vol. XVIII. Copyright 1955 by Hogarth Press, Ltd., London, and used by their permission. In the United States, permission granted by Liveright Publishing Corp., New York.

Bartlett's book was titled *Remembering,* not *Forgetting*). Freud's orientation, on the other hand, had been predominantly negative—i.e., why we forget or fail to perceive—providing, therefore, a more immediate point of departure for theories of perceptual defense.

McGinnies' Experiment

The general topic of selective perception is an interesting chapter in the history of psychology, but only those segments of it treating the negative or defensive functions are pertinent here. Although the notion had been introduced earlier, McGinnies' "Emotionality and Perceptual Defense" (1949) was the first article exclusively devoted to the thesis that individuals, without any conscious intent, purposefully fail to perceive.

Using, as stimuli, words presumed to be emotionally toned—socially taboo words (e.g., "whore") and supposedly comparable neutral words (e.g., "stove")—McGinnies presented each tachistoscopically to his subjects, college students, at speeds well above that at which correct report could be made. On each exposure prior to recognition, the subject's galvanic skin response (GSR) was recorded, and he was asked to say what he had seen. Each word was presented with increasing exposure times until correct identification was reported. McGinnies found that the GSR's accompanying emotionally toned words but preceding their reported recognition were significantly larger than those obtained under similar conditions for neutral words, and that the recognition threshold for taboo words, as measured by duration of exposure, was significantly longer than that for neutral words. These findings he offered as evidence for a perceptual defense mechanism, or repression at the perceptual level. More specifically, he concluded:

> Perceptual defense apparently is based upon conditioned avoidance of unpleasant or dangerous stimulus objects. That the individual actually discriminates the stimulus before he fully perceives it is evident in his increased emotionality before recognition. Inimical stimuli, then, may serve as cues which are appropriately evaluated by the central nervous system even though the integration of the afferent impulses is such as to delay recognition, either through distortion or an increase in threshold or both. Almost without exception, the galvanic skin response of the observers was greatest following the final exposure of the critical words; that is, the one during which recognition occurred. Clearly the process of perceptual defense is designed to delay the greater anxiety that accompanies actual recognition of the stimulus.[3]

[3] From E. McGinnies, "Emotionality and Perceptual Defense," *Psychol. Rev.,* 1949, 56, 250. Used by permission of the American Psychological Association.

With the appearance of McGinnies' article the battle flags went up. Because the very notion of perceptual defense was antithetical to the description of man's behavior furnished by most academic psychologists, widespread opposition to McGinnies' treatise was voiced. Especially distasteful, of course, was the notion of an unconscious emotional determination of perceptual recognition which was purportedly demonstrable in the experimental laboratory. In a sense, home territory was being invaded. The concept was repugnant to associationists and configurationists alike, for their principles were subordinated to more dynamic ones (repression, etc.).

Examination of the major points of objection will demonstrate the extent and degree of the dissension.

The Frequency Controversy

WORD COUNT CONTROLS. Almost immediately, D. H. Howes and R. L. Solomon ("A Note on McGinnies' 'Emotionality and Perceptual Defense,'" *Psychol. Rev.*, 1950, 57) challenged McGinnies' explanation for the threshold differences in terms of defense, invoking in its place the frequency hypothesis. "Our contention here is that McGinnies' taboo words might be expected to have far higher duration thresholds than his neutral words because the relative frequencies of the former are far lower" (p. 229). Using Thorndike-Lorge counts as an index of frequency of word usage, they plotted McGinnies' threshold data against log word-frequencies. On the basis of these plots they maintained that "the taboo words behave pretty much as if their Lorge-Thorndike frequencies predicted their duration thresholds adequately" (p. 230).

In his rebuttal McGinnies ("Discussion of Howes' and Solomon's note on 'Emotionality and Perceptual Defense,'" *Psychol. Rev.*, 1950, 57) objected that literary sources did not provide a valid index of the frequency of taboo words. Furthermore, when he made separate scatterplots for neutral and taboo words, neither exhibited the relationship predicted by Howes and Solomon. McGinnies suggested therefore that the Howes-Solomon effect "could be merely an artifact resulting from the combining of two sets of threshold data the respective means of which have been determined by word meaning rather than by frequency of occurrence in conservative literary sources" (p. 237). He did, however, concede that "a possible confounding effect introduced by frequency cannot entirely be discounted without further investigation. But no such effect has been demonstrated with our data by the technique employed by Howes and Solomon" (p. 237).

Pursuing the frequency hypothesis still further, Solomon and Howes (1951) determined visual duration thresholds for high frequency and low frequency words representing each value area of the Allport-Vernon *Study of Values*. Their data showed that differences between duration threshold of words representing extreme differences in value rank as determined by performance on the *Study of Values* were negligible when compared with differences between the thresholds of words representing extreme differences in word frequency. On the basis of their findings they suggested that *value, interest,* and similar concepts are often inferences from word frequencies and generalized, apropos of McGinnies' work, that

> Emotional factors undoubtedly operate to an important extent in the *building* of word frequencies in a given life history. In this way they would be related to word frequency and, indirectly, to duration threshold. . . . But to date we can find no evidence to suggest that emotional factors operate in the tachistoscopic situation independently of their effect upon word frequency.[4]

LACK OF EXPLANATORY CHARACTER.   Postman and Schneider (1951) challenged this reduction of value effects to frequency of usage. Varying both frequency and value in experiments on word recognition and recall, they obtained data which indicated that frequency and the interaction of frequency and value were significant sources of variance for recognition thresholds, and value a significant source in recall. Their conclusion was

> . . . that it will not be profitable at this stage of theoretical development to cast the laws of all cognitive processes into a uniform mold of stimulus-response correlations and response probabilities. When we have measured the relative frequency with which words occur in the English language, we have not exhausted the determinants of their perceptual recognition. . . .
>
> Although general frequency of usage may be practically useful in predicting responses to verbal stimuli in a variety of situations, we do not believe that response probability is a basic psychological variable which will advance general cognitive theory. . . . An empirical correlation between response probability and duration thresholds for verbal stimuli, for example, does not explain the duration thresholds at all. It merely poses the question as to the general psychological principles under which both the general and the specific response probabilities can be subsumed.[5]

[4] From R. L. Solomon and D. H. Howes, "Word Frequency, Personal Values, and Visual Duration Thresholds," *Psychol. Rev.*, 1951, 58, 267. Used by permission of the American Psychological Association.

[5] From L. Postman and B. H. Schneider, "Personal Values, Visual Recognition, and Recall," *Psychol. Rev.*, 1951, 58, 283. Used by permission of the American Psychological Association.

LABORATORY CONTROL OF FREQUENCY. Viewing the tachisto-scopic situation as similar to most reading situations, Solomon and Post-man (1952) considered inappropriate McGinnies' reply that the Thorndike-Lorge word counts are not actually representative of fre-quency. According to the principles of stimulus generalization, they as-serted, frequency of occurrence in literature should predict duration thresholds at least as well as verbal response frequency in conversation. They did admit, however, that a *population index* like the Thorndike-Lorge count of frequency of word usage provides only rough estimates of individual subjects' frequency of usage. Any method which relies on such an index, they recognized, entails a lack of control over this crucial independent variable, since frequencies are always determined prior to the experiment and their values for an individual are unknown.

To remedy this inadequacy they used nonsense words and "built in" differential frequencies of usage by presenting the various words dif-fering numbers of times before the recognition test. Under this condi-tion, frequency, as in the Howes and Solomon experiment, was found to be inversely related to recognition thresholds.

RANGE OF OPERATION. Re-examination of the Solomon-Postman and other similar data which support the frequency-hypothesis led Lazarus (1954) to conclude

> . . . that the correlations between word frequencies and visual recog-nition thresholds are minimal, particularly at the higher word frequen-cies which are typically found in most experiments. Most of the co-variation seems to occur when words of zero frequency are compared with words with slightly greater frequencies and over a very wide range. . . . Little covariation seems to occur when highly frequent words of differing frequency value are used, and it is these high-frequency words which are typically employed in perceptual studies. There is not much doubt that word frequency is a variable in per-ceptual recognition under certain conditions, but it is not a variable of such great importance and generality as has been suggested.[6]

In a critical review of the role of frequency in perceptual recog-nition, C. W. Eriksen ("The Case for Perceptual Defense," *Psychol. Rev.*, 1954, 61) summarily argued, "Even if familiarity could be shown to be a major determinant of recognition thresholds, it still would be unable to explain the evidence for perceptual defense" (p. 179). He then cited findings from several experiments in which individual dif-ferences in reaction to success or failure, completion or incompletion

[6] From R. S. Lazarus, "Is There a Mechanism of Perceptual Defense? A Reply to Postman, Bronson, and Gropper," *J. abnorm. soc. Psychol.*, 1954, 49, 397. Used by permission of the American Psychological Association.

experiences, produced significant variation in perceptual sensitivity to words associated with those experiences. He stated, for example, that "an explanation in terms of familiarity would be hard put to explain why subjects who recall completed tasks [better than incompleted ones] have high recognition thresholds for words with long association times, while subjects who recall incompleted tasks do not" (p. 179). Eriksen (1952) had previously interpreted these results as demonstrating the role of different ego defenses in the perception of ego-threatening stimuli.

CONSTANT FREQUENCY, VARIABLE THRESHOLD. But perhaps the most crucial demonstration of the inadequacy of the frequency factor alone to explain threshold variability was provided by M. Wiener ("Word Frequency or Motivation in Perceptual Defense," *J. abnorm. soc. Psychol.*, 1955, 51). Questioning the Howes-Solomon hypothesis, Wiener selected four critical words which had both neutral and "threat" meaning (e.g., "fairy") and embedded them in two lists of fifty words, one of which emphasized the neutral meaning of the words, the other the "threat" meaning. After exposing one group of subjects to the neutral list, another to the threat list, he presented them with booklets, one for each critical word and for two added neutral words. Each booklet contained thirty successive carbon copies of the test words, beginning with the least clear copy and continuing by degrees to the clearest. He instructed the subjects to decipher the words as quickly as possible, the score being the page number on which they identified the word. The group who had been given the "threat" list, he discovered, needed significantly fewer trials than the group who had been exposed to the neutral list to decipher the critical words, whose frequencies, of course, were constant. This led him to conclude "that with structural determinants held constant, word meaning and therefore motivational factors are important determinants in perceptual behavior and word frequency hypotheses alone cannot account for the results" (p. 217).

BRIEF SUMMARY. Although many issues pertinent to the frequency hypothesis as it related to word usage and recognition were still being argued (e.g., *how* it influences thresholds, the relationship between frequency and familiarity, etc.), by 1955 the controversy over the role of frequency in "perceptual defense" had largely subsided. Some consensus seemed to be reached to the effect that while word frequency is important enough in threshold determination to require control in experimental designs, it does not supplant motivational-emotional factors.

This controversy, like most others in the history of science, arose because a given set of empirical results confirmed at least two different hypotheses. In the present instance, the obtained difference between recognition thresholds for emotional and neutral words could be viewed as supporting either a "frequency" or a "defense" hypothesis. The trend toward resolution was the typical one of introducing controls which "untied" the effects of the confounded variables—e.g., word counts, experimentally determined frequency and emotionality, *et al.*

Suppression or Repression?

Another line of attack launched by Howes and Solomon (1950) against McGinnies' defense hypothesis was their contention that his subjects were doubtless recognizing but not immediately reporting the critical words; i.e., that they were suppressing verbal response rather than repressing threatening perception. They claimed:

> The subject's "set" in the usual tachistoscopic experiment tends to "inhibit" his actually speaking a taboo word. McGinnies' study appears to be no exception. Suppose a long exposure has raised the probability of the taboo word far above the probabilities of any other word, so that it would be reported if the inhibitory "set" were not present; overt report of the word will tend to be held back in the atmosphere of scientific respectability that surrounds the experiment . . .[7]

They suggested that the degree to which this kind of inhibition operates might be determined by experimental manipulation of subject-experimenter relationship (friend, male-female, etc.).

PRERECOGNITION DATA. Although McGinnies (1950) admitted that the possibility of deliberate withholding does "constitute one of the knottier problems in this type of research" (p. 237), he in reply cited the content analysis of his subjects' volunteered, prerecognition hypotheses—the guesses or speculations they made about what the word might be, even though quite uncertain. For the neutral words, prerecognition hypotheses were categorized predominantly either as being structurally *similar* to the stimulus word or as bearing a *part-whole* relationship to it (e.g., recognizing some letters); for the taboo words the prerecognition hypotheses were more often either structurally *unlike* the stimulus or *nonsensical*, i.e., a word without dictionary meaning. He asserted, "It seems improbable, as Howes and Solomon would have to maintain, that the observers spontaneously and consistently adopted these patterns of hypothesis formation when faced with taboo words and reverted to a different pattern of verbal-report behavior when viewing the neutral stimuli" (p. 238). He in turn criticized them for

[7] From D. H. Howes and R. L. Solomon, "A Note on McGinnies' 'Emotionality and Perceptual Defense,' " *Psychol. Rev.*, 1950, 57, 232. Used by permission of the American Psychological Association.

their failure to avail themselves of this type of data (prerecognition hypotheses) in evaluating their assertions about suppression.

Postman, Bronson, and Gropper (1953) argued, however, that Mc-Ginnies' findings about prerecognition hypotheses hardly constituted unequivocal evidence for a perceptual-defense hypothesis, since, they contended, one might equally well reconcile exactly opposite findings with the hypothesis of perceptual defense. For example, more structurally similar and part responses to charged words could, they pointed out, be interpreted as evidence that perceptual defense delays the final correct organization of the word.

"DEFENSE" GENERALIZATION.   As a further check on the suppression hypothesis, McGinnies and Sherman (1952) attempted to create a situation in which subjects would have no hesitancy in verbalizing their perceptions. Each of eight neutral words was presented tachistoscopically and recognition thresholds determined. Half of these words were always preceded by a full exposure of another neutral word, the other half by a full exposure of a taboo word. Because thresholds obtained under the latter condition (taboo-pairing) were higher than those under the former, and since all the test words were neutral, the reporting of which should elicit no anxiety, McGinnies and Sherman concluded that the raised thresholds indicated a genuine delay in *recognition*, not merely in reporting.

Here again Postman, Bronson, and Gropper (1953) objected that these findings neither represented cogent evidence for perceptual defense nor disposed of the problem of selective report. They maintained that since perceptual defense has been alleged to be an avoidance reaction specific to threatening stimuli, it must be demonstrated *as such* before it is appropriate to assert its generalization to neutral stimuli.

CONTROLS FOR SUPPRESSION.   Studies which made use of Howes and Solomon's suggestion to manipulate inhibitory tendencies experimentally by varying the subject-experimenter relationship did not yield consistent results. For example, in a recognition-threshold test, administered sometimes by a Negro, sometimes by a white experimenter, to both white and Negro subjects, and including stimulus words like "nigger" and "darky," Whittaker, Gilchrist, and Fischer (1952) reported evidence of suppressed reports. Cowen and Beier (1954), on the other hand, with both male and female experimenters and subjects in a recognition test which included sexually oriented threat words, purportedly demonstrated an absence of differential inhibition.

BRIEF SUMMARY.   The last word has not been written on the suppression-repression controversy, but it has become less virulent as research designs minimize factors which might produce withholding of verbal report. Here again the argument centered around two different explanations for the same event, viz., the delayed reporting of taboo words. In this instance, however, because psychologists have not yet devised reliable operations for distinguishing the two processes, repression and suppression, evidence advanced for either explanation is more suggestive than conclusive. To the scientist working in the marginal zone where precise controls are lacking, the question of what constitutes acceptable evidence becomes acute. The research psychologist would probably never present the kind of evidence regularly employed by one of the seamen in Paul Gallico's *The Abandoned:* Mr. Strachan habitually "proved" that he had witnessed some remarkable event by producing a burnt match stick or small bit of paper which he had with him at the time the phenomenon supposedly occurred. But, convinced that a certain hypothesis is tenable and lacking definitive confirmation, the psychologist might offer as evidence data which to an objective or differently biased observer were irrelevant (e.g., McGinnies' generalization evidence for perceptual defense to Postman, Bronson, and Gropper). Such evidence is usually speedily challenged.

The Set Explanation

A further group of psychologists took issue with the defense interpretation of McGinnies' data, objecting not so much to the likelihood that the experimental situation and the subject's past experience cause him to withhold purposefully his responses to the taboo words, as to the possibility that such factors work toward the creation of a *set* or a predisposition to organize stimuli in a certain fashion, which, without unconscious intent to protect himself or conscious inhibition of response to avoid embarrassment, may result in the raised thresholds. Luchins, for example, early asserted that

> . . . if a general explanation must be forthcoming, it seems to us that it can be found more parsimoniously in the concept of set.
>
> If the concept of set can help to explain why selectivity for certain stimulus objects is enhanced, it can also help to explain why selectivity for other objects is lessened. . . . While a set may focus one on certain aspects of the stimulus field, it may blind him to others.

As an illustration he cited his own experiment on problem-solving in which he found that

> an *Einstellung* or mental set, by tending to favor the utilization in subsequent problems of an oft-repeated method of solution, prevented the use of another, simpler method. Yet we did not find it necessary

or helpful to postulate that the subject was defending himself against this simpler method, that he was consciously or unconsciously excluding it, nor did the subjects' reports bear out such an interpretation. Organization of the perceptual situation in line with the prevailing set militated against its reorganization in line with what was required by the simpler method of solution.[8]

Eriksen ("The Case for Perceptual Defense," *Psychol. Rev.*, 1954, 61) dismissed Luchins' criticism without much ado: "He [Luchins] has also suggested that the concept of perceptual defense could be handled in terms of 'set,' and this is quite probably true. The concept of set has shown itself in the history of psychology to be both broad and ambiguous enough to hide many important problems" (p. 180).

PERCEPTUAL HYPOTHESES.   Rejecting repression as the factor responsible for the elevated thresholds for threatening words, Postman (1951) also offered an explanation in terms of set or—to use his term—hypotheses. But his account of hypotheses—which can be identified here as perceptual expectancies—incorporated enough safeguards to avoid being labeled "broad" and "ambiguous." He repeatedly insisted that any assumed determinant of selective perception must be properly anchored in definable antecedent and consequent conditions, i.e., in the measurable physical stimulus and the objective aspects of an organism's behavior. He therefore attempted to relate hypothesis development to the rather well established laws of associative learning—frequency and recency of confirmation and emphasis resulting from motivational relevance.

In a level-of-aspiration situation, Postman and Brown (1952) allowed the members of one group to exceed their announced goals on most trials and seldom permitted members of another group to attain their stated goals. The findings demonstrated that hypotheses related to success gain strength in a situation associated with success, while those related to failure gain in a failure situation. In a context of success, thresholds were lower for success words, and similarly for a failure context and failure words. They claimed:

> It seems to us that theoretical arguments relating perception to such general personality factors (as "repression" and "autistic tendencies") hold out little promise for the precise specification and experimental manipulation of the conditions under which variations in perceptual behavior occur. It would be difficult, for example, to vary repressive tendencies experimentally in order to demonstrate their perceptual consequences. Our formulation which relates perceptual selec-

---

[8] From A. S. Luchins, "On an Approach to Social Perception," *J. Personality*, 1950, 19, 77. Used by permission.

tivity to principles of learning is capable of experimental tests and will stand or fall with the results of such tests.[9]

Extending this argument Postman, Bronson, and Gropper (1953) posed the question of whether, after the effects of frequency, suppression, and set have been taken into account, any mechanism of perceptual defense exists. Their reply was clearly negative.

> . . . the processes described by such terms as "defense" or "repression" surely are not to be conceived as subject to significant manipulation by means of preparatory instructions! If they were so manipulable, such defenses or repressions would, indeed, be very different from those described by personality theorists. . . .
> We conclude that the experimental findings to date have failed to lend support to the concept of perceptual defense. The results have been either indeterminate or can be explained in terms of more general principles. It may, of course, be argued that stimuli such as those used by McGinnies and ourselves are not appropriate for testing the hypothesis of perceptual defense. Such may or may not be the case; the possibility of future positive evidence cannot, of course, be excluded. At the present, however, perceptual defense has, at best, the status of an unconfirmed hypothesis.[1]

RELEVANT VS. IRRELEVANT DATA.   This attempt to eliminate the defense aspect of perceptual defense by reducing the effects to the operation of non-emotional (or "non-personality") determinants did not go unchallenged. Lazarus (1954) accused Postman, Bronson, and Gropper of attacking perceptual defense on the basis of a few inappropriate experiments. He expressed "no doubt that findings in terms of mean differences in thresholds for emotional and neutral words could be made to go in either direction by the appropriate selection of words on the basis of such variables as context, contrast, sequential probabilities, and a host of other factors not directly related to word frequency. We have no way of knowing which variables were operating in this type of study. But this is irrelevant to the concept of defense" (p. 397). Relevant data, he continued, "include differential thresholds in the perception or recall of emotional and non-emotional stimuli which have been found to correlate with clinical typologies, or with the results of additional exposure to different kinds of stresses" (p. 397). As an example, he cited Lazarus, Eriksen, and Fonda's finding (1951) that patients classified as intellectualizers on the basis of case history and interview

[9] From L. Postman and D. R. Brown, "The Perceptual Consequences of Success and Failure," *J. abnorm. soc. Psychol.*, 1952, 47, 219–20. Used by permission of the American Psychological Association.

[1] From L. Postman, W. C. Bronson, and G. L. Gropper, "Is There a Mechanism of Perceptual Defense?" *J. abnorm. soc. Psychol.*, 1953, 48, 222–3. Used by permission of the American Psychological Association.

perceive threatening material with greater accuracy than do those classified as repressers.

REPRESSION REAFFIRMED.   Blum (1955) objected to Postman's "vociferous denouncement" of the concept of perceptual defense, and promptly responded by conducting an experiment, the design of which purportedly controlled for Postman's "incisive criticisms," to test the hypothesis that

> Subjects predisposed to use the mechanism of repression in conjunction with a given conflict will, when confronted subliminally with a conflict-relevant stimulus, show defensive behavior directly traceable to the perceptual process itself.[2]

By means of his Blacky Pictures, Blum assessed subjects for conflict and repression in the various areas represented by the test pictures (e.g., oral sadism, masturbation guilt, etc.). He then flashed four of the pictures simultaneously for .03 seconds duration, one each at the left, right, top, and bottom of the exposed field, instructing the subjects to identify the pictures in each of the four positions. Although the instructions indicated that no picture would be presented in the same pattern twice and that the pattern would vary from flash to flash, the same four pictures were flashed forty-eight times, six different patterns being repeated eight times. Under this arrangement the responses could be classified according to whether the picture called was present or absent, and for each of these, whether it represented an area of conflict and repression for the subject, or specifically:

Condition 1—Picture present, conflict and repression
Condition 2—Picture present, neutral
Condition 3—Picture absent, conflict and repression
Condition 4—Picture absent, neutral.

Analysis of the distribution of calls revealed, consonant with Blum's hypothesis, that with the pictures actually present, the number of calls of pictures associated with conflict and repression was significantly fewer than that of calls of neutral pictures, while no differences between the calls of neutral and conflict pictures were found when the pictures were absent.

On the basis of these findings, Blum argued:

> About the only even remote way we can try to reconcile the hypothesis theory with our data is to say that the individual in Condition 1 has a *strong hypothesis not to perceive* the negative stimulus, and the response of not perceiving is tripped off by the actual appear-

---

[2] From G. S. Blum, "Perceptual Defense Revisited," *J. abnorm. soc. Psychol.*, 1955, 51, 25. Used by permission of the American Psychological Association.

ance of that stimulus in the tachistoscope. Having gone this far, we are confronted once again with what would have to be a $64 question for Postman—Why does the individual develop a hypothesis not to perceive?—a question easily answered if we look to psychoanalytic theory and perceptual defense.[3]

In conclusion he asserted that ". . . current attempts to abandon perceptual defense in the interests of 'theoretical parsimony' may very well be premature" (p. 29).

Smock (1956), however, immediately cast doubt on the reliability of Blum's demonstration, pointing out that the similarity between the criterion used to assess repression and the method of testing the perceptual manifestations of repression make interpretation of the data equivocal.

The previously cited experiment by Wiener (1955; cf. p. 718) also raised some questions for a set explanation. The group who had been exposed to two critical words in a context of threat words had, in a later tachistoscopic test, lower recognition thresholds for the critical words than did the group who had experienced them in a neutral context. This Wiener recognized as being in accord with the operation of set. But since the "threat-context" group was not proportionately slower than the "neutral-context" group in recognizing neutral test words, as Wiener assumed a set explanation would predict, he concluded that set or the use of threat hypotheses did not account for the data.

BRIEF SUMMARY. No final answer is at present available to the question of which hypothesis, set or defense, better explains the data on differences in recognition thresholds. Perhaps in some instances the seemingly divergent hypotheses are referring to the same mediating mechanisms; conceivably they may be complementary, or even tautological. Certainly in many instances they both intend some inferred motivational determinant.

This controversy exemplifies rather clearly the manner in which psychological concepts "evolve" or "mature" through critical scrutiny. The challengers here complained of the lack of rigor in experimental procedure which led to indeterminate results. When they applied their precise, efficient "tools," they rejected the defense interpretation as superfluous. The charges were met with countercharges; the challengers (and the early investigators as well) were accused of searching in the wrong places and were reminded that no degree of refinement in operations would be productive unless relevant behavior were sampled. Hence an attempt was made (in this instance by Blum) to attain a "sharper"

[3] From G. S. Blum, "Perceptual Defense Revisited," *J. abnorm. soc. Psychol.*, 1955, 51, 28. Used by permission of the American Psychological Association.

concept by heeding both the criticism of lack of rigor and that of lack of relevance. On a larger scale this interplay between the methodological ideals of maintaining strict controls in the observation of responses and selecting significant segments of behavior for conceptualization, is much of the history of modern psychology.

The Logical Paradox of "Subliminal Perception"

SEMANTIC ASPECTS.   In his critique of perceptual defense, Howie (1952) called attention to the semantic problem involved in the concept, maintaining that it entailed a simultaneous process of knowing and avoiding knowing. Bruner and Postman (1949) had been well aware of the paradox and had even suggested its resolution— namely, that veridical report has one threshold, and affective avoidance response another. Postman (1953), however, replied further to Howie's comment that semantic issues do not bar the use of a concept, pointing out that the only contradictions providing serious grounds for objection to a given concept are incompatible operations or incompatible deductions entailed by its use. Postman indicated that since the history of perceptual defense made it clear that neither of these conditions applied, Howie's objection was hardly appropriate.

SUBCEPTION.   Related to the semantic issue just outlined was the more fundamental question of how awareness, which can not be verbalized or reported, is mediated? Soon after the first barrage of objections was hurled at perceptual defense, published research by Lazarus and McCleary (1951) on discrimination without awareness provided data which McGinnies considered corroborative evidence for his interpretation of elevated GSR's as prerecognition responses to emotionally toned words. Independently of McGinnies they established that when nonsense syllables which had been associated with electric shock were presented tachistoscopically at exposures too rapid for recognition, higher GSR's were obtained than for nonshock syllables. They coined the term "subception" to identify this observed phenomenon and the process which they believed it implied:

> The major finding of the present research, the subception effect, has implications not only for perceptual theory, which we have mentioned earlier, but may also have relevance in the field of personality and clinical psychology. The unconscious determination of behavior is a concept of considerable importance in present-day clinical thinking. In so far as autonomic activity can be regarded as a form of behavior, we believe that we may have here an experimental instance of such an unconscious process. . . . This kind of mechanism is all the more suggestive when coupled with the possibility that "recognition

thresholds" might be subject to influence by the "needs" of the individual.[4]

The evidence which Lazarus and McCleary presented has been interpreted as providing an answer to how a person can "know" what to defend against.

SUBCEPTION: EFFECT VS. PROCESS. But any encouragement which the perceptual-defense camp may have received from the subception hypothesis was relatively short-lived, since it too was soon the object of onslaught.

Bricker and Chapanis (1953) and Murdock (1954), for example, questioned the validity of the interpretation that lawful autonomic responses occur to stimuli without any conscious recognition of these stimuli. Specifically, they objected to the assumption that no information was obtained from stimulus presentations which were incorrectly identified. By allowing subjects additional guesses when the first response to the tachistoscopically presented stimulus word was incorrect, these experimenters established that these stimuli could be correctly identified with better-than-chance accuracy (e.g., Bricker and Chapanis found that fewer guesses were needed to identify incorrectly perceived stimuli than to arrive at the correct response by random guessing). Howes (1954) argued that the postulation of a subception *process* was unnecessary; as an alternative, he presented a statistical model from which the subception effect could be derived on the basis of response probabilities.

Eriksen (1956) claimed that subception is an artifact resulting from the comparison of a response system having a discrete distribution, the verbal responses, with one that for all practical purposes is continuously distributed, the GSR's. The unavailability of a sufficient number of verbal responses to reflect all the discriminations which the subjects are capable of making, he contended, produced the subception effect. That is, in the typical subception experiment, verbal responses are scored on an all-or-none basis, no differentiation being made between possible degrees of recognition (e.g., no credit is allowed for responses such as "the middle letter was a 'u' "); GSR's, on the other hand, may have a near infinity of values, possibly reflecting many different degrees of awareness.

To these objections, Lazarus retorted:

It is not at all necessary to assume that the physiological response system of the organism is a more precise mirror of the physical stimuli

[4] From R. S. Lazarus and R. A. McCleary, "Autonomic Discrimination without Awareness: A Study of Subception," *Psychol. Rev.*, 1951, *58*, 121. Used by permission of the American Psychological Association.

than the verbal response system. A perfectly logical alternative is that the autonomic response system reflects the presence or absence of danger—that is, the shock or nonshock consequences of the stimulus— even though the level of discrimination is not sharp enough to identify the specific components of the stimulus. In this event, the process does not involve a one-to-one correspondence of the autonomic response with the stimulus, but a categorical one. Such a relationship may be based upon the direct response of the organism to the stimulus, or may be mediated by a process of inference in which the nature of the stimulus is built up from the stimulus elements. . . .

Eriksen's argument is based on a statistical rather than a psychological analysis of the problem. It could be also argued that restriction in one response system (verbal) in contrast to the other (autonomic) is quite close to the conditions prevailing in actual life, and that what we refer to as "lack of awareness" can be dependent upon (although not necessarily identical with) just such restriction in the verbal processes. . . .

Psychologists find great, and I believe often fruitless, sport in examining data which arise out of theoretical frameworks which have real fertileness for generating hypotheses and in showing that these data can be explained, *post hoc*, by some other system. Of course it can. In this sense, Eriksen's argument misses the point, as do those of Bricker and Chapanis, of Murdock, and of Howes. The issues dealing with such postulates as perceptual defense and the process of subception cannot be decided solely on the basis of laboratory experiments. These issues have to be cast in the much broader frame of one's entire conceptual view of human behavior.[5]

Further experimentation led Eriksen both to modify his theory in the direction of Lazarus' comment and to reject Lazarus' suggestion that the threshold for danger discrimination is lower than that for specific identification. He concluded:

. . . the subception effect as an effect is real enough but it has nothing to say and offers no proof concerning the capacity of the GSR to reflect a more sensitive discrimination than that which is available through the Ss' verbalizations. Instead the subception effect focuses attention upon the limitations of verbal responses in conveying the individual's perceptual experiences. . . .

There is reason to suspect that a considerable amount of the evidence that the clinician finds for unconscious processes is in the nature of discrepancy between concurrent responses. The clinician may note the Ss' autonomic responses and evidences of emotion do not correspond, i.e., do not correlate very well, with his verbal statements. This lack of correlation is a basis for the clinician's inference of un-

[5] From R. S. Lazarus, "Subception: Fact or Artifact? A Reply to Eriksen," *Psychol. Rev.*, 1956, 63, 344–7. Used by permission of the American Psychological Association.

conscious processes or defensive mechanisms at work. A concurrent response system model would seem the efficient way of conceptualizing this situation and suggesting ways of experimentally investigating the clinical phenomena.[6]

BRIEF SUMMARY. The analyses of subception effectively illustrate a typical trend in science—viz., the correction of oversimplifications. The history of psychology is replete with examples of discarded "constancy hypotheses" (e.g., the phrenologist's hypothesis about brain areas and character traits, the early behaviorist's notion of learning as the acquisition of a series of *specific* movements, etc.). Here the dichotomous *knowing-not knowing* approach, together with the tacit assumption of verbal report as the most sensitive indicator of awareness, was demonstrated to be inadequate. It was established that perception has a variety of indicators which are only partially related.

Defense vs. Vigilance

Still another line of attack questioned the relationship between perceptual defense and the complementary mechanism, vigilance. Luchins (1950) objected that "the principles of perceptual selectivity, in the manner in which they are formulated, are not amenable to experimental verification. Where does the process of resonance cease and the process of defense begin? And at what point does defense give way to vigilance?" (p. 75). Developing this argument still further, D. Howie granted that apparently contradictory principles *per se* do not constitute grounds for *a priori* objection, but contended that the Bruner-Postman principles "do not make it possible for an investigator to determine from the concrete data where one principle gives place to another. As they stand, the principles of resonance, defense and vigilance do not permit of clear functional demarcation and rigorous testing, and there is, too, a smack of 'saving hypotheses' about them" ("Perceptual Defense," *Psychol. Rev.*, 1952, 59, 310).

Admitting that "some of the early statements of the three principles made their precise demarcation difficult when they were used in the speculative interpretation of observed perceptual responses," Postman ("On the Problem of Perceptual Defense," *Psychol. Rev.*, 1953, 60, 301) argued that "they can, however, be given adequate and mutually exclusive definitions. . . . Using the thresholds for standard 'neutral' stimuli as points of reference, thresholds for stimuli from specific meaning classes which are significantly higher would define defense, thresh-

[6] From C. W. Eriksen, "Discrimination and Learning without Awareness: A Methodological Survey and Evaluation," *Psychol. Rev.*, 1960, 67, 290. Used by permission of the American Psychological Association.

olds which are significantly lower would define vigilance" (p. 301). He did, however, acknowledge that lacking certain controls of antecedent conditions, "alternative explanations of the threshold differences are possible and a precise demarcation of significantly 'vigilant' and significantly 'defensive' thresholds must remain difficult" (p. 301).

A number of psychologists have subsequently addressed themselves to the question of the differential antecedents of defense and vigilance.

LEVEL OF AWARENESS.   One of the most ingenious differentiations was that formulated in psychoanalytic terms by Blum (1954). According to him:

> . . . sexual and aggressive impulses, denied conscious expression by the ego, still continue to strive actively to break through into consciousness. In other words, repressed psychosexual impulses, of which the individual is not consciously aware, are always pushing and seeking for an outlet in conscious behavior. If this theoretical formulation is correct, then *everyone* should, at the unconscious level, be sensitive and responsive to cues relevant to these potentially threatening impulses . . .

This process, he pointed out, is familiarly labeled, "vigilance," "subception," "selective sensitization," etc.

> This process, however, is expected to operate only at a level below conscious awareness, for when the impulses do begin to approach the surface, we have a second process, ego defense. Now, that which the organism basically desires must be warded off because of its threatening quality. At this point, rather than being vigilant for psychosexual cues, the individual seeks devious ways not to perceive them—a mechanism currently labeled "perceptual defense." [7]

His specific operations included: (1) A pretest series involving simultaneous tachistoscopic presentations of four Blacky pictures at .03 seconds duration for the subject to indicate which one "stood out" the most; (2) a sensitization period during which two of the stimulus pictures were presented in full view, their contents explained, and the subjects asked to recall when they might have felt as Blacky did in the pictures; (3) a test series identical with the "base line" series described in (1) above, the .03 second exposure representing a level well below conscious recognition; (4) a test presentation at .20 seconds duration (a level approaching conscious recognition), the subjects being instructed to indicate the position (top, bottom, right, left) in which a

[7] From G. S. Blum, "An Experimental Reunion of Psychoanalytic Theory with Perceptual Vigilance and Defense," *J. abnorm. soc. Psychol.*, 1954, 49, 94. Used by permission of the American Psychological Association.

particular picture appeared. As predicted by his hypothesis, subjects in the rapid-exposure situation responded relatively more often to critical pictures than they did in the pretest series; and they made fewer correct locations of critical than neutral pictures at the near-conscious level.

In a replication of Blum's work, however, C. C. Smock ("Replication and Comments: 'An Experimental Reunion of Psychoanalytic Theory with Perceptual Vigilance and Defense,'" *J. abnorm. soc. Psychol.*, 1956, 53) was unable to duplicate the defense phenomenon, although the vigilance effects were confirmed. He questioned whether, even with positive "defense" data, "it would be necessary to postulate an active avoidance mechanism (repressed impulse and/or defense) in order to account for such results. Since the critical stimulus had been associated with anxiety, an alternative explanation in terms of the effects of anxiety on the generalization gradient seems to be an equally plausible interpretation" (p. 72).

OTHER DIFFERENTIATIONS. Two other examples of attempts to disentangle perceptual defense and vigilance were those (1) of Murphy and Solley (1957), who indicated that the results obtained depend upon the sheer intensity of the unpleasant and the degree of freedom permitted the subject in the experimental situation, and (2) of Osgood (1957) who stated:

> *Perceptual vigilance*, it would appear, is obtained with materials that only mildly threaten or perhaps even titillate the subjects employed. . . .
> *Perceptual defense*, on the other hand, has been obtained where the materials can be assumed to produce fairly intense anxiety, as indicated either by the selection of subjects or by other behavioral measures.[8]

BRIEF SUMMARY. Investigators have begun to identify with some degree of success the variables determining which complementary mechanism, defense or vigilance, operates at a given time—e.g., the intensity of threat, the degree of freedom allowed in responding, etc. This search for a principle or principles which will yield valid differential predictions of vigilance and defense furnishes some insight into how science progresses by reducing the "error term"—i.e., in psychology one explanatory principle will be invoked (e.g., intensity of threat) to account for some observed behavior; its application to a set of data will no doubt leave some unexplained variance. The differing responses of individual subjects are then analyzed and a new principle deduced

[8] From C. E. Osgood, "Motivation Dynamics of Language Behavior," in M. R. Jones (ed.), *Nebraska Symposium on Motivation*, 1957, p. 395. Used by permission of University of Nebraska Press, Lincoln, Nebraska.

(e.g., degree of freedom allowed in responding) which will further reduce the unexplained variance. This process is repeated until predictions approach perfection.

Individual Differences

Finally McGinnies' work and the host of similar experiments were attacked for their neglect of individual differences. Relatively early in the functionalistic perception movement, Klein and Schlesinger (1949) had raised the question, "Where is the perceiver in perceptual theory?" Unfortunately, a large proportion of those interested in perceptual-defense research, perhaps themselves "victims" of the mechanism which they so assiduously studied in others, seldom applied the question to their own designs. Lazarus made it clear that it was especially applicable to investigators of perceptual defense:

> . . . it was recognized long ago that the concept of defense as we now use it does not predict that all persons will deal with threat in the same way. It appears that we have not even caught up with Freud himself, who long ago decided that repression was not the only mechanism of defense. The only experiments which are relevant to the notion of a process of defense are those which look, not for main effects (e.g., mean differences in group perception of emotional vs. nonemotional material), but for interactions between different kinds of personalities and different ways of dealing with threat. The McGinnies-type experiment is therefore not an appropriate empirical relationship with which to test the notion of psychological defense.[9]

Concurrently Eriksen also assailed the McGinnies-type of experiment:

> The methodology and logic of the procedure are such that the method as a whole is incapable of testing the perceptual defense hypothesis. The implicit assumption that the taboo words chosen are anxiety-arousing for all or even a majority of the subjects is extremely gratuitous. Even if this assumption were substantially correct, the studies using this procedure make no provision for individual differences among subjects in terms of how they respond to or handle this anxiety. If one wishes to determine whether psychological defenses can affect recognition thresholds, it would seem obvious that a first requisite is to show that the particular stimuli give rise to defensive behavior as determined by other independent criteria.[1]

[9] From R. S. Lazarus, "Is There a Mechanism of Perceptual Defense? A Reply to Postman, Bronson, and Gropper," *J. abnorm. soc. Psychol.*, 1954, 49, 396. Used by permission of the American Psychological Association.

[1] From C. W. Eriksen, "The Case for Perceptual Defense," *Psychol. Rev.*, 1954, 61, 177. Used by permission of the American Psychological Association.

BRIEF SUMMARY.   Despite these strong criticisms the "dirty-word" technique is still being employed, although an increasing number of experiments tend to determine or establish the anxiety aspect of the stimulus for the subjects within the confines of the laboratory rather than depend upon assumed general socialization procedures to create emotionality. In its evolution from a subjective to an objective science, psychology has repeatedly faced this problem of redefining response-based terms (e.g., taboo, anxiety-producing, threatening). Where predictions concern meanings, the psychologist has, as here, had to determine through a set of independent operations that the meaning of a stimulus intended by the experimenter was in fact that experienced by each subject.

Some Perspectives on Perceptual Defense

If the history of psychology were divided into decades, and these identified according to major problems investigated, the "Decade of Perceptual Defense" would surely be one label applied to the 1950's. As a new decade begins, however, it can hardly be said that perceptual defense is an established concept in general psychological theory or that the repression hypothesis is generally acceptable in perceptual theory. Whereas McGinnies' data have been reproduced under a variety of circumstances, the interpretations have also been varied. Under the banner of parsimony, the perceptual defense effect has been explained in terms of set (Luchins, 1950), *Praegnanz* (Rosenstock, 1951), the dominance of strong alternative hypotheses (Postman, 1951), response suppression (Lysak, 1954), cue-drive theory (Putsell, 1957)—or essentially the effect has been translated from psychoanalytic or functionalistic principles to those of other systematic positions. But the principle of parsimony itself leaves room for equivocalities, and the questions, "What is simple?" and "What is adequate?" are usually ultimately answered in terms of temperament rather than of logic.

Toward the end of the decade one of the main contributors to the perceptual-defense literature, Eriksen asserted that nearly all the better controlled studies of perceptual defense could be interpreted along the following lines:

The perceptual defense phenomenon is obtainable only in the narrow range of values around the recognition threshold or in situations where the stimulus is ambiguous. Under these circumstances the perceptual process itself is weak or incomplete, as can be determined by allowing the subject the freedom of the English language to describe his perception. This weak perceptual process, however, may be assumed to activate various response tendencies. If certain of these responses, or in the case of words, the words themselves, have in the past been conditioned stimuli for anxiety arousal, then it is to be expected that these responses will be less apt to occur relative to other non-anxiety responses that are activated by the perceptual process. The perception has to become much more definite or less ambiguous before the anxiety responses will occur. In this case the perceptual defense phenomenon does not require the assumption of an unconscious manikin who screens the unconscious perceptions and determines what the conscious mind will perceive. It depends upon nothing more mysterious than the empirically derived laws of the effect of punishment or anxiety upon behavior.[2]

Later, in the wake of this reductionism Klein grimly pictured the status of perceptual defense in these words:

> . . . recent studies may have interred the corpse of perceptual defense and muted claims for distinctive discriminative agencies in and outside of awareness; they have not ruled out the possibility that behavior is affected on various levels, in various modes of experience, and in various states of consciousness by the activations induced by subliminal stimuli.[3]

Scoring the investigators in subliminal research for their "wizened perspective" and for their obscuring and restrictive questions, Klein pointed out that "inadequate for discrimination" is not equivalent to "no activating effects," and attempted to free this research from what might be termed "fixation at the threshold stage" by suggesting more fruitful regions in which to study the effects of subliminal stimulation. He expressed the opinion that most of the research had obscured rather than illuminated the basic issues, namely:

a) that an incidental stimulus may activate meanings (or trace systems or schema) quite *independently* of those which are pertinent to the main directions of a person's thought at the moment;

b) that such incidentally or even subliminally activated meanings will affect *different* levels of behavior and *different* modes of experience than the ones to which conscious selective effort is directed;

c) that the incidentally or subliminally activated meanings may have *delayed* effects; they may persist and affect behavior in situations and in states of consciousness quite removed from those in which the excitations originally occurred;

d) that such incidental stimuli may acquire special properties by the very fact of their peripheral status in the field of stimulation, making it possible for such subliminal activations to have *distinctive*

[2] From C. W. Eriksen, "Unconscious Processes," in M. R. Jones (ed.), *Nebraska Symposium on Motivation*, 1958, p. 207. Used by permission of University of Nebraska Press, Lincoln, Nebraska.

[3] From G. S. Klein, "On Subliminal Activation," *J. nerv. ment. Dis.*, 1959, 128, 298. This and the following excerpt used by permission of Williams and Wilkins Co., Baltimore, Maryland.

effects on thought as compared to stimuli which claim full attention [p. 294].

Summary and Comment

An impartial observer of this decade-long battle over the question of repression operating in perception would likely be unable, Klein's pessimistic summary to the contrary, to identify any victors or vanquished.

Despite settlement or clarification of some propaedeutic issues (e.g., the role of frequency and the precision of GSR discrimination vs. verbal recognition), the protagonists, with respect to the basic controversy seem to remain somewhat like Omar in the *Rubaiyat* who

> . . . heard great argument
> About it and about: but evermore
> Came out by the same door where in [he] went.

In short, those who are convinced that repression serves as a shield in perception have discovered ample evidence to justify their belief, while those who reject the notion have found no convincing data to support it.

The observer of the perceptual-defense controversy is, moreover, almost certain to have *déjà vu* feelings, for the logic and import of the arguments and counter-arguments are much the same as those which characterized the repressed-memory controversy—e.g., "Are the stimulus situations personally relevant?" "Is the demonstrated cognitive failure due to anxiety?" etc. There are nonetheless some shifts of emphasis in the experimental studies of repression conducted during the last decade.

To begin with, the process under investigation has ceased almost entirely to be called repression. Instead, it now goes by the name of perceptual defense. A poet might say that "a rose by any other name would smell as sweet." But in science such is not the case, for the history of science is replete with recorded instances in which the approach to the study of the same phenomenon has changed markedly with the discarding of an earlier term freighted with all kinds of emotional connotations and overtones and the substitution for it of another name. One example will suffice: the tremendous difference in attitudes toward and approaches to the study of hypnosis which followed upon Braid's substitution of the term "hypnotism" to refer to those behavioral manifestations which had earlier been referred to as mesmerism.

This substitution of perceptual defense for repression has a further consequence. The researches of the 1950's have been spared attack and criticism at the hands of the psychoanalysts, who appear to be interested only in the sanctity of their own concepts. If any non-psychoanalytic psychologist claimed to have investigated repression, he was almost certain to be told by some psychoanalyst that he had not. But the work on perceptual defense has gone unnoticed and uncriticized by psychoanalysts.

This, of course, does not imply that the investigation of perceptual defense has been noticeably less free of controversy and acrimonious debate than the earlier attempts to study repression. But this time the argument has been more among psychologists than between psychologists and psychoanalysts. In a curious and interesting way, though, most of the criticism of these later researches boils down to a denial that the investigator has indeed dealt with a demonstrated process or mechanism of perceptual defense.

Earlier the psychoanalysts denied that the experimental investigations had indeed done what was claimed, namely, investigated repression because, as they saw it, the essential dynamics of repression had not been reproduced. The experiences associated with failure or guilt induced in the experimental subjects might indeed be demonstrated to be less well recalled than experiences free from associated overtones of failure and guilt, but these experiences, just because less well recalled, could not properly be said to have been repressed. In one sense they seemed to the psychoanalytic critics to be not sufficiently unconscious. It is conceivable, they would admit, that the experimental material might be unconscious in the sense of possessing those attributes or characteristics of preconscious unconsciousness but not those of the dynamic unconscious.

The criticism leveled in the last decade against experimental studies of perceptual defense has been that they have assumed the existence of perceptual processes outside of consciousness or awareness and have thus in effect assumed the existence of unconscious psychological processes, a notion which is alarming to most experimental psychologists. If earlier studies of repression were damned by psychoanalysts as failing to have anything to do with dynamic unconscious processes, the later studies of perceptual defense are damned by experimental psychologists for implicitly assuming the existence of unconscious perceptual processes.

Another difference between the earlier studies of repression and the later investigations of perceptual defense is that while the former were more often concerned to demonstrate that repression does occur and that it is possible for it to do so under conditions of controlled observation and experimental manipulation, the studies of perceptual defense have been much more often directed toward demonstrating that perceptual defense does not occur or is at best an experimental artifact.

There is still a further difference between the experimental studies of repression and perceptual defense. Whereas the former were largely aimed at demonstrating the conditions under which repression could be shown to occur, the latter, when executed by experimentalists genuinely

interested in the phenomenon of perceptual defense rather than concerned to demonstrate its nonexistence, have sought to elucidate the
processes which mediate it.

OVERVIEW

IN MANY RESPECTS the history of psychology, like that of any
other science, is a chronicle of conquest and expansion. The scientist is
continually striving to conquer the unknown and bring it within the
domain of the known. Usually his attempts at territorial extension are
rather gradual, somewhat like homesteading just across the border. But
sometimes scientists push forward in a "panzer-thrust," cutting deep
within the territory of the unknown: Freud's theory of personality, of
which the repression hypothesis is the mainstay, was such a spearhead.

Similarly, one finds, in the events subsequent to Freud's formulation of this hypothesis, parallels to the aftermath of a panzer drive. Thus
the first half of this century has produced many instances of attempts to
consolidate the gains, to strengthen the position by providing objective
data obtained under controlled conditions from a variety of sources.
There have also been repeated suggestions for retrenchments with such
persistent questions as, "Have we not gone too far?" "Can we not more
profitably attack in another direction?" "Can we as scientists justify
such a position?" etc.

Questions such as these are still very real and timely, and the current army of psychologists seems to fall into one of four camps with respect to repression: those completely indifferent to the problem; those
who contend that the position is secure and needs no further defense;
those who believe the spearheaded territory worth keeping but in need
of bolstering; and those who consider it indefensible.

REFERENCES

ALEXANDER, F. *The medical value of psychoanalysis.* New York:
Norton and Co., 1932.

ALPER, T. G. Memory for completed and incompleted tasks as a
function of personality: An analysis of group data. *J. abnorm.
soc. Psychol.*, 1946, 41, 403–20.

———. The interrupted task method in studies of selective recall:
A re-evaluation of some recent experiments. *Psychol. Rev.*, 1952,
59, 71–88.

BARTLETT, F. C. *Remembering, a study in experimental and social
psychology.* Cambridge: Cambridge University Press, 1932.

BLANCHARD, P.   A psycho-analytic study of Auguste Comte. *Amer. J. Psychol.*, 1918, *29*, 159–81.

BLUM, G. S.   An experimental reunion of psychoanalytic theory with perceptual vigilance and defense. *J. abnorm. soc. Psychol.*, 1954, *49*, 94–8.

———.   Perceptual defense revisited. *J. abnorm. soc. Psychol.*, 1955, *51*, 24–9.

BRENNER, C.   The nature and development of the concept of repression in Freud's writings. *Psychoanal. Stud. Child*, 1957, *12*, 19–46.

BREUER, J., AND FREUD, S.   On the psychical mechanism of hysterical phenomena, 1893. Translated in *Collected papers*. Vol. I. London: Hogarth, 1924. Pp. 24–41.

———.   Studies in hysteria, 1895. (Translated.) New York: *Nerv. ment. Dis. Monogr.*, 1936, No. 61.

BRICKER, P. D., AND CHAPANIS, A.   Do incorrectly perceived tachistoscopic stimuli convey some information? *Psychol. Rev.*, 1953, *60*, 181–8.

BROWN, J. F.   Psychoanalysis, topological psychology, and experimental psychopathology. *Psychoanal. Quart.*, 1937, *6*, 227–37.

BRUNER, J. S.   Perceptual theory and the Rorschach test. *J. Pers.*, 1948, *17*, 157–68.

BRUNER, J. S., AND POSTMAN, L.   Emotional selectivity in perception and reaction. *J. Pers.*, 1947, *16*, 69–77.

———.   Perception, cognition, and behavior. *J. Pers.*, 1949, *18*, 14–31.

BRUNSWIK, E.   *Wahrnehmung und Gegenstandswelt*. Vienna: Deuticke, 1934.

———.   The conceptual framework of psychology. *Int. Encyclopedia of Unified Sci.* Vol. I, No. 10. *Foundations of the Unity of Science.* Chicago: University of Chicago Press, 1952.

BUNKER, H. A.   "Repression" in pre-Freudian American psychiatry. *Psychoanal. Quart.*, 1945, *14*, 469–77.

COWEN, E. L., AND BEIER, E. G.   Threat expectancy, word frequencies, and perceptual prerecognition hypotheses. *J. abnorm. soc. Psychol.*, 1954, *49*, 178–82.

DOOLEY, L.   Psychoanalytic studies of genius. *Amer. J. Psychol.*, 1916, *27*, 363–416.

———.   Psychoanalysis of Charlotte Brontë, as a type of the woman of genius. *Amer. J. Psychol.*, 1920, *31*, 221–72.

ERIKSEN, C. W.   Defense against ego-threat in memory and perception. *J. abnorm. soc. Psychol.*, 1952, *47*, 230–5.

———.   The case for perceptual defense. *Psychol. Rev.*, 1954, *61*, 175–82.

————. Subception: Fact or artifact? *Psychol. Rev.*, 1956, 63, 74–80.

————. Unconscious processes. In M. R. Jones (Ed.), *Nebraska symposium on motivation, 1958*. Lincoln: University of Nebraska Press, 1958. Pp. 169–227.

————. Discrimination and learning without awareness: A methodological survey and evaluation. *Psychol. Rev.*, 1960, 67, 279–300.

FRENCH, T. M. Interrelations between psychoanalysis and the experimental work of Pavlov. *Amer. J. Psychiat.*, 1933, 12, 1165–1203.

FREUD, A. *The ego and mechanisms of defence*, 1936. (Translated) London: Hogarth, 1937.

FREUD, S. *Further remarks on the defence neuro-psychosis*, 1896. Translated in *Collected papers*, Vol. I. London: Hogarth, 1924. Pp. 155–82.

————. *The psychopathology of everyday life*, 1901. (Translated.) New York: The Macmillan Company, 1948.

————. The origin and development of psychoanalysis. *Amer. J. Psychol.*, 1910, 21, 181–218.

————. *Psycho-analytic notes upon an autobiographical account of a case of paranoia (dementia paranoides)*, 1911. Translated in *Collected papers*. Vol. III. London: Hogarth, 1925. Pp. 387–470.

————. *On the history of the psycho-analytic movement*, 1914. Translated in *Collected papers*. Vol. I. London: Hogarth, 1924, Pp. 287–359.

————. *Repression*, 1915. Translated in *Collected papers*. Vol. IV. London: Hogarth, 1925. Pp. 84–97.

————. *Beyond the pleasure principle*, 1920. Translated in J. Strachey (Ed.), *The standard edition of the complete psychological works of Sigmund Freud*. Vol. XVIII. London: Hogarth, 1955. Pp. 7–64.

————. *Analysis terminable and interminable*, 1937. Translated in *Collected papers*. Vol. V. London: Hogarth, 1950. Pp. 316–57.

GERÖ, G. The concept of defense. *Psychoanal. Quart.*, 1951, 20, 565–78.

GLIXMAN, A. F. An analysis of the use of the interruption-technique in experimental studies of "repression." *Psychol. Bull.*, 1948, 45, 491–506.

————. Recall of completed and incompleted activities under varying degrees of stress. *J. exp. Psychol.*, 1949, 39, 281–95.

GOULD, R. Repression experimentally analyzed. *Charact. and Pers.*, 1942, 10, 259–88.

HARTMANN, H., AND KRIS, E. The genetic approach in psychoanalysis. *Psychoanal. Stud. Child*, 1945, 1, 11–30.

HILGARD, E. R. Experimental approaches to psychoanalysis, 1952. In E. Pumpian-Mindlin (Ed.), *Psychoanalysis as science*. Stanford: Stanford University Press. Pp. 3–45.

HOLT, E. B.   *The Freudian wish.* New York: Henry Holt and Co., 1915.

HOWES, D.   A statistical theory of the phenomenon of subception. *Psychol. Rev.*, 1954, *61*, 98–110.

HOWES, D. H., AND SOLOMON, R. L.   A note on McGinnies' "Emotionality and perceptual defense." *Psychol. Rev.*, 1950, *57*, 229–34.

HOWIE, D.   Perceptual defense. *Psychol. Rev.*, 1952, *59*, 308–15.

HULL, C. L.   Modern behaviorism and psychoanalysis. *Trans. N.Y. Acad. Sci.*, 1939, *1*, Ser. II, 78–82.

HUMPHREY, G.   The conditional reflex and the Freudian wish. *J. abnorm. Psychol.*, 1919–20, *14*, 388–92.

————.   The child's unconscious mind. *J. abnorm. Psychol.*, 1920–1, *15*, 387–402.

————.   Education and Freudianism. *J. abnorm. Psychol.*, 1920–1, *15*, 350–86.

HUSTON, P. E., SHAKOW, D., AND ERICKSON, M. H.   A study of hypnotically induced complexes by means of the Luria technique. *J. gen. Psychol.*, 1934, *11*, 65–97.

JAMES, W.   Review of J. Breuer and S. Freud, Über den psychischen Mechanismus hysterischer Phänomene. *Psychol. Rev.*, 1894, *1*, 199.

JANET, P.   Psychoanalysis. *J. abnorm. Psychol.*, 1914–15, *9*, 1–35; 153–87.

JONES, E.   The psychopathology of everyday life. *Amer. J. Psychol.*, 1911, *22*, 477–527.

————.   Professor Janet on psychoanalysis: A rejoinder. *J. abnorm. Psychol.*, 1914–15, *9*, 400–10.

————.   *The life and work of Sigmund Freud.* Vol. 2. New York: Basic Books, 1955.

JUNG, C. G.   *Studies in word-association.* London: Heinemann, 1918.

KLEIN, G. S.   On subliminal activation. *J. nerv. ment. Dis.*, 1959, *128*, 293–301.

KLEIN, G. S., AND SCHLESINGER, H.   Where is the perceiver in perceptual theory? *J. Pers.*, 1949, *18*, 32–47.

KOHS, S. C.   The association method in its relation to complex and complex indicators. *Amer. J. Psychol.*, 1914, *25*, 544–95.

KRIS, E.   The nature of psychoanalytic propositions and their validation, 1947. In S. Hook and M. R. Kowitz (Eds.), *Freedom and experience: Essays presented to Horace Kallen.* Ithaca: Cornell University Press. Reprinted in M. H. Marx (Ed.), *Psychological theory: contemporary readings.* New York: The Macmillan Company, 1951. Pp. 332–51.

KUBIE, L. S.   Problems and techniques of psychoanalytic validation and progress. In E. Pumpian-Mindlin (Ed.), *Psychoanalysis as science*. Stanford: Stanford University Press, 1952. Pp. 46–124.

LAZARUS, R. S. Is there a mechanism of perceptual defense? A reply to Postman, Bronson, and Gropper. *J. abnorm. soc. Psychol.*, 1954, 49, 396–8.

————. Subception: Fact or artifact? A reply to Eriksen. *Psychol. Rev.*, 1956, 63, 343–7.

LAZARUS, R. S., ERIKSEN, C. W., AND FONDA, C. P. Personality dynamics and auditory perceptual recognition. *J. Pers.*, 1951, 19, 471–82.

LAZARUS, R. S., AND MCCLEARY, R. A. Autonomic discrimination without awareness: A study of subception. *Psychol. Rev.*, 1951, 58, 113–22.

LEWIN, K. *Die Entwicklung der experimentellen Willenspsychologie und die Psychotherapie*. Leipzig: S. Hirzel, 1929.

————. The conflict between Aristotelian and Galilean modes of thought in contemporary psychology. *J. gen. Psychol.*, 1931, 5, 141–77.

————. *A dynamic theory of personality*. New York: McGraw-Hill Book Co., 1935.

LUCHINS, A. S. On an approach to social perception. *J. Pers.*, 1950, 19, 64–84.

LURIA, A. R. Die Methode der abbildenden Motorik bei Kommunikation der Systeme und ihre Anwendung auf die Affektpsychologie. *Psychol. Forsch.*, 1929, 12, 127–79.

————. Die Methode der abbildenden Motorik in der Tatbestandsdragnostik. *Z. angew. Psychol.*, 1930, 35, 139–83.

————. *The nature of human conflicts*. New York: Liveright, 1932.

LYSAK, W. The effects of punishment upon syllable recognition thresholds. *J. exp. Psychol.*, 1954, 47, 343–50.

MCGINNIES, E. Emotionality and perceptual defense. *Psychol. Rev.*, 56, 244–51.

————. Discussion of Howes' and Solomon's note on "Emotionality and perceptual defense." *Psychol. Rev.*, 1950, 57, 235–40.

MCGINNIES, E., AND SHERMAN, H. Generalization of perceptual defense. *J. abnorm. soc. Psychol.*, 1952, 47, 81–5.

MACKINNON, D. W. *The violations of prohibitions in the solving of problems*. Unpublished doctoral dissertation. Cambridge: Harvard University Library, 1933.

MADISON, P. Freud's repression concept: A survey and attempted clarification. *Int. J. Psychoanal.*, 1956, 37, 75–81.

MELTZER, H. Present status of experimental studies on the relationship of feeling to memory. *Psychol. Rev.*, 1930, 37, 124–39.

MURDOCK, B. B., JR. Perceptual defense and threshold measurements. *J. Pers.*, 1954, 22, 565–71.

MURPHY, G., AND SOLLEY, C. M.   Learning to perceive as we wish to perceive. *Bull. Menninger Clinic*, 1957, 21, 225–37.

MURRAY, H. A., *et al.   Explorations in personality*. New York: Oxford University Press, 1938.

OSGOOD, C. E.   Motivation dynamics of language behavior. In M. R. Jones (Ed.), *Nebraska symposium on motivation*, 1957. Lincoln: University of Nebraska Press. Pp. 348–424.

PAGE, C. W.   The adverse consequences of repression. *Amer. J. Insan.*, 1892–3, XLIX, 373.

PERRY, R. B.   *The thought and character of William James*. Briefer version. Cambridge: Harvard University Press, 1948.

POSTMAN, L.   Toward a general theory of cognition. In J. H. Rohrer and M. Sherif (Eds.), *Social psychology at the crossroads*. New York: Harper & Bros., 1951. Pp. 242–72.

———.   On the problem of perceptual defense. *Psychol. Rev.*, 1953, 60, 298–306.

POSTMAN, L., BRONSON, W. C., AND GROPPER, G. L.   Is there a mechanism of perceptual defense? *J. abnorm. soc. Psychol.*, 1953, 48, 215–24.

POSTMAN, L., AND BROWN, D. R.   The perceptual consequences of success and failure. *J. abnorm. soc. Psychol.*, 1952, 47, 213–21.

POSTMAN, L., BRUNER, J. S., AND MCGINNIES, E.   Personal values as selective factors in perception. *J. abnorm. soc. Psychol.*, 1948, 43, 142–54.

POSTMAN, L., AND SCHNEIDER, B. H.   Personal values, visual recognition, and recall. *Psychol. Rev.*, 1951, 58, 271–84.

PROCTER-GREGG, N.   Schopenhauer and Freud. *Psychoanal. Quart.*, 1956, 25, 197–214.

PRUETTE, L.   A psycho-analytical study of Edgar Allan Poe. *Amer. J. Psychol.*, 1920, 31, 370–402.

PUTSELL, T. E.   The experimental induction of perceptual vigilance and defense. *J. Pers.*, 1957, 25, 425–38.

RAPAPORT, D.   Freudian mechanisms and frustration experiments. *Psychoanal. Quart.*, 1942, 11, 503–11.

RIKLIN, F.   Jung's association test and dream interpretation. *J. proj. Tech.*, 1955, 19, 226–35.

ROSENSTOCK, I. M.   Perceptual aspects of repression. *J. abnorm. soc. Psychol.*, 1951, 46, 304–15.

ROSENZWEIG, S.   The recall of finished and unfinished tasks as affected by the purpose with which they were performed. *Psychol. Bull.*, 1933, 30, 698.

———.   Types of reaction to frustration. *J. abnorm. soc. Psychol.*, 1934, 29, 298–300.

———.   The experimental study of repression. In H. A. Murray *et al., Explorations in personality.* New York: Oxford University Press, 1938. Pp. 472–90.

————. An experimental study of "repression" with special reference to need-persistive and ego-defensive reactions to frustrations. *J. exp. Psychol.,* 1943, 32, 64–74.

————. The investigation of repression as an instance of experimental idio-dynamics. *Psychol. Rev.,* 1952, 59, 339–45.

ROSENZWEIG, S., AND MASON, G. An experimental study of memory in relation to the theory of repression. *Brit. J. Psychol.,* 1934, 24, 247–65.

ROSENZWEIG, S., AND SARASON, S. An experimental study of the triadic hypothesis: Reaction to frustration, ego-defense, and hypnotizability. I. Correlational approach. *Charact. and Pers.,* 1942, 11, 1–19.

SANFORD, R. N. The effect of abstinence from food upon imaginal processes; a further experiment. *J. Psychol.,* 1937, 3, 145–59.

SANFORD, N., AND RISSER, J. What are the conditions of self-defensive forgetting? *J. Pers.,* 1948, 17, 244–60.

SCHOPENHAUER, A. *The world as will and idea,* 1819. Vol. III. Translated by R. B. Haldane and J. Kemp. London: Trübner, 1886.

SEARS, R. R. Functional abnormalities of memory with special reference to amnesia. *Psychol. Bull.,* 1936, 33, 229–74.

————. Initiation of the repression sequence by experienced failure. *J. exp. Psychol.,* 1937, 20, 570–80.

————. *Survey of objective studies of psychoanalytic concepts.* Bull. 51. New York: Social Science Research Council, 1943.

————. Personality. *Annu. Rev. Psychol.,* 1950, 1, 105–18.

SHARP, A. A. An experimental test of Freud's doctrine of the relation of hedonic tone to memory revival. *J. exp. Psychol.,* 1938, 22, 395–418.

SMITH, P. Luther's early development in the light of psychoanalysis. *Amer. J. Psychol.,* 1913, 24, 360–77.

SMOCK, C. D. Replication and comments: "An experimental reunion of psychoanalytic theory with perceptual vigilance and defense." *J. abnorm. soc. Psychol.,* 1956, 53, 68–73.

SOLOMON. R. L., AND HOWES, D. H. Word frequency, personal values, and visual duration thresholds. *Psychol. Rev.,* 1951, 58, 256–70.

SOLOMON, R. L., AND POSTMAN, L. Frequency of usage as a determinant of recognition on thresholds for words. *J. exp. Psychol.,* 1952, 43, 195–201.

TANNENBAUM, S. A. Some current misconceptions of psychoanalysis. *J. abnorm. Psychol.,* 1917–18, 12, 390–422.

WELLS, F. L. Critique of impure reason. *J. abnorm. Psychol.* 1912–13, 7, 89–93.

WHITTAKER, E. M., GILCHRIST, J. C., AND FISCHER, J. W. Perceptual defense or response suppression. *J. abnorm. soc. Psychol.*, 1952, 47, 732–3.

WIENER, M. Word frequency or motivation in perceptual defense. *J. abnorm. soc. Psychol.*, 1955, 51, 214–18.

WITMER, L. Is the psychology taught at Harvard a national peril? *Current Literature*, 1909, 46, 434–8.

WOODWORTH, R. S. Some criticisms of the Freudian psychology. *J. abnorm. Psychol.*, 1917–18, 12, 174–94.

ZEIGARNIK, B. Über das Behalten von erledigten und unerledigten Handlungen. *Psychol. Forsch.*, 1927, 9, 1–85.

ZELLER, A. F. An experimental analogue of repression. I. Historical summary. *Psychol. Bull.*, 1950a, 47, 39–51.

———. An experimental analogue of repression. II. The effect of individual failure and success on memory measured by relearning. *J. exp. Psychol.*, 1950b, 40, 411–22.

ZIEHEN, T. Review of Jung's "Über die psychologie der Dementia Praecox," 1908. *Mschr. Psychiat. Neurol.*, XXIII, 565–6.

CHAPTER 12

Attempts to Understand Hypnotic Phenomena[1]

THEODORE R. SARBIN

INTRODUCTION

NEGLECTED IN RECENT YEARS, the study of the history of hypnosis may illuminate many of the dark corners of contemporary psychology. Hypotheses generated by the controversies about the nature of the hypnotic state continue subtly to influence today's psychological theorizing. Such social psychological phenomena as suggestion and imitation, conforming behavior, the effects of mass media, to name but a few, have some of their roots in the nineteenth-century arguments about how "one mind influences another." Scientific interest in clairvoyance, extrasensory perception, and psychical research can be traced to the same problem. Medical psychological problems, including the baffling psychosomatic diseases, are somewhat better understood in the light of the history of hypnosis and its contribution to the explanation of hysteria. The study of unconscious processes is traceable directly to the efforts of earlier scientists to understand the hypnotic state.

To the student of the history and philosophy of science, the devel-

---

[1] This chapter can only be titled a Sketch. Because of space limitations, I have been unable to write even a brief history. I have had to omit many important contributors, among them Colquhoun (1844), Elliotson (1843), Carpenter (1875), Janet (1901), Breuer and Freud (1895), and Schilder and Kauders (1927). The writers I have selected for attention, however, do serve the purpose of illustrating the major trends in the development of the problem.

opment of theories about hypnosis is particularly fascinating. Few other psychological problems provide such clear-cut examples of the effect of the *Zeitgeist* on theory and practice, of the influence of contemporary scientific models on the explanation of observed phenomena, of the interpenetration of ideas developed by philosophers, neurologists, psychologists, and practitioners of the healing arts. In few other areas can one find such strong partisanship for theories, producing challenges and counterchallenges.

It is important to recognize, at the beginning, that the scientific study of hypnotism originated in the attempts of medical and other healers to treat and cure illness. It is also important to recognize that theories about the cause and cure of illness are products of local culture and that healing practices are rationalized in terms of the prevailing system of beliefs and values. For example, Mesmerism and animal magnetism, antecedents of hypnosis, were spun out of observations embedded in the particular theory of illness which guided the efforts of a specific healing practitioner.

The prestige of different theorists must also be considered. Acknowledged authorities and leaders of schools utter pronouncements which profoundly influence the direction of research and conceptualization. A catalogue of contributors to the study of hypnosis is a veritable "Who's Who" in the life sciences. Among the eminent names are such luminaries as Freud, Charcot, Wundt, Janet, Hull, Broca, Heidenhain, Binet, Babinski, Féré, Dessoir, Maudsley, and Tuke.

All scientific theories begin with raw observations of regularities or uniformities in nature. Theories of hypnosis, no exception to the rule, began with observations of regularly appearing changes in the behavior of persons (usually suffering from some somatic or psychological illness). The changes, furthermore, appeared as a result of the gestural and verbal behavior of another person (usually a healing practitioner). These changes in behavior were frequently so dramatic, so remarkable, that standard theories of physiology and pathology were feebly inappropriate to account for the phenomena. New, radical theories were proposed to explain the mystifying behavior that seemed to be elicited by the utterances, gesticulations, and manipulations of the healer.

THE BASIC PHENOMENA OF HYPNOTISM

A QUICK REVIEW of some of the observed regularities of behavior will set the stage for our study of this chapter in the history of science.

Historically, two broad areas of investigation have been labeled "hypnotism." One of these is concerned with changes in the behavior of the "normal" subject as a result of the intervention of the hypnotist. The rigidities, catalepsies, somnambulisms, automatic writing, and other behavior usually demonstrated in a normal subject fall into this class. The second area of investigation occurs in the therapeutic setting. Here we find a patient (in contrast to the so-called normal volunteer) who seeks to be relieved of symptoms. Often such symptoms are indistinguishable from the *effects* produced in experimental hypnosis, e.g., amnesia. The arbitrary inclusion of both areas of study under the single term "hypnosis" presents some difficulty. For this reason we shall try to indicate when we are referring to hypnosis as therapeusis or as experimental condition.

Because all the phenomena of hypnosis were not discovered at the same time, the early theorists' job was somewhat different from the later theorists'. Mesmer, for instance, had to account for convulsions but not for somnambulism. The latter effect was first reported by a successor of Mesmer, Marquis de Puysegur. In this historical sketch, no space is available for recording the discovery of the various hypnotic phenomena. Suffice it to say that by 1825 nearly all the behavior that today we subsume under the term "hypnosis" had been recognized and described. Except for the early "magnetizers," then, "what to explain" has been substantially the same for nearly all theorists.

Observations to Be Explained

The observations that required explanation may be grouped as follows:

(1) The discrepancy between the magnitude of the stimulus and the intensity of the response.

(2) The apparent increase in the limits of volitional behavior.

(3) The apparent automaticity of the response.

(4) Individual variation in responsiveness to hypnotic suggestions.

STIMULUS-RESPONSE DISCREPANCY.   The first class of observations has to do with the fact that dramatic, intense behavior may be instigated by simple verbal, gestural, or postural actions of the hypnotist. In most instances the hypnotist merely talks to the subject. Unlike extreme stimulating conditions, such as narcosis, fevers, disease, fatigue, trauma, etc., where marked changes in behavior are expected, "suggestions" and other verbalizations of the hypnotist are relatively benign.

Surgical anesthesia may be cited as an example of this class of hypnotic behavior. Insensibility to pain induced by hypnosis has been a subject that has frequently excited the interest of physiologically minded psychologists. The work of the British surgeon, Esdaile, in the 1840's (Esdaile, 1902), in which hypnosis was used as a surgical anesthetic, has become a classic in hypnotic literature. The following surgical report is representative:

June 12th—Lokee, a peasant woman, aged 60, has a tumor on the calf of the leg of nine years' standing; it is full of deep ulcerations and maggots. I tried to subdue her yesterday, but the pain did not allow her to get beyond common sleep. Today, after much trouble, first by one person, and then another, she was entranced, and I cut out the tumor in the presence of Captain Elder, without her feeling it, and we left her sleeping.

June 13th.—She awoke three hours after the operation; felt no pain on waking, and asked me today, "Who cut off the tumor?" [p. 57].

APPARENT INCREASE IN THE LIMITS OF BEHAVIOR.   The second class of behavior which has aroused the interest of experimenters is the apparent extension of the limits of normal behavior. This is most dramatically shown in the cure of hysterical symptoms. In hysteria a patient cannot perform certain specific acts under waking conditions. For example, a patient may have a paralysis of the arm which will not respond to conventional medical treatment. Under hypnotic instructions he may gain the use of the otherwise useless limb. Recovery of lost childhood memories; changes in self-perception and in body-image; apparent increase in muscular strength; changes in functions served by the autonomic system—these are other illustrations of this class of observations.

APPARENT AUTOMATICITY.   The third class of behavior which must be considered is what appears to be the automatic nature of the behavior. To the casual observer, the person who has been placed in the hypnotic trance will appear to perform actions in an automatic way. The exercise of his critical faculties and of his normal voluntary processes seems to be in abeyance during the hypnotic session. Remarkable instances of automatic behavior are related by some of the earlier workers in the field. Some of the automatisms were considered a function of the "imitative faculty," which was thought to become more pronounced during hypnosis.

One striking example of behavior which led observers to the inference of automaticity is that of automatic writing. A hypnotized person will be given a pencil and paper and engaged in conversation on one subject. At the same time he will write meaningful words and sentences on some unrelated subject.

INDIVIDUAL VARIATION IN RESPONSIVENESS.   The fourth class of phenomena that must be analyzed and explained is that of individual differences. In the early writings no attention was paid to the fact of variation in responsiveness to hypnotic stimulation. Failure to respond was attributed to inappropriate technique, or to the hypnotist's inability to direct the magnetic fluid or thought processes into the appropriate channels. For the most part, little systematic attention was paid to individual differences. It was not until fairly recently that differential responsiveness became a focus of scientific interest. Even as late as 1933, Hull, in his monumental work on hypnosis and suggestibility, failed to regard individual differences as an important subject of study. In direct line of descent from the earlier magnetizers, he was interested in the *state* brought about by hypnotic suggestion, not in the characteristics of persons who were responsive as compared to those who were not.

Variations in Theoretical Formulations

To explain these observations, theorists have advanced various mechanisms which presumably intervene between the behavior of the hypnotist and the behavior of the subject. Here the theorist is allowed a great deal of freedom inasmuch as the mechanism is not available to direct observation but must be inferred from observations and (usually) must be consistent with currently acceptable theoretical considerations. The earlier workers in this field identified the mechanism as an invisible force or fluid, an analogy from the then current notion of the ether as an invisible physical substance necessary to Newtonian mechanics. Later the mechanism was located in the ganglia of the nervous system, which distributed the vital fluid to appropriate effector organs. At one point, mineral magnetism with its positive and negative attractions served as an analogue for a theory that emphasized sympathy and antipathy between hypnotist and subject as responsible for success and failure as a hypnotic subject. The mechanism of hypnotic sleep as introduced by Braid (1843) in his theory of monoideism had to do with the antecedents of suggestion, learning, and transfer. Although the nervous system was seen as the important mediating structure, the placement of hypnosis on a psychological continuum was an achievement. Neurological doctrine was introduced by other writers based in part upon work in comparative behavior. Here the observations of Preyer and Czermak (Heidenhain, 1899, p. 27) on catalepsy in animals were employed as analogues to human hypnosis. As we shall see, the nature of the intervening mechanism or construct has changed from time to time and from one writer to another.

Having described some of the persisting phenomena that are subsumed under the term "hypnosis," we now turn to attempts of scientists and scholars to explain these phenomena. At first it should be mentioned that the historian of science, particularly of social science, has two problems: (1) He must try to explain why the phenomena occurred in the individual or in the group, that is to say, he must set out the conditions that were antecedent and probably causal to the phenomena under observation; and (2) he must analyze and point to the conditions that led to the contemporary scientific explanation of the phenomena. In short, his two problems are: (1) To describe the phenomena under study, and (2) to describe the changing scientific climate which led to successive explanations of the behavior.

MESMER AND ANIMAL MAGNETISM

THE USE OF MAGNETS in the treatment of disease goes back to antiquity. The magnet was regarded as having healing powers and was widely employed as a remedial agent. The notion that the human body has magnetic properties of its own is credited to Paracelsus (Boring, 1929), a sixteenth-century writer. He held that the human organism was possessed of two kinds of magnetism. The first kind attracted the planets and this provided the organism with wisdom, judgment, and other psychological properties. The other attracted material elements and produced the somatic aspect of the organism. Following Paracelsus, many writers of the sixteenth and seventeenth centuries continued to develop the notion that there is an all-pervading principle of magnetism by which it is possible to explain the phenomena of nature. Such ideas were in the air, so to speak, when Franz Anton Mesmer began his studies in Vienna. He received his doctorate in medicine in 1766. For his doctoral dissertation, "The Influence of the Planets in the Cure of Disseases," he set out to demonstrate that the heavenly bodies act upon living beings through the agency of a subtle fluid. He called this animal magnetism because it was similar to the effects of mineral magnetism as then understood. He demonstrated animal magnetism on sick persons in Vienna, using magnetic steel instruments. He soon discovered that curative effects could be produced without magnets. From this he inferred that the magnetic properties were within his own body and could be transmitted to others.

Evolution of Mesmer's Theory

The development of Mesmer's theory is neatly described by an early critical advocate of animal magnetism.

> He observed that, in the case of nervous patients, in particular, he was enabled to produce a variety of phenomena of a very peculiar character, which were not reconcilable with the usual effects of the magnet. This induced him to suppose that his magnetic rods, perhaps, did not operate merely by attraction, but that they, at the same time, served as the conductors of a fluid emanating from his own body. This conjecture seemed to him to be converted into a certainty, when he became satisfied, by repeated experiments, that he could produce the very same effects without using the magnet at all, by merely passing his hands from the head of the patient towards the lower extremities,

or even by making these motions at some distance from the body of the patient; and that he could also communicate to inanimate objects, by merely rubbing them with his hand, the power of producing similar effects upon such nervous patients as came in contact with them. Partly swayed by the fact ascertained by previous experiments, that, in like manner, by repeated friction in certain directions, a magnetic attraction could be excited in iron, without the application of any magnet, and partly seduced, also, by the supposed fact, that, in the process above mentioned, the animal body exhibited a certain polarity and inclination, Mesmer now jumped at once to the conclusion that there exists in the animal frame an original and peculiar species of magnetism, which is capable of being set in activity without the aid of the artificial magnet. He then extended this magnetic power over all nature, formed theories upon this assumed fact, and, in so far as this alleged influence was manifested in the animal body, he gave it the name of *animal*, to distinguish it from the *mineral*, magnetism [Colquhoun, 1844, Vol. 1, pp. 218–20].

MESMER'S PROPOSITIONS.   Mesmer migrated to Paris, the intellectual capital of the world at that time, where he hoped to gain recognition and support for his theory from the medical profession. In 1779 he published a paper in which he announced that he had discovered a principle which was capable of curing all diseases. This discovery was stated in the form of twenty-seven propositions, a few of which are reproduced below.

1. A responsive influence exists between the heavenly bodies, the earth, and animated bodies.
2. A fluid universally diffused, so continuous as not to admit of a vacuum, incomparably subtle, and naturally susceptible of receiving, propagating, and communicating all motor disturbances, is the means of this influence.
5. This reflux is more or less general, more or less special, more or less compound, according to the nature of the causes which determine it.
7. The properties of matter and of organic substance depend on this action.
8. The animal body experiences the alternative effects of this agent, and is directly affected by its insinuation into the substance of the nerves.
9. Properties are displayed, analogous to those of the magnet, particularly in the human body, in which diverse and opposite poles are likewise to be distinguished, and these may be communicated, changed, destroyed, and reinforced. Even the phenomenon of declination may be observed.
10. This property of the human body which renders it susceptible of the influence of the heavenly bodies and of the reciprocal action of those which environ it, manifests its analogy with the magnet, and this has decided me to adopt the term of animal magnetism.

11. The action and virtue of animal magnetism, thus characterized, may be communicated to other animate or in-animate bodies. Both these classes of bodies, however, vary in their susceptibility.

20. The magnet, whether natural or artificial, is like other bodies susceptible of animal magnetism, and even of the opposite virtue: in neither case does its action on fire and on the needle suffer any change, and this shows that the principle of animal magnetism essentially differs from that of mineral magnetism.

22. It teaches us that the magnet and artificial electricity have, with respect to diseases, properties common to a host of other agents presented to us by nature, and that if the use of these has been attended by some useful results, they are due to animal magnetism.

23. These facts show, in accordance with the practical rules I am about to establish, that this principle will cure nervous diseases directly, and other diseases indirectly.

24. By its aid the physician is enlightened as to the use of medicine, and may render its action more perfect, and he can provoke and direct salutary crises, so as completely to control them [Binet and Féré, 1901, pp. 5–7].

MESMER'S TECHNIQUES.   As is well known, patients flocked to Mesmer. He was most successful as a practitioner. In order to accommodate the large numbers of patients who came to him, he invented the famous *baquet* (see Figure 79). This is a trough around which more than thirty persons could be magnetized at the same time. Iron filings and other minerals, as well as bottles, were placed in the bottom of the

FIGURE 79.   Mesmer's *baquet*.

trough. Through holes in the top of the case protruded a number of iron rods. The patients were connected to the baquet by means of cords which passed around their bodies and were attached to the baquet. In addition the patients all joined hands. Mesmer, wearing a dramatic gown, would pace through the crowd along with his associates and students. He would sometimes carry an iron rod with which he touched the bodies of patients. Other times he would magnetize them with his eyes or apply his hands to portions of the abdomen. A critical scientific observer of the time described one of these sessions.

Some patients remain calm, and experience nothing; others cough, spit, feel slight pain, a local or general heat, and fall into sweats; others are agitated and tormented by convulsions. These convulsions are remarkable for their number, duration, and force, and have been known to persist for more than three hours. They are characterized by involuntary, jerking movements in all the limbs, and in the whole body, by contraction of the throat, by twitchings in the hypochondriac and epigastric regions, by dimness and rolling of the eyes, by piercing cries, tears, hiccough, and immoderate laughter. They are preceded or followed by a state of languor or dreaminess, by a series of digressions, and even by stupor. Patients are seen to be absorbed in the search for one another, rushing together, smiling, talking affectionately, and endeavouring to modify their crises. They are all so submissive to the magnetizer that even when they appear to be in a stupor, his voice, a glance, or sign will rouse them from it. It is impossible not to admit, from all these results, that some great force acts upon and masters the patients, and that this force appears to reside in the magnetizer. This convulsive state is termed the *crisis*. It has been observed that many women and few men are subject to such crises; that they are only established after the lapse of two or three hours, and that when one is established, others soon and successively begin.

When the agitation exceeds certain limits, the patients are transported into a padded room; the women's corsets are unlaced, and they may then strike their heads against the padded walls without doing themselves any injury.

Mesmer, wearing a coat of lilac silk, walked up and down amid this palpitating crowd. Mesmer carried a long iron wand, with which he touched the bodies of the patients, and especially those parts which were diseased; often, laying aside the wand, he magnetized them with his eyes, fixing his gaze on theirs, or applying his hands to the hypochondriac region and to the lower part of the abdomen. This application was often continued for hours, and at other times the master made use of passes. He began by placing himself *en rapport* with his subject. Seated opposite to him, foot against foot, knee against knee, he laid his fingers on the hypochondriac region, and moved them to and fro, lightly touching the ribs. Magnetization with strong currents was substituted for these manipulations when more energetic results were to be produced. The master, erecting his fingers in a pyramid, passed his hands all over the patient's body, beginning with the head, and going down over the shoulders to the feet. He then returned again, to the head, both back and front, to the belly and the back; he renewed the process again and again, until the magnetized person was saturated with the healing fluid, and was transported with pain or pleasure, both sensations being equally salutary. Young women were so much gratified by the crisis, that they begged to be thrown into it anew; they followed Mesmer through the hall, and confessed that it was impossible not to be warmly attached to the magnetizer's person [Binet and Féré, 1901, pp. 9–11].

CRISIS AND CURE.   So far as we are now able to judge, Mesmer excited in his patients hysterical crises. Silence, darkness, excitement, and the *expectation* of some extraordinary phenomenon are conditions known to encourage hysterical attacks in predisposed subjects, especially when facilitated by the presence of a group.

It is most important to underscore the fact that violent crises were the rule and, further, that the cure of the nervous patient was attributed to the crisis. Moreover, the crisis could be developed by the magnetizer according to his diagnosis and observations. The high degree of organismic involvement attests to the fact that these crises were genuine phenomena and not sham behavior. A century later, Charcot labeled the same phenomenon *la grande passion*, and included it as symptomatic of hysteria. Even later, Freud showed the relationship of what he called "cathartic abreaction" to symptom relief. In any case, convulsions and violent behavior often resulted in the patients' cure.

The challenge thrown down by Mesmer centered around the postulation of a subtle fluid analogous to ether in its form and to mineral magnetism in its action. This fluid, entering the body of a person not in magnetic equilibrium, would throw the patient into a convulsive crisis. This in turn would lead to a re-establishment of magnetic equilibrium and to relief from symptoms.[2]

Systematic Tests of Animal Magnetism

In 1784 two commissions were nominated to inquire into the claims of Mesmer and his followers. The first commission was made up primarily of members of the Academy of Sciences, the second was composed of members of the Royal Academy of Medicine.

The members of the commissions allowed themselves to be used as subjects. Except for some irritation due to fatigue and perhaps hostility

[2] The employment of methods to induce convulsions and other extreme behavior has a long history. Examples are exorcism in primitive tribes and in medieval times; shock therapies in modern times.

to the whole enterprise, they experienced none of the phenomena which were claimed by the magnetizers. The commissioners also made a number of observations of patients who were somnambulistic. One fact stood out. The crises occurred in the patient *only* if he knew that he was being magnetized. One woman, a sensitive subject, responded to the heat of the hypnotizer's hand as it approached her body. She was then blindfolded, magnetized, and told she would experience the same sensation of warmth. She responded accordingly. When she was magnetized without being informed that she was the object of the magnetizer's efforts, she experienced nothing.

Another demonstration of the invalidity of the theory of magnetism was the following. According to theory, if a tree were magnetized, a person would have a convulsive crisis if he touched it. A youth who was known to be a very susceptible subject was blindfolded and told to approach a group of trees. He had a convulsion almost immediately upon entering a wooded area, although he was still some twenty-four feet from the magnetized tree. His expectations of a crisis were fulfilled although he was far from the magnetized tree.

The concluding remarks of the commissioners' report are worth reproducing:

> The commissioners have ascertained that the animal magnetic fluid is not perceptible by any of the senses; that it has no action, either on themselves or on the patients subjected to it. They are convinced that pressure and contact effect changes which are rarely favorable to the animal system and which injuriously affect the imagination. Finally, they have demonstrated by decisive experiments that imagination, apart from magnetism, produces convulsions, and that magnetism without imagination produces nothing. . . . There is nothing to prove the existence of the animal magnetic fluid; that this fluid, since it is non-existent, has no beneficial effect; that the violent effects observed in patients under public treatment are due to contact, to the excitement of the imagination, and to the mechanical imitation which involuntarily impels us to repeat that which strikes our senses. . . . [Binet and Féré, 1901, pp. 16–17].

The effect of this report was to throw out the baby with the bath water. On the basis of observation and experiment, animal magnetism was justifiably rejected as a scientific principle, but at the same time the dramatic effects of imagination were cavalierly dismissed as objects of inquiry. The report, in a sense, was only partly relevant to the issue. The theory of animal magnetism was found unwarranted, to be sure. But the events were genuine and called for further study.

Although animistic notions similar to Mesmer's continued to be propounded and accepted by many scholars who were trying to integrate the mind-body dualism with Newtonian mechanics, some scientists looked upon the effects of magnetism in a more common-sense way as a characteristic of the human organism. Outstanding as a scientific pioneer who tried to approach hypnosis in such a naturalistic way was James Braid.

BRAID AND NEURYPNOLOGY

IN 1841 JAMES BRAID, a Manchester surgeon, witnessed a demonstration of Mesmerism. Until that time Braid had regarded Mesmerism as a "system of collusion or delusion, or of excited imagination, sympathy, or imitation" (1899, p. 98). At the demonstration he reported, "I saw nothing to diminish, but rather to confirm, my previous prejudices" (*ibid.*). At a later demonstration, "*One* fact, the inability of the patient to *open his eyelids*, arrested my attention. I considered this to be a real phenomenon, and was anxious to discover the physiological [3] cause of it" (*ibid.*).

I instituted a series of experiments to prove the correctness of my theory, namely, that the continued fixed stare, by paralyzing nervous centres in the eyes and appendages, and destroying the equilibrium of the nervous system, thus produced the phenomenon referred to.
My first object was to prove that the inability of the patient to open his eyes was caused by paralyzing the levator muscles of the eyelids, through their continued action through the protracted fixed stare, and thus rendering it *physically* impossible for him to open them. With a view of proving this, I requested . . . a young gentleman present to sit down, and maintain a fixed stare at the top of a wine bottle, placed so much above him as to produce a considerable strain on the eyes and eyelids, to enable him to maintain a steady view of the object. In three minutes, his eyelids closed, a gush of tears ran down his cheeks, his head dropped, his face was slightly convulsed, he gave a groan, and instantly fell into a profound sleep, the respiration becoming slow, deep and sibilant, the right hand and arm being agitated by slight convulsive movements" [pp. 99f.].

Braid performed additional experiments, using the method of ocular fixation, and produced many of the phenomena already described by the magnetizers. He interpreted the phenomena as a "derangement of the state of the cerebro-spinal centres, and of the circulatory, and respiratory, and muscular systems, induced . . . by a fixed stare, absolute repose of the body, fixed attention, and suppressed respiration, concomitant with that fixity of attention. That the whole depended on the physical and psychical condition of the patient, arising from the causes

[3] Note that the search for causes in science is not free but is constrained by the preconceptions of the scientist. Braid, trained as a surgeon, and familiar with the work of such physiologists and anatomists as Müller and Sir Charles Bell, first sought a physiological rather than a psychological explanation.

referred to, and not at all on the volition, or passes of the operator, throwing out a magnetic fluid, or exciting into activity some mystical universal fluid or medium" (p. 101).

Braid's Physiological Orientation

Braid turned his attention to monitoring the physiological components of hypnosis. He noted, for example, changes in respiration, in blood volume in certain organ-systems, etc. All these changes were initiated by "overexerting the attention, by *keeping it riveted to one subject or idea which is not of itself of an exciting nature,* and overexercising one set of muscles, and the state of the strained eyes, with the suppressed respiration and general repose . . . which excites in the brain and in the whole nervous system . . . Hypnotism or nervous sleep" (p. 126).

Although Braid focused on the physiological effects in this theory, his conception of the instigating conditions was essentially psychological. He regarded the induction of hypnosis as due to fatigue of the nerve substance following prolonged attention to some object or event. He was concerned with the physiological components of attention; he ignored antecedent conditions that would lead to fixed attention.

In some ways he anticipated later attempts (his and others') at psychological explanations of hypnosis. Not only did he recognize the importance of attention, but also of imagination and expectancy. "It is important to remark that the oftener patients are hypnotized, from association of ideas and habit, the more susceptible they become; and in this way they are liable to be affected *entirely through the imagination.* Thus, if they consider or imagine there is something doing, although they do not see it, from which they are to be affected, they *will become affected;* but, on the contrary, the most expert hypnotist . . . may exert all his endeavours in vain, if the party does not expect it, and mentally and bodily comply, and thus yield to it" (p. 116f.).

In his first theory he further anticipates later psychological explanations when he adds personality traits to the notions of imagination and expectancy. Hypnotizability is seen as a trait of the subject, not of the hypnotist.

> It is this very circumstance, coupled with the extreme docility and mobility of the patients, and extended range and extreme quickness of action, at a certain stage, of the ordinary functions of the organs of sense, including heat and cold, and muscular motion, the tendency of the patients in this state to approach to, or recede from, impressions, according as their intensity or quality is agreeable or to the contrary, which I consider has misled so many, and induced the animal magnetizers to imagine they could produce their effects on patients at a distance, through mere volition and secret passes [p. 117].

Unlike most of his predecessors, Braid was aware of individual differences in susceptibility to hypnosis. He did not resort to animistic explanations but rather saw such variation as parallel with variations in susceptibility to drugs, fatigue, and other physical excitants or depressants. Individual susceptibility was entirely a property of the subject.

To Braid goes the credit, not only for suggesting the psychological nature of the antecedents of hypnosis (fixed attention) and the physiological components of the reaction, but also for giving a more acceptable name to the phenomena. He summarized his finding and theory with the term "nervous sleep" (distinguished from true sleep). As was customary in his time, a Greek word was coined as a label—neurohypnology (the study of nervous sleep). He shortened this to neurypnology and later suppressed the prefix and gave us such terms as hypnotic, hypnotize, dehypnotize, etc.

Braid's Psychological Theory

On the basis of further study and observation, Braid was led to propound in 1847 a second theory which minimized physiological findings but emphasized psychological conditions. Here he attempted to explain all hypnotic phenomena as due to mental concentration or monoideism. Braid found his physiological theory of nervous sleep inadequate for several reasons: not all subjects fell asleep, visual or auditory fixation was not a *sine qua non* of hypnosis, and physiological effects varied from patient to patient. He was impressed by the finding that the various methods of inducing hypnosis all had one aspect in common, viz., concentration of attention, or, in the language of the newer theory, the dominance of one idea over others. His first theory anticipated the second by recognizing the psychological nature of the conditions that instigated the trance, i.e., fixed attention.

MONOIDEISM.   The dominant idea influenced bodily functions and produced the physiological effects which had been the focus of his earlier work. Braid further related monoideism in hypnosis to monoideism in other situations, such as the prolonged trance of Indian fakirs and involuntary muscle action involved in table-turning, in the use of magnets, divining-rod phenomena, etc. In this presentation Braid made clear again that the trance was a subjective state brought about either by dominant ideas suggested directly by the operator, or by dominant ideas which had been dormant but which were activated by suggestions.

This psychological theory, while less widely circulated than the physiological theory, was sophisticated for Braid's time. It was a first attempt at translating complex behavior into concepts which were not

animistic and at the same time not grossly physiological. It was an attempt at explaining conduct with the meager psychological tools then
available. Ideas, as the elements of the mind, had been an integral
part of British philosophy since Locke and were now being employed
as "intervening variables" by Braid.[4]

The absence of convulsions or crises in Braid's reports merits attention. One wonders why Mesmer and other magnetizers were able to
excite dramatic, intense, and violent behavior while Braid's subjects were
more constrained. Two answers are suggested: (1) Mesmer was operating during a period of unrest and violence in France, just before the
revolution. Violent behavior was, in a manner of speaking, a way of life.
Braid worked during a period of relative tranquillity in England where
violent or extreme behavior was eschewed. (2) The attitudes of the two
investigators toward their patients were radically different. Mesmer
apparently believed that he had some invisible fluid which he felt compelled to transmit to all his patients, most of whom were hysterical
women. He would attempt to excite them by various means, including
contact, until a convulsion was achieved. Braid believed that the power
to be hypnotized resided in the patient, that the hypnotist had little
to do with it. He did not believe that hypnosis was a cure-all, but like
any other medical treatment, had its indications and contraindications.
His patients were not limited to female hysterics.

THE SALPÊTRIÈRE: NEUROPATHOLOGY AND HYPNOSIS

THE FAST-DEVELOPING science of neurology had not ignored explanations of hypnosis. The development of knowledge about the
anatomy and physiology of the nervous system brought in its wake
neurological explanations of human behavior in general and hypnosis
in particular. The age-old attempt to resolve the mind-body problem
now appeared to have a real chance of success. The mechanism of interaction was in the nervous system, operating according to the model of
telegraphic communication; the cerebral cortex was the switchboard and
the locus of the mind. Further, the cerebrum was capable of reflex actions in the same way as other parts of the body.

Numerous theories based on the new neurology were advanced. An
example of such theorizing was one proposed by Heidenhain, a physiologist of great eminence. By rejecting at the outset the employment of
psychological conceptions and looking at the hypnotized subject as a

---

[4] According to Bramwell (1903), Braid had worked out, before his death, a third
theory based on the notion of a "double consciousness." This theory used the notion
of alternating foci of attention, and anticipated by nearly a half century the work of
Janet, Prince, Goddard, and others on multiple personalities.

specimen for study in a physiological laboratory, Heidenhain came forward with the following hypothesis:

> . . . The cause of the phenomena of hypnotism lies in the inhibition of the activity of the ganglion cells of the cerebral cortex. . . . the inhibition being brought about by gentle prolonged stimulation of the sensory nerves of the face, of the auditory, or of the optic nerve [1899, p. 46].
> . . . Movements in hypnotized individuals are caused by sensory impressions calling forth, in some parts of the brain situated below the cerebral cortex, changes which act immediately as stimuli upon the motor apparatus; . . . hence the apparently voluntary movement of imitation is carried out, like a reflex action, independently of the will [p. 50].

In a sense, this was the beginning of the Golden Age in neurology. This was the period when the work of Flourens, Bell, J. Müller, and Helmholtz was being advanced and applied. Like Heidenhain, Charcot, chief at the famous Salpêtrière hospital in Paris, was a part of this age. His interest, however, was in the *pathology* of the nervous system. His method was the clinical neurological examination. The existing procedures for examining a patient suspected of pathology of the central nervous system were not dissimilar from today's procedures. The examiner would look for physical signs of tissue loss or destruction through the meticulous study of reflexes, paralyses, contractures, and anesthesias.

Charcot began his studies in hypnosis in 1878. He looked upon the hypnotic subject as a neuropathological patient. In fact, in the decade or more that he worked on hypnosis, all his subjects were female patients suffering from hysteria. Unknown to himself and his students, he arbitrarily imposed limitations on his findings by studying hypnosis as manifested in one class of psychopathological persons. From his silent presupposition that the clinical neurological examination was the only scientific way to study the mechanism of hypnosis, he rejected *a priori* any possible contribution of psychological science. Constrained by this neuropathological bias, he set out to discover the stages of hypnosis and their physical manifestations in the same way that he studied such disorders as tabes, aphasia, paralysis, or other pathological conditions.

The official position on hysteria at the time was a vestigial remnant of the theory proposed by the ancients that hysteria is a disorder of the uterus. Therefore hysteria could only be found in women. These women were subject to convulsive attacks which superficially resembled the attacks of epilepsy. Charcot was aware that these seizures were not identical with genuine epileptic seizures and referred to them as hystero-epileptic convulsions. Unlike current views that hystero-epilepsy is primarily of psychogenic origin, Charcot's theory treated it as a morbid condition of the nervous system. A dozen such patients served as the only subjects for Charcot's studies of hypnosis.

STAGES OF HYPNOSIS.   From his studies of these women, he drew the conclusion that certain physical excitants could produce definite syndromes of reaction which he called "stages of hypnosis." These excitants were treated as parallel to physical stimuli, such as striking a tendon, which were used to elicit responses in the standard neurological examination. Although he acknowledged that these stages were sometimes hard to define, nonetheless he wrote as if they were quite distinct one from the other and had specific excitants. Any psychological symptoms, if noted at all, were regarded as the by-products of neuropathology.

In 1882, in the spirit of the times, Charcot presented his nosographic essay in which he attempted to distinguish three different morbid conditions which were subsumed under the term hypnotism: catalepsy, lethargy, and artificial somnambulism. The following quotations illustrate the main points of the essay:

1. *The Cataleptic State.* This may be produced: . . . primarily, under the influence of an intense and unexpected noise, of a bright light presented to the gaze, or again, in some subjects, by the more or less prolonged fixing of the eyes on a given object; . . . The subject thus rendered cataleptic is motionless, and, as it were, fascinated. The eyes are open, the gaze is fixed, the eyelids do not quiver, the tears soon gather and flow down the cheeks. Often there is anesthesia of the conjunctiva, and even of the cornea. The limbs and all parts of the body may retain the position in which they are placed for a considerable period, even when the attitude is one which is difficult to maintain. The tendon reflex disappears. Neuromuscular hyperexcitability is absent. There is complete insensibility to pain, but some senses (in part) retain their activity . . . the muscular sense and those of sight and hearing. This continuance of sensorial activity often enables the experimenter to influence the cataleptic subject in various ways, and to develop in him by means of suggestion automatic impulses, and also to produce hallucinations. . . .

2. *The Lethargic State.* This is displayed: (a) primarily, under the influence of a fixed gaze at some object . . . (b) or it may succeed . . . the cataleptic state, simply by closing the eyelids, or by leading the subject into a perfectly dark place.

At the moment when he falls into the lethargic state, the subject often emits a peculiar sound from the larynx, and at the same time a little foam gathers on his lips. He then becomes flaccid, as if plunged in a deep sleep; there is complete insensibility to pain in the skin, and in the mucous membrane in proximity with it. . . . There is an exaggeration of the tendon reflex; neuromuscular excitability is always present although it varies in intensity. It may be general, extending to all the muscles of the animal system, the face, the trunk, and the limbs. . . . This phenomenon is displayed when mechanical excitement stimulation is applied to a nerve-trunk by means of pressure with a rod or quill; this causes the muscles supplied by this nerve to contract.

The muscles themselves may be directly excited in the same way; somewhat intense and prolonged excitement of the muscles of the limbs, trunk, and neck produces contracture of the muscles in question; on the fact, however, the contractures are transitory. . . . Contracture may also be produced in the limbs by means of repeated percussion of the tendons. These contractures . . . are rapidly relaxed by exciting the antagonistic muscles. . . .

3. *The State of Artificial Somnambulism.* This state may, in some subjects, be immediately produced by fixity of gaze, and also in other ways. . . . It may be produced at will in subjects who have first been thrown into a state of lethargy or catalepsy, by exerting a simple pressure on the scalp, or by a slight friction. This state seems to correspond to what has been termed the magnetic sleep. . . .

. . . The eyes are closed or half-closed; the eyelids generally quiver; when left to himself the subject seems to be asleep, but even in this case the limbs are not in such a pronounced state of relaxation as when we have to do with lethargy. Neuromuscular hyperexcitability, as it has been defined above, does not exist. . . . On the other hand, various methods, among others, passing the hand lightly and repeatedly over the surface of a limb (mesmeric passes), or again breathing gently on the skin, causes the limb to become rigid, but in a way which differs from the contracture due to muscular hyperexcitability, since it cannot, like the latter, be relaxed by mechanical excitement of the antagonistic muscles. . . .

The skin is insensible to pain, but this is combined with hyperesthesia of some forms of cutaneous sensibility, of the muscular sense, and of the special senses of sight, hearing, and smell. It is generally easy, by the employment of commands or suggestions, to induce the subject to perform very complex automatic actions. . . . [Binet and Féré, 1901, pp. 155–9].

This lengthy quotation is reproduced to indicate the meticulous attention to overt responses and the failure to recognize the interpersonal nature of the stimuli for hypnosis. The student of history sees in Charcot's work a return to the theories and practices of the mesmerists and magnetizers. They, too, believed in the efficacy of specific physical stimulation to produce convulsions in the patient. (Parenthetically, another similarity is the belief in the direct hypnogenous influence of certain metals and magnets on the nervous system without the mediation of expectancy or belief.) To Charcot, suggestion in normal life was unrelated to hypnosis. Suggestibility was a physiological (normal) event. Hypnosis was a pathological event, an artificially produced hysteria and regarded as a definite form of neuropathology.

The Pathological Bias

Charcot was not at all influenced by Braid's later work or by the extensive work of his contemporaries of the Nancy School. He was interested in disease, in pathology. His thinking had no room for the inchoate concepts of psychology, such as monoideism, expectancy, or attention. His model was the clinical neurological examination and the known functions of the central nervous system. From our viewpoint, his naïveté in regard to the use of hysterical patients as subjects appears to be inexcusable. He acknowledged that his hysterical patients were suggestible, but the suggestibility was due to the morbid condition of the central nervous system. He did not accept the criticism that his few patient-subjects were, in effect, trained subjects who performed according to his explicitly announced theories. Believing that the patients were unconscious, i.e., unaware of what was going on, he would discuss his theories and expectations in their presence. The idea of a controlled experiment was foreign to him. He was a master of clinical observation and—as indicated in the quotations above—paid careful attention only to overt responses.

His contributions are only of historical interest. Because he limited his studies to a small number of selected subjects, his generalizations were invalid. By not employing control experiments, he failed to see that the physical excitants were, in effect, signals which both he and his docile cooperative patients had unwittingly agreed upon. Had he followed up his original essay with experiments on nonpathological cases, he might have elaborated the psychological features which differentiated hysterical patients from normals.[5]

THE NANCY SCHOOL: SUGGESTION

BRAID'S FIRST THEORY received wide circulation and influenced later neurological theorizing. The fatigue imposed on the ocular muscles was something concrete that physiologists could recognize and which served as a physiological point of departure for explanations of hypnosis. However, implicit in Braid's first theory (and explicit in his second) was a psychological component. Hidden behind the veil of premature physiologizing was a recognition that the hypnotic subject was responding to something in his social environment—that he was not only a vehicle for a nervous system.

[5] It remained for two of his students, Janet and Freud, to describe in detail the *psychology* of hysteria. Janet, who succeeded Charcot at the Salpêtrière, wrote the classic volume, *The Mental State of Hystericals* (1901). Freud, as a young neuropathologist, had studied with Charcot, but was unimpressed with his approach. He was more influenced by the work of Bernheim, which is reflected in his own early work with Breuer, *Studien über Hysterie* (1899).

The Nancy School [6] proposed a set of principles which, in effect, was an extension of Braid's. The work of the Nancy group had its beginnings with the investigations of a country doctor, A. A. Liébeault. In 1860 he began systematically to study hypnotism. In order to have subjects for his studies, he appealed to the parsimonious character of the French peasant. He told them that he would charge a fee if he treated them by drugs and other standard methods, but that hypnotic treatment was free. The response was gratifying. He had plenty of subjects. In 1864 he settled at Nancy and continued working exclusively among the peasantry. In 1866 he published a book, *Sleep and Analogous States Considered from the Point of View of the Action of the Mind on the Body*. Only one copy was sold. He was regarded by other practitioners as a fool, but the country folk among whom he worked regarded him with affection and respect. His clinic was always crowded; he helped many patients who had been unsuccessfully treated by standard methods. In 1882 Bernheim came to work with him. Two years later, Bernheim published his first book, *Suggestion*, in which he supported and developed Liebeault's theories. A sequel, *Suggestive Therapeutics*, appeared in 1886. As a result, medical men from all countries came to study the new therapeutic methods.

Suggestive Therapeutics

The work of the members of the Nancy School was aimed exclusively at cure. A competent first-hand observer reported on the methods used.

> The quiet, ordinary, everyday tone of the whole performance formed a marked contrast to the . . . morbid excitement shown at the Salpêtrière. The patients told to go to sleep apparently fell at once into a quiet slumber, then received their dose of curative suggestions, and when told to awake, either walked quietly away or sat for a little to chat with their friends; the whole process rarely lasting longer than ten minutes. The negation of all morbid symptoms was suggested; also the maintenance of the conditions upon which general health depends, i.e., sleep, digestion, etc. I noticed that in some instances curative suggestions appeared to be perfectly successful, even when the state produced was only one of somnolence. . . . Liébeault took especial pains to explain to his patients that he neither exercised nor possessed any mysterious power, and that all he did was simple and capable of scientific explanation [Bramwell, 1903, p. 31].

[6] The Nancy School is somewhat of a misnomer. The name arose probably for purposes of distinction between the work at Paris (Salpêtrière) and the work of Liébeault and Bernheim at Nancy. Because of their cogent arguments and demonstrations aimed at invalidating the neuropathological ideas of Charcot, they were described as a "school." Other writers who shared their point of view were Beaunis, Liégois, and later, in Switzerland, Forel.

Bernheim's theoretical views may be taken as representative of the Nancy School. His hypotheses reflect two important considerations: (1) the continuity of hypnosis with behavior in everyday life, and (2) its psychological nature.

The Psychological and Non-pathological Orientation

Bernheim maintained that hypnotic acts are analogous to, if not identical with, acts performed in daily life which are of an automatic, involuntary, and unconscious nature. Hypnosis, to the Nancy School, was a "psychical condition, which one can produce, and in which suggestibility is increased" (Bernheim, quoted by Forel, 1907, p. 54). The psychological condition was one of concentration of attention on a single idea. It is important to note that Bernheim was expanding Liébeault's theory of suggestion during the same period that Wundt was developing his structural psychology. The "idea" was one of the elemental units of mental life. Ideas had an independent existence and could be intense or weak, enduring or transitory, focal or marginal. Ideas could lead to action. In fact the hypothesis of ideomotor action was a cornerstone of Bernheim's theory. In everyday life, Bernheim argued, we are subject to all sorts of errors of perception, hallucinations, and illusions. These errors, unless checked by ratiocination, lead to motoric action, to conduct. Such conduct may follow from ideas produced by sensory impressions, sometimes from ideas suggested by others through the medium of gesture and language. Although the tendency exists for such ideas to activate behavior, there is an inhibitory influence which allows the person time to evaluate the consequences of the behavior. The same kind of process is seen in hypnosis, except that the tendency to activate conduct through suggested ideas is increased. The condition responsible for this increased suggestibility is that of suggestion itself. By suggesting the "idea" of sleep, the patient's entire "nervous force" focuses on the idea of sleep and the body complies. To Bernheim, hypnotic sleep and normal sleep were identical.

THE CONCEPT OF SUGGESTION.   Suggestion was the key to understanding the same phenomena which the Mesmerists thought was activated by a vital fluid. Suggestion, however, was not easy to define. Forel (1907), who follows Bernheim closely, defined suggestion with the aid of the structuralistic terms then in vogue.

> By suggestion one means the production of a dynamic change in the nervous system of a person, or of such functions which depend upon his nervous system, by another person by means of the calling forth of representations or ideas . . . that such change is taking place, has taken place or will take place. . . . Verbal suggestion, or "persua-

sion," may be taken to express suggestion produced by spoken words.
. . . Many persons are extremely suggestible even in the waking condition. . . . The conception of hypnosis in this respect can scarcely
be limited, since the normal condition of these people during waking
passes by imperceptible degrees into the condition of hypnosis. Everyone is, however, to a certain extent suggestible during the period of
waking . . . [p. 54].

To the Nancy School, nearly everyone was hypnotizable. This followed both from the results of their observations and from the theoretical statement that suggestibility is a characteristic of the normal person.
Liébeault, for example, in a three-year period attempted to hypnotize
1,756 cases, of which 97 per cent were influenced. Bernheim reported
success in inducing hypnosis in over 80 per cent of 10,000 cases. The
criteria of hypnosis are not specifically given—but it is apparent that any
responsiveness, from mild somnolence to deep somnambulism, is taken
as an indication of hypnotic influence. Pathological cases, according to
Bernheim, were the most difficult to hypnotize. This result was to be expected because the patient must be able to concentrate attention, to
allow the one suggested dominant idea automatically to activate the behavior associated with that idea. Contrary to Charcot, who saw hypnosis
as an artificial hysteria capable of being produced only in neuropathological cases, Bernheim saw hypnosis as a form of behavior continuous
with normal waking behavior, capable of being produced in nearly everyone.

The Nancy School may be credited with introducing and developing the notion of suggestion, a notion which later was picked up by the
sociologists, psychoanalysts, and social psychologists, and further refined
into the concepts of imitation, identification, and role-taking. The mem-
oirs of the Nancy School failed to explain, however, why some suggestions do not produce an idea which activates behavior, or why some
suggestions activate behavior contrary to the intent of the suggestions.
The constructs of mentalistic, dualistic psychology were not adequate to
pin down the nature of suggestion.

Another contribution was the insistence upon the subjective nature
of the hypnotic state (after Braid), the recognition that the important
factor in the interaction was the subject, not the operator. The equating
of normal sleep with hypnotic sleep was an error, but not crucial to the
argument.

In the debate between Charcot and Bernheim, the issue was not
primarily one of method—although differences in method contributed
to their respective findings. The debate was centered around differences
in the conception of the human organism, in the context of the mind-
body problem. On the one hand, Charcot saw the organism as a mechanistic bundle of muscles and nerves, capable of being roused to action

by physical stimuli. So-called mental phenomena were epiphenomena. His conceptions were influenced, no doubt, by the classificatory and nosographic emphases then operating in anatomy and physiology. On the other hand, Bernheim saw the organism in a more humanistic way. His dualism was an interactional one. The mediating agency, of course, was the nervous system, but a plastic system that responded to excitants thrown out by other persons. Implicit in the theory and in the practice of suggestive therapeutics was the notion of interpersonal relations, of social psychological events. From a historical point of view, it appears that the Nancy School was influenced by the same events which led to Comte's formulation of the sciences, giving a special place to the "morale" sciences, which included psychology and sociology. The human organism was more than a vehicle for a nervous system, it was capable of having "ideas" and of having its "ideas" influenced by other human beings.

HULL AND THE CONTROLLED EXPERIMENT

UNTIL THE SECOND QUARTER of the twentieth century, little if any controlled experimentation was attempted. Theorizing was based on clinical reports about the effects of hypnosis when used for healing purposes. In addition to the clinical records, anecdotal reports of unsystematic observations cluttered the literature. Dissatisfied with such observations as a background for a theory of hypnosis, Clark L. Hull, in the late 1920's, set out to design and perform experiments in order to discover the psychological characteristics of hypnotism and its relationship to waking suggestibility.

The Experimental Orientation

Hull was not interested in psychopathology, nor was he interested in the use of hypnosis in the treatment of mental or somatic illness. Unlike most of his predecessors, Hull used adult "normal" subjects, usually student volunteers. As an experimental psychologist, Hull was interested in discovering the stimulus variables which elicited certain classes of responses. His theoretical orientation was behavioristic. His concepts were continuous in form and scope with his later and better-known contributions to learning theory: habit, stimulus, and response.

In contrast to the clinical observation, the controlled experiment—derived from Mills' "method of differences"—was Hull's method of choice. Hull quotes Mills' principle and it bears repetition here.

> If an instance in which the phenomenon under investigation occurs and an instance in which it does not occur have every circumstance in common save one, that one occurring only in the former; the cir-

cumstance in which alone the two instances differ is the effect, or the cause, or an indispensable part of the cause, of the phenomenon [Hull, 1933, p. 19].

The main feature of the work of Hull and his collaborators was the use of control subjects or control conditions. Waking, unhypnotized subjects served as controls and were exposed to the same kinds of stimuli or experimental circumstances as were the hypnotized subjects. In this way, differences between the responses of hypnotized subjects and waking subjects could be attributed to the hypothesized hypnotic state.

Not only was Hull's work experimental, it was programmatic. He and his collaborators published more than thirty papers prior to the appearance of his book, *Hypnosis and Suggestibility*, in 1933. In the present chapter, only one or two of these studies will be sketched to illustrate the experimental method and to show the application of his theory that hypnosis is a state of heightened suggestibility. Hull had broad interests in hypnotic phenomena. He and his collaborators performed experiments which demonstrated that true sleep and hypnosis are unrelated; that posthypnotic suggestions lose their strength over a period of time; that recently acquired memory material is recovered as well in the waking state as in hypnosis.

THE POSTURAL-SWAY TEST.   As one measure of suggestibility, Hull employed the postural-sway technique. This procedure is now widely used as a standard demonstration of waking suggestibility. The subject is blindfolded and told in a variety of ways that he is falling forward. The measure that Hull employed was "suggestion time," defined as the number of seconds required to elicit the maximum postural reaction to the repeated suggestions. Both the latency of response and the amount of the postural sway varied for subjects and for conditions of the experiment, i.e., waking suggestion or hypnotic suggestion.

In one of a series of experiments designed to determine the relationship of hypnotic to waking suggestibility, Hull and Huse (1930) used the postural-sway test as follows. Using a counterbalanced order and observing other standard laboratory precautions, they gave the postural-sway test to eight subjects in the waking and in the hypnotic conditions. The protocols were in the form of tracings obtained by attaching the end of a recording device to the subject's collar. Figure 80 is a reproduction of a tracing shown in Hull's book.

The "suggestion time" is represented by the distance between marks *A* and *B* in 5-sec. intervals. Note that in the trance state the suggestion time for the second trial is about 5 sec. as compared with the suggestion time in the waking state for the second trial, about 30 sec. The data of the experiment are summarized in Table 1. Compare the average "suggestion time" in the trance state, 10.55 sec., with the aver-

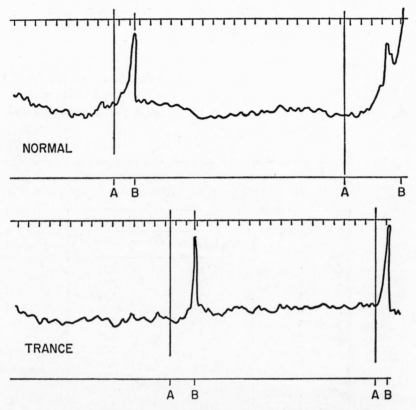

NORMAL

A B   A   B

TRANCE

A   B   A B

FIGURE 80. Typical record from the experiment to determine the relative suggestibility to postural movements of normal adults in the trance and the waking state. (From Hull and Huse, 1930, p. 283. Used by permission of the *American Journal of Psychology*.)

age "suggestion time" in the waking state, 23.67 sec. The implication of this finding, of course, is that the hypnotic trance increases suggestibility. Also note the correlation between suggestion time in the two conditions, $r = .96$. The implication of this second finding is that those persons who are most suggestible in the waking state are most suggestible in the hypnotic state. It is interesting to note that Hull made little of this second finding—probably because he was interested in the *state* or *process* rather than in individual differences.

The relationship of increased suggestibility to hypnosis was regarded by Hull as a matter of "considerable theoretical importance." "A plausible hypothesis which would make hypnosis but a special case of direct prestige suggestion is that whenever a direct prestige suggestion is reacted to positively there is generated within the reacting organism a heightened susceptibility to react positively to all other prestige suggestions. . . . These experimental results show that waking suggestions seem to facilitate closely subsequent trance inductions" (Hull, 1933, p. 331).

When we appraise Hull's work after twenty-five years, it becomes apparent that he thought of hypnosis as somewhat parallel to a physiological or chemical state. He regarded the subject of a hypnotic experiment as a laboratory specimen. His model for experimentation was the physiological laboratory. Stimuli are presented, responses measured and

TABLE 1

CONDENSED TABLE SUMMARIZING THE RESULTS OF
HULL AND HUSE CONCERNING SUGGESTIBILITY
IN THE TRANCE AND THE WAKING STATE *

Subject No.	Mean suggestion time in seconds	
	Waking state	Trance state
1	17.63	4.13
2	13.00	5.38
3	12.25	5.38
4	80.50	42.50
5	19.00	10.75
6	9.75	4.38
7	7.13	5.38
8	30.13	6.50
Mean........	23.67	10.55
PE_M.........	5.36	2.92
Correlation (r)	0.96	

* From Clark L. Hull, *Hypnosis and Suggestibility*, p. 292. Copyright 1933 D. Appleton-Century Co., Inc. Used with permission of Appleton-Century-Crofts, Inc. Adapted from material in C. L. Hull and P. Huse, "Comparative Suggestibility in the Trance and Waking States," *Amer. J. Psychol.*, 1930, *52*, 279–86. Reprinted with permission of the *American Journal of Psychology*.

recorded. Because of the restrictions imposed by the laboratory model, he could only study easily measured motor responses or simple memory functions. Complex affective and motivational determinants were ignored.

That Hull regarded the hypnotic state as something analogous to a state induced by physiological or chemical processes is shown by his attempts to study "problems concerning the rise and decay of hypnotic suggestibility." The purpose of the studies was to plot the curves showing decreases in latency to repeated postural-sway suggestions.

In one experiment (Patten, Switzer, and Hull, 1932), the plan was to analyze these curves representing latency decreases into two components. (1) hypersuggestibility and (2) facilitation due to practice effects. The experimental design was this: Three postural-sway suggestions were given to each of sixteen susceptible subjects for twenty successive days. A period of one minute elapsed between the termination of each suggestion and the beginning of the next, for the three suggestions given

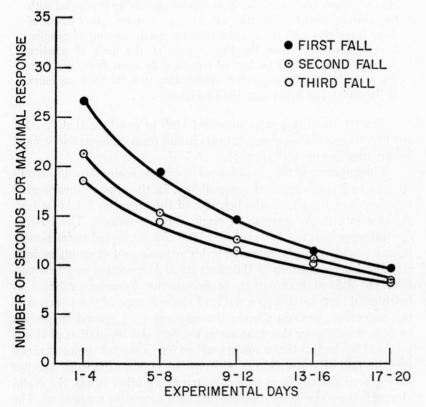

FIGURE 81. Graph showing the decrease in the immediate facilitation of suggestibility as the amount of permanent facilitation decreases with practice. (From Patten, Switzer, and Hull, 1932, p. 547.)

each day. The hypothesis was that the two components, "hypersuggestibility" and "facilitation," would be demonstrated in the curves by (1) some distance between the curves and (2) a drop in the curves, respectively (see Figure 81). This approach regarded facilitation as having at least twenty-four hour permanency, while temporary facilitation (such as "warm-up" effects) was assumed to be inoperative or operative to an unknown degree.

In Hull's own words, the experiment was expected to isolate the two components as follows:

The effects of practice could be avoided by testing some form of suggestion behavior for homoactive hypersuggestibility after the activity in question had been practiced until it had ceased to show permanent facilitation. Such a procedure should reveal unambiguously any hypersuggestibility which is genuinely distinct from practice effects [1933, p. 321]. Our present hypothesis assumes . . . that at the limit of practice these curves must converge in such a way as to coincide as a single horizontal line if no hypersuggestibility is mingled with the obviously existent practice effects. . . . On the other hand, if there is mingled with the practice effects a certain amount of genuine hypersuggestibility, then the three curves at the limit of practice should become horizontal but be separated by some finite distance, the magnitude of the separation constituting in some sense an index of the amount of hypersuggestibility present. . . .[7]

The results of this experiment led Hull to conclude that ". . . if any hypersuggestibility whatever exists in this form of suggestion it must be very small in amount" (p. 325).

The influence of the physiological laboratory is also shown in Hull's attempt to identify types of suggestibility. In the typical physiological experiment of the 1920's, the behavior of the organism would be fractionated into single response, or single response systems. The modern dynamic approach was in its infancy. Hull also attempted to fractionate behavior—this is amply illustrated by his measurement of simple motoric acts and his formulation of the concepts of homoaction and heteroaction. He defined homoaction, or homoactive hypersuggestibility, as heightened suggestibility as a result of the influence of the response to one suggestion procedure upon the response to a second suggestion procedure calling for the same act as the first. An illustration of this is provided by the fact that a subject will go into a second trance as measured by rate of eyelid closure with special rapidity immediately after having been aroused from a previous trance. In other words, the eyelid closure is the response manipulated by both successive suggestions. The homoactive effect is the decrease in latency from the first to the second suggestions of eyelid closure. Heteroaction, or heteroactive hypersuggestibility, was defined as heightened suggestibility to a second but different response from the first. For instance, the effect of responding to the suggestion of eyelid closure upon such a response as forward movement of the arm, quite dissimilar acts from the anatomist's and the physiologist's point of view, is an example of heteroaction. The reduction in latency or "suggestion time" was taken as a measure of heteroaction.

Incidentally, Hull pointed out the parallel between these concepts and direct training and transfer of training. As theoretical constructs and as experimental variables, these notions proved fruitless in trying to understand the nature of the hypnotic phenomena.

The failure of attempts at fractionating the hypnotic behavior, however, did not lead Hull to a study of the "whole person." To Hull, the behaviorist and experimental psychologist, the subject came into the experimental laboratory somewhat like a subject who had to memorize a list of nonsense syllables rather than as an organism with conscious and unconscious preconceptions, motives, attitudes, and skills. Not only was the subject *qua* person ignored, but differences among persons in reactivity were looked upon as accidents of the laboratory, as error. The *process* was the important thing, individual differences could be overlooked. But this was the tenor of the times. Dynamic psychology and social psychology had not yet made any inroads into the psychological laboratory.

This is not to say that Hull did not recognize the fact of individual variation. He was restricted by the state of psychological measurement, however, as were other investigators of his time, in finding personality correlates of hypnotizability. The methods available at that time allowed for only the grossest measurement of personality traits by means of inventories of doubtful validity.

Hypnosis as Prestige Suggestion

In one respect, however, Hull broke away from the model of the physiological laboratory, viz., in regarding hypnosis as the effect of *prestige* suggestion. Implicitly, Hull was here acknowledging an interpersonal, social element in the situation. In this connection, he confirmed hypotheses of earlier investigators, notably Binet, that suggestibility as inferred from responses to illusions of length, illusions of weight, perceptual perseveration, etc., was not necessarily related to prestige suggestibility. In distinguishing hypnosis from tonic immobility in animals, erroneously called animal hypnosis, Hull hints at the learned nature of hypnotizability:

> . . . hypnosis and prestige suggestion appear to originate in habits which must previously have been acquired, whereas the tendency of animals to pass into a state of tonic immobility seems to be innate and unlearned [p. 388].

On the basis of his experiments with relatively simple motoric phenomena, Hull rejected nearly every belief about hypnosis. He had shown that everything that could be done under hypnosis could also be done in waking suggestibility, but in a somewhat attenuated form. All that was left of hypnosis was prestige suggestion which, incidentally, was not exclusive to the trance state. Summarizing, Hull said:

The mere susceptibility to prestige suggestion, no matter in what degree, is not hypnosis. Its essence lies in the experimental fact of a quantitative *shift* in the upward direction which may result from the hypnotic procedure. So far as the writer can see, this quantitative phenomenon alone remains of the once imposing aggregate known by the name of hypnosis. But this undoubted fact is quite sufficient to give significance and value to the term hypnosis for the upper level, and to prevent its application to the lower or normal (waking) level . . . [p. 392].

In trying to relate prestige suggestion to the body of existing psychological knowledge, Hull said:

The experimental evidence indicates that whatever else prestige suggestion may be, it at least is a habit phenomenon. That both hypnosis and waking suggestion manifest the classical behavior of habituation in remarkable detail has been shown by [three experiments]. . . . Learning the ordinary habitual responses to language stimuli is an essential component of acquiring the tendency called suggestibility [p. 394].

The reader will at once recognize the similarity between Hull's formulation and Bernheim's. The latter explained hypnosis in terms of suggestion defined mentalistically as the association of ideas. Hull explained hypnosis also in terms of suggestion, but defined it in more behavioristic terms as the association between stimulus and response, "ideas" being regarded as "physical symbolic acts."

Hull's Contributions

In any historical review, the contributions of a scientist ought to be evaluated. What did Hull contribute to the solution of the problem of hypnosis? He demonstrated that phenomena of hypnosis were not discontinuous from the main stream of psychological data. Hypnotic phenomena could be studied with the same objectivity and with the same laboratory procedures as other phenomena. His insistence on regarding hypnotic suggestibility and waking suggestibility as habit phenomena was another way of showing that hypnosis was not something esoteric but was amenable to experimental analysis directed at testing specific hypotheses. He thus removed hypnosis from the clinic where discovery is incidental to therapeutics, where the vitiating effects of patients as subjects are unknown, where the controlled experiment is practically impossible.

By isolating prestige suggestion as an explanatory formulation, Hull (probably unwittingly) laid part of the groundwork for later attempts at regarding hypnosis as an interpersonal or social-psychological phenomenon. His insistence on controlled experimentation removed a lot of the hocus-pocus that, like a barnacle, had fastened itself to the basic structure of hypnosis.

In a sense, Hull was a little ahead of his time. The progress of psychological science had not yet produced the techniques or the concepts for a thorough investigation of hypnosis. The behavioristic laboratory of the 1920's with its operations centered on the elicitation of simple responses was ill-equipped to deal with complexities of interpersonal relations. Furthermore, existing stimulus-response theories could not adequately conceptualize the complexities inherent in the now apparent social psychological nature of hypnosis.

Working during the zenith of the behavioristic movement, Hull rejected any method that resembled introspection. He was thus left without the self-report data which had made up the raw material for some of the earlier theorists. He could contribute little, for example, to confirm or refute the hypothesis that hypnosis made possible the recall of otherwise inaccessible memories or the hypothesis of increased organismic involvement. In the case of Hull's work as that of any other scientist's, the method used dictated the type of solution obtained. The final paragraph in Hull's book is a fitting recognition of this essential historical fact:

> We have done our best to see the problems with a fresh eye, to avoid the omnipresent experimental pitfalls, to devise really adequate experimental controls, and to be docile in the face of facts. The history of the subject teaches us to have no illusions in regard to the success of such efforts. No worker can wholly escape the ideology of his time. Many of the things here gravely put down as securely established will be rejected with reason by investigators of the future, just as we have found reason to reject more or less of what many earlier workers have regarded as certain. This is both inevitable and proper, for science is to a certain extent a trial-and-error process. [p. 403].

CONTEMPORARY HYPNOTIC THEORY

SINCE THE PUBLICATION of Hull's work, the experimental literature of hypnosis has expanded. Interest in therapeutic aspects of hypnosis has continued apace, but current theorizing flows more from the implications of systematic observation and controlled experimentation than from the study of therapeutic effects.

In a review of recent theories of hypnosis, Pattie (1956) asserts that the most widely accepted theory places hypnotic behavior on a continuum of role-taking. Briefly stated, this theory asserts that hypnotic behavior is *not* discontinuous from other behavior. It is the result of the subject's striving to achieve a role, the role having been defined through prior learning and modified by present social events, including the instructions of the hypnotist. Individual differences in responsiveness to the hypnotic instruction are accounted for by (1) motivational variables (the hypnotic situation must meet some needs of the subject); (2) perceptual variables (the subject must achieve a valid perception of the hypnotic role according to the expectations of the hypnotist or other observers); (3) aptitude variables (the subject must have some skill in role-enactment, i.e., in shifting implicit sets and performing accordingly; these skills are a product of prior learning). Behavior in the hypnotic experiment which is mediated through the skeletal musculature, i.e., overt movements, speech, etc., requires no different explanation from nonhypnotic behavior. Behavior mediated through the autonomic nervous system is explained as a by-product of the hypnotic situation. Thus autonomic and other physiological and humoral changes may be attributed to muscular effort, frustration, vicarious excitement, hypoxia due to muscular relaxation, change in respiration, etc.[8]

Analysis of Individual Variation in Hypnotizability

The role-taking theory begins with the observation of individual differences in responsiveness to identical stimulation. By using scales of depth of hypnosis based upon the individual's disposition to accept such suggestions and commands as amnesia, anesthesia, posthypnotic compulsions, catalepsy, etc., it becomes at once apparent that human beings vary greatly in responsiveness (susceptibility in the language of Bernheim, sensitivity in the language of the magnetizers.). The question of first importance has become: What are the characteristics of persons who perform the hypnotic role according to the expectations of the hypnotist?[9] Currently, the expectations of researchers comprise the phenomena classified on page 747. The subject is supposed to (1) respond automatically and without conscious volition (changes in motility);

[8] Many investigators from the early nineteenth century to the present have distinguished between the effects that could be stimulated by contact, expectation, and/or imagination. Autonomic effects and hyperamnesia for early events, however, could not easily be explained on this basis. Therefore, animistic notions were introduced such as "odylic" force, vibratory motions of the ether, clairvoyance, psychic control, etc.

[9] The expectations of the hypnotist vary from time to time and from one theoretical orientation to the other. At the Nancy School, the expectations were apparently a mild somnolence or relaxation, or, in the absence of any noticeable change in overt behavior, therapeutic effects of suggestion. At the Salpêtrière, the expectations were lethargy, catalepsy, somnambulism, and hysterical symptoms. The depth of hypnosis as an experimental variable was first explored by Barry, MacKinnon, and Murray (1931). Hull utilized a scale in order to test his subjects for depth. Friedlander and Sarbin (1938) later combined scales from several observers and provided some information on scoring and standardization. Hilgard and his collaborators (1958) have refined the latter scale and modified the scoring procedure.

(2) exceed the limits of his waking behavior; (3) shift his attention from object-perception to self-perception and exhibit hyperamnesia. Experiments in which the preconceptions (expectations) of the subjects were known have demonstrated rather conclusively that the automatism is apparent and not real. If a subject believes that eye-closure is prerequisite to accepting, say, a posthypnotic suggestion, then he will not accept the suggestion if offered when the eyes are open. The subject performs in an apparently automatic way because he believes that such change in motility is part of his role. The frequently encountered resistances to performing certain acts as well as the spontaneous additions to the hypnotist's instructions further point to the conative and volitional rather than the automatic character of the performance. From the time of Braid to the present nearly all investigators have observed such changes in motility. The older explanations failed to take into account the subject's preconception of the role. The preconception is acquired through experiences of many kinds, such as listening to others report on hypnosis, observing others in the hypnotic state, acquiring the belief that the hypnotic state is the same as sleep or drowsiness, and so on.

The increase in the limits of one's abilities, such as strength, knowledge, memory, etc., which astounded the early magnetizers (and led to such ideas as clairvoyance) turns out to be more apparent than real. Systematic studies of behavior in hypnosis and in the waking state show none of the "miraculous" differences noted by earlier workers who had failed to employ controlled experimentation. Those differences which are systematically observed are explicable on the basis of increased motivation, freedom from distraction, and/or aptitude in role-taking. As an illustration, the phenomenon of age regression may be cited. It has often been claimed that hypnosis facilitates the recall of childhood memories. This facilitation is attributed to the subject's capacity for age regression —for "reliving" the childhood event. The hypnotist instructs the subject "to go back to such-and-such an age." The predisposed subject will perform according to the instruction. He will exhibit mannerisms, gestures, language, and other conduct characteristic of the suggested age. This phenomenon was investigated by Sarbin (1950). Subjects (average age nineteen) were instructed to regress to age eight, once in hypnosis and once in the waking state in counterbalanced order. Then they were administered the Stanford-Binet test. Available to the investigator were the actual Stanford-Binet records for these subjects at age eight. None of the subjects repeated his performance at age eight, although there were wide invidual differences. When the depth of hypnosis was introduced as a variable, a large segment of the individual differences could be accounted for. Those subjects who could take the role of the hypnotic subject most convincingly (as measured by ratings on the Friedlander-Sarbin scale) came closer to their IQ at age eight than did those subjects who were less able to accept the hypnotic role. In other words, those subjects who demonstrated an aptitude for role-taking in hypnosis could imaginatively take the role of a young child. However, the idea of accurately "reliving" a former age was not demonstrated.

Motivational Analysis

The first serious attempt to study the influence of motivational variables was made by R. W. White (1941). He related success at achieving the hypnotic role to certain personality traits as assessed through the analysis of ratings and fantasy productions. He found a positive correlation between hypnotizability and the need for deference, and a negative correlation between hypnotizability and the need for autonomy .White's article makes it clear that many other motives may determine success in achieving the hypnotic state, such as the need for recognition, need for sex, need for sharing in the hypnotist's supposed power, etc. An extension of this statement was developed by the present author (Sarbin, 1950): motivation favorable to the achievement of the hypnotic role is present when the behavioral requirements of the role and the subject's self-concept are not incongruent. When the requirements of the role violate the subject's self-image, the subject cannot achieve the hypnotic role. To be sure, the motives are inferred from the analysis of behavior and may not be accessible to the subject's own examination.

Continuity of Hypnosis with Other Behavior

Taking a hard-headed attitude toward hypnotic phenomena, current theorists see the catalepsies, the paralyses, the anesthesias, the amnesias, the posthypnotic performances as a matter of role-taking on the part of the subject. These manifestations also make up the syndromes of hysteria. This does not mean that role-taking or hysteria is to be interpreted as sham or fraudulent conduct. Modern theory sees the hypnotic interaction as continuous with other social interactions. It begins with the postulate that social groups are organized around positions, or units, of a social structure. Such units are defined by a consensus of expectations. Certain positions call for certain behaviors. These behaviors make up the content of the role. In hypnosis the hypnotist and the subject occupy positions; each expects certain behaviors from the other. Instead of leaning on a model taken from physics, current hypnotic theory is continuous with theories of other forms of social behavior, such as the drama. The subject acts in relation to the hypnotist as the actor does in relation to the stage director. Each has a conception of his own role and each of these conceptions may be modified through social interaction. Both the hypnotist and the director instruct the occupant of the reciprocal position how to behave. The success of the subject's or actor's performance depends upon his preconception of the role, the degree of favorable motivation, and the amount and quality of role-taking aptitude or skill. In short, the hypnotic subject, like the actor, strives to fill a specified social position, to enact a given role.

The implications of regarding hypnotic behavior as role-taking are sweeping. Hypnosis, on this view, is *not* a special "state" of the organism. The observed behaviors are artifacts of the role as prescribed by the experimenter and interpreted by the subject. Pertinent here is a recent paper by Orne (1959), which describes several attempts at isolating the "essence" of hypnotic behavior from its role artifacts. He adapted the "blind" technique from pharmacology, where the physician responsible for evaluating the effects of a drug is ignorant of which patients were administered drugs. Orne used two groups of subjects, (1) deeply hypnotizable subjects and (2) simulators. The latter were instructed by an associate of the experimenter to *pretend* to be hypnotized. The experimenter was unable to differentiate by any of the usual tests between the hypnotic role-takers and the simulating role-takers. From these findings, Orne generalized that explanations of the behavior of subjects in hypnosis (and in other experimental settings) must take into account the "demand character" of the interactional setting. The demand character of both the hypnotic instruction and the simulating instruction are substantially the same. In both, the subject becomes committed to the enactment of a role.[1]

Psychophysiological Aspects

This explanation in terms of role-taking, without further refinement, cannot account for such psychosomatic effects as changes in blood-sugar levels under hypnosis, changes in glandular secretions, changes in menstrual functioning, etc. At the present time, two hypotheses are advanced to account for organismic changes which are mediated by the autonomic nervous system. Both hypotheses begin with the assumption that the subject strives to enact a role. In the first hypothesis (Sarbin, 1956), the autonomic effects are regarded as by-products of the motoric actions produced by the subject in enacting his role. Such organismic conditions as muscular effort, excitement, or frustration may produce

[1] Orne reported some casual data which suggests that the "essence" of hypnosis lies in the ability to transcend logic. Some of the hypnotized subjects resolved conflicts induced by hallucinatory behavior by the use of a different logic from that used by simulators. It should be pointed out, however, that the simulators were selected because they were *nonresponsive* to the hypnotic role induction procedures. Hence the difference in the use of logical forms might be a corollary of personality characteristics which accounted for individual differences in responsiveness to the hypnotic induction situation.

autonomic side effects. For example, when the subject strains to produce a certain response, autonomic concomitants of such strain may be observed, e.g., increased respiration, pulse rate, etc. These physiological changes may, in turn, trigger off other visceral responses. If the investigator focuses exclusively on the physiological *effects*, he may fail to note the antecedent stimulating events.

The second hypothesis (Sarbin, 1956) offered to explain autonomic effects as well as shifts in attention from object-perception to self-perception will now be considered. When an individual takes the role of a hypnotic subject, shifts in cerebral circulation occur as a by-product of the somnolence or of the emotional excitement produced by the effort to enact the role. This shift in circulation results in reduction in the oxygen supply in the cerebral cortex, which, in turn allows subcortical centers to achieve temporary dominance so that behavior mediated by the subcortex and the autonomic nervous system may be observed. The latter hypothesis follows from the work of Papez (1937) and MacLean (1949) on the physiology and neurology of emotional behavior.[2]

The role-theory of hypnosis, then, attempts to explain certain hypnotic behavior (catalepsy, amnesia, anesthesia, etc.) as the *direct* effect of role-enactment, and other responses (autonomic changes) as the *indirect* effects of role-enactment.

The form and content of this current theory reflect the influences that have modified personality theory generally. The most important of these influences are (1) the development of sociology and social psychology; (2) the growth of interest in motivational psychology; and (3) attempts at resolving the mind-body dualism through research in psychosomatic medicine.

From sociology and social psychology have come the knowledge about the social determinants of behavior. The two participants—hypnotist and subject—are not without social characteristics. The behavior of the subject is determined to a degree by the position of the hypnotist, often a scientist, a member of the healing profession, or one perceived as a "possessor of occult powers." The importance of social structure in defining the behavior of participants in a social interaction was first systematically explored by Cooley (1922) and by Mead (1934). Each participant in a social relationship responds to the other in terms of the other's role. Socially valid behavior depends upon the accuracy of the subject's role perception. The application of this conception to the hypnotic situation is obvious. In order to enact the role of the hypnotized

[2] Barber (1959) has recently added data and argument to demonstrate how changes in psychophysiological functioning in hypnosis are continuous with changes observed in other conditions. His observations add support to contemporary social-psychological formulations which place explanations of hypnosis in a naturalistic setting.

person, the subject must have some knowledge of that role. This he may acquire through hearsay, rumor, reading, authoritative declarations, observation, etc. The hypnotic interaction is regarded in current theory as continuous with any other social interaction: the positions of the two participants are defined beforehand. Each tries to perform so as to validate his occupancy of the position.

The continuing interest in motivation, the "why's" of behavior, has similarly affected the development of hypnotic theory. Rejecting the notion of automaticity, so important to the proponents of animal magnetism, current theory sees hypnotic behavior as goal-directed striving. The subject tries to perform in certain ways in order to fulfill certain needs—most of which, of course, are unconscious, i.e., inaccessible to self-examination.

Social psychology and motivational psychology have placed the overt behavior of the hypnotic subject on a continuum with waking behavior. The psychosomatic (i.e., autonomic) effects observed in hypnosis required examination by means of concepts not a part of traditional psychology. The work on psychosomatic medicine of the past three decades has formulated concepts and methods applicable to the study of autonomic responses to symbolic stimuli. Solid work on the neurophysiology of the emotions has also markedly influenced the course of modern theorizing about hypnosis (Sarbin, 1956).

RECAPITULATION

THE STUDY OF HYPNOTISM began with the problem of identifying the mechanism by which one person influences another. In this chapter I have tried to sketch how scientists, working in different historical periods, have tried to answer that question. No theorist, as Hull pointed out, can wholly escape the influence of his times. Each is influenced by his philosophical orientation as to the nature of man, by current and recent developments in other areas of knowledge—notably the more prestigeful natural sciences, and by implicit goals. Whoever became concerned with the problem had to start from his own particular way of handling the mind-body dualism.

Mesmer and the other magnetizers located the mechanism of transmission in a vital fluid regarded as analogous to (or identical with) the ether as postulated by Newton. Here was an attempt at finding a physicalistic solution to the mind-body problem—the mechanism being the postulated fluid. Animal magnetism as a theory could flourish before empirical science became concerned with human beings *qua* social-psychological entities as objects of study and experiment. Braid, a half-century later, had an advantage over the magnetizers in that he had been exposed to such neurological discoveries as those of Bell and Müller.

His first theory reflected the assimilation of his observations to current knowledge and interest in the workings of the central nervous system. Braid's second theory, monoideism, arose, first, out of his recognition of the inadequacies of his neurological theory for the explanation of hypnosis without ocular fixation. Monoideism was an outgrowth of the doctrines of the British empiricists, particularly the notion of the "idea" as a structural entity of mind. In the mid-nineteenth century, as a result of the discoveries of Flourens, Müller, Bell, Helmholtz, and others, mental functions were increasingly related to nerve impulses and brain mechanisms. Helmholtz's discovery of the speed of the nervous impulse, for example, demonstrated that the nervous impulse was a physical event. Ideas could be conceived as analogous to, or the products of, nerve impulses. This was a manifestation of the emphasis on empirical, naturalistic science and led the way toward reducing the mind-body dualism to a physicalistic monism.

From the work of the competing schools of Bernheim and Charcot, we can infer the influence of two distinct social contexts. At Nancy, the patient was first and foremost a human being. He was more than a bundle of nerves and muscles. As a product of natural selection, man occupied a special place in nature. The attitude of Liébeault and Bernheim reflected this notion. This was the period of Huxley's advocacy of Darwinism (1863). Behavior could be understood by studying man naturalistically; this meant more concern with the context (social and physical) and less concern with speculations about unobservables and unknowables.

Charcot's work illustrates clearly the proposition that modern neurology began in the social context of telegraphic and telephonic communication. The first successful trans-Atlantic cable was laid in 1866, the first successful telephone instrument was invented in 1876. Charcot's conceptual model (like those of other neurologists) was the telegraphic system with its wires, trunks, connections, induction, etc. The concern of the neurologist was in the transmission of "messages" via the nervous system to the central switchboard. As a neuropathologist, of course, Charcot was interested in those events which interfered with the systematic transmission of nervous impulses. The human being was only a vehicle for the transmission networks.

Hull's model, nearly a half-century after Charcot, was the physiological laboratory. But, for the first time, the emphasis was not on therapeusis. The subject was a psychological entity, to be sure, but the stimulus-response methods of the physiological laboratory were preferred. As pointed out earlier, Hull implicitly recognized the social-psychological nature of hypnosis when he employed the concept of prestige suggestion. The mind-body dualism could be reduced to a physicalistic monism by following the lead of Watson and rejecting concepts, phenomena, and methods that were not sanctioned by physical science. The revolt against mentalism and against speculative philosophy was reflected in Hull's rejection of the methods of self-report.

The rise of psychology as an independent discipline freed investigators from the necessity of employing physical or physiological models. The interactional nature of hypnosis had been hinted at as early as 1784 in the report of the first French Commission. A systematic theory based on social interaction could not be developed without social-psychological concepts. For example, the notion of role, drawn from everyday life and from the theater, has served as an aid in understanding social interaction in general and hypnosis in particular. The concept of *aptitude*, developed by psychologists in recent decades in the context of vocational selection for an industrial society, had a ready application to hypnosis in the form of role-taking aptitude.

In the mid-twentieth century, no psychological theory is complete without the concept of motivation. To the biological emphasis derived from Darwinism has been added a social or interpersonal emphasis. Influenced by early twentieth-century writers such as Cooley, Baldwin, Mead, and James, psychologists have formulated the concept of the self as an aid in studying the person's strivings. From Freud and other therapeutically oriented scholars has come the parallel concept of the ego. The underlying notion to both formulations is that a cognitive organization, a set of concepts or beliefs, serves as the base line for behavior. In hypnosis we see the application of such a motivational theory. Favorable motivation is one of the requirements for successfully performing the hypnotic role. It is obvious that such a concept would not have occurred to the nineteenth-century investigators whose subjects were, for the most part, well-motivated patients. When working with non-patient subjects unselected for motivation, individual variation in responsiveness is observed and must be explained. Motivation is one of the cornerstones of contemporary explanations of hypnosis.

The history of hypnosis, like any other chapter in science, is the history of trial and error by human beings. The explanations put forth at different times are dependent upon the concepts and the tools available to the investigator. These concepts and tools he assimilates to his own needs and refines for the next generation of scientists. Thus each scientist, in his own unique way, responds to the challenge laid down by his predecessors.

REFERENCES

BARBER, T. X. Toward a theory of pain: relief of chronic pain by prefrontal leucotomy, opiates, placebos and hypnosis. *Psychol. Bull.*, 1959, 56, 430–60.

BARRY, H., JR., MACKINNON, D. W., AND MURRAY, H. A., JR. Hypnotizability as a personality trait and its typological relations. *Hum. Biol.*, 1931, 3, 1–36.

BINET, A., AND FÉRÉ, C. *Animal magnetism.* New York: Appleton Co., 1901.

BORING, E. G. *A history of experimental psychology.* New York: Century Co., 1929.

BRAID, J. *Neurypnology; or, the rationale of nervous sleep, considered in relation with animal magnetism.* London: Churchill, 1843.

————. *Neurypnology; or, the rationale of nervous sleep considered in relation to animal magnetism or mesmerism,* 2nd ed. London: G. Redway, 1899.

BRAMWELL, J. M. *Hypnotism, its history, practice, and theory.* London: P. Richards, 1903.

BREUER, J., AND FREUD, S. *Studien über Hysterie.* Leipzig: F. Deuticke, 1909.

CARPENTER, W. B. *Principles of mental physiology.* London: King, 1875.

COLQUHOUN, J. C. *Isis revelatus: an inquiry into the origin, progress, and present state of animal magnetism,* 3rd ed. Edinburgh: W. Wilson, 1844. 2 vols.

COOLEY, C. H. *Human nature and the social order.* New York: C. Scribner's Sons, 1922.

ELLIOTSON, J. *Surgical cases in Mesmerism without pain.* London: Baillière, 1843.

ESDAILE, J. *Mesmerism in India and its practical application in surgery and medicine.* Chicago: Psychic Research Co., 1902.

FOREL, A. *Hypnotism; or suggestion and psychotherapy.* (Rev. American ed.) New York: Rebman, 1907.

FRIEDLANDER, J. W., AND SARBIN, T. R. The depth of hypnosis. *J. abnorm. soc. Psychol.*, 1939, 33, 453–75.

HEIDENHAIN, R. *Hypnotism or animal magnetism.* London: Paul, Trench, Trübner, 1899.

HILGARD, E. R., WEITZENHOFFER, A. M., AND GOUGH, P. Individual differences in susceptibility to hypnosis. *Proc. Nat. Acad. Sci.*, 1958, 44, 1255–9.

HULL, C. L. *Hypnosis and suggestibility: an experimental approach.* New York: Appleton-Century, 1933.

HULL, C. L., AND HUSE, B. Comparative suggestibility in the trance and waking states. *Amer. J. Psychol.*, 1930, 52, 279–86.

JANET, P. *The mental state of hystericals.* (Tr. by C. R. Corson) New York: Putnam, 1901.

MACLEAN, P. D. Psychosomatic disease and the "visceral brain": recent developments bearing on the Papez theory of emotion. *Psychosom. Med.*, 1949, 11, 338–53.

MEAD, G. H. *Mind, self and society.* Chicago: University of Chicago Press, 1934.

ORNE, M. The nature of hypnosis: Artifact or essence. *J. abnorm. soc. Psychol.*, 1959, 58, 277–99.

PAPEZ, J. W. A proposed mechanism of emotion. *Arch. Neurol. and Psychiat.*, 1937, 38, 725–38.

PATTEN, E. F., SWITZER, ST.C. A., AND HULL, C. L. Habituation, retention, and perseveration characteristics of direct waking suggestion. *J. exp. Psychol.*, 1932, 15, 539–49.

PATTIE, F. A. Theories of hypnosis. In R. M. Dorcus (Ed.), *Hypnosis and its therapeutic applications.* New York: McGraw-Hill Book Co., 1956.

SARBIN, T. R. Contributions to role-taking theory: I. Hypnotic behavior. *Psychol. Rev.*, 1950, 57, 255–70.

———. Physiological effects of hypnotic stimulation. In R. M. Dorcus (Ed.), *Hypnosis and its therapeutic applications.* New York: McGraw-Hill Book Co., 1956.

———. Mental age changes in experimental regression. *J. Pers.*, 1950, 19, 221–8.

SCHILDER, P. F., AND KAUDERS, O. *Hypnosis.* (Tr. by S. Rothenberg.) New York: Nervous and Mental Disease Publishing Co., 1927.

WHITE, R. W. A preface to a theory of hypnotism. *J. abnorm. soc. Psychol.*, 1941, 36, 477–505.

Name Index

Subject Index